TRACING TECHNOLOGY

# BABESCH

*Annual Papers on Mediterranean Archaeology*

*Supplement 42 — 2021*

**BABESCH FOUNDATION**
*Stichting Bulletin Antieke Beschaving*

# TRACING TECHNOLOGY

# FORTY YEARS OF ARCHAEOLOGICAL RESEARCH AT SATRICUM

Edited by

Marijke Gnade and Martina Revello Lami

**PEETERS**

Leuven - Paris - Bristol, CT

2021

BABESCH Supplement Series
edited by
G.J. van Wijngaarden

Cover designed by Loes Opgenhaffen

*All volumes published in the BABESCH Supplements are subject to anonymous academic peer review.*

© 2021 Peeters, Bondgenotenlaan 153, B-3000 Leuven

*All rights reserved, including the right to translate or reproduce this book or parts in any form.*

ISBN 978-90-429-4664-4
eISBN 978-90-429-4665-1
D/2021/0602/168

CONTENTS

Marijke Gnade, Martina Revello Lami
Introduction: Tracing Technology. *Forty years of archaeological research at Satricum* — 1

## CONTEXTUALIZING TECHNOLOGY

Jan Sevink, Peter Attema, Evelien Witmer
The Astura river valley and Satricum, an assessment of current environmental and landscape archaeological data — 13

Luca Alessandri, Clarissa Belardelli, Peter Attema, Francesca Cortese, Mario Federico Rolfo, Jan Sevink, Wouter van Gorp
Bronze and Iron Age salt production on the Italian Tyrrhenian coast. *An overview* — 25

Gabriele Cifani
Tecniche edilizie e societá nel Lazio Arcaico — 41

Tymon De Haas
Contextualising ceramic production at Satricum
*An economic perspective on Archaic and early Roman South Latium* — 51

## MATERIALIZING TECHNOLOGY (BUILDINGS & INFRASTRUCTURES)

Marijke Gnade
Satricum: studio delle tecniche edilizie fra *chaîne opératoire* ed analisi del paesaggio — 71

Seth Bernard
A *chaîne opératoire* approach to the development of early ashlar masonry at Rome — 85

Sophie Helas
Le fortificazioni di Gabii (dal X al VI sec. a.C.).
*Tecniche di costruzione e riflessioni sulle modalità di trasferimento di tecnologia* — 97

Barbara Belelli Marchesini
Il santuario monumentale nell'insediamento marittimo di Pyrgi.
*Edilizia e procedimenti costruttivi* — 107

## MATERIALIZING TECHNOLOGY (MOBILE OBJECTS)

Martina Revello Lami
Fluctuation and stability
*Materialising technological knowledge among Satricum potters* — 129

Alessandro M. Jaia
Produzioni di ceramica a vernice nera nell'area costiera del Latium Vetus — 145

Valeria Acconcia, Serafino Lorenzo Ferreri
Ironworking between the Early Iron Age and the Archaic period
*A view from the Middle-Adriatic region* — 153

Romina Laurito
Technology and tradition of textile production during the first millennium BC in southern Etruria — 169

Artemios Oikonomou
The core formed glass from Satricum
*An overall assessment* — 179

## VISUALIZING TECHNOLOGY

Loes Opgenhaffen
Identifying past building practices through 3D modelling
*The case of the late Archaic temple of Satricum* — 191

Jesús García Sánchez, Jitte Waagen
Built environment in Satricum
*Tracing technology and Archaic society using Remote Sensing tools* — 213

Wieke de Neef, Burkart Ullrich
Tracing protohistoric technology using geophysical techniques in Italy and the Crimea — 227

## POSTERS

Sadi Maréchal, Nathalie de Haan, Tim Clerbaut
Manufacturing *tubuli*
*An experimental reconstruction of the chaîne opératoire based on archaeological evidence* — 243

Amanda Sengeløv, Giswinne van de Wijdeven, Marijke Gnade,
Andrea Waters-Rist, Jason Laffoon
Buried in Satricum
*A bioarchaeological examination of isotopes ($^{87}Sr/^{86}Sr$ and $\delta^{18}O$) and dental nonmetric traits to assess human mobility in a Post-Archaic context* — 249

Agostino Sotgia
Vasai di montagna
*Ricostruire i modelli di sapere condiviso tra le comunità artigianali dei monti della Tolfa nel Bronzo Finale. Spunti di ricerca* — 255

List of Contributors — 265

# Tracing Technology
## *Forty years of archaeological research at Satricum*

*Marijke Gnade, Martina Revello Lami*

Introduction

To celebrate the 40th anniversary of the Satricum Project, a three-day international conference was held in Rome in October 2017 under the aegis of the University of Amsterdam and the Royal Netherlands Institute in Rome. This volume gathers the contributions presented during the symposium and aims to showcase the recent activities carried out at Satricum alongside other relevant sites in Central Italy as well as to share new challenges and innovative lines of inquiry that will direct future archaeological research in the region and beyond.*

Over the years, the diverse nature of archaeological evidence brought to light at Satricum provided all scholars involved in the project with the unique opportunity to pursue different research paths, to investigate a wide range of themes and to experiment with as many methodologies and analytical approaches. To acknowledge to the variety of topics addressed during such a long-term research program, the three-day conference was concentrated on the multifaceted subject of technology, which encompasses in its broadest meaning all social, economic and cultural aspects of human agency.

Technology has played a key role in archaeology since its inception, being generally considered a major causal motor for cultural evolution. The reconstruction of technological systems figures prominently in most research on ancient communities because of the intrinsic nature of the archaeological record, mainly consisting of the material remains produced by past human activities. Artefacts, structures and even landscapes created and shaped by people have multiple physical dimensions that prompt technical description and analysis. To provide such detailed descriptions, archaeology has developed a wealth of theoretical approaches and high-end technical gadgetry to retrieve and analyse those artefacts and tools that testify to the technological knowledge of ancient communities. In this sense, the long research history of the Satricum project epitomizes the salient developments of archaeology as a discipline.

Looking back: archaeological research at Satricum between Tradition and Technological Innovation

*The discovery of Satricum*

Forty years of systematically conducted archaeological research in the Latin settlement of ancient Satricum (nowadays Le Ferriere) have produced an outstandingly rich and varied archaeological record, which shows evidence of uninterrupted habitation over a period of nearly 900 years, from the early Iron Age to the early Imperial Period. Huts, houses, burial grounds, a road system with associated dwellings and votive deposits which belong to the city's main sanctuary of Mater Matuta, represent the chief material sources that allow us to reconstruct the complex and multi-layered biography of this settlement. At the same time, it offers a wide range of possibilities to explore aspects of technology, the subject of the international symposium organised in October 2017 at the Royal Dutch Institute in Rome, and the very place where the project started on invitation of the *Comitato per l'Archeologia Laziale* in 1977.

The Satricum excavations began as an emergency excavation. Modern agricultural activities seriously endangered the ancient site, which had been discovered already in 1896 by the French archaeologist Henri Graillot and subsequently excavated by the Italian excavator, Raniero Mengarelli.[1] Over the following two years, Mengarelli and his team unearthed the remains of the temple complex of Mater Matuta as well as the remains of large buildings around the sanctuary and part of an ancient road leading to it. Underneath these remains he discovered a rich record of Iron Age traces, amongst which were several huts. He excavated the votive deposit belonging to the earliest phases of the Mater Matuta sanctuary - one of the richest votive deposits of Latium - and discovered a second one from the Hellenistic period opposite the temple complex. An inscribed cippus from the late republican period with a dedication to Mater Matuta was found in its surroundings and confirmed the identification of the temple with the one mentioned in the written sources.[2] In the area northwest of the acropolis he found an Iron Age burial ground with cremation and inhumation graves and some very rich chamber tombs dating to the 7th century BC.[3] After some preliminary publications in the *Notizie degli Scavi* and renewed excavations between 1907-1910, during which Mengarelli found a small sanctuary in the southwest area of the settlement, all data disappeared into a drawer and the remains became overgrown.[4] Small-scale excavations in the thirties and fifties remained unpublished. All that remained visible of Satricum were the selected finds exhibited in two rooms of the National Museum of the Villa Giulia and many more finds in its store rooms.[5]

*The re-discovery of Satricum and the beginning of Dutch archaeological research*

It was this exceptionally rich archaeological record, which was 'rediscovered' in 1976 with the exhibition *Civiltà del Lazio primitivo*,[6] as well as the growing awareness that Satricum and other ancient Latin settlements were about to be destroyed by large scale agricultural activities and modern urbanisation, that led to the decision to resume archaeological research in Satricum. Its main aim was to document and save what could still be saved of the neglected archaeological remains. The Dutch Institute in Rome was invited by the Italian authorities to reopen research in Satricum, and in October 1977 a combined team of archaeologists of the Dutch Institute in Rome and the Rijksuniversiteit of Groningen, led by Conrad Stibbe and Marianne Maaskant-Kleibrink respectively, resumed the excavation activities at the site. For more than 10 years the teams conducted systematic archaeological research on the acropolis in which they combined the new results with the old data of Mengarelli and at the same time studied the huge collections stored and exhibited in the Villa Giulia Museum.[7] In these early years several new Iron Age huts were discovered, which brought the total to circa 47 and thereby made Satricum one of the best documented sites of the Iron Age in Latium.[8]

One hut was conspicuous because of its position between the walls of the first stone temple. This special position led to its interpretation as the oldest cult place,[9] an interpretation which is, however, not shared by everyone. At the same time, three consecutive stone temple buildings could be identified in the mass of foundational tufa blocks which had been found during the excavations of the 19th century.[10] During the cleaning of the blocks an exceptional discovery was made: one of the tufa blocks of the foundation of Temple II (500-480 BC) revealed a monumental inscription in archaic Latin in two lines which arguably contained the name of Publius Valerius, one of the founding fathers of the Roman Republic.[11] The publication of the inscription in 1980 led to a spate of studies which mainly discussed the missing letters at the beginning of the text or the identification of the person mentioned.

Directly related to the re-excavation of the sanctuary was the meticulous research conducted in the store rooms of the Villa Giulia Museum, which resulted in thousands of fragments of architectural terracottas being attributed to the three main temple phases; each phase brought new types, styles and techniques of terracotta.[12] Most spectacular was the reconstruction of a series of nearly life-size terracotta statues which were mounted along the ridge-pool of the roof of the late Archaic temple and represented pairs of gods in combat with giants in a *gigantomachy*.[13]

Apart from evidence about the earliest Iron Age settlement, the excavations also revealed many remains of large buildings - courtyards as well as smaller buildings - from the Archaic period, bringing the total number of buildings around the temple to at least 23.[14]

With regard to the cult practices of Mater Matuta, it became clear that the large votive deposit associated with the earliest cult activities of Mater Matuta had been thoroughly removed by the team of Mengarelli without leaving any visible trace. However, several smaller votive pits containing votive offerings dating to the same period were found in its direct surroundings beneath the stone foundations of the sanctuary.[15] The Hellenistic votive deposit, also known from the 19th-century excavations, was re-excavated in the period between 1986-1990. These excavations revealed that its original function was that of a cistern constructed in the first half of the 7th century BC, which was converted into a deposit for votive offerings only at the end of the 3rd century BC.[16] In 1983, a third deposit, for chronological reasons known as votive deposit II, was discovered in a long natural depression northwest of the temple. Instead of the primarily terracotta votive offerings found in the Hellenistic deposit, the objects in deposit II consisted mainly of pottery, mostly domestic wares dating from the 5th-3rd centuries BC. The interpretation of the deposit as an open votive deposit in which objects were put during special ritual occasions has been discussed.[17]

Simultaneously with the discovery of the new deposit, a small burial ground with circa 30 inhumation graves dating from the 5th century BC was found at the southwest side of the temple.[18]

The burial ground showed many similarities with a 5th-century burial ground containing more than 200 inhumation graves that was excavated between 1980-1986 in the southwest area of the archaic town, within its 6th-century city boundaries.[19] Both burial grounds were attributed to the Volscians, people from the mountainous hinterland of Latium, who according to the historical sources occupied the town of Satricum at the beginning of the 5th century BC.

Though the attention of the excavators in these years increasingly turned towards the lower settlement area as the result of several unexpected discoveries, excavations on the acropolis hill continued at a steady pace resulting in still more discoveries, such as the remains of a mid-Republican villa from the 3rd-2nd centuries in the southeast area of the hill.[20]

*The most recent past: the research conducted by the University of Amsterdam*

In 1991 the excavation project was transferred to the University of Amsterdam and came under the direction of Marijke Gnade. Where the first two decades of the project had been mainly interested in the acropolis of the town, from the late nineties the focus shifted more and more to the lower settlement area, west of the acropolis. Already in 1984 an emergency excavation was organized in order to save the remains of a monumental road which appeared during levelling activities in the northern part of the ancient town, known as *Poggio dei Cavallari*.[21] Presumably the road led to the acropolis and therefore to the sanctuary, where its end had already been discovered in the 19th century. The excavation of the road was resumed in the late nineties and since 2004 constitutes, together with its surrounding area, the main focus of the archaeological research. So far the road has been documented over a length of 440 metres revealing continuation in a westerly direction towards the central gate of the settlement.[22] It shows at least two crossroads that lead to the southern part of the town and two large buildings alongside its south side, which are of the courtyard-type known from the acropolis. The road and its associated buildings form part of a large-scale renovation of the town, which was undertaken in tandem with the construction of the late-Archaic monumental temple dated to 500-480 BC. With a width of c. 5-6 meter and its particular way of construction (the pavement is supported at the sides by foundation walls of circa 1 m high which consist of two stacked tufa blocks), the road is considered a technical masterpiece.[23] Excavations of its deepest levels revealed clear traces of Iron Age occupation similar to those found on the acropolis. These recent findings will certainly change the traditional ideas about the settlement's development from a small hut village on the acropolis to a fully-fledged town of circa 55 hectares.

In the same area, a third necropolis has recently been discovered that consists of circa 50 inhumation graves of the same cultural background as the burial grounds which were earlier found in the southwest part of the settlement and on the acropolis.[24] The graves were either on the north side of the road or were dug through the walking level of the road itself and the foundations of the buildings alongside, both of which appear to have been abandoned after having undergone severe destruction. The presence of burial grounds inside the archaic settlement boundaries indicate how the appearance of the archaic town must have radically changed in the first half of the 5th century BC. Such a radical change accords well with the historical record, which relates the movement of non-Latin mountain-dwelling groups from the Apennine hinterlands towards the Latium area in search of new territory.[25]

Another conspicuous change in the life of Satricum can be observed in the second half of the 4th century BC, when the Volscian cemeteries seem to be no longer in use and even to be obliterated in some zones by new building activities (such as the mid-Republican villa found on the acropolis). In addition, the excavation of the top layers of the road area has clearly revealed occupation traces of this period, as is also underlined by the presence of the Hellenistic votive deposit on the acropolis. The archaeological evidence can be linked with some caution to the historical account that relates numerous encounters between Latin, Volscians and Romans at Satricum, which ultimately led to the installation of a Roman colony in 346 BC.

*Present and Future Research at Satricum*

Today, archaeological research in Satricum is still in full swing. Attention is now directed to the northwest part of the town where the badly preserved remains of a Roman villa from the 1sth century AD are presently being excavated.[26] The villa had been noted already during the 19th-century excavations but at that time had not been considered important enough for further archaeological research.[27] The site is heavily overgrown with large trees and at risk of further damage due to the many roots that affect the foundations of the villa without proper documentation been carried out.

In the last decade, the Satricum excavations have developed from a simple rescue excavation into a valuable and multi-faceted heritage project directed at a wider public. It is within this context that the desire to establish a local archaeological museum should be seen. The initiative for such a museum was taken in 2014, when a semi-permanent exhibition was opened in the local iron factory. This exhibition presents a diachronic panorama of the town's archaeological heritage in close harmony with the historical record. The picture is illustrated by some 750 objects which were carefully selected from the then 35 years of excavations. The idea is to make this museum part of a larger archaeological park centred around the temple complex of Mater Matuta, which since 2000 has been protected by a wooden roofing and open to the public. Both the exhibition (which has been extended every year since the opening) and the acropolis with its covered temple remains have been the focus of cultural events in recent years, such as a performance of Shakespeare's Coriolanus, organised in 2016 and 2017 by the University of Amsterdam and performed by local authors and musicians.

Meanwhile, archaeological research continues and spans from landscape and geomorphological analysis to the study of the settlement's organisation, infrastructures, monumental architecture, domestic buildings, funerary contexts and material culture. Keeping in theme with the volume, the ongoing research at Satricum is now assisted by cutting edge technologies such as geophysical prospection, LiDAR and drone exploration, as well as 3D visualization applied to landscape, buildings and artefacts. The study of artefacts in particular is central to the project and is characterised by the integration of several analytical techniques such as petrographic and chemical analysis, use wear and experimental studies. The combination of all these methods increases exponentially the quality and quantity of data available for Satricum, continuously adding to our knowledge of the town. Thanks to the systematic application of 3D technology it will be possible to interpret and visualize old and newly acquired archaeological evidence within a virtual environment, ultimately bringing to life the unearthed remains of ancient Satricum.

The archaeological research has, more than anything else, been made possible by the trust the Italian Ministry of *Beni Culturali* has put into the Dutch teams and the constant positive cooperation by the *Soprintendenza archeologica del Lazio*. Moreover, the support and cooperation by the owner of the terrain that hides the remains of the northern urban area of ancient Satricum, *Casale del Giglio*, has been of immense value in saving the archaeological heritage. Last but by no means least, the municipality of Latina and the inhabitants of Le Ferriere must be thanked for their constant support.

LOOKING FORWARD: TRACING TECHNOLOGICAL INNOVATION AND SOCIAL LEARNING IN THE ARCHAEOLOGICAL RECORD

*Archaeological approaches to technology in a nutshell*

From Binford's "man's extrasomatic means of adaptation"[28] to Dobres's "mutual becoming of people and products",[29] the definition of technology has been a complex matter in archaeology, which inevitably mirrors the many theoretical turns taken by the discipline. The materialistic and positivist standpoints underpinning New Archaeology interpreted technology as synonymous with culture and thus tracing the history of technology through the material record came to equate the possibility of writing the history of culture. Even though processual archaeologists provided a solid scientific method to connect artefacts, sites, landscapes and environment to societies, they also favoured a deterministic view of the past that drew upon grand narratives such as "progress" or "economic efficiency" all hinting to the special character inherent to Western civilization. The resulting explanatory models are based on the social and biological concepts of evolution and the underlying assumption that "the history of technology has been one of inevitable and accelerating progress toward modernity".[30] The emergence of behavioural approaches to the archaeology of technology, though deeply rooted in the processual construct, contributed to broaden the interpretative framework by including analytical methods borrowed from neighbouring disciplines such as anthropology and ethnography.[31] The description of performance characteristics of raw materials and manual dexterity of tool makers became central to behavioural archaeologists paving the way to more fine-grained analysis of manufacturing processes. However, an idea of inevitability and/or progress toward modernity survives in their interpretation of technological developments, thus revealing that evolutionary concepts were still looming in the background.

The ensuing major theoretical shift toward a humanistic interpretation of technology has been inspired by a number of different intellectual traditions such as structuralism, symbolic studies, social anthropology, gender and agency theory.

Within these approaches, technology is seen as the materialisation of prevailing worldviews, social values and cultural attitudes dictating how to live and act in a community. In other words, according to Kohring, technology can be understood as "a knowledge system which we use to construct our world but at the same time, technology shapes us, constructs our world and becomes a principle avenue for communicating social meanings".[32] This definition emphasises the interaction between people and artefacts, the way in which people have control over the material world and how the material world influences them.

Methodologically, archaeologists interpreting technology as a social construct contributed to the development of a powerful conceptual framework conventionally referred to as *chaîne opératoire*,[33] which aims to reconstruct the sequence of events and human choices leading to the creation, use and discard of an object. Translated as operational sequence and more generally defined as "life history" research, it documents in extraordinary detail the ordered train of actions, bodily gestures, instruments and agents leading the transformation of a given material toward the manufacture of a product. The relevance of the agent joining the chaîne opératoire becomes central to this formulation, highlighting how the succession of technological actions connecting materials, humans or other sources of energy, practices, tools and knowledge can be studied together in a continuum. The focal point shifts from the end-product to the process of making it and extends further to include the whole life cycle of an artefact and its interaction with the community that produced and used it.[34] However, considering the chaîne opératoire just as an object of study would be a narrow definition. In fact, the broad spectrum of topics possibly addressed through this notion have gradually turned it from a subject to a line of research, or as Dobres puts it "an interpretative methodology and analytical method capable of forging robust inferential links between the material patterning of technical acts and the sociopolitical relations of production accounting for them".[35]

This volume offers a range of contributions highlighting how valuable the chaîne opératoire has become as a conceptual framework: from changes in landscape dynamics and settlement patterns (Sevink et al., Alessandri et al., De Haas, Gnade, Garcia Sanchez & Waagen, De Neef & Ullrich), to the development of innovative building techniques (Cifani, Gnade, Bernard, Helas), construction systems (Belelli Marchesini, Opgenhaffen), glass making and pottery production (Oikonomou, Jaia, Marechal et al., Revello Lami, Sotgia), metalworking (Acconcia & Ferreri) and weaving (Laurito). A wide array of analytical techniques are applied across these studies to attain a comprehensive reconstruction of the operational sequence, including: petrographic and chemical analysis (Revello Lami, Jaia, Oikonomou, Sengelov et al.) use-wear, waste products, refitting, experimentation and diacritical studies (Laurito), identification of late reshaping or functional changes (Helas, Opgenhaffen. Belelli Marchesini). In addition, long-term frameworks such as settlement pattern analysis to identify dynamics of production, consumption, use and discard (De Haas) and depositional and post-depositional processes (Alessandri, Sevink et al., Gnade) are also considered.

Within this broad framework, all papers bring to the fore an understanding of technological systems as socially and contextually situated phenomena, where the relationship between people and artefacts is mediated through the technological process. Any variation along such process reflects the agency of both people (individuals and communities) and objects.[36] Not surprisingly, the analysis of episodes of change and innovation, adoption and rejection of new technological systems – particularly visible in the material record thanks to the diachronic perspective - lies at the core of much archaeological research on technology carried out at Satricum and represents a common thread running through this volume.

*The adoption of innovation and its social context: a view from Satricum*

Technological innovations – as aptly described by Fogarty, Creanza and Feldman - can occur via multiple interacting processes and at multiple scales.[37] In many models of social learning new information penetrates into a population via trial and error or individual interaction with natural and social environment, which is then culturally transferred. The accumulation of newly acquired information may explain for instance some of the bursts of building activity that are observed in the archaeological record at Satricum, like the consecutive increases in complexity near the transitions from the 7th to the 6th century BC and from the mid-6th to the early 5th BC as reflected in the succeeding temple phases excavated on the acropolis or in the sophisticated road system implemented in the lower settlement at the turn of the 6th BC. The introduction of new ideas and information may provide an account of the dynamics of technological development at Satricum also in historical times, if we think for instance of the dramatic changes that intensive agriculture and uncontrolled urbanization caused to the area in the last century.

The ways in which new information travels have been the subject of sociological research since the 30s, when diffusion of innovations and contagion theories were formulated and used to examine the spread of new ideas and techniques. One such study by Everett Rogers focused the discussion on the variability in uptake of new technologies within a community. In his seminal work on the mechanism triggering the diffusion of innovation, he demonstrated the importance of interpersonal relationships and social interaction as opposed to knowledge. From this follows Roger's well-known interpretative model that splits adopters into different categories depending on their predisposition toward novel information and technology. From the cosmopolitan and adventurous innovators eager to try new ideas, through the early adopters, usually profiled as respectable local elites with the highest degree of opinion leadership, innovation spreads to the early majority, whose innovation-decision period is relatively longer, but play a fundamental role in the diffusion network. They are in fact an important link between the innovators and the more sceptical late majority up to the last ones in the social system to surrender to new information, lagging far behind in the innovation-decision process.[38]

Such classification is admittedly a simplification; however, it serves to break into different stages the diffusion process and visualize a focal point, i.e. the gap in innovation uptake at both community and individual level. The distance between knowing about an innovation and adopting it represents the gap, and the size of the gap will vary through time depending on the attitude toward that innovation (either positive or negative) manifested by various groups. The eventual adoption (or rejection) of the innovation proves to be a socially and culturally situated practice, thus reiterating the significance of interpreting technology as a social construct.[39]

Archaeology, then, is in a privileged position to understand how ancient communities perceived and transferred new ideas and techniques, because observing phenomena over a longer span of time provides greater awareness, if not necessarily understanding of the pre-requisites for the adoption of innovation. The research carried out at Satricum and presented in this book enables us to observe the way in which ancient communities have changed and adapted to their environment, the emergence of technological knowledge among Satrican communities and how those communities shared that technological knowledge, with new techniques and styles adopted and adapted to both the material locally available as well as the skilfulness of people. Technology is our window onto change at Satricum, and bringing together such a diverse range of scholarship allows us to see and understand the ancient Satrican community in a way they have never been seen before.

VOLUME OVERVIEW

The papers in the present volume grapple with technology as a complex cultural phenomenon embedded in specific worldviews, social practices and human agency. At the same time, they establish the important role that investigating technological knowledge systems plays in crafting the history of not only single technical events and choices, but more broadly the social and cultural context in which they took place. The contributions have been organised according to four different themes, each one representing a different angle through which technology might be addressed, namely:

- Contextualizing Technology
- Materializing Technology #1 (Buildings and Infrastructures)
- Materializing Technology #2 (Mobile Objects)
- Visualizing Technology

The geographical context revolves mainly around Central Italy, including case studies from both the Tyrrhenian and Adriatic regions and spanning the Bronze Age to the late republican period. Satricum serves as the focal point in all sections, alongside other major settlements in Etruria and Lazio, such as Rome, Gabii and Pyrgi, as well as Marche, Abruzzo and Calabria.

*Contextualizing Technology*

Landscape and different environmental conditions are central to our understanding of long-term settlement and land use dynamics and essential indicators of the mutual relationship occurring between people and the material world. The evidence archived in archaeological and sedimentological data testifies to the constant interplay between man and environment through technology. This section opens with the research by J. Sevink, P. Attema and E. Witmer in the Agro Pontino, which brings to the fore the peculiar role played by river valleys in terms of human frequentation and population growth across the region. Through the integration of survey, excavation and palaeoenvironmental studies, the authors show how the river Astura profoundly impacted the way in which ancient communities have adapted to and have changed their environment, setting the pace for infrastructural development (bridges, drainages systems etc.) and nautical engineering (as in the case of the flat-bottomed boats "sandali"). A similar call for the integration of palaeoenvironmental data to extant archaeological evidence is made by Luca Alessandri et al. in their analysis of salt production in Tyrrhenian Italy. Too often the identification of production sites overlooks contextual data such as distance from salt sources, availability of large quantities of fuel to carry out the *briquetage* process, highlighting a knowledge gap in the chaîne opératoire of salt producing systems.

Gabriele Cifani's overview of the innovations characterising architecture and building technologies in Latium Vetus at the turn of the 6th century BC provides further evidence for the interdependence of available raw sources, technological choices and artisanal skills. The shift from structures mostly made of wood and mudbricks to masonry highlights not only a change in the raw material procurement strategy (from short to long distance) and the emergence of shared metric standards, but more generally attests to the close connection between changing socioeconomic and technological systems.

The last contribution in this section reviews the extant evidence for pottery production to explore the dynamic interaction between context, technology and people. In his multi scalar analysis of ceramic workshops at Satricum and its surroundings, Tymon De Haas addresses the sociopolitical and economic variables affecting technological choices, focusing in particular on the fluctuations in potters' output, production volume, market demand and consumption levels recorded from the Archaic to the late Republican period.

*Materializing Technology, 1# Buildings and Infrastructures*

The second and third sections of the volume shift the attention from the context within which technological choices take place to their outcome, i. e. the artefact. Section two in particular turns the spotlight on the building industry and architectural engineering. The scale of analysis of all papers is site-related and shares the common aim to demonstrate how the detailed identification of technical sequences underlying ancient building craft practices may contribute to bridge the gap between artifice and artefacts, people and products.

Marijke Gnade and Seth Bernard adopt a chaîne opératoire approach in order to reconstruct the entire series of technical actions through which infrastructures and monumental buildings have been constructed respectively in Archaic Satricum and Rome. In particular, Gnade offers a detailed account of the technological endeavour spent to build the elaborate road system in the lower settlement of the city, an operation that perfectly represents the mutual influence between the Satrican community and its environment.

Bernard observes the changes in the raw materials used in ashlar masonry to evaluate shifts in technological knowledge and labour organisation in Archaic Rome. The development of ashlar masonry at Gabii is the common denominator also in Sophie Helas contribution. The thorough review of the technical developments recorded in the ensuing defensive structures of the town enables the author to trace not only the emergence of innovative building practices and specialised craftmanship, but also the wider artisanal network through which such innovations reached Gabii, arguing in favour of a close connection between the Latial town and Southern Italy.

Lastly, Barbara Belelli Marchesini brings to the fore Etruscan architecture by using the monumental temple A and B at Pyrgi as a case study. Belelli Marchesini presents the two well-known sacred buildings in an original perspective: her attention focuses in particular on the elusive traces left by the machinery used at the site in order to construct both temples. This too often neglected evidence allows the author to suggest the type of leverage systems and devices utilised during the erection of the structures, a key factor for understanding technical skills, organisation of labour and knowledge transfer between artisanal communities.

*Materializing Technology, 2# Mobile Objects*

The third thematic area keeps the focus on the end-product of technology, but in this case with particular reference to mobile objects (pottery, metals, textiles and glass). The case studies presented address the reconstruction of technological systems by exploiting several different analytical techniques spanning from petrographic and chemical analysis integrated with geoprospection of raw sources (Revello Lami, Oikonomou), use-wear analysis and experimental research (Laurito), archaeometallurgical analysis (Acconcia & Ferreri), chrono-typological and macroscopic fabric analysis (Jaia).

Martina Revello Lami and Alessandro Jaia open the section with two works addressing pottery production systems. Revello Lami's contribution uses a specific case study, the red slipped ware produced at Satricum, to illustrate how visible and invisible characteristics of ceramic artefacts tell different stories in terms of adoption of innovative techniques or perpetuation of traditions among Satricum potters. Alessandro Jaia provides a detailed analysis of the production of black gloss wares at Lavinium and Ardea in order to reconstruct the transmission of new ideas and technologies among the potting community located on the Latial littoral and the impact that a growing market and production centre like Rome exerted on them.

Based on the extant archaeological evidence for bronze and iron metallurgy in the Middle-Adriatic area and the unfortunately scanty metallographic data available in the region, Valeria Acconcia and Lorenzo Ferreri provide a detailed description of the metalworking chaîne opératoire in the study area, from raw material extraction to transport, processing and manufacturing. By comparing earlier bronzeworking to ironworking activities, they shed new light on the ways in which technical knowledge and practices were transferred among craftsmen.

The search for tradition and innovation, local and foreign inputs as expressed through the material record lies at the core of both Laurito's and Oikonomou's works. Romina Laurito in particular records continuities and discontinuities within Etruscan textile production relying on the wealth of data retrieved from the often-understudied record of tools utilised to spin and weave fabrics. Lastly, Artemios Oikonomou presents the results of the chemical analysis conducted on the glass fragments found in the Hellenistic Votive Deposit at Satricum, which has contributed to pinning down the provenance of the diverse raw materials used and outline a very diverse glass manufacturing tradition as well as a wide trade network in Mid- and Late Republican Satricum and Central Italy.

As a corollary of this section, two short essays in the appendix of the volume address material culture and technology from two different perspectives: Sandi Maréchal, Nathalie De Haan and Tim Clerbaut walk us through all the phases of the elaborate manufacture of Roman *tubuli*. The series of experiments they conducted demonstrate a complex, risky and time-consuming production process, which explains why *tubuli* were highly valued and expensive artefacts in ancient Rome. Lastly, Agostino Sotgia illustrates the potential of embedding the concept of "community of practice" within more traditional approaches to pottery studies in order to unravel the social dynamics underlying technological choices among the potters of the Tolfa Mountains in Bronze Age South Etruria.

*Visualizing Technology*

The last section of the volume addresses the issue of visualizing ancient technological systems for research and dissemination purposes. Loes Opgenhaffen's fine-grained reconstruction of the Temple of Mater Matuta offers a great example of the potential of applying 3D technology to the study of ancient building practices. In addition to the established value in terms of musealisation, the process of visualizing every single element of the sacred complex allows the author not only to revise the tangible architectural data at our disposal, but also to reconstruct the intangible sequence of choices and events underlying the technical process of building the temple.

Turning to landscape reconstruction, Jesús García Sánchez and Jitte Waagen call for a more systematic application of geospatial and remote sensing methods to archaeological research in Latium Vetus. By using Satricum as a case study, the authors demonstrate how the combination of LiDAR data, LAU Photogrammetry and aerial imagery can integrate archaeological and survey evidence in a non-invasive way and add to our understanding of land-use, episodes of extension or contraction of ancient settlements and more generally the level of technical endeavour spent in order to modify the environment. In the same vein is the work of Wieke De Neef and Burkart Ullrich, who illustrate how geophysical techniques contribute to archaeology when it comes to characterising technological traditions and production strategies in protohistoric societies. In particular, the case studies presented from Southern Italy (Marche and Calabria) and Crimea investigate both large-scale operations requiring the effort of a community, and medium-scale operations at a household level and demonstrate how geophysical surveys combined with surface collections and soil studies can reveal complex processes of construction and production. Lastly, the essay by Amanda Sengelov, Giswinne van de Wijdeven and Marijke Gnade in the appendix of this volume reviews the bioarchaeological data yielded from several funerary contexts at Satricum, providing another example of how cutting-edge analytical technologies contribute to visualizing a more detailed picture of ancient communities, their mobility and connectivity.

All case studies represent a first effort to consolidate a theoretical approach favouring a humanistic interpretation of technology and to demonstrate how such an approach might be applied to current archaeological research in the history and protohistory of Central Italy. In doing so, the whole volume seeks to emphasize the pivotal role of the social aspects of technology as they embed the cognitive frameworks where demands for goods and information are developed and expressed, knowledge is transferred, ideas are developed, and innovation happens.

NOTES

* The conference was made possible thanks to the generous financial support of the Amsterdam Universiteits Fonds and the research funding of the Amsterdam Centre of Ancient Studies and Archaeology of the University of Amsterdam. The Villa Giulia Museum hosted the opening lectures of the conference as well as the reception and musical performance in its beautiful garden. The Royal Dutch Institute in Rome hosted the conference of the following two days and accommodated the organisational committee. Casale del Giglio kindly offered the wine for lunches and receptions.
1. For the preliminary reports of the Italian excavations published in the *Notizie degli Scavi*, see Barnabei 1896a-c; Barnabei/Cozza 1896; Barnabei/Mengarelli 1896; Mengarelli 1898; see also Waarsenburg 1998; Cifani 2010.
2. Barnabei/ Mengarelli 1896, 195-196.
3. Waarsenburg 1995, for the publication of the excavations of the graves of the Northwest Necropolis by Mengarelli.
4. Ginge 1996, for the publication of the 1907-1910 excavations.
5. Della Seta 1918 for the finds exhibited in the Museum of the Villa Giulia.
6. *CatLazio primitivo* 1976.
7. For an overview of the new and old excavations on the acropolis, see *CatSaticum* 2007.
8. Stobbe in *CatSatrium* 2007, 20-28
9. Stibbe 1980.
10. De Waele 1981; also Knoop/Lulof in *CatSatricum* 2007, 32-36.
11. Stibbe *et al.* 1980 for the *editio princeps* of the Lapis Satricanus.
12. Knoop 1987 for the publication of the antefixes of the first two temple buildings; see also Knoop/Lulof in *CatSatricum* 2007, 36-42.
13. Lulof 1996; see also Knoop/Lulof in *CatSatricum* 2007, 36-42.
14. Maaskant-Kleibrink 1987; 1992. A third volume on the excavations conducted by the University of Groningen on the acropolis is now in preparation. See also Gnade 1997, 2003, 2004; Gnade/Stobbe 2012.
15. Stobbe in *CatSatricum* 2007, 24-26.
16. Heldring in *CatSatricum* 2007, 78-81; Kruijf, van der, in *CatSatricum* 2007, 82-84; also Gnade 2016
17. Bouma 1996 for the publication of the deposit; Gnade 2002, 31-49 for the discussion.
18. Maaskant-Kleibrink 1992, 101-105.
19. Gnade 1992.
20. Louwaard in *CatSatricum* 2007, 75-77.
21. Heldring 1985, 75; Heldring/Stibbe 1987.
22. Gnade 2002; see also Gnade 2006, 2007, 2009, 2011.
23. Gnade 2017.
24. Gnade 2011, 2012. The publication of this third necropolis is now in preparation.
25. See infra Sengelov et al.
26. Heldring 1985, 72-75, for the report on the first research on the Roman villa in 1984; also Raaymakers in *CatSatricum* 2007, 86-90.
27. Barnabei/Mengarelli 1896, 199.
28. Binford 1965, 209.
29. Dobres 2009, 104
30. Adams 1999, 131.
31. Schiffer 2001.
32. Kohring 2013, 2.
33. Balfet 1991; Cresswell 1983; Edmonds 1990; Martinon Torres 2002.
34. Sillar and Tite 2000.
35. Dobres 1999, 124.
36. See Revello Lami in this volume.
37. Fogarty *et al.* 2015, pp. 736-754.
38. Rogers 1983.
39. This is the so called "Knowledge-Attitude-Practice Gap" (KAP Gap) theorized by Rogers, which highlights how the "attitude" or social reaction may affect the spread of new ideas and technologies. The effectiveness of the KAP gap as an analytical tool has been however profoundly revised by sociologists, arguing that it only treats attitude as a dichotomy of positive or negative and in that it only examines relationships and time. Such a limitation has been overcome by incorporating space into the equation. In fact, understanding how environment and space affect the transmission of ideas is key to understanding social and technological transmissions (Barash 2011, 15).

BIBLIOGRAPHY

Adams, R.M. 1999, Book review of T. Ingold, Paths of Fire: An Anthropologist's Inquiry into Western Technology, *Technology and Culture* 40(1), 130-131.

Balfet, A. (ed.) 1991, *Observer l'action technique: De chaînes opératoires, pour quoi faire?*, Paris.

Barash, V. 2011, *The Dynamics of Social Contagion*. Unpublished Ph.D.) Cornell University, Ann Arbor.

Barnabei, F. 1896a, Conca, *NSc* 1896, 69.

Barnabei, F. 1896b, Conca. Nuove scoperte nell'area dell'antico tempio presso le Ferriere, *NSc* 1896, 99-102.

Barnabei, F. 1896c, Conca. Nuove indagini nell'area dell'antico tempio presso le Ferriere, *NSc* 1896, 167.

Barnabei, F./A. Cozza 1896, Conca. Di un antico tempio scoperto presso Le Ferriere nella tenuta di Conca, dove si pone la sede della città di Satricum, *NSc* 1896, 23-48.

Barnabei, F./R. Mengarelli 1896, Conca. Nuovi scavi nel tempio satrican di Mater Matuta, scoperto sulla collina presso le Ferriere di Conca, *NSc* 1896, 190-200.

Binford, L.R. 1965, Archaeological Systematics and the Study of Culture Process, *American Antiquity* 31.2 (1), 203-210.

Bouma, J.W. 1996, Religio Votiva. *The Archaeology of Latial Votive Religion. The 5th-3rd c. BC votive deposit south west of the main temple at <Satricum> Borgo Le Ferriere*. PhD thesis, Rijksuniversiteit Groningen, Groningen.

*CatLazioPrimitivo* 1976: G. Colonna (ed.), Satricum, in *Civiltà del Lazio primitivo* (Exh. cat. Rome 1976), Rome.

*CatAreaSacra* 1985: P. Chiarucci/T. Gizzi (eds.), *Area sacra di Satricum tra scavo e restituzione* (Exh. cat. Albano 1985), Rome.

*CatSatricum* 2007: M. Gnade (ed.), *Satricum. Trenta anni di scavi olandesi*. (Exh. cat. Le Ferriere 2007-2008), Amsterdam.

Cifani, G. 2010, Satrico (Satricum), in Ch. Michelini/C. Cassanelli (eds.), *Bibliografia topografica della colonizzazione greca in Italia e nelle isole tirreniche* 18, Pisa/Rome/Naples, 382-410.

Cresswell, R. 1983, Transferts de techniques at chaines operatoires, *Technique et Culture* 2, 145-163.

Della Seta, A. 1918, *Il Museo di Villa Giulia*, Rome.

De Waele, J.A.K.E. 1981, I templi della Mater Matuta di Satricum, *MededRom* 43, 7-68.

Dobres, M.A. 1999, Technology's links and chaînes. The processual unfolding of technique and technician, in M.A, Dobres/C.R. Hoffman (eds.) *The social dynamics of technology: practice, politics and world views*, Washington, 124-146.

Dobres, M.A. 2009, Archaeologies of technology, *Cambridge Journal of Economics* 34, 103–114.

Fogarty, L./N. Creanza/M.W. Feldman 2015, Cultural evolutionary perspectives on creativity and human innovation, *Trends in ecology & evolution* 30(12), 736-754.

Ginge, B. 1996, *Excavations at Satricum (Borgo Le Ferriere) 1907-1910: Northwest Necropolis, Southwest Sanctuary and Acropolis*, Amsterdam.

Gnade, M.1992, *The Southwest Necropolis of Satricum. Excavations 1981-1986*, Amsterdam.

Gnade, M. 1997, Le ricerche olandesi a Satricum dal 1977 ad oggi, *MededRom* 56, 37-55.

Gnade, M. 2002, *Satricum in the Post-Archaic Period. A Case Study of the Interpretation of Archaeological remains as Indicators of Ethno-Cultural Identity*, Leuven 2002.

Gnade, M. 2003, Satricum: la prosecuzione delle ricerche, *Lazio & Sabina* 1, 213-220.

Gnade, M. 2004, Resoconto degli scavi olandesi a Satricum nel 2002, *Lazio & Sabina* 2, 265-272.

Gnade, M. 2006, La ventottesima campagna di ricerca a Satricum dell'Università di Amsterdam nel 2004, *Lazio & Sabina* 3, 255-260.

Gnade, M. 2007, I risultati della campagna di scavi 2005 e 2006 a Satricum, *Lazio & Sabina* 4, 191-200.

Gnade, M. 2011, Nuovi risultati della ricerca archeologica dell'Università di Amsterdam a *Satricum*, *Lazio & Sabina* 7, 453-463.

Gnade, M. 2012, Satricum 2011: proseguimento delle ricerche, *Lazio & Sabina* 8, 451-457.

Gnade M. 2016, Il Santuario di Satricum. Connessioni mediterranee riflesse nei suoi depositi votive, in A. Russo/F. Guarneri (eds.), *Santuari mediterranei tra oriente e occidente. Interazioni e contatti culturali*, Rome, 73-80.

Gnade M. 2017, Satricum in the Age of Tarquinius Superbus: cambiando prospettiva, in P.S. Lulof/C. Smith, *The Age of Tarquinius Superbus. History and Archaeology. Atti Convegno Internazionale Scuola Britannica Roma (Rome, 09-11-2013)* (Supplement BABESCH 29), Leuven, 249-258.

Gnade, M./J. A. Stobbe 2012, Riflessioni sul santuario di Mater Matuta sull'acropoli di Satricum alla luce delle recenti scoperte archeologiche, in E. Marroni (ed.), *Sacra nominis latini: i santuari del Lazio arcaico e repubblicano. Atti del convegno internationazionale (Roma 2009)* (Volume speciale di Ostraka), Naples, 453-463.

Heldring, B. 1985, L'ottava campagna di scavo dell'Istituto Olandese di Roma a Satricum, *QuadAEI* 11, 72-76.

Heldring, B. 2007, Il deposito votivo III: ua cisterna prima, un deposito votivo dopo, in *CatSatricum* 2007, 78-81.

Heldring, B./C.M. Stibbe 1987, Breve comunicato sulla settima e ottava campagna di scavi a Satricum eseguite nel 1983 e nel 1984, *MededRom* 47, 231-241.

Knoop, R.R. 1987, *Antefixa Satricana. Sixth-century Architectural Terracottas from the Sanctuary of Mater Matuta at Satricum (Le Ferriere)*, Amsterdam.

Knoop, R.R./P.S. Lulof 2007, L'architettura templare, in *CatSatricum* 2007, 32-42.

Kruijf, L.van der 2007, Le terrecotte votiva rinvenute nel deposito votivo III, in *CatSatricum* 2007, 82-84.

Louwaard, M. 2007, L'acropoli: l'edificio di età medio repubblicano, in *CatSatricum* 2007, 75-77.

Lulof, P.S. 1996, *The Ridge-Pole Statues from the Late-Archaic Temple at Satricum*, Amsterdam.

Maaskant-Kleibrink, M. 1987, *Settlement excavations at Borgo Le Ferriere "Satricum" 1. The campaigns 1979, 1980, 1981*, Groningen.

Maaskant-Kleibrink, M. 1992, *Settlement excavations at Borgo Le Ferriere "Satricum" II. The campaigns 1983, 1985 and 1987*, Groningen.

Martinon Torres, M. 2002, Chaîne opératoire: The concept and its applications within the study of technology, *Gallaecia* 21, 29-43.

Mengarelli, R. 1898, Nuove scoperte nella tenuta di Conca nel territorio dell'antica città di Satricum, *NSc* 1898, 167-171.

Raaymakers, R. 2007, La villa romana, in *CatSatricum* 2007, 86-90.

Rogers, E.M. 1983, *Diffusion of innovations*, New York.

Sillar, B./Tite, B. 2000, The challenge of the technological choices for materials science approaches in archaeology, *Archaeometry* 41 (1), 2-20.

Stibbe, C.M. 1980, Il tempio di Satricum ed il luogo di culto sottostante, *ArchLaz*, 3, 172-176.

Stibbe, C.M. et al 1980, *Lapis Satricanus. Archaeological, Epigraphical, Linguistic and Historical Aspects of the New Inscription from Satricum*, 's Gravenhage.

Stobbe, J. 2007, L'inizio di una comunità sull'acropoli, in *CatSatricum* 2007, 20-28.

Waarsenburg, D.J. 1995, *The Northwest necropolis of Satricum. An Iron Age Cemetery in Latium Vetus*, Amsterdam.

Waarsenburg, D.J. 1998, *Satricum. Cronaca di uno scavo*, Rome.

# Contextualizing Technology

# The Astura river valley and Satricum, an assessment of current environmental and landscape archaeological data

*Jan Sevink, Peter Attema, Evelien Witmer*

*Abstract*

*This paper presents landscape archaeological and sedimentological data on the Astura valley, with Satricum as its focal point. The progress in the study of the changing environmental conditions in this valley, which connects the Alban Hills with the Tyrrhenian coast, is described and the constraints for adequate $^{14}C$ dating of the sedimentary phases distinguished. We reflect on the relations that the observed changes in environmental conditions may have had with long-term settlement and land use dynamics in and around the valley. This is placed in the wider context of results from studies on the Agro Pontino.*

INTRODUCTION

Over the last decades a number of landscape archaeological river valley surveys have been carried out in Central and South Italy that give insight into long-term settlement and landscape dynamics. Examples are the Potenza valley study, the Biferno valley, the Raganello valley, and the Cecina valley.[1] These surveys show how river valleys from their earliest human frequentation onwards functioned as important corridors connecting uplands and mountainous areas with coastal lagoonal and wetland environments. River valleys can therefore be considered important archives of material data concerning long-term human and animal mobility, exchange and trade connections, and changing settlement and land use technologies.

Archaeological research has shown that by the Final Bronze Age over large parts of Italy early complex settlement organizations and advanced ways of dividing up and working the land were in place.[2] The evidence is mounting that the Italic cultures, in doing so, transformed their environment at a rapid pace.[3] From an environmental point of view this transformation is especially evident in increased erosion rates in upland areas and in sedimentation in river valleys and coastal plains. River valleys should therefore also be considered as important archives of the increased human impact that was exerted on the landscape in the more elevated parts of the landscape upstream of the rivers.

To fully understand the interplay between settlement and land use intensity, and the resulting increase of human impacts on the natural landscape, interdisciplinary landscape archaeological research is needed. This should involve a combination of regional settlement archaeology and palaeoenvironmental studies, as these in combination provide information on local and regional socio-economic and political changes in the middle and long-term perspective of man-environment interactions.

Such interdisciplinary approach forms the core of the Dutch interdisciplinary research that since the 1970s has been going on in the Pontine region and which aims at the reconstruction of the protohistoric and Roman human landscapes of this region. In this paper, its results at regional level are summarized. This review forms the background for the study of the Astura valley (north and south of Satricum), which connects the Alban Hills with the Tyrrhenian coast (*fig. 1a-b*). Such study is of specific importance for the landscape archaeological contextualization of protohistoric Satricum that due to its location on the river Astura was an important node between coast and hinterland. Satricum has been under excavation by archaeologists from Dutch universities since 1977.

The main aim of the paper is to give insight into the progress that is being made in the study of the changing environmental conditions in the valley both up- and downstream of Satricum and to reflect on the relations such changes may have had with long-term settlement and land use dynamics in and around the valley, and how this links to the dynamics at more regional scale.

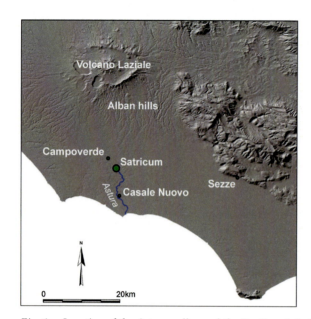 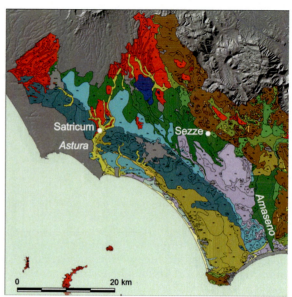

*Fig. 1a. Location of the Astura valley and the Pontine plain towards the southeast.*
*Fig. 1b. Soil map of the Astura valley and Pontine plain towards the southeast (from Arnoldus-Huyzendveld et al., 2009; based on Sevink et al., 1984, 1991; Duivenvoorden, 1985; and for the Agro Romano on Arnoldus-Huyzendveld et al. (2009).*

## The Agro Pontino: a regional review

Dutch researchers have explored human impacts in the Pontine Region ever since the soils of Southern Lazio and Campania were mapped.[4] The soil map (*fig. 1b*) appeared instrumental for archaeologists, notably for studies on the early cultures.[5] Especially the Late Holocene alluvial and colluvial deposits, and the river valley fills were deemed indicators of human impact, and later on their origin and development became object of study of an on-going collaboration between physical geographers and archaeologists.[6]

Relevant results for the Agro Pontino *sensu stricto* are summarized below and illustrated by the soil map (*fig. 1b*) and a palaeogeographical reconstruction (*fig. 2*).

- By the first millennium BC a colluvial cover had buried large tracts of land in the northwest of the Pontine plain. Canal-like extensions of former rivers, the dark green areas on the soil map, had gradually filled in the western part of an inland lake with gravelly to coarse sandy channel fills and associated thick sheets of reddish-brown clays.
- In the southern part of the Pontine Region the Amaseno river had built up a large cone of eroded reddish-brown clays and coarse-textured channel fills already from the Late Bronze Age onward. Sedimentation continued, as evidenced by the declining ages of peat found underneath these clays southwards toward Terracina, but since Roman times seems to have been of minor importance.[7]
- Throughout the Agro Pontino, the colluvial cover had already largely reached its current configuration, both in extension and thickness, before the Imperial Roman period, and probably even earlier (before the construction of the Via Appia and associated land division system). Later deposits were of minor dimensions, implying that archaeological remains of the Roman Imperial period are generally found near or at the surface.[8]

In the currently running project "The Avellino event: distal palaeoecological effects of the great Bronze Age eruption of Mount Vesuvius on the Pontine landscape" (http://avellino.gia-mediterranean.nl) further palaeogeographical reconstructions are being carried out in the central and SE part of the Pontine plain by the Universities of Groningen and Leiden. A recent reconstruction of the development of this area, also based on palaeoecological data, is presented by van Gorp and Sevink and illustrates that the *terminus post quem* for the onset of the colluviations indeed dates from the Late Bronze Age to Early Iron Age as postulated on basis of earlier research (*fig. 3*).[9]

The Astura valley system was hardly dealt with in the soil surveys (*fig. 1b*). Its pre-Holocene

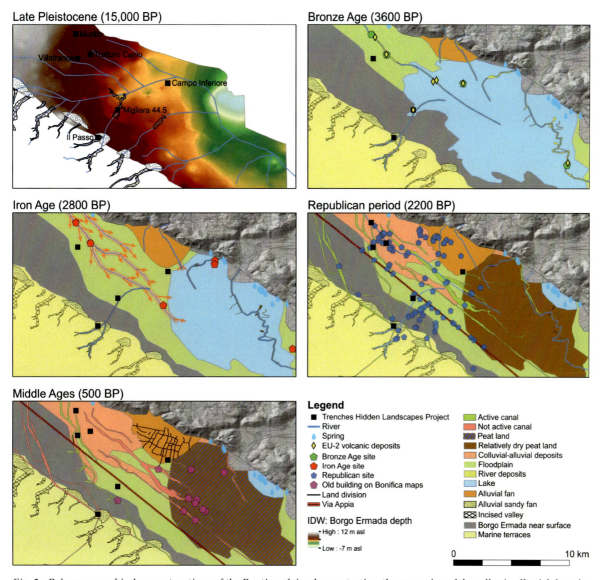

*Fig. 2. Palaeogeographical reconstructions of the Pontine plain, demonstrating the expansion of the colluvio-alluvial deposits over time (from Feiken, 2014).*

geology was studied by de Wit *et al.* who produced a detailed analysis and geological map, with emphasis on the Pleistocene formations exposed in its steep banks.[10] Far less attention was paid to the Holocene fill of the valley. Situated in the northern part of its catchment, the Campoverde area with its major votive site received more attention. Veenman produced a highly interesting pollen record, pointing to an increase in Cerealia simultaneous with a reduction in tree pollen, which we may interpret as deforestation in favour of agriculture. Unfortunately, $^{14}$C ages for this record were not reliable and conclusions drawn regarding the phasing of its sedimentary fill, and its vegetation and land use history were open to serious discussion.[11]

THE ASTURA VALLEY: CURRENT RESEARCH

Interest in the Holocene fill of the Astura valley revived in 2008 when Sevink, Kalkers and van Milligen executed a series of corings. $^{14}$C analyses of organic material found in the various corings and some pits served to constrain the ages of the sedimentary units encountered, but results were often confusing and forced us to repeat the sampling.[12] In a follow-up campaign by the authors carried out in 2016 and 2017 new corings were

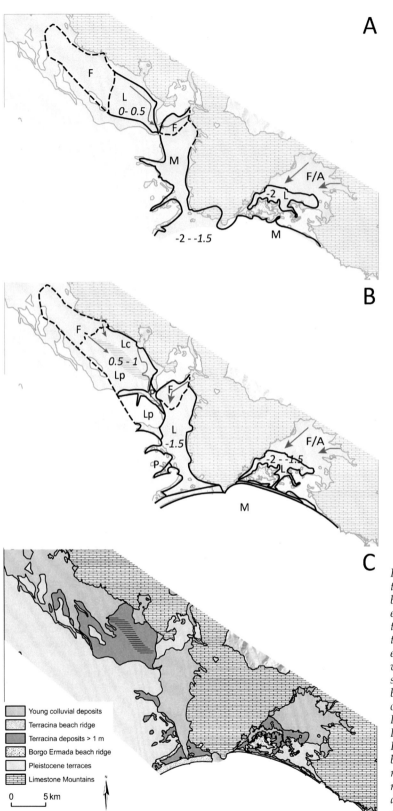

Fig. 3. Palaeogeographical reconstruction of the Agro Pontino and Fondi basin around the time of the Avellino eruption. A: Schematic reconstruction of the situation before the Avellino eruption. B: Schematic reconstruction of the environment in which the AV-tephra was deposited. C: Reconstruction of the situation after the Avellino eruption, based on soil map units. Explanation of symbols: F . Fluvial/Alluvial, L . Lacustrine, Lc . Ca-rich (aerobic) lake, Lp . Pyritic (anoxic) lake, M. Marine, P. Peat. Dashed area indicates boundary between aerobic and pyritic lake. Italic numbers indicate approximate lake or marine level. Grey arrows indicate main discharge directions. (from Van Gorp and Sevink, 2018).

added along the same transects to obtain samples for further [14]C dating and palaeoecological reconstruction. The corings and results from these are described below, while the radiocarbon datings are dealt with separately. The section ends with the interpretation of the results, in terms of the genesis of the fill, its phasing and the implications for the study of the interaction between man and his environment. The coring locations are indicated in *fig. 4a*.

CORINGS

We start out by a discussion of the corings at Campoverde, which is in the upper reach of the Astura catchment. Previous results have been published, but as also stated by Veenman the results from the [14]C datings are questionable.[13] In 2012, Sevink resampled a core from the sediments to the S of the lake, with a stratigraphy that resembled the stratigraphy encountered in the previous studies, and collected macro plant remains from this core for [14]C dating (mostly *Alnus* seeds). These allowed for an assessment of the reliability of the earlier datings of bulk samples.[14]

The sedimentary sequence encountered covers a considerably longer period of time than earlier assumed and started with an Early Holocene lacustrine phase with diatomaceous sediment, followed by reduced, poorly ripened clay (about 3 m) and followed by about 1 m of presumably 'alluvio-colluvial' material that is lesser sorted, far less plastic and reduced, and loamier. In the upper 4 m, coarse wood fragments abound, but on closer examination these could be identified as fairly recent (completely fresh) large woody root fragments, probably mostly from *Alnus* and *Populus* trees. This may well explain the aberrant age sequence observed in the earlier core, since in 2012 such wood fragments were found in several corings in the area.

The corings of transect 3 were located just to the north of Satricum (*fig. 4b*). Here the Astura has incised deeply into the Tufo Lionato bedrock and reaches the underlying far less resistant volcanic rocks (pozzolane). These are highly permeable, in contrast to the dense Tufo Lionato, and act as an important aquifer. The soil stratigraphy features a stratigraphy consisting of palude (sediments formed in marsh conditions) with on top riverbed and fluvial sediments, and finally

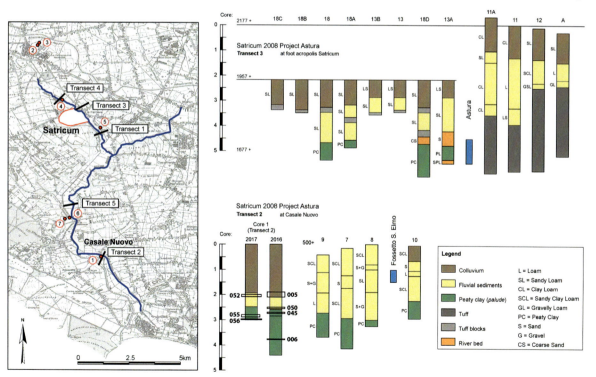

*Fig. 4a. The Astura river (blue) and the coring locations of the 2008 transects (rectangles) and 2016 corings (red dots).*
*Fig. 4b. Sections of the corings of transect 3 just north of Satricum (after van Milligen, 2008)*
*Fig. 4c. Sections of the corings of transect 2 near Casale Nuovo. The two leftmost bars represent our recent corings (2016/2017) and show the depth of our radiocarbon-dated samples (partly after van Milligen, 2008).*

colluvio-alluvial sediments (indicated in the transects as 'colluvium').

This change, just as at Campoverde, reflects an increased input of eroded soil material, which in the case of colluvium without significant further sorting is transported downslope into the river and subsequently transported downstream, largely as soil aggregates. It is this well-conserved aggregation, poor sorting and the characteristic reddish-brown to yellowish-brown colour, which are the properties that characterize the material 'inherited' from the original soils. They allow for its identification as 'colluvio-alluvium', though its colour may change to more greyish blue due to later reduction under waterlogged conditions. In more truly fluvial material, aggregates have fallen apart and lost their soil colour, and individual mineral particles are transported, being deposited as well-sorted layers, i.e. with specific grain size classes, such as fine gravel, coarse sand, fine sand and loam.

The actual grain size of a specific layer of fluvial sediment depends on the velocity (carrying capacity) of the stream at the time of its deposition and the extent to which aggregates have fallen apart. When seasonal discharge becomes larger, e.g. because of the destruction of the vegetation on slopes and increase in cultivated land and sizes of fields, discharge peaks become more common and larger, and the transport capacity of the river in flood will increase, with large amounts of soil aggregates being transported and eventually lesser sorting. As a consequence, transitions between palude and fluvial material, and between fluvial and colluvio-alluvial material are often gradual. The transition between palude, with very low stream velocities and consequently very minor transport of coarser size fractions (sand or coarser), and colluvio-alluvial deposits thus indicates an increase in sedimentation rates in the lower Astura valley, which points to enhanced and presumably human-induced erosion in the hinterland.

Near to transect 3, a test pit was excavated at the foot of the acropolis of Satricum. The stratigraphy in this pit was somewhat puzzling, since charcoal found in stratified position in colluvio-alluvial material about 50 cm below an archaeological layer, at about 3 m depth below the natural land surface, showed a $^{14}$C age of 918-806 cal BC. The colluvio-alluvial sediment extended to considerable depth, still containing ceramic fragments (e.g. Late Archaic tiles) to about 6 m below the land surface. A wood sample from about that depth provided a $^{14}$C age of 790-490 cal BC, while another large wood fragment (also from deep in this section) turned out to be from a large tree root, having the relatively recent $^{14}$C age of 52 cal BC-71 cal AD. In conclusion, the datings are conflicting and might indicate that the colluvio-alluvial sediment dates from the Late Republican period and is composed of reworked older materials, of which the oldest components may date back to the early part of the first millennium BC.

The considerable thickness of the colluvio-alluvial deposit at this site may in part be explained by the position of the pit, right below and close to the steep slope, and be due to a considerable downslope transport of debris and soil from this slope or even straightforward dumped material. In transect 1, slightly further down the Astura valley, close to the valley slope palude deposits were also deeply buried (> 3.5 m) below the colluvio-alluvial fill, whereas in the more central part of the valley and further downstream the palude deposits generally occurred at considerably lesser depth.

Downstream a further two transects were cored, 5 and 2, of which we discuss the southernmost (2) located near the Late Bronze Age site of Casale Nuovo. As at location 3, cores show a sharp transition between palude and colluvio-alluvial to fluvial deposits (*fig. 4c*). As this transect is located more downstream the Astura river, the colluvium (brown) is more reworked into fluvial deposits, compared to upstream transects. This implies that stratification is more prominent as well as sorting of the transported material. Nevertheless, the deposits here still consist of coarse unsorted volcanic material, linked to upstream erosion, as indicated by the presence of olivine and other volcanic minerals. Also here we would expect a dating of the transition towards palude deposits somewhere in the first millennium BC, but due to the downstream position, slightly later than at Satricum itself.

RADIOCARBON DATING

The results for Campoverde are quite straightforward and show that the transition from clay to more colluvio-alluvial deposits (at about 1 m depth) dates from 798-521 cal BC. Given the truly early age of the lower sample, the sedimentation rate in the lake initially must have been very low as can be expected in a period with far lesser land use and concurrent erosion (2 m sediment over a period of about 4500 years).

The two leftmost cores depicted in fig. 4c concern recent corings obtained from Casale Nuovo (coring1), which are within a distance of a few meters from the earlier coring from transect 2 (see *fig. 4a*), that was studied.[15] Depths where samples for radiocarbon dating were taken are indicated. Below about 370 cm the palude deposits are true peats, while upward they become more clayey. At about 320 cm depth, they grade into more sorted humic fluvio-colluvial sediment, which from about 180 cm depth becomes truly gravelly and even more poorly sorted. Both earlier and recent cores are virtually identical regarding their stratigraphy.

Charcoal samples (EW) at depths ranging from 2 to 4 m gave dates between the 15th and 17th centuries AD (table 1, highlighted in blue). The earlier datings on wood by Sevink (JS) exhibit the same young ages. A study of the nature of this wood revealed that it is from tree roots of relatively recent trees. Datings on plant remains from between 190 and 263 cm depth in contrast had yielded dates between the start of the 4th and end of 3rd centuries BC, i.e. the mid-Republican period (Sevink, unpublished data).

A deposition of 2-4 m of colluvial sediment over the past few centuries, as might be suggested by the recent ages of the charcoal, is extremely unlikely and it is very hard to explain why this sediment would contain so much older well-conserved plant material (which is easily destroyed upon transport). We therefore assume the dates on plant remains to be reliable and the dates on the fine charcoal to be unsuited for dating the sediments that contain this charcoal. It should be mentioned that the same fine charcoal was encountered in virtually all cores and its presence thus is rather a standard feature of the valley fill.

The most likely explanation for the recent dates obtained for the fine charcoal is that it has been brought into the soil by bioturbation through soil fauna. Earthworms are known to move up and down over great vertical distances in connection with seasonal variations in soil moisture and to transport soil including fine charcoal over these distances.[16] Earlier the valley floor of the Astura was poorly drained (prior to its reclamation in the early 20th century) and the reclamation and associated deep drainage may well have been accompanied by massive deepening of the bioturbated zone and thus hamper proper $^{14}$C dating based on small charcoal fragments.

It should be emphasized that for a hypothesis that the disturbance during the Bonifica was of such magnitude that the upper meters of the valley fill should be considered as land fill,

| Location and number sample ID | Gr number | Age in cal yr AD | Depth (cm) |
|---|---|---|---|
| Campoverde | | | |
| JS-1 (seed) | GrA-57042 | 798-521 BC | 90-100 |
| JS-2 (seed) | GrA-57043 | 5294-5020 BC | 380-390 |
| Pit below acropolis | | | |
| JS 2010-1 (CK) | GrA-51291 | 915-806 BC | 200 cm |
| JS 2010-2 (wood) | GrA-51292 | 790-490 BC | 350 cm |
| JS 2012-1 (wood*) | GrA-56495 | 52 BC-71 AD | 350 cm |
| Casale Nuovo | | | |
| JS 52568 (plant) | GrA-52568 | 380-198 BC | 190-193 |
| EW-005 (CK) | GrA-69329 | 1690-1925 AD | 190-210 |
| EW-052 (CK) | GrM-10467 | 1666-1948 AD | 200-210 |
| EW-050 (CK) | GrA-69546 | 1650-1955 AD | 250-255 |
| JS 52569 (plant) | GrA-52569 | 372-204 BC | 260-263 |
| EW-045 (CK) | GrA-69545 | 1415-1515 AD | 275-280 |
| EW-055 (seed) | GrM-12267 | 1664-1954 AD | 283-293 |
| EW-056 (CK) | GrM-10468 | 1666-1948 AD | 300-301 |
| JS 53849 (wood*) | GrA-53849 | 863-1020 AD | 350-352 |
| JS 53154 (wood*) | GrA-53154 | 1449-1634 AD | 373-381 |
| EW-006 (CK) | GrA-69327 | 1485-1650 AD | 375-378 |
| JS 53848 (wood*) | GrA-53848 | 40 BC-142 AD | 420-423 |

*Table 1. Radiocarbon ages of samples from Campoverde, the test pit below Satricum, and the corings near Casale Nuovo. Unreliable young ages are highlighted in blue. Calibration by Oxcal 4.3, based on IntCal 13.*
*\* = wood from large root; CK = charcoal.*

explaining the presence of recent charcoal at considerable depth, there is not the slightest indication: in the corings there is no indication for a disturbed stratigraphic sequence, nor for an anthropogenic origin of the sediment ('land fill'). Furthermore, the colluvium can be subdivided into a more recent colluvium containing hematite, which originated from the former iron-industry at la Ferriere, overlying earlier colluvium without such hematite, thus evidencing a distinct stratification of the colluvium into a pre-medieval and a younger colluvium[12].

The conclusion is that only the ages obtained for macro plant remains are reliable and those on small charcoal fragments are not, unless they are obtained on charcoal from closed stratified sections, such as was the case in the test pit at Satricum that we discussed, and which gave a date between 918 and 806 cal BC. That $^{14}$C datings for woody root fragments are completely unreliable as indicator for the age of the sediment that contains these roots, is extremely clear and stresses that wood fragments are only suited for dating, if they can be identified as above ground plant parts.

In summary, reliable dates for the transition from palude type deposits to colluvio-alluvial sediment in the Astura valley so far come from:

- Transect 3 at Campoverde: here the top of the palude was dated on plant remains (*Alnus*) to the Iron Age/Archaic period (798-521 cal BC).
- Transect 5 near Casale Nuovo gave a reliable date obtained from plant remains for the transition palude to truly colluvio-alluvial deposits between the 2$^{nd}$-4$^{th}$ century BC.

DISCUSSION AND INTEGRATION OF RESULTS

These dates provide us with a hypothesis of an in time and space progressing sedimentation starting upstream in full protohistory (likely the Final Bronze Age/Early Iron age transition) and extending downstream, where sedimentation started to cover the palude following the Archaic period. This scenario would chronologically overlap with the datings we obtained in the past for the colluvium covering parts of the Pontine plain. Here radiocarbon datings were foremost done on plant macro remains from peats formed in a marsh environment and we can consider these to be reliable.[17]

A major question then is 'How likely is a causal relationship between progressing sedimentation in the Astura valley and pressure on the landscape in the catchment of the Astura?' Desktop research, field survey and excavation have now generated a good insight in settlement development in the Alban Hills and the Astura basin (*fig. 5*). Luca Alessandri's inventory[18] and subsequent phasing of protohistoric occupation shows that the Alban hills were a favoured location for settlement from the Middle Bronze Age onwards. By the time of the Final Bronze Age / Early Iron Age transition the slopes of the Alban hills were densely settled. This process of infill of the landscape with settlement and agricultural fields continued in the Iron Age and Archaic period and resulted in increased deforestation as recorded in the regional pollen record.[19] This in turn resulted in continuing erosion, as documented in the corings of the Astura valley sedimentary fill in the form of coarse textured reddish-brown colluvium that gradually covered the initially marshy river environment. Judging from the dates that we consider reliable, this was a process that was already underway at the time that in the 9$^{th}$ century BC the first people started to live on the hill of Satricum.

Zooming out, we can say that the case of the Astura valley fits the image of increasing human impact on the landscape of the Pontine region from especially the later Bronze Age onwards, as shown in the palaeogeographical reconstructions[20] for the plain below Sezze (*fig. 2*). Here parts of the former inland lake became available for intensive farming in the course of the first millennium BC as a result of this severe colluviation.

GENERAL DISCUSSION AND CONCLUSIONS

As a case study the Astura valley adds to the wider palaeogeographical reconstruction of the Pontine region that is being developed in the on-going work of the Pontine region project. Palaeogeographical reconstruction will – as stated in our introduction – help us to evaluate in space and time how environmental change enabled and restrained settling and exploitation of the land, and the possibilities of moving through the landscape.

Technology plays an important role here and the study of the environment and environmental change will prompt questions how local communities adapted to their surroundings in view of demographic growth and corresponding economic demands. Such questions range from the navigability of the rivers in the Pontine region, like the Amaseno and Astura, for transport and commerce, to the suitability of the soils for various types of cultivation and grazing. As to the former, we should not imagine that large vessels going upstream could reach inland archaic settlements, like Satricum and Ardea. To navigate rivers winding through marshy and silting up val-

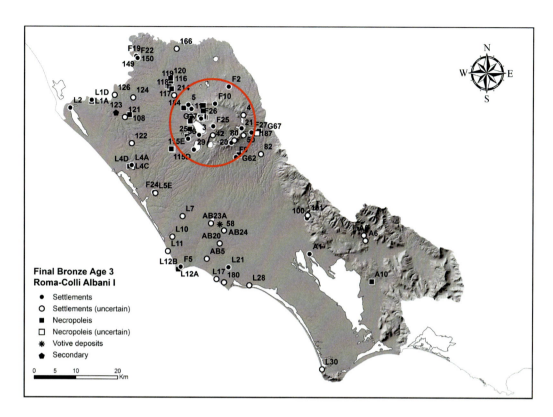
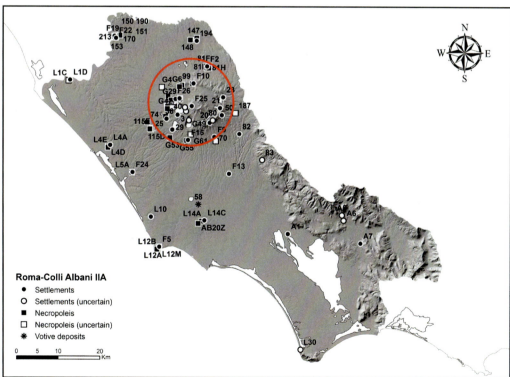

*Fig. 5. Site distribution pattern between the Final Bronze Age 3 (upper) and Early Iron Age (lower), illustrating a high site density in the Alban hills (from Alessandri, 2013).*

ley environments, one would have to rely on flat-bottomed boats, such as the 'sandali' known from recent history or make use of transport over land (*figs 5-6*).

Moving through the landscape overland would in the Pontine region be conditioned by roads that avoided the ubiquitous marshy zones in the coastal plain.

*Fig. 6a Flat-bottomed boat (sandali) as a means of transportation through shallow waters (Giulio Aristide Sartorio, Lo spurgo dei canali, 1913, Galleria Nazionale d'arte moderna, Roma).*

*Fig. 6b Historical map depicting the ubiquitous marshy zones in the coastal plain of the Pontine region prior to the 20th-century land reclamations (Carte représentant l'état des marais Pontins en 1777, avant le commencement des travaux ordonnés par le pape Pie VI, Bibliothèque Nationale de France).*

Reliable reconstructions of infrastructure can only be provided combining palaeogeography and settlement distribution, and using sophisticated GIS analysis.

As to the agricultural potential of the region we should consider how erosion and sedimentation changed the soil conditions over large areas as well as drainage patterns. For the Astura valley, several archaeological studies provide background for such analysis of the impacts of agriculture and its spatial pattern.[21]

More in general, it is important to know the degree of landscape degradation in the uplands and when and where well-drained land became available for tillage due to sedimentation, always considering the use of simple ploughs and available crop choices. Concluding we can state that a critical interdisciplinary landscape archaeological approach is useful to read human impact on the landscape at various scales: that of the region to identify trends in landscape development and that of the individual site, as at Satricum.

In view of the on-going research at Satricum, the reconstruction of the palaeoenvironmental conditions in the Astura river valley and its catchment is fundamental to increase our understanding of how Satricum functioned in its setting. However, as shown, there are methodological issues in obtaining robust [14]C datings that affect chronological interpretation. In our future work we will therefore concentrate on further strengthening the chronological framework of our sedimentological and palaeoecological work of the Astura valley.

ACKNOWLEDGEMENTS

Thanks are due to Rogier Kalkers (RUL), Paul van Milligen (UvA), and Nikolaas Noorda (RUG), who assisted us in the field, particularly in the execution of the corings. Several colleagues helped with the identification and selection of organic materials for [14]C dating, including Bas van Geel (UvA), Wim Kuijper (RUL), Arnoud Maurer (RUG), and Rita Palfenier-Vegter (RUG). [14]C datings were performed at CIO (RUG, Groningen). Sanne Palstra from CIO aided us in the interpretation of the results for samples taken in 2017. Sander Tiebackx assisted us in the production of the figures and we thank Paul van Milligen (UvA), Rik Feiken (RUG), Luca Alessandri (RUG) and Wouter van Gorp (RUG) for the use of their figures. Special thanks are due to the Soprintendenza Archeologica del Lazio e dell'Etruria Meridionale, who allowed us to execute the corings, and to Marijke Gnade for her hospitality and continued support.

The research was funded by a number of organisations: the 'Fundatie van de Vrijvrouwe van Renswoude', the Koninklijk Nederlands Instituut in Rome (KNIR), the Groningen Institute of Archaeology (GIA), and last but not least, the Institute for Biodiversity and Ecosystem Dynamics (IBED) and the Archaeological Institute of the University of Amsterdam (UvA).

NOTES

[1] The studies mentioned include the Potenza Valley study by Vermeulen/Boullart 2005; the early benchmark study of the Biferno valley by Barker 1995; the RPC project in Calabria, described by Attema/van Leusen 2004 and, more recently, by Feiken 2014. Lastly, the study of the Cecina valley by Terrenato/Ammerman 1996.

[2] Relevant studies include Pacciarelli 2001 and Attema *et al.* 2010.

[3] A review of this evidence can be found in the chapter by Attema and Sevink within the forthcoming (2019) *Oxford Handbook of Pre-Roman Italy (1000-49 BCE)*.

[4] A reconnaissance soil survey at scale 1:100.000 was published by Sevink *et al.* in 1984, preceded by a detailed soil survey of a much smaller area to the SE of the Astura valley by Sevink *et al.* 1982. In 1991, Sevink *et al.* published a 1:100.000 soil map of the Agro Pontino, which extended further NW than the earlier 1984 map. The soil map of the province of Latina, published by Arnoldus-Huyzendveld *et al.* in 2009, was to a very large extent based on the earlier maps described above.

[5] The Agro Pontino Survey Project was based on close cooperation between archaeologists and physical geographers, as evidenced by the book on this project by Voorrips *et al.* 1991 and the PhD thesis by Kamermans 1993.

[6] This collaboration is most evident from the PhD theses of van Joolen 2003 (focusing on archaeological land evaluation and further developing the approach by Kamermans for more recent periods) and Feiken 2014 (more oriented towards landscape archaeology and its methodology).

[7] Van Joolen 2003 was the first to systematically study the phasing of the human induced infill of the Agro Pontino graben by dating the peat underneath the alluvio-colluvial fill. Results are reviewed in Attema *et al.* 2010.

[8] De Haas 2011 extensively studied the early Roman colonization in the Pontine region, confirming the earlier preliminary conclusions of Sevink *et al.* 1984 on the phasing of the colluvial cover.

[9] Results from the Avellino project (http://avellino.gia-mediterranean.nl) include studies by van Gorp/Sevink 2019, on the palaeogeography of Early Bronze age and later landscape of the Agro Pontino graben and Fondi basin, and by Doorenbosch/Field 2019, on the palaeoecology of these areas. Results regarding anthropogenic impacts on these areas are in line with those from the earlier research, summarized by Attema *et al.* 2010.

[10] The study by de Wit *et al.* 1986 was the first detailed study of the geology of the Satricum area and still forms the basis for understanding the geological setting of Satricum.

[11] It is particularly because of the votive site that this area received attention e.g. by van Loon *et al.* 2015. The pollen record of a lake section – the lake which held this votive depot – was studied by Veenman 1996, 2002. Sevink *et al.* 2013 showed that the $^{14}C$ datings published by Veenman (1996) were indeed unreliable and provided new datings.

[12] Preliminary results of the coring campaign were published by Sevink in 2009. Hematite is an iron ore, likely imported from Tuscany (Elba or Colline Metallifere) or even from further away, since there are no local sources of this ore in Lazio or Campania. It is easily identified in sand and gravel fractions by its colour (black) and metallic lustre, and probably was an important ore used in the medieval and later iron industry at Le Ferriere.

[13] Here we refer to Veenman 1996 and her remarks concerning the reliability of the $^{14}C$ datings.

[14] Reference is made to Sevink *et al.* 2013 for a full discussion on the problems with these datings.

[15] See note 12.

[16] Quite some studies have been published on soil bioturbation and its potential impacts on the distribution of charcoal and its use for $^{14}C$ dating. Carcaillet 2001 demonstrated the major impact bioturbation may have, while Topoliantz and Ponge 2003 published an excellent case study on this phenomenon.

[17] The limitations of $^{14}C$ datings for bulk samples and the reliability of such datings when using macro remains from terrestrial plants are extensively described by Sevink *et al.* 2013, to which reference is made for details.

[18] The study by Alessandri 2013 points to an early rather massive impact of settlement in this sloping area, in the upstream catchment of the Astura river.

[19] Land use related changes in vegetation in that period were studied by van Joolen 2003. The Avellino project (http://avellino.gia-mediterranean.nl) focused on the earlier vegetation and land use (Early Bronze Age).

[20] In his palaeogeographical reconstruction Feiken 2014 produced a detailed overview of the various phases in the development of the central Agro Pontino graben, depicted in fig. 2.

[21] These studies include Attema *et al.* 2011, de Haas 2011 and Tol 2012.

BIBLIOGRAPHY

Alessandri L. 2013, *Latium Vetus in The Bronze Age and Early Iron Age* (BARIntSer 2565), Oxford.

Arnoldus-Huyzendveld, A./C. Perotto/P. Sarandrea (eds.) 2009, *I suoli dell Provincia di Latina. Provincia di Latina* (Settore Pianificazione Urbanistica e Territoriale), Rome.

Attema, P.A.J./G-J. Burgers/P.M. van Leusen 2010, *Regional Pathways to Complexity: settlement and land-use dynamics from the Bronze Age to the Republican period*, Amsterdam.

Attema, P.A.J./T.C.A. de Haas/G.W. Tol 2011, *Between Satricum and Antium, Settlement Dynamics in a Coastal Landscape in Latium Vetus* (BABESCH Suppl. 18), Leuven.

Attema, P.A.J./P.M. van Leusen 2004, Intra-regional and inter-regional comparison of occupation histories in three Italian regions: the RPC project, in S.E. Alcock/J.F. Cherry (eds.), *Side by side survey. Comparative regional studies in the Mediterranean world*, Oxford, 86-100.

Attema, P.A.J./J. Sevink 2019, The Peoples and Landscapes of Protohistoric and Classical Italy, in F. de Angelis/M. Maiuro M. (eds.) *The Oxford Handbook of Pre-Roman Italy (1000-49 BCE)*, Oxford, in press.

Barker, G. 1995, *A Mediterranean Valley: Landscape archaeology and Annales history in the Biferno Valley*, London.

Carcaillet, C. 2001, Soil particles reworking evidences by AMS 14C dating of charcoal, *Earth and Planetary Science* 332(1), 21-28.

De Wit, H.E./J. Sevink/P.A.M. Andriessen/E.H. Hebeda 1986, Stratigraphy and radiometric datings of a Mid-Pleistocene Transgressive complex in the Agro Pontino (Central Italy), *Geologica Romana 26*, 449-460.

Doorenbosch, M./M.H. Field 2018, A Bronze Age palaeoenvironmental reconstruction from the Fondi basin, southern Lazio, central Italy, *Quaternary International* 499, part B, 221-230.

Duivenvoorden, J. 1985, *Soils and landscape development of the area NW of Latina, Agro Pontino. Italy*. Internal report, Rome: Istituto Olandese.

Feiken, H. 2014, *Dealing with biases: three geo-archaeological approaches to the hidden landscapes of Italy* (Groningen Archaeological Studies 26), Groningen.

Kamermans, H. 1993, *Archeologie en landevaluatie in de Agro Pontino (Lazio, Italië)*, PhD thesis, University of Amsterdam.

Pacciarelli, M. 2001, *Dal villaggio alla città. La svolta protourbana del 1000 a. C. nell'Italia tirrenica*, Florence.

Sevink, J. 2009, Het Astura-dal: ontstaan en kenmerken, bezien vanuit aardkundig oogpunt, *Nieuwsbrief van de Vereniging Vrienden van Satricum en de Stichting Nederlands Studiecentrum voor Latium (dec. 2009)* 16(1), 8-18.

Sevink, J./J. Duivenvoorden/H. Kamermans 1991, The soils of the Agro Pontino, in A. Voorrips/S.H. Loving/H. Kamermans (eds.), *The Agro Pontino Survey Project* (Studies in Prae- en Protohistorie 6), Amsterdam, 31-47.

Sevink J./J. van der Plicht/H. Feiken/P.M. van Leusen/ C.C. Bakels 2013, The Holocene of the Agro Pontino graben: Recent advances in its palaeogeography, palaeoecology, and tephrostratigraphy, *Quaternary International* 303, 153-162.

Sevink, J./A. Remmelzwaal/O.C. Spaargaren 1984, *The soils of southern Lazio and adjacent Campania* (Publicaties van het Fysisch-Geografisch en Bodemkundig Laboratorium van de Universiteit van Amsterdam 38), Amsterdam.

Sevink, J./P. Vos/W.E. Westerhoff/A. Stierman/ H. Kamermans 1982, A sequence of marine terraces near Latina (Agro Pontino, Central Italy), *Catena* 9, 361-378.

Terrenato, N./A.J. Ammerman 1996, Visibility and site recovery in the Cecina Valley Survey, Italy, *JFieldA* 23(1), 91-109.

Tol, G.W. 2012, *A fragmented history: a methodological and artefactual approach to the study of ancient settlement in the territories of Satricum and Antium* (Groningen Archaeological Studies 18), Groningen.

Topoliantz, S./J.F. Ponge 2003, Burrowing activity of the geophagous earthworm *Pontoscolex corethrurus* (Oligochaeta: Glossoscolecidae) in the presence of charcoal, *Applied Soil Ecology* 23(3), 267-271.

Van Gorp, W./J. Sevink 2019, Distal deposits of the Avellino eruption as a marker for the detailed reconstruction of the Early Bronze Age depositional environment in the Agro Pontino and Fondi Basin (Lazio, Italy), *Quaternary International* 499, part B, 245-257.

Van Joolen, E. 2003, *Archaeological land evaluation: a reconstruction of the suitability of ancient landscapes for various land uses in Italy focused on the first millennium BC*, PhD thesis, University of Groningen.

Van Loon, T./S.L. Willemsen/G.W. Tol 2015, Sites and finds of the Campoverde and Padiglione surveys of the Pontine Region Project (2005), *Palaeohistoria* 56, 105-147.

Van Milligen, P. 2008, *Booronderzoek naar de fysischgeografische kenmerken van het Astura-dal bij Le Ferriere, 2008*. Unpublished MSc-thesis, Amsterdam.

Veenman, F. 1996, Landevaluatie in de Pontijnse regio (Zuid-Latium, Italië), dateringsproblemen rond een bronstijdakkerbouwfase, *Paleo-aktueel* 8, 59-62.

Veenman, F. 2002, *Reconstructing the pasture: a reconstruction of pastoral land use in Italy in the first millennium BC*. PhD thesis, Free University of Amsterdam.

Vermeulen, F./C. Boullart 2005, *The Potenza Valley Survey*, BABesch 76, 1-18.

Voorrips, A./S.H., Loving/H. Kamermans (eds.) 1991, *The Agro Pontino Survey Project* (Studies in Prae-en Protohistorie 6), Amsterdam.

# Bronze and Iron Age salt production on the Italian Tyrrhenian coast
## *An overview*

*Luca Alessandri, Clarissa Belardelli, Peter Attema,
Francesca Cortese, Mario Federico Rolfo, Jan Sevink, Wouter van Gorp*

*Abstract*

*A synthesis of the current knowledge of the so-called Italian giacimenti a olle d'impasto rossiccio (reddish jar potsherd deposits) is presented. These sites are common along the Tyrrhenian side of Central Italy and are usually interpreted as salt-production sites, because of parallels with similar European specialised sites. In the latter, salt was obtained by boiling a brine in special disposable pottery, a technique known as briquetage. However, the analogies are not straightforward and alternative hypotheses, e.g. fish-processing, and a more complex intertwined economy have also been put forward. To solve the interpretation issues, we advocate to use a multidisciplinary approach involving quantification of the ceramics encountered, establishment of their morphological and functional typologies, and physico/chemical analyses to identify their use.*

INTRODUCTION

Salt is an essential part of the human diet, although the necessary intake has been controversial.[1] At the moment the physiological adequate intake for an adult is estimated at 1.5 gr per day.[2] The need of domestic animals for salt is much greater: according to Bergier, a cow needs around 90 grams per day and a horse 50 grams.[3] In a meat-based diet, the necessary intake of salt can probably be obtained from food, but in an agricultural diet possibly not. That is why hunter-gatherer tribes generally do not trade salt but agricultural societies sometimes do.[4] However, in antiquity salt was also used for other purposes: to preserve foodstuffs through its antimicrobial property, as part of ritual activities, and in the tanning process.[5] Only three sources of salt can be exploited all over the world: rocks, brine springs, and sea water. Only the latter is available in Italy, with a few small exceptions of halite deposits in Sicily and Calabria.[6] Salt can be extracted from the sea water in two ways: by means of solar evaporation or boiling a brine, which can be obtained by partial solar evaporation. In Italy, evidence for saltworks has been traced only from the Roman period onward, but these works leave scanty traces on the ground and the precise technique used is hard to establish.[7]

Several different techniques have been used all around the world to obtain salt from brine. The *briquetage* technique is the most widespread in Europe.[8] Basically, the process consists of boiling the brine in earthenware vessels and then to break the containers to extract the salt cakes. In the secondary firing, the jars are thought to acquire a reddish hue due to some chemical processes. This explains the at times huge amount of reddish broken pottery that characterizes these specialised sites. Combustion structures onto which the brine boiling containers were placed and vats placed around such structures to store and/or evaporate brine are typical features of these workshops. Typical examples of the latter are Landrellec and Enez Vihan (so-called *ateliers de briquetage*, in French), in Bretagne (*fig. 1*).[9] However, evidence of *briquetage* has been found in almost all continental Europe and along the English coastline.[10] The earliest evidence comes from some Neolithic sites in Romania,[11] although the peak of the phenomenon is to be placed in the Iron Age and Roman period, especially in northern Europe.

*The first salt hypothesis*

Along the Italian Tyrrhenian coast, accumulations of sherds of reddish-brown earthenware jars, mostly dated to the Final Bronze Age (FBA) and/or Early Iron Age (EIA), have long been considered as traces of "industrial" sites. In the Italian literature, they are referred to as *giacimenti a olle d'impasto rossiccio*[12] or *installazioni funzionali*, as opposed to settlements with a domestic function that show a much wider variety of pottery wares and shapes (*fig. 2; table 1*). Already in 1991, Marco Pacciarelli[13] suggested that these accumulations of FBA and EIA impasto sherds might be evidence for salt production. Pacciarelli based his hypothesis on the strong predominance of these jars within the archaeological assemblages found at these sites and on their reddish colour, which he tentatively attributed to secondary firing. He noted that this pottery assemblages resembled the deposits of the *ateliers de briquetage*. Another possible parallel is provided by the Iron Age salting mounds of Essex, large heaps of burnt and broken potsherds that were discovered at the end of the 19$^{th}$ c. CE[14], and the Bronze Age/Iron Age evidence from Lincolnshire.[15] Interesting is the recurring use of locations for salt production such as in the modern saltern of Tarquinia (Saline di Tarquinia) where accumulations of reddish-brown potsherds were found that, according to Pacciarelli, could be related to EIA salt production (Fig 2, 22).[16] Below we give an overview of recent evidence brought to light since the phenomenon was first defined by Pacciarelli, followed by a discussion about the interpretation of the *giacimenti a olle d'impasto rossiccio* as salt production sites.

*Evidence north of the Tiber*

Over the last two decades, many sites characterized by accumulations of reddish-brown sherds of jars have been found along the Tyrrhenian coast (table 1). The northernmost location is Isola di Coltano (Fig 2, 1).[17] Here the University of Pisa excavated thousands of sherds found in layers on the banks of an ancient lagoon. About 70% of the pottery sherds of the deposit belonged to large ovoid or half-conical locally made vessels.

Between 2001 and 2008, excavations carried out by the archaeological service of Tuscany (*Soprintendenza per i Beni Archeologici della Toscana*) on the shores of the Baratti Gulf[18] (*fig. 2, and 6*) and on the southernmost shores of the Gulf of Follonica[19] (*fig. 2, 8-14*) led to the discovery of several furnaces, characterized by both single and double compartments having either vertical or horizontal draft channels (*fig. 3*). G. Baratti interpreted the furnaces from Baratti and Puntone Nuovo – Le Chiarine (kiln B) as salt production facilities,[20] noting their similarity with the French *briquetage* kilns of Enez-Vihan, Landrellec[21] and Moyenvic, Les Crôleurs, in the Seille valley.[22] However, the kilns can, according to us, also be compared with the Minoan cross-draft channel kilns known from Haghia Triada[23] (LM IB) and Kommos[24] (LM IA) that were used for firing pottery.[25] Two recently explored Iron Age sites from Tombolo di Feniglia – Poggio Pertuso[26] (*fig. 2, 19*) and Duna Feniglia,[27] dated to the 9$^{th}$-8$^{th}$ c. BCE – feature the presence of typical reddish-brown potsherds as well. Here the excavations led to the discovery of a kiln similar to the one from Baratti and different types of pits (elliptical, rectangular) sometimes associated with layers of pure clay – probably to produce vessels – and reddish-brown impasto sherds (*fig. 4*). Prior to the Tombolo di Feniglia discoveries, similar structures were found in 1994 at Marangone (*fig. 2, 30*) where a pit filled with ash and potsherds was found.[28] Comparable structures were found in excavations at Acque Fresche[29] (*fig. 2, 25*) at Torre Valdaliga[30] (*fig. 2, 26*) and at La Mattonara.[31]

*Evidence South of the Tiber*

Between 2001-2002, the Groningen Institute of Archaeology excavated the FBA site of Pelliccione (also known as P13) on the Tyrrhenian coast (*fig. 2, 38*).[32] The archaeological deposit consisted of a huge amount of reddish-brown impasto jar sherds, found together with fragments of tufa chunks bearing traces of fire. The tufa chunks were interpreted as provisional stands for the vessels that, filled with brine, would have been placed over a fire. In the same area, numerous other sites with the presence of the reddish-brown sherds (Le Grottacce, Saracca, Area Stop 4, Fosso Moscarello) have been identified[33] (with references. *Fig. 1, 37* and *39-42*, respectively).

In 2017, in a joint excavation of the universities of Groningen and Rome Tor Vergata on two small islands in the lagoon of Caprolace, a number of ceramic pedestals were found in combination with Middle Bronze Age (MBA) ceramics (*fig. 5*). Similar pedestals have been found in England, at the site of Brean Down[34] and in France, where they are called *piliers*.[35] The pedestals have a slightly rounded base with a concave centre and, where preserved (rarely), a set of three lobes on the top. The shank is circular in section. Such features are usually found in the *briquetage* sites, all over Europe, and are usually interpreted as pedestals on which the vessels were placed during the brine evaporating process.[36] The chronology of the Bronze Age phase at the Caprolace site spans the MBA to Recent Bronze Age,[37] although the age of the context with the pedestals is restricted to the beginning of the MBA (subphases 1 and 2). Elsewhere on the islands, also the characteristic reddish-brown potsherds, mostly belonging to half-conical vessels, are quite common, but pedestals were absent. The chronology of the layer

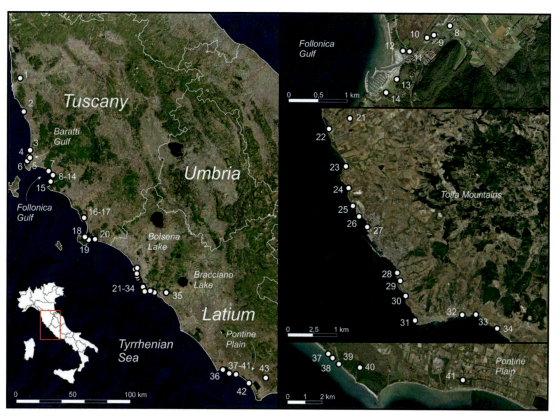

*Fig. 1. Map of Tyrrhenian sites featuring the presence of accumulations of reddish-brown jars discussed in the text. See table 1 for the related toponyms. Background imagery: Esri, DigitalGlobe, GeoEye, Earthstar Geographics, CNES/Airbus, DS, USDA, USGS, AeroGRID, IGN, GIS User Community.*

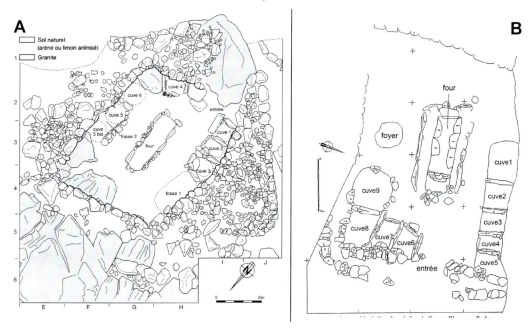

*Fig. 2. A, plan of the briquetage atelier of Enez Vihan, (from Daire et al. 2001). B, plan of the briquetage atelier of Landrellec (from Daire 2002).*

| Num. | Site | Reddish jar potsherds | Pit(s) | Kiln(s) | Hearths | Ash layer | Fire-dogs | Stands | Settlement ev. | Chronology |
|---|---|---|---|---|---|---|---|---|---|---|
| 1 | Isola di Coltano | 70%, local prod. | | | Yes | | Yes | | | MBA1-2 to FBA |
| 2 | Galafone | Majority, local. prod. | | | | | Yes | | | FBA?, EIA |
| 3 | Riva degli Etruschi | Majority | | | | | | | | FBA |
| 4 | Poggio del Molino | Majority | | | | | | | Yes | RBA, FBA |
| 5 | La Torraccia | Majority | | | | | | | | FBA3 or EIA |
| 6 | Baratti | Majority | Clay deposit | 1 | | | | | | FBA or EIA |
| 7 | Torre Mozza | Majority | | | | | | | | FBA or EIA |
| 8 | Puntone Nuovo-Le Chiarine | Majority | Clay deposit | 3 | | | | | | FBA |
| 9 | Puntone Nuovo-Campo da Gioco | 95%, local production | With CaCO3 layer | 3 | | | | | | EIA |
| 10 | Puntone Nuovo-Meleta | Majority | | 3 | | | | | | EIA |
| 11 | Puntone Nuovo-Fiumara | Majority | | | | | | | | MBA, FBA |
| 12 | Puntone Nuovo-Fosso del Fico | Only | | | | | | | | FBA |
| 13 | Portiglioni - Campo da Gioco | Majority | "Some with CaCO3 layer; one lined with burnt clay" | | | | | | | FBA3 or EIA |
| 14 | Portiglioni | Majority | | | | | | | | |
| 15 | Poggio Carpineta | Majority | | | | | | | | |
| 16 | Tombolello | Only | | | | | | | | FBA or EIA |
| 17 | Casa San Giuseppe | Only (and one amphora) | | | | | | | | EIA |
| 18 | Punta degli Stretti | 65,9% | | | | | | | | FBA3 |
| 19 | Poggio Pertuso | Majority | | | | | 2 | | | EIA |
| 20 | Duna Feniglia | Majority | Often lined with clay, often with CaCO3 layer | 1 | | | | | | EIA |

| Num. | Site | Reddish jar potsherds | Pit(s) | Kiln(s) | Hearths | Ash layer | Fire-dogs | Stands | Settlement ev. | Chronology |
|---|---|---|---|---|---|---|---|---|---|---|
| 21 | Fontanile delle Serpi | Majority? | | | | | | | Yes | FBA or EIA |
| 22 | Le Saline di Tarquinia | Majority | | | | | | | | EIA |
| 23 | Bagni Sant'Agostino | Only | | | | | | | | EIA |
| 24 | La Frasca | Majority | Yes | | | | | | Yes | EIA |
| 25 | Acque Fresche | Majority | | 1 | | | | | Yes | EIA |
| 26 | Torre Valdaliga | 51% | Lined with clay | | | | | | Yes | EIA |
| 27 | La Mattonara | 63% | Some lined with clay | | | | | | | FBA?, EIA |
| 28 | Punta del Pecoraro | Only | | | | | | | | EIA |
| 29 | Malpasso | Only (in the EIA) | | | | | | | | EIA |
| 30 | Marangone | Only (in the EIA) | | | | | | | | EIA |
| 31 | Torre Chiaruccia/ Foce Guardiole | Majority | Lined with clay | | | | | | | EIA |
| 32 | Colonia dei Calabresi | Only reddish fragments | | | | | | | | EIA |
| 33 | Quartaccia | Only, and one bowl | | | | | | | | FBA?, EIA |
| 34 | Grottini | Only, and one bowl | | | | | | | Yes | EIA |
| 35 | Greppa della Macchiozza | Majority | | | | | | | | FBA or EIA |
| 36 | Cretarossa/San Rocco | Majority | | | | | | | | EIA |
| 37 | Le Grottacce | Majority | | | | | | | | FBA |
| 38 | Pelliccione | 80-85% | | | | | | | | FBA |
| 39 | Saracca | Majority | Clay deposit | | | | | | | RBA |
| 40 | Area Stop 4 | Majority | | | | | | | | EBA?, MBA?, FBA? |
| 41 | Fosso Moscarello | Majority | | | | | | | | FBA |
| 42 | Caprolace | Majority | | | | | | Yes | | MBA |
| 43 | La Cotarda | Majority | | | | | | | | ? |

*Table 1. Briquetage sites shown in figure 2: characteristics and chronology (see Alessandri* et al. *2019 for the references).*

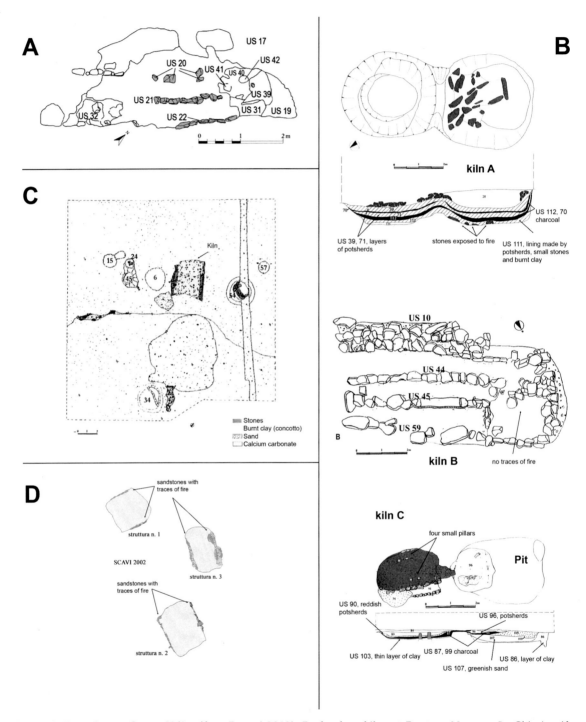

*Fig. 3. A, Baratti, area Centro Velico (from Baratti 2010). B, the three kilns at Puntone Nuovo – Le Chiarine (from Aranguren 2009); C, 'Saggio A' at Portiglioni – Campo da Gioco (from Aranguren & Castelli 2011); D, the three kilns at Puntone Nuovo – Campo da Gioco (from Aranguren et al. 2014).*

30

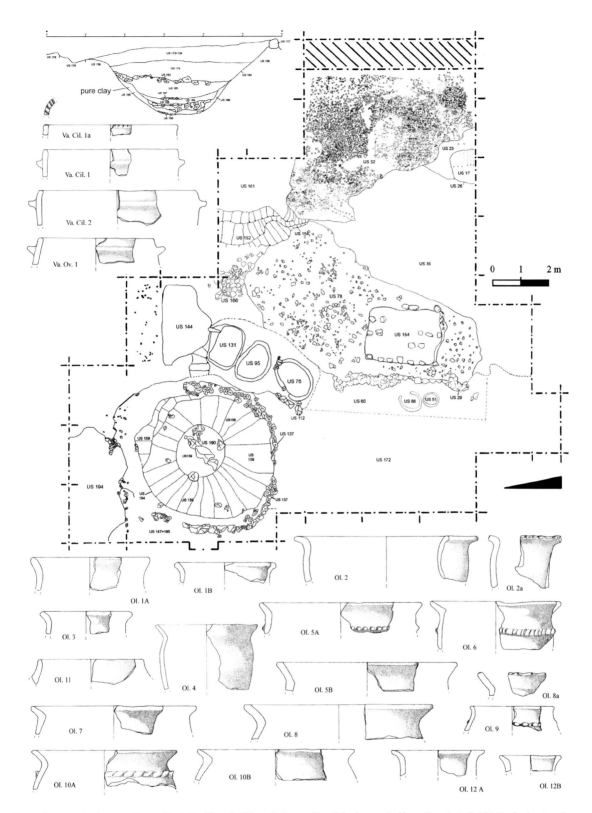

Fig. 4. Excavation area at Duna Feniglia (Saggio D) and the profile of the large pit (from Rossi et al. 2014); the jar typology: Va.Cil., cilindrical vessels; Va.Ov., ovoidal vessels; Ol., jars; scale 1:8 (from Benedetti et al. 2008).

with the reddish-brown jars is uncertain, due to the lack of diagnostic fragments: at the moment only one decorated potsherd could be dated to the final stage of MBA (subphase 3).

To conclude this overview, we mention a group of FBA sites from Campania, at San Marco, Agropoli,[38] and Napoli, Duomo,[39] where considerable quantities of reddish-brown sherds of impasto jars were found on the ancient shoreline, in combination with pits, fire traces, and a vat lined with white concretions.

Discussion

*Pottery production and dating*

At the moment, a presumed local provenance of the vessels at the various sites mentioned can only be hypothesised. Preliminary chemical analyses of a number of potsherds from Puntone Nuovo – Campo da Gioco and Isola di Coltano, however, did point to a local origin of the clay.[40] At the site of La Saracca, two vats filled with clay (ready to use?) were found in a sandy profile.[41] The location was at only a short distance from an exposure of Marne Azzurre, exposed by marine erosion, which could have been used to obtain the clay. Finally, in Duna Feniglia, a very large vat was excavated, partially filled with a layer of clay (SU 186). The feature has been interpreted as a clay deposit for pottery making (*fig. 4*).[42]

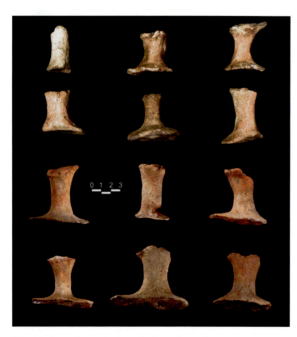

*Fig. 5. Selection of pedestals from Caprolace.*

Almost all the jars from the Bronze and EIA Age sites north and south of the Tiber have been studied and classified (*fig. 4* and *6*). North of the Tiber most of the potsherds come from sites located at the foot of the Tolfa Mountains and are dated to the EIA.[43] The ceramic assemblage includes many reddish-brown coarse ware jars, with a fairly rough surface, frequently with a horizontal cord decoration, and occasionally with a semi-circular, rectangular or trapezoidal saddle grip. Because of the large number of horizontal angular handles of the same type of impasto, we think that many jars had handles. Most of the rims, either unclassifiable or of uncertain origin, probably belong to this group of jars. South of the Tiber, the majority of the reddish potsherds come from the Pelliccione site.[44] Here, the ceramic assemblage is characterized by 80/85% jars, half-conical or ovoidal in shape. The vessels are often decorated just below the rim by horizontal notched ribs with sometimes incorporated grips. The published vessels from Duna Feniglia show a very similar typology.[45]

The dating of these sites is mostly based on ceramic typology and spans from the Isola di Coltano and Caprolace MBA layers to the EIA, although the peak of the phenomenon has to be placed within the latter. Only a few radiocarbon dates are available. These includes two dates on animal bones from Pelliccione (*fig. 1, n. 38*) which were 2945 ± 45 BP (GrA 22090, 1278-1012 calBC) and 3005 ± 45 (GrA 22092, 1399-1113 calBC) and confirm the FBA chronology of the site.[46] Another radiocarbon date, on charcoal, comes from Portiglioni–Campo da Gioco (*fig. 1, n. 13*): 2660 ± 40 BP (Beta 215476, 901-792 calBC), placing the context in the EIA.[47] All dates mentioned are calibrated using OxCal 4.3, IntCal 13, with a probability of 95,4%.

*Content*

On the content of the jars there are no decisive data yet. So far chemical analyses are only available for some potsherds from Puntone Nuovo – Campo da Gioco. These analyses, however, did not yield unequivocal evidence for their use in a salt production process.[48] Following on Pacciarelli's initial hypothesis that the coastal sites mentioned above might be related to salt production, other scholars have suggested other possible uses for the jars, for example to boil food products containing fish and salt.[49] In this context it is worth noting that small ports for fish breeding and/or the production of *garum* were built during the Roman period at four Iron Age coastal sites

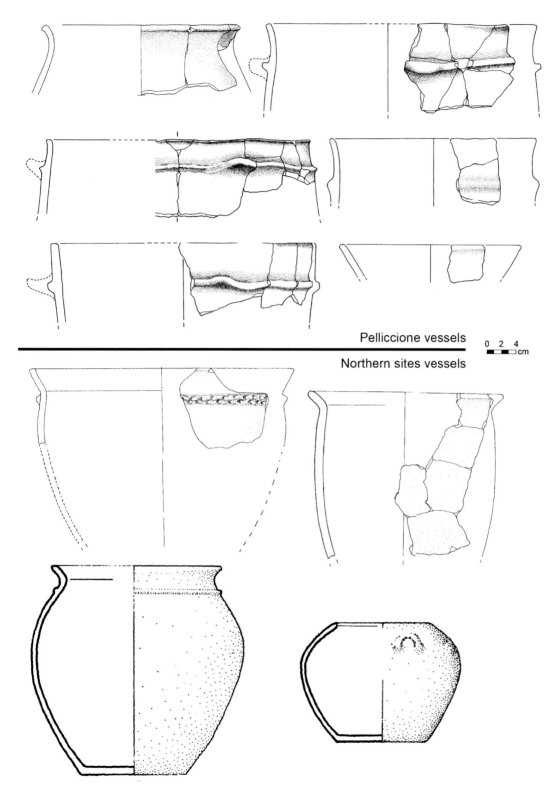

*Fig 6. Representative samples of the "briquetage" vessels North of the Tiber (from Belardelli, 2013) and South of the Tiber (Pelliccione, from Nijboer et al., 2006).*

33

north of the Tiber (Torre Valdaliga, La Mattonara, Punta Pecoraro, Torre Chiaruccia/Foce Guardiole).[50] Similarly, south of the Tiber several fishponds have been found on the coast between Nettuno and Torre Astura[51] at locations where several sites with reddish-brown jars have been found (Le Grottacce, Pelliccione, Saracca, Area Stop 4). This observation has led some authors to postulate that the Romans may have built further on a fish industry that had its roots in the protohistorical period, benefitting from the same environmental conditions to produce a comparable commodity.[52] Obviously there is a chronological hiatus here, but in support of this hypothesis we may mention that at the site of Cretarossa/San Rocco (also known as Nettuno, Depuratore) deposits of reddish-brown pottery dating from the 7th century BCE to the Archaic period have been recorded and published,[53] while the current excavations of the Groningen Institute of Archaeology, the Soprintendenza of Etruria and the University of Naples at Puntone di Scarlino have revealed ceramic deposits dating to the Orientalising period (7th century BCE, pers. comm. M. R. Cinquegrana).

*Nature of the production sites*

From the contexts cited we can deduce that the specialised activity indicated by the pottery debris heaps and related excavated structures took place either in specific areas within settlements or completely separated from settlements. In the former case, the evidence is the presence of other shapes and wares than reddish-brown impasto jars, i.e. both open and closed shapes and fragments of a finer coarse ware, usually smoothed and burnished. In such cases functional elements other than furnaces and vats were also present, like building remains and objects related to domestic activity (*i.e.* kilns, bobbins, and spindle whorls). This is the case, for example, at Torre Valdaliga[54] and Caprolace (unpublished). Differentiation within the archaeological assemblages can be used to discern between residential and specialized activities, even when dealing with surface finds, like at Le Saline di Tarquinia.[55]

However, when the pottery debris heaps occur without clear evidence of domestic use in the form of a minimal presence of tableware potsherds, which north of the Tiber often have Iron Age Villanovan decoration, we likely deal with veritable special activity sites whose location is separated from domestic sites. We note, however, that up to now sites have only been partially excavated.

*Socio-economic context*

The sites listed here mainly date to the later stages of the Bronze and initial stages of the Iron Age, which is a period characterized by fundamental changes in settlement organization, both north and south of the Tiber. In southern Etruria, a network of nearly 70 settlements, with an average size of 5-6 hectares, was abandoned with the population concentrating in five vast settlement areas of more than 100 hectares.[56] Also for northern Etruria, a similar process of synoecism has been hypothesised, especially for the coastal area around the Iron Age settlement of Populonia.[57] In the same time span, in *Latium Vetus* the subcoastal inland settlements expanded, for example Lavinium, Ardea and, slightly afterwards, Rome.[58] Moreover, south of the Tiber the grave inventories become richer, featuring indicators of political-military and religious functions, which are commonly interpreted as signs of an emerging elite.[59] The expansion of the settlement areas, notably in Etruria, reflects population growth and increasing food demands, among which probably marine products. Hence, the common hypothesis is that these contemporary specialized coastal sites were organized by the elites of the developing urban settlements as part of a new territorial organisation.[60]

Paradoxically, later in the Iron Age, in a period of concomitant economic and demographic growth as is evident from burial grounds and settlement sizes, the number of specialized sites decreases. As far as salt production is concerned, we note that to produce large quantities of salt, solar evaporation of salt water in artificial basins in coastal lagoons is a mode of production that is more efficient and less labour intensive than the *briquetage* technique. Interestingly, traces of Roman saltworks, dated to the first century BCE, have recently been excavated near the Maccarese lagoon, at the mouth of the Tiber river.[61] This is in a location where many Roman authors placed the salterns of the Etruscan city of Veio and, later, the *Campus Salinarum Romanarum*.[62] In this formerly wet area, which was only seasonally submerged, also FBA artificial mounds together with clear evidence for cooking and/or boiling activities (kilns and fireplaces) have been found. The area has already been interpreted as a specialized area where agricultural and artisanal practices took place: mostly breeding but also dairy activities, tissues and bone processing.[63] It is well possible that briquetage-like activities took place here alongside solar evaporation to obtain salt. Since the solar evaporation of seawater produces unrefined salt (with other impurities and minerals like magnesium and calcium carbonates), which is bitter and has an unpleasant taste,[64] the specialized activities detected on the mounds may have been partially related to a subsequent phase of salt-refinement.

CRITICAL ISSUES

In the interpretation of the evidence discussed so far, several critical issues remain to be further investigated, especially the salt production hypothesis.[65]

*Absence of typical briquetage equipment*

It must be noted that, at a number of sites, the typical *briquetage* equipment (e.g. pedestals, furnace grids, firedogs) is absent. Firedogs have been found only at Isola di Coltano and Galafone. The chronology of the former covers the beginning of MBA up to the FBA;[66] Galafone is an Iron Age site with possible FBA and/or 7th/6th century BCE layers.[67] Tufa chunks with traces of fire come from the FBA Pelliccione.[68] On the Tyrrhenian side of Italy, pedestals have only been collected in Caprolace. On the Adriatic side, a large quantity of pedestals has been found at Castelliere degli Elleri, together with some half-conical vessels that might be connected with the production of salt.[69]

*The presence of reddish colour in no briquetage-related pottery*

In a modern replica of the briquetage process, the vessels indeed acquired a reddish hue after secondary exposure to high temperatures in the presence of oxygen.[70] Analyses carried out on some potsherds from two Chalcolithic Romanian briquetage sites, Hălăbutoaia à Țolici and Cacica[71] led to the same conclusions. However, the red colour could also be due to an oxidising atmosphere during the pottery production process itself, as seems to be the case at Puntone Nuovo – Campo da Gioco.[72] Moreover, some other presumably domestic vessels, not involved in the salt production process, have the same colour, like those from Pelliccione, Saracca and Fosso Moscarello (Fig 2, 38, 39 and 41, respectively).[73] This would imply that a direct connection between the jar colour and their use in the boiling phase cannot be established with certainty.

*Inconclusiveness of the chemical analyses*

Several attempts have been made to develop an analytic method for assessing the involvement of the jars – and thus their sherds - in the *briquetage* process. All of them focus on anomalous quantities of both Chlorine (Cl) and/or Sodium (Na) in the ceramic fabrics. At the sites of Champ-Durand (Vandée, France) and Barycz (Poland), for example, XRF analyses did reveal a very high concentration of chlorine in the pottery in which the brine was supposedly boiled.[74] Moreover, at the Chinese site of Zhongba, SEM-EDS studies of potsherds revealed a relatively high concentration of both Na (0.7-0.8 wt%) and Cl (0.2-0.3 wt%), progressively decreasing from the interior surfaces towards the exterior, approaching zero at a depth of about, respectively, 1.7-2.1mm and 1.1mm.[75] A SEM-EDX analysis in a modern replica of the briquetage process gave essentially the same results, with Cl virtually absent at 2mm.[76] However, advanced chemical analyses (XRDP and SEM-EDS) carried out on a number of potsherds from Puntone Nuovo – Campo da Gioco, supposedly used to boil brine, failed to find Na or Cl in such concentrations that they should be ascribed to salt production. However, Na and Cl are highly mobile elements, which after the deposition of the potsherds may be easily washed out by meteoric or phreatic waters.[77]

*Different shapes of containers*

The Italian reddish jars are often different from the usual central and Atlantic European briquetage vessels, in both shape and in size. Vessels known from briquetage sites from the latter areas are quite small and half-conical or cylindrical, to enhance the evaporation process, like the ones which have been found at Castelliere di Elleri, on the Adriatic side of Italy. The vessels from the sites described in this paper, which are all on the Tyrrhenian side of Italy, are usually much bigger and some shapes do not seem fit for the evaporation process. Besides, some of them seem too refined for being disposable containers. Even if it is likely that other kinds of vessels were in use, for example for transporting brine or even salt, their percentage seems too high.

*Distance of salt source*

Finally, it should be noted that sites with large quantities of reddish-brown pottery also occur in inland contexts at significant distance from the coastline or coastal lagoons. Only recently, J. Sevink and W. van Gorp identified in the Pontine plain a new yet unpublished site at La Cotarda, (*fig. 1, 43*) featuring large quantities of reddish-brown impasto sherds – almost all jars and dolia – at the surface level. La Cotarda may prove to be a key site in the interpretation of this class of containers, since there are no salt sources in the nearby area (the sea is at 14 km distance). Thus, at least in this case, the hypothesis of salt production must be ruled out. Unfortunately, at the moment, the potsherds collected so far are not suitable for a precise dating.

CONCLUSION

Following Pacciarelli's hypothesis in 1991, the availability of new data has given rise to new questions – as this usually goes – instead of answering the initial one. In fact, several lines of research are still needed to test the hypotheses which have been brought forward so far. In particular, more physical/chemical analyses are needed to assess both the provenance and the contents of the reddish impasto jars. Some analyses are currently being executed by the Groningen Institute of Archaeology at the site of Puntone Nuovo di Scarlino, north of the Tiber, and in the site of Caprolace, south of the Tiber.

Next, we call for more consistent quantitative studies concerning the number of vessels to assess the scale of production.[78] Even though some authors refer to "quasi industrial" processes,[79] this statement needs to be more solidly substantiated. Without doubt, the concentration and quantity of reddish jars in Isola di Coltano, Duna Feniglia and Pelliccione are remarkably high. Unfortunately, none of these sites have been completely excavated, hence the impossibility to assess the overall quantity of potsherds debris and to quantify the estimated output. However, as a comparison we can recall here the "proto-industrial" (Iron Age 7th- 1st centuries BCE) *briquetage* sites in the Seille Valley where 3-4 million m³ of *briquetage* potsherds have been identified in 12 meters high mounds.[80] Here the term "industrial" has been used with a different meaning. Additional evidence in this sense might also be obtained from environmental studies since for the heating process, when the *briquetage* technique is used, substantial quantities of fuel (probably wood) are needed, which should have resulted in a serious environmental impact on the surrounding landscape.[81]

Moreover, the current resolution of the chronologies is too large to determine the intensity of production. Hence, we are not able to distinguish between protracted but seasonal (or occasional) and very intensive but short activities.

As for the shapes of the vessels, a comprehensive morphological and functional typology which encompass all the collected potsherds together, at least on a regional basis, has never been attempted. Such a typology would serve as a basis to assess both the function and the circulation of vessels and/or ideas.

At the moment, the accumulations of the typical reddish jars along the Tyrrhenian coast cannot be explained only with the 'salt hypothesis' and in fact a more diversified coastal economy may have existed at the sites discussed north and south of the Tiber, especially between the FBA and the EIA. In fact, even assuming that most of the sites were related to fisheries and fish processing, another part must have been devoted to salt production for storage and preservation. If that was the case, part of the jars might have been used to transport salt from the production sites to the places where fish was processed. Moreover, if a large part of the products was traded, as suggested by many authors,[82] the differences in shape between the jars may be explained by the different traded products: fish, sauces, salt. It must be noted that many of the sites we discussed are located in or near lagoons, which could mean that access to inland fresh water was necessary, as is the case with seafood production.[83] The exact nature of the content of the jar and the possible trading networks would also shed new light on the relationships between these sites and the emerging early states, both in Etruria and in *Latium Vetus*. The very existence of an intertwined and complex organization for the exploitation of both fish and salt would assume, for example, the presence of labour division and coordination, and a flow of information which would have required the presence of a ruling class i.e. the emerging elite of the early states.

ACKNOWLEDGEMENTS

We would like to thank F. di Gennaro, A. Guidi and M. R. Cinquegrana for their suggestions and comments.

NOTES

1. Harding 2013.
2. Cappuccio/Capewell 2010.
3. Bergier 1982.
4. Kurlansky 2002.
5. Harding 2013; Heth 2015.
6. Lugli *et al.* 2007; Roveri *et al.* 2014; Harding 2014.
7. Lanciani 1888; Grossi *et al.* 2015.
8. Harding 2013; Weller/Brigand 2015.
9. Daire/Le Brozec 1990; 1991; Daire *et al.* 2001; Daire 2002.
10. Kinory 2012.
11. Weller *et al.* 2008; Sordoillet *et al.* 2018.
12. Pacciarelli 2001.
13. Pacciarelli 1991.
14. Lane and Morri, 2001.
15. Chowne *et al*, 2001.

[16] Mandolesi 1996; Pacciarelli 2001.
[17] Di Fraia/Secol, 2002; Di Fraia 2006.
[18] Baratti 2010.
[19] Aranguren 2001; 2002; 2003; Aranguren/Castelli 2006; Aranguren 2008; Aranguren *et al.* 2014; Aranguren/Cinquegrana, 2015.
[20] Baratti 2010.
[21] Daire/Le Brozec 1990; 1991; Daire *et al.* 2001; Daire 2002.
[22] Laffite 2002.
[23] Levi/Laviosa 1986; Puglisi 2011.
[24] Shaw *et al.* 2001.
[25] Belardelli *et al.* forthcoming.
[26] Negroni Catacchio/Cardosa 2002; Cardosa 2004.
[27] Benedetti *et al.* 2008; 2010; Rossi *et al.* 2014; Rossi 2017.
[28] Belardelli/Pascucci 2002; Trucco, di Gennaro/D'Ercole 2002.
[29] Mandolesi/Trucco 2002.
[30] Belardelli 1999.
[31] Pascucci 1998; 1999; Belardelli/Trucco/Vitagliano 2008.
[32] Attema/Nijboer/Rooke 2002; Attema/de Haas/Nijboer 2003; Nijboer/Attema/van Oortmerssen 2006.
[33] Alessandri 2013.
[34] Bell 1990.
[35] Weller 2000 figs 47–49.
[36] Nenquin 1961; Weller 2000 fig. 83.
[37] Alessandri 2013. Pending the draft of this contribute, Alessandri *et al.* 2019 has been published which confirms the chronology of the briquetage phase.
[38] Albore Livadie *et al.* 2010.
[39] Belardelli et al. forthcoming.
[40] Di Fraia/Secoli 2000; Aranguren *et al.* 2014.
[41] Alessandri 2007.
[42] Ross, 2017.
[43] Belardelli 2013.
[44] Nijboer/Attema/van Oortmerssen 2006.
[45] Benedetti *et al.* 2008.
[46] Attema/de Haas/Nijboer 2003.
[47] Aranguren/Castelli 2011.
[48] Aranguren *et al.* 2014.
[49] Belardelli/Pascucci 1996; Belardelli 2013.
[50] Belardelli 2013.
[51] Higginbotham 1997.
[52] Belardelli 2013.
[53] Alessandri/Tol 2007; Tol *et al.* 2012.
[54] Maffei 1981; Belardelli/Pascucci 1996.
[55] Mandolesi 1996; 1999.
[56] di Gennaro/Peroni 1986; Pacciarelli 2001; Barbaro 2010.
[57] Bartoloni/Rossetti 1984; Milletti 2015.
[58] Guidi 2006; Alessandri 2013; Fulminante 2014.
[59] Bietti Sestieri 2005; Guidi 2010; De Santis 2011; Alessandri 2016.
[60] Pacciarelli 2001; Negroni Catacchio/Cardosa 2002; Alessandri 2013; Belardelli 2013.
[61] Ruggeri *et al.* 2010; Grossi *et al.* 2015.
[62] Pavolini 1989; Camporeale 1997; Morelli/Forte 2014.
[63] De Castro *et al.* 2018.
[64] Harding 2013.
[65] Di Fraia, forthcoming.
[66] Pasquinucci/Menchelli 2002.
[67] Pasquinucci/Del Rio/Menchelli 2002.
[68] Attema/Alessandr, 2012.
[69] Càssola Guida/Montagnari Kokelj 2006; Montagnari Kokelj 2007.
[70] Tencariu *et al.* 2015.
[71] Sandu *et al*, 2012.
[72] Aranguren *et al.* 2014.
[73] Nijboer/Attema/van Oortmerssen 2006; Alessandri 2007.
[74] Ard/Weller 2012.
[75] Flad *et al.* 2005.
[76] Tencariu *et al.* 2015.
[77] Flad *et al.* 2005; Horiuchi *et al.* 2011; Sandu *et al.* 2012.
[78] Costin 1991; 2001.
[79] Pacciarelli 2001; Alessandri 2013.
[80] Olivier/Kovacik 2006; Olivier 2009; Jusseret *et al.* 2015.
[81] Villalobos/Ménanteau 2006; Riddiford *et al.* 2012.
[82] Pacciarelli 2001; Alessandri 2013; Belardelli 2013.
[83] Belardelli/Pascucci 1996; Thurmond 2006.

BIBLIOGRAPHY

Albore Livadie, C. et al. 2010, Torre S. Marco: un insediamento costiero del Bronzo finale ad Agropoli (SA), *Annali dell'Università degli Studi Suor Orsola Benincasa*, 7–74.

Alessandri, L. 2007, *L'occupazione costiera protostorica del Lazio centromeridionale* (BAR Int. Ser. 1592), Oxford.

Alessandri, L. 2013, *Latium Vetus in the Bronze Age and Early Iron Age / Il Latium Vetus nell'età del Bronzo e nella prima età del Ferro* (BAR Int. Ser. 2565), Oxford.

Alessandri, L. 2016, Hierarchical and federative polities in protohistoric Latium Vetus. An analysis of Bronze Age and Early Iron Age settlement organization, in P.A J. Attema/J/ Seubers/S. Willemsen (eds), *Early states, territories and settlements in protohistoric Central Italy. Proceedings of a specialist conference at the Groningen Institute of Archaeology* (Corollaria Crustumina 2), Groningen, 67–82.

Alessandri, L./G.W. Tol 2007, Cretarossa/San Rocco, in C. Belardelli et al., *Repertorio dei siti protostorici del Lazio - province di Roma, Viterbo e Frosinone*, Borgo San Lorenzo (FI), 215–218.

Alessandri, L./ K.F. Achino/P.A.J. Attema/M. de Novaes Nascimento/M. Gatta/M.F. Rolfo/J. Sevink/G. Sottili/W. van Gorp, 2019. Salt or fish (or salted fish)? The Bronze Age specialised sites along the Tyrrhenian coast of Central Italy: New insights from Caprolace settlement. PLoS One 14. https://doi.org/10.1371/journal.pone.0224435

Aranguren, B.M. 2001, Il comprensorio delle Colline Metallifere in età pre-protostorica, in *Atti della XXXIV Riunione Scientifica dell'Istituto Italiano di Preistoria e Protostoria, Preistoria e Protostoria della Toscana*, Firenze, 489–502.

Aranguren, B.M. 2002, Il Golfo di Follonica in età protostorica: l'idrografia antica e i sistemi insediamentali, in *Atti del V incontro di studi Preistoria e Protostoria in Etruria. Paesaggi d'acque*, Firenze, 111–122.

Aranguren, B.M. 2003, ll sistema insediativo del territorio di Scarlino in età protostorica, in *Scarlino. Arte, Storia e Territorio*, Firenze, 9–23.

Aranguren, B.M. 2008, Una fornace per ceramica dell'età del bronzo finale in località Le Chiarine, Puntone Nuovo, Scarlino (GR). Nota preliminare, in N. Negroni Catacchio (ed.), *Atti dell'VIII incontro di studi preistoria e protostoria in Etruria. Paesaggi reali e paesaggi mentali*. Milano, 593–602.

Aranguren, B.M., 2009. Un insediamento produttivo per ceramica dell'età del Bronzo finale in località Le Chiarine, Puntone Nuovo, Scarlino (GR), *Off. Etruscologia* 1, 9–22.

Aranguren, B.M. et al. 2014, Le strutture e lo scarico di olle del Puntone Nuovo di Scarlino (GR), e i siti costieri specializzati della protostoria mediotirrenica, *RScPreist* 64, 227–259.

Aranguren, B.M./S. Castelli 2006, Scarlino (GR). Testimonianze di attività produttive a Portiglioni, *Notiziario della Soprintendenza per i Beni Archeologici della Toscana* 1, 293–299.

Aranguren, B.M./S. Castelli 2011, Fra mare e laguna: ipotesi interpretative per il sito produttivo di Portiglioni, Scarlino (GR), in F. Lugli/A.A. Stoppiello/S. Biagetti (eds), *Atti del 4° Convegno Nazionale di Etnoarcheologia* (BAR Int. Ser. 2235), Oxford, 9–16.

Aranguren, B.M./M.R. Cinquegrana 2015, Siti industriali del litorale marino del Golfo di Follonica tra il Bronzo finale e il primo Ferro, in *Atti della L Riunione Scientifica dell'Istituto Italiano di Preistoria e Protostoria, Preistoria del Cibo*. Available at: www.preistoriadelcibo.it/contributi/3_39.pdf.

Ard, V./O. Weller 2012, Les vases de 'type Champ-Durand': témoins d'une exploitation du sel au Néolithique récent dans le Marais poitevin, in R. Joussaume (ed.), *L'enceinte néolithique de Champ-Durand à Nieul-sur-l'Autise (Vendée)*, Chauvigny, 309–333.

Attema, P.A.J./L. Alessandri 2012, Salt production on the Tyrrhenian coast in South Lazio (Italy) during the Late Bronze Age: its significance for understanding contemporary society, in V. Nikolov/K. Bacvarov (eds), *Salz und Gold: die Rolle des Salzes im prähistorischen Europa / Salt and Gold: The Role of Salt in Prehistoric Europe*, Provadia/Veliko Tarnovo, 287–300.

Attema, P.A.J./T. de Haas/A.J. Nijboer 2003, The Astura Project, interim report of the 2001 and 2002 campaigns of the Groningen Institute of Archaeology along the coast between Nettuno and Torre Astura (Lazio, Italy), *BABesch* 78, 107–140.

Attema, P.A.J./A.J. Nijboer/M. Rooke 2002, Piccarreta 13, een late Bronstijdnederzetting op de kust van zuid-Latium (Italië), *Paleoaktueel*, 13, 65–69.

Baratti, G. 2010, Un sito per la produzione del sale sulla spiaggia di Baratti (area Centro Velico) alla fine dell'età del Bronzo, in *Materiali per Populonia 9*, Pisa, 243–260.

Barbaro, B. 2010, *Insediamenti, aree funerarie ed entità territoriali in Etruria meridionale nel Bronzo finale*, Firenze.

Bartoloni, G./C. Rossetti 1984, L'insediamento protostorico di Scarlino. Relazione preliminare, *RiScPreist* 39, 223–246.

Belardelli, C. 1999, Torre Valdaliga, in *Ferrante Rittatore Vonwiller e la Maremma, 1936-1976. Paesaggi naturali, umani, archeologici*, Grotte di Castro, 79–90.

Belardelli, C. 2013, Coastal and underwater Late Urnfield sites in South Etruria, *Skyllis* 1, 5–17.

Belardelli, C. et al. forthcoming, Il Sale. Record archeologico, produzione e manipolazione, in *Atti della L Riunione scientifica dell'Istituto Italiano di Preistoria e Protostoria. Preistoria del Cibo*.

Belardelli, C./P. Pascucci 1996, I siti costieri del territorio di Civitavecchia e S. Marinella nella prima età del ferro. Risultati preliminari di una revisione critica dei dati, *Bollettino della Società Tarquiniese di Arte e Storia* 25, 343–398.

Belardelli, C./P. Pascucci 2002, Lo sfruttamento delle risorse marine nell'età del ferro: il caso di Marangone (Santa Marinella, Roma), in N. Negroni Catacchio (ed.), *Atti del V incontro di studi Preistoria e Protostoria in Etruria. Paesaggi d'acque*, Milano, 241–255.

Belardelli, C./F. Trucco/S. Vitagliano 2008, Installazioni funzionali costiere della prima età del Ferro: elementi moderni di un paesaggio protostorico, in N. Negroni Catacchio (ed.), *Atti dell'VIII incontro di studi preistoria e protostoria in Etruria. Paesaggi reali e paesaggi mentali*, Milano, 353–365.

Bell, M. 1990, *Brean Down. Excavations 1983–1987*, London.

Benedetti, L. et al. 2008, Paesaggi d'acque. Duna Feniglia, loc. Ansedonia. Scavo di un insediamento del Primo Ferro: risultati e prospettive, in N. Negroni Catacchio (ed.), *Atti dell'VIII incontro di studi preistoria e protostoria in Etruria. Paesaggi reali e paesaggi mentali*, Milano, 261–284.

Benedetti, L. et al. 2010, Nuovi dati dallo scavo di Duna Feniglia (Orbetello, GR), in N. Negroni Catacchio (ed.) *Atti del IX incontro di studi Preistoria e Protostoria in Etruria. L'alba dell'Etruria. Fenomeni di continuità e trasformazione nei secoli XII-VIII a.C.*, Milano, 157–167.

Bergier, J.-F. 1982, *Une histoire du sel*, Fribourg.

Bietti Sestieri, A.M. 2005, A reconstruction of historical processes in Bronze and Early Iron Age Italy based on recent archaeological research, in, P.A.J. Attema/A.J. Nijboer/A. Zifferero (eds), *Papers in Italian Archaeology VI, Communities and Settlements from the Neolithic to the Early Medieval Period*, Oxford, 9–24.

Camporeale, G. 1997, Il sale e i primordi di Veio, in G. Bartoloni (ed.), *Le necropoli arcaiche di Veio. Giornata di studio in memoria di Massimo Pallottino*, Roma, 197–199.

Cappuccio, F./S. Capewell 2010, A sprinkling of doubt, *New Scientist* 2758, 22–23. Available at: https://www.newscientist.com/article/dn18835-theres-no-doubt-about-the-health-dangers-of-salt/.

Cardosa, M. 2004, 'Paesaggi d'acque' al Monte Argentario, in N. Negroni Catacchio (ed.), *Atti del VI incontro di studi preistoria e protostoria in Etruria. Miti simboli decorazioni*, Milano, 405–415.

Càssola Guida, P./M. Montagnari Kokelj 2006, Produzione del sale nel Golfo di Trieste: un'attività probabilmente antica, in A. Cardarelli/M. Pacciarelli/A. Vanzetti (eds) *Studi di Protostoria in onore di Renato Peroni*, Firenze, 327–332.

Chowne, P. et al. 2001, *Excavations at Billingborough, Lincolnshire, 1975–8: A Bronze-Iron Age Settlement and Salt-Working Site. East Anglian Archaeology, Report 94*, Salisbury.

Costin, C.L. 1991, Craft Specialization: Issues in Defining, Documenting, and Explaining the Organization of Production, *Archaeological Method and Theory* 3, 1–56. Available at: http://www.jstor.org/stable/20170212.

Costin, C.L. 2001, Craft Production Systems, in G.M. Feinman/T.D. Price (eds), *Archaeology at the Millennium: A Sourcebook*, Boston, MA, 273–327. doi: 10.1007/978-0-387-72611-3_8.

Daire, M.Y. et al. 2001, Un complexe artisanal de l'Age du Fer à Enez Vihan en Pleumeur-Bodou, Côtes d'Armor, *Revue archéologique de l'ouest* 18, 57–93.

Daire, M.Y. 2002, Ateliers de bouilleurs de sel en Trégor (Bretagne). Données récents et inédites, in O. Weller (ed.), *Archéologie du sel: techniques et sociétés dans la pré- et protohi-stoire européenne, Actes du Colloque 12.2 du XIVe Congrès de UISPP et de la Table ronde du Comité des salines de France*, Rahden/Westf., 31–51.

Daire, M.Y./M. Le Brozec 1990, Un nouvel atelier de bouilleur de sel à Landrellec en Pleumeur-Bodou, *Revue archéologique de l'ouest* 7, 57–71.

Daire, M.Y./M. Le Brozec 1991, L'atelier de bouilleur de sel de Landrellec en Pleumeur-Bodou, *Association Man-*

*che Atlantique pour la Recherche Archéologique dans les Iles. Bulletin d'information* 4, 47–52.

De Castro, F. R. *et al.* 2018, La sponda destra del Tevere, presso la foce, prima dei Romani: gli insediamenti, in M. Cébeillac-Gervasoni/N. Laubry/F. Zevi (eds), *Atti del Terzo seminario ostiense. Ricerche su Ostia e il suo territorio*, Roma: doi: 10.4000/books.efr.3642.

De Santis 2011, L'ideologia del potere: le figure al vertice delle comunità nel Lazio protostorico, in V. Nizzo (a cura di ), *Dalla Nascita alla morte: Antropologia e Archeologia a confronto, Atti dell'Incontro Internazionale di Studi in onore di Claude Lévi-Strauss*, Roma Museo Nazionale Preistorico Etnografico L. Pigorini 21 maggio 2010, 171-197.

Di Fraia, T. 2006, Produzione, circolazione e consumo del sale nella protostoria italiana: dati archeologici e ipotesi di lavoro, in *Atti della XXXIX Riunione Scientifica dell'Istituto Italiano di Preistoria e Protostoria, Materie Prime e Scambi nella Preistoria Italiana*, Firenze, 1639–1649.

Di Fraia, T. forthcoming, Reddish ollas and production and use of salt: an open question, in Caliniuc, Ştefan et al. (eds) *First International Congress on the Anthropology of Salt*.

Di Fraia, T./L. Secoli 2000, Un contributo alla conoscenza della produzione e del consumo del sale nella preistoria. Il sito di Isola di Coltano presso Pisa, *Naturalmente*, 13/3(settembre), 62–67.

Di Fraia, T./L. Secoli 2002, Il sito dell'età del Bronzo di Isola di Coltano, in N. Negroni Catacchio (ed.), *Atti del V incontro di studi Preistoria e Protostoria in Etruria. Paesaggi d'acque*, Milano, 79–93.

Di Gennaro, F./R. Peroni 1986, Aspetti regionali dello sviluppo dell'insediamento protostorico nell'Italia centro-meridionale alla luce dei dati archeologici e ambientali, *DialA* 2, 193–200.

Flad, R.K. *et al.* 2005, Archaeological and chemical evidence for early salt production in China, *Proceedings of the National Academy of Sciences of the United States of America*, 102(35), 12618–12622. doi: 10.1073/pnas.0502985102.

Fulminante, F. 2014, *The Urbanisation of Rome and Latium Vetus: From the Bronze Age to the Archaic Era*, Cambridge.

Grossi, M.C. *et al.* 2015, A complex relationship between human and natural landscape: a multidisciplinary approach to the study of the roman saltworks in 'Le Vignole - Interporto' (Maccarese, Fiumicino - Roma, in *Archaeology of salt. Approaching an invisible past*, London, 83–101.

Guidi, A. 2006, The Archaeology of Early State in Italy, *Social Evolution & History*, 5(2), 55–89.

Guidi, A. 2010, The Archaeology of Early State in Italy: New Data and Acquisitions, *Social Evolution & History*, 9(2), 12–27.

Harding, A. 2013, *Salt in Prehistoric Europe*, Leiden.

Harding, A. 2014, The prehistoric exploitation of salt in Europe, *Geological Quarterly*, 58(3), 591--596. doi: 10.7306/gq.1164.

Heth, C.L. 2015, The Skin They Were In: Leather and Tanning in Antiquity, in S.C. Rasmussen (ed.), *Chemical Technology in Antiquity*, Washington, 181–196. doi: 10.1021/bk-2015-1211.ch006.

Higginbotham, J. 1997, *Piscinae. Artificial fishponds in Roman Italy*, Chapel Hill.

Horiuchi, A. *et al.* 2011, Detection of chloride from pottery as a marker for salt: A new analytical method validated using simulated salt-making pottery and applied to Japanese ceramics, *Journal of Archaeological Science*, 38(11), 2949–2956. doi: http://dx.doi.org/10.1016/j.jas.2011.06.003.

Jusseret, S. *et al.* 2015, Le Briquetage de la Seille (Moselle): géoarchéologie et archéogéographie d'un complexe d'exploitation intensive du sel à l'âge du Fer, in F. Olmer/R. Roure (eds), *Les Gaulois au fil de l'eau : actes du 37e colloque international de l'Association Française pour l'Étude de l'Âge du Fer*. Montpellier, 515–537.

Kinory, J. 2012, *Salt production, distribution and use in the British Iron Age* (BAR British Series 559), Oxford.

Kurlansky, M. 2002, Salt: A world history, New York.

Laffite, J. D. 2002, Le briquetage de la Seille à Moyenvic (Moselle, France), au lieu-dit 'Les Crôleurs', in O. Weller (ed.), *Archéologie du sel: techniques et sociétés dans la pré- et protohi-stoire européenne, Actes du Colloque 12.2 du XIVe Congrès de UISPP et de la Table ronde du Comité des salines de France*, Rahden/Westf., 197–207.

Lanciani, R. 1888, Il Campus Salinorum Romanorum, *BCom*, 83–91.

Lane, T./I. Morris 2001, *A millennium of saltmaking: prehistoric and Romano-British salt production in the Fenland*, Exeter.

Levi, D./C. Laviosa 1986, Il forno minoico da vasaio di Haghia Triada, *ASAtene* 57, 7–47.

Lugli, S. *et al.* 2007, Messinian halite and residual facies in the Crotone basin (Calabria, Italy), *Geological Society, London, Special Publications*, 285(1), 169 LP – 178. doi: 10.1144/SP285.10.

Maffei, A. 1981, Il complesso abitativo proto-urbano di Torre Valdaliga, in *La preistoria e la protostoria nel territorio di Civitavecchia*, Civitavecchia, 96–217.

Mandolesi, A. 1996, L'insediamento Villanoviano, *Teknos*, 6, suppl.(September), 35–37.

Mandolesi, A. 1999, *La 'prima' Tarquinia: L'insediamento protostorico sulla Civita e nel territorio circostante*, Firenze.

Mandolesi, A./F. Trucco 2002, L'abitato costiero della prima età del ferro di Acque Fresche (Civitavecchia - RM), in N. Negroni Catacchio (ed.), *Atti del IV incontro di studi Preistoria e Protostoria in Etruria. Paesaggi d'acque*, Milano, 495–503.

Milletti, M. 2015, La nascita di Populonia: dati e ipotesi sullo sviluppo della città etrusca all'alba del primo millennio a.C., in M. Rendeli (ed.), *Le città visibili. Atti del Seminario Internazionale in onore di Gilda Bartoloni e Alberto Moravetti*, Roma, 59–96.

Montagnari Kokelj, M. 2007, Salt and the Trieste karst (North-Eastern Italy) in prehistory: some consideration, in D. Monah, D. et al., *L'exploitation du sel à travers le temps*, Piatra Neamt, 161–189.

Morelli, C./V. Forte 2014, Il Campus Salinarum Romanarum e l'epigrafe dei conductores, *MEFRA [En ligne]*, 126(1). doi: 10.4000/mefra.2059.

Negroni Catacchio, N./M. Cardosa 2002, Dalle sorgenti al mare. Rapporti tra l'area interna e le lagune costiere nel territorio tra Fiora e Albegna, in N. Negroni Catacchio (ed.), *Atti del V incontro di studi Preistoria e Protostoria in Etruria. Paesaggi d'acque*, Milano, 157–177.

Nenquin, J.A.E. 1961, *Salt. A Study in Economic Prehistory* (Dissertationes Archaeologicae Gandenses,6), Gent.

Nijboer, A.J./P.A.J. Attema/G.J.M. van Oortmerssen 2006, Ceramics from a Late Bronze Age saltern on the coast near Nettuno (Rome, Italy), *Palaeohistoria*, 47/48, 141–205.

Olivier, L. 2009, Contribution à l'étude de l'évolution techno-typologique des modes de production du sel dans la vallée de la Seille (Moselle) à l'âge du Fer, *Antiquités Nationales* 40, 1–19.

Olivier, L./J. Kovacik 2006, The 'Briquetage de la Seille': proto-industrial salt production in the European Iron Age, *Antiquity* 80, 558–566.

Pacciarelli, M. 1991, Insediamento, territorio, comunità in Etruria meridionale agli esordi del processo di urbanizzazione, *ScAnt* 5, 163–208.

Pacciarelli, M. 2001, *Dal villaggio alla città. La svolta protourbana del 1000 a.C. nell'Italia tirrenica*, Firenze.

Pascucci, P. 1998, L'insediamento costiero della prima età del ferro de 'La Mattonara' (Civitavecchia), *ACl* 50, 69–115.

Pascucci, P. 1999, La Mattonara, in *Ferrante Rittatore Vonwiller e la Maremma 1936-1976: paesaggi naturali, umani, archeologici, Atti del convegno*, Grotte di Castro, 91–102.

Pasquinucci, M./s. Menchelli 2002, The Isola di Coltano Bronze Age village and the salt production in North coastal Tuscany (Italy), in O. Weller (ed.), *Archéologie du sel: techniques and sociétés. Colloque 12.2, XIVe congrés UISPP*, Rahden/Westf., 177–188.

Pasquinucci, M./A. Del Rio/S. Menchelli 2002, Terra e acque nell'Etruria nord-occidentale, in N. Negroni Catacchio (ed.), *Atti del V incontro di studi Preistoria e Protostoria in Etruria. Paesaggi d'acque*, Milano, 51–61.

Pavolini, C. 1989, *Ostia*, Bari.

Puglisi, D. 2011, La fornace da vasaio TM IB di Haghia Triada. Le ceramiche e il sistema di produzione, distribuzione e consumo, *Creta Antica* 12, 199–271.

Riddiford, N.G. et al. 2012, Holocene palaeoenvironmental history and the impact of prehistoric salt production in the Seille Valley, Eastern France, *The Holocene*, 22, 831–845.

Rossi, F. et al. 2014, Duna Feniglia (Orbetello, GR). I risultati delle ultime campagne di scavo (2011-2012) nell'area nord-occidentale, in N. Negroni Catacchio (ed.), *Atti dell'XI incontro di Preistoria e Protostoria in Etruria. Paesaggi cerimoniali*, Milano, 681–688.

Rossi, F. 2017, Duna Feniglia – Sede Forestale (sito TF01). Un sito produttivo villanoviano, in N. Negroni Catacchio/M. Cardosa/A. Dolfini (eds), *Paesaggi d'Acque. La Laguna di Orbetello e il Monte Argentario tra Preistoria ed Età Romana*, Milano, 230–251.

Roveri, M. et al. 2014, The Messinian Salinity Crisis: Past and future of a great challenge for marine sciences, *Marine Geology*, 352, 25–58. doi: https://doi.org/10.1016/j.margeo.2014.02.002.

Ruggeri, D. et al. 2010, Località Le Vignole, Maccarese (Fiumicino, Roma): risultati preliminari dello scavo protostorico, in N. Negroni Catacchio (ed.), *L'alba dell'Etruria. Fenomeni di continuità e trasformazione nei secoli XII-VIII a.C. Atti del IX incontro di studi Preistoria e Protostoria in Etruria*, Milano, 327–338.

Sandu, I. et al. 2012, Analyses archéométrique sur les moules à sel chalcolithiques de l'est de la Roumanie, in V. Nikolov/K. Bacvarov (eds), *Salz und Gold: die Rolle des Salzes im prähistorischen Europa / Salt and Gold: The Role of Salt in Prehistoric Europe*, Provadia/Veliko Tarnovo, 143–154.

Shaw, J. W. et al. 2001, *A LM IA ceramic kiln in South-Central Crete: function and pottery production*, Princeton. Available at: http://hdl.handle.net/1807/3306.

Sordoillet, D. et al. 2018, Earliest salt working in the world: From excavation to microscopy at the prehistoric sites of Țolici and Lunca (Romania), *Journal of Archaeological Science*, 89, pp. 46–55. doi: https://doi.org/10.1016/j.jas.2017.11.003.

Tencariu, F.-A. et al. 2015, Briquetage and salt cakes: an experimental approach of a prehistoric technique, *JASc* 59, 118–131. doi: 10.1016/j.jas.2015.04.016.

Thurmond, D. L. 2006, *A Handbook of Food Processing in Classical Rome. For Her Bounty No Winter*, Leiden.

Tol, G. W. et al. 2012, Protohistoric sites on the coast between Nettuno and Torre Astura (Pontine Region, Lazio, Italy), *Palaeohistoria*, 53/54, 161–193.

Trucco, F./F. di Gennaro/V. D'Ercole 2002, Contributo alla conoscenza della costa dell'Etruria meridionale nella protostoria. Lo scavo 1994 al Marangone (S. Marinella - RM), in N. Negroni Catacchio (ed.), *Atti del V incontro di studi Preistoria e Protostoria in Etruria. Paesaggi d'acque*, Milano, 231–240.

Villalobos, C.A./I. Ménantau 2006, Paléoenvironnements et techniques de production du sel marin (par ignition ou insolation) durant l'Antiquité: les cas des baies de Bourgneuf (France) et de Cadix (Espagne), in J.-C. Hocquet/J.-L. Sarrazin (eds) *Le sel de la Baie: Histoire, archéologie, ethnologie des sels atlantiques*, Rennes, 87–103. doi: 10.4000/books.pur.7598.

Weller, O. 2000, Le matériel de briquetage des ateliers sauniers de Sorrus (Pas-de-Calais), in Y. Desfosses (ed.), *Archéologie préventive en Vallée de Canche. Les sites protohistoriques fouillés dans le cadre de la réalisation de l'autoroute A. 16*, Berck sur Mer, 272–279.

Weller, O. et al. 2008, Première exploitation de sel en Europe: Techniques et gestion de l'exploitation de la source salée de Poiana Slatinei à Lunca (Neamț, Roumanie), in O. Weller/A. Dufraisse/P. Pétrequin (eds), *Sel, eau et forêt: hier et aujourd'hui*, Besançon, 205–230.

Weller, O./R. Brigand (eds) 2015, *Archaeology of Salt: approaching an invisible past*, Leiden.

# Tecniche edilizie e societá nel Lazio Arcaico

*Gabriele Cifani*

*Abstract*

*Technology can be effect and cause of social and cultural change. An example is offered by the widespread diffusion of the opus quadratum building technique in Rome as well as in the whole Tyrrhenian Italy, from the 6th century onward. It has been noted that such a phenomenon entails an increase in the sophistication of building activities, but one should also consider the deep social and political transformations that occurred in Latium and Etruria in the course of the 6th century BC as the background for such long term technological innovation. Within this historical framework, this paper discusses the evidence of the most ancient squared stone buildings and some aspects of their social significance.*

E' merito degli organizzatori di questo convegno per il quarantennale delle ricerche su *Satricum* aver posto l'attenzione sul ruolo dello sviluppo tecnologico in rapporto alle culture dell'Italia antica, in particolare per l'epoca preromana.

E' necessario ricordare infatti che il caso di *Satricum* è forse uno dei più positivi esperimenti di collaborazione tra istituzioni italiane ed estere, nell'ottica della ricerca scientifica e della tutela di un territorio, tramite un approccio interdisciplinare.[1]

Alle équipes olandesi impegnate nell'area pontina dobbiamo non solo la magistrale documentazione di importanti siti archeologici, ma anche il contributo ad un dibattito metodologico sull'archeologia dei paesaggi intesa in senso globale: dalla geologia alla pedologia, alle analisi paleoambientali finalizzate a ricostruzioni storiche di ampio respiro.

Il tema proposto per questo quarantennale non poteva essere più attuale: il ruolo della tecnologia antica come causa ed effetto di processi storici e sociali.

Siamo oggi in un'epoca di grandi trasformazioni legate ad un'evoluzione della tecnologia sempre più frenetica. La dimensione altamente specialistica dei vari rami della tecnologia attuale conduce alla percezione di uno sviluppo autonomo della scienza rispetto al mercato e alla società ed addirittura alla concezione di una tecnologia avulsa dalla società.

In realtà ogni sviluppo tecnologico presuppone una domanda da parte della società che la motiva nella ricerca e la finanzia nello sviluppo ed applicazione.

Se poi gli effetti di tale sviluppo vadano a vantaggio di tutta la società o solo di una parte di essa, ciò può essere oggetto di un dibattito storico, oltre che politico, che l'archeologia può concorrere a chiarire.

ARTIGIANATO E POLEOGENESI

Lo sviluppo tecnologico, in particolare della metallurgia, con i suoi correlati fenomeni di accumulo di ricchezza, necessità di protezione degli impianti produttivi e dei depositi di metallo, oltre che di combustibile necessario alla lavorazione, è certamente uno dei fattori che possono aver influenzato le dinamiche insediative fin da epoca protostorica.

La concentrazione insediativa che si attua nell'Italia centro-tirrenica a partire dal Bronzo Recente è causa ed effetto di una progressiva concentrazione delle produzioni artigianali entro luoghi relativamente sicuri, quali gli insediamenti fortificati o in prossimità di essi; tale processo si accentua nel Bronzo Finale e si manifesta ulteriormente con lo sviluppo degli abitati di tipo urbano tra IX e VIII secolo a.C.[2]

Nella strategica area dello stagno di Maccarese, presso la foce del Tevere, sono state da tempo individuate diverse aree produttive attive già in epoca eneolitica[3] e quindi una frequentazione del Bronzo Recente e Finale che comprendeva certamente la metallurgia del bronzo, la produzione di pasta vitrea, oltre alla lavorazione di strumenti in osso, in parallelo allo sviluppo di prodotti agricoli locali, in particolare caseari e verosimilmente alla produzione del sale.[4]

Per quanto concerne il sito di Roma, la presenza di fornaci per la ceramica e forge per la lavorazione dei metalli appare ben evidente al più tardi dall'VIII secolo a.C., come rivelano una serie di contesti sul *Capitolium*, Palatino e area del

| Contesto | Evidenza | Prodotti | Cronologia | Bibliografia | Fig. 2 |
|---|---|---|---|---|---|
| Capitolium | Forgia | Oggetti di bronzo e ferro | VIII-VI secolo a.C. | Mura Sommella et al. 2001, 314-317. | N. 1 |
| Area del Foro di Cesare | Fornace | Ceramica | IX-VIII secolo a.C. | De Santis et al. 2010, 172-173. | N. 2 |
| Area del Foro di Cesare | Forgia | Oggetti in ferro | VII secolo a.C. | De Santis et al. 2010, 172-173. | N. 3 |
| Palatino, pendici settentrionali | Fornace | Ceramica | Fase laziale II b | Carandini, Carafa 2000, 112-113, 119. | N. 4 |
| Palatino, pendici settentrionali | Scorie di fusione | Oggetti in ferro | VI secolo a.C. | Capodiferro et al. 1986, 411. | N. 5 |
| Villa Villa Patrizi | Cava in sotterraneo | Blocchi di tufo granulare grigio | VI-V secolo a.C. | Lanciani 1918; Cifani 2008, 226 | N. 6 |
| Stazione Termini | Cava in sotterraneo | Blocchi di tufo granulare grigio | VI-V secolo a.C. | Cifani 2008, 229 | N. 7 |
| S. Bibiana | Cava in sotterraneo | Blocchi di tufo granulare grigio | VI-V secolo a.C. | Cifani 2008, 232 | N. 8 |
| Vigna Querini | Cava in superficie | Blocchi di tufo granulare grigio | VI-V secolo a.C. | Cifani 2008, 229 | N. 9 |

*Fig. 1. Luoghi di produzione a Roma e suburbio, VIII-V secolo a.C.*

*forum Caesaris*[5] (*figg. 1-2*), quest'ultima poco distante dal santuario del *Volcanal*, il cui culto, per le sue analogie con quello greco di Efesto, può aver incluso anche aspetti tecnologici e produttivi mediante l'impiego del fuoco.[6]

Sempre nel corso dell'VIII secolo a Roma, abbiamo l'attestazione di ceramica depurata lavorata al tornio e di complesse lavorazioni coroplastiche, come i ben noti sarcofagi fittili dal sepolcreto del Quirinale,[7] mentre a specifiche officine metallurgiche romane della fasi Laziali III e IVA è stata ascritta la produzione di armi e vasellame metallico, in particolare una specifica classe di tripodi bronzei (e più raramente in ferro)[8] insieme a quella di ciste cilindriche di lamina di bronzo lavorata a sbalzo, tipiche delle sepolture femminili.[9]

Occorre ricordare inoltre come anche la tradizione letteraria antica, associasse l'istituzione delle corporazioni di artigiani allo stesso mito della fondazione urbana, riferendole all'operato del pacifico re Numa Pompilio.[10]

LE TECNICHE EDILIZIE DELLA PRIMA ETÀ DEL FERRO (IX-VIII )

Analogamente agli altri centri medio tirrenici, la tecnica edilizia di questa fase per il Lazio comprende murature con basamento in scheggioni di tufo cementati con argilla completati da alzati lignei. Ne fanno fede diverse fortificazioni di abitati latini, tra cui quelli di *Gabii*, Ficana, Castel di Decima e Acqua Acetosa Laurentina,[11] insieme alle fortificazioni urbane di Veio risalenti alla prima Età del Ferro,[12] ma anche l'eccezionale sequenza del basamento del muro della seconda metà dell'VIII secolo a.C. rinvenuto alle pendici settentrionali del Palatino e ai primi del VII secolo a.C. e nella metà del VI secolo a.C.[13]

Un esempio di apparati lignei edilizi è stato rinvenuto a Colle Rotondo presso Anzio, nell'ambito degli scavi condotti dalle Università di Roma Tor Vergata, La Sapienza e Roma Tre tra il 2009 e il 2014 che hanno documentato due *aggeres*; il più

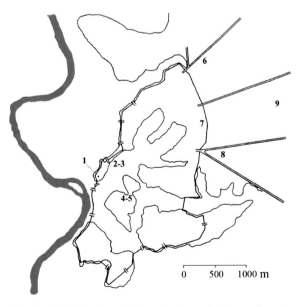

*Fig. 2. Distribuzione dei luoghi di produzione a Roma e suburbio, VIII-V secolo a.C.*

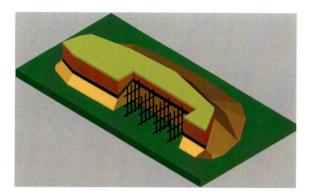

*Fig. 3. Ricostruzione schematica dell'aggere orientale di Colle Rotondo, IX-VIII secolo a.C. (da CIFANI et al. 2012).*

antico dei questi (esattamente quello orientale) è stato realizzato con un imponente riporto di depositi sabbiosi, rinforzati da un'armatura interna in legno di quercia, la cui datazione tramite C14 è risultata compresa tra la fine del X e gli inizi dell'VIII secolo a.C. (*fig. 3*).[14] Si tratta di un sistema non altrimenti noto in area centro tirrenica e che trova confronto in aree caratterizzate dall'assenza di risorse litiche idonee a costruire una solida struttura muraria.

Un riferimento diretto viene dalla tradizione erudita nota tramite Varrone e quindi nella letteratura di età romana imperiale sulla castrametazione, in particolare da Igino Gromatico (o pseudo Igino), che ricorda la necessità di rinforzare i riporti di terra friabile mediante pali di legno detti *cervoli*.[15]

Un parallelo a livello tecnico può anche essere visto nelle fortificazioni celtiche del c.d. *murus gallicus* descritto da Giulio Cesare (*De bello Gallico* VII, 23) e ben documentato sul piano archeologico, ovvero di murature in pietrame e terra con pali inseriti all'interno della struttura.

Un ulteriore esempio delle tecniche edilizie basate su apparati lignei è offerto dalla casa di *Fidenae* databile alla III fase Laziale. L'edificio presenta una pianta rettangolare, con mura perimetrali in pisè, montanti lignei e tetto straminneo.[16]

Una tecnica analoga con murature in pisé e armatura lignea è attestata per l'edificio della c.d. *domus regia* rinvenuta nell'area del santuario di Vesta, relativamente alle fasi riferite ai periodi laziale III B e IV A (750-650 a.C.).[17]

Questi dati lasciano comprendere le caratteristiche della tecnica edilizia nella prima fase dell'urbanizzazione: strutture a carattere stabile, prevalentemente lignee, con impiego di risorse geolitiche ottenibili in loco (o a breve distanza), ridotta specializzazione delle maestranze, ad eccezione forse dei carpentieri per la struttura lignea e l'approvvigionamento dei principali elementi di palificazione.

LA TECNOLOGIA EDILIZIA NEL VI SECOLO A.C.

A partire dalla fase laziale IV b (ca 640 / 30 - 580 a.C.) abbiamo le più antiche attestazioni di edifici con tetti rivestiti da tegole fittili,[18] con muri composti da alzati lignei e basamenti in scheggioni di tufo e progressivamente in pietrame squadrato e quindi in opera quadrata, la cui prima importante attestazione a Roma è da individuarsi nella c.d. cisterna Vaglieri sul Palatino,[19] mentre ad una tecnica assimilabile all'opera quadrata potrebbero rientrare anche le murature in blocchi di tufo grigio litoide alti cm 15, ma di lunghezza variabile, documentati c.d. regia di *Gabii* (inizi VI secolo a.C.).[20]

La diffusione delle tegole con il loro correlato di stabili trabeazioni lignee oblique (e pertanto tetti di tipo spingente), muri portanti e fondazioni in muratura, implica anche una nuova organizzazione dei cantieri insieme alla pianificazioni dei drenaggi superficiali spesso correlati alla realizzazione di grandi cisterne.

Le premesse tecniche dello sviluppo architettonico ed urbanistico del VI secolo a.C. sono pertanto da riferirsi già alla fine del VII secolo a.C.

Ciò che si verifica nel corso del VI secolo a.C. è piuttosto un impiego perfezionato e su ampia scala di tali tecniche, che a livello storico ci obbligano a considerarne le possibili implicazioni sociali ed economiche.

E' noto come la seconda metà del VI secolo rappresenti il momento di attuazione a Roma di una serie di grandi progetti edilizi, quali il tempio di Giove Capitolino, il sistema di collettori idraulici noti dalla tradizione letteraria come *Cloaca Maxima* e il nuovo perimetro di fortificazioni della città, identificati dalla moderna antiquaria come "mura serviane".[21]

La pietra impiegata per queste opere è costantemente il tufo granulare grigio, denominato nella Carta Geologica d'Italia come Tufo del Palatino.[22]

Si tratta di un litotipo di facile lavorazione ed alta resistenza alla compressione, particolarmente idonea per fondazioni e terrazzamenti.

Il suo impiego su ampia scala dovette richiedere l'organizzazione di una serie di coltivazioni in sotterraneo o in superficie, poste poco fuori le mura o in aree periferiche della città, come esemplificano gli impianti documentati presso la Stazione Termini, S. Bibiana, Villa Patrizi, Vigna Querini.[23]

Con l'adozione dell'opera quadrata si delinea pertanto una specifica riforma organizzativa ed urbanistica collegata alla nuova tecnica, che implica un importante progresso: la standardizzazione degli elementi litici.

I blocchi di tufo granulare grigio sono infatti tagliati su multipli del modulo di un piede: sia del tipo osco italico da 27,2 cm attestato già dalla fine del VII - inizi VI secolo a.C. o più frequentemente del tipo c.d. attico, da 29,7 cm, note a partire dalla fine del VI secolo a.C. (*fig. 4*).

L'introduzione di un'unità di misura per lavori pubblici di grande estensione implica una più estesa razionalizzazione amministrativa interna alla comunità romana, che trova un adeguato parallelo nella tradizione letteraria secondo la quale il re Servio Tullio "*mensuras, pondera classes centuriasque constituit*" (*De vir. ill.*, 7, 8).

Blocchi squadrati e tegole fittili standardizzate sono pertanto espressione della razionalità della società urbana di VI secolo e dell'impiego di elementi prefabbricati nella nuova tecnologia edilizia, funzionale anche all'impiego di masse di manodopera non qualificata per l'estrazione, il taglio e il trasporto del materiale, sotto forma di *corveè*, meglio note come *munera* nella tradizione letteraria.[24]

Evidenza dell'avanzata organizzazione delle coeve figline urbane connesse all'edilizia sono anche i grandi *kalypteres heghemones* che caratterizzano i tetti di fase arcaica rinvenuti in più punti della città[25] (*fig. 5*), nonché la produzione di vere da pozzo e anelli di rivestimento in ceramica delle canne dei grandi pozzi, come quello rinvenuto presso il lato orientale del podio del tempio di Giove[26] (*fig. 6*) che testimoniano una produzione su ampia scala per le necessità della comunità urbana.

Sempre nel corso del VI secolo a.C. sono attestati sarcofagi monolitici in tufo granulare grigio, in particolare per sepolture infantili quali la tomba 1 degli scavi del *Capitolium* ed un *suggrundarium* dall'area della domus 3 della pendice settentrionale palatina.[27]

Sul finire del VI secolo a.C., la realizzazione del monumentale tempio di Giove Capitolino (il più grande tempio colonnato a Roma fino all'età adrianea) implica un'elevata specializzazione delle maestranze ed in particolare un complesso sistema di conoscenze tecniche connesse soprattutto alla gestione dei grandi carichi del tetto. Questo deve aver contemplato sistemi spingenti di travi lignee, verosimilmente delle capriate, atti a coprire intercolumni larghi fino a 12 metri.[28]

La conoscenza tecnica di sistemi spingenti su questo orizzonte cronologico è inoltre corroborata dalla presenza delle prime strutture voltate in opera quadrata identificabili nel collettore a duplice ghiera rinvenuto nella valle del Colosseo e nella cisterna con volta a botte sempre in opera quadrata, della casa 3 della pendice settentrionale palatina, che rappresentano l'inizio dell'architettura voltata a Roma.[29]

Nella Roma di fine VI secolo a.C., la realizzazione di decine di migliaia di blocchi in tufo granulare grigio, con misure standard di 1 piede x 2 x 3 (m 0,29 x 0,58 x 0,87), di peso relativamente limitato (1,1 - 1,4 g/cm3 a seconda della qualità e grado di umidità) e ancora manovrabili da una coppia di operai, rende bene l'idea di un sistema di produzione su ampia scala basato su una manodopera di base non qualificata, reclutata tramite corvée ed affiancata da pochi artigiani altamente specializzati e retribuiti.

Lo sviluppo delle tecniche di idraulica condiziona anche la modalità di realizzazione dei rivestimenti parietali. Accanto all'impego di intonaci argillosi fin da epoca preistorica, sul finire dell'VIII-inizi VII secolo abbiamo le prime attestazioni di intonaci a base di calce, in un contesto abitativo di Caere.[30]

Circa l'impiego della calce a Roma troviamo la prima attestazione accertata in un contesto della fine del VI secolo a.C. alle pendici settentrionali del Palatino (US 2961), dal quale sono stati raccolti frammenti di intonaco dipinto in rosso che, sottoposti ad analisi termo-differenziale, hanno rivelato una componente di carbonato di calcio (CaCO3) corrispondente a circa l'85 % del conglomerato.[31]

Questo dato consente di inquadrare l'uso della calce a Roma a partire almeno dal VI secolo a.C. e permette di riferire ipoteticamente ad età arcaica anche l'uso di rivestimenti di intonaco idraulico composto da calce e argilla per alcune opere idrauliche, quali ad esempio le cisterne palatine. Va notato inoltre che litotipi calcarei utilizzabili per la produzione di calce sono facilmente reperibili sotto forma di depositi travertinosi nel territorio prossimo alla Roma arcaica, in particolare, per la zona nord il Monte dei Parioli, il Pincio, e quindi a sud nella zona del Torrino e della valle del fosso Galeria.[32]

Occorre ricordare a riguardo che lo sviluppo della tecnica edilizia in età arcaica è funzionale ad una serie di innovazioni sia nel campo della tecnica idraulica (condotti ipogei, scavati o costruiti, canalizzazioni ecc.),[33] sia delle costruzioni stradali; queste prevedono carreggiate e delle, spesso di larghezza sufficiente al passaggio di due carri, realizzate con strati compatti pezzame d tufo, argilla e sabbia contenute entro filari di blocchi.

Ne sono evidenza i tratti rinvenuti in più punti del suburbio (es. Tenute della Muratella, Tor di Mezzavia) o anche la monumentale via glareata (larghezza 4,4 - 5 metri) contenuta tra due crepidini, documentata sull'acropoli e nell'area urbana di *Satricum*.[34]

| Unità di misura | Valore | Principali attestazioni | Cronologia | Bibliografia |
|---|---|---|---|---|
| Piede italico | 272.4 mm | - Roma: Blocchi del muro sotto l'Equus Domitiani.<br>- Roma: blocchi del tempio arcaico di S. Omobono.<br>- Roma: blocchi di alcuni segmenti delle fortificazioni urbane.<br><br>- Gabii: planimetria della c.d. Regia.<br>- Satricum: planimetria del tempio I (c.d. sacellum), 550-540 a.C. (m 6 x 10,4 = 22 x 38 piedi).<br><br>- Satricum: planimetria del tempio II, 530-520 a.C. (m 27 x 16,2 = 100 x 60 piedi). | Fine del VII - VI secolo a.C | Roma:<br>Cifani 2008, 239-240 con bibl.<br><br>*Gabii:*<br>Fabbri 2017, 229.<br><br>*Satricum:*<br>Knoop, Stibbe 1997.<br>Colonna 2005. |
| Piede attico | 296 mm | - Planimetria del podio e blocchi del tempio di Giove Capitolino.<br>- Blocchi del podio del tempio dei Dioscuri<br>- Blocchi degli edifici domestici delle pendici settentrionali del Palatino.<br>- Blocchi della maggior parte dei segmenti delle mura urbane. | Dalla seconda metà del VI secolo a.C. in poi. | Cifani 2008, 239-240 con bibl. |
| Libbra | 320 gr. | Peso dal Lapis Niger, Roma. | VI secolo a.C. | Nijboer 1998, 302-307.<br>Crawford 2003, 67-69. |
| Libbra | 360 gr | Peso da Satricum | VI secolo a.C. | Nijboer 1998, 302-307.<br>Crawford 2003, 67-69. |

*Fig. 4. Unità di misura attestate nel Lazio arcaico.*

*Fig. 5. Kalypteres heghemones dall'Esquilino (Musei Capitolini, foto dell'autore, 2018).*

*Fig. 6. Anelli di rivestimento interno del pozzo sul lato orientale del podio del tempio di Giove Capitolino (Musei Capitolini, foto dell'autore, 2018).*

La crescita del paesaggio agricolo è favorita dalla rete stradale e verosimilmente da una serie di infrastrutture tese a valorizzare il potenziale produttivo del suburbio. Nascono infatti in questo periodo le fattorie isolate, quale prodotto delle riforme sociali ed economiche di età arcaica, garantite dalla presenza di un esercito stabile in grado di proteggere il territorio e dal ruolo politico di un ceto sociale di piccoli proprietari.[35]

Lo sviluppo dell'olivicoltura a Roma è di questa fase (VI secolo a.C.) insieme alla prima attestazione di una pressa olearia, rinvenuta nella villa dell'Auditorium Flaminio (inizi V secolo a.C.), costituita da un blocco squadrato di tufo grigio (m 1,4 x 1,3), con ancora inciso il canale di deflusso del liquido di spremitura.[36]

L'INTRODUZIONE DEI TUFI LITOIDI: IMPLICAZIONI TECNICHE E ORGANIZZATIVE

A partire dalla fine del VI secolo cominciano ad essere lavorati a Roma anche i tufi litoidi, sia nell'edilizia che per realizzazione di contenitori in ambito funerario. Lo testimoniano il grande muro di terrazzamento tardo arcaico in opera quadrata dell'area sacra di S. Omobono, nonché una serie di sarcofagi o custodie di urne rinvenuti nella necropoli Esquilina.[37]

I principali depositi di questo litotipo presso Roma sono documentati nella zona di Marino e a nord del lago Albano, da cui deriva l'appellativo di *lapis albanus*,[38] quindi nell'area della città di *Tusculum*, da cui la denominazione di tufo di Tuscolo o sperone[39] e nel circondario di valle Castiglione, presso l'antica *Gabii*, da cui deriva anche la denominazione di *lapis gabinus* (Tac., *Ann.* XV.43; Strab. V.3.10),[40] mentre un ulteriore deposito (riferito alle colate piroclastiche dei vulcani sabatini) è segnalato al chilometro 8,5 della via Flaminia.[41]

Va comunque tenuto presente che a livello di economia di trasporti le cave maggiormente avvantaggiate risultano quelle collegate a corsi di acqua navigabili.

In questa prospettiva i depositi della via Flaminia, prossimi al Tevere e soprattutto quelli del cratere vulcanico della Valle di Castiglione, occupato dalla città di *Gabii* e collegati all'Aniene tramite l'affluente fosso dell'Osa, risulterebbero i più indiziati per il rifornimento di questo materiale in età arcaica a Roma, mentre quelli dell'entroterra (Colli Albani) appaiono come i meno convenienti.

Tuttavia una recente ricerca petrografica effettuata sulle murature dell'area sacra di S. Omobono ha rivelato come i blocchi del terrazzamento tardo arcaico siano in peperino proveniente dai Colli Albani.[42]

Tale scoperta lascia intuire come la ricerca della pietra di migliore qualità, anziché l'economia di trasporto potessero occasionalmente animare la scelta del litotipo per l'edilizia e conferma anche il complesso sistema di approvvigionamento litico instaurato nella Roma di fine VI secolo a.C. per rifornire i grandi cantieri edilizi urbani.

Un momento di svolta nella tecnica cantieristica è segnato infine dal restauro delle mura urbiche tra il 378 e non oltre il 353 a.C., quando le precedenti mura in opera quadrata di tufo granulare grigio vengono ricostruite o rialzate mediante blocchi di tufo giallo litoide alti due piedi romani (175 x 66 x 60 cm) (*fig. 7*).[43]

Il cantiere si avvale di uno specifico finanziamento pubblico, anziché delle corveè imposte alla popolazione tipiche del VI secolo a.C., e ciò implica il ruolo di gruppi di privati per l'esecuzione dell'opera.[44]

La nuova fortificazione si avvale di un complesso sistema di approvvigionamento del materiale litico, proveniente da cave ubicate lungo il Tevere, a 20 km a nord dalla città e trasportato via fiume.[45]

Il carattere di produzione su ampia scala si evince dalla presenza di numerosi marchi di cava, necessari verosimilmente alla gestione e al computo dei vari lotti di blocchi.

Il peso e il volume di tali apparecchiature litiche (vedi sopra ) implicano verosimilmente l'impiego di *machinae tractoriae* per la movimentazione[46] e posa in opera, unitamente all'impiego di maestranze specializzate.

Tale ristrutturazione dell'impianto difensivo urbano può essere giustificata sul piano tecnico per realizzare strutture più resistenti agli agenti atmosferici, sia anche per costruire in questo modo un'apparecchiatura litica più idonea a contrastare le nuove tecniche di poliorcetica del IV secolo a.C. che contemplavano l'impiego dei primi mezzi di artiglieria sia in difesa che in attacco.[47]

Questo aspetto è anche provato dal fatto che il riallestimento medio repubblicano in tufo giallo litoide sembra interessare particolarmente i tratti più esposti delle mura, mentre, al contrario, i muri di contenimento interno dell'aggere furono lasciati per lunghi tratti in blocchi di tufo granulare grigio. Anche la presenza di torri documentate presso l'aggere esquilino, verosimilmente per l'alloggiamento di macchine balistiche,[48] testimonia l'adeguamento di Roma alle nuove dottrine in tema di fortificazioni, con il passaggio da una approccio difensivo tipico della fase arcaica ad uno offensivo, diffuso a partire dal IV secolo a.C.

L'evoluzione tecnologica nel Lazio arcaico, in particolare nell'edilizia, ribadisce come ogni innovazione si affermi quale risposta ad una specifica richiesta.

L'alta densità demografica, la presenza di ampi centri urbani, unita all'interazione mediterranea di questo territorio dell'area centro-tirrenica contribuiscono a farne un laboratorio di punta della tecnologia e dei saperi e, dal punto di vista archeologico, un osservatorio privilegiato per la ricostruzione delle cultura di età arcaica.

In particolare, l'adozione di alcune innovazioni tecniche collima con precisi momenti di evoluzione sociale ed economica.

La crescita insediativa di Roma, nel corso della c.d. III fase Laziale, si verifica in concomitanza con un incremento delle conoscenze tecnologiche, ravvisabili a livello archeologico, soprattutto

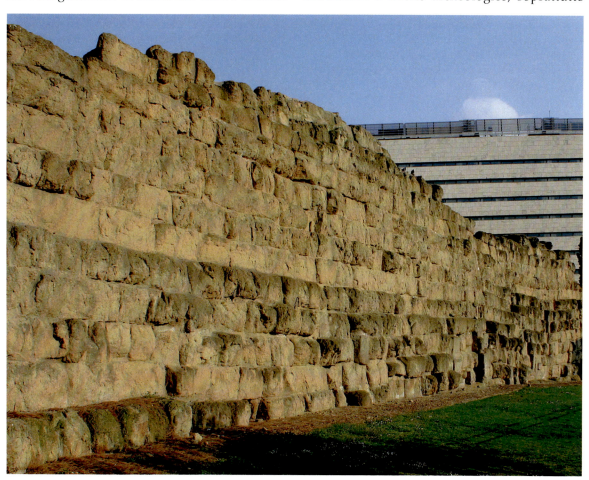

*Fig. 7. Muro dell'aggere esquilino (visto dall'interno) presso piazzale della Stazione Termini, nella fase repubblicana in blocchi di tufo giallo litoide (foto dell'autore, 2011).*

nella produzione ceramica e metallurgica. La concentrazione di artigiani e mercanti va pertanto considerata tra i principali motori economici connessi ai processi di poleogenesi che si attuano nell'VIII secolo a.C.

Lo sviluppo dei sistemi viari nel corso del VI secolo va altresì inquadrato in un ulteriore sviluppo dei commerci via terra che trova il proprio parallelo nell'intensificazione dei traffici marittimi tirrenici dello stesso periodo, con la comparsa, tra la fine del VI e gli inizi del V secolo a.C. di navi di maggiore tonnellaggio, ovvero fino ad almeno 40 tonnellate, e con doppia vela.[49]

La grande cantieristica arcaica è la più evidente espressione del miracolo economico del VI secolo a.C. ed è a sua volta sia causa che effetto di importanti innovazioni tecnologiche in campo edilizio. Lo testimoniano in particolare la diffusione dell'opera quadrata, dei sistemi di copertura spingenti quali volte e capriate, oltre che, sul finire del VI secolo a.C., di un generale rinnovamento dei sistemi decorativi coroplastici.[50]

Sono queste le grandi innovazioni tecniche in ambito edilizio che rimarranno di fatto inalterate, o con poche modifiche, fino all'avvento, nel II secondo secolo a.C., dell'edilizia in calcestruzzo, in un quadro storico e sociale ormai del tutto distante dagli orizzonti di epoca arcaica.

## Note

[1] Ringrazio la prof.ssa Marijke Gnade per il cortese invito a questo convegno sui quaranta anni degli scavi di *Satricum*.
[2] Alessandri 2013 con bibl.
[3] Manfredini 2002.
[4] Acconcia *et al.* 2018
[5] Area del *Forum Caesaris*: De Santis *et al.* 2010, 172-173; Campidoglio: Mura Sommella *et al.* 2001, 314-317; Palatino, pendice settentrionale: Mura Sommella *et al.* 2001, 314-317.
[6] In generale: Capdeville 1995 con bibl.
[7] Pinza 1905; Colonna 1988, 299 con bibl. sulle produzioni di impasto a Roma e nella bassa valle del Tevere tra VIII e VII secolo a.C. si rimanda a: Carafa 1995 e Ten Kortenaar 2011 con bibl.; Damiani, Parisi Presicce 2019; Cifani 2020b.
[8] Colonna 1977, 481; Bedello Tata *et al.* 2016, 67-72 with bibl.
[9] Colonna 1988; Bietti Sestieri 1992 a, 415, n. 82, tav. 43; Bettelli 1997, 131 con bibl.
[10] Plut. Numa, XVII, 1-4, su cui Gabba 1984 con bibl.
[11] *Gabii*: Helas 2016; *Ficana*: Fischer-Hansen 2016; Castel di Decima: Guaitoli 1981, 118-122; Acqua Acetosa Laurentina: Bedini 2016.
[12] Boitani *et al.* 2016.
[13] Carandini, Carafa 2000.
[14] Cifani *et al.* 2012; Cifani, Guidi 2016 con bibl.
[15] Varr., LL, V. 24: *Cervi ab similitudine cornuum cervi* ; Hyg. Grom. *De munitionibus castrorum* LI: "*Cervoli trunci ramosi. Ad hos decurritur, si soli natura nimia teneritate cespes frangitur neque lapide mobili nisi copiosum vallum extrui potest nec fossa fieri, ut non ripae decidant*", inoltre: Polyb. XVIII, 18; in generale: Cascarino 2007, 152 ss
[16] De Santis *et al.* 1998, Bietti Sestieri, De Santis 2001, di Gennaro *et al.* 2001, 201, n. 70.
[17] Carandini *et al.* 2017, 363-368,: Carafa *et al.* 2018.
[18] Wikander 2017 con bibl., sui sistemi decorativi: Winter 2008.
[19] Cifani 2008,157-162 con bibl.
[20] Fabbri 2016, 229-230.
[21] Cifani 2008; Ziółkowski 2016 con bibl.
[22] Funiciello 1995.
[23] Cifani 1994; 2008, 226-232 con bibl.; sull'approvvigionamento litico nel territorio veiente: Arizza, Rossi 2018 con bibl.
[24] Milazzo 1993, Palombi 1997, Cifani 2008, 326-333; 2010 con bibl.
[25] Due esemplari provenienti del Cispio (Roma, Antiquarium Comunale, n.inv. 4400; 2296), uno dall'area sacra di S. Omobono, tre esemplari dalla Regia, insieme alla segnalazione di ulteriori due esemplari dalla zona 4a di Ficana: Cifani 2008, 249 con bibl.
[26] Cifani 2008, 316 con bibl.
[27] *Capitolium*: Mura Sommella *et al.* 2001, 334-336, figg. 11 e 13 (misure della cassa del sarcofago: cm 163 x 60); Palatino: Carandini, Carafa 2000, 250-256 (misure del sarcofago: cm 35 x 65 x 42). Sulle sepolture di epoca regia e repubblicana in sarcofagi monolitici: Pinza 1905, quindi Colonna 1977, 138-139 con bibl.; recenti segnalazioni di sepolture alto e medio repubblicane in sarcofagi monolitici da sepolcreti prossimi all'aggere esquilino: Barbera *et al.* 2006 (Piazza Vittorio); Menghi *et al.* 2006 (via Goito).
[28] Cifani 2016 con bibl.
[29] Cifani 2008, 320-323 con bibl.
[30] Colivicchi *et al.* 2016, 371-372 con bibl.
[31] Analisi effettuate nel 1994 dalla dott.ssa M. L. Santarelli nei laboratori della Facoltà di Ingegneria dell'Università di Roma "La Sapienza", allora sotto la direzione del Prof. G. Torraca (1927-2010).
[32] Carrara *et al.* 2012 con bibl.
[33] A riguardo mi permetto di rimandare a: Cifani 2020a, e 2021 con bibl.
[34] Cifani 2008, pp. 305-307 con bibl. Sulla strada dell'acropoli di *Satricum*: Maaskant-Kleibrink 1984, 356-357, quindi Gnade 2002, 5-29 e Gnade 2017, 254-257 con bibl.
[35] Cifani 2009.
[36] Carandini *et al.* 2007.
[37] Farr 2014; Farr *et al.* 2015 con bibl.
[38] Camponeschi, Nolasco 1982, p. 459 ss. con bibl.; con riferimento anche a formazioni recenti: Funiciello *et al.* 2002 con bibl.
[39] Jackson *et al.* 2005, p. 498 con bibl.
[40] In generale vedi anche Blake 1947, pp. 34-35 e Lugli 1957, pp. 306-308; per una caratterizzazione delle differenti colate piroclastiche vedi anche: Karner *et al.* 2001 con bibl.
[41] Funiciello 1995, pp. 96-97.
[42] Farr *et al.* 2015.
[43] Lugli 1957, 195; per un'introduzione storica si veda ora anche: Bernard 2018 con bibl.
[44] Liv. VI, 32.1: " *Parvo intervallo ad respirandum debitoribus dato, postquam quietae res ab hostibus erant, celebrari de integro iuris dictio et tantum abesse spes veteris levandi fenoris, ut tributo novum fenus contraheretur in murum a censoribus locatum saxo quadrato faciundum; cui succum-*

*bere oneri coacta plebes, quia quem dilectum impedirent non habebant tribuni plebis"*.

[45] Lombardi, Meucci 2006; Volpe 2014 con bibl. e inoltre Bernard 2018, 76-117.
[46] L'impiego di *machinae tractoriae* è negato da Lugli 1957, p. 260 che sottolinea l'assenza di fori in posizione centrale per i *ferri forfices*. Tuttavia l'imbraco dei blocchi potrebbe essere stato effettuato anche semplicemente tramite corde che possono non aver lasciato particolari tracce.
[47] Sulla poliorcetica ellenistica e le innovazioni in campo militare nel IV secolo a.C.: Garlan 1974, p. 66 ss., con analisi delle fonti, quindi: McNicoll 1986 e Bettalli 1998, pp. 736-740 con bibl. Sul possibile impego di catapulte già nell'assedio siracusano di Mozia del 397 a.C.: Lawrence 1979, pp. 49-50 con fonti letterarie. A riguardo anche la grande ristrutturazione delle fortificazioni siracusane promossa da Dionigi I a partire dal 405 a.C. (da ultimo Mertens 2006, pp. 424-433 con bibl.) può aver fornito nuovi modelli difensivi urbani per Roma.
[48] Säflund 1932, Agger K, pp. 56-67; 265-266.
[49] Pomey 2006, 2011, Nantet 2017 con bibl.
[50] Da ultimo Colonna 2016.

## Bibliografia

Acconcia, V. *et al.* 2018, I materiali, in Cébellac-Gervasoni 2018, http://books.openedition.org/efr/3667
Alessandri, L. 2013, *Latium vetus in the Bronze Age and Early Iron Age / Il Latium vetus nell'età del Bronzo e nella prima età del Ferro* (B.A.R. Int. Seri.), Oxford.
Arizza, M./D. Rossi 2018, Tuff quarrying in the territory of Veii: a "status" activity of the landowning aristocracy of the Archaic period, from construction to craft, *ScAnt* 24, 101-110.
Barbera, M. *et al.* 2005, Ritrovamenti archeologici in Piazza Vittorio Emanuele II, *BCom* 106, 302-337.
Bedello Tata, M. *et al.* 2016, Scoperte e restauri a Ficana tra vecchie e nuove collaborazioni, in Mangani/Pellegrino 2016, 63-80.
Bedini, A. 2016, Laurentina Acqua Acetosa (Roma). Il sistema difensivo dell'abitato protostorico: i dati di scavo 1976-1980, in Fontaine/Helas 2016, 139-176.
Bernard, S. 2018, *Building Mid-Republican Rome: Labor, Architecture, and the Urban Economy*, Oxford.
Bettalli, M. 1998, L'esercito e l'arte della guerra, in S. Settis (ed.), *I Greci. Storia, arte, cultura e società* 2. III, Torino, 729-742.
Bettelli, M. 1997, Roma. La città prima della città: i tempi di una nascita. La cronologia delle sepolture ad inumazione di Roma e del Lazio nella prima età del ferro, Roma.
Bietti Sestieri, A.M. 1992 (ed.), *La necropoli di Osteria dell'Osa*, Roma.
Bietti Sestieri, A.M./A. De Santis 2001, L'edificio della I età del ferro di Fidene (Roma): posizione nell'abitato, tecnica costruttiva, funzionalità in base alla distribuzione spaziale dei materiali e degli arredi, in Brandt/Karlsson 2001, 211-221.
Blake, M.E. 1947, *Ancient Roman Construction in Italy from the Prehistoric Period to Augustus*, Washington.
Boitani, F. *et al.* 2016, Le fortificazioni a Veio tra Porta Nord Ovest e Porta Caere, in Fontaine/Helas 2016, 19-35.
Brandt, R./L. Karlsson 2001 (ed.), *From huts to houses. Transformation of ancient societies* (Proceedings of an International Seminar organized by the Norwegian and Swedish Institutes in Rome, September 1997), Stockholm.

Camponeschi, B./F. Nolasco 1982, *Le risorse naturali della Regione Lazio 7. Roma e i Colli Albani*, Roma.
Capdeville, G. 1995, *Volcanus. Recherches comparatistes sur les origines du culte de Vulcain*, Paris.
Carafa, P. 1995, *Officine ceramiche di età regia. Produzione di ceramica di impasto a Roma dalla fine dell'VIII alla fine del VI secolo a.C.*, Roma.
Carafa, P. *et al.* 2018, Il primo santuario di Vesta, *ScAnt* 24, 47-100.
Carandini, A. *et al.* 2007, *La fattoria e la villa dell'Auditorium nel quartiere flaminio di Roma*, Roma.
Carandini, A. *et al.* 2017, *Santuario di Vesta, pendice del Palatino e via Sacra*, Roma.
Carandini, A./P. Carafa 2000, *Palatium e Sacra via* I, Roma.
Carrara, C. *et al.* 2012, I travertini meteogenici dei Monti Parioli-Valle Giulia (Roma): aspetti geologici e geomeccanici in relazione ad eventi franosi, in *Geoingegneria Ambientale e Mineraria* 49, n. 3, 5-22.
Cascarino, G. 2007, *L'esercito romano. Armamento e organizzazione*, Rimini.
Cébellac-Gervasoni, M. *et al.* 2018, *Ricerche su Ostia e il suo territorio. Atti del terzo seminario ostiense*, Roma 2015, Roma. http://books.openedition.org/efr/3637
Cifani, G. 2008, *Architettura romana arcaica. Edilizia e società tra monarchia e repubblica*, Roma.
Cifani, G. 2009, Indicazioni sulla proprietà agraria nella Roma arcaica in base all'evidenza archeologica, in Jolivet *et al.* 2009, 311-324.
Cifani, G. 2016, The fortifications of Archaic Rome: social and political significance, in R. Frederiksen *et al.*, *Focus on Fortifications*. Acts of the Conference, Athens 2012, Oxford, 82-93.
Cifani, G. 2020a, Osservazioni su bonifiche e opere idriche in area centro tirrenica tra VIII e VI secolo a.C., in E. Bianchi/M. D'Acunto (ed.), *Opere di regimentazione delle acque in età arcaica*. Atti della conferenza, Roma 2017, 339-356.
Cifani, G. 2020b, La Roma dei Re: su una recente mostra, in *Mediterraneo Antico. Economie società culture* 23, 2020, 535-546.
Cifani, G. 2021, *The origins of the roman economy*, Cambridge.
Cifani, G. *et al.* 2012, Colle Rotondo (Anzio), risultati della campagna di scavo 2011, *Lazio e Sabina* 8, 371-384.
Cifani, G./A. Guidi 2016, Le fortificazioni nel territorio di Anzio, in Fontaine/Helas 2016, 111-124.
Colivicchi, F. *et al.* 2016, New excavations in the urban area of Caere (2012-2014), *Mouseion* 13.2, 359-450.
Colonna, G. 1977, Un aspetto oscuro del Lazio antico. Le tombe del VI - V secolo a.C., *PdP* 32, 131-165.
Colonna, G. 1988, La produzione artigianale, in Momigliano/Schiavone 1988, 291-316.
Colonna, G. 2005, Tra architettura e urbanistica. A proposito del tempio di Mater Matuta a Satricum, in Mols/Moorman 2005, 111-119.
Colonna, G. 2016, Tarquinio il Superbo e la Roma "Etrusca": novità dal Campidoglio e dalle pendici nord-orientali del Palatino, *StEtr* 78, 61-75.
Crawford, M.H. 2003, Land and people in republican Italy, in D. Braun/C. Gill (eds.), *Myth, History and Culture in republican Rome. Studies in honour of T.P. Wiseman*, Exeter, 56-72.
Damiani, I/C. Parisi Presicce 2019 (eds.), *La Roma dei Re: il racconto dell'archeologia* (catalogo della mostra), Roma.
De Santis, A. *et al.* 1998, *Fidene. Una casa dell'età del ferro*, Milano.

De Santis, A. et al. 2010, Un'area artigianale dell'età del Ferro nel centro di Roma: l'impianto produttivo del Foro di Cesare, *Officina Etruscologia* 3, 169-195.

di Gennaro, F. et al. 2001, Fidenae. Contributi per la ricostruzione topografica del centro antico. Ritrovamenti 1986-1992, *BCom* 102, 197-250.

Fabbri, M. 2016, La Regia di Gabii nell'età dei Tarquini, in P.S. Lulof/C. Smith (ed.), *The age of Tarquinius Superbus. A paradigm shift?* Atti Convegno Internazionale (Roma, 7-9 novembre 2013) (Babesch, Supplement 29), 225 - 241.

Farr, J.M. 2014, *Lapis Gabinus: tufo and the economy of urban construction in ancient Rome*, Phd Thesis at the University of Ann Arbor.

Farr, J.M. 2015, Geochemical identification criteria for "peperino" stones employed in ancient Roman buildings: A Lapis Gabinus case study, in *JAS: Reports* 3, 41-51.

Fischer-Hansen, T. 2016, Ficana (Monte Cugno). The fortifications from the early history of the settlement, in Fontaine/Helas 2016, 177-198.

Fontaine, P./S. Helas 2016, *Fortificazioni arcaiche del Latium vetus e dell'Etruria meridionale*. Atti delle giornate di studio, Roma, Accademia Belgica, 2013, Brussels/Roma.

Funiciello, R. 1995, *Memorie descrittive della carta geologica d'Italia L. La geologia di Roma. Il centro storico*, Roma.

Funiciello, R. et al. 2002, L'attività recente del cratere del Lago Albano di Castelgandolfo, *RendLinc* n.s. 9, 13, 113-143.

Gabba, E. 1984, The Collegia of Numa: Problems of Method and Political Ideas, *JRS* 74, 81-84.

Garlan, Y. 1974, *Recherches de Poliorcètique Grecque*, Athens/Paris.

Gnade, M. 2002, *Satricum VI. Satricum in the post-archaic period. A case study of the interpretation of Archaeological remians as indicators of ethno-cultural identity*, Leuven/Paris/Dudley, Ma.

Gnade, M. 2017, Satricum nel periodo di Tarquino Superbo: cambiando prospettiva, in P.S. Lulof/C. Smith (eds.), *The age of Tarquinius Superbus. Central Italy in the late sixth century BC*. Proceedings of the conference, Rome 2013s (BABESCH suppl. 29), Leuven/Pari/Bristol, CT, 249-257.

Guaitoli, M. 1981, Castel di Decima. Nuove osservazioni sulla topografia dell'abitato alla luce dei primi saggi di scavo, in *Quaderni dell'Istituto di Topografia Antica* 9, 127-150.

Helas, S. 2016, Nuove ricerche sulle fortificazioni di Gabii. Le indagini sul versante orientale dell'acropoli e sul lato meridionale della città, in Fontaine/Helas 2016, 91-109.

Jackson, M.D. et al. 2005, The judicious selection and preservation of tuff and travertine building stone in ancient Rome, *Archaeometry* 47, 485-510.

Karner, D.B. et al. 2001, Age of the Ancient Monuments by means of Building stones Provenance: a case study of the Tullianum, Rome, Italy, *JASc* 28, 387-393.

Knoop, R.R./C.M. Stibbe 1997, Satricum, *EAA. II supplemento* VII, 75.

Lanciani, R. 1918, Delle scoperte di antichità avvenute nelle fondazioni degli edificii per le Ferrovie di Stato nella già Villa Patrizi in Via Nomentana, *Rivista Tecnica delle Ferrovie Italiane*, 14, 118, nn. 2-4, 3-36.

Lawrence, A.W. 1979, *Greek aims in fortification*, Oxford.

Lombardi, G./C. Meucci 2006, Il Tufo giallo della Via Tiberina (Roma) utilizzato nei monumenti romani, *RendLinc*, 263-287.

Lugli, G. 1957, *La tecnica edilizia dei Romani*, Roma.

Jolivet, V. et al. 2009, *Suburbium II. Il suburbio di Roma dalla fine dell'età monarchica alla nascita del sistema delle ville (V-II secolo a.C.)*, Rome.

Maaskant Kleibrink, M. 1984, L'urbanistica: il caso di Satricum, *Archeologia Laziale* 6, 351 - 357.

Manfredini, A. (ed.) 2002, *Le dune, il lago e il mare. Una comunità di villaggio del'età del Rame a Maccarese*, Firenze.

Mangani, E./A. Pellegrino (ed.) 2016, για το φίλο μας. *Scritti in ricordo di Gaetano Messineo*, Roma.

McNicoll, A. 1986, Developments in techniques of siegecraft and fortification in the Greek world ca. 400-100 B.C., in P. Leriche/H. Tréziny (eds.), *La fortification dans l'histoire du monde Grec*. Actes du Colloque International, Valbonne 1982, Paris, 305-313.

Menghi, O. et al. 2006, La necropoli di epoca repubblicana in via Goito a Roma, in *The Journal of Fasti Online* 2006, www.fastionline.org/docs/FOLDER-it-2006-53.pdf

Mertens, D. 2006, *Städte und Bauten der Westgriechen. Von der Kolonisationszeit bis zur Krise um 400 vor Christus*, München.

Milazzo, F. 1993, *La realizzazione delle opere pubbliche in Roma arcaica e repubblicana. Munera e Ultro tributa*, Napoli.

Mols, S.T.A.M./E.M. Moormann (ed.) 2005, *Omni pede stare. Saggi architettonici e circumvesuviani in memoriam Jos de Waele*, Napoli.

Momigliano, A./A. Schiavone 1988, *Storia di Roma I. Roma in Italia*, Torino.

Mura Sommella, A. et al. 2001, Primi risultati delle indagini archeologiche in Campidoglio nell'area del Giardino Romano e del Palazzo Caffarelli, *BCom* 102, 261-364.

Nantet, E. 2016, *Phortia. Le tonnage des navires de commerce en Méditerranée du VIIIe siècle av. l'ère chrétienne au VIIe siècle de l'ère chrétienne*, Rennes.

Nijboer, A.J. 1998, *From household production to workshops. Archaeological evidence for economic transformation, pre-monetary exchange and urbanisation in central Italy from 800 to 400 BC*, Groningen.

Palombi, D. 1997, Cic. 2 Verr., V, 19, 48 e Gloss. Ps. Plac. f5 (=GL, IV, p.61) sulla costruzione del tempio di Giove Capitolino, *BCom* 98, 7-14.

Pinza, G. 1905, Monumenti primitivi di Roma e del Lazio antico, *MonAnt* 15, 1-844.

Pomey, P. 2006, Les navires Étrusques: mythe ou réalité, in *Gli Etruschi da Genova a Empurias*. Atti del XXIV Convegno di Studi Etruschi ed Italici (Marseille – Lattes 2002), Pisa/Roma, 423-433.

Pomey, P. 2011, Les conséquences de l'évolution des techniques de construction navale sur l'économie maritime antique: quelques exemples, in W. V. Harris/K. Iara (eds.), *Maritime technology in the ancient economy: ship design and navigation*, Portsmouth, Rhode Island, 39-55.

Säflund, G. 1932, *Le mura di Roma repubblicana*, Lund.

Ten Kortenaar, S. 2011, *Il colore e la materia. Tra tradizione e innovazione nella produzione dell'impasto rosso nell'Italia medio-tirrenica*, Roma.

Volpe, R. 2014, Dalle cave della via Tiberina alle Mura repubblicane di Roma, in *Arquelogía de la Construcción IV. las canteras en el mundo antiguo: sistemas de explotación y procesos productivo*. Convegno Internazionale di Studi Padova, 22-24 novembre 2012 (Anejos de Archivo Espanol de Arqueologia 69), Madrid/Mérida, 61-71.

Wikander, Ö. 2017, *Roof-tiles and tile-roofs at Poggio Civitate (Murlo). The emergence of Central Italic tile industry*, Stockholm.

Winter, N 2008, *Symbols of Wealth and Power. Architectural Terracotta Decoration in Etruria and Central Italy, 640-510 B.C.*, Ann Arbor.

Ziółkowski, A. 2016, The Servian enceinte: should the debate continue ?, *Palamades* 11, 151-170.

# Contextualising ceramic production at Satricum
## *An economic perspective on Archaic and early Roman South Latium*

*Tymon de Haas*

*Abstract*

*This paper contextualises the evidence for ceramic production at Satricum within regional developments in settlement, demography and social organisation between the Archaic and mid-Republican period. It is argued that concepts from economic theory (friction of distance, agglomeration effects and transaction costs) provide a useful perspective on the economy of Archaic Latium, and that besides reciprocity and redistribution, market exchange played a considerable role in the economy. Furthermore, the regional archaeological record suggests that both economic conditions (demand/market potential) and socio-political circumstances changed over time, and that these changes had a profound impact on the scale and organisation of ceramic production.*

INTRODUCTION

The site of Satricum is one of the best known centres of early craft production in central Tyrrhenian Italy. Since systematic investigations were initiated by Dutch universities under the aegis of the Dutch Institute in Rome in the 1970s, evidence for ceramic and other artisanal production has been found in various parts of the ancient settlement (fig. 1).[1] The evidence for production (kilns and related infrastructure, wasters, moulds etc.) has been supplemented by extensive ceramic studies aimed at identifying the characteristics of the pottery and architectural terracottas produced locally between the 7th and 3rd centuries BC.[2] Together, the evidence has allowed a reconstruction of the main technological and typological developments in local ceramic production through time.

Such reconstructions have been used to better understand changes in the organisation and scale of production, and more broadly the role of craft specialisation in relation to religious institutions ('temple economies') and urbanization processes.[3] More recently, they have also been used to better understand the choices producers made, and the social practices behind such choices.[4] Thanks to the quantity and quality of archaeological evidence, we thus know relatively much about the technology of ceramic production and its social and organisational implications - not only at Satricum, but also in Archaic Latium more generally.[5]

Less well understood is the way in which the socio-economic context affects ceramic production. This context, which includes the mechanisms through which goods are exchanged, the volume and nature of demand, and ultimately consumption practices, defines both which types of ceramics need to be produced and in which quantities. Especially where it concerns (non-elite) daily-use goods, which were needed in large volumes, these parameters largely define the ways in which they were produced (the extent to which specialisation occurred), and ultimately also

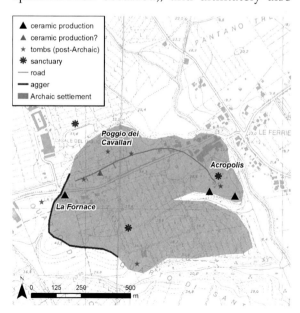

*Fig. 1. A map of Satricum showing the main a of ceramic production (T. de Haas).*

affect the technological choices involved in the production process.

In order to complement studies focusing on ceramic production from a technological perspective, this paper therefore contextualises the evidence for ceramic production at Satricum in light of consumption demand. Using concepts from different strands of economic theory, I review regional developments in settlement, demography and social organisation as the context in which ceramics were produced. It should be stated on the outset that the use of such economic theory is explicitly not intended to offer a modernizing interpretation of an economy that was fundamentally defined by context-specific institutions (such as sanctuaries and elites), and in which market exchange (the existence of which is assumed in such theories) was surely not the only or even the primary mode of exchange. However, it is argued that such theory can provide us with new and useful perspectives on production and exchange in Archaic Latium, and that market exchange indeed played a considerable role in the period under discussion. As we will see, both economic circumstances (demand and market potential) and socio-political conditions changed considerably within the period under consideration. This had a clear impact on the scale and organisation of production, with potential implications for technological choices as well.

CERAMIC PRODUCTION AND EXCHANGE: AN ECONOMIC PERSPECTIVE

*Economic theory and ancient societies*

Economic theory is not often explicitly applied in the study of production and exchange in early Latium, and more generally there has been much discussion over the applicability of modern economic theory and models to pre-modern societies. This debate in essence evolves around two fundamentally different scholarly perspectives on past societies, "[..] between those that believe that the difference between Western-type market economies and primitive-subsistence economies is one of degree, and those who believe it is one of kind [...]".[6] Thus, some ('Formalists') would argue that markets governed by price-setting mechanisms may also have existed and that the principle of profit maximizing behaviour may also have applied in the pre-modern World, others ('Substantivists') would argue that ancient mentalities and practices would have been so fundamentally different that such models cannot be applied.[7] In this perspective, states, elites and religious institutions rather than an abstract market would be the key agents in exchange. Their behaviour should either conform to other modes of exchange (e.g., reciprocity or redistribution), or, even worse, would be too culturally specific to allow the identification of any underlying mechanisms or rules.

These positions may be considered two abstract and extreme ends of a broad and diverse spectrum of possible economic behaviours: in reality both past and modern economies were much more complex. Archaeologists, historians and anthropologists working in different chronological and regional contexts have pointed at the crucial role of markets in many (though not all) pre-modern states and empires - without denying that alternative modes of exchange existed side by side with market exchange.[8] Conversely, various schools in modern economics acknowledge the cultural embeddedness of market economies; we can think of New Institutional Economics with its emphasis on institutions and their role in lowering or increasing transaction costs;[9] or Behavioural Economics, which uses psychological experiments to highlight the irrationality of individual (consumer) behaviour. Without denying the usefulness of models from (Neo-)classical economic theory, such schools of thought do problematize the assumed rational and optimizing behaviour which underlies some of these models.[10]

In sum: while modern economic theory has criticised the 'modernising' assumptions of rational behaviour in the context of present-day market economies, scholars of pre-modern societies increasingly acknowledge that past behaviour (and by extension economies) may not have been so fundamentally different from the present as sometimes thought. Without denying that there are indeed major differences between pre-industrial and modern economies, all this does suggest that there is no *a priori* reason not to apply theories and principles from modern economics to the ancient world, as a heuristic tool to help explain observed patterns in the past.

*The economy of Archaic Central Italy*

Key to the economy of Archaic Rome and Latium are the links between agricultural surplus production, craft specialisation (iron working and ceramic production), urbanisation and elite consumption and display.[11] The agricultural economy generated substantial surpluses, which were put to various uses: they sustained an increasing urban population, in part specialised in non-agricultural production; they were used by elites for status display, both through the supply of imported goods and the deposition of goods in elite burials and votive contexts; and they were used in the construction of communal monuments such as fortifications, roads and temples.[12] At Rome, but also at other urban sites, such construction works suggest the control over large surpluses and hence quite substantial economic development.[13]

In this economic context various modes of exchange complemented each other. Redistribution and reciprocity (gift exchange) had a central role within early Latial exchange systems: the exchange of imports may have entailed a combination of highly regulated trade at coastal entrepots (controlled by elites and religious institutions), and redistributive and/or reciprocal exchange within the region.[14] Exchange of foodstuffs and other goods may have taken place through similar mechanisms, with a central role for the clan or *gens*. However, market exchange certainly played a role as well: indications for this include the rise of rudimentary central place systems and the existence of weight standards and standardised metal objects, which suggest a pre-monetary trade system.[15] Also, both written and archaeological sources point out that in the context of urbanization processes, craft production attained increasing levels of standardization, specialisation and labour division, suggesting that market mechanisms operated from the 7th and 6th centuries BC onwards.[16]

Such a complementary understanding of the Archaic economy fits well with two recent studies that have approached the Archaic economy from different perspectives. From an anthropological perspective, Cristiano Viglietti has pointed out the culturally embedded nature of the economy of Archaic Rome, but also acknowledges that Romans were already familiar with market exchange and associated price-setting mechanisms.[17] Drawing mainly on written sources, Neil Coffee has similarly argued that although reciprocity was central to Roman social and economic behaviour, there is also ample evidence (the first treaty with Carthage, references to the regulation of *nundinae* in the Twelve Tables) that trade and market exchange were already an important feature of the economy.[18]

CONTEXTUALISING CERAMIC PRODUCTION IN SATRICUM: GEOGRAPHICAL ECONOMICS, INSTITUTIONS AND TRANSACTION COSTS

From the above, it may be clear that although it is generally acknowledged that market exchange played a significant role in Archaic central Italy, it is less clear what the scale and scope of market exchange was.[19] Were non-prestige items for day-to-day use, such as ceramics, primarily exchanged through market exchange? And would this have been a constant, or were there changes in the scale and scope of market exchange between the Archaic period and Roman Republican times? To help answer these questions, and in light of what I argued above, I consider models and concepts derived from economic theory a useful means and therefore employ them in the following review of the changing socio-economic context of ceramic production in Satricum.

An economic systems perspective (*fig. 2*) provides a useful starting point to this end, as it not only considers production processes, but also the circulation, distribution and consumption of goods and services, as well as the potential regulatory processes.[20] In other words, this perspective frames the technological and infrastructural evidence for craft production in its broader economic context without losing sight of the societal (cultural) context.

While it is beyond the scope of this paper to fully analyse these systems, I here focus on three crucial aspects of the economic system: production, consumption and regulation. In analysing production and consumption, I draw on Neoclassical Location Theory and New Geographical Economics, which focus on two ordering principles in the spatial organisation of economic activities: the costs of distance, and the benefits of agglomeration or increasing returns to scale.

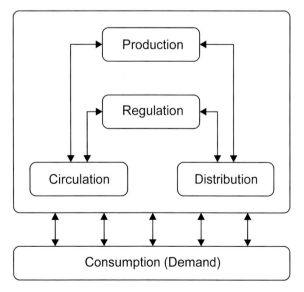

*Fig. 2. Organization of the production system (after Dicken/Lloyd 1990, fig. I.3).*

The former states that the intensity of economic exchange will decline with increasing transportation costs; the latter that the concentration of productive activities and demand in specific places provide an incentive for economic growth.[21] In light of these principles, I discuss spatial aspects of the production process such as the availability of raw materials, and the role of infrastructure in lowering transport costs and promoting economic integration. I will also consider demographic change and patterns of urbanization, which define the volume and variability in demand. In different configurations they may also stimulate an increase in the scale and level of specialisation of production and thus lead to agglomeration effects.

As already alluded to, one cannot properly understand patterns of production and consumption without considering regulatory processes, more specifically the social and political frameworks of Archaic society that define to what extent and under which restraints market exchange could take place. At an abstract level we may think of the role of religious beliefs and social attitudes towards exchange; more concretely we may think of the role of states, warfare, religious institutions (temples) or clan leaders in enhancing different forms of exchange. It is useful to consider how these institutions affected *transaction costs*, a concept central to New Institutional Economics, as a restraint on the development of market exchange. Thus, because of religious beliefs the purchase of certain goods may be deemed inappropriate, or kinship ties may enforce that goods are exchanged reciprocally. In such conditions, transaction costs are simply too high for market exchange to take place. On the other hand, social norms regarding conspicuous consumption or religious practices (e.g., the deposition of prestige goods) may also stimulate the acquiring of traded goods or the local production and purchase of votive objects and may thus enhance market exchange. Political or religious institutions may have provided formal rules and regulations or introduced weight standards with the objective of making exchanges more reliable, thus lowering transaction costs and stimulating market exchange.[22]

These considerations imply that changes in the regional population size, settlement system and associated socio-political organisation and its external interactions may explain changes in the systems of production, at both Satricum and the regional level. To evaluate such links, this paper presents a review of this regional context, structured chronologically in three main phases: the Archaic period (c. 580-480 BC), the post-Archaic period (c. 480-350 BC), and the mid- to late Republican period (c. 350-30 BC). While these are coarse chronological divisions, they roughly reflect distinct phases in the historical and socio-economic development of Satricum and the surrounding region.

With regard to the production process, I review the evidence for ceramic production at both the regional level and for Satricum. While this evidence is far from complete, and targeted research will for sure uncover many new production sites[23], it provides a good starting point for understanding the scale and organisation of ceramic production. The evidence is considered in light of:

1. the accessibility of raw materials, which for ceramic production are mainly clay, water and fuel. As both fuel and clay are bulky, production will as a rule not take place too far away from these resources.

2. transport costs, which in pre-industrial societies were a major limitation in the marketing of goods. Thus, the development of constructed roads, river transport and associated infrastructure would have enhanced the distribution of goods over larger distances.

3. population size and processes of urbanization, which condition the volume and nature of demand, and therefore fundamentally define the scale and level of specialisation of production.

In evaluating changes in demand, I also consider the size and distribution of the population, as population growth would arguably lead to larger demand, the upscaling and specialisation of production, and increased productivity. In addition, the spatial concentration of population (urbanization) would enable the rise of specialised labour and, knowledge and if multiple producers are active in one location, agglomeration effects or economies of scale.

To reconstruct population changes (as a proxy for demand), I draw on both the rural settlement data collected within the Pontine Region Project, and a recent inventory of nucleated settlements in the region. These data form the basis for reconstructing relative changes in population, but also rough estimations of absolute population levels. Although such estimates are notoriously problematic, they are important to assess the order of magnitude of demand, which ultimately must be the basis for any reconstruction of ancient economies, especially when dealing with changes over time.[24]

THE ARCHAIC PERIOD

*The regional context: settlement patterns and demography*

As other parts of central Italy, the Pontine region witnessed the flourishing of many urban centres in the Archaic period (*fig. 3*). Satricum ranks as the largest and best known of these, but sites like Caracupa, Caprifico, Antium, Velitrae, Lanuvium, Colle della Coedra and Cora (perhaps slightly later also Norba) were probably of similar importance and order of size. In addition, a series of smaller, secondary centres existed (e.g., Colle Rotondo, Contrada Casali). While small numbers of isolated farms seem to have been established in the countryside in the late 7th century, the 6th century witnessed a major increase in rural settlement numbers in many parts of the Pontine region.[25] It is widely accepted that these processes of urbanization and rural infill relate to the rise of small, fairly independent socio-political units ('city-states') exercising some degree of control over their surrounding rural territories.[26]

To evaluate the demographic characteristics of these Archaic polities, the size estimates we have for many of the larger settlements provide a good starting point. As shown in figure 4, the larger centres measured between c. 25 and 51 hectares, whereas secondary sites range in size between c. 1 and 7 hectares. Using methods more commonly applied to estimate the population of

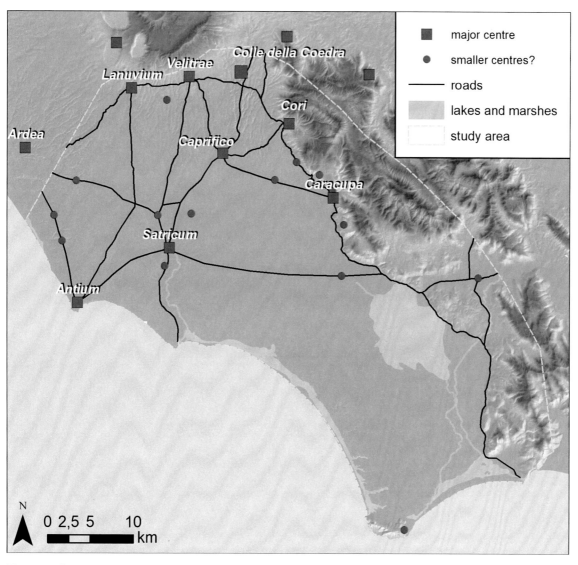

*Fig. 3. Archaic nucleated settlements in the Pontine region (T. de Haas).*

Roman cities, we may cautiously use these data to estimate the order of magnitude of the population of the Archaic settlements.[27] With relatively low density estimates of 50 to 120 people per hectare and using the average size of larger and secondary centres, we arrive at a minimum estimate of c. 18,500 and a maximum estimate of some 43,000 persons living in primary and secondary settlements (*fig. 4, table 1*). It should be noted that such calculations use a low size estimate for several sites that later became major centres (Norba, Privernum, Circeii), but for which we do not know the size in the Archaic period.[28] Furthermore, it seems doubtful whether all secondary settlements in the region have been identified, which means that probably more people lived in such sites. All in all, the figures in table 1 give a realistic range of population levels in nucleated settlements, although these more likely approached the higher end of the range.

Estimating rural population levels is arguably more difficult. Although PRP surveys show beyond doubt that rural infill occurred, the ceramic dating evidence has substantial margins of error and allows for quite different reconstructions of Archaic rural settlement densities.[29] On one extreme, it seems possible that in some surveys too many sites have been assigned an Archaic phase, leading to an overrepresentation; on the other hand, it is generally accepted that because of visibility biases and post-depositional processes (destruction and covering of sites by erosion and sedimentation), field surveys only recover a fraction of the rural sites that were originally present in a certain area.

The potential effects of such different scenarios on rural population reconstructions are explored in Table 2. If we assume an (over)complete recovery of sites and small household sizes, our data would translate into a modest regional rural population of less than 40,000 people; if we believe in a low recovery rate and assume households were rather larger, we end up with a much larger rural population (more than 110,000). Although admittedly based more on gut feeling than actual evidence, I suggest that a most likely reconstruction would account for a slight net (recovery minus false identifications) underrepresentation of Archaic rural sites in our dataset combined with intermediate average household size, as illustrated in the final column of table 2. I acknowledge that there are quite a lot of assumptions in this reconstruction: besides the recovery biases already discussed, these include the representativity of our survey data (which only cover c. 2% of the entire region) and the potential variation in rural site classes (perhaps there were more small hamlets our surveys have not been able to identify). But despite the tentative nature of the figures, I would argue that they again do provide a broad yet reasonable order of magnitude; the 'reasonable' figure of slightly over 50,000 people also aligns pretty well with the calculated populations in nucleated settlements.

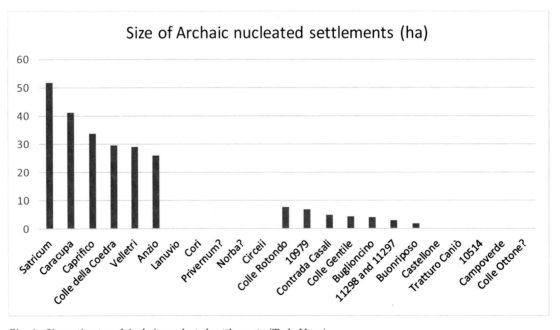

*Fig. 4. Size estimates of Archaic nucleated settlements (T. de Haas).*

| Size of centre | N identified | Average Size | Area total (Ha) | Minimum population estimate (50 persons/ha) | Maximum population estimate (120 persons/ha) |
|---|---|---|---|---|---|
| Large centres (Satricum, Caracupa, Colle della Coedra, Caprifico, Velitrae, Antium, Lanuvium, Cori) | 8 | 35.2 (based on 6 estimates) | 281.5 | 14,073 | 33,776 |
| Small centres (>1 ha) | 15 | 4.7 (based on 7 estimates) | 70,9 | 3,546 | 8,511 |
| Total | | | | 18,026 | 43,263 |

Table 1. Minimum and maximum population estimates for Archaic nucleated settlements.

| Landscape zone | Inhabitable area (km2) | Area surveyed in km2 (% of inhabitable area) | Settlements in surveyed area | Minimum rural Population (5 persons per site, assuming 25% "overidentification" of Archaic rural sites in the surveyed areas | Maximum rural population (8 persons per site, assumed recovery rate in surveyed areas is 50%) | 'reasonable' rural population (6 persons per site, assumed recovery rate 80%) |
|---|---|---|---|---|---|---|
| Coastal plain | 544.4 | | | | | |
| | 10.8 (2.0%) | 47 | 11,846 | 37,906 | 17,769 | |
| Interior plain | 623.3 | 18.3 (2.9%) | 88 | 14,986 | 47,957 | 22,480 |
| Uplands | 151.7 | 2.3 (1.5%) | 28 | 9,234 | 29,549 | 13,851 |
| Total | | | | 36,066 | 115,412 | 54,100 |

Table 2. Extrapolation of Archaic rural site numbers and populations.

To sum up, a rough approximation based on the archaeological evidence suggests that in demographic terms the Archaic period was one of considerable population levels, with a first substantial peak in the regional population. In the northern part of the Pontine region a hierarchically organised landscape had arisen, with a series of regularly distributed urban centres surrounded by (in what may loosely be defined their respective hinterlands) smaller secondary centres and dispersed rural sites. On aggregate, we deal with a population in the range of c. 60,000 to 100,000 persons that provided for a considerable volume of demand. The urban and many of the secondary centres were connected through a network of roads – although we cannot really tell whether these were well-constructed and maintained.[30] Certainly, sites along the coast (Antium, perhaps Astura) were equipped with port facilities and provided connections to external trade networks, being therefore particularly important for access to prestige goods. However, it seems likely that most exchange took place at the micro-regional and regional scale. The urban centres provided relatively stable and safe contexts for producing, buying and selling products.

This brings us to the role of regulatory systems in the economy. In this centralised settlement system, institutional control over production and exchange was relatively firm, and this probably had a positive effect on the development of market exchange. Even if the urban centres had no strong public institutions that controlled the actions of individual members of the elite (clan leaders),[31] some form of common mobilisation of surpluses certainly occurred, and a pre-monetary system that required a broad acceptance of standards arose. Sanctuaries may well have stimulated the production and selling of votive offerings, and the occurrence of weight standards in votive deposits may reflect a role of religious authorities in guaranteeing the value of these standards.[32]

*Satricum*

As one of the larger (if not the largest) of these polities, Satricum formed a major central place, and with its relatively densely occupied hinterland it also served a substantial population.[33] In terms of central place functions, the sanctuary of Mater Matuta probably formed a point of attraction for not only local visitors, but also for people from further away. These visitors would need to eat, drink, be provided with offerings and probably required other services as well. They thus added substantially to the potential demand for goods and services. In addition, Satricum had a strategic position within regional transport networks and probably was a crucial hub in regional traffic and exchange: the Astura river formed a direct link towards the coast with its maritime connections, and the site occupied one of the few easy passes across the Astura, connecting the northern part of the pontine plain towards areas further south.

How does this general context tie in with pottery production? For the Archaic period, evidence for ceramic production has been identified in two locations on the acropolis. The oldest of these contexts dates to the late 7th century and suggests only the production of domestic pottery wares as a household industry, being run by one household, supplying a local market. The second context dates to the (late) 6th century, and produced a range of ceramics, including roof tiles, storage containers, various kitchen wares, fine wares and, presumably, bucchero and architectural terracotta's (temple decorations). This context is interpreted as an example of workshop industry, where production takes place at a larger scale, in dedicated facilities, by specialised potters.[34] The proximity of this workshop to the sanctuary of Mater Matuta may indeed suggest control over production by the sanctuary.

The development of such centralised and specialised production fits in well with the observed patterns of population growth and urbanisation, which entailed the construction of monumental architecture. These developments had created demand for a range of ceramic products, including cooking and storage wares, and more expensive table wares (such as bucchero), commonly used building materials as well as architectural materials destined specifically for the urban sanctuaries. Rural demand was less varied (bucchero table wares are hardly known from rural contexts, and tiles were probably not a standard feature of all farms), but still considerable. As no rural ceramic production centres are known and the fabrics and shapes occurring in the countryside are similar to those found at Satricum, it is likely that urban workshops also supplied rural populations.

Whether such urban producers typically served local markets is hard to tell. For sure, many major urban centres in central Tyrrhenian Italy had ceramic workshops,[35] but such remains have so far not been attested for most of the centres in the Pontine region.[36] In fact, there are reasons to believe that Satricum's ceramic industry operated also on a regional level. This is suggested, first, by the fact that the site probably imported marine clays for the production of chiaro sabbioso ceramics from Lavinium. At a distance of some 20 km, this implies considerable transport costs that would perhaps also suggest that the production served a larger regional market.[37] Second, clay prospections show that Satricum occupies a particularly favourable position in terms of proximity to clay resources: it is situated at the intersection of various geological zones and thus had access to a range of clays, including marine, volcanic, colluvial and lagoonal deposits, with different technical properties, at relatively low costs (*fig. 5*). Finally, fabric analyses on materials from small rural sites seem to confirm that Satrican *impasto rosso* was indeed distributed over considerable distances. All this would suggest that Satricum had a major role in ceramic production in the Pontine region.[38]

The post-Archaic period

*The regional context*

Written sources suggest that the 5th and early 4th centuries were a turbulent period with continued struggles between Rome, Latins and Volcians. We still have a limited understanding of the archaeology of this period: at only few sites clear 5th century phases are attested, and we also have difficulties in identifying settlements of this period in our field survey assemblages.[39]

Both the fact that the archaeological evidence is scarce and the limited evidence we do have, suggest that important changes occurred. First, field surveys at urban sites (Caracupa and Caprifico) and secondary centres (Contrada Casali) show that these contracted or disappeared in this period, and as we will see below the excavations at Satricum equally highlight fundamental changes in the urban fabric. Second, field surveys also suggest that rural settlement patterns changed: the numbers of small rural settlements (farms) declined in various parts of the region, and some areas (for example south of Satricum) that were settled in the Archaic period seem to have been abandoned.[40] Also, in some areas there is evidence for the rise of nucleated settlements (villages) of a few hectares in size, indicating local shifts from dispersed to more nucleated rural settlement patterns. Finally, the limited presence of typical coarse ware ceramics in rural contexts, and the scarce occurrence of imports in both urban and rural contexts as well as a reduction in major construction works -especially temples- in urban contexts are suggestive of economic decline. One could suggest that in the historical context

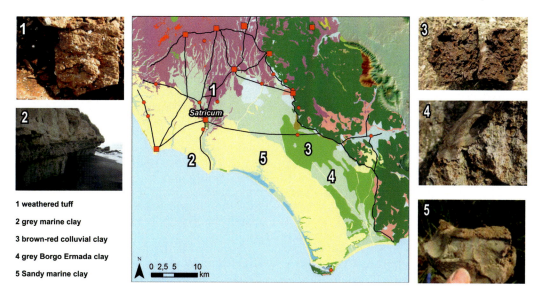

*Fig. 5. Location of Satricum in relation to geological deposits (T. de Haas).*

of the 5th century it is not surprising that decreasing central control from the urban polities went hand in hand with economic decline: with regular raiding and warfare, agricultural surpluses became smaller and/or more difficult to control, and the supply of prestige goods (and their deposition in votive contexts) decreased.

The demographic dimension of this 5th century decline remains unclear: to what extent the scarcity of archaeological evidence reflects a decrease of the population (there are few sites) or only economic decline (we can't see the sites because people don't consume pottery) is difficult to say. Although it is beyond doubt that population levels decreased, it is therefore impossible to assess this decline quantitatively. I would argue that we should account for a considerable decrease of both urban and rural populations, that this caused a drop in demand for foodstuff and craft items, and hence affected the scale and organisation of production.

The general picture sketched here would also have negative implications for regional connectivity and regulation of exchange. As urban centres contracted and centralised socio-political organisation weakened, it seems likely that the regional infrastructure was also less well maintained due to a lack of central management. Under such conditions, exchange at the regional and supra-regional level certainly became more costly; the aforementioned decrease in the consumption of imported wares is in this light perhaps not surprising. At the level of individual sites, contraction and/or clustering of habitation may equally reflect a less centralised organisation of these centres, perhaps with a more autonomous role of individual social groups (clans).[41] Thus, not only did overall demand decrease, but it also became more difficult to centrally mobilise surpluses, and hence the conditions that had stimulated processes of specialisation and labour division in the Archaic period became less favourable. From an institutional perspective, the decreasing role of public and religious institutions in production and exchange, would also have increased transaction costs.

*Satricum*

Satricum represents the by far best known post-Archaic site in south Latium, although its development in this period is quite complex and debated. It is beyond the scope of this paper to review these developments and debates in detail, but it is beyond doubt that the site underwent profound changes in its urban organisation and its ethnic composition. Major monuments such as the main road and its temples were destroyed in the 5th century, and parts of the urban area were now in use as cemeteries. These cemeteries contain graves and gravegoods that display non-local characteristics and pertain to Volscian immigrants. At the same time, there are also elements of continuity, as the deposition of votives seems to have continued, and there is also continuity in ceramic traditions.[42] Thus, it seems that the Archaic urban settlement broke up into separate smaller habitation clusters, perhaps reflecting social groups of both Volscian descent and local lineages.[43] In terms of population size, these changes may also have implied considerable decline, perhaps from several thousands of inhabitants to several hundreds.[44] In line with what is observed in the countryside, the more humble votives of this period equally suggest economic decline (with a recovery from the late 5th/early 4th century onwards).[45]

The evidence at Satricum indicates that changes also occurred in its ceramic production. The workshops on the acropolis ceased to exist, and new workshops sprang up in the countryside south of Satricum, producing a more limited range of ceramic building materials (tiles) and domestic coarse wares.[46] In line with the broader context sketched above, these developments seem to reflect a shift of centralised and specialised urban production towards more dispersed, smaller scale production, perhaps to be interpreted as household industry or estate production.[47] However, the story is more complex, as new production sites also arose at Satricum after the transformation of the site in the late Archaic period. Recent investigations in the area of Poggio dei Cavallari have yielded evidence of another ceramic workshop dating to the 5th century, probably producing red-firing coarse wares. In addition, white firing chiaro sabbioso ceramics continued to be produced as well, using marine clays imported from the area of Lavinium.[48] This suggests that investments in transportation of raw materials continued to be made and hence it seems likely that Satricum's ceramic production continued to have considerable outputs targeted at regional markets.[49] Moreover, in the (early?) 4th century yet another workshop arose on the edge of the former city in the area of La Fornace, producing tiles, domestic pottery and votive materials.[50] This context, with its more varied output and substantial infrastructure, seems to be compatible with workshop industries.

Thus, although the context for ceramic production became less favourable with a decrease in aggregate demand and a less favourable institutional context, this only in part affected Satricum's ceramic industry: apparently the production of (bucchero) table wares stopped and no other fine table wares were produced anymore. At the same time, production remained substantial: the sanctuaries may well have provided for enough local demand to maintain production at a considerable scale, and it seems that specific vessels were also produced to be deposited in burial contexts.[51] On the other hand, Satricum's favourable geographical position also guaranteed its continued importance as a regional production centre.

## THE MID AND LATE REPUBLICAN PERIOD

### The regional context

From the mid-4th century BC, the stability that resulted from Rome's more firm control over south Latium, brought major changes in the regional settled landscape (*fig. 6*). Pre-existing towns expanded and monumentalised, while new towns and secondary centres also arose. In many areas, rural settlement numbers increased considerably, and previously marginal areas were once again settled. The most prominent of these was the southern part of the Pontine plain, a marsh that was now reclaimed, allowing a major expansion in rural settlement.[52]

Throughout the region new roads were constructed, most importantly the Via Appia, but also transversal roads that linked coastal and inland areas. Canals such as the Decennovium and the Rio Martino connected the inner plain with the coast, accommodating faster and cheaper transport within the region. New ports at sites such as Tarracina, Circeii, Astura and Antium integrated the region in maritime networks, whereas the aforementioned canals and roads with associated roadside settlements and smaller ports (as at Forum Appii) enhanced connectivity within the region.

The increased archaeological evidence again allows us to roughly estimate the demographic characteristics of the region in the mid and late Republican period (*fig. 7, tables 3-4*). Using the methods already applied for the Archaic period, the population of nucleated settlements was probably somewhere between 15,000 to 45,000 people. A most plausible estimate, assuming that the main urban centres became more densely settled than the less structured secondary centres, and assuming that not all of these smaller centres are known to us, would suggest a population of around 30,000.[53] These figures are quite comparable to the urban population reconstruction for the Archaic period, but now more people lived in small centres (such as the aforementioned newly founded roadside settlements). To reconstruct rural population levels, I have adapted the methods described above for the Archaic period slightly: as in the Republican period larger rural estates developed, we may assume that maximum and average households are slightly larger. Furthermore, as our dating evidence for this period is solid, there is no allowance made in the minimum estimate for overrepresentation of sites in the dataset. With these slightly different parameters, we end up with rural population estimates between c. 44,000 and 176,000; allowing for an average household that is slightly larger than for the Archaic period and similar recovery rates, we end up at a plausible rural population of c. 80,000 people (table 4). The PRP survey data therefore clearly suggest that the increase in urban populations is matched by a substantial increase in rural populations.

Thus, in the Republican period several factors contributed to fundamental economic changes. Population growth led to a substantial rise in demand, agricultural expansion and increasingly large surpluses, as well as the rise of nucleated settlements, providing a hierarchical system of central places servicing rural areas. Investments in infrastructure reduced transport costs and contributed to the integration of the region in larger trade networks.

Roman imperial expansion was of course fundamental to these changes, not only through investments financed by conquests, but also through laws and regulations regarding market rights and regulating trade relations between Roman citizens and Latins, which reduced transaction costs as well.[54] Together these conditions laid the ground for an expansion and diversification of the regional economy. If we consider the occurrence of black gloss table wares on rural sites as a reflection of rising standards of living for rural non-elites, the widespread occurrence of such table wares in our PRP surveys throughout the region indicate quite favourable economic circumstances leading to increasing prosperity for peasant farmers.[55]

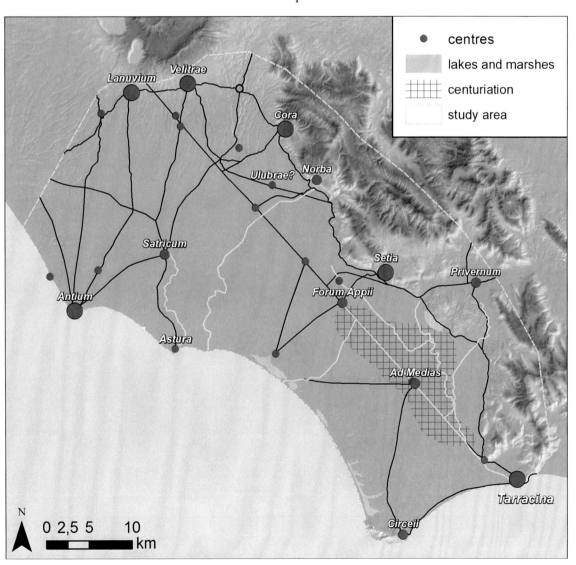

Fig. 6. Republican nucleated settlements and infrastructure in the Pontine region (T. de Haas).

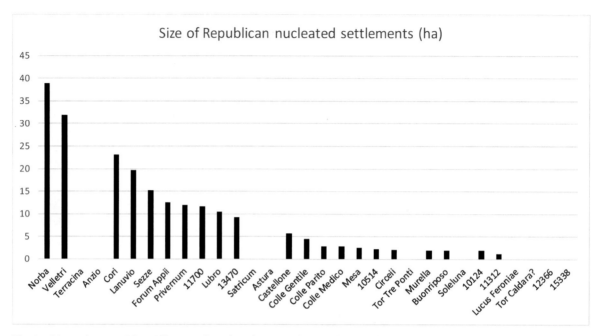

*Fig. 7. Size estimates of Republican nucleated settlements. Sites without such an estimate are inserted according to their assumed approximate size (T. de Haas).*

| Size of centre | N identified | Average Size | Area total (Ha) | Minimum population estimate (50 persons/ha) | Minimum population estimate (150 persons/ha) | 'reasonable' population estimate (50 persons/ha for small centres, 120 persons/ha for large centres, recovery of 75% of small centres) |
|---|---|---|---|---|---|---|
| Large centres (Norba, Cora Velitrae, Antium, Lanuvium, Tarracina, Setia) | 7 | 25.8 (based on 5 estimates) | 180,6 | 9,030 | 27,090 | 21,672 |
| Small centres (>1 ha) | 24 | 5.4 (based on 16 estimates) | 129,6 | 6,480 | 15,552 | 8,640 |
| Total | | | | 15,510 | 42,642 | 30,312 |

*Table 3. Minimum and maximum population estimates for Mid- to Late Republican nucleated settlements.*

| Landscape zone | Inhabitable area (km2) | Area surveyed in km2 (% of inhabitable area) | Settlements in surveyed area | Minimum rural Population (5 persons per site, assuming full recovery) | Maximum rural population (10 persons per site, assumed recovery rate in surveyed areas is 50%) | 'reasonable' rural population (7 persons per site, assumed recovery rate 75%) |
|---|---|---|---|---|---|---|
| Coastal plain | 566.7 | 10.8 (1.9%) | 49 | 12,856 | 51,423 | 23,997 |
| Interior plain | 676.6 | 18.3 (2.7%) | 124 | 22,903 | 91,611 | 42,790 |
| Uplands | 152.5 | 2.3 (1.5%) | 25 | 8,288 | 33,152 | 15,471 |
| Total | | | | 44,047 | 176,186 | 82,258 |

*Table 4. Extrapolation of Republican rural site numbers and populations.*

*Satricum*

While levelling and deep ploughing have largely destroyed the site's later phases of occupation and recent excavations may suggest more substantial 4th century and possibly even later remains, Satricum by this time probably played a modest role on the regional scene and was certainly no longer a major regional centre.[56] However, production of a broad array of ceramics (tile, domestic wares, fine wares, anatomical votives and possibly black gloss pottery) continued in the area of la Fornace into the 3rd century BC. This diverse production, perhaps including higher-value table wares and material produced specifically for religious purposes, is suggestive of workshop-industry level, specialised production; this level may well have been sustained by the demand generated by the sanctuaries and surrounding rural populations.[57]

At the regional level, the evidence for ceramic production becomes more substantial and diverse. Republican production sites are more numerous compared to previous periods, and they also occur in more diverse contexts including urban centres, secondary centres and rural villas and farms. These sites also show a greater diversification of production: some mainly focused on tiles and domestic coarse wares, while others produced black gloss table wares or dolia; yet others produced broader ranges of ceramics, also including amphorae to transport locally produced wine and olive oil.[58] Many of these production sites are situated on either road crossings or waterways, suggesting that their products were indeed traded over longer distances within and perhaps beyond the region – as is also suggested by the common occurrence of kitchen wares of probable extra-regional origin.[59]

The evidence for rural ceramic production ties in with contemporary changes in agriculture, which witnessed the development of specialised, market-oriented production of cash crops such as wine and olive oil. It thus seems that ceramic production was part of a broader attempt to increase labour productivity at rural estates, reflecting both an increasing dependence on an integrated market economy, and economic growth, probably to the benefit of not only the elites.

CONCLUSION

The diachronic contextualisation of Satricum´s ceramic industry presented in this paper will hopefully have made clear that an economic perspective can indeed fruitfully complement the study of ancient crafts and associated technological developments. Issues of demand (how much pottery was required by a community? What types of ceramics could be afforded by whom?) are relevant considerations as much as social preferences and norms. Technological choices can thus not be seen as separate from the broader social and economic context in which they were made.

Furthermore, without denying a fundamental role for redistribution and reciprocity between and within social groups, I have argued that markets formed an important aspect of Archaic and early Roman society, and that modern economic theory can provide a useful contribution to the study of the economy of Archaic Latium. To underline this point, let us return to the three main concepts derived from economic theory underpinning my preceding diachronic analysis. The extant evidence clearly shows dramatic changes in terms of costs of distance, agglomeration effects, and transaction costs, which fundamentally impacted the scale and nature of ceramic production as identified in the archaeological record.

In the Archaic period, processes of urbanization and population growth went hand in hand with specialisation, diversification and centralization of production, which in turn imply increased (concentration of) demand, and decreased transaction costs. Therefore, aggregate economic growth occurred, and conditions for the rise of market exchange were favourable.[60] Even if the costs of distance may not have reduced as much as in later phases in Roman history, these conditions seem to have led to some degree of regional integration in the Archaic period, in which Satricum, judging from the ceramic evidence, may have played a pivotal role.

Socio-economic developments in the post-Archaic period provided much less favourable conditions: in this period, south Latium is characterised by ongoing socio-political and military struggles, a contraction in both urban and rural populations and decreasing levels of centralization. These circumstances imply a drop in demand, a lack of potential for agglomeration effects, and rising transaction costs - a context partly reflected in the evidence for ceramic production, which became more dispersed and less diversified. While this certainly implies economic stagnation, and possibly even a return to alternative modes of exchange for daily use goods such as ceramics, this is not the whole story: it seems indeed that Satricum due to its favourable location, exceptional local demand generated by the sanctuaries and perhaps also its long tradition of ceramic production, remained a production centre of regional importance.

By Mid-Republican times, increasing levels of state control, population growth and urbanization once again provided the conditions for higher demand, larger potential for specialisation and lower transaction costs. However, crucial for the further development of the economy were investments in infrastructure: road building and port construction lowered transport costs and stimulated the integration at the regional level, and also increasingly connected the regional economy to broader exchange networks. These circumstances led to specialisation and market oriented production in agriculture, and stimulated the spread of ceramic production in both urban and rural contexts, raising labour productivity and contributing to economic growth – arguably now also with a positive effect on living standards.

By this time, Satricum no longer ranked among the major urban centres of the region, and its prominent role in the history of South Latium had ended. However, it is not by chance that along with the sanctuary of Mater Matuta, around which the settlement had developed centuries earlier, ceramic production seems to have been the primary economic activity to endure into Republican times.

NOTES

[1] For the earlier excavations, see Waarsenburg 1998. For overviews and extensive references to more recent research, see Gnade 2007a; Cifani 2010. Besides ceramic production there is also evidence for Iron, Bronze and amber working (Nijboer 1995; Smith 2001).

[2] For the ceramic production facilities, see Nijboer 1998 and Revello Lami 2017. For the ceramic studies carried out by the University of Groningen: Attema et al. 2003; http://www.lcm.rug.nl/lcm/teksten/teksten_uk/fabric_analysis_on_ceramics_uk.htm; For the ongoing ceramic studies by the University of Amsterdam's Satricum Project: Revello Lami 2017.

[3] On the links between temples and the economy: Smith 1996. On the links with centralisation and urbanization processes: Nijboer 1998 and 2004; on the Archaic economy see now also Cifani 2021.

[4] Revello Lami 2019; cf. Sillar/Tyte 2000.

[5] Carafa 1995; Biella et al. 2017.

[6] Cook 1966 cited in Isaac 1993, 219.

[7] On the formalist-substantivist debate and Polanyi's rejection of both neoclassical and Marxist economic theory: Isaac 1993. It should be noted that even in their initial formulation, these positions were not so clear-cut: Polanyi already acknowledged that different modes of exchange, including markets, existed side by side in the past; vice versa, it is widely acknowledged that other allocation mechanisms operate in the modern world besides markets (North 1977).

[8] Garraty/Stark 2010. Debates on the Roman economy now revolve around the degree of integration of markets rather than their existence (Bang 2008; Temin 2012).

[9] On New Institutional Economics, see North 1977 and 1981. For applications to the Roman world, Verboven/Laes 2016.

[10] Behavioural Economics speaks of 'bounded rationality, self-interest and willpower (Thaler 2015).

[11] Smith 1996; Nijboer 1998; Roselaar 2018, 173-176.

[12] Cornell 1995; Smith 1996;

[13] Bradley 2017.

[14] "[…] for the larger-scale and regional exchanges in the archaic period, we should think more in terms of gift-exchanges and personal relationships rather than trade as it later developed […]." (Smith 2001, 19). See also Nijboer 1998, 35/43.

[15] Smith 1996, 120-122; Smith 2001 with references; Nijboer 1998, 233/234.

[16] Nijboer 2004.

[17] Viglietti 2011 and 2017.

[18] "From its earliest discernable origins, Rome was not a culture like Mauss's Polynesia, with an economy wholly dominated by reciprocal exchange. Nor was it like societies of the modern West, where market interactions, supported by a network of laws and institutions, have marginalized gift giving. Rome was instead deeply invested in both gift and gain." Coffee 2017, 28/29.

[19] "[…] the advance of market exchange in central Italy requires further research." (Nijboer 1998, 44)

[20] Dicken/Lloyd 1990; De Haas 2017a. Production systems consider besides technology, the theme of this volume, the inputs needed for ceramic production, that is the production factors, which include land and natural resources, the labour applied to acquire and transform these inputs, and the capital needed to acquire inputs, labour and related infrastructure. Processes of circulation concern the ways in which products are transported from their place of production to markets. Processes of distribution deal with how products are made available to consumers. Regulation processes describe how institutions (laws, administrative and juridical systems, customs) control or regulate economic activities in a given social context. Consumption or demand, finally, concerns the needs of consumers, which will vary according to demographic, economic and social conditions.

[21] Dicken/Lloyd 1990; Brakman et al. 2011.

[22] For regulations concerning *nundinae* in the Twelve Tables, see Coffee 2017, 28/29. For the introduction of weight standards, see Nijboer 1998.

[23] Tol/Borgers 2016.

[24] On issues related to population estimation based on settlement data: Drennan et al. 2015 and Bowman/Wilson 2011. My approach combines the estimation of populations in nucleated settlements on the basis of site size estimates and of dispersed rural settlements through multiplying corrected settlement numbers with average household size figures (cf. Attema/de Haas 2011). A more extensive discussion of the approach and results are currently in preparation.

[25] De Haas 2017b.

[26] Fulminante 2014; cf. Seubers 2018 for a critical review.

[27] Fulminante (2014) and Bradley (2017) use ranges of 120-300 and 150-200 persons per hectare for Archaic Rome. I find these densities high as average figures (especially for the smaller Latial sites), and would suggest lower densities comparable to those of Greek poleis (cf. Hansen 2006, using 150 persons per ha excluding public space and 75 persons per ha on average).

[28] I only include sites with archaeological evidence of their existence in Archaic times, and therefore Tarracina and Astura are missing from the calculations. If these were indeed also nucleated settlements, this would all the more suggest population levels tend towards the higher end of the range.
[29] Seubers/Tol 2016; Attema et al. 2017; Seubers 2018.
[30] The evidence from Satricum shows that roads within the town were well-built (Gnade 2006). Investments in road construction outside urban centres are archaeologically attested in both Latium and Etruria (Izzet 2007, 193-196).
[31] Smith 2001, 19.
[32] Nijboer 1998, 228; Nijboer 2004, 149.
[33] Satricum´s urban surface is commonly estimated at c. 40 ha, but it is unclear how this estimate came about. GIS-based calculations using the reconstructed area shown in fig. 1 suggest the site was considerably larger, at c. 50 ha.
[34] Nijboer 1998, 79-89; Revello Lami 2017, 402.
[35] Nijboer 1998; Biella et al. 2017.
[36] The well-investigated site of Ardea had similar workshops. This site was situated near some particularly well-suited clay sources.
[37] Revello Lami, personal comment.
[38] Mater 2005, 90-95.
[39] For the historical context: Cornell 1995. For the archaeology: Crise et transformation 1990; Coarelli 1990; De Haas 2011.
[40] De Haas 2011, 161.
[41] Cf. Smith 2006 and most recently Terrenato 2019, who argues for a particularly strong and relatively independent role for such groups within and between city-states.
[42] Nijboer 1998, 30 with references. Nijboer (87-88) assumes that the production of temple decorations took place locally, by itinerant craftsmen working here temporarily; cf Knoop/Lulof 2007, 41/42.
[43] Such a reading would be in line with recent understandings of the workings of elite networks that transcend ethnic and polity-boundaries (Terrenato 2019).
[44] Cf. Nijboer 1998, 30.
[45] For votive deposit 2: Bouma 1996 and 2001; for evidence from the graves: Gnade 2013.
[46] Tol/de Haas 2013, 151.
[47] Cf. Mater 2005, 99.
[48] Revello Lami 2017.
[49] Revello Lami 2017, 397-399. Ethnographic data suggest potters usually procured clays from within 1 km of production facilities, and seldom from further than 7 km (Arnold 2000, 343 with references).
[50] Nijboer et al. 1995; Nijboer 1998, 89-91. Nijboer et al. (1995, 5) suggested that the white-firing ceramics here were produced with local weathered tuffs and not with imported clays.
[51] Gnade 2013.
[52] De Haas 2017c.
[53] These population figures probably rose further towards the late Republic, when cities such as Tarracina and Antium developed into major towns with substantially higher population densities.
[54] Cornell 1989, esp. 365 -367; cf. Cornell 1995.
[55] For the PRP data: De Haas et al. 2011. On the use of such proxies: Wilson 2014. Such an economic reading does of course not deny that the consumption of black gloss fine wares also reflects major cultural changes (Roth 2007; Scopacasa 2015, esp. 273-275).
[56] The most recently excavated necropolis contains 4th century graves, and a thick deposit of pebbles may also pertain to a Republican phase of the site (Gnade 2013). Pending full publication of the most recent results, it remains unclear what the implications for the overall size and status of the site are or how this evidence might connect to the foundation of a Roman colony in 385 BC. The presence of what is presumably a rural farm building of the 3rd century BC on the acropolis is, however, indicative for the changing character of the site (Gnade 2007b and Louwaard 2007).
[57] Nijboer 1998, 89-90.
[58] See Tol/de Haas 2013; Tol/Borgers 2016.
[59] Borgers et al. 2018.
[60] On the distinction between aggregate and per capita growth, see Jongman 2014.

BIBLIOGRAPHY

Arnold, D. 2000, Does the Standardization of Ceramic Pastes Really Mean Specialization?, *Journal of Archaeological method and Theory* 7-4, 332-375.

Attema, P./A. Beijer/M. Kleibrink/N. Nijboer/G. van Oortmerssen 2003, Pottery classifications: ceramics from Satricum and Lazio, Italy, 900-300 BC, *Palaeohistoria* 43/44, 321-96.

Attema, P./T. de Haas 2011, Rural settlement and population extrapolation, a case study from the ager of Antium, central Italy (350 BC - AD 400), in A. Bowman/A. Wilson (eds), *Settlement, Urbanisation and Population*, Oxford, 97-140.

Attema, P./T. de Haas/J. Seubers,/G. Tol 2017, In search of the Archaic countryside. Different scenarios for the ruralisation of Satricum and Crustumerium, in: P. Lulof/C. Smith, The Age of Tarquinius. Central Italy in the Late 6th century, Leuven, 195-204.

Bang, P. 2008, *The Roman Bazaar. a Comparative Study of Trade and Markets in a Tributary Empire*, Cambridge.

Biella, M./R. Cascino/A. Ferrandes/M. Revello Lami (eds) 2017, Gli artigiani e la città. Officine e aree produttive tra VIII e III a.C. nell'Italia centrale tirrenica, *Scienze dell'Antichità* 23-2, Roma.

Borgers, B./G. Tol/T. de Haas 2018, Roman cooking vessels (ollae): a preliminary study of the material from the Pontine region, Central Italy, *STAR: Science & Technology of Archaeological Research*, DOI: 10.1080/20548923.2018.1445824.

Bouma, J. 1996, *Religio Votiva: The archaeology of latial votive religion. The 5th - 3rd century BC votive deposit south west of the main temple at 'Satricum' Borgo le Ferriere*, Rijksuniversiteit Groningen.

Bouma, J. 2001, Understanding local economy: a 5th-3rd c. BC votive deposit at Satricum, Borgo le Ferriere (Italy), *Caeculus* 4, 57-68.

Bowman, A./A. Wilson (eds) 2011, *Settlement, Urbanization, and Population* (Oxford studies on the Roman economy 2), Oxford.

Bradley, G. 2017, The Rome of Tarquinius Superbus. Issues of Demography and Economy, in P. Lulof/C. Smith (eds), *The Age of Tarquinius Superbus: Central Italy in the Late 6th Century*, Leuven, 123-134.

Brakman, S./H. Garretsen/C. Van Marrewijk 2011, *The New Introduction to Geographical Economies*, Cambridge.

Carafa, P. 1995, *Officine ceramiche di età regia: produzione di ceramica in impasto a Roma dalla fine dell'VIII alla fine del VI secolo a.C*, Roma.

Cifani, G. 2010, Satrico (Satricum), in G. Nenci/G. Vallet (eds), *Bibliografia topografica della colonizzazione greca in Italia e nelle isole tirreniche*, Pisa.

Cifani, G. 2021, *The Origins of the Roman Economy: From the Iron Age to the Early Republic in a Mediterranean Perspective*, Cambridge.

Coarelli, F. 1990, Roma, I Volsci e il lazio antico, in *Crise et transformation des sociétés archaïques de l'Italie antique au Ve siècle av. J.C.*, Rome, 135-154.

Coffee, N. 2017, *Gift and Gain. How Money Transformed ancient Rome*, Oxford.

Cornell, T.J. 1989, The conquest of Italy, in Astin *et al.* (eds) *Cambridge Ancient History Volume 8: Rome and the Mediterranean to 133 BC*, Cambridge, 351-419.

Cornell, T. 1995, *The beginnings of Rome: Italy and Rome from the Bronze Age to the Punic Wars (c. 1000 - 264 BC)*, London.

*Crise et transformation* 1990. *Crise et transformation des sociétés archaïques de l'Italie antique au Ve siècle av. JC. Actes de la table ronde de Rome (19-21 novembre 1987)*, Collection de l'École française de Rome 137, Rome.

De Haas, T. 2011, *Fields, farms and colonists. Intensive field survey and early Roman colonization in the Pontine region, central Italy*, Groningen.

De Haas, T. 2017, The economic geography of Roman Italy and its implications for the development and integration of rural economies, in: T. De Haas/G. Tol (eds), *The Economic Integration of Roman Italy. Rural Communities in a Globalizing World*, Leiden, 51-82.

De Haas, T. 2017b, The Ager Pomptinus and Rome: the impact of Roman colonization in the late Regal and early Republican period, in: P. Lulof/C. Smith, *The Age of Tarquinius. Central Italy in the Late 6th century*, Leuven, 261-268.

De Haas, T. 2017c, Managing the marshes: An integrated study of the centuriated landscape of the Pontine plain, *Journal of Archaeological Science: Reports* 15, 470-481.

De Haas, T./G. Tol/P. Attema 2011, Investing in the colonia and ager of Antium, *Facta* 5, 111-144.

Dicken, P./P. Lloyd 1990, *Location in Space. Theoretical perspectives in economic Geography*, New York.

Drennan, R./A. Berrey/C. Peterson 2015, *Regional Settlement Demography in Archaeology*, New York.

Fulminante, F. 2014, *The Urbanisation of Rome and Latium Vetus. From the Bronze Age to the Archaic Era*, Cambridge.

Garraty, C./B. Stark (eds) 2010, *Archaeological Approaches to Market Exchange in Ancient Societies*, Boulder.

Gnade, M. 2006, La Ventottesima campagna di ricerca a Satricum dell'Università di Amsterdam nel 200, *Lazio & Sabina* 3, 255-260.

Gnade, M. 2007a, *Satricum. Trenta anni di scavi olandesi*, Amsterdam.

Gnade, M. 2007b, Satricum nell'età medio-repubblicana, in M. Gnade (ed.), *Satricum. Trenta anni di scavi olandesi*, Amsterdam, 74.

Gnade, M. 2013, A new burial ground from Satricum. Preliminary results of the excavations in 2010, *Caeculus* 8, 139-152.

Hansen, M. 2006, *The Shotgun Method: The Demography of the Ancient Greek City-State Culture*, Columbia.

Isaac, B. 1993, Retrospective on the Formalist-Substantivist debate, *Research in Economic Anthropology* 14, 213-233.

Izzet, V. 2007, *The archaeology of Etruscan Society*, Cambridge.

Jongman, W. 2014, Re-constructing the Roman economy, in L. Neal/J. Williamson (eds), *The Cambridge History of Capitalism*, Cambridge, 75-100.

Knoop, R./P. Lulof 2007, L'architettura templare, in M. Gnade (ed.), *Satricum. Trenta anni di scavi olandesi*, Amsterdam, 32-42.

Louwaard, M., 2007, L'acropoli: l'edificio di età medio-repubblicana, in M. Gnade (ed.), *Satricum. Trenta anni di scavi olandesi*, Amsterdam, 75-77.

Mater, B. 2005, *Patterns in Pottery. A comparative study of pottery production in Salento, Sibaritide and Agro Pontino in the context of urbanization and colonization in the first millennium BC*, PhD thesis, Vrije Universiteit Amsterdam.

Nijboer, A. 1995, Craft Specialization during the Orientalizing period in central Italy, *Caeculus* 2, 33-42.

Nijboer, A. 1998, *From household production to workshops. Archaeological evidence for economic transformations, pre-monetary exchange and urbanisation in central Italy from 800 to 400 BC*, PhD thesis, Rijksuniversiteit Groningen.

Nijboer, A. 2004, Characteristics of emerging towns in central Italy, 900/800 to 400 BC., in P. Attema (ed.), *Centralization, early urbanization and colonization in first millennium BC Italy and Greece. Part 1: Italy*, Leuven, 137-156.

Nijboer, A./P. Attema/J. Bouma/R. Olde Dubbelink 1995, Notes on artifact and pottery production at Satricum in the 5th and 4th centuries BC, *Mededelingen van het Nederlands Instituut te Rome Antiquity* 54, 1-38.

North, D.C. 1977, Markets and Other Allocation Systems in History. The Challenge of Karl Polanyi, *The Journal of European Economic History* 6-3, 703–716.

North, D.C. 1981, *Structure and change in economic history*, New York/London.

Revello Lami, M. 2017, Evidenze dirette, indirette, o circostanziali? Topografie e archeometria della produzione ceramica a Satricum durante il period arcaico, in Biella *et al.* 2017, 389-411.

Revello Lami, M. 2019, Il materiale e il culturale. La produzione ceramica antica tra saperi tecnici, scelte artigianali e tradizioni culturali, in M. Modolo/S. Pallecchi/G. Volpe/E. Zanini (eds.), *Una lezione di archeologia globale. Studi in onore di Daniele Manacorda*, Bari, 413-419.

Roselaar, S. 2018, Economy and demography of Italy, in G. Farney/G. Bradley (eds), *The peoples of ancient Italy*, Boston/Berlin, 173-190.

Roth, R. 2007, *Styling Romanisation. Pottery and society in Central Italy*, Cambridge.

Scopacasa, R. 2015, *Ancient Samnium: settlement, culture, and identity between history and archaeology*, Oxford.

Seubers, J.F. 2018, *Scratching through the surface: Revisiting the archaeology of city and country in Crustumerium and north Latium Vetus between 850 and 300 BC*, PhD thesis, Rijksuniversiteit Groningen.

Seubers, J./G. Tol 2016, City, country and crisis in the *ager crustuminus*. Confronting legacy data with resurvey results in the territory of ancient Crustumerium, *Palaeohistoria* 57/58, 137-234.

Sillar, B./M. Tyte 2000, The challenge of 'technological choices' for material science approaches in archaeology, *Archaeometry* 42-1, 2-20.

Smith, C. 1996, *Early Rome and Latium. Economy and Society c. 1000 to 500 BC*, Oxford.

Smith, C. 2001, Ritualising the economy, *Caeculus* 4, 17-23.

Smith, C. 2006, *The Roman Clan. The Gens from Ancient Ideology to Modern Anthropology*, Cambridge.

Temin, P. 2012, *The Roman Market economy*, Princeton.

Terrenato, N. 2019, *The Early Roman Expansion into Italy. Elite Negotiation and Family Agendas*, Cambridge.

Thaler, R. 2015, *Misbehaving: the making of behavioral economics*, New York.

Tol, G./T. de Haas 2013, Pottery production and distribution in the Pontine region: A review of data of the Pontine Region Project, in: G. Olcese (ed.), *IMMENSA AEQUORA: Atti del convegno Roma 24-26 gennaio 2011.* Edizioni Quasar, Roma, 149-161.

Tol, G./B. Borgers 2016, An Integrated Approach to the Study of Local Production and Exchange in the lower Pontine Plain, *Journal of Roman Archaeology* 29, 349-370.

Verboven, K./C. Laes (eds) 2016, *Work, Labour, and Professions in the Roman World*, Leiden.

Viglietti, C. 2011, *Il limite del bisogno: antropologia economica di Roma arcaica*, Bologna.

Viglietti, C. 2017, Tarquinius Superbus and the purchase oft he Sybilline books. Conflicting models of Price formation in Archaic Rome, in P. Lulof/C. Smith (eds), *The Age of tarquiniuis Superbus, central Italy in the late 6th century BC*, Leuven, 49-56.

Waarsenburg, D. 1998, *Satricum, cronaca di uno scavo. Ricerche archeologiche alla fine dell'Ottocento*, Roma.

Wilson, A. 2014, Quantifying Roman Economic Performance by Means of Proxies: Pitfalls and Potential, in F. De Callatay (ed.), *Quantifying the Greco-Roman Economy and Beyond*, Bari, 147-167.

# Materializing Technology
# (Buildings & Infrastructures)

# Satricum: studio delle tecniche edilizie fra *chaîne opératoire* ed analisi del paesaggio

*Marijke Gnade*

*Abstract*

*More than forty years of archaeological research in Satricum have revealed much information related to construction techniques and the procurement and use of environmental resources. At the same time the research has provided important data regarding the ancient landscape which dramatically changed appearance in recent times. The original geomorphology of the area appears to have been exploited in numerous ways for a complex system of constructions that characterised the 6th century BC and accordingly reflects the close relationship between human behavior and the built and natural environment. This contribution will focus on the changing settlement profile over time, revealing technological progress which involved societal and political decisions.*

INTRODUZIONE

Durante la sua lunga esistenza l'antica Satricum, ubicata nell'area pontina, 60 km a sud di Roma, fu ristrutturata completamente almeno tre volte. Grazie alla continuità della ricerca archeologica è stato possibile documentare in dettaglio le varie fasi di ristrutturazione dell'insediamento, a partire dal complesso templare sull'acropoli con le sue quattro fasi edilizie successive, compresa quella capannicola sottostante alle strutture di pietra, fino alla zona circostante che sembra dimostrare uno sviluppo architettonico analogo.[1] Negli ultimi venti anni le indagini archeologiche sono state estese verso le zone limitrofe, nell'area della cosiddetta città bassa, con l'obiettivo di salvaguardare i resti che sospettavamo essere conservati in quest'area e che hanno rilevato di volta in volta scoperte inaspettate. Sono stati messi in evidenza numerosi resti di abitazioni e di infrastrutture che hanno cambiato fondamentalmente l'immagine dell'insediamento antico e, nello stesso tempo, hanno fornito una rilevante quantità di nuovi dati che permettono di arricchire l'inquadramento storico dell'insediamento.[2] Anche qui sono state riconosciute almeno tre fasi costruttive consecutive collegabili a quelle osservate sull'acropoli.

Un aspetto di continuo interesse nelle ricerche è stato lo studio dei particolari tecnici delle strutture nonché l'analisi di queste in rapporto con il paesaggio antico. Paesaggio che, come tutti sappiamo, è radicalmente cambiato in tempi recenti, sia a causa dei sempre più intensi lavori agricoli sia a causa dell'urbanizzazione moderna. Anche oggi gli scassi a larga scala – spesso di carattere abusivo – stanno continuando, in molti casi con effetti devastanti. Inoltre, poco o niente è rimasto delle grandi cave di tufo nei dintorni di Satricum utilizzate nell'antichità per l'estrazione del materiale edilizio. Satricum non è un caso unico per quanto concerne i danni causati dalle attività agrarie, ma certamente, grazie alla continua presenza di archeologi nell'area, un caso ben seguito e documentato.

EVIDENZE RISALENTI ALL'ETÀ DEL FERRO FUORI DELL'ACROPOLI

Durante l'estate del 2012 è stata effettuata una ricognizione geologica ed archeologica nel terreno attorno al ponte sull'Astura a Le Ferriere quando furono condotti lavori per la costruzione di una rotatoria e un nuovo ponte a fianco di quello vecchio. In considerazione del fatto che qui si trova il punto più stretto del letto del fiume Astura, quindi una probabile zona di attraversamento anche nell'antichità, i lavori di costruzione sono stati supervisionati, per quanto possibile, da parte della nostra équipe.

I lavori accompagnati da enormi scassi e movimenti di terra lungo i bordi dell'Astura riguardavano anche il terreno ad est del fiume, cioè fuori dei limiti presunti dell'antica città. Già nel 2008, durante una ricognizione in questa zona dopo intense attività agricole, erano stati recuperati molti reperti risalenti al periodo arcaico e postarcaico. Tali ritrovamenti mostrano grandi somiglianze con i reperti documentati durante gli scavi sistematici della strada principale che percorreva l'area urbana di Satricum e potrebbero indicare la continuazione di questa strada fuori del limite urbano.[3] I primi saggi superficiali eseguiti nell'area dei lavori di costruzione non hanno portato alla luce tracce del presunto percorso della strada, plausibilmente perché gli strati antichi si trovano ad un livello inferiore, come sembra essere confermato dai reperti emersi da alcuni dei carotaggi in profondità eseguiti per i lavori di fondazione della rotatoria. Infatti, ad una profondità di circa 4,50 m sotto il piano di campagna, sono emersi alcuni reperti ceramici risalenti all'età del Ferro.

Si tratta di una concentrazione di circa 20 frammenti ben conservati di ceramica d'impasto databile al periodo laziale IVA o poco prima ancora nel periodo laziale III. Alcuni dei frammenti diagnostici trovano un confronto preciso nei contesti di abitazione dell'età del Ferro sull'acropoli.[4] La scoperta di questi frammenti ceramici in una zona esterna rispetto a quella che di solito è considerata l'area di abitazione in questo periodo risulta di grande importanza per la ricostruzione dell'insediamento più antico. Non doveva essere occupata solo l'acropoli, ma anche l'altra riva dell'Astura che apparentemente doveva trovarsi ad un livello molto profondo inferiore a quello odierno, a giudicare dai risultati dei carotaggi.

Un altro caso più chiaro dell'estensione dell'insediamento fuori dei limiti dell'acropoli durante l'età del Ferro è emerso durante gli scavi del 2013 nell'area inferiore della citta antica, detta Poggio dei Cavallari (*fig. 1*).

Tale area, oggetto di ricerche sistematiche dal 2004 (dopo lo scasso dei terreni) in poi, ha rivelato un ricchissimo archivio archeologico nonché una più chiara immagine del paesaggio antico e del suo cambiamento nel corso del tempo. Oltre ai resti monumentali della strada principale che collegava la città bassa con l'acropoli e il santuario centrale, sono state trovate due strutture (edificio A e B) sul lato sud della strada nell'area di scavo occidentale (area 3), entrambe attribuite al periodo tardo arcaico. Inoltre sono state messe in evidenza due strade laterali in direzione sudest verso l'interno della città ad una distanza rispettiva di circa m 140 (aree 2 e 3) (*fig. 1*).[5]

Fino a poco tempo fa mancavano nell'area urbana tracce evidenti della prima fase dell'insediamento che conosciamo così bene dagli scavi dell'acropoli, benché qualche indicazione di attività precedente alla fase arcaica fosse stata già notata in precedenza. Ci si riferisce in particolare ai reperti dell'età del Ferro, cioè frammenti ceramici d'impasto orientalizzante, buccheri sottili ed etrusco-corinzi, uniti a quelli arcaici, rinvenuti negli strati più profondi compresi fra i muri arcaici. In un primo momento non era stato possibile stabilire la loro provenienza originaria. La situazione è mutata nel 2009, quando abbiamo proseguito lo scavo in profondità raggiungendo in vari punti il terreno vergine. In quell'occasione sono venuti alla luce resti risalenti all'età del Ferro sotto l'edifico A (*fig. 6*, nel saggio IIB), lungo il lato sud della strada.[6] Si tratta di una fossa poco profonda (cm 20-30) di forma circolare irregolare, evidenziata come una macchia grigio-nerastra nella terra vergine giallastra, delle dimensioni di 1,60 x 4,80 m. La macchia risultava essere stata tagliata dal muro 6 dell'edificio A fino al fondo, mentre gli strati superiori apparivano assenti a causa del livellamento eseguito per la costruzione dell'edificio, i cui resti del piano di calpestio coprivano quanto conservato dello strato dell'età del Ferro.

La fossa conteneva un gran numero di frammenti ceramici con superficie lucidata, rossa e nera, databili al tardo periodo laziale III e IVA, e numerosi frammenti di ossa di animali. Da notare inoltre la presenza di alcuni frammenti di ceramica depurata dello stesso periodo. Al momento della sua scoperta la fossa fu identificata come uno scarico e, malgrado fosse l'unica testimonianza del genere finora nota nell'area bassa della città, non è stato interpretato come un fenomeno isolato.

Questa impressione, infatti, è stata confermata recentemente dalla scoperta nell'area 2, a distanza di c. 160 m dalla fossa dell'età del Ferro, di un nuovo contesto risalente allo stesso periodo. Sotto un pavimento di ciottoli all'interno di un edificio tardo-arcaico (*fig. 2, C; fig. 3, n.2*), è stato messo in evidenza uno strato bruciato di spessore c. 0,10 m che copriva uno spesso strato di ceramica databile alla prima metà del VII secolo a.C. fra cui frammenti ceramici d'impasto orientalizzante ed etrusco-corinzi depositato sopra il terreno vergine. Inoltre, lo strato conteneva numerosi frammenti di grandi dolii con delle rimanenze di ferro lavorato e molte scorie di ferro, chiare evidenze di attività metallurgiche.

Un'ulteriore conferma di attività umana in zona durante l'età del Ferro consiste nel ritrovamento di una tomba infantile sotto l'edifico B, a c. 16 m di distanza, in direzione ovest rispetto alla fossa menzionata prima, sotto l'edificio A (*fig. 6*, trincea 345). Sotto uno spesso strato di argilla, quasi al livello della terra vergine, è stata messa in luce la parte inferiore di una ricca sepoltura di un infante di circa 9 mesi[7] databile al primo quarto del VII sec. a. C.[8] La tomba è stata interpretata come una tomba del tipo a *suggrundario*.[9] Oltre all'importanza della tomba in se stessa visto il ricchissimo corredo, altrettanto fondamentale è la sua associazione con i resti dell'età del Ferro.

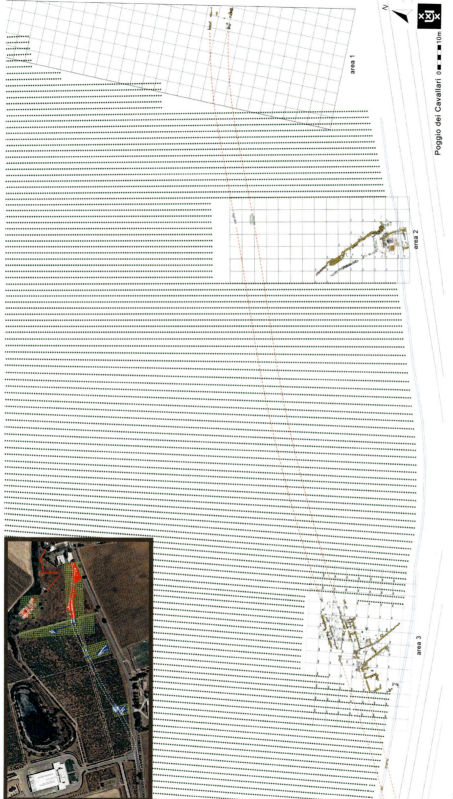

Fig. 1. Pianta delle aree di scavo 1-3 (da destra a sinistra) a Poggio dei Cavallari II.

Senza dubbio i fenomeni sui livelli più profondi della terra vergine indicano l'esistenza di un nucleo capannicolo anche in questa zona e non solo sull'acropoli. Una conclusione legittimata dalle nuove scoperte che rivelano come l'insediamento satricano fosse costituito probabilmente da più nuclei abitativi ciascuno dei quali dislocato in diverse zone dell'area poi occupata dalla cittá arcaica.[10]

## Le evidenze dell'età arcaica

Grazie al fatto che negli ultimi anni è stato raggiunto in più punti il terreno vergine è stato possibile approfondire la conoscenza del terreno originale il cui andamento altimetrico era molto più irregolare di quanto si poteva immaginare. Nel frattempo siamo stati in grado di approfondire la conoscenza delle tecniche edilizie arcaiche in zona.

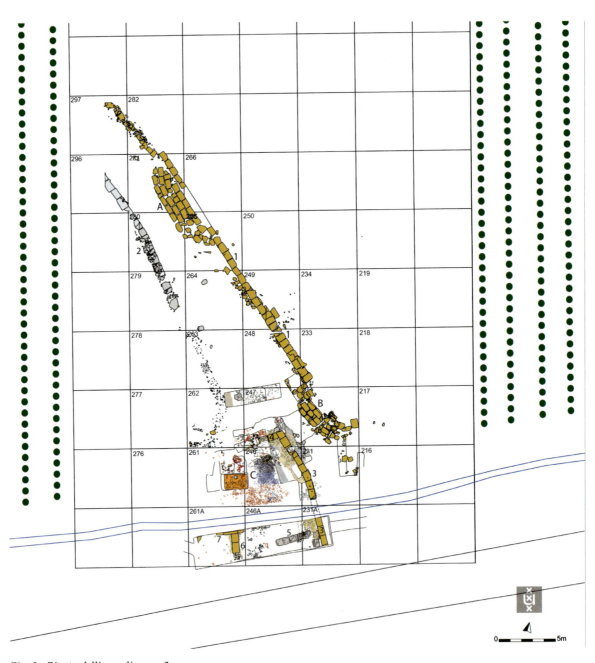

*Fig. 2. Pianta dell'area di scavo 2.*

È stato stabilito che quasi tutti i muri, sia quelli della strada principale che percorre l'area urbana in direzione est-ovest che quelli degli edifici lungo il suo lato sud, sono stati costruiti direttamente sulla terra vergine, adattandosi al suo andamento irregolare, mentre sono state utilizzate depressioni naturali per la costruzione delle strade. E ciò vale sia per la strada principale sia per quelle secondarie in direzione sudest.

Un chiaro esempio di un tale utilizzo nonché dell'adattamento al terreno naturale è emerso dalla ricerca sulla costruzione della strada principale. La sua tecnica di costruzione è stata ampiamente discussa durante il convegno recente su Tarquinio il Superbo,[11] per cui passiamo alle aree meridionali direttamente a fianco della strada (*fig. 1*, aree 2 e 3) dove corrono le due strade laterali in direzione sud-est verso l'interno della città. Erano ambedue affiancate da edifici risalenti allo stesso periodo di costruzione della strada principale. Ci concentriamo ora in specifico sui vari livelli di calpestio che sono stati rinvenuti nei saggi in profondità eseguiti per indagare la stratigrafia spesso complessa. In tutte le aree indagate ci sono grandi somiglianze nelle applicazioni tecniche per la costruzione dei pavimenti e nel loro rapporto con l'architettura, ma ci sono anche differenze tra le diverse situazioni dovute alle ristrutturazioni ed ai rialzamenti intermedi dei livelli.

L'AREA 2

Sono presenti in ambedue le zone di scavo livelli di calpestio impostati direttamente sulla terra vergine, probabilmente interpretabile come la prima fase della strada laterale.

Il livello meglio conservato, che può essere seguito per una lunghezza di circa 33 m e larga 3 m, si trova nell'area 2 (*fig. 3, n.1*). Giace direttamente sul fondo della depressione nella terra vergine che mostra un forte sconscendimento verso sud-est, con una differenza di quota di quasi due metri fra nord e sud su tutta la lunghezza indagata. Il calpestio che è stato adattato all'andamento del terreno, presenta una consistenza molto compatta costituita da pezzi di tufo bianco smussati frammisti con ciottoli fluviali di varie dimensioni, piccoli frammenti di dolii spezzati appositamente per tale scopo e altri frammenti di ceramica fra cui bucchero.

Il calpestio assomiglia molto alla pavimentazione della strada principale che corre qui a circa 30 m di distanza verso nordest. Però, non è sorretta da muri laterali in blocchi di tufo, un sistema di costruzione straordinario che è stato invece osservato per l'intero percorso della strada principale.[12] Fu proprio questa somiglianza tra le due pavimentazioni che ci ha portato nel 2007 alla proposta di attribuire i due calpestii allo stesso

*Fig. 3. Veduta della parte sud dell'area di scavo 2 (2018, foto realizzata con drone).*

periodo di costruzione malgrado il fatto che non si fosse potuto verificare il loro collegamento a causa del vigneto che copre questa area (vedi *fig. 1*).[13] Tale interpretazione sembra tuttora ancora valida.

Un collegamento tra il calpestio della strada laterale con un grande edificio (C) costruito nella parte meridionale dell'area sembra evidente (*figg. 2-3*). Si tratta di una grande struttura con fondazioni costituite da due filari sovrapposti di blocchi rettangolari di tufo lionato. Ci sono conservati un lungo muro orientale (*fig. 2, n.3*) con andamento curvilineo e l'angolo nordest dell'edificio. I muri sono impostati direttamente sul fondo della depressione stradale, mentre il livello del calpestio corre all'altezza del lato superiore del blocco inferiore. I muri delimitano un ambiente dotato di un calpestio formato da piccoli ciottoli frammisti a numerosi grandi frammenti di ceramica grezza tardo-arcaica che sono stati anche pressati sopra lo stesso strato di ciottoli. Sotto il calpestio di ciottoli è stato rinvenuto il contesto dell'età del Ferro sopra descritto che risultava tagliato dai muri dell'edificio C. L'area circoscritta dai muri era sepolta sotto uno strato di tegole, forse pertinenti al tetto crollato oppure da interpretare come le rimanenze di un semplice scarico di tegole. Fra i reperti ceramici vi sono tante forme di uso domestico fra cui diverse scodelle quasi complete con orlo a fascia e fondo piano e bacini dei quali uno in impasto chiaro sabbioso con orlo ingrossato esternamente e con maniglia verticale sopraelevata. Vista la pavimentazione in ciottoli, si potrebbe identificare l'ambiente come un cortile oppure un ambiente di lavoro appartenente ad un più grande edificio che purtroppo è stato obliterato a causa della costruzione della strada provinciale Nettuno-Cisterna. L'edificio ha un confronto abbastanza preciso nella struttura i/g posta sul lato nord della strada principale a Poggio dei Cavallari I e scavata negli anni novanta, dove sono state ritrovate simili tipi di ceramica in associazione con il livello del calpestio interno.[14] Quest'edificio fu eretto poco dopo la costruzione della strada ed dovrebbe risalire alla fine del VI oppure all'inzio del V secolo a.C. quando fu rialzato il primo livello della strada principale con uno strato di sabbia.

L'uso di sabbia quasi sterile per i rialzamenti connessi a processi di ristrutturazione è un aspetto tecnico molto ricorrente nel sistema di costruzione studiato nell'area di Poggio dei Cavallari. Già documentata in diversi punti nella parte orientale della strada principale scavata negli anni novanta, la sabbia è anche presente nella sua continuazione verso ovest come anche nelle costruzioni nelle aree adiacenti dove gli strati di sabbia possono raggiungere un spessore di addirittura 0,60-0,70 m. In quasi tutti i casi, i depositi di sabbia giacciono sopra uno strato di grandi frammenti di tegole rosse arcaiche, non sempre identificabili come resti di crolli in situ ma soprattutto come scarico di materiali edilizi riusati per garantire stabilità oppure drenaggio.

Uno spesso strato di sabbia è stato messo in opera anche per il rialzamento del primo livello di calpestio della strada laterale nell'area 2. Sono state documentate immense quantità di sabbia quasi sterile (*fig. 5*) spesso contenenti grandi blocchi irregolari di tufo bianco e blocchi rettangolari di tufo

*Fig. 4. Concentrazione nord dei blocchi di tufo lionato sistemati in filari paralleli sopra il primo calpestio lungo il lato interno del muro n. 1.*

*Fig. 5. Foto in sezione dello strato di sabbia rinvenuto nell'area di scavo 2 addossato alla concentrazione di blocchi di tufo lionato. Sono ancora visibili i 'pacchetti di sabbia' come sono stati deposti sopra il calpestio inferiore. Sopra lo strato di sabbia si notano i resti del calpestio di tufo lionato pressato.*

lionato. I blocchi bianchi sono stati collocati contro il lato est del muro n. 3 e poggiano sul calpestio sottostante (*fig. 2*). Quelli di tufo lionato sono invece disposti lungo il lato opposto del piano di calpestio, in due grandi concentrazioni sistemate in filari paralleli al lato interno di un ulteriore muro di blocchi di tufo lionato (n. 1) impostato sul bordo della depressione ove è stata alloggiata la strada. I blocchi posti a nord corrispondono più o meno all'inzio del muro e consistono in quattro filari paralleli di tufo lionato con andamento leggermente curvilineo (*fig. 2, A; fig. 4*). I blocchi seguono in altezza l'andamento del calpestio sottostante, aumentando in altezza da 0,20 m a 0,50/0,70 m procedendo da nordovest a sudest (*fig. 4*).[15]

La seconda messa in opera di blocchi, sempre immersi e parzialmente coperti dalla sabbia, si trova in coincidenza della parte finale del muro principale (n. 1) dove si nota un grande blocco messo a testa. Anche questi filari sono stati disposti in linee parallele ricurve, tre in questo caso (*fig. 2, B; fig. 3, n.3A*). Diversamente però dall'altra messa in opera posta a nord, questi filari parelleli giacciono a quote diverse e mostrano una forte inclinazione verso ovest e sud. Non è chiaro se i blocchi siano scivolati verso il livello inferiore oppure se fossero stati appositamente collocati in questo modo.

È anche notevole come i blocchi si trovino nel punto in cui l'avvallamento nel terreno vergine compie una curva verso est, come si evince anche dalla presenza di un grande blocco di tufo messo di testa con un orientamento diverso, come controparte del blocco finale posizionato nello stesso modo del muro n. 1 (*Figg. 2 e 3*). Tale blocco fa probabilmente messo in connessione con un altro tratto murale che correva verso est, purtroppo non conservato.

*Un grandioso rialzamento e un nuovo livello stradale*

A prima vista le due messe in opera di blocchi sembravano far parte di strutture monumentali simili a fondamenta, vista la regolarità della posizione dei blocchi nonchè la loro ubicazione quasi strategica lungo il lungo muro n. 1. Per ora, però, questa idea rimane ipotetica. I livellamenti moderni del terreno hanno cancellato ogni traccia di eventuali strutture sui livelli più alti.

È tuttavia chiaro che i filari paralleli in blocchi messi in opera con la sabbia e posti come possibile rinforzo delle parti iniziali e finali del muro n.1 facevano parte di un grandioso rialzamento sul quale fu sistemato un nuovo livello di calpestio, questa volta costituito da uno spesso e durissimo strato di tufo lionato pressato mischiato con grandi frammenti di tegole (*fig. 3, n.3B; fig. 5*).

Tale strato è talmente compatto e duro da assomigliare in consistenza a una specie di cemento. Infatti, dagli esperimenti che abbiamo eseguito per capire la composizione di questo livello di calpestio, realizzati mischiando pezzi di tufo lionato pestati con sabbia fine ed acqua, abbiamo ottenuto un materiale durissimo che si potrebbe facilmente denominare malta-tufo. Solo con grande forza, usando il piccone, si riesce a demolire tale strato. In questo senso, l'antica Satricum si dimostra precorritrice per quanto riguarda le teniche costruttive.

Tale massicciata stradale è stata documentata per tutto il percorso stradale laterale ed è da associare con il muro n. 1 contro il cui lato inferiore il calpestio appoggiava mentre il muro 1 possibilmente funzionava come muro di contenimento dell'area retrostante che senz'altro era più alta prima delle attività agricole moderni.

Non si è potuto stabilire se l'edificio C sia stato abbandonato dopo la costruzione della nuova strada oppure se continuasse ad essere utilizzato. Il nuovo livello della strada non fu attestato sopra i suoi resti; infatti pare che il livello di tufo si fermasse proprio presso i muri di fondazione dell'edificio. Dall'altra parte, lo strato di tegole rinvenuto sopra l'ambiente con il calpestio di piccoli ciottoli risultava coperto da un sottile strato di sabbia posto subito sotto l'arato, un'indicazione che molto probabilemte anche l'edificio fu obliterato dallo strato di sabbia e che eventuali resti del calpestio di tufo soprastante sono stati cancellati in epoca moderna.

La datazione del rialzamento non è del tutto precisabile perchè lo strato di sabbia si presenta in generale abbastanza sterile. Fra i pochi reperti, però, vi sono alcuni ritrovamenti interessanti che meritano di essere menzionati qui. Per esempio, abbiamo frammenti di un bacino in impasto chiaro sabbioso con maniglia sopraelevata e decorazione a fascia trovati sopra i blocchi lionati della messa in opera a sud del muro 1 (vedi *fig. 3, n.3A*). Il ritrovamento trova confronto con il bacino rinvenuto sul calpestio di ciottoli citato sopra. Inoltre vi sono diversi grandi frammenti di un'anfora di tipo Corinzio B rinvenuti sparsi nello strato di sabbia e un frammento notevole di un grande bacino con orlo ingrossato e decorato con elementi geometrici e figurativi dipinti in rosso su fondo bianco, ugualmente trovato nello strato di sabbia. Purtroppo, la produzione di questi oggetti copre un lungo arco di tempo, cioè dalla metà del VI fino alla fine del V sec. a.C., il che non permette di precisare meglio la datazione del rialzamento.[16] Riguardo alla cronologia dobbiamo prendere in esame la situazione documentata nell'area di scavo 3.

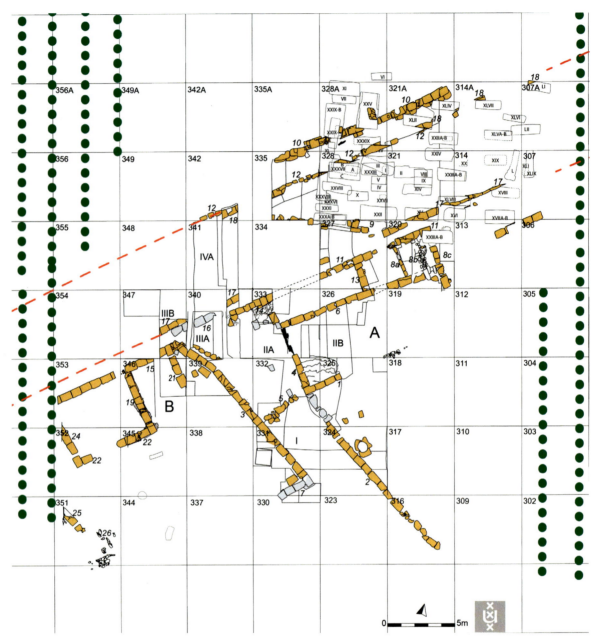

Fig. 6. Pianta dell'area di scavo 3.

L'AREA 3

Come nell'area 2, una simile complessità di attività costruttive si è presentata nell'area 3 dove sono stati rinvenuti i due edifici A e B costruiti all'incrocio della strada principale con quella laterale (*fig. 6*).[17] Anche in questa zona è stata documenta una forte differenza di quota del suolo naturale sotto gli edifici: almeno 2,10 m fra le aree meridionali della zona di scavo e l'area direttamente a fianco della strada principale. Tale salto di quota è specialmente evidente verso la depressione usata per la costruzione della strada principale. Il bordo della depressione si trova sotto gli ambienti settentrionali dei due edifici A e B e corre parellelamente alla strada stessa ad una distanza di circa 3-4 m (*fig. 7*).

È stata osservata una grande cura nel collocamento dei muri degli edifici A e B durante il processo di costruzione. Essi si addattano all'inclinazione del terreno, aumentando i filari di blocchi per avere un livello in piano come base dell'elevato degli edifici (*fig. 7*). Consequentemente, i muri settentrionali degli edifici direttamente a fianco della strada (*fig. 6*, muri 6, 3 e15) consistono di tre filari di blocchi sovrapposti, il cui numero diminuisce verso sud a due e poi ad uno solo nelle parti meridionali degli edifici A e B, in specifco nei muri 2 e 3.

Per garantire la stabilità dei muri più alti posti lungo il bordo della depressione, fu modellato il livello inferiore della terra vergine nel punto di posa praticando un taglio, che dà origine ad una parete di terra verticale contro la quale sono stati alloggiati i lati posteriori dei blocchi inferiori.

Durante le ricerche degli anni passati è apparso chiaro che l'area 3 ha subito notevoli cambiamenti, nel senso che la strada laterale e gli edifici sono caduti in disuso a causa di una distruzione drammatica. Sono documentati ammassi di tegole - talvolta intere- rinvenute in uno spesso strato lungo il lato esterno del muro 3, grandi pezzi di argilla cotta, alcuni a forma di blocchi rettangolari, interpretabili come mattoni crudi cottisi durante un forte incendio e provenienti dagli elevati dei muri, insieme a numerosi grandi resti di legno bruciato fra cui una trave di dimensioni notevole, tutti trovati sopra il probabile livello di calpestio della strada laterale (*fig. 8*). Sia il livello con le macerie che le rimanenze degli edifici stessi furono coperti in una fase di costruzione posteriore da uno spesso strato di sabbia quasi sterile sopra la quale fu alloggiato un nuovo pavimento consistente di grandi ciottoli frammisti con frammenti di tegole (*fig 7; fig 9*). Tale rialzamento artificiale di sabbia corrisponde con quello documentato nella zona di scavo 2 sopra descritto. Solo il tipo di pavimento appare diverso, cioè ciottoli invece del duro strato di malta-tufo

Differenze tecniche sono anche osservate nella sistemazione della strada laterale. Il livello sul quale furono trovati gli elevati ed altri elementi dei tetti è stato documentato in vari saggi in profondità condotti nella zona di incrocio della strada principale e quella laterale (saggi IIA, IIIA e IIIB; vedi *fig. 6*). Tale livello appoggiava al lato esterno del muro 3 all'altezza del lato superiore del secondo filare di blocchi, mentre sul lato opposto continuava quasi indistinguibile, senza

*Fig. 7. Vista generale dell'edificio B, da est. A sinistra si può notare l'andamento inclinato della depressione naturale nel suolo caratterizzato da numerose fossette forse atribuibili a costruzioni anteriori oppure interpretabili come tracce di vegetazione. L'inclinazione corre in una linea dritta sotto l'ambiente settentrionale dell'edificio B, parallela al tratto della strada principale della quale si vede un blocco del suo muro laterale meridionale, in primo piano all'angolo destro del saggio IIIA.*

*Fig. 8. Macerie rinveute sopra il calpestio composto da uno pseudo-cocciopesto.*

*Fig. 9. Sezione ovest del saggio IIIB. Sotto si vede lo strato di pseudo-cocciopesto che procede dal muro 3 (a sinistra) verso nord, dove continua sopra il muro laterale 17 pertinente alla strada principale (a destra). Lo strato è coperto dallo spesso livello di sabbia coperto a sua volta dai ciottoli del piano di calpestio superiore.*

netti margini di definizione, nello strato di calpestio della strada principale (*fig. 9*). Quest'osservazione conferma l'idea che la strada e gli edifici che l'affiancano apppartengano ad un unico momento di costruzione.

Lo strato di color grigio ha uno spessore di almeno 0,30 m ed è costituito da tantissimi piccoli frammenti consumati di ceramica grezza frammisti con pezzi di tufo, ciottoli e chiazze di sabbia. Come tale, lo strato mostra una forte asssomiglianza alla tecnica di cocciopesto, per cui si potrebbe prudentemente chiamarlo un cocciopesto *avant la lettre* vista la sua datazione alla fine del VI secolo a.C.

Va notato che lo strato mostra una stratigrafia interna: al di sotto dello strato superiore di materiale eterogeneo (*fig. 10, n.1A*) si trova un secondo strato costituito da macerie fra cui pezzi di argilla cotta di dimensioni molto più piccoli di quelli caduti sulla sua superficie, ma anche frammenti di ceramica e di tegole arcaiche (*fig. 10, n.1B*). I pezzi di argilla sono durissimi, essendo cotti ad alte temperature e mostrano diverse impronte di incannucciato. La loro quantità e il loro ottimo stato di conservazione ne permettono uno studio approfondito e sistematico. Finora sono stati studiati più di mille frammenti che rappresentano solo una percentuale modesta del materiale rinvenuto.

Lo strato tipo cocciopesto copriva una serie di blocchi irregolari di tufo lionato di funzione sconosciuta disposti in linea retta lungo la base del muro 3 (vedi *fig. 10*, a destra). Possibilmente tali blocchi si trovano ancora in posizione originaria e risalgono ad una fase costruttiva anteriore a quella delle grandi strutture di tufo lionato. Lo strato tipo cocciopesto copriva a sua volta un ulteriore calpestio sottostante che mostra caratteristiche molto diverse rispetto a quelle dello strato soprastante (*fig. 10, n.2*). È talmente compatto e duro nella sua consistenza che può essere identificato come il vero e primo livello di calpestio. Mostra allo stesso tempo una grande somiglianza con il pavimento della strada principale. Tale livello di tufo copriva a sua volta una serie di quattro grandi blocchi rettangolari di tufo bianco che giacevano lungo il lato sud del muro laterale della strada principale (*fig. 6; fig. 10*). L'intercapedine compresa fra i due tratti murari

*Fig. 10. Saggio IIIA nell'area di scavo 3 (da ovest). Sono visibili i vari strati di calpestio l'uno sopra l'altro (1A-B; 2; 3), le macerie di tegole e mattoni cotti caduti sopra il calpestio detto cocciopesto (4; sopra, a destra), il muro no. 3 (a destra) e i blocchi irregolari disposti in linea retta lungo la sua base, i blocchi bianchi (a sinistra) appoggiati contro i blocchi del muro laterale della strada principale.*

fu appositamente riempita con frammenti di tufo e di tegole, mentre l'altro lato dei blocchi bianchi fu rinforzato da un accumulo di altri blocchi, bianchi e di tufo lionato, ma di forma irregolare e misure più piccole, quasi con l'intenzione di evitare lo spostamento dei blocchi grandi. Nel saggio IIIB si è potuto osservare in seguito che il tratto dei blocchi bianchi consisteva in un filare solo di uno spessore di 0,20 m. È venuto fuori che questi blocchi funzionavano come una copertura sotto la quale era uno spazio probabilmente appartenente ad un canale di drenaggio che correva lungo il muro della strada.

Sotto il livello inferiore tufaceo del saggio IIIA, infine, è stato documentato un ulteriore strato spesso e compatto di macerie, costituito da tantissimi grandi pezzi di argilla cotta, frammenti di tegole e ceramica (*fig. 10, n.3*). Tale strato a sua volta era posto direttamente sulla terra vergine sottostante che si trova ad una profondità di quasi 1,60 m al di sotto del livello superiore del muro 3 dell'edificio B.

Sulla base di quanto si è descritto la conclusione preliminare è che tutti gli strati, malgrado le loro composizioni diverse, facessero parte di un unico processo di costruzione, cioè la creazione di una massicciata stradale che si doveva unire a quella della strada principale. Per ora gli strati si distinguono fra di loro solo dal punto di vista tecnico e di composizione ma non nel senso della loro datazione. Un elemento costante che ricorre in tutti gli strati sono i frammenti di tegole risalenti al periodo arcaico, un periodo che trova conferma nella ceramica grezza presente negli stessi strati.

Conclusione

I saggi descritti dentro l'area 3, per quanto di piccoli dimensioni, dimostrano come costruire in zona era un lavoro alquanto impegnativo, come già si è potuto osservare nella ricostruzione delle attività di realizzazione della strada principale.[18] Tali lavori impegnativi dimostrano nello stesso tempo una cura costante profusa nei particolari costruttivi e nell'estrema precisione adoperata nella loro realizzazione. Sembra che nessun particolare costruttivo sia stato dimenticato, anche se oggi non capiamo sempre il perché delle operazioni. È tuttavia chiaro che la scelta dei diversi strati alternati e ben distinti è stata fatta con una profonda conoscenza dei materiali e delle loro caratteristiche.

Tutta questa esperienza non è andata persa con la distruzione della città arcaica. È difficile dire il momento preciso, ma dopo un lungo periodo di abbandono enormi quantità di sabbia furono gettate sopra i resti degli edifici distrutti e, in seguito, ricoperti da nuovi livelli stradali. Nel caso dell'area di scavo 3, il nuovo livello consisteva di grandi ciottoli misti con frammenti di tegole bianche e rosate.[19] Nell'area di scavo 2, come abbiamo visto, questa nuova fase si presenta in un livello compatto duro di tufo lionato. Anche in questi due casi sono state prese delle decisioni di usare altri tipi di pavimenti che difficilmente si spiegano oggi, ma sicuramente possono essere capite meglio una volta chiarite le specifiche destinazioni d'uso dei vari livelli di calpestio messi in evidenza durante lo scavo.

Note

[1] Per una panoramica delle varie fasi di costruzione sull'acropoli indagate dal 1977 fino al 2014, vedi *CatSatricum* 2007, 20-23 (età del Ferro); 32-42 (complesso templare); 43-50 (architettura arcaica intorno ai templi); 75-77 (l'edificio di età medio-repubblicano). Vedi anche De Waele 1981 (per i templi); Maaskant-Kleibrink 1987; Maaskant-Kleibrink 1992; Gnade-Stobbe 2012, 453-463.
[2] Per una panoramica dei resti di abitazioni e di infrastrutture scoperti fino al 2007 nell'area della cosiddetta città inferiore, vedi *CatSatricum* 2007.
[3] Per la strada all'interno dell'area urbana, Gnade 2002, 5-29; 51-94; *CatSatricum* 2007, 51-56; Gnade 2017.
[4] Per esempio, un frammento di un holmos di impasto rosso levigato con decorazione a doppio cordone ad impressioni verticali riempite con pasta bianca (inv. SA12 S1/B1-2). Cf. Beijer 1991, 26 con riferimenti a Decima, La Rustica e Ficana); vedi anche Maaskant-Kleibrink 1992, 218, cat.n. 2286; rinvenuto nello strato di distruzione della struttura AA, databile nel VII sec. a.C.; *Ibidem* 251, cat.n. 2803
[5] Per gli edifici A e B e le due strade laterali, vedi le relazioni biennali di Gnade negli *Atti dell'Incontro di Studi sul Lazio e Sabina* dal 2006 fino al 2011.
[6] Gnade 2011, 453.
[7] L'età dell'individuo stabilita alla morte è di circa 9 mesi +/- 3 mesi (Infante 1). L'analisi dei denti è stata eseguita da dott.ssa Paola Zaio.
[8] Gnade 2018.
[9] Per il fenomeno del *suggrundarium* vedi Modica 2007, 218-224.
[10] *Cf.* Kleibrink 1997/1998, 442. Con il suggerimento dell'esistenza di tre nuclei abitativi sparsi nell'area satricana.
[11] Gnade 2017 per l'analisi tecnica della costruzione della strada.
[12] Gnade 2017; per l'evoluzione della tecnica stradale nell'Italia centrale, vedi Quilici 1992, 19-32.
[13] *CatSatricum* 2007, 53-54.
[14] Gnade 2002, 52-53, Fig. III.
[15] Evidentemente va preso in considerazione il fatto che non conosciamo le altezze originarie dei blocchi a causa delle attività di livellazione moderna.
[16] Ringrazio Martina Revello Lami per la prima analisi del bacino con la decorazione in rosso. La presenza di ingubbiatura biancastra e la tipologia decorativa trovano confronti abbastanza vicini con le produzioni

etrusche dell'area di Spina e del mantovano, in particolare: Tipo 1-B1 rinvenuto al Forcello di Bagnolo S. Vito nel mantovano (S. Casini, P. Frontini, E. Gatti "Gli Etruschi a Nord del Po", Mantova 1988, vol. I, p. 253, fig. 152, n.1-B1) datato su confronto al V secolo; Tipo 38a rinvenuto a Spina (S. Patitucci Uggeri, "Classificazione preliminare della ceramica dipinta di Spina", Studi Etruschi 51, 1983, p. 116, fig 10, n. 38a) datato all'ultimo quarto del V secolo.

[17] Vedi la nota 5.
[18] Gnade 2017.
[19] Vedi Gnade 2019 per la proposta di associare il rialzamento delle due zone al periodo dopo la installazione della colonia romana nel 346 a. C., cioè alla seconda metà del IV secolo a.C. oppure alla prima metà del III secolo a.C.

BIBLIOGRAFIA

Beijer, A. 1991, Impasto Pottery and Social Status in Latium Vetus in the Orientalising Period (725–575). An Example from Borgo Le Ferriere ("Satricum"), in E. Herring et al., *The Archaeology of Power, Papers of the Fourth Conference on Italian Archaeology* (BAR. Int. Ser.), n.p. [Oxford], I, 21–39.

CatSatricum 2007: M. Gnade (ed.), *Satricum. Trenta anni di scavi olandesi*. (Exh. cat. Le Ferriere 2007-2008), Amsterdam.

Cifani, G. 2008, *Architettura romana arcaica. Edilizia e società tra Monarchia e Repubblica*, Roma.

De Waele, J.A.K.E. 1981, I templi della Mater Matuta di Satricum, *MededRom* 43, 7-68.

Gnade, M. 2002, *Satricum in the Post-Archaic Period. A Case Study of the Interpretation of Archaeological remains as Indicators of Ethno-Cultural Identity*, Leuven.

Gnade, M. 2006, La ventottesima campagna di ricerca a Satricum dell'Università di Amsterdam nel 2004, *Lazio & Sabina* 3, 255-260.

Gnade, M. 2007, I risultati della campagna di scavi 2005 e 2006 a Satricum, *Lazio & Sabina* 4, 91-200.

Gnade, M. 2009, La ricerca a Satricum dell'Università di Amsterdam nel 2007, *Lazio & Sabina* 5, 363-368.

Gnade, M. 2011, Nuovi risultati della ricerca archeologica dell'Università di Amsterdam a Satricum, *Lazio & Sabina*, 7, 453-463.

Gnade, M. 2012, Satricum 2011: proseguimento delle ricerche, *Lazio & Sabina*, 8, 451-457.

Gnade, M. 2017, Satricum in the Age of Tarquinius Superbus: cambiando prospettiva, in P.S. Lulof/C. Smith (eds.), *The Age of Tarquinius Superbus: Central Italy in the Late 6th Century*, Leuven, 249-258.

Gnade, M. 2018, A new Iron Age child burial from Satricum, in J. Talbolli (ed.), *From Invisible to Visible. New Data and Methods for the Archaeology of Infant and Child Burials in pre-Roman Italy and Beyond* (SIMA), Jonsered, 59-68.

Gnade, M. 2019, Satricum as a mid-Republican town, in F.M. Cifarelli/S. Gatti/D. Palombi (eds.), *Oltre "Roma Medio Repubblicana". Il Lazio fra i Galli en la battaglia di Zama*, Roma, 185-194.

Gnade, M./J.A. Stobbe 2012, Riflessioni sul santuario di Mater Matuta sull'acropoli di Satricum alla luce delle recenti scoperte archeologiche, in E. Marroni (ed.), *Sacra nominis latini. I santuari del Lazio arcaico e repubblicano. Atti del convegno internazionale, Roma 2009*, vol. spec *Ostraka*, Napoli, 453-463.

Kleibrink, M. 1997/1998, The Miniature Votive Pottery Dedicated at the 'Laghetto del Monsignore', Campoverde, *Palaeohistoria: Acta et Communicationes Instituti Archaeologici Universitatis Groninganae* 39/40.

Maaskant-Kleibrink, M. 1987, *Settlement Excavations at Borgo Le Ferriere <Satricum> I. The campaigns 1979, 1980, 1981*, Groningen.

Maaskant-Kleibrink, M. 1992, *Settlement excavations at Borgo Le Ferriere <Satricum> II. The campaigns 1983, 1985 and 1987*, Groningen.

Modica, S. 2007, *Rituali e Lazio Antico. Deposizioni infantili e abitati*, Milano.

Quilici, L. 1992, Evoluzione della tecnica stradale nell'Italia centrale, in L. Quilici/S. Quilici Gigli (eds.), *Tecnica stradale romana 1*, Roma, 19-32.

# A *chaîne opératoire* approach to the development of early ashlar masonry at Rome

*Seth Bernard*

*Abstract*

*This chapter traces technological developments in ashlar masonry at Rome from the Archaic period through the Mid-Republic, focusing on a comparison of construction in blocks of tufo del Palatino and tufo giallo. Attention is paid to the entire series of technical actions (chaîne opératoire) through which stone was extracted, moved, transformed into architecture, and then maintained or reused. This more complete view highlights differences between the use of the two stones, and such differences are then related to early Rome's changing socioeconomic institutions.*

INTRODUCTION

In the early decades of the sixth century BCE, Roman builders began to use regularly squared stone blocks of *tufo* or volcanic tuff in monumental architecture.[1] Such *opus quadratum* masonry using tuff blocks would become a mainstay of the city's architecture and remained so for centuries, forming an essential ingredient of urban construction through the High Empire.[2] Early Roman ashlar thus represents one end of a long thread in the technological basis of urban production, while the durability of stone as compared to other, more perishable materials presents a relatively full archaeological corpus with which to trace this thread's development. This chapter describes ashlar masonry technology at Rome over the first few centuries of its use and situates the technology's development within its sociohistorical context from about 600 to 300 BCE.

While there can be no denying historical change at Rome from Archaic to Early- and Mid-Republican periods, the productive technologies of Roman architecture remain poorly integrated into this narrative. Moreover, while scholarship reveals a great deal about the initial appearance of ashlar masonry, there is less focus on subsequent developments. Such oversight may be seen to continue a discourse established by Giuseppe Lugli's fundamental work on Roman building technology, *La tecnica edilizia Romana* (1957). Lugli often systematizes Roman building techniques on the basis of stylistic or physical features: he identifies four manners of polygonal masonry, eleven periods of brickwork, and so forth. However, his discussion of *opus quadratum* takes a different form, analyzing the technique based on cultural and geographical aspects and dividing discussion into categories of Greek, Etruscan, and Roman ashlar. While he allows for the use of different stones, the implied view is that, within larger categories of Greek, Etruscan, or Roman, the underlying technical practice remained more or less the same. However, as I argue here, a close reading of the evidence from Rome reveals more continuous development in the production of stonemasonry over time.

To account for technological changes in ashlar masonry in their complexity, I want to expand our perspective on early Roman ashlar to encompass the wider *chaîne opératoire* or operational sequence of its production and use, from the extraction of stone, to its movement and handling, to its maintenance or reuse as it entered the archaeological record. This approach follows the lead of a body of scholarship ultimately derived from the work of the anthropologist Leroi-Gourhan, who investigated the sequence of human actions that transformed raw material into tools.[3] His work has been particularly influential in the study of prehistorical lithic technology, but more recently one encounters similar approaches applied to a range of technological artifacts. What particularly interests me is the method's delineation of the stages involved in an object's production and use, as well as the insistence that each stage carries its own set of social contexts and implications. As with the manufacture of all artifacts, the making of architecture using stone blocks results from a sequence of actions, each involving the activation of particular knowledge. Focusing on these actions, and not simply on the object itself, calls attention to human agency and helps bridge the gap between artifact and social history. This approach holds particular value, I would argue, in the study of ashlar masonry because we are dealing with a technology that remained highly similar on a formal level. That is, throughout its long history at Rome, ashlar masonry involved stone blocks of more or less identical rectangular shape. As I point out, however, while the objects themselves may have appeared more or less the same, differences emerge over time once we start to think about how blocks were obtained, shaped, maneuvered, and maintained.

For the purpose of this paper I compare the manufacture of ashlar architecture in two different building stones (*figs. 1-2*).[4] The first is *tufo del Palatino*, the olive-green stone of Rome's earliest ashlar architecture, sometimes referred to as *tufo granulare grigio* or *cappellacio*. As the name suggests, the extent of this geological formation includes the Palatine, where there is evidence of early quarrying, but facies of the stone outcrop throughout much of central Rome, and quarries were located around the city.[5] The second material is *tufo giallo della via Tiberina*, often called *Grotta Oscura tufo* after prominent quarries on the Tiber's right bank in the territory of Veii. This yellowish, friable stone was first exploited on a large-scale for Rome's Republican walls in the first quarter of the fourth century following the conquest of Veii, with some limited urban use prior to that.[6]

Focus on these two stones is to some extent reductive, as even the earliest Roman ashlar masonry employed a greater variety of materials. The first phases of the Archaic Temple of Sant' Omobono, for example, used a hard local variant of *tufo lionato* not otherwise known in early Roman architecture and possibly from the Anio valley.[7] By the early fifth century, we find *tufo lionato* from Monteverde as well as *peperino* from the Alban Mount, while *tufo lionato* from Anio appears again in Rome's archaeological record in the late-fourth century.[8] Nonetheless, *tufo del Palatino* and *tufo giallo* were used in significant quantities and in more or less chronologically successive phases of urban construction, and this makes for a useful comparison. In what follows,

Fig. 1. *Tufo del Palatino* blocks in the podium of the Capitoline Temple of Jupiter Optimus Maximus (509 BCE). Chisel marks are visible on the face of several blocks. Photo by author.

Fig. 2. *Tufo giallo della via Tiberina* blocks in the external wall of the Esquiline agger (378 BCE). Seam in the masonry is visible just to the right of the cypress tree where blocks in courses on the right do not bond to those in courses on the left. Photo by author.

I describe the stages of each material's production in sequential order before returning to the question of socioeconomic context.

DEPOSITION AND EXTRACTION

The extraction of stone for urban construction in this period was shaped in the first place by the physical geology of Rome and its surrounding region. *Tufo del Palatino* belongs to the class of Alban Hills volcanic rocks, which tend to be better lithified then stones like *tufo giallo* erupted from the Monte Sabatini volcanoes. Importantly, both stones were formed not by pyroclastic surges of molten rock coming into contact with ground or surface water, but rather as ignimbrites, massive and often poorly sorted deposits of erupted particulate matter, which flowed down and came to rest along the sides of valleys.[9] In contrast to pyroclastic rocks formed by surge deposits, and also to those frequently used sedimentary rocks like travertine, tuff ignimbrites contain little to no internal stratification. This geological quality held significant implications for builders, as blocks could be cut to any desired depth up to the extent of the ignimbrite. Quarrymen needed only to clear away or tunnel through softer, eroded material to access thick deposits of usable rock.

*Tufo del Palatino* quarry pits were made to take advantage of rock exposed by erosion on hillsides. Quarries were often open to the sky, as those at vigna Querini on the via Tiburtina, or they could take the form of subterranean tunnels into cliff faces, such as at Villa Patrizi on the Quirinal, or in gallery tunnels noted on the Esquiline, Palatine, and Capitoline.[10] *Tufo giallo* was sometimes accessed as surface outcroppings, as evident in some quarried facies along the Cremera river. More often, though, the stone was extracted from large underground quarries like those at Grotta Oscura or Fosso del Drago, where crisscrossing galleries were cut underground and blocks were mechanically raised to the surface for transport to Rome along the Tiber river (*fig. 3*).[11]

Once good stone was exposed, the manner of extracting blocks was to start by carving a rectangular trench in the surface of the quarry floor, then to continue this channel downward to the desired depth. The practice is evinced by grooves representing the start of blocks found in many quarries. This cut would form the sides of a block, which was then freed from the natural rock beneath it. Picks could be used to separate blocks from the quarry floor, but wedges are attested in tuff quarries around Rome, including those at Grotta Oscura, and were probably the preferred technique for both materials.[12]

*Fig. 3. Plan of the tufo giallo quarry galleries at Grotta Oscura. Reprinted from Bernard 2018, fig. 2.3.*

This extraction technique meant that most of a block's six faces were cut to flat surfaces during quarrying, and the squaring process was largely accomplished before blocks left the quarry. Thus, block size was determined at this initial operational stage, and we should assign technical decisions relating to metrology or modularity to this stage of the operational sequence. Scholarship recognizes two distinct feet in these stones: blocks of *tufo del Palatino* display both an earlier 0.272 m "Osco-Italic" foot and a later 0.296 m "Attic-Syracusan" or Roman foot, while blocks of *tufo giallo* mostly display the 0.296 m foot. The transition from one unit to the other across *tufo del Palatino* architecture is documented by Cifani, who demonstrates a period of metrological fluidity in the late sixth century, when both feet appear in structures of *tufo del Palatino*.[13] Such units were ideals, and even blocks in single monuments show considerable variability (*fig. 4*). Nonetheless, the fact that *tufo del Palatino* quarries produced material based on two different metrological units over time, while *tufo giallo* quarries did not, is noteworthy.

There is also somewhat more fluid modularity exhibited by blocks of *tufo del Palatino* than those of *tufo giallo*. By and large, *tufo del Palatino* blocks were cut to an ideal size of 1 × 2 × 3 Roman feet (RF), while *tufo giallo* blocks were larger, measuring 2 × 2 × 4 RF. *Tufo giallo* blocks often varied in length, sometimes extending to 5 or 6 RF, but headers were cut with great regularity to a size of 2 × 2 RF. This tendency appears from the first large-scale use of *tufo giallo* in the fourth-century

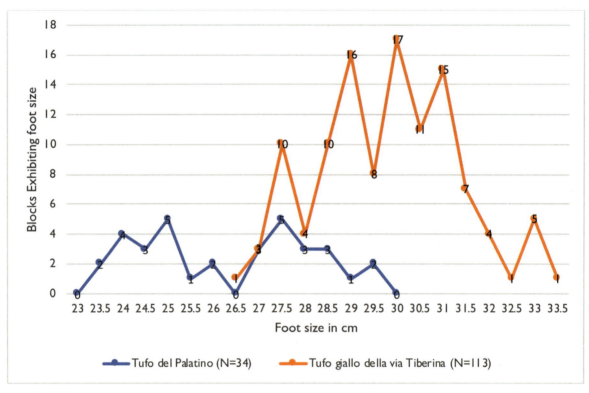

*Fig. 4. Metrological distribution chart of tuff block sizes from the Esquiline agger.*

circuit walls down to the last monuments making significant use of the stone in the second century. By contrast, it is possible to point to several buildings constructed entirely from *tufo del Palatino* blocks not cut to the 1 × 2 × 3 RF standard.[14]

TRANSPORT AND MANEUVERING

Once blocks were extracted and shaped in the quarry, the next step was to move them to construction sites. Practices of handling and transporting material were dictated in part by blocks' size and weight and so were also influenced by decisions made during the quarrying process. In their ideal module, *tufo giallo* blocks were larger and almost three times heavier than *tufo del Palatino* blocks, weighing 624 kg to 229 kg. Difficulties implied by handling larger, heavier blocks were mitigated by the introduction of a new feature to the supply chain: *tufo giallo* was the first building material imported to Rome on a large scale by waterway, as Romans shipped blocks from quarries in the Tiber Valley to the city's port in the Campus Martius. *Tufo del Palatino* blocks were transported overland from urban quarries to nearby building sites.[15]

While shipping stone via river allowed for the convenience of water power, it also seems to have spurred further complexity in the supply system. For one thing, it seems that *tufo giallo* was stockpiled or staged at some intermediate point between quarry and construction site. Vitruvius advocates for curing stone from the *lapicidinae Pallenses*, very likely the *tufo giallo* quarries, for two years to assess the stone's durability before using it for *opus quadratum*.[16] This shows awareness that *tufo giallo* contained significant "quarry sap" or moisture and hardened while drying.

Such intermediate staging of material may be reflected in the material evidence. Mason's marks appear in early Roman ashlar masonry almost exclusively on *tufo giallo* blocks from their earliest to latest use and, where we may observe large numbers of marks on monuments, their distribution suggests a relationship to a staging component to the stone's supply chain.[17] In particular, within the long *tufo giallo* ashlar walls of the Esquiline *agger* still standing outside Termini station there is a panel of 36 m of wall bounded on both sides by neat seams in the masonry (cf. *fig. 2*). As Säflund recognized, these seams likely indicate the efforts of a single work group. On the blocks of the panel of wall between the two seams, two mason's marks, *eta* and *tau*, make up 21 of 26 signs on the lowermost eight courses but do not appear on the upper courses, where *pi* instead comprises 23 of 25 marks. On the walls' continuation on either side of the panel, all three marks are extremely rare, with different marks predominating to the north and south. The distribution is distinctive and suggests that marks corresponded to shipments of blocks arriving to builders as they proceeded from lower to upper courses and from one section of walls to the next.[18] No similar marks have been found at or around the *tufo giallo* quarries, while many instances of single marks are greater than could be carried by single boats. These factors make it unlikely that marks relate to quarries or to boatloads of stone. Instead, marks were inscribed on blocks in the city at some stage between the urban delivery of stone and its onward delivery to building sites. Thus, the intermediary stockpiling described by Vitruvius would form a reasonable explanation for their appearance.

Further complexity in the supply of *tufo giallo* can be seen in other regular cuttings on blocks, this time for the insertion of lifting devices. Blocks of *tufo giallo* display the first known holes for lifting tongs, *ferrei forfices*, in Roman architecture. Similar cuttings appear somewhat earlier in some select instances in Etruscan architecture; I return to the possibility of technological diffusion from Etruria below. By contrast, *tufo del Palatino* blocks show no cuttings for lifting devices, and this would suggest that the application of lifting technology was conditioned by the type of stone. Possibly *tufo del Palatino* blocks were lifted using cranes and rope cradles, which left no mark on blocks; however, ramps used to raise blocks of *tufo del Palatino* are attested in several monuments by a correspondence between course height and the earthen stratigraphy adjacent to walls.[19] Notably, Boni observed similar correspondence between the earthen mound of the Esquiline agger and abutting courses of *tufo giallo* blocks, suggesting that at least some *tufo giallo* blocks were maneuvered with ramps in conjunction with cranes and lifting tongs.[20]

Once transported to site, structures built of both materials were assembled in similar fashion. Romans built in what Vitruvius refers to as *alternis coriis*, with alternating courses entirely of headers or stretchers, as opposed to the Greek *emplekton* technique in which in-facing headers were used within stretcher courses to bind a wall's face to its core.[21] While some scholarship detects aspects of Greek influence in Rome's stonemasonry of this early period, masons at Rome exclusively employed this Italic placement of blocks, and nowhere did urban monuments use the *emplekton* masonry of Western Greek architecture.

TOOLS

Chisel marks or other surface features observable across joins of *tufo del Palatino* blocks confirm that masons worked blocks during the assembly process, refining material shaped in the quarry (*fig. 5*). The same was true of *tufo giallo* blocks, which occasionally display anathyrosis. *Tufo giallo* blocks also often have a slightly trapezoidal profile but are closely fit in an almost pseudo-polygonal style, suggesting careful attention to individual block shapes during assembly.[22]

In terms of the tools used to achieve on-site finishes, scholarship focuses on direct percussion instruments such as pickaxes described by ancient sources.[23] When still soft with moisture from the quarry, tuff could be squared entirely with a hand-axe. The thin, slightly radial lines photographed in the early twentieth century on the walls of the Grotta Oscura quarries were produced by a worker swinging an axe with a pointed tip.[24] However, it is not true as some claim that tuff architecture shows no evidence of indirect percussion tools such as chisels or punches struck with a mallet.[25] These tools have left those straight, not radial, marks on *tufo del Palatino* blocks from Archaic structures at the Porta Esquilina (cf. *fig. 5*), or on blocks from the Capitolium platform (cf. *fig. 1*). Mason's marks on *tufo giallo* blocks were likewise cut with pointed chisels. While these examples come from finished monuments, plenty of comparative evidence for mallet-driven tools at quarries in Iron Age Italy makes it likely such tools also were used in tuff quarries around Rome – the aforementioned use of wedges, for example, to free blocks from the quarry floor fit within this category of tool.[26]

Chisels and other indirect percussion tools were more precise and produced finer finishes than axes. This bears stressing, as it is sometimes assumed that early tuff architecture required minimal tooling, but architectural ornament does appear at Rome in tuff architecture already by the Archaic period. The first temple at Sant' Omobono had a torus molding, while molded cornices and fragments of a fluted column drum have been identified from *tufo giallo* monuments of the late fourth century.[27]

STRATEGIES OF PRIMARY USE

While a certain skill level was brought to bear on finishing monuments of both stones, both *tufo del Palatino* and *tufo giallo* were too friable to hold highly intricately carved ornament as sometimes seen by the third century in harder tuffs like *peperino di Marino*, and in marble and travertine by

*Fig. 5. Detailed view of straight chisel marks across blocks joins from a section of the Archaic Porta Esquilina (6th – 5th century BCE). Photo by author.*

the next century. The earlier, softer tuffs were poorly cemented, making them susceptible to environmental degradation. Ancient masons, keenly aware of these stones' physical limitations, developed strategies from an early date to protect monuments built of blocks of such tuffs. In the Archaic temple at Sant' Omobono, one of the city's first ashlar monuments, the choice to employ a unique and highly lithified tuff may have been driven by the need to protect the monument from Tiber flood waters at a site near the riverbank. Vitruvius advocated for restricting tuff blocks to covered places, *locis tectis*, to preserve them from frost and water damage (*De Arch.* 2.7.2). One way of providing such protection was to shield friable stone beneath more durable stone as a sort of cladding. This practice is somewhat more common with *tufo giallo* than *tufo del Palatino*, as there are more identifiable monuments of purely *tufo del Palatino* construction.[28] The practice, of course, depended on Rome's access to a greater selection of building stones, something which became progressively possible with the conquest of Central Italy during the Mid-Republic, but both *tufo del Palatino* and *tufo giallo* blocks were protected with more durable materials from an early date. In the early fifth century, masons built the platform of the twin temples at Sant' Omobono with a core of *tufo del Palatino* blocks concealed within more lithified tuffs, while the nearby temple of Apollo Medicus was made of a similar two-stone construction with a *tufo del Palatino* core.[29] Meanwhile, the podium of Largo Argentina Temple C had internal walls of *tufo giallo* and an exterior facing of durable *tufo lionato*, now demonstrated by petrochemical study to be stone from the Anio Valley.[30] The practice became increasingly regular into the Mid-Republic, and by the second century it was normal to restrict blocks of *tufo giallo* or *tufo del Palatino* to below-ground foundations or otherwise to protect them with facings of other stones.[31]

Another option was to cover stones with a decorative and protective coat of plaster. Direct evidence for this practice at Rome is not as forthcoming as outside the city, where traces of plaster appear on stone architecture at Pyrgi, Lanuvium, or the Castrum Inui sanctuary at Ardea, but fragments of plaster have been found at Rome in the excavation of several Archaic monuments, and a piece of a plastered *tufo del Palatino* block was found reused in the later *caementa* of the Temple of the Castores in the Roman forum.[32] Marchetti Longhi excavated large areas of plaster, no longer extant, on the podium wall of Large Argentina Temple C, applied and then scored to look like the underlying joins of the stonemasonry. Notably, Temple C shows multiple strategies of maintenance at once, as the temple's podium had a core of *tufo giallo* blocks clad in harder Anio tuff, which was then covered in plaster.[33]

STRATEGIES OF SECONDARY USE

The basic picture suggests greater reuse of *tufo giallo* than *tufo del Palatino* in both classical and post-classical periods. It is not easy to identify the reuse of *tufo del Palatino* blocks as blocks.[34] Rubble of *tufo del Palatino* appears within the *caementa* of concrete structures such as the Metellan temple of the Castores, the houses along the Via Sacra, or the Late Republican phases of the *domus Vestae*.[35] Tufo del Palatino rubble was found in the earthen fill of the podium of Largo Argentina Temple C, perhaps from earlier structures in that area of the Campus Martius.[36] So far as can be discerned, recycling in these cases used material on site or nearby. Provenance is less clear for *tufo del Palatino* rubble in the lower courses of the *navalia*, which is not located near any known archaic structures.

*Tufo giallo* appears more extensively in secondary use, both as recycled blocks and commonly as rubble in *caementa* cores of concrete monuments, something which may reflect ancient awareness of the pumice-rich material's comparatively light weight.[37] The stone also appears in the facing of concrete structures of reticulate or *opus incertum*, a use for which *tufo del Palatino* is unattested. Several medieval structures, mostly churches built under papal commission, utilized *tufo giallo* blocks for foundation courses (fig. 6).[38] These blocks do not seem to have been reworked but were simply salvaged from ancient contexts and laid in courses in later monuments.[39] This is not to say that reused *tufo giallo* ashlars were common in early medieval Roman architecture, but the impression is of greater availability of *tufo giallo* than *tufo del Palatino* blocks by that date.[40]

DISCUSSION

Bringing all of these steps together, we may sketch the complete operational sequence of ashlar masonry in both *tufo del Palatino* and *tufo giallo* in early Roman architecture (fig. 7). The chart represents something of an historical progression since, as noted above, the use of *tufo giallo* expanded significantly after Rome's conquest of Veii in 396 BCE, at which date the use of *tufo del Palatino* started to decline, even as the latter stone was not entirely phased out of urban architecture for centuries. Recent work on the *chaîne opératoire* of craft technologies stresses common interactions between the manufacture of one type of object and another, or between technical knowledge applied at different stages in an operational sequences.[41] In the case of early Rome's architecture, interaction between different technologies has been observed before: above all, ashlar appeared in the city's monuments around the same time as the first fired tiles, and it makes sense to link the emergence of heavier roofs and more solid foundations.[42] Obviously, it is unsurprising to find points of overlap between the production of ashlar in one or another stone, since both tuffs were worked within the wider tradition of Roman ashlar masonry. Closer and more particular affinities in the technical knowledge applied to these stones are also detectable: I have noted that Roman masons regularly used more durable tuffs to clad and protect blocks of softer tuff in the interior or foundations of monuments. While both *tufo del Palatino* and *tufo giallo* were frequently used in tandem with harder tuffs, neither material was used in this way with the

*Fig. 6. Reused tufo giallo ashlar blocks incorporated into a medieval structure beside the church of S. Gregorio on the Caelian Hill. Photo by author.*

other, and both normally formed the core of monuments. From an early point, then, Roman masons classed both stones among those particularly susceptible to environmental damage.

If technological overlap may be expected, this makes differences in the respective operational sequence of both tuffs all the more interesting. While both stones followed similar sequences of production, the individual stages of that sequence were noticeable more elaborate for *tufo giallo* than for *tufo del Palatino*. The difference arose from a geographic shift: while *tufo del Palatino* was quarried around the *urbs* and closer to building sites, *tufo giallo* was imported to Rome over a longer distance down the Tiber. But the change was not merely geographical: *tufo giallo* blocks were also larger and somewhat more standardized. Such standardization combined with the possibility that *tufo giallo* was staged at some point between quarry and worksite make the entire *tufo giallo* production sequence seem more dislocated, resembling what economists would call a factor market, with production of raw material operating without close coordination with centers of demand, in this case construction sites. Tentatively, I raise the possibility that these aspects also may have resulted in more of this material in monuments and even possibly intermediary stockpiles for post-primary use.

We can also focus on the different lifting technologies, *ferrei forfices*, used to raise of *tufo giallo* blocks, while blocks of *tufo del Palatino* show no such signs of lifting machines. To understand technological innovation in the sequence of production, *chaîne opératoire* theory would focus on agency, and on the possibility that novel practices in *tufo giallo* ashlar architecture reflected the

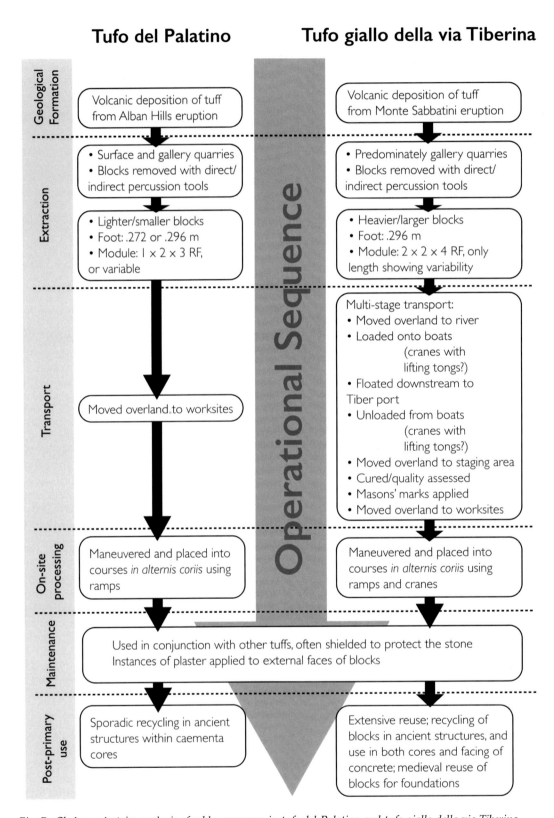

*Fig. 7. Chaîne opératoire analysis of ashlar masonry in tufo del Palatino and tufo giallo della via Tiberina.*

influx of new technical knowledge traveling along with new workers who were not part of the earlier production of *tufo del Palatino* ashlar.[43] In turn, this encourages us to situate such change within a supply-side analysis of Rome's labor force. Of course, demand-side concerns also mattered: in 378 BC, the building of the Republican walls alone required some million blocks of *tufo giallo*, which will have driven investment and specialization.[44] Meanwhile, the late-sixth century – the putative period of the Tarquinian monarchy – was also a time of energetic urban building and increased demand for stone.[45] However, it cannot be coincidence that both these periods were crucial moments for the development of Roman labor. Roman tradition ascribed the Tarquins' grand public works to the monarchs' brutal efficiency in extracting citizen labor for construction while, according to Dionysius of Halicarnassus, Tarquinius Superbus even forced Romans to work in stone-quarries.[46]

Sources also described citizen corvées in 378 BCE for the construction of *tufo giallo* city walls, but Rome's labor supply was at that moment entering a period of dramatic change.[47] The fourth century saw the installation of the slave mode of production at the center of the Roman economy as the initial stages of imperial expansion brought tens if not hundreds of thousands of slaves into Roman hands. In particular, the large-scale exploitation of *tufo giallo* from the territory of Veii closely followed Rome's first recorded mass enslavement, as the surviving population of the conquered Etruscan capital were sold. Quarries were common destinations in antiquity for war-slaves, and Frank first suggested that Veian prisoners of war worked in *tufo giallo* quarries.[48] Slavery thus provides a potential conduit by which new workers and new technological knowledge entered the Roman building industry. This context makes it highly intriguing that *tufo giallo* blocks carried the earliest holes for *ferrei forfices*. As noted, Etruscan masons used this technology at a somewhat earlier date, raising the possibility that the technology moved from Etruria to Rome alongside skilled slaves.

Lifting technology was not the only aspect of *tufo giallo*'s production, which accompanied changes to Rome's labor supply. In particular, the production of *tufo giallo* ashlar required a significant increase of workers involved in transporting stone, and this aspect of the operational sequence implies a significant increase in workers who were not necessarily skilled at stonemasonry. A simple quantification of the manpower to ship stone on rafts downstream from quarries in the *ager Veientanus* to the city's port on the Campus Martius is instructive. Assuming a capacity per raft of 18 blocks, the production of enough *tufo giallo* blocks for the Republican walls alone necessitated 55,000 raft trips along the Tiber from quarries to port.[49] Each trip demanded pilot and crew, porters to on- and offload material at various points, carpenters and shipwrights to build and maintain rafts, and drivers and oxen to tow vessels upstream back to the quarries. Later evidence describes the river port in the Forum Boarium as a place where carpenters congregated and draught animals were dependably found.[50] Considering the quantity of stone blocks reaching the city from the fourth century onward, some of these qualities may have featured at the Tiber port already in an earlier period.

Overall, the implication is that of a much-expanded sector of the urban economy involved both directly and indirectly in the operational sequence of *tufo giallo* ashlar masonry as compared to that of *tufo del Palatino*. Since this expanding supply of workers was involved in something other than primary food production, this in turn raises questions about how they were fed, or where they lived. We might therefore relate the more expansive production sequence of *tufo giallo* architectural production to a host of concomitant changes in the structure of the urban economy, from early evidence for intensive agriculture in the *suburbium* seemingly targeted at urban markets, to signs of a rising population domiciled at Rome around the same time.[51] These are larger themes than can be treated here, but this discussion shows the possibilities of thinking through the socioeconomic context of technological changes in urban stone architecture: not only did the practice of ashlar masonry at Rome change over time, but changes can be seen to reflect the city's historical dynamics.

NOTES

1. I am grateful to the conference organizers for the warm welcome in Rome and Satricum. I also thank Prof. Carrie Atkins for guiding me through bibliography on *chaîne opératoire*, and Prof. Margaret Andrews for sharing unpublished work on post-classical ashlar masonry in Rome.
2. For the emergence of ashlar at Rome, see Cifani 1994; 2008, 238; cf. Hopkins 2016, 32 for possible ashlars from the seventh century.
3. Leroi Gourhan 1964; also relevant is Kopytoff 1986 on biographical approaches to objects; for subsequent scholarship and critiques, see Sellet 1993; Bar Yosef and Van Peer 2009; Brysbaert 2011.
4. Geological introduction in Jackson and Marra 2006; I follow their geological terminology for various stones.
5. Cifani 2008, 226-36; 2010, 42-4; for Palatine quarries, see Tomei 1998.

6. Volpe 2014.
7. Diffendale *et al.* 2016; Brocato *et al.* in press.
8. Farr, Marra, and Terrenato 2014; Marra, D'Ambrosio, Gaeta, and Mattei 2018.
9. Jackson and Marra 2006, 413.
10. Cifani 2008, 226-36 with further bibliography.
11. Carbonara and Messineo 1996; Sisani 2005, 22-4; Bernard 2018, 29-30. For the apparatus used to raise blocks, see Cristofani and Boss 1992 on Caere.
12. For picks: Previato 2016, 54, in reference to quarries on Sardinia; closer to Rome, Ashby 1924, 136 notes holes for their setting at Grotta Oscura; Farr 2014, 121 publishes an iron wedge from the tuff quarries at Gabii.
13. Cifani 2008, 239-40.
14. Examples: early temenos of *curiae veteres* sanctuary (Zeggio 2005, 69); first phase of the Archaic temple at Sant Omobono, albeit in a unique variety of stone (Diffendale *et al.* 2016, 12); wall abutting the Archaic Porta Esquilina built of regular 45 x 61 cm. blocks, (Andrews and Bernard 2017, 248-9). Also note deviation in *tufo del Palatino* blocks from the Archaic Porta Collina (Cifani and Fogagnolo 1998, 384).
15. The identification of *tufo lionato* from Anio in Archaic architecture discussed above suggests a certain amount of stone arrived by river already in an earlier period, but the scale of important seems much smaller.
16. *De Arch.* 2.7.5; repeated by Plin. *NH* 36.50.170; for identification of these quarries, see Jackson and Marra 2006: 410-1.
17. While almost unknown on *tufo del Palatino*, two mason's marks on blocks of that stone are reported from the *curiae veteres* sanctuary by Zeggio 2006, 69.
18. Further discussion of the marks at Bernard 2018, 93.
19. Ioppolo 1989, 31; Cifani 2008, 241-2; Bernard 2018, 94-6.
20. Boni 1910, 510-14.
21. *De Arch.* 2.3.4; Lugli 1957, 181–83; Castagnoli 1974, 431–32; Säflund 1932, 119.
22. Säflund 1932, 117.
23. For ancient names, see Cifani 2008, 241; 2010, 38. Problematically, one option, *upupa*, appears once in Latin literature as a quarry tool at Plaut. *Capt.* 1004, where context suggests the playwright chose the term to pun on the name of a bird; cf. Plin. *NH* 10.44. What made the *upupa* bird-like is impossible to say. *Dolabra* appears more commonly in Latin as an excavation tool.
24. Säflund 1932, 117, fig. 56; these quarries were badly damaged in WWII, cf. Carbonara and Messineo 1996, 294-5.
25. Cf. Säflund 1932, 118-9; a much-reproduced image by Adam 1984, fig. 30 shows a worker in a tuff quarry using only a pickaxe.
26. For general introduction, see Bessac 1996; Camporeale and Pais 2009 offer detailed presentation of tool marks from contemporary Etruscan quarries near Populonia; cf. Farr, here note 12
27. Brocato and Terrenato 2017, 100-1; for *tufo giallo*, see Diosono 2016, 84 on the Temple of Portunus.
28. Several late-sixth and early-fifth century temples have foundations and stone elements entirely of *tufo del Palatino* including temples of Jupiter Optimus Maximus, of the Castores, and possibly of Saturn, and the recently discovered structure on the Quirinal published by Arizza and Serlorenzi 2013. By comparison, the only temple exclusively of *tufo giallo* is the Mid-Republican phase of the temple of Portunus, on which see Colini and Buzzetti 1986; Diosono 2016. The first phase of Largo Argentina Temple A may have been exclusively *tufo giallo*, as see Coarelli 1981, 16.
29. Sant' Omobono: Diffendale *et al.* 2016, 23-5; Apollo: Ciancio Rossetto 1997-98, 184.
30. Marra, D'Ambrosio, Gaeta, and Mattei 2018.
31. Bernard 2018, 194-212.
32. Cifani 2008, 246-7; for the Temple of the Castores, see Nielsen and Poulsen 1992, 78.
33. Marchetti Longhi 1932, 298-9; Marra, D'Ambrosio, Gaeta, and Mattei 2018.
34. Tucci 2018, 42-3, notes reuse of *tufo del Palatino* blocks and rubble in Imperial structures beneath the Aracoeli on the Capitoline, but not in any systematic manner. Another possible exception is a structure of *tufo del Palatino* blocks on via del Teatro Marcello laid unusually entirely in headers and supported by brickwork; perhaps originally from the circuit walls, these blocks appear reused for unknown purposes; see Ruggiero 1990, 23.
35. Cf. the table in Mogetta 2015, 8.
36. Marchetti Longhi 1932, 284-85.
37. For reuse of blocks, see Colini 1940, 50 on the Temple of Veiovis; for awareness of weight, see Jackson *et al.* 2005, 506.
38. Krautheimer 1980, 124, interpreting this as material from the walls; Barelli 2007; Andrews in press.
39. Barelli 2007, 67.
40. The phenomenon must have been shaped in part by accessibility to monuments of each stone. The Republican walls made copious amounts of *tufo giallo* available. However, monuments of *tufo del Palatino* must also have existed for spoliation: the ruins of the Capitolium, e.g., were visible into the fifteenth century, as cf. the description at the start of Poggio Bracciolini's *De Varietate Fortunae* (1447).
41. Brysbaert 2011.
42. Cifani 1994; Hopkins 2016.
43. It is unlikely that technical knowledge circulated to Rome at this date through theoretical manuals instead of alongside labor, as see Bernard 2018: 220-2 with Vitr. *De Arch.* 7.pr.18. The Roman tradition of architectural writing remained underdeveloped into the Late Republic.
44. Estimates: Cornell 1995, 462 n. 11; Cifani 2010, 37-8; Volpe 2014, 61-2; Bernard 2018, 97.
45. For this period of architectural production at Rome, see Hopkins 2016.
46. Dion. Hal. 4.81.2; 4.44.2; Cifani 2008, 236, 240.
47. Liv. 6.32 with Bernard 2018, 108-14.
48. Frank 1918, 183.
49. Bernard 2018, 98, 107, assuming a capacity for flat-bottomed boats of 18 blocks (7.38 m$^3$ of stone) after Volpe 2014, 53.
50. Cf. Liv. 35.40.8 for a *porticus inter lignarios* in the area; for draught animals and boats by the *portus Tiberinus*, see Proc. *Goth.* 5.26.
51. For the intensification of viticulture in the *suburbium* in this moment, see Volpe 2009; Panella 2010; see also Piranomente and Ricci 2009 for wool-working. Evidence for market-exchange and demographic growth at Rome is detailed in Bernard 2018, 159-92.

BIBLIOGRAPHY

Andrews, M. in press, The Reuse of Ancient Tuff Blocks in Early Medieval Ecclesiastical and Residential Construction in Rome

Andrews, M./S.G. Bernard 2017, The long durée urban development of the Porta Esquilina and the church of San Vito in Rome (6th c. B.C. – A.D. 15th c.), *JRA* 30, 244-265.

Arizza, M./M. Serlorenzi (eds.) 2015, *La scoperta di una struttura templare sul Quirinale presso l'ex Regio Ufficio Geologico*, Rome.

Ashby, T. 1924, La via tiberina e i territori di Capena e del Soratte nel periodo romano, *MemPontAcc* 1,2, 129-175.

Bar Yosef, O./P. Van Peer 2009, The Chaîne Opératoire Approach in Middle Paleolithic Archaeology, *Current Anthropology* 50.1, 103-131.

Barelli, L. 2007, La diffusione e il significato dell'*opus quadratum* a Roma nei secoli VIII e IX, in M.P. Sette *et al.*, *Saggi in Onore di Gaetano Miarelli Mariani* (*QISA* 44-50), Roma, 67-74.

Bernard, S. 2018, *Building Mid-Republican Rome: Labor, Architecture, and the Urban Economy*, Oxford.

Bessac, J.-Y. 1996, *La pierre en Gaule narbonnaise et les carrières du Bois des Lens (Nîmes): histoire, archéologie, ethnographie, et techniques* (*JRA* Suppl. 16), Portsmouth, RI.

Boni, G. 1910, Mura urbane tra la Porta Collina e la Viminale, *NSc* 7, 495–513.

Brocato, P/N. Terrenato 2017, The Archaic Temple of S. Omobono: New Discoveries and Old Problems, in P. Lulof/C. Smith (eds.), *The Age of Tarquinius Superbus: Central Italy in the Late 6th Century*, Leuven, 97-106.

Brocato, P. *et al.* in press, Identification of a Previously Unknown Tuff for the Construction of the Archaic Temple Podium at Sant'Omobono, Rome, *JMedArch*.

Brysbaert, A. 2011. Introduction: Tracing Social Networks through Studying Technologies, in A. Brysbaert (ed.), *Tracing Prehistoric Social Networks through Technology: A Diachronic Perspective on the Aegean*, London, 1-11.

Camporeale, S./A. Pais 2009, Analisi e interpretazione delle tracce di cavatura, in F. Cambi/F. Cavari/C. Mascione (eds.), *Materiali da costruzione e produzione del ferro: studi sull'economia populoniese fra periodo etrusco e romanizzazione*, Bari, 47-64.

Carbonara, A./G. Messineo 1996, Via Tiberina: Nuove acquisizioni lungo il tracciato della antica via. II. Cave antiche presso il Fosso di Grotta Oscura e il Fosso del Drago, *BCom* 97, 294-297.

Castagnoli, F. 1974, Topografia e urbanisitica di Roma nel IV secolo a.C., *StRom* 22, 425-443.

Ciancio Rossetto, P. 1997-1998. Tempio di Apollo. Nuove indagini sulla fase repubblicana, *RendPontAcc* 70, 177-195.

Cifani, G. 1994, Aspetti dell'edilizia romana arcaica, *StEtr* 60, 185-226.

Cifani, G. 2008, *Architettura romana arcaica: edilizia e società tra Monarchia e Repubblica*, Rome.

Cifani, G. 2010, I grandi cantieri della Roma arcaica: aspetti tecnici ed organizzativi, in S. Camporeale/H. Dessales/A. Pizzo (eds.), *Arqueología de la construcción II. Los procesos constructivos en el mundo romano: Italia y provincias orientales*, Madrid/Mérida, 35-49.

Cifani, G./S. Fogagnolo 1998, La documentazione archeologica della mura arcaiche a Roma, *RM* 105, 359-389.

Coarelli, F. 1981, *Topografia e storia, L'area sacra di Largo Argentina* I, Rome.

Colini, A.M. 1940, *Il tempio di Veiove*, Rome.

Colini, A.M./C. Buzzetti 1986, Aedes Portuni in Portu Tiberino, *BCom* 91, 7-30.

Cornell, T.J. 1995, *The Beginnings of Rome 1000-264 B.C.*, London.

Cristofani, M./M. Boss 1992, La struttura, in M. Cristofani (ed.), *Caere 3.1. Lo scarico arcaico della Vigna Parrocchiale*, Rome, 5-17.

Diffendale, D./P. Brocato/N. Terrenato/A. Brock 2016, Sant'Omobono: an interim status quaesitionis, *JRA* 29, 7-42.

Diosono, F. 2016, La porta e il porto. Il culto di Portunus nella Roma arcaica e repubblicana, in V. Gasperini (ed.), *Vestigia: Miscellanea di studi storico-religiosi in onore di Filippo Coarelli nel suo 80° anniversario*, Stuttgart, 81-98.

Farr, J.M. 2014, *Lapis Gabinus: Tufo and the Economy of Urban Construction in Ancient Rome*. Unpublished PhD diss. University of Michigan.

Farr, J./F. Marra/N. Terrenato 2015. Geochemical identification criteria for 'peperino' stones employed in ancient Roman buildings: A Lapis Gabinus case study, *JASc* 3, 41-51.

Frank, T. 1918, Notes on the Servian wall, *AJA* 22, 175-188.

Hopkins, J.N. 2016, *The Genesis of Roman Architecture*, New Haven.

Ioppolo, G. 1989, Il tempio arcaico, in *Il viver quotidiano in Roma arcaica : materiali dagli scavi del tempio arcaico nell'area sacra di S. Omobono*, Rome, 29-33.

Jackson, M./F. Marra 2006, Roman stone masonry: Volcanic foundations of the ancient city, *AJA* 110.3, 403-426.

Jackson, M./F. Marra/R. Hay/C.A. Cawood/E.M. Winkler 2005, The Judicious Selection and Preservation of Tuff and Travertine Building Stones in Ancient Rome, *Archaeometry* 47, 585-510.

Kopytoff, I. 1986, The cultural biography of things: commoditization as process, in A. Appadurai (ed.), *The Social Life of Things: Commodities in Cultural Perspective*, Cambridge, 64-91.

Krautheimer, R. 1980, *Rome: Profile of a City, 312-1308*, Princeton.

Leroi Gourhan, A. 1964, *Gesture and Speech*, Cambridge, MA.

Marra, F./E. D'Ambrosio/M. Gaeta/M. Mattei 2018, The Geochemical Fingerprint of Tufo Lionato Blocks from the Area Sacra di Largo Argentina: Implications for the Chronology of Volcanic Building Stones in Ancient Rome, *Archaeometry* 60, 641-659.

Marchetti Longhi, G. 1932, Gli scavi del Largo Argentina I, *BCom* 60, 253-346.

Mogetta, M. 2015, A New Date for Concrete in Rome, *JRS* 105, 1-40.

Nielsen, I./B. Poulsen 1992. *The Temple of Castor and Pollux 1. The pre-Augustan temple phases with related decorative elements* (LSA 17), Rome.

Panella, C. 2010, Roma, il suburbio e l'Italia in età medio- e tardo- repubblicana: cultura materiale, territori, economie, *Facta* 4, 11-123.

Piranomonte, M./G. Ricci 2009, L'edificio rustico di viale Tiziano e la fonte di Anna Perenna. Nuovi dati per la topografia dell'area Flaminia in epoca repubblicana, in V. Jolivet et al. *Suburbium II. Il Suburbio di Roma dalla fine dell'età monarchica alla nascità del sistema delle ville*, Rome, 413-435.

Previato, C. 2016, *Nora. Le cave di pietra della città antica*, Rome.

Ruggiero, I. 1990, La cinta muraria presso il Foro Boario in età arcaica e medio repubblicana, *ArchLaz* 10, 23-30.

Säflund, G. 1932 (repr. 1998), *Le mura di Roma repubblicana*, Rome.

Sellet, F. 1993, Chaîne opératoire; the concept and its applications, *Lithic Technology* 18.1-2, 106-112.

Sisani, S. 2005, Cave del Lazio in età etrusco-romana, in *Le Cave nel Lazio*, Rome, 11-32.

Tomei, M.A. 1998, Cave e cavità sotterranee del monte Palatino, in C. Giavarini (ed.), *Il Palatino. Area sacra sud-ovest e Domus Tiberiana*, Rome, 155-176.

Tucci, P.L. 2018, A funerary monument on the Capitoline: architecture and painting in mid-Republican Rome, between Etruria and Greece, *JRA* 31.1, 30-52.

Volpe, R. 2009, Vini, vigneti ed anfore in Roma repubblicana, in V. Jolivet (ed.), *Suburbium II. Il Suburbio di Roma dalla fine dell'età monarchica alla nascità del sistema delle ville*, Rome, 369-381.

Volpe, R. 2014, Dalle cave alla Via Tiberina alle mura repubblicane di Roma, in *Arqueologia de la construcción IV. Las canteras en el mundo antiguo: sistemas de explotación y procesos productivos* (Anejos de Archivo Español de Arqueologia) Mérida, 61-73.

Zeggio, S. 2005, Un santuario alle pendici nord-orientali del Palatino ed i suoi depositi votivi fra età arcaica e medio-repubblicana, in A.M. Comella/S. Mele (eds),. *Depositi votivi e culti dell'Italia antica dall'età arcaica a quella tardo-repubblicana*, Atti del Convegno di Studi, Perugia, 1-4 giugno 2000, Bari, 63-76.

Zeggio, S. 2006, Dall'indagine alla città: un settore del Centro Monumentale e la sua viabilità dalle origini all'età neroniana, *ScAnt* 13, 61-122.

# Le fortificazioni di Gabii (dal X al VI sec. a.C.)
## Tecniche di costruzione e riflessioni sulle modalità di trasferimento di tecnologia

*Sophie Helas*

*Abstract*

*As early as the Early Iron Age (Latial II), Gabii's citadel (arx) was protected by fortifications which underwent several phases of improvement and renovation. The initial, 2m-strong mud wall was soon reinforced with wooden beams. Following a second mud wall on a high socle of quarry stones, an agger – i.e. a defensive embankment made of earth and stones – was constructed in the 8th cent. BC, which probably encircled the entire settlement by the following century. In the 6th cent. BC, the northern section of the agger was finally faced with large ashlars.*

*Compared with the neighbouring regions, the building techniques employed by the Iron Age builders seem rather experimental. The sudden, sophisticated use of ashlar masonry, however, points to the possibility that craftsmen and architects from Magna Graecia might have been commissioned or consulted. The city walls of Kyme and Megara Hyblaia resemble those of Gabii in many aspects of the blocks' finishing and the way they were offset from their lower courses. It seems therefore unlikely that these walls were simply copied without the benefit of personal instruction and guidance. The adaptation of this particular type of ashlar masonry at Gabii may therefore serve as an example for the both intensive and extensive intra-regional technology transfer taking place during the 7th/6th cent. BC, which served as a catalyst for the process of urbanisation already in progress in central Italy.*

INTRODUZIONE

Gabii è situata sulla strada che porta da Roma a Palestrina. Il lago di Castiglione, ormai prosciugato da più di cento anni, è un cratere vulcanico, mentre il pianoro tufaceo si è formato durante l'attività sismica. Le sponde del lago di Castiglione erano occupate da insediamenti fin dalla media Età del Bronzo.[1] Come dimostra la necropoli di Osteria dell'Osa, il sito doveva avere un ruolo significativo già a partire dal IX secolo a.C.,[2] benché ci sfuggano conoscenze precise sull'insediamento. All'inizio dell'Età del Ferro venne probabilmente abitato il pianoro tufaceo adiacente al lago, sul quale, nel corso dell'VIII secolo a.C., si stabilì un insediamento protourbano.[3]

I nostri lavori[4] si sono concentrati intorno a due nuclei principali (*fig. 1*): quello delle mura settentrionali, nel punto in cui queste appaiono identiche a quelle pertinenti l'acropoli, e, dal 2011 in poi, anche quello che comprende i sistemi difensivi a sud dell'insediamento.[5]

DESCRIZIONE DELLE MURA SULL'ARX SECONDO LE SUE FASI (X-VI SEC. A. C.)

Con il sostegno della *Deutsche Forschungsgemeinschaft* abbiamo svolto otto campagne di scavo a partire dal 2008 a nord della città, le quali ci hanno permesso di individuare almeno sette fasi principali nel processo formativo delle mura, incominciando con una costruzione in argilla nel X secolo e concludendo con un rinforzo nel III secolo a. C. costituito da un muro eretto davanti all' esistente.[6]

*I. Le mura in argilla (periodo laziale IIA)*

Il muro più antico[7] è costituito da un basso zoccolo di pietre appena sbozzate, che poggiava sulla roccia levigata sul quale è impostato un muro in argilla (*fig. 2*). Finora non sono stati ritrovati resti di mattoni crudi, quindi supponiamo che l'alzato del muro sia stato eretto con la tecnica del pisé. Fra lo zoccolo e la massa argillosa, che contiene frammiste delle piccole pietre, insisteva un compatto strato di schegge tufacee dalla probabile funzione di equiparatore fra i due elementi costruttivi: il piano in schegge tufacee infatti serviva sia ad ottenere un piano orizzontale per l'alzato in argilla, sia a migliorare le facoltà di drenaggio. Al di sopra dello zoccolo sono comparsi nel saggio accanto, a una distanza di 1 m ca. l'una dall'altra, due concentrazioni isolate di schegge tufacee che fungevano da platea per i pali. Al di sopra di una di queste si sono

*Fig. 1. Sito di Gabii visto da Sud con indicazione dei saggi archeologici dell'università di Bonn. Foto: Robinson Krämer, Projekt Gabii.*

conservati i resti di un palo carbonizzato di forma rettangolare. Il muro fu evidentemente assicurato per mezzo di pali verticali, che forse erano ancorati gli uni agli altri, conferendo all'intera struttura maggiore stabilità.

## II. Le Mura in argilla e legno (periodo laziale IIA)

In un secondo momento il muro in pise' fu allestito da un'impalcatura consistente in pali verticali, probabilmente fissati con assi orizzontali (*figg.* 2-4). Tale incorniciatura strutturale doveva avere la funzione di fronteggiare lo sfaldamento della struttura. L'interspazio tra le impalcature verticali fu probabilmente riempito tramite larghe pietre, venendo a creare una solida facciata esterna in pietra. Questa tecnica costruttiva può essere messa a confronto con fortificazioni in pietra e travi, caratteristiche delle strutture difensive tardo celtiche rinvenute al di nord delle Alpi: si pensi ad esempio al cosiddetto *murus gallicus* (Pfostenschlitzmauer).[8]

## III. Le Mura in pietra (periodo laziale IIB)

In questa terza fase costruttiva il muro in argilla e travi divenne il nucleo di una nuova fortificazione allorché la cinta fu nuovamente ricostruita (*figg.* 3-4). Durante questo processo i costruttori si rifecero alla tecnica precedentemente adottata in pali lignei interni a sostegno di un muro in terra battuta. Tali pali tuttavia, questa volta avevano un diametro generalmente più ampio ed insistevano più solidamente in fosse di fondazione riempite di pietrame. Così come in fase I, queste

*Fig. 2. Saggio B. Muro in argilla visto da ovest alla fine dello scavo in 2014. Foto: Heide Behrens, DAI Rom, D-DAI-ROM-2014.1526.*

*Fig. 3. Saggio B visto da Ovest con il muro in pietra dopo la campagna di scavo di 2012. Nel piano inferiore si riconosce la fornace della bottega di metalli. Foto: Daniela Gauss, DAI Rom, D-DAI-ROM-2012.3191.*

pietre erano informi e ammassate irregolarmente le une sulle altre. La larghezza del muro venne incrementata ulteriormente raggiungendo circa i 5 metri.

*IV. Le Mura ad aggere (periodo laziale III)*

Nell' VIII secolo questo muro venne coperto da un aggere molto più massiccio. La copertura in pietre di tufo non lavorate obliterò la struttura precedente (*fig. 4*). L'aggere risulta essere costituito da tre elementi principali: il paramento settentrionale in pietre di dimensioni più grandi, il terrapieno inclinato verso l'insediamento, che nel nostro caso consiste soprattutto in pietre alloggiate abbastanza regolarmente e circondate da poca terra argillosa, infine nel muro di controscarpa quale terzo elemento. La larghezza complessiva della costruzione misura 10 m ca.

*V. Le Mura a conci (VI sec. a. C.)*

La fase successiva all' aggere consiste in una modernizzazione della facciata (*fig. 5*). Senza alcun legame costruttivo, direttamente davanti all'aggere venne eretto un muro dal paramento regolare e ben fatto, in blocchi squadrati. Questo muro, chiamato il 'muro bello', è in blocchi di tufo rettangolari che presentano bordi lisciati e facce lavorate a scalpello. I blocchi, irregolari in lunghezza, hanno margini smussati da un taglio netto a forma di V (*fig. 6*), mentre le superfici laterali di contatto presentano anatirosi.

La datazione di questo muro è problematica, in quanto esso è impostato sulla roccia e non disponiamo di materiale proveniente da un'eventuale trincea di fondazione. Inoltre sul lato meridionale della città mancano i piani di frequentazione attigui al muro. Tali strati non sono conservati in quanto l'attuale piano di campagna si trova al di sotto del livello antico di questa fase. Non è quindi possibile definire con la sola stratigrafia il momento della costruzione del 'muro bello' – a cui però il muro ad aggere fornisce un terminus post quem.

*VI. Il rinforzo delle Mura a conci (III sec. a. C.)*

Come fase più recente si incontra una riparazione effettuata davanti al muro bello (*figg. 4, 5, 7*), in

*Fig. 4. I saggi A e B sull'Arx di Gabii dopo la campagna di scavo dell'autunno di 2011. Foto: Stefan Kiel, Magdeburg.*

*Fig. 5. Le mura settentrionali dell'Arx di Gabii viste da Nord dopo la ripulitura di 2011. Foto: Daniela Gauss, DAI Rom, D-DAI-ROM-2011.2695.*

*Fig. 6. Dettaglio delle Mura a conci: margini smussati a forma di V. Foto: Daniela Gauss, DAI Rom, 2007.*

cui vennero utilizzati gli antichi blocchi del muro evidentemente distrutto in alcune parti. In gran fretta vennero collocati l'uno sopra l'altro, tanto che per esempio gli incassi erano visibili sul lato esterno. Dagli strati creati durante la costruzione del muro provengono molti materiali, sufficienti a permetterne una classificazione cronologica. L'ultima riparazione fu, dunque, realizzata all'inizio del III sec. a.C.[9]

Questa datazione fornisce allo stesso tempo il *terminus ante quem* per la costruzione del muro in blocchi squadrati. Tuttavia, negli strati smossi nel III sec. sembrano prevalere materiali di VII e VI secolo, mentre mancano reperti di V e IV sec. A mio avviso questo va interpretato come indizio del fatto che il "muro bello" vada datato piuttosto al VI secolo, anche perché dagli strati più bassi provengono frammenti ceramici risalenti al medesimo.[10]

DESCRIZIONE DEL FOSSATO PIÙ ANTICO DELLA FORTIFICAZIONE MERIDIONALE (VI SEC. A. C.)

A sud del grande insediamento, che occupava un'area di ca. 75 ettari, abbiamo svolto 4 campagne di scavo dal 2011 in poi. Tramite carotaggi e prospezioni geofisiche siamo riusciti a dimostrare che anche a sud dell'insediamento molto probabilmente esisteva una grande opera difensiva parimenti costruita secondo il sistema dell'aggere.[11] Per ragioni legate alla strategia di intervento, e considerata l'ampiezza della cinta muraria, abbiamo deciso di scavare solo i fossati difensivi.

Il saggio ha raggiunto una lunghezza di 36 metri con una profondità, in alcuni punti, di più di 3 metri. Abbiamo potuto individuare almeno 10 fossati di cui presenteró qui solo la fase più antica (*fig. 8*).

Possiamo presumere in questa zona un insediamento stratigraficamente anteriore al primo fossato già in avanzata età del Ferro, vale a dire durante la fase laziale IV. Il primo fossato I (US 106) fu scavato all'inizio del sesto secolo tagliando uno stato argilloso di colore molto scuro. Il fossato I Nord ha forma trapezoidale con pareti ripide e fondo piatto ("Sohlgraben"). Forma e larghezza sono confrontabili con quelle della fortificazione ad aggere di Ficana,[12] datata tra la metà dell' VIII sec. a.C. e il VI sec. a.C.

CONFRONTI PER LE PRIME FASI DAL DECIMO ALL'OTTAVO SECOLO AVANTI CRISTO

L'osservazione delle strutture difensive dell'Italia centrale induce a ipotizzare che furono escogitate soluzioni diversificate a dimostrazione di una certa sperimentazione sia nelle tecniche costruttive sia nei materiali. Nel caso di Colle Rotondo, ad esempio, vi era probabilmente un'impalcatura lignea interna costruita al fine di fornire ulteriore contenimento alla terragettatavi sopra.[13] Il muro ai piedi del Palatino viene ricostruitocon pali lignei interni, i quali erano circondati da terra e pietrame.[14] A Veio, invece, sembra sia stato praticato un consolidamento dell'aggere per mezzo di pietre posizionate verticalmente.[15] A differenza di queste soluzioni, che hanno come scopo il consolidamento di masse di terra, troviamo ad Acqua Acetosa,[16] a Castel di Decima,[17] a Castellina di Marangone[18] e, forse, anche a La Rustica,[19] muri in pietre addossati a pendii. Muri in pietra si ritrovano anche a Lavinio,[20] non appoggiati ad un pendio, bensì costruttivamente staticamente autonomi.

Una concezione omogenea, e generalmente valida, per le fasi Laziale II e III non è dimostrata.[21] Piuttosto si sperimentava per mezzo di materiali a disposizione quali pietre, terra e legno, realizzando così diverse strutture.

*Fig. 7. Le mura settentrionali dell'Arx di Gabii viste da Est dopo la pulitura di 2007 (A = anathyrosis; O = orlatura). Foto: Daniela Gauss, DAI Rom, 2007.*

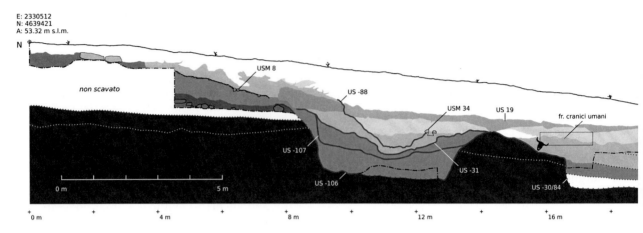

*Fig. 8. Sezione orientale del saggio D con i diversi fossati. Disegno: Eva Träder, Projekt Gabii.*

## Confronti laziali per l'aggere

A partire dall'ottavo secolo si diffonde, in particolare in ambito latino, una soluzione difensiva riscontrabile in diversi luoghi, vale a dire l'aggere.[22] Questo consiste in due elementi principali: un ampio fossato e un imponente terrapieno, la cui parte superiore è inclinata verso l'insediamento. In aggiunta, possono esservi un muro di contenimento lungo il lato esterno dell'insediamento, e un muro di controscarpa ai piedi dell'aggere. L'esempio più noto sono le cosiddette mura Serviane di Roma.[23] In Italia Centrale i predecessori sul piano cronologico sono di solito impiantati su livelli tufacei e seguono analoghi principi, così come dimostrano i casi di Gabii,[24] Lavinio[25] o Anzio.[26] Il sistema difensivo basato sull'aggere ben si adattava in modo particolare a cinte murarie afferenti ad aree di ampie dimensioni. L'aggere poteva essere costruito sia in piano sia in avvallamenti naturali, in situazioni, quindi, che non necessitavano di pendenze. Per l'erezione di tali opere venivano risparmiate costruzioni a ridosso dei pendii, mentre i cumuli di terra erano resi più stabili e assicurati per mezzo di muri spesso realizzati in blocchi che potevano essere leggermente sbozzati.

## Confronti e classificazione delle mura in opera quadrata nel sesto secolo

L'utilizzo di conci, quindi di pietre lavorate e preparate, rappresenta una notevole innovazione che si può constatare in molte località nello stesso arco di tempo, cioè nel corso del sesto secolo.[27] Questa tecnica permetteva la costruzione di mura in opera quadrata già note in alcune colonie greche occidentali, come Megara Hyblea,[28] ma anche Leontini,[29] Selinunte[30] e in particlare Cuma.[31] È significativo il fatto che l'opera quadrata schermava sovente gli aggeri: esempi ne sono Lavinio,[32] Anzio[33] e Castel di Decima.[34] Non è, quindi, la situazione topografica ad accomunare i muri in blocchi riscontrabili in Italia Centrale con quelli delle regioni meridionali e della Sicilia, piuttosto: a) una simile lavorazione della pietra e b) un'analoga messa in opera dei blocchi, che rendeva l'effetto ottico dei muri molto affine.

Nella presentazione della quinta fase costruttiva sono stati già menzionati i dettagli caratteristici come gli angoli smussati, l'anatirosi e il bugnato, così come la superficie lisciata (*figg. 6, 7*). A tali tracce si aggiungano poi fori per il sollevamento e incisioni sulle superfici superiori dei blocchi, indizio rispettivamente dell'uso da parte degli operai di inserire assi in ferro e da parte dei capomastri di apporre graffiti. Inoltre i filari rientrano progressivamente, cosicché il muro mostri una lieve pendenza verso l'interno, ovvero dalla parte della città (muro a scarpa). A Megara Hyblea,[35] e allo stesso modo a Cuma,[36] incontriamo questo particolare nella cinta settentrionale. La pendenza del muro verso l'interno infatti serviva a controbilanciare la pressione del cumulo terroso evitandone dunque il possibile crollo o scivolamento.

Entrambe le messe in opera sono costituite da semplici filari con conci posizionati di taglio e, come il cosiddetto 'muro bello' di Gabii, non sono erette in opera isodoma. Sebbene i blocchi si distinguano in lunghezza, i giunti verticali non aderiscono, in modo tale da conferire una buona stabilità. Sia a Megara sia a Cuma si riscontrano angoli smussati, che come l'anatirosi sulle facce di

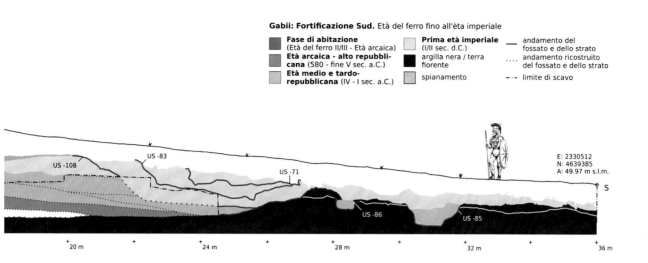

giunzione, garantiscono un migliore adattamento delle componenti edilizie in fase di messa in opera. A Megara Hyblea e a Cuma si può riconoscere, inoltre, nella superficie superiore dei singoli blocchi e talvolta anche in quella laterale, una sorta di orlatura che facilitava l'aderenza tra i componenti edilizi. I medesimi dettagli sono riscontrabili anche a Gabii (*fig. 7*). Il posizionamento delle pietre e le indicazioni circa la messa in opera dei blocchi rivelano la presenza di maestranze esperte ed specializzate. A Gabii il principio della costruzione modulare con pietre lavorate probabilmente non si sviluppò progressivamente bensì fu introdotto in forma già elaborata.

Almeno a Gabii non è riconiscibile un'evoluzione lenta o un processo graduale. Appaiono tutti gli elementi insieme e la lavorazione dei blocchi è subito su un alto livello di qualità. Può darsi che abbiamo da fare con una lacuna nel record archeologico, ma é più probabile un repentino cambio di tradizione tecnologica.

ALCUNE LINEE TEORICHE SULLA LA TRASMISSIONE DI CONOSCENZE TECNOLOGICHE

Per poter redigere una classificazione delle murature qui presentate dal punto di vista tecnologico, vorrei offrire alcune riflessioni di carattere generale. Per tecnologia si intende la scienza della trasformazione della materia prima in prodotto, nel nostro caso la scienza della trasformazione dei materiali da costruzione in cinta muraria.

Volendo articolare le modalità in cui questo sapere tecnologico si possa trasmettere da un posto ad un altro, è possibile distinguere tre livelli principali, i quali non si escludono a vicenda, bensì si integrano reciprocamente.

a) Il sapere può essere trasportato da individui in movimento, quindi attraverso migrazioni su grande o piccola scala. In tale caso dunque il sapere "viaggia" insieme con le persone.
b) Il sapere può essere conservato in un medium, ad esempio su supporti scritti o illustrati, e dunque viaggiare tramite il medium stesso.
c) Il sapere può essere letto e appreso dal prodotto stesso, in quanto inerente ad esso. In tale caso il sapere tecnologico si diffonde con il diffondersi del prodotto stesso. La cinta con i suoi blocchi lavorati possa essere stata copiata attraverso la diretta osservazione.

Per comprendere meglio i complessi meccanismi di diffusione/ricezione delle conoscenze tecniche è opportuno distinguere due livelli: quello del sapere teorico e quello della realizzazione pratica, ovvero la competenza e abilità nel realizzare tecnicamente un determinato prodotto. È molto probabile che il sapere teorico inerente la tecnica di lavorazione litica e relativa messa in opera sia stato "salvato", per dirla in termini moderni, in forma di testi, piante, disegni e modelli che viaggiavano con capomastri e architetti, ma ovviamente non disponiamo delle relative testimonianze archeologiche in proposito (caso b). È altrettanto ipotizzabile una imitazione di concezioni difensive e materiali da costruzione attraverso l'osservazione in loco. Ma probabilmente il know how specializzato nella lavorazione, ossia la competenza artigianale, può essere trasmesso esclusivamente tramite contatto diretto tra maestranze, ovvero attraverso forme di apprendistato (caso a).

Indizi di trasmissione tecnologica avvenuta per contatto diretto tra artigiani sono rintraccia-

*Fig. 9. Le mura settentrionali dell'Arx di Gabii viste da Nord. Relievo: Antje Werner, Projekt Gabii.*

bili in specifici dettagli della lavorazione litica quali smussature, anatirosi, orlature e altri dettagli relativi alla messa in opera come l'elevazione a scarpa, l'inserimento di assi, le incisioni e i segni di riconoscimento apposti sui blocchi. Quanto più specifico appare il dettaglio artigianale, tanto meno appare probabile un meccanismo di semplice imitazione, una copiatura avvenuta tramite osservazione diretta (transfer legato al prodotto, caso c). Altrettanto improbabile appare l'invenzione autonoma di un perfetto equivalente, di conseguenza tanto più plausibile diventa il transfer del know how per mezzo di contatto diretto fra le persone. I dettagli della lavorazione della pietra rivelano piuttosto l'utilizzo di utensili e attrezzi idonei i quali, così come il sapere teorico e la competenza pratica, venivano trasmessi dal trasferente al ricevente.

Per quanto riguarda Gabii da queste riflessioni possiamo quindi ipotizzare che alle fasi di costruzione delle mura difensive in blocchi abbiano partecipato operai e capomastri altamente specializzati (caso a). Poiché i confronti che seguono afferiscono a contesti dalla Campania e dalla Sicilia, cioè da colonie greche occidentali, la trasmissione delle conoscenze nel caso dell'opera quadrata avveniva attraverso artigiani greci o attraverso artigiani formati da o in contesti greci.[37] Mi sembra non troppo audace ipotizzare che le autorità gabine abbiano affidato la costruzione della cinta a maestranze alloctone (greche in questo caso) con lo scopo di fornire alla porzione settentrionale della città un aspetto più "moderno". Dal punto di vista difensiva questo muro non è neccessario visto che il muro d'aggere è molto stabile. Di conseguenza questa parte della mura crea solo una facciata nuova, è solo un ornamento. Probabilmente fu costruito per motivi estetici mostrando che anche i Gabini si sono resi conto della nuova moda di costruire alla grecque.

OSSERVAZIONI CONCLUSIVE SULL'URBANIZZAZIONE

Grazie alle nuove competenze artigianali e al nuovo sapere teorico e dei suoi presupposti matematici[38] che è possibile postulare, furono rese attuabili innovative soluzioni costruttive, che superavano le forme edilizie tradizionali. Ad esempio, il principio modulare secondo unità (edilizie) regolari e reciprocamente complementari che si riflette nell'opera quadrata, venne realizzato anche nelle piante degli edifici.[39]

Ipotizziamo che l'erezione di strutture quadrangolari sia sostanzialmente connessa con l'apprendimento di tecniche edilizie artigianali e i loro modelli matematico-teorici. Le conseguenze di tale trasmissione tecnologica, in ambito architettonico, non vanno certo sopravvalutate. Il nuovo sapere teorico e le nuove capacità artigianali vanno verosimilmente di pari passo e fungevano insieme come catalizzatore di una nuova ostentazione. Nel sesto secolo seguirono i primi complessi edilizi monumentali così come impianti stradali e disposizione degli spazi urbani conformi a una progettazione.[40]

Come noto, la ricerca scientifica sui processi di urbanizzazione del Latium, in particolare di Roma, risale già a tempi remoti. Essa ci ha richiesto un'intensa discussione e nel corso degli ultimi decenni si sono configurate posizioni addirittura opposte a riguardo.[41] Un punto cruciale nel dibattito concerne il ruolo giocato nella prima Età del Ferro da persone alloctone inseritesi tra le popolazioni del Latium. Le opposte posizioni sono quindi, da una parte, l'ipotesi di una 'indigenous urbanisation', relativamente disgiunta da influssi esterni e sorta organicamente in seno alla cultura laziale. Dall'altra parte, invece, si sottolinea la convinzione di una 'foreign urbanisation', intesa come diretta conseguenza del decisivo impulso, per l'urbanizzazione del Latium, dei vicini Etruschi, Greci e Fenici.

Ritornando al caso di Gabii, è da constatare da un lato l'alta datazione delle prime fortificazioni: le mura in tufo sono un elemento costitutivo della fase protourbana del Lazio. Dall'altra parte, è necessario sottolineare l'influsso del mondo della Magna Grecia sulla lavorazione della pietra e sull'architettura a partire del sesto secolo.

È tuttavia plausibile una conciliazione tra le due posizioni grazie alle aggiornate sequenze cronologiche fornite da dati recenti:[42] da una parte sicuramente i contatti con l'esterno hanno inciso nel processo di urbanizzazione, dall'altra parte lo sviluppo all'interno degli agglomerati era in fieri già nella prima età del Ferro. Una certa autonomia di tali processi a livello locale nel Lazio dalla tarda età del Bronzo va considerata altrettanto decisiva quanto l'effetto catalizzatore di culture esterne – sul piano delle idee, del know-how tecnologico nell'architettura e nell'artigianato – che influenzarono profondamente il processo di urbanizzazione.

NOTE

Trad. Carla Cioffi (italiano), Eva Träder (inglese).
[1] Bietti Sestieri 2014, 134.
[2] Bietti Sestieri 1992.
[3] Guaitoli 1981.
[4] Il progetto è stato finanziato dalla Deutsche Forschungsgemeinschaft e accolto dall'Università di Bonn nella persona di Martin Bentz che ha condiviso e sostenuto sempre l'iniziativa. Ringrazio di tutto cuore l'allora assessore della Soprintendenza di Roma Stefano Musco prematuramente scomparso per il suo supporto scientifico e l'aiuto pratico-organizzativo.
[5] Vorrei esprimere la mia sincera gratitudine ai curatori di questo volume Marijke Gnade e Martina Revello Lami che ringrazio per aver accolto il mio contributo.
[6] I risultati sono il frutto di un intenso scambio di informazioni e discussioni avvenute durante e dopo le campagne di scavo. Responsabile per la supervisione dei saggi erano Petra Fleischer, Sandra Münzel, Eva Träder e Alexander von Helden. Il laboratorio dei reperti é stato gestito da Robinson Krämer, Lucia Lecce, Alessia Mancini e Marzia Zingaretti. Si veda a questo proposito Helas 2010, Helas 2013, Helas 2014, Helas 2016, Helas 2018.
[7] Per la datazione, basata sull'analisi del materiale ceramico proveniente dagli scavi, rimandiamo alla pubblicazione finale dello scavo attualmente in preparazione. Per quanto riguarda il problema della cronologia laziale: Nijboer 2005; Bietti Sestieri - De Santis 2008. In questa sede ci atteniamo alle sequenze riviste e di conseguenza poniamo la nostra prima fase già nel decimo secolo (Laz. IIA.: 1020-900 a.C.).
[8] Ballmer 2018.
[9] Helas 2016, 99-100.
[10] Helas 2016, fig. 16.
[11] Helas 2016, figg. 17, 19, 20.
[12] Fischer-Hansen - Algreen-Ussing 2013; Fischer-Hansen 2016, fig. 9.
[13] Guidi - Nomi 2014; Cifani - Guidi 2016, 114, figg. 8, 9.
[14] Bruno 2012, 220.
[15] Boitani - Biagi - Neri 2016, 24.
[16] Bedini 2016, fig. 14, 15.
[17] Guaitoli 1979.
[18] Fontaine 2016.
[19] De Santis - Musco 2016.
[20] Jaia 2016.
[21] Bartoloni - Michetti 2014, Fontaine - Helas 2016.
[22] Miller 1995, 13.
[23] Nijboer 2018, 117.
[24] cfr. anche Fabbri - Musco 2016, fig. 2.
[25] Jaia 2016, fig. 5, C1-C4.
[26] Cifani - Guidi 2016, 122.
[27] Gatti - Palombi 2016, 240.
[28] Gras - Treziny - Broise 2004.
[29] Rizza 1957, 69 fig. 10; Frasca 2009, 68 tavv. V, VI.
[30] Mertens 2003, 71-72.
[31] Fratta 2002; D'Agostini - Fratta - Malpede 2005; D'Agostini 2014.
[32] Jaia 2016, fig. 3-5.
[33] Cifani - Guidi 2016, 121-123, fig. 16-17.
[34] Miller 1995, 371.
[35] Gras - Treziny - Broise 2004, 271 fig. 298, 299.
[36] Fratta 2002, 52, tratto 604, fig. 25 "Entrambe le cortine hanno un profilo a scarpa ed i blocchi presentano un trattamento molto accurato delle superfici; infatti su entrambe le facce a vista ciascun blocco ha una fascia lievemente ribassata presso i margini e un bugnato centrale con un trattamento a spina di pesce. Essi presentano inoltre un'accentuata *anathyrosis* concava sulle testate dei blocchi, con fascia levigata presso i margini."; 59, tratti 803 e 808, fig. 29. - D'Agostini - Fratta - Malpede 2005, 23.
[37] Müller Wiener 1988, 41. 72. 73.
[38] Pitagora di Samo che traslocò a Crotone verso 530, ma probabilmente egli fu solo un personaggio famoso. Verosimilmente la matematica era già ben conosciuta dai Greci formati in generale, visto che furono in grado di contruire città a strighe e case a blocchi giá nel settimo secolo, come per esempio a Megara Hyblaia. cfr. Treziny 2016.
[39] Lindenhout 2016.
[40] Lindenhout 1997.
[41] Fulminante - Stoddart 2010, 12-14, 17-18.
[42] Fontaine - Helas 2016.

BIBLIOGRAFIA

Ballmer, A. 2018, The Introduction of the Pfostenschlitz Concept in the Fortification Architecture of the North-West Alpine Hallstatt Circle, in Ballmer/Fernández-Götz/Mielke 2018, 135-146.
Ballmer, A./M. Fernández-Götz/D.P. Mielke 2018 (ed.), *Understanding ancient fortifications. Between Regionality and Connectivity*, Oxford.
Bartoloni, G./L.M. Michetti 2014, *Mura di legno, mura di terra, mura di pietra: fortificazioni nel Mediterraneo antico*. Convegno internazionale a Roma = ScAnt 19,2/3.
Bedini, A. 2016, Laurentina Acqua Acetosa (Roma). Il sistema difensivo dell'abitato protostorico: i dati di scavo 1976-1980, in Fontaine/Helas 2016, 139-176.
Bietti Sestieri, A.M. (ed.) 1992, *La necropoli laziale di Osteria dell'Osa*, Roma.
Bietti Sestieri, A.M. 2014, *L'Italia nell'età del bronzo e del ferro: dalle palafitte a Romolo (2200 - 700 a.C.)*, Roma.
Bietti Sestieri, A.M./A. De Santis 2008, Relative and Absolute chronology of Latium vetus from the Late

Bronze Age to the transition to the Orientalizing Period, in D. Brandherm/M. Trachsel, *A New Dawn for the Dark Age*. Convegno Lisabon 2006, Oxford, 119-133.

Boitani, F./F. Biagi/S. Neri 2016, Le fortificazioni a Veio tra Porta Nord-Ovest e Porta Caere, in Fontaine/Helas 2016, 19-35.

Bruno, D. 2012, Regione X. Palatium, in A. Carandini (ed.), *Atlante di Roma antica. Biografia e ritratti della città*, Milano, 215-280.

Cifani, G./A. Guidi 2016, Le fortificazioni del territorio di Anzio, in Fontaine/Helas 2016, 111-124.

D'Agostini, B. 2014, Le fortificazioni di Cuma, in Bartoloni/Michetti 2014, 207-227.

D'Agostini, B./D. Andrea (ed.) 2002, *Cuma. Nuove forme di intervento per lo studio del sito antico*. Atti della Giornata di Studio, Napoli 2001 (AIONArch 14), Napoli.

D'Agostini, B./F. Fratta/V. Malpede 2005, *Cuma. Le Fortificazioni 1. Lo Scavo 1994-2002*, Napoli.

De Santis, A. 2016, Vecchi e nuovi dati sui sistemi difensivi della città latina di Collatia, in Fontaine/Helas 2016, 125-138.

Fabbri, M./S. Musco 2016, Nuove ricerche sulle fortificazioni di Gabii. I tratti nord-orientale e settentrionale, in Fontaine/Helas 2016, 71-90.

Fischer-Hansen, T. 2016, Ficana (Monte Cugno). The fortifications from the Early History of the Settlement, in Fontaine/Helas 2016, 177-198.

Fischer-Hansen, T./G. Algreen-Ussing 2013, *Excavations at Ficana III. The iron Age Fortifications*, Rome.

Fontaine, P. 2016, Castellina del Marangore. Sondages stratigraphiques sur l'einceinte «Bastianelli», in Fontaine/Helas 2016, 51-70.

Fontaine, P./S. Helas (ed.) 2016, *Le fortificazioni arcaiche del Latium Vetus e dell'Etruria meridionale (IX-VI sec. a. C.). Stratigrafia, cronologia e urbanizzazione*. Convegno Roma 2013, Bruxelles/Roma.

Frasca, M. 2009, *Leontinoi. Archeologia di una colonia greca*, Roma.

Fratta, F. 2002, Per una rilettura del sistema di fortificazioni di Cuma, in D'Agostini/Andrea 2002, 21-73.

Fulminante, F./S. Stoddart 2010, Formazione politica a confronto in Etruria e Latium vetus: status quaestionis e nuove prospettive di ricerca, *BollArch* Vol. Speciale. Roma 2008 - International Congress of Classical Archaeology, 11-22.

Gatti, S./D. Palombi 2016, Le città del Lazio con mura poligonali: questioni di cronologia e urbanistica, in Fontaine/Helas 2016, 233-249.

Gra, M./H. Treziny/H. Broise 2004, *Mégara Hyblaea 5. La ville archaïque*, Roma.

Guaitoli, M. 1979, L'abitato di Castel di Decima, ArchLaz II (QuadAEI 3), 37-40.

Guaitoli, M. 1981, Gabii. *Osservazioni sulle fasi di sviluppo dell'abitato*, Quaderni dell'Istituto di topografia antica 10, 23-57.

Guidi, A./F. Nomi 2014, Colle Rotondo (Anzio, RM): Un aggere difensivo protostorico con armatura lignea, ScAnt 19.2-3, 35-38.

Helas, S. 2010, Prospezioni geofisiche a Gabii: interpretazioni e prospettive per uno studio delle mura, *Lazio & Sabina* 6, 249-258.

Helas, S. 2013, Gabii/Latium. Die Befestigungen von archaischer bis in mittelrepublikanische Zeit. Erster Vorbericht, *Kölner und Bonner Archaeologica* 3, 145-166.

Helas, S. 2014, Gabii. Gli impianti difensivi dell'insediamento urbano (VIII-III. sec. a.C.). ScAnt 19.2-3, 234-241.

Helas, S. 2016, Nuove ricerche sulle fortificazioni di Gabii. Le indagini sul versante orientale dell'acropoli e sul lato meridionale della città, in Fontaine/Helas 2016, 91-109.

Helas, S. 2018, The Iron Age Fortifications of Gabii/Latium (Italy), in Ballmer/Fernández-Götz/Mielke 2018, 123-133.

Jaia, A.M. 2016, Le mura di Lavinium, in Fontaine/Helas 2016, 199-212.

Mertens, D. 2003, *Selinus 1. Die Stadt und ihre Mauern*, Mainz.

Miller, M. 1995, *Befestigungsanlagen in Italien vom 8. bis 3. Jahrhundert vor Chr.*, Hamburg.

Müller-Wiener, W. 1988, *Griechisches Bauwesen in der Antike*, München.

Njiboer, A.J. 2005, La cronologia assoluta dell'età del Ferro nel Mediterraneo, dibattito sui metodi e sui risultati, in G. Bartoloni/F. Delpino (ed.), *Oriente e occidente. Metodi e discipline a confronto. Riflessioni sulla cronologia dell'età del ferro italiana*. Convegno Roma 2003 (=Mediterranea 1), Roma, 527-556.

Nijboer, A.J. 2018, Fortifications in and Around Rome, 950-300 BC, in Ballmer/Fernández-Götz/Mielke 2018, 111-122.

Rizza, G. 1957, Leontini. Scavi e ricerche degli anni 1954-1955, *BdA* 42, 63 -73.

Van 't Lindenhout, E. 1997, Architectural and Spatial Organization of the First Towns in the Coastal Plain of Latium, 6th Century B.C. Towards a General Scheme, *ActaHyp* 7, 297-315.

Van 't Lindenhout, E. 2016, Taking courage: from huts to houses. Reflections on changes in early archaic Architecture in Latium vetus (Central Italy), in P. Attema/J. Seubers/S. Willemsen, W. (ed.), *Early states, territories and settlements in protohistoric Central Italy*. Convegno Groningen 2013, Eelde, 143-152.

# Il santuario monumentale nell'insediamento marittimo di Pyrgi
## Edilizia e procedimenti costruttivi

*Barbara Belelli Marchesini*

*Abstract*

*The excavations funded by the Sapienza University of Rome since 1957 have focussed the southern district of Pyrgi's settlement (late VIIth-IIIrd century BC), which is featured by the arrival of the main road connecting the mother- town Caere to the coastline. The district includes two different sanctuaries (the Monumental Sanctuary of Uni-Astarte, a demetriac cult place dedicated to the couple of deities Śur/Śuri and Cavatha) and several buildings- some of them provided with decorated roofs –erected along a pebbled road that departs from the Caere-Pyrgi and leads towards the harbor. Archaeological evidence allows a full analysis of the architectural features and building techniques of monumental, public and private buildings/infrastructures of Caere's outpost, based on the choice of local and/or imported raw material, shedding light on the urban asset of the maritime settlement itself.*

Introduzione

Il Santuario Monumentale di Pyrgi è un contesto di fondamentale importanza e imprescindibile punto di riferimento per lo studio dell'architettura templare di epoca preromana, grazie alla puntuale pubblicazione degli scavi condotti dalla Sapienza a partire dal 1957[1] con l'accurata analisi delle strutture offerta da Giovanni Colonna, e alla ricostruzione volumetrica dei templi A e B, ottenuta attraverso calcoli strutturali basati sulle indicazioni di Vitruvio e proposta sotto forma di modellini in scala 1:50.[2]

In anni recenti, grazie al coinvolgimento della Facoltà di Architettura della Sapienza di Roma, è stato possibile realizzare la modellazione in formato tridimensionale dei due edifici templari e del loro apparato decorativo,[3] finalizzata non soltanto a fornire un contributo per un approfondimento di studio, ma anche al *Cultural Heritage*, essendo la conservazione del santuario sempre più minacciata dall'ingressione marina. Il lavoro di virtualizzazione ha interessato l'elevato degli edifici, utilizzando come base di partenza i dati editi e le planimetrie in scala 1:50 realizzati all'epoca degli scavi dallo studio Di Grazia. Nel 2017, in seguito a un intervento straordinario di pulizia che ha riportato entrambi gli edifici a una ottimale condizione di visibilità, è stato inoltre possibile eseguire la documentazione tridimensionale delle fondazioni, tramite l'impiego del *laser scanning* e una battuta fotografica da drone,[4] ed effettuare misurazioni e osservazioni sulla loro tessitura.

L'attività di scavo della Sapienza ha inoltre permesso di inserire il Santuario all'interno di una più ampia cornice topografica, attraverso l'esplorazione dell'area santuariale a carattere demetriaco dedicata alla coppia di divinità Suri e Cavatha sul versante meridionale (1985-2008), e della fascia a N del Tempio A (2009-2018)[5] (*fig. 1b*).

In questo contributo, intendo discutere in primo luogo il rapporto tra il Santuario e il comprensorio archeologico, in termini di pianificazione degli spazi e di scelte edilizie operate nei diversi settori; quindi ricordare il significato dei templi A e B nei confronti dell'edilizia di età arcaica, con particolare riferimento all'Etruria; infine, trattare sinteticamente gli aspetti progettuali e costruttivi dei due edifici, basandomi sull'osservazione dei resti conservati e proponendo qualche piccola novità rispetto alla progettazione e ai procedimenti di cantiere. Non intendo in questa sede occuparmi delle coperture che, con parte degli elevati, sono state oggetto di uno smontaggio sistematico negli anni intorno all'impianto della colonia romana (ca. 273 a.C.), fattore che ha consentito di ricostruire in maniera puntuale gli apparati decorativi.

1. Il contesto topografico

Il complesso santuariale di Pyrgi si colloca all'estremità meridionale di un insediamento marittimo (10 ha) fondato verso la fine del VII sec.a.C., quale principale scalo portuale di Caere (*fig. 1a*).

L'insediamento era collegato alla città-madre da una strada glareata larga 10 metri che, dopo aver percorso obliquamente la pianura costiera con un drittofilo, descriveva una curva assumendo un andamento parallelo alla costa e assolvendo la doppia funzione di limite sul lato dell'entroterra e di asse generatore della viabilità urbana. La conoscenza complessiva dell'insediamento si basa sull'osservazione della sezione occasionale progressivamente intagliata dall'erosione marina:[6] l'abitato non presentava un impianto urbanistico regolare, ma condizionato dall'andamento della linea di costa, e si articolava in due settori principali, delimitati da strade glareate (largh. 350/380) convergenti verso il litorale;[7] il settore settentrionale dell'insediamento, sede di edifici pubblici e interpretabile come *arx*, è stato significativamente ricalcato dall'impianto della colonia romana del 273a.C.. Nei due settori si osservano sino a cinque livelli di case, separate da strade in terra battuta (largh. cm 200) e *ambitus*. Maggiori informazioni sul tessuto insediativo derivano

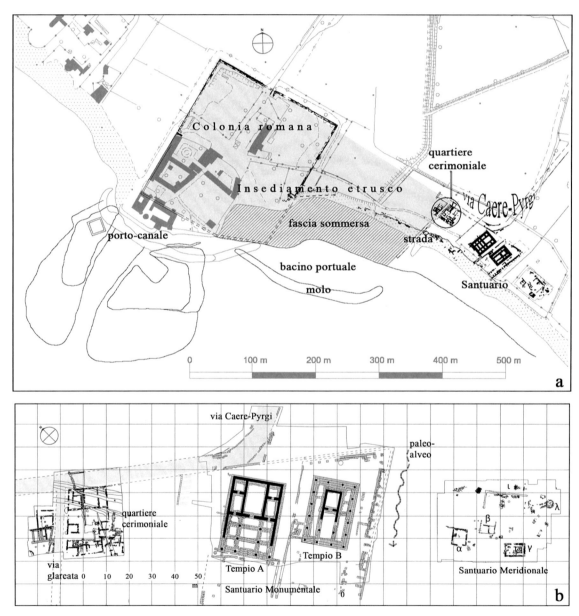

*Fig. 1a-b a) Pyrgi. Il comprensorio archeologico di Pyrgi; b) Settore di indagine dell'Università La Sapienza, presso l'arrivo della via Caere-Pyrgi (archivio Sapienza).*

dallo scavo condotto a partire dal 2009 a nord del Tempio A, in corrispondenza del raccordo tra il tratto urbano della Caere-Pyrgi e una strada glareata diretta verso il bacino orientale del porto (*Figg. 1b, 2a-b*).[8] Il raccordo non ortogonale dei due percorsi ha condizionato l'assetto degli isolati contigui, occupati da edifici che, impiantati nei decenni finali del VII sec.a.C., hanno svolto a partire dalla metà del secolo successivo un ruolo di rappresentanza, sottolineato dalla presenza di tetti decorati con sistemi di tipo campano e ceretano (530-520 a.C.) e dalla reiterazione di atti rituali intesi a sottolinearne le trasformazioni planimetriche e altimetriche. In particolare, sul versante meridionale della strada è stato portato alla luce un complesso edilizio a pianta trapezoidale (mq 550) che, nella fase di V sec., appare incentrato su un'area cortilizia e include sul lato orientale una serie di vani preceduti da un portico, con basi di colonna in tufo grigio. Sul lato opposto della strada, spicca la presenza di un edificio bipartito a pianta trapezoidale con fondazione in blocchi di tufo, per il quale è stata proposta l'interpretazione di casa-torre (*fig. 2c*), impiantato negli anni intorno al 500 a.C. ma preceduto da un edificio a sviluppo assiale.

Allo stato attuale delle indagini, una fascia di rispetto sembra separare il quartiere in corso di scavo nei confronti del distretto sacro, che si sviluppa in corrispondenza della curva della strada di collegamento con Caere.

Com'è noto, il distretto sacro di Pyrgi comprende due santuari, fisicamente separati da un corso d'acqua che raccoglieva le acque di una sorgente perenne dall'immediato entroterra, e nettamente contrapposti tanto dal punto di vista architettonico quanto del regime del culto[9] (*fig. 1b*).

Il Santuario Monumentale, frutto di un ambizioso progetto edilizio concepito per esprimere il ruolo politico e commerciale svolto da Caere a livello internazionale, fondato e donato ad Astarte intorno al 510 a.C. dal re-tiranno Thefarie Velianas, è stato inizialmente collocato nella fascia prossima al corso d'acqua, occupata in precedenza da sacelli, impiantando un muro di témenos di forma allungata, aperto sul lato dell'entroterra con un portale a quadruplice fornice. All'interno del recinto venne innalzato il tempio B a pianta ellenizzante, affiancato dall'area di culto attrezzata C; al muro meridionale del recinto, vennero addossate venti celle precedute da altari. Con l'innalzamento del Tempio A (460 a.C.), la superficie del Santuario fu più che raddoppiata in direzione dell'abitato e leggermente ampliata in direzione dell'entroterra con l'arretramento del muro di peribolo orientale; in concomitanza, fu apportata una modifica anche alla Caere-Pyrgi, convertendo la curva precedentemente descritta dalla strada in un piazzale, in funzione della visione frontale dell'altorilievo dei Sette contro Tebe.

In ambedue le fasi del Santuario, l'andamento obliquo del muro di témenos orientale costituisce una anomalia rispetto all'orientamento rituale degli edifici di culto, ma risponde all'orientamento del tracciato urbano della Caere-Pyrgi; è possibile dunque ipotizzare il condizionamento di una maglia stradale preesistente,[10] o piuttosto una scelta intenzionale di pianificazione degli spazi monumentalizzati, in accordo con la griglia urbanistica. Di estremo interesse è la scoperta, avvenuta nel 2018, di un muro in blocchi di tufo per taglio, orientato come gli edifici templari (*fig. 1b*): si tratta con ogni probabilità della crepidine di un asse stradale che, diramandosi dalla Caere-Pyrgi, delimitava o costeggiava il Santuario sul versante settentrionale.

In posizione volutamente marginale, il Santuario Meridionale, dedicato alla coppia di divinità Suri e Cavatha, è stato fondato intorno al 540 a.C. con la costruzione di un sacello (β) in blocchi di tufo, a doppia cella con vestibolo in *antis*, impiantato al di sopra di un dosso artificiale. L'area sacra è stata progressivamente ampliata attraverso operazioni di bonifica del suolo, con l'aggiunta di una serie di altari di diversa tipologia e di sacelli,[11] caratterizzati da ingressi decentrati e banchine e realizzate con le stesse tecniche delle case. A fronte della distribuzione apparentemente disorganica delle diverse strutture, si è proposto di ricostruire procedimenti di tipo rituale nella definizione degli interventi sul terreno, riconoscendo la presenza di un *templum in terris* al centro dello spazio sacro.[12]

2. Pyrgi: l'edilizia di tipo abitativo

Gli edifici scavati a N del Tempio A, come le case di abitazione, sono costruiti con l'impiego quasi esclusivo di materiali reperibili localmente (*fig. 2d*): le fondazioni e gli zoccoli murari (largh cm 45-60) sono di norma realizzati in ciottoli e/o pietrame spaccato, disposti a incastro su due filari e rincalzati con schegge litiche, e livellati con frammenti di tegole marcapiano, solo talvolta conservati; gli alzati e i muri divisori sono realizzati in mattoni crudi di formato sesquipedale rettangolare (cm 41-46 x 31-33) e intonacati; i piani pavimentali degli interni sono generalmente in terra battuta, mentre l'impiego di battuti in tufo è riservato alle aree cortilizie e alle pavimentazioni stradali; fin dai primi livelli di case, è documentato l'impiego di coperture fittili. L'impiego del tufo, importato dall'entroterra ceretano, costituisce il

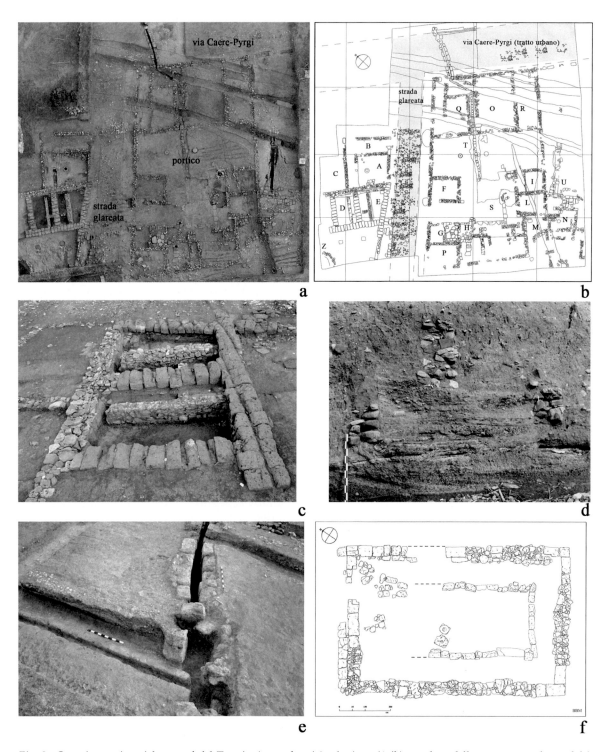

*Fig. 2. Quartiere cerimoniale a nord del Tempio A: ortofoto (a), planimetria (b) e veduta della casa-torre, da nord (c); opere idrauliche che costeggiano e attraversano il tratto urbano della via Caere-Pyrgi (e). Abitato di Pyrgi: strutture sezionate dall'erosione marina (d). Santuario meridionale: planimetria dell'edificio gamma (f) (archivio Sapienza).*

significativo segnale del controllo esercitato dalla città-madre sull'urbanizzazione del litorale ed è documentato *in primis* dal tracciato della Caere-Pyrgi, delimitata da crepidini in blocchi, e dalle tombe di età arcaica costruite lungo il suo percorso in loc. Quarto di Monte Bischero.[13] L'impiego di blocchi di tufo in associazione al pietrame è per lo più inteso come espediente per rafforzare i punti critici dei fabbricati, quali le porzioni cantonali e i varchi di ingresso, e trova massima espressione nei sacelli α e γ nel Santuario Meridionale (*fig. 2f*); solo occasionalmente, è possibile osservare il ricorso a schemi costruttivi basati su criteri di alternanza dei materiali, che trovano confronto con la tecnica orvietana a scacchiera di tipo A.[14] L'impiego di blocchi caratterizza le fondazioni di taluni edifici di spicco, quali la casa-torre del quartiere cerimoniale (*fig. 2c*) e ricorre nelle principali opere di drenaggio, nelle strade e nel sottosuolo dei complessi edilizi (*fig. 2e*).

3. L'EDILIZIA PUBBLICO-MONUMENTALE

Grazie all'esplicito riferimento alla committenza da parte di Thefarie Velianas contenuto nelle lamine d'oro bilingui affisse sullo stipite del portale del tempio B,[15] il Santuario di Pyrgi costituisce un eccezionale esempio, in territorio etrusco, dello stretto collegamento tra l'emergere di figure di re-tiranni e il decollo dell'edilizia pubblica stigmatizzato dalla Roma dei Tarquini;[16] ma anche del fondamentale significato del tempio, che nel periodo arcaico assurge al ruolo di categoria architettonica a sé stante,[17] quale massima forma di (auto-)rappresentazione del potere politico a livello internazionale e quale riflesso del clima concorrenziale tra le diverse *poleis*.[18]

Com'è noto, la realizzazione di opere urbanistiche su larga scala e la piena strutturazione delle città arcaiche,[19] si collega alla capacità, da parte del nuovo regime politico, di un pieno controllo della progettazione e della programmazione degli interventi attraverso la gestione centralizzata delle risorse, l'investimento di disponibilità finanziarie provenienti dai bottini di guerra, il convogliamento di grandi masse di manodopera (anche sotto forma di lavoro coatto), e il coinvolgimento di maestranze altamente specializzate:[20] significativo il reclutamento di artigiani dal Lazio e da tutta l'Etruria (Livio, I.56.1), in particolare da Veio,[21] per il cantiere di Giove Capitolino.

Se il decollo dell'architettura pubblica si deve al nuovo clima politico, le capacità tecniche dispiegate in epoca arcaica sono l'esito di un lungo processo di affinamento dei procedimenti costruttivi, anche attraverso la recezione e l'elaborazione di imprestiti culturali dall'esterno, che affonda le sue radici nel secolo precedente.

Indubbio elemento di rottura nella tradizione edilizia è l'introduzione in Italia della coroplastica architettonica, attribuita alla équipe leggendaria giunta da Corinto al seguito di Damarato intorno al 650 a.C.,[22] con la conseguente specializzazione delle maestranze addette alle opere di carpenteria (i *fabri tignari*, inseriti da Plutarco al terzo posto della lista di Numa[23]), affiancati da bronzisti, e il perfezionamento del sistema di sostegno delle coperture, a partire dalle incastellature lignee documentate dalle tombe medio-orientalizzanti di Caere[24] fino al presunto ricorso alla capriata,[25] di cui è stata ipotizzata la comparsa in Sicilia nel VI sec.a.C.[26]

Alla realizzazione di opere pubbliche di epoca arcaica si collega l'impiego generalizzato dell'opera quadrata, intesa come tecnica idonea a garantire la costruzione di murature massive[27] attraverso lo svolgimento simultaneo del lavoro da parte di diverse squadre di operai, grazie alla possibilità di ottenere ricorsi livellati e di altezza omogenea e di utilizzare i blocchi in direzioni alternate. Al controllo pubblico dell'attività estrattiva si deve l'adozione di sistemi metrologici di riferimento per le operazioni di taglio, in possibile sostituzione di quelli locali; tale fenomeno è chiaro per Roma, seppure a fronte di una iniziale applicazione promiscua.[28] Ben più complesso è il quadro offerto dalle città dell'Etruria meridionale, per le quali sono riconoscibili altrettanti criteri locali di taglio (vedi *infra*) e, a seconda dei campi di applicazione, una grande variabilità di soluzioni formali, con ampio ricorso all'adattamento del materiale costruttivo agli apparecchi murari.[29]

L'impiego dell'opera quadrata non coincide con un progresso tecnico, ma risponde alla necessità di razionalizzare e semplificare i procedimenti costruttivi. La capacità di squadratura dei blocchi è infatti documentata in Etruria almeno a partire dal primo quarto del VII sec.a.C., nei muri a pilastri di tipo fenicio della Civita di Tarquinia;[30] in epoca orientalizzante l'impiego dell'opera "quadrata", anche in associazione a tecniche basate sull'incernieramento di blocchi disomogenei mediante riseghe e tasselli,[31] trova massima espressione nei grandi tumuli funerari, per la formulazione dei quali è ben noto l'apporto di modelli vicino-orientali e il contributo di artigiani immigrati.[32]

L'acquisizione dei principi teorici alla base delle grandi opere pubbliche di epoca arcaica trova massima espressione nel campo dell'ingegneria idraulica, per il quale fondamentale è stato l'apporto ionico,[33] attraverso la padronanza di tecniche di geodetica e del connesso strumentario (livelle, diottrie e corobati).[34] Per quanto concerne l'edilizia templare, la redazione di trattati di architettura, ricordati dalle fonti a proposito dei grandi cantieri della Ionia arcaica (Vitr. VII,12), ha certamente contribuito alla diffusione di modelli di progettazione, trovando riscontro nell'adozione in ambito italico del piede ionico-attico di cm 29,6.[35]

Per quanto riguarda il rapporto tra progetto architettonico e realizzazione dei templi etrusco-italici, in mancanza di indicazioni da parte di Vitruvio, gli studi hanno in genere privilegiato- come nel caso di Pyrgi- il riconoscimento di griglie modulari e di rapporti proporzionali tra i vari elementi dell'edificio, mentre negli ultimi decenni si è dato risalto alla possibilità di ricondurre la pianta degli edifici e le loro partizioni a figure geometriche:[36] il Cherici, in particolare, ha evidenziato la corrispondenza di misure e rapporti forniti da Vitruvio per il tempio tuscanico con un tipo di edificio composto, tanto nella *pars antica* che nella *pars postica*, da due identici rettangoli aurei.[37] L'attuale tendenza è quella di utilizzare un approccio di tipo geometrico-proporzionale nell'interpretazione del cantiere antico,[38] analizzando il rapporto tra progetto e possibile applicazione di procedimenti geometrici nella fase esecutiva.

In quest'ottica, la trasposizione sul terreno dello schema progettuale poteva avvenire con il semplice impiego di corde e paletti,[39] a partire dal cerchio e dal quadrato in esso inscritto, ottenendo rettangoli dinamici - regolati da valori numerici irrazionali- attraverso il ribattimento della diagonale del quadrato di partenza e dei rettangoli da essi derivati, sistema cui allude Vitruvio (VI,3,3); con l'impiego di una corda annodata a intervalli modulari si potevano materializzare sul terreno i cosiddetti triangoli pitagorici, da cui derivano figure geometriche regolate da un numero intero di unità.[40]

La corretta esecuzione del progetto veniva controllata attraverso il ricorso a linee-guida incise sui piani di attesa e l'impiego del regolo, l'asta graduata, che connota l'architetto etrusco Vel Rafi, rappresentato sull'urna da Perugia.[41]

I due edifici templari di Pyrgi offrono la possibilità non soltanto di ricostruire il progetto generale dell'architetto, ma anche di tracciare le principali operazioni di cantiere; lo sfruttamento in epoca antonina come cava a cielo aperto ne ha intaccato le fondazioni, evidenziandone la tessitura alle diverse quote.

Per realizzare gli edifici è stato necessario trasportare i blocchi di tufo dall'entroterra, lungo il tragitto di 12 km della via Caere-Pyrgi, che prende avvio dall'area del Manganello; non ci sono tuttavia elementi per stabilire l'ubicazione della cava, se immediatamente all'interno o all'esterno dell'area urbana (cfr. *infra*). Allo stato attuale delle indagini, manca inoltre una diretta evidenza dello svolgimento in loco di attività artigianali strettamente collegate al cantiere edilizio, quali la fabbricazione delle terrecotte architettoniche e dello strumentario metallico.[42]

Nella descrizione che segue, mi atterrò al criterio di numerazione delle assise - dall'alto verso il basso - utilizzata nell' *editio princeps*.

### 4. Il Tempio B[43]

I muri di fondazione del tempio periptero B (*fig. 3*) si sviluppavano per un numero massimo di quattro assise di blocchi -due delle quali abbastanza conservate- e risultano completamente asportati in corrispondenza del lato breve orientale e della porzione d'angolo meridionale. Alla quota di impianto (assisa IV), l'edificio appare definito da un robusto muro perimetrale ripartito da due muri longitudinali più esili, che frazionano il rettangolo interno in tre parti, quella centrale larga il doppio di quelle laterali; i muri longitudinali sono collegati da due traverse, quella posteriore saldata al muro perimetrale, quella anteriore ricadente al centro dell'edificio. Alla medesima quota si impostano briglie murarie che ricadono tra i muri longitudinali interni e quelli perimetrali (*fig. 3: i, l, m, n*): a destra se ne contano due, all'altezza della parete frontale della cella e a metà circa della sua lunghezza; a sinistra è presente quella posteriore, mentre la seconda, non portata a termine, appare sotto forma di ammorsatura. Per tali strutture, annegate nel terrapieno, si è proposta una funzione di stabilizzazione del fabbricato in corso d'opera, trovando confronto nell'Heraion alla foce del Sele;[44] ma, anche in virtù della parziale realizzazione, si è anche proposto di considerarle la spia di un radicale cambiamento del progetto - inizialmente concepito in funzione di un tempio di tipo tuscanico - nella fase di stipula del trattato tra Roma e Cartagine.[45] Ulteriori strutture in blocchi con funzione di contrasto, impostate a quota più superficiali e rimosse nel IV sec.a.C., sono state documentate nella parte anteriore dell'edificio.

La cella risulta interamente delineata alla quota della III assisa, attraverso la contrazione del muro perimetrale di fondo (*fig. 3: g*) e la creazione di una intercapedine; all'interno di essa era presente una platea superficiale di blocchi, anch'essa asportata nel IV sec.a.C..

All'alzato del tempio sono riferibili i sette blocchi reimpiegati, insieme alle sime, per costruire la

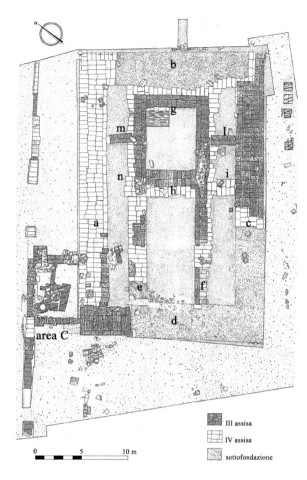

Fig. 3. Tempio B, planimetria: muri perimetrali nord (a), est (b), sud (c) e ovest (d); muri longitudinali (e-f) e trasversali (g-h); contrasti (i-n) (da Pyrgi 1992, fig. 139, elab. Belelli Marchesini).

vasca delle lamine nell'area C:[46] quattro di essi sono intonacati su facce contigue e dunque attribuibili alla testata di muri d'anta.[47] L'intonaco[48] impiegato è quello di tipo B (sp. 0,2): bianco, a base di calce, ben aderente a una preparazione di stucco impastato con detriti silicei. Alle colonne si riferiscono poche schegge di tamburi, in tufo grigio.[49]

All'interno della cella è ipotizzabile la presenza di una struttura in mattoni crudi, cui si riferiscono i frammenti di intonaco dipinti in rosso porpora[50] del tipo A: uno stucco (sp. 0,1) tenero e gessoso, impastato con fibre vegetali.

### 4.1 Il progetto

Il tempio B si configura come un tempio a pianta ellenizzante elevato su basso podio o crepidoma, con cella in antis addossata al muro di fondo, porticato posteriore notevolmente più stretto che ai lati e sulla fronte, provvisto di una peristasi di 6 colonne sui lati e 4 sulle fronti; si tratta del più antico esempio in territorio etrusco della variante centro-italica del periptero greco, che corrisponde al tempio definito "aerostilo" da Vitruvio (III, 3,5).[51]

Le dimensioni dell'edificio, un *hekatompedon* alla quota di fondazione, sono state progressivamente calibrate arretrando il ciglio esterno del fabbricato lungo tutto il perimetro, per la larghezza di cm 18 tra IV e III assisa, di cm 7 tra la III e la II; quest'ultima riduzione è indicata dalle linee-guida osservabili all'angolo ovest.
Le dimensioni[52] sono le seguenti:

|  | metri | piedi attici | rapporto |
|---|---|---|---|
| IV assisa | 20,10 x 29,65 | 68 x 100 | 1:1,475 |
| III assisa | 19,80 x 29,35 | 67 x 99 | 1:1,482 |
| II assisa | 19,65 x 29,20 | 66,5 x 98,5 | 1:1,486 |
| stilobate (ric. 1985) | 18,648 x 28,416 | 63 x 96 | 1:1.523 |

Dal punto di vista geometrico, il rapporto di circa 1:1,5 permette di assimilare lo stereobate a un rettangolo 3:2 e di avvicinare il Tempio B ad altri templi ellenizzanti dell'Italia centrale.[53] Una perfetta corrispondenza si ottiene ipotizzando dimensioni "ideali" di 64 x 96 piedi,[54] da cui deriva una griglia di quadrati da 32 piedi o sottomultipli.[55] Applicando questa griglia alla pianta, osserviamo una sostanziale corrispondenza con l'ingombro delle strutture murarie, fatta eccezione per il settore di fondo; è inoltre possibile osservare che, in base a questo schema, il limite esterno dei muri laterali e frontali della cella, alla quota della III assisa, ricadono all'interno di rettangoli dinamici √2 (*fig. 4a*).

Se il ricorso a figure geometriche nella trasposizione sul terreno dell'edificio può essere solo ipoteticamente dimostrato, lo studio metrologico ha riconosciuto l'impiego di un modulo costruttivo di 3 piedi attici (cm 88,8):[56] nella ricostruzione proposta nel 1985, il tempio si inserisce all'interno di un reticolo di 21 x 32 moduli, di cui 8 x 10 assegnati alla cella, 6 agli intercolumni e 7 all'intercolumnio centrale sui lati corti[57] (*fig. 4b-c*).

### 4.2 I procedimenti costruttivi[58]

I muri di fondazione sono stati impiantati su un riporto di argilla gialla spesso 60 cm; lo schema geometrico è stato riportato sul terreno ritagliando trincee per una profondità non superiore a cm 40 e successivamente colmandole con una

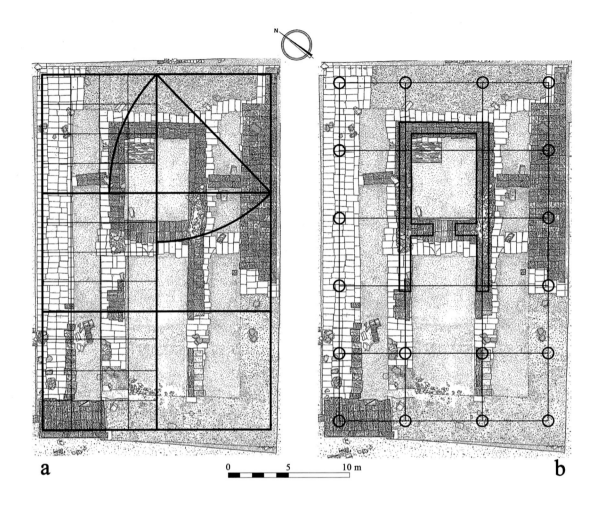

Fig. 4. Tempio B: schema geometrico (a) e ricostruzione (da Pyrgi 1992, fig. 139, elab. Belelli Marchesini); modellino ricostruttivo in scala 1:50 (archivio Sapienza).

sottofondazione in tritume di tufo, utile a offrire un piano livellato di appoggio per i muri e a garantire il drenaggio;[59] a quest'ultima funzione si riferisce anche la fodera in tritume di tufo che fascia il perimetro dell'edificio, per l'altezza della prima assisa di blocchi.

I blocchi sono stati ritagliati in funzione della tessitura e larghezza dei muri. Le dimensioni medie, rilevate sulla base di un campione di 230 unità (*fig. 5*), sono: lunghezza compresa tra cm 78 e 90, massima di cm 134; larghezza di cm 45-48; altezza, pari a quelle delle assise, di cm 40-42. I blocchi risultano accuratamente accostati, utilizzando nelle commessure ciottoli delle dimensioni di un pugno, a mo' di zeppe (*fig. 6c*): tale espediente, assente nel tempio A, ricorre anche nel tempio di Giove Capitolino.[60] L'impiego di linee-guida incise è documentato soltanto per delineare il limite esterno dello stereobate. I piani di attesa delle assise si presentano perfettamente livellati.

Alla quota di imposta (IV assisa), si osserva un impiego quasi esclusivo di blocchi per testa e una rigida gerarchia tra le strutture: nel muro perimetrale, i lati corti si compongono di quattro filari (largh. cm 340-350), i lati lunghi di tre filari per testa abbinati ad uno per taglio, che ne definisce il ciglio interno (largh. 300). A questa quota, il lato corto est è saldato al muro di fondo della cella e da esso prendono avvio i due muri interni longitudinali, realizzati con due-tre filari di blocchi sotto-misura, per testa: quello nord presenta larghezza costante (cm 200), quello sud è irregolare e si assottiglia verso il mare (largh. cm 250-120). Il muro anteriore della cella si compone di tre filari per testa (largh. cm 250-280).

Alla quota della III assisa, i muri perimetrali (largh. cm 280-300) presentano tre filari per testa, abbinati a un filare per taglio in corrispondenza del ciglio esterno. I muri interni delineano una sorta di U e si compongono di un filare per testa

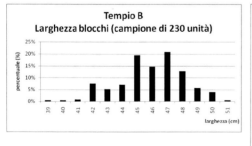
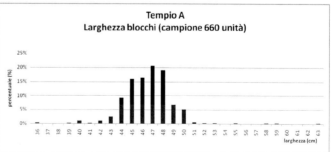

*Fig. 5. Misure dei blocchi del Tempio A e del Tempio B.*

115

Fig. 6. Tempio B: a) distribuzione delle zeppe calcaree (pallini neri), punto di avvio del lavoro e segmentazione del muro perimetrale nord (ortofoto A. Jaia; elab. Belelli Marchesini); b-c) dettagli della tessitura del muro perimetrale nord e dell'angolo occidentale.

e di uno per taglio (largh. cm 120-150); il filare per taglio, regolarmente allineato, è rivolto verso l'interno nei muri longitudinali, verso l'esterno nel muro di fondo della cella. Il muro anteriore della cella si compone invece di due filari per testa, con drittofilo sul lato interno, ed è largo cm 150-200.

La costruzione dell'edificio ha preso avvio dai muri perimetrali. In assenza di tracce relative all'impiego di leve metalliche, l'andamento del cantiere è stato ricostruito osservando la disposizione dei blocchi sul ciglio esterno, soprattutto in posizione d'angolo, ipotizzando che le maestranze abbiano operato in senso orario, a partire dall'angolo occidentale del lato lungo nord, tanto al livello della IV che della III assisa (*fig. 6a*). Tuttavia, considerando la priorità assegnata invece alla tessitura dei muri corti in corrispondenza degli angoli,[61] non escluderei la possibilità dello svolgimento simultaneo del lavoro da parte di più squadre di operai, muovendo anche in direzione opposta.[62]

Per quanto riguarda le operazioni di montaggio, particolarmente interessante nei muri perimetrali è il costante frazionamento delle giunture dei blocchi esterni, rispetto a quelli che compongono il nucleo, quale espediente per garantire una maggiore coesione: a tale accorgimento si collega con ogni probabilità l'impiego di una coppia di blocchi sotto-misura all'angolo nord. Si può inoltre osservare, sul ciglio esterno del muro nord, l'impiego di blocchi con lunghezze progressivamente scalate, alcuni dei quali provvisti di riseghe per ammorsare i blocchi del nucleo (*fig. 6b*), disposti a cadenze regolari: il tipo di tessitura evidenzia la segmentazione del muro in tratti della lunghezza di cm 300-350, composti da 6-7 blocchi (*fig. 6a*), forse corrispondenti ad altrettante tappe del lavoro. Il fenomeno di adattamento del materiale costruttivo si osserva in particolare nel muro di fondo della cella, realizzato dopo quelli laterali, che esibisce alle estremità tasselli e conci appositamente ritagliati.

I muri in alzato della cella, rastremati verso l'alto, dovevano essere composti alla base da due filari di blocchi per taglio alternati a ricorsi per testa (largh. cm 90 ca); la larghezza alla quota di imposta del tetto, pari a cm 75,[63] è data dai blocchi reimpiegati nella vasca della lamine, di cui si è detto sopra.

## 5. Il Tempio A[64]

Il basamento dell'edificio si compone di una griglia di strutture elevate fino ad un massimo di otto assise, quella più alta divelta dalle arature; l'attività dei cavatori di blocchi ha quasi totalmente cancellato la seconda e raggiunto, ma non divelto, l'assisa più profonda in corrispondenza dell'angolo ovest (*figg. 7, 8a*).

Il tipo di fondazione a griglia, sperimentata nel tempio di Giove Capitolino e nel tempio dei Castori a Roma, rappresenta un'alternativa rispetto alle fondazioni isolate[65] e si collega ad esigenze di tenuta statica, soprattutto in presenza di terreni di base poco solidi.

La griglia è definita da un robusto anello murario perimetrale suddiviso internamente da due muri longitudinali e da quattro muri trasversali diversamente intervallati, da cui deriva la presenza di 14 vani di fondazione di forma quadrangolare. L'innalzamento delle strutture murarie è avvenuto in concomitanza con il riempimento dei vani e con la realizzazione di un terrapieno esterno. Sulla fronte dell'edificio, il terrapieno era contenuto da due bracci murari ad L a delimitazione di una ampia terrazza e inglobava due pozzi-serbatoio con camicia e imboccatura in blocchi di tufo sagomati.

Rispetto al livello di calpestio, il basamento emergeva per l'altezza di due assise di blocchi; ad esso è stata attribuita una modanatura composta da cuscino e toro schiacciato, rappresentate rispettivamente da una scheggia e da un frammento di blocco d'angolo in tufo cinerognolo.[66] Relativamente all'alzato, sulla base della distribuzione di frammenti di intonaco di diverso tipo (vedi *supra*), si è potuto riconoscere l'impiego dell'opera quadrata di tufo nei muri perimetrali, prolungati verso la facciata, e dei mattoni crudi nei muri divisori.

Alle colonne rastremate del tempio si riferiscono poche schegge di tamburi in tufo, del diametro superiore al metro, e un frammento di tamburo con sommoscapo e capitello (diam. cm 66) in peperino: quest'ultimo reca sul piano superiore due rettangoli proporzionali, incisi l'uno dentro l'altro, quello di minori dimensioni inscritto all'interno della circonferenza del capitello, interpretati come guida per l'intonacatura.[67]

### 5.1 Il progetto

Il tempio A si configura come tempio di tipo tuscanico, con tre celle che ne occupano la *pars postica*, quelle laterali provviste sul fondo di due vani di diseguali dimensioni; nella *pars antica* è stata riconosciuta, sulla base dei dati di scavo, la presenza di un pronao con quattro colonne racchiuse tra ante e di una fila di quattro colonne sulla fronte.

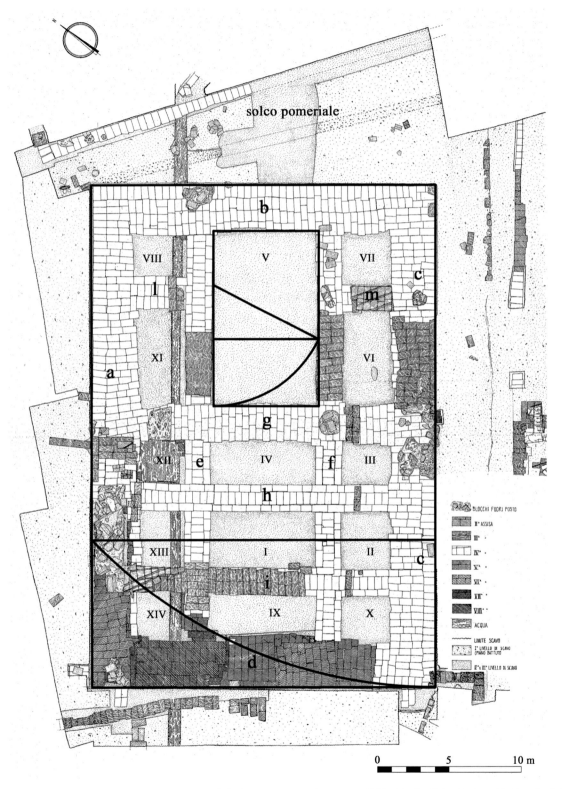

*Fig. 7. Tempio A: planimetria, con indicazione delle figure geometriche riconoscibili a livello di fondazione (da Pyrgi 1970, figg. 5-6, elab. Belelli Marchesini).*

Le dimensioni[68] sono:

|  | Metri | Piedi attici | Rapporto |
|---|---|---|---|
| IV assisa | 23,98 x 34,47 | 81 x 116,5 | 1,437 |
| III assisa | 23,98 x 34,33 | 81 x 116 | 1,431 |
| Ricostruzione alzato[69] | 21,9 x 25,75 (modello) | 74 x 87 (modello) | 1,17 |
|  | 21,75x 25.9 (teorico) | 73,5 x 87,5 (teorico) | 1,19 (=5:6) |

Dal punto di vista geometrico, è stato osservato che, aggiungendo un piede alla larghezza della III assisa (m 24,27 x 34,33), il podio è assimilabile a un rettangolo √2,[70] e che lo spazio racchiuso dalla cella corrisponde a un rettangolo aureo[71] (*fig. 7*).

Per l'alzato, è stato riconosciuto l'impiego del piede ionico-attico ma non di un modulo costruttivo.[72] Nella ricostruzione proposta nel 1985, che fa riferimento al canone vitruviano ed è stata utilizzata per il modellino in scala 1:50 (*fig. 8c*), l'edificio è suddiviso in due metà, quella posteriore occupato da una cella centrale (30 piedi) e da celle laterali (22 piedi) in rapporto di circa 3:4:3; il diametro inferiore delle colonne è di 3,5 piedi.[73]

Partendo dalle dimensioni considerate per il modello ricostruttivo, è possibile riconoscere il ricorso a rettangoli √2 in ciascuna metà dell'edificio, che presenterebbe in tal modo cella e intercolumnio centrali misuranti 31 piedi (*fig. 8b*).[74]

In rapporto alla pianificazione del cantiere del tempio A, di estremo interesse è inoltre la presenza di un solco di tipo "pomeriale" colmato di detrito tufaceo compattato, che corre alle spalle del tempio parallelamente al muro di peribolo delimitando una fascia di rispetto larga cm 350/400[75] (*Fig. 8b*).

## 5.2 I procedimenti costruttivi

La griglia di fondazione si compone di strutture murarie reciprocamente incernierate, tutte con funzione portante ma gerarchicamente distinte, che sono state impiantate su un terreno di base scosceso in direzione ovest e presentano dunque un diverso sviluppo in altezza, descrivendo in senso longitudinale due principali salti di quota e presentando un numero variabile di sei-otto assise di blocchi (*fig. 8a*); il livellamento dei piani di imposta dei muri è ottenuto, all'occorrenza, attraverso l'impiego di una assisa di blocchi dimezzata e/o di una sottofondazione in tritume di tufo. I muri longitudinali risultano impiantati a quota più profonda rispetto a quelli trasversali.

Una distinzione gerarchica dei muri è data dalla diversa larghezza, maggiore (in media, cm 300) nei muri perimetrali, media (cm 240) nel muro trasversale mediano e minore (cm 180) nei restanti muri longitudinali e trasversali, con impiego di multipli di un piede di circa cm 30[76] avvicinabile a quello utilizzato per la progettazione.

I blocchi risultano dimensionati in funzione della larghezza dei muri o ritagliati in funzione della tessitura: sulla base di un campione di 144 unità (*fig. 5*), la lunghezza media è di cm 80-90, massima di cm 135; la larghezza oscilla tra cm 44-50, con prevalenza dei valori di cm 45 e 48; l'altezza, pari a quella delle assise, si attesta tra cm 42 e 45.

Quanto alla tessitura, i muri perimetrali si compongono di tre-quattro filari di blocchi per testa, cui si aggiunge un filare posto generalmente per taglio; soltanto il ciglio esterno dei muri perimetrali presenta un drittofilo, a partire dalla quinta assisa verso l'alto, ottenuta anche attraverso riseghe orizzontali scalpellate sui blocchi ("*anathyrosis*").[77] Il muro trasversale mediano si compone di tre filari per testa, a giunti sfalsati; nei restanti muri, si applica l'alternanza di due filari per testa, e di un filare per testa delimitato da filari per taglio (*fig. 9a*).

La concatenazione delle strutture murarie è ottenuta attraverso ammorsature e dando precedenza, alternativamente, alla stesura dei muri trasversali o longitudinali interni.

La solidità dello scheletro murario, caratterizzato alle diverse quote da aggetti e rientranze dei blocchi, è inoltre garantita dall'intima connessione con i terrapieni, composti da gettate di argilla alternate a livelli di detrito tufaceo.

In mancanza di tracce relative alla messa in opera, osservando la disposizione dei blocchi del muro perimetrale alla quota della IV assisa, si è ipotizzato che il cantiere abbia preso avvio dal lato sud, procedendo con andamento a tenaglia lungo i lati corti[78] (*fig. 9b*). A fronte del costante adattamento del materiale disponibile alla tessitura, si osservano criteri di messa in opera diversificati: in particolare, all'angolo est si riscontra l'impiego di blocchi sotto-misura, che permette di riconoscere il lavoro di maestranze operanti da ovest; in corrispondenza, il raccordo tra le pareti contigue è risolto con una linea spezzata, a fronte della giustapposizione osservabile agli angoli nord e sud; lungo le pareti, sono riconoscibili porzioni di muratura caratterizzate dall'allineamento o dallo sfalsamento dei giunti, e dalla disposizione talvolta obliqua, a indizio della segmentazione in più lotti o tappe di lavorazione (*fig. 9c*).

Quanto ai muri interni longitudinali, incernierati a una sola estremità a quelli trasversali, è

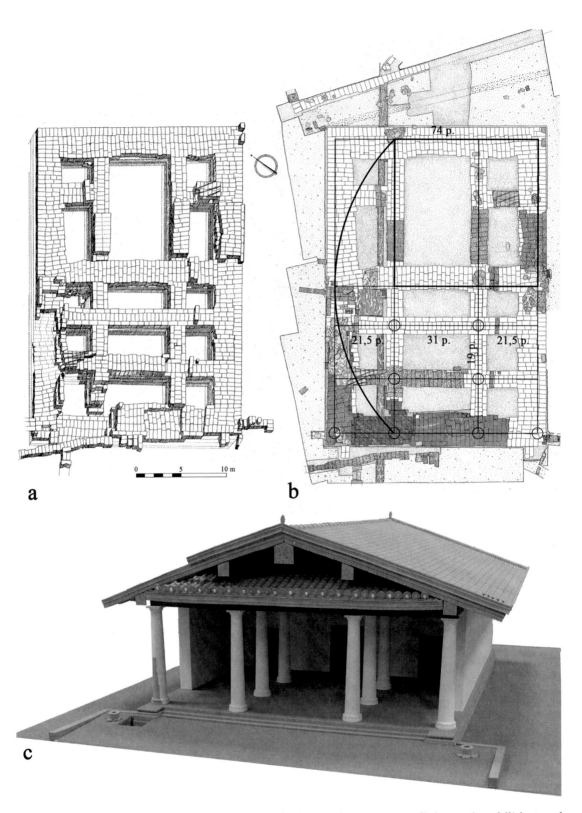

*Fig. 8. Tempio A: a) assonometria (da Pyrgi 1970, fig. 17); b) planimetria, con proposta di ricostruzione dell'alzato su base geometrica (da Pyrgi 1970, figg. 5-6, elab. Belelli Marchesini); c) modellino ricostruttivo in scala 1:50 (archivio Sapienza).*

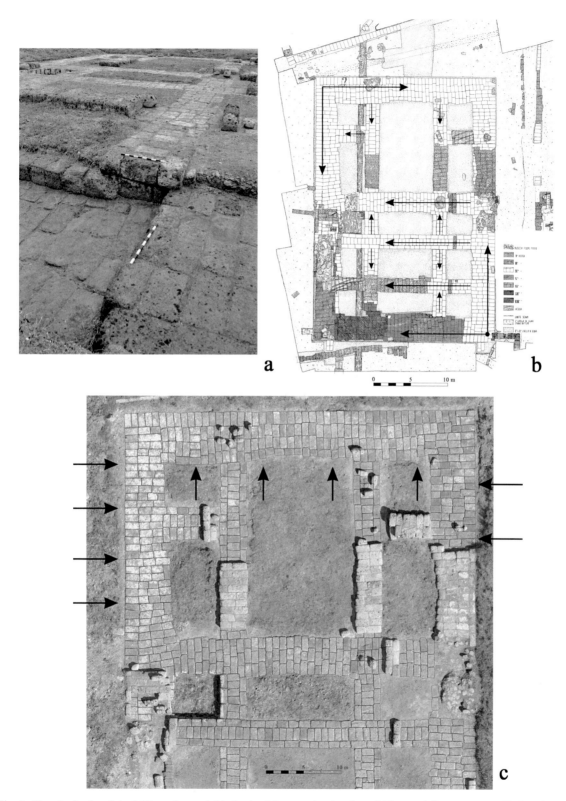

*Fig. 9. Tempio A: a) veduta dell'angolo ovest; b) planimetria, con ricostruzione del lavoro delle maestranze (da Pyrgi 1970, figg. 5-6, elab. Belelli Marchesini); c) ortofoto, con proposta di segmentazione del muro perimetrale (ortofoto A. Jaia; elab. Belelli Marchesini).*

possibile stabilirne la direzione di allettamento, riconoscendo il lavoro simultaneo di più squadre (*fig. 9b*).

## 6. Osservazioni conclusive: Pyrgi e Caere

I due edifici templari di Pyrgi rappresentano i due modelli architettonici, decorati *tuscanico more*, che si affermano in ambito centro-italico a partire dal VI sec.a.C. trovando un connubio nel tempio di Giove Capitolino, quale che sia lo sviluppo della peristasi.[79] L'associazione, che trova confronto in area urbana nella Regio I di Marzabotto,[80] a quanto pare è stata replicata a Caere nell'area sacra di S. Antonio. Questo santuario comprende due edifici paralleli a pianta rettangolare, affacciati su una ampia terrazza: il tempio A, che ingloba al suo interno un precedente sacello e una fontana monumentale, è stato interpretato come tempio di tipo tuscanico, databile tra la fine VI-inizio V sec.a.C.;[81] il tempio B, assai mal conservato, è stato di recente interpretato come tempio periptero.[82] Per questi edifici, come per l'edificio tripartito di Vigna Parrocchiale[83] e le strutture indagate a Valle della Mola,[84] non disponiamo di informazioni sufficienti a un confronto puntuale con le architetture pyrgensi.

Non mi risulta tuttavia che a Caere, come a Pyrgi, sia segnalato l'impiego di leve metalliche per la messa in opera,[85] peraltro documentato sporadicamente in ambito medio-tirrenico: nel Lazio ricorre almeno nelle diverse fasi del tempio di Satricum[86] e nella fase arcaica dell'ara IX di Lavinium;[87] a Roma nel tempio di Giove Capitolino[88] e nella seconda fase del tempio di S. Omobono.[89] In Etruria la tecnica, precocemente documentata nella crepidine del tumulo della Cuccumelletta di Vulci (decenni finali del VII sec.a.C.),[90] è attestata con due tipi di tracce: piccoli solchi, talvolta di forma allungata e reiterati, riferibili allo slittamento dei blocchi nella sede prestabilita; cavità rettangolari o stondate utilizzate per leve metalliche con interposizione di ciocchi di legno, adatte a ospitare eventuali perni lignei. In epoca arcaica e tardo-arcaica, incassi di questo tipo trovano ulteriori esempi almeno a Tarquinia,[91] nella tomba monumentale di Castro,[92] a Veio - Casale Pian Roseto;[93] negli templi A e C di Orvieto.[94] In questa fase l'impiego di perni lignei verticali ricorre in particolare nelle colonne lapidee, come ben esemplificato dai frammenti di basi e tamburi dalla Vigna Parrocchiale di Caere.[95] Le grappe di collegamento trasversale, dapprima lignee e poi plumbee, che sono strettamente collegate all'impiego del paletto, sono documentate per lo più dal IV sec.a.C.: ne sono esempio la fase in tufo litoide delle mura di Roma[96] e, in Etruria, l'altare di Pieve a Socana.[97]

In assenza di tracce di leve metalliche, la movimentazione dei blocchi alla quota di fondazione doveva avvenire manualmente, con l'ausilio di una pertica e del cordame. Per la realizzazione delle parti in elevato, oltre alla messa in opera di impalcature lignee, dobbiamo pensare all'impiego di meccanismi per il sollevamento quali le gru, utilizzate nelle attività delle aree portuali,[98] con ausilio di corde o di eventuali dispositivi metallici.[99] Per l'architettura della Grecia occidentale, l'impiego di tali meccanismi, perfezionati con la sperimentazione precoce della carrucola, è stata collegata all'introduzione delle colonne a rocchi al posto di quelle a fusto monolitico a partire dalla metà del VI sec.a.C. (tempio C di Selinunte, Basilica di Paestum).[100]

A Caere, la presenza di un argano collegato a una struttura lignea autoportante è stata riconosciuta nella cava di Vigna Parrocchiale[101] e ipotizzata in quella presso le mura urbiche, in loc. Bufolareccia:[102] entrambe esemplificano la conduzione dell'attività di tipo estrattivo a Caere, caratterizzata dall'apertura di cave estemporanee a cielo aperto, tanto nell'area urbana quanto in area di necropoli,[103] che talvolta subiscono una riconversione d'uso (idraulico, o funerario).

Da un punto di vista metrologico, le dimensioni medie dei blocchi impiegati nelle fondazioni dei templi A e B di Pyrgi (*fig. 5*) corrispondono al criterio di taglio registrato nella cava di Vigna Parrocchiale (cm 80-85 x 45-50 x 40-45)[104] trovando generico riscontro anche nell'edilizia pubblica ceretana,[105] seppure con fenomeni di adattamento del materiale costruttivo ai contesti specifici.[106]

In generale, va detto che, a fronte del tentativo di riconoscere un piede etrusco,[107] gli esempi di opera quadrata disponibili nelle diverse città dell'Etruria meridionale[108] e nell'agro falisco[109] mostrano una certa fluidità dimensionale, seppure con la possibilità di riconoscere criteri metrologici locali, riflettendo sistemi di sfruttamento delle risorse non pienamente standardizzati.

Sul rapporto tra attività estrattiva ed edilizia, come sul rapporto tra progetto architettonico e fase di realizzazione sul cantiere, deve essere necessariamente indirizzata la futura ricerca nel campo dell'architettura monumentale etrusca al fine di comprendere le modalità e la capacità di gestione delle risorse locali da parte delle singole città, ma anche la permeabilità nei confronti di imprestiti culturali dall'esterno. A fronte dell'elaborazione di un linguaggio decorativo che a partire dalla fase tardo-arcaica accomuna i tetti dell'area medio-tirrenica, colpisce infatti non riscontrare una analoga diffusione di procedimenti di cantiere, quale l'impiego delle leve per la messa in opera: in particolare a Caere, città etrusca particolarmente legata al mondo greco tanto da avere un thesauros a Delphi, e nel suo scalo portuale di Pyrgi.

NOTE

1 *Pyrgi* 1959, 1970, 1992.
2 F. Melis, in *Arezzo 1985*, 7.1B, p. 130; 7.1.G, pp. 134-136. I calcoli strutturali sono stati eseguiti dall'arch. G. Foglia.
3 La ricostruzione è stata realizzata attraverso due Tesi di Laurea Magistrale (relatore prof. arch. A. Ippolito), incentrate rispettivamente sul tempio A (M. Attenni, *Rilievo e archeologia. Documentazione digitale e modellazione 3d per la divulgazione e la ricostruzione del santuario di Pyrgi*, a.a. 2013-2014) e sul tempio B (E. Valente, *Dalla conoscenza alla virtualizzazione: acquisizione, gestione e comunicazione del dato archeologico. L'area sacra di Pyrgi*, a.a. 2015-2016).
4 Rispettivamente eseguite dall'équipe del prof. Ippolito e, con la consueta amichevole disponibilità, dal prof. A.M. Jaia; per recenti interventi di documentazione 3d, cfr. Alvaro 2021.
5 Per una lettura di insieme dei contesti indagati dalla Sapienza: Baglione/Michetti 2017; Michetti/Belelli Marchesini 2018. Per i più recenti dati di scavo e la ripresa delle indagini nel santuario: Michetti *et al.* 2021.
6 Belelli Marchesini 2001, 2013a; B. Belelli Marchesini, in Baglione *et al.* 2017b, 204-206.
7 Altri insediamenti marittimi etruschi, quali Regisvilla (Morselli/Tortorici 1983, Figg. 1-2) e Fonteblanda (Ciampoltrini 2003, 281-283, fig. 5), sembrano presentare una urbanistica di tipo regolare; schemi con orientamenti flessibili, seppure improntati a criteri di ortogonalità, sono documentati ad esempio a Massalia (Moliner 2001).
8 Baglione *et al.* 2010, 2017a, 2017b; Baglione/Belelli Marchesini 2015; Colonna 2013, 87-95.
9 Per un bilancio complessivo delle evidenze: Colonna 2000; Baglione 2014.
10 Colonna 2000, 276.
11 Colonna 1991-1992; 2006; Belelli Marchesini 2013b. Sugli altari di Pyrgi: Baglione/Belelli Marchesini 2013.
12 Belelli Marchesini 2013b, 23-24, fig. 9.
13 Colonna 1968.
14 Belelli Marchesini 2001, 403, fig. 10. Sulla tecnica orvietana: Stopponi 2006, 209-215.
15 Colonna 2010, 276-277, figg. 4-5.
16 Sintesi del quadro archeologico in Cifani 2008.
17 G. Colonna, in *Arezzo 1985*, 60-61.
18 Rendeli 1989.
19 Per Caere: Rizzo 2008; Belelli Marchesini 2014.
20 Cifani 2010.
21 Colonna 2008.
22 Torelli 1983; Colonna 1986, 423-424. Da ultimo, sulla figura di Damarato e la sua équipe, Ampolo 2018.
23 Significativa, se non frutto di una tradizione elaborata nel I sec.a.C. (Gabba 1984), è la precoce organizzazione di artigiani in corporazione di mestieri, attribuita dalle fonti all'iniziativa del re Numa (Plutarco, Vita di Numa, 17; Plinio, N.H. 34.I, 35.46) o all'epoca del re Servio Tullio (Florus I.6.3).
24 Colonna 1986, 402-403, fig.275

25 Ipotizzata per l'edilizia monumentale di epoca arcaica, in base al calcolo dei carichi, in Mac Intosh Turfa/Steinmeyer 1996. Sull'impiego in questa fase delle false capriate: Zamperini 2015, 630-631, fig. 1.
26 Hodge 1980, 38-44; Klein 1998, 351.
27 Lugli 1957, 169.
28 Cifani 2008, 239-240, con riferimenti.
29 Per le opere di fortificazione: Fontaine 2008, 211.
30 Bonghi Jovino 1991, 176-177.
31 A Caere, il miglior esempio di impiego delle due tecniche è offerto dalle tombe di San Paolo (Rizzo 2001, 2015, 14-23, figg. 8-10, 29).
32 Colonna 1986, 397-398; Naso 1998.
33 Coarelli 1991, 39-40; Cifani 2008, 319-323.
34 Cherici 2006, 13, nota 4.
35 Dinsmoor 1961, 357.
36 In generale, Cherici 2006, 2007. Per Tarquinia: Bonghi Jovino 2000, Invernizzi 2001 (complesso della Civita); Cavalieri 2008 (Ara della Regina). Per Marzabotto: Sassatelli/Govi 2005, 26-30, fig. 30; Ranieri 2005. Per l'architettura greca: Leonardis 2016.
37 Cherici 2006, 19-20, fig. 4.
38 Barresi 1990, Baronio 2012.
39 Barresi 1990, 255. Per l'applicazione nell'ambito dell'architettura domestica, Maaskant Kleibrink 1992, 134, fig. LI.
40 Baronio 2012, 12-13, fig. 2.
41 Bigi 2017.
42 Ne è esempio lo scarico di fonderia a Caere, Vigna Parrocchiale: Bellelli 2005. Sull'organizzazione del cantiere edilizio: Cifani 2008, 326-332, fig. 271
43 Sui dati archeologici: Colonna 1970b, 1992.
44 Krauss 1951, 87-88
45 Gentili 2013, 228-232.
46 G. Colonna, in Pyrgi1970, 597, figg. 448-454.
47 Un ulteriore spezzone di blocco intonacato è stato rinvenuto all'interno di un cavo di asportazione dei muri: Colonna 1992, 180, fig. 150.
48 Per la classificazione degli intonaci: Pyrgi 1959, 228.
49 Colonna 1966b, fig. 2; 1992, 180, fig. 151
50 G. Colonna, in Pyrgi 1970, 440-441.
51 Sul modello architettonico: Colonna in Pyrgi 1992, 181-183; Colonna, in Sassatelli/Govi 2005, 317
52 Precisate in Colonna 1992, 171.
53 In questo *range* rientrano i templi di Pompei, Foro Triangolare di Pompei (1,6), Satricum II (1,57), Marzabotto (1,616) e Vulci (1,47) (E.Govi, in Sassatelli/Govi 2005, nota 44); Orvieto Campo della Fiera, tempio C (1:465) (Stopponi 2017, 124). Un rapporto di 1,6 si riscontra anche nel Tempio II di Tarquinia (Bonghi Jovino in *Tarchna IV*, 47).
54 De Waele 1981, 51, figg. 25-26.
55 Barresi 1990, 268, fig. 7. Analoga proporzione si ottiene ipotizzando dimensioni di 66 x 99 piedi alla quota di fondazione, con griglia da 33 piedi.
56 Colonna 1965, 194; Colonna 1966a, 277, nota 31; Colonna 1992, 289.
57 Melis 1985b.
58 Colonna 1992, 177-178.
59 Anche a Satricum, il podio del tempio pseudoperiptero riposa su uno strato di preparazione in schegge tufacee: de Waele 1981, 30.
60 Ringrazio la collega Sophie Helas per la segnalazione.
61 Anche nell'angolo nord, all'altezza della IV assisa, la cui tessitura non è riprodotta fedelmente nelle planimetrie edite.

[62] Nei templi greci e magno-greci, ricorrente è l'avvio del lavoro da un punto, da cui si opera lateralmente, anche se non mancano casi di edifici realizzati impiegando simultaneamente più squadre di operai: Hodge 1975, 142.
[63] Colonna 1965.
[64] Sui dati archeologici: Colonna 1959, 1970a.
[65] Belelli Marchesini 1997, 633-634; Colonna 2000, 316.
[66] Colonna 1966b, 275-277, fig. 4; 1970a, 40-41, fig. 3.
[67] Colonna 1966b, 268-269, fig. 1-2; 1970a, 43, figg. 30, 32
[68] Colonna 1970a, 23.
[69] Melis 1985a.
[70] Baronio 2012, 29, nota 32.
[71] Cherici 2007, 14, fig. 6.
[72] Colonna 1965.
[73] Melis 1985a.
[74] Il risultato ottenuto collima con la ricostruzione proposta in Colonna 1965, che considera un diametro inferiore delle colonne pari a 4 piedi.
[75] G. Colonna, in *Pyrgi* 1970, 451-452, figg. 5 e 352.
[76] Considerato come piede progettuale in De Waele 1981, 51, figg. 23-24.
[77] Tale espediente trova riscontro nel tempio di Giove Capitolino, nel cosidetto "muro romano": Cifani 2008, 89, fig. 72.
[78] Colonna 1970a, 36.
[79] Sommella Mura 2009, 343-344.
[80] Govi 2017.
[81] Rizzo 2009, 95-100; Maggiani 2017, 75-76, fig. 2. Il tempio, misurante m 24 x 16,5, presenta proporzioni (1:1,5) simili al tempio B di Pyrgi.
[82] Maggiani 2017, 76-77, Figg. 2-3, che ne corregge le dimensioni (m 20 x 28; rapporto 1:1,4) rispetto a quanto pubblicato in precedenza.
[83] M. Cristofani, in *Caere 4*, 17-21.
[84] Attribuite a un tempio periptero sine postico, di cui le terrecotte architettoniche segnalano una fase tardo-arcaica e un rifacimento di età ellenistica: Nardi 2001, 157-158.
[85] Sulla tecnica: Adam 1984, 54-56; Lugli 1957, 231-235. Per la Grecia: Martin 1965, pp.236-237
[86] Colonna 2005, 112. A Satricum la tecnica è documentata anche nella struttura J adiacente alla strada in località Poggio Cavallari (Gnade 2002, 54-58, tavv. 20-22).
[87] Cozza 1975, 126, fig. 157.
[88] Cifani 2008, 87, fig. 74.
[89] Colonna 1991, 52.
[90] Sgubini Moretti 1994, 23-24, nota 80, fig. 25.
[91] Ad esempio, nel tempio dell'Ara della Regina (osservazione personale) e nell'altare (struttura 14) antistante la terrazza del tempio (Bagnasco Gianni 1986, p. 365, fig. 361); nella crepidine del tumulo 6183 (osservazione personale: pianta in Cataldi 1993, 76, fig. 90).
[92] Sgubini Moretti 1980, tavv. XCIX-C (fori circolari).
[93] Murray Threipland/Torelli 1970, fig. 1.
[94] Cortese informazione prof. S. Stopponi (cfr. Stopponi 2018, figg. 7, 14).
[95] Moscati 1992.
[96] Lugli 1957, 235-237.
[97] Colonna 1986, 474.
[98] Landels 1978, 84-98.
[99] L'impiego di *ferrei forfices* è ipotizzato per la messa in opera dei conci in chiave delle coperture dei Meloni del Sodo e di Camucia (VI sec.a.C.) a Cortona: Colonna 1986, 430. Tracce relative a sistemi di sollevamento sono presenti sugli edifici di Campo della Fiera a Orvieto (cortese informazione prof. Simonetta Stopponi): in particolare sul tempio A, analizzato da Giovanni Virgineo.
[100] Gullini 1990, 95-98.
[101] M. Boss, in *Caere 3.1*, 15-17, fig. 20.
[102] Mitro/Salvadori 2017.
[103] Per un esempio sull'altopiano della Banditaccia: Benedettini/Cosentino/Russo Tagliente 2018, 119-120.
[104] M. Cristofani, in *Caere 3.1*, 15. Nella cava della Bufolareccia si conserva la traccia del distacco di un blocco misurante cm 85 x 50 x 45 (Graziadei *et al.* 2014, 92).
[105] Ad esempio, nell'edificio tripartito tardo-arcaico di Vigna Parrocchiale: M. Cristofani, in *Caere 4*, 17.
[106] In particolare,per le mura urbiche: Graziadei/Iannaccone/Salvadori 2014, 84, fig. 9.
[107] Vinaccia 1926.
[108] Sull'argomento, che ho affrontato nell'ambito della mia ricerca di Dottorato (Belelli Marchesini 1995), tornerò in altra sede.
[109] Per il rapporto tra attività estrattiva e monumenti: Chilini/de Lucia Brolli 2017.

BIBLIOGRAFIA

Adam, J.P. 1984, *La construction romaine, materiaux et techniques*, Paris.

Alvaro, C. 2021, Appendice. Attività di rilievo laser scanner a Pyrgi, in Michetti et al. 2021, 211-218.

Ampolo, C. 2017, Demarato di Corinto 'bacchiade' tra Grecia, Etruria e Roma: rappresentazione e realtà fonti, funzione dei racconti, integrazione di genti e culture, mobilità sociale arcaica, in S. Struffolino (ed.), *Scritti per il decimo anniversario di Aristonothos*, Aristonothos 13.2, 25-134.

*Arezzo* 1985: G. Colonna (ed.), *Santuari d'Etruria* (catalogo della mostra, Arezzo 19 maggio-20 ottobre 1985), Milano.

Baglione, P. 2014, Pyrgi. Un santuario nel cuore del Mediterraneo, in F. Gaultier/L. Haumesser (eds), *Gli Etruschi e il Mediterraneo. La città di Cerveteri* (catalogo della mostra, Roma, Palazzo delle Esposizioni, 15 aprile-20 luglio 2014), Roma, 204-220.

Baglione, M.P./B. Belelli Marchesini 2013, News from the field. Altars at Pyrgi, *EtrSt* 16.1, 229-243.

Baglione, M.P./B. Belelli Marchesini 2015, Nuovi dati dagli scavi a nord del Santuario nella seconda metà del VI sec.a.C., *ScAnt* 21.2, 131-152.

Baglione, M.P./M.D. Gentili 2013 (eds), *Riflessioni su Pyrgi. Scavi e ricerche nelle aree del santuario* (Supplementi e Monografie ACl 11, n.s. 8), Roma.

Baglione, M.P./L. Michetti 2017, Tra Caere e Pyrgi. I grandi santuari costieri e la politica di Caere, in Govi 2017, 97-120.

Baglione, M.P./B. Belelli Marchesini/C. Carlucci/L.M. Michetti 2010, Recenti indagini nel comprensorio archeologico di Pyrgi (2009-2010), *ScAnt* 16, 541-560.

Baglione, M.P./B. Belelli Marchesini/C. Carlucci/L.M. Michetti/M. Bonadies/E. Cerilli/A. Conti/B. Giuliani/M. Zinni, Pyrgi, l'area a nord del santuario: nuovi dati dalle recenti campagne di scavo, *ScAnt* 23.1,135-172.

Baglione, M.P./B. Belelli Marchesini/C. Carlucci/L.M. Michetti, Pyrgi, harbour and sanctuary of Caere: landscape, urbanistic planning and architectural features , *Archeologia e calcolatori* 28, 39-48.

Bagnasco Gianni, G. 1986, Un maestoso tempio per gli dei: l'Ara della Regina. Gli interventi recenti, in M. Bonghi Jovino (ed.), *Gli Etruschi a Tarquinia* (catalogo della

mostra, Milano 14 aprile-29 giugno 1986), Modena, 364-372.
Baronio, P. 2012, Un architetto per il tempio di Tina a Marzabotto. Studio dell'antico procedimento geometrico-proporzionale utilizzato nel progetto del tempio urbano della città etrusca di Kainua, *Ocnus* 20, 9-32.
Barresi, P. 1990, Schemi geometrici nei templi dell'Italia centrale, *ACl* 42, 251-285.
Belelli Marchesini, B. 1997. Tempio. Etruria, *EAA. II supplemento* V, 628-638.
Belelli Marchesini, B. 1995, *L'edilizia in Etruria Meridionale dal VII al IV sec.a.C: tecniche e accorgimenti costruttivi*. Tesi di Dottorato, Sapienza Università di Roma.
Belelli Marchesini, B. 2001, L'abitato costiero di Pyrgi, in J.R. Brandt/L. Karlsson (eds), *From huts to houses. Transformation of ancient societies*, Proceedings of the International Seminar organized by the Norwegian and Swedish Institutes in Rome, 21-24 September 1997), Stockholm, 395-405.
Belelli Marchesini, B. 2013a, Considerazioni sull'abitato etrusco di Pyrgi, in Baglione/Gentili 2013, 247-262.
Belelli Marchesini, B. 2013b, Le linee di sviluppo topografico del santuario meridionale, in Baglione/Gentili 2013, 11-40.
Belelli Marchesini, B. 2014, L'architettura monumentale di Cerveteri in epoca arcaica, in F. Gaultier/L. Haumesser (eds), *Gli Etruschi e il Mediterraneo. La città di Cerveteri* (catalogo della mostra, Roma, Palazzo delle Esposizioni, 15 aprile-20 luglio 2014), Roma, 154-155.
Benedettini, M.G./R.Cosentino/A. Russo Tagliente 2018, La necropoli della Banditaccia: rapporto preliminare su un nuovo quartiere funerario sull'altopiano delle Onde Marine, in A. Naso/M. Botto (eds), *Caere orientalizzante. Nuove ricerche su città e necropoli*, Roma, 109-122.
Bigi, D. 2017, Di professione architetto. Sull'urna di Vel Rafi, nel tentativo di restituire dignità ad un ipogeo dimenticato, in C. Masseria/E. Marroni (eds.), *Dialogando. Studi in onore di Mario Torelli*, Pisa, 39-48.
Bonghi Jovino, M. 1991, Osservazioni sui sistemi di costruzione a Tarquinia: tecniche locali ed impiego del "muro a pilastri" fenicio, *ACl* 43, 171-191.
*Caere* 3.1: M. Cristofani (ed.), *Caere 3.1. Lo scarico arcaico della Vigna Parrocchiale*, Roma 1992.
*Caere* 4: M. Cristofani (ed.), *Caere 4. Vigna Parrocchiale. Scavi 1983-1989. Il santuario, la "residenza" e l'edificio ellittico*, Roma 2003.
Cataldi, M. 1993, *Tarquinia*, Roma
Cavalieri, M. 2008, *Genus numeri*, relations mathématiques sous-jacentes à l'architecture étrusque. Le cas du temple de *l'Ara della Regina à Tarquinia*, Res antiquae 5, 3-14.
Cherici, A. 2006, Per una scienza etrusca, *Science and Technology for Cultural Heritage* 15 (1-2), 9-28.
Cherici, A. 2007, Per una scienza etrusca, 2. Templum, templi e rettangolo aureo, *Science and Technology for Cultural Heritage*, 9-30.
Chilini, G./M.A. de Lucia Brolli, Una cava di tufo alle porte di Faleri, *ScAnt* 23.2, 181-198.
Ciampoltrini, G. 2003, L'insediamento arcaico di Fonteblanda e l'urbanistica "ippodamea" tra Orvieto e Vulci, *AnnFaina* 10, 279-299.
Cifani, G. 2008, *Architettura romana arcaica. Edilizia e società tra Monarchia e Repubblica*, Roma.
Cifani, G. 2010, I grandi cantieri della Roma arcaica: aspetti tecnici e organizzativi, in S. Camporeale/H. Dessales/A. Pizzo (eds.), *Arqueología de la construcción II. Los processos constructivos en el mundo romano: Italia y provincias orientales*, Madrid/Mérida, 35-49.
Coarelli, F. 1991, Gli emissari dei laghi laziali: tra mito e storia, in M. Bergamini (ed.), *Gli Etruschi maestri di idraulica*, Perugia, 35-41.
Colonna, G. 1959, Descrizione dello scavo, in *Pyrgi 1959*, 154-170.
Colonna, G. 1965, Il santuario di Pyrgi alla luce delle recenti scoperte, *StEtr* 33, 191-219.
Colonna, G. 1966a, Nuovi elementi per la storia del santuario di Pyrgi, *ACl* 18, 85-102.
Colonna, G. 1966b, Elementi architettonici in pietra dal santuario di Pyrgi, *ACl* 18, 268-278.
Colonna, G. 1968, La via Caere-Pyrgi, in *La via Aurelia da Roma a Forum Aurelii* (Quaderni Istituto di Topografia Antica Università di Roma 4), Roma, 75-87.
Colonna, G. 1970a, Il Tempio A. Le strutture, in *Pyrgi 1970*, 23-47.
Colonna. G. 1970b, Il Tempio B. Le strutture, in *Pyrgi 1970*, 275-289.
Colonna, G. 1984, I templi del Lazio fino al V secolo compreso, *ArchLaz* 6, 396-411.
Colonna, G. 1986, Urbanistica e architettura, in *Rasenna. Storia e civiltà degli Etruschi*, Milano, 371-530.
Colonna. G. 1991, Le due fasi del tempio di S.Omobono, in M. Gnade (ed.), *Stips votiva. Papers presented to C.M. Stibbe*, Amsterdam, 51-59.
Colonna, G. 1991-1992, Altari e sacelli. L'area sud di Pyrgi dopo otto anni di ricerche, *RendPontAcc* 64, 63-115.
Colonna, G. 1992, Il Tempio B. Le strutture, in *Pyrgi 1992*, 171-183.
Colonna, G. 2000, Il santuario di Pyrgi dalle origini mitistoriche agli altorilievi frontonali dei Sette e di Leucothea, *ScAnt* 10, 251-336.
Colonna, G. 2005, Tra architettura e urbanistica. A proposito del Tempio di Mater Matuta a Satricum, in S.T.A.M./Mols,/E.M./Moorman (eds.), *Omni pede stare. Saggi architettonici e circumvesuviani in memoriam Jos de Waele*, Napoli, 111-117.
Colonna, G. 2006, Sacred architecture and the religion of the Etruscans, in N. de Grummond/E. Simon (eds), *The religion of the Etruscans*, Austin, 132-168.
Colonna, G. 2008, L'officina veiente: Vulca e gli altri maestri di statuaria arcaica in terracotta, M. Torelli/A.M. Moretti Sgubini (eds), *Etruschi. Le antiche metropoli del Lazio* (catalogo della mostra, Roma, Palazzo delle Esposizioni 20 ottobre 2008- 6 gennaio 2009), Verona, 53-63.
Colonna, G. 2010, A proposito del primo trattato romano-cartaginese (e della donazione pyrgense ad Astarte), *AnnFaina* 17, 275-303.
Colonna, G. 2013, Nuovi dati sui porti, sull'abitato e sulle aree sacre della Pyrgi etrusca, *StEtr* 76, 81-109.
De Waele, J. 1981, I templi della MaterMatuta a Satricum, *MededRom* 43, 7-68.
Fontaine, P. 2008, Mura, arte fortificatoria e città in Etruria. Riflessione sui dati archeologici, in *La città murata in Etruria*. Atti del XXV Convegno di Studi Etruschi ed Italici, Chianciano Terme, Sarteano, Chiusi, 30 marzo-3 aprile 2005, Roma/Pisa, 203-220.
Gabba, E. 1985, The Collegia of Numa: Problems of Method and Political Ideas, *JRS* 74, 81-86.
Govi, E. (ed.) 2017, *La città etrusca e il sacro. Santuari e istituzioni politiche*. Atti del Convegno, Bologna 21-23 gennaio 2016, Bologna.
Govi, E. 2017a, La dimensione del sacro nella città di *Kainua*-Marzabotto, in Govi 2017, 145-179.
Hodge, A.T. 1960, *The woodwork of Greek roofs*, Cambridge.

Hodge, A.T. 1975, Bevelled joints and the direction of laying in Greek architecture, *AJA* 79, 333-347.

Graziadei, A./P. Iannaccone/Y. Salvadori 2014, La tecnica costruttiva delle fortificazioni ceriti, in V. Bellelli (ed), *Caere e Pyrgi: il territorio, la viabilità e le fortificazioni*. Atti della Giornata di Studio, Roma CNR, 1 marzo 2012 (Caere 6), Pisa/Roma, 81-96.

Gullini, G. 1990, Ingegneria e artigianato industriale, in *Magna Grecia. Arte e artigianato*, Milano, 80-102.

Invernizzi, E. 2001, Il complesso monumentale: osservazioni sulla natura geometrica dell'edificio, in A.M. Moretti Sgubini (ed.), *Tarquinia etrusca: una nuova storia* (Catalogo della Mostra, Tarquinia 2001)», Roma, 44.

Landels, J.C. 1978, *Engineering in the ancient World*, London.

Leonardis, R. 2016, Geometry in Greece The Use of Geometry by Ancient Greek Architects, in M.M. Miles (ed), *A Companion to Greek Architecture*, 92-104.

Lugli, G. 1957, *La tecnica edilizia dei Romani*, Roma.

Klein, N.L. 1998, Evidence for West Greek Influence on Mainland Greek Roof Construction and the Creation of the Truss in the archaic period, *Hesperia* 67, 335-374.

Krauss F. 1951, L'architettura, in P. Zancani Montuoro/U. Zanotti Bianco (eds), *Heraion alla foce del Sele* I. *Il santuario. Il tempio della dea. Rilievi figurati vari*, Roma, 83-119.

Maaskant Kleibrink, M. 1992, *Settlement excavation at Borgo Le Ferriere(Satricum)* II, Groningen

Maggiani, A. 2017, Il sacro in Etruria: dentro e fuori la città, in Govi 2017, 75-96.

MacIntosh Turfa, J./A.G. Steinmeyer 1996, The comparative structure of Greek and Etruscan monumental buildings, *BSR* 64,1-39.

Martin, R. 1965, *Manuel d'architecture grecque* I, Paris.

Melis, F. 1985a, Modello di ricostruzione del tempio A, in *Arezzo 1985*, scheda 7.1G, 134-136.

Melis, F. 1985b, 7.1.G. Modello di ricostruzione del tempio B, in *Arezzo 1985*, scheda 7.1B, 130.

Michetti, L./B. Belelli Marchesini 2018, Pyrgi, porto e santuario di Caere. Tra conoscenze acquisite e ricerche in corso, AnnFaina 25, 333-365.

Michetti, L.M./B. Belelli Marchesini/M. Bonadies/A. Conti/R. Zaccagnini/M. Zinni 2021, Pyrgi, porto e grande santuario marittimo di Caere. Scavi nell'area dell'abitato e nel Santuario (campagne 2017-2020), *ScAnt* 27.1, 175-210.

Mitro, R./Y. Salvadori 2017, Cerveteri, cave a cielo aperto nell'area urbana, *ScAnt* 23.2, 223-231.

Moliner, M. 2001, *Orientations urbaines dans Marseille antique, in Marseille. Trames et paysages urbains de Gytis au Rai René*. Actes du colloqu de Marseille, 3-5 novembre1999 (Etudes Massaliètes 7), Marseille,101-120.

Morselli, C./E. Tortici 1985, La situazione di Regisvilla, in *Il commercio etrusco arcaico*. Atti dell'incontro di studio, 5-7 dicembre 1983, *QuadAEI* 9, 27-40.

Moscati, P. 1992, Strutture lapidee, in *Caere 3.1*, 21-27.

Mura Sommella, A. 2009, Il tempio di Giove Capitolino: una nuova proposta di lettura, *AnnFaina* 16, 333-372.

Murray Threipland, L./M. Torelli 1970, A semi-subterranean Etruscan building in the Casale Pian Roseto (Veii) area, *BSR* 31, 62-121

Nardi, G. 2001. Il santuario sulla Valle della Mola, in A.M. Sgubini Moretti (ed), *Veio, Cerveteri, Vulci. Città d'Etruria a confronto* (catalogo della mostra, Roma 2001), Roma, 157-161.

Naso, A. 1998, I tumuli monumentali in Etruria meridionale: caratteri propri e possibili ascendenze orientali, in *Archäologische untersuchungen zu den beziehungen zwischen altitalien und der zone nordwärts der Alpen während der frühen eisenzeit alteuropas* (Atti del colloquio, Regensburg 3-5 nov. 1994), Regensburg, 117-157.

*Pyrgi* 1959: *Santa Severa (Roma). Scavi e ricerche nel sito dell'antica Pyrgi (1957-1958)*, NSc 1959, 143-263.

*Pyrgi* 1970: *Santa Severa (Roma). Scavi del santuario etrusco di Pyrgi (1959-1967)*, NSc 1970, II supplemento.

*Pyrgi* 1992: *Santa Severa (Roma). Scavi del santuario etrusco di Pyrgi (1969-1971)*, NSc 1988-1989, II supplemento.

Ranieri, M. 2005, La geometria della pianta del tempio urbano di Marzabotto (Regio I, insula 5), in Sassatelli/Govi 2005, 73-87.

Rendeli, M. 1989, "Muratori, ho fretta di erigere questa casa" (Ant. Pal. 14, 136). Concorrenza tra formazioni urbane dell'Italia centrale tirrenica nella costruzione di edifici di culto arcaici, *RIA* s. III, 12, 49-68.

Rizzo, M. A. 2001, Le tombe orientalizzanti di San Paolo, in A.M. Sgubini Moretti (ed), *Veio, Cerveteri, Vulci. Città d'Etruria a confronto* (catalogo della mostra, Roma 2001),163-176.

Rizzo, M.A. 2008, Cerveteri. Le grandi architetture dei vivi e dei morti, in M. Torelli/A.M. Moretti Sgubini (eds), *Etruschi. Le antiche metropoli del Lazio* (catalogo della mostra, Roma, Palazzo delle Esposizioni 20 ottobre 2008- 6 gennaio 2009), Verona, 78-87.

Rizzo, M.A. 2009, Scavi e ricerche nell'area sacra di S.Antonio a Cerveteri, *Mediterranea* 5, 91-120

Rizzo, M.A. 2016, *Principi Etruschi. Le tombe orientalizzanti di San Paolo a Cerveteri. Bollettino d'Arte* - Volume Speciale.

Sassatelli, G./E. Govi 2005, Il tempio di Tinia in area urbana, in G. Sassatelli/E. Govi (eds), *Culti, forma urbana e artigianato a Marzabotto. Nuove prospettive di ricerca*. Atti del Convegno di Studi, Bologna, S. Giovanni in Monte 3-4 giugno 2003, Bologna, 9-62.

Sgubini Moretti, A. M. 1980, Castro, *StEtr* 48, 523-526.

Sgubini Moretti, A.M. 1994, Ricerche archeologiche a Vulci: 1985-1990, in M. Martelli (ed.), *Tyrrhenoi philotechnoi*. Atti della Giornata di Studio organizzata dalla Facoltà di Conservazione dei Beni Culturali dell'Università degli Studi della Tuscia in occasione della mostra "Il mondo degli Etruschi. Testimonianze dai Musei di Berlino e dell'Europa orientale", Viterbo, 13 ottobre 1990, Roma, 9-49.

Stopponi, S. 2006, Tecniche edilizie di tipo misto a Orvieto, in M. Bonghi Jovino (ed.), *Tarquinia e le civiltà del Mediterraneo* (Convegno Internazionale, Milano 22-24 giugno 2004), *Quaderni di Acme* 77, 207-245

Stopponi, S. 2017, Orvieto, Campo della Fiera: forme del sacro nel "luogo celeste", in Govi 2017, 121-144.

Stopponi, S. 2018, Orvieto- località Campo della Fiera: la scoperta del *Fanum Voltumnae*, AnnFaina 25, 9-36.

Tarchna IV: M. Bonghi Jovino/G. Bagnasco Gianni (eds), *Tarquinia. Il santuario dell'Ara della Regina. I templi arcaici*, Roma 2012.

Torelli, M. 1983, Polis e "palazzo". Architettura, ideologia e artigianato greco in Etruria tra VII e VI sec., in *Architecture et société de l'archaisme grec à la fin de la république romaine*. Actes du Colloque International, Rome 1980, Rome, 471-492.

Vinaccia, M. 1926, Saggio di metrologia etrusca, *RendAcLinc*, 532-542.

Zamperini, E. 2015, Timber trusses in Italy: the progressive prevailing of open-joint over closed-joint trusses, in *Proceedings of the 5th International Congress on Construction History* (Chicago, june 2015) 2, 629-636.

# Materializing Technology
# (Mobile Objects)

# Fluctuation and stability.
## *Materialising technological knowledge among Satricum potters*

*Martina Revello Lami*

*Abstract*

*This paper discusses the potential of applying a chaîne opératoire approach to the study of technology to bridge the traditional divide between materialistic and structuralist ontologies. Using pottery making systems in Archaic Satricum as a case study, this analysis brings to the fore aspects of continuity and discontinuity detectable in the ceramic record as a valuable tool to reconstruct technological knowledge and practice within potting communities and society at large.*

INTRODUCTION

Twentieth-century studies on ancient technology have provided an excellent framework for disentangling the complex interactions between technical knowledge, choices and practices.[1] These approaches are as diverse as their theoretical underpinnings and are usually categorized in this binary: technological determinism or the social construction of technology.[2] Technological determinism relies explicitly on a positivist standpoint and interprets technology as a set of material things and knowledge that shape almost all aspects of human culture, including economics, politics, and social organization. Archaeological research adopting such a materialist approach is grounded in formalist economic models, and is mostly concerned with patterns of production, efficiency and labor organization.[3] On the other hand, archaeologists viewing ancient technology as a social construct usually place particular emphasis on the people within the human-material culture relationship, drawing heavily on social anthropology, structuralism and agency theory. Within this framework, technology is understood as materialized cultural systems that influence the entire life cycle of an artefact, from manufacture through use, repair and discard.

A valuable common ground between these two opposing interpretations is provided by research dedicated to the detailed reconstruction of artefacts' productive sequence, which is crucial to our understanding of past technological practices and bodily gestures performed by artisans in the manufacturing process. Too often, however, such an approach focuses only on the mechanics of techniques without making them explicitly social.[4] Technical systems are embedded within broader social dynamics. Because the chaîne opératoire concept allows multiple scales of analysis - from the individual agent to larger communities of practice – it may greatly contribute to unraveling how technological knowledge influences society and vice versa. In this respect, discussing the degree of artefacts variability can be very useful in order to move beyond deterministic interpretations of chaînes opératoires. Stability in specific attributes of pottery assemblages is usually approached in terms of increased economic efficiency; in reality, a certain degree of homogeneity may reflect particular learned behaviors, which lead to more standardized outputs even in a non-industrial setting.[5] Clearly, by excluding the social dimension from technology our definition of variability becomes less meaningful, demonstrating how changes in technological knowledge and practice need to be interpreted within their socio-cultural systems.

ARCHAEOLOGY OF TECHNOLOGY BETWEEN MATERIALISM AND STRUCTURALISM

We shape the world in which we live in both material and symbolic ways, and technology is involved in this dynamic process on a daily basis.[6] Through the activities and social relations involved in material production, we create things. In turn, such creative processes and their end products become material and symbolic structures through which the world is perceived and responded to.[7] Cultural evolutionary theory has long described human progress in terms of innovation and change in the technology at hand, being considered as a major causal motor of human evolution. Not surprisingly, technology forms the centerpiece of practically all research into ancient past, as the archaeological record comprises the material remains of ancient lifeways. Despite the turn to more social and cultural concerns of related disciplines such as anthropology, social sciences and geography, archaeology has continued to engage with material things,[8] in particular those things that we (in the present) typically equate with technology, such as lithic tools, ceramic vessels, metal artefacts, weaving devices, production discards etc. Since the inception of the discipline these things have been imbued with meaning by researchers and recognized as cultural historical markers thorough analogy and comparison.

Archaeology has been deeply affected by the shifting intellectual conceptions of technology in both academia and society at large, resulting in a wealth of different theoretical approaches. To focus on the recent past: throughout the ensuing decades of processual and postprocessual archaeology, the question of how to interpret the material record and technological variability became a matter of heated debate. At its core one may discern two polarizing perspectives on the archaeological record relying respectively on materialistic and humanistic ontologies. On the one hand, proponents of New Archaeology were mainly concerned with explaining the functional, technological and adaptive importance of things, whilst postprocessualists placed particular emphasis on unraveling the social and symbolic meaning of artefacts. From such divergent understandings of material culture follow equally divergent interpretations of technology; one aiming at the definition of its physical characteristics, the other one its cultural dimensions, which perfectly epitomizes the great divide between practical and cultural paradigms sketched above.

Diving into practical reasons, a great part of traditional scholarship on ancient technologies is deeply rooted in materialistic and positivistic knowledge systems, and New Archaeology standpoint is no exception. In line with the formulation of one of its most influential proponents, Lewis Binford, the definition of technology overlaps with that of culture interpreted as "man's extrasomatic means of adaptation".[9] In Binford's view, the primary way in which cultures adapt to their environments happens by means of economic, social, and ideological subsystems mediated by technology (hence his technomic, sociotechnic, and ideotechnic categories).[10] Technology therefore acts as the physical, practical and rational buffer between cultural systems and the external world. The theoretical framework underpinning such an approach borrows from Marx's historical materialism, where history is defined as the dialectics of the mode of production and where the essence of individuals coincides with their way of producing. Historical change is thus triggered by the opposition between productive forces – such as means of production, labor conditions and power – and the social relations connected to production. The latter are based upon the ownership of the means of production and the ability to purchase labor power to create a surplus, at least in a capitalistic realm. Building on historical materialism and its several variants, archaeological interpretations promoting a practical interpretation of technology have often taken a marked political economic perspective. Closer to classical economic principles, such a perspective considers the logic of ancient technological systems ruled by factors such as competition, efficiency and management of organizational complexity. Within this framework modern cost/benefit and performance analyses are commonly applied to evaluate strengths and weaknesses of ancient craft production systems in general, but also to explain in more detail the strategies put in place by the maker for procuring, designing, manufacturing and using a tool.[11]

Likewise grounded in materialism, behavioral research lines drawing on Schiffer's work focus on deterministic aspects of specific techniques, placing emphasis on the universality of artefacts physics. Inquiry into basic causes of artefact variability takes centre stage here and has been actively pursued by proponents of behavioral archaeology by applying explanatory models developed in other fields such as biology and evolutionary ecology. Despite the distance from the theoretical underpinnings of economy driven perspectives described above, behavioral research into technology exploits similar analytical tools, as it is demonstrated by the attention paid to the performance characteristics inherent in raw materials and their impact on makers' choices.[12]

Research favoring materialist ontologies, of which the overview above makes no claim of completeness, is characterized by excellent fine-grained studies of craft techniques, innovations and artefacts variability and provides solid explanatory models to untangle the complex interaction between tools and tools-makers. However, by relying heavily on positivist and evolutionary standpoints it has tended to focus more on what is knowable of ancient technologies (the physics of artefacts) to the detriment of the social relations and cultural contexts, which are essential components for the definition of any technosystem. The political economic variant in particular, by applying analytical frameworks derived from modern economy theory, can lead to a biased interpretation of ancient production systems.

Such a claim lies at the core of the shift toward analytical frameworks adopting humanistic ontologies in order to investigate ancient technology. Since the 90s by merging two broad streams of scholarship, namely social anthropology and STS, archaeological research has increasingly concentrated its efforts onto unravelling the social dynamics of material culture production and use. This line of work approaches science and technology as social institutions possessing distinctive structures, commitments, practices, and discourses that vary across cultures and change over time. Structuralism, agency theory, symbolic and gender studies, all encouraged archaeologists to interpret the technological record differently, moving beyond the traditional separation between technology intended as ecological adaptation to the environment and art as the cultural filter through which sensory experiences are communicated. The shifting perspective to more abstract components of technology highlighted how intelligence, sensibility and expression "are essential to the accomplishment of any craft from the actual bodily movement of the practitioner in his or her environment".[13] Technical actions do not provide information only on practical material matters and their mechanical ways, but convey information about how those mechanical ways are communicated, transferred and understood by the groups that produce and use them. In this sense, the contribution of ethnoarchaeology in depicting a broader picture of technological (social) systems has been pivotal in overcoming issues of theory and methodology as well as the divide between practical and cultural ontologies. Carrying out research on living, usually pre-industrial, craft communities allows the direct documentation of the social dimension of people-artefacts interaction, showing that as much as technology seeks control over the physical world, it also *influences* and *is influenced by* the non-physical world. Any technical action is shaped and reinforced by belief systems and cultural constraints and can therefore be considered as the materialization of prevailing worldviews, social values and cultural attitudes.[14]

Examples derived from ethnoarchaeological works on ceramic production systems illustrate well the limitations encountered when less attention is paid to the socio-cultural end of the technological equation. Focusing for instance on the very first stage of pottery making – i.e. raw materials' procurement - studies conducted on several potters' communities scattered across the globe, spanning from Papua New Guinea to New Mexico and Madhya Pradesh, demonstrate how such an activity is often charged with symbolic, ritualistic meaning.[15] Among the Azera potters of Morobe Province in Papua New Guinea for instance, the act of extracting clay is traditionally strictly ruled and no outsiders are allowed to observe the procedure. Only married women – not yet mothers – can collect clay and only at certain time periods provided that they comply with several prescriptions, such as wearing a traditional dress and using a particular container typical of the area to carrying the clay. As documented by May and Tuckson in their extensive survey across the country, in several potting communities there seems to be an underlying connection between good blood, good health, the ability for procreation and good potters' clay as much as sickness, bad blood and infertility are believed to cast a curse causing the soil to be unsuitable for potting activities.[16] The choices and norms listed above would most definitely not fit well with any theoretic construct built on cost/benefit or performance analysis.

Similarly, the way in which the Jicarilla Apaches exploit the micaceous clay crops in northern Rio Grande (New Mexico) to manufacture the majority of their pottery defies Western economic supply and demand laws. Deeply connected with their land, the Jicarilla hold micaceous clays sacred and blessed with divine power since they provide for their daily needs. Every clay pit is taken care of by the whole community that uses it, embodying in a way the health and status of that community. Traditionally offerings are brought to the crops where potters wait "to sense whether the time is opportune to dig or whether more offerings should be made. Sensing that the time is correct, the potter has the responsibility to gather enough material to make his or her creations and no more".[17]

The cases described above are but two examples of how research based on a methodological hierarchy, which prompt archaeologists to focus on the material aspects of ancient technology and exclude social relations and beliefs may lead to potentially misleading interpretations. Adopting a humanistic and structuralist view on technology, where knowledgeable practice and practical knowledge are embedded in any bodily routine of tool making, develops a far more meaningful account of the socially and environmentally situated practices of real human agents.[18]

## Chaîne Opératoire as a Reconciling Factor

To summarise the conflicting views illustrated above, according to deterministic ontologies technology and productive forces shape and have control over the physical world, while those grounded in structuralism and social theory state the opposite, i. e. it is our world (intended as a complex system of social and cultural values) that controls and has a major influence over technological knowledge and practice. However divergent, if we zoom out the traditionally opposing philosophical underpinnings, we might notice that the two lines of work share a common ground. At their core lies the dynamic relationship between people and artefacts, or the "stickiness of human-thing entrapments" as Hodder puts it.[19] Depending on whether emphasis is placed on the "people" or "artefact" part of the equation, one will end up supporting either the structuralist or materialist side of the discourse. As rightly pointed out by Sheila Kohring in an innovative work on the Beaker phenomenon in Western Europe between Late Neolithic and early Iron Age (ironically titled "Let's NOT talk technology?"):

"Technology is a knowledge framework which we use to construct our world but at the same time, technology shapes us, constructs our world and becomes a principle avenue for communicating social meanings".[20]

Building on structuralism and humanistic ontologies brought forward by Latour, Lemonnier, Dobres and Ingold, Kohring calls for a shift in approach towards the study of technology, placing more emphasis on the dialectic between production events and broad cultural systems and how such events are executed in socially meaningful manners. The underlying assumption is that humans and material culture are inseparable and interdependent entities, and so investigating their technological systems is central in order to understand how they influence each other.

A particularly powerful tool to approach technology and bridge the gap between determinism and humanism is provided by research dedicated to the detailed reconstruction of artefacts' productive sequence. Conventionally referred to as chaîne opératoire, the concept was first outlined for archaeology by Leroi-Gourhan in the 60s and applied to Palaeolithic research in France. In his formulation technology is intended as a "total social phenomenon" where any technological activity is constituted within an influent social and historical context and thus both realms cannot be analysed in isolation. When man creates and transforms the physical world he is also creating and transforming himself. The recognition and analysis of every stage along an operational sequence "becomes therefore relevant, since it provides information about the subject of that action and, moreover, about the society within which the given action is inscribed".[21] From this starting point, the notion of chaîne opératoire and its many interpretations is capable of merging the two opposing epistemologies described above. Even in its narrower sense of "a series of technological operations which transforms a raw material into a usable project"[22], chaîne opératoire entails a shift of scholarly attention from the examination of the end-product to the process of manufacturing. Previous approaches to technology revolved mostly around the description of ancient tools in order to address issues related to their dissemination through time and space (diffusionism/evolutionism) or to explain the laws of human adaptation to the environment. The spotlight was on the object, whilst the particular human activity that had originated it was completely missing from the picture. In contrast, the notion of chaîne opératoire emphasises every step, and every choice, of tool making. The object of study therefore becomes a longer sequence instead of just one item, thus enhancing the possibility of reaching more accurate reconstructions of ancient technological systems. Following the works of Sellet, Grace, Sillar and Tite, it is now widely agreed that this conceptual chain does not end with the realisation of the manufactured product, but when the artefact is finally discarded after different uses and reuses.[23] The target of attention lengthens further and the analysis extends to the whole life cycle of an artefact and its interaction with the community that produced and used it. Along this ordered sequence of actions, gestures, instruments, the agents leading the transformation of a given material towards the manufacture and use of a product through a series of recurrent and predictable steps move to centre stage. The two latter components (the relevance of the agent as well as the degree of predictability of a project) are key topics in assessing technological knowledge. Reconstructing the operational sequence reveals the technical choices made by the individuals in a group, thus allowing the characterisation of the technical traditions within a social group.

Over the last three decades the chaîne opératoire ceased to be simply an object of study and became an approach, an interpretative methodology "capable of forging robust inferential links between the material patterning of technical acts and the sociopolitical relations of production accounting them".[24] Such an approach entails the application of a wide range of analytical techniques spanning from those borrowed from the hard sciences in order to identify the physical factors influencing the manufacture, shape, use and discard of an object, to those grounded in anthropology, ethnography and social sciences in order to identify the cultural factors determining the technological action and charging the resulting end-products with meaning. In this light, the dynamic enactment of the technical process takes place in connection with static concepts or sets of rules, but it goes beyond the simple interaction between knowledge and skill. The focal point is recognizing that the interaction between the technical gesture (the manner of carrying the body) seats at the confluence of the mind, body, social and material world. Moving from the detailed description of the sequence of motions performed by a potter to shape the rim of a jar, to the more universal narrative of the choices made by a community when it comes to the acquisition of raw materials or the style of a decorative pattern, a chaîne opératoire approach enables archaeologists to go beyond the redundancies of the material record and look at the system of values and beliefs that individuals share when shaping and using the material world. In short, incorporating a chaîne opératoire approach helps to mend the scholarly tear between practice and culture.

The Chicken or the Egg: Technology Shaping Society or Society Shaping Technology?

The knowledge that a maker translates into production events materializes a whole suite of social as well as technical sets of information which depend on the different roles, statuses and genders experienced by the individual. Though embodied individually, knowledge systems occur in social contexts, so are also shared, modified, restricted and replicated within a community. Bodily and conceptual knowledge are inseparable as both are made meaningful within a specific social environment. In other words, we perceive and understand the world through our body not only through the way we materially engage with things, but mostly through the complex of customs and practices we learn from and share with our community. The groups in which we live or align with set the path and boundaries of our knowledge experience by structuring the learning process of specific techniques and their meanings. Through repetition and interaction within the community, such techniques become established ways of doing and along the process they contribute to establish a communal understanding of the world. Socially established practices, however flexible, dynamic and susceptible to change, construct around us a safe space made of collectively learned and shared beliefs as well as a shared way of making and doing things.

Knowledge systems – social as well as technological – are structured by and within communities and depending on the group we decide to assimilate into those conceptual frameworks will vary accordingly. Technological knowledge and practice are contextually and socially situated, and by extension also our physical engagement with them, i.e. any technical action carried out to produce material culture, largely also depend on people and context. The dynamic interaction between people and artefacts is mediated through the technological process, therefore any variation along such process reflects the agency of both people (individuals and communities) and objects.[25]

Due to the diachronic perspective, change and innovation in manufacturing techniques and styles of production are particularly noticeable in the archaeological record. Small wonder then, that the painstaking documentation of continuities and discontinuities in artefacts lies at the core of much archaeological research into ancient technological systems. In fact, the material remains of variation – or lack thereof - in craft production narrate the perpetuation, reproduction, rejection and adaptation of learned customs and information as expressed through technological processes.

From the introduction at Çatalhöyük of clay pots used as cookware in place of clay balls, to the emergence of the potter's wheel in Southern Levant, to the Carolingians' adoption of the stirrup in the early 8th century AD,[26] there are innumerable examples in archaeological scholarship illustrating the interdependency between innovations in technological knowledge and practice and changes in socio-cultural systems.

The visual impact of changes detectable in the material world plays a crucial role in giving substance to changes of meanings, behaviours and relationships occurring in a community. In this sense approaching material culture by tracing back the chain of technological events and choices resulting in a product allows us to understand not only the information and actions involved in the making, but also the shared norms that trigger either replication or variation within established models.

*Artefacts Variability: The Visible and The Invisible*

The formal characteristics of artefacts, such as shape, style and decoration, are visible to both the maker and the user, and are therefore well suited to explore both technological actions and social meanings within a community. On the other hand, technical features such as the raw sources exploited, tools used and technical gestures carried out are visible only to the makers and their restricted community, and completely invisible to the users.

The collective choices determining whether or not to conform to shared standards, thus influencing the degree of variability of objects, depends equally upon the physical features of raw materials and tools available to manufacture those objects as well as on the ways of making and using them chosen by the community. In fact, the identification of which part within the technological endeavour allows the maker to have more space for creativity and individuality, provides us with a good starting point in order to infer to what extent a community can agree with innovation and accept more or less significant variations to an established model. At the same time, assessing variability enables us to grasp how well the level of experimentation sought by the maker is received socially and considered appropriate within the community. At the other end of the spectrum, when an artefact's visual attributes and production techniques reveal increasing degrees of standardization, they may reflect adherence to aesthetic and technical canons deeply rooted in both craft communities and society at large. Any deviation from the norm would then have a significant impact on technological and social knowledge systems. When a community innovates, accepts, and incorporates new technologies and subsequent changes in their knowledge systems, the coefficient of variation within the technological practice increases accordingly, thus leading to proportionally more varied end-products and broadening the meanings and uses associated with them.

In this light, ancient pottery craft systems are fertile sources of investigation, providing direct evidence of technological knowledge and practice, and embodying the material expression of established styles, aesthetics and behaviours as determined by society and time. By going beyond the mechanistic reconstruction of potters' operational sequences, it is possible to trace phenomena of innovation or tradition in both craft communities and society at large, thus contributing to disentangling the complex interaction between material and culture.

In his classic work on craft traditions among African potters, Olivier Gosselain warned researches about the dangers of considering pottery chaînes opératoires "simply as functionally oriented and monolithic systems".[27] According to his formulation, potting traditions are "heterogeneous cultural aggregates"[28] which articulate "mix of inventions, borrowed elements, and manipulations that display an amazing propensity to redefinition by individuals and local groups".[29] Due to their heterogeneous nature, these aggregates are not equally susceptible to innovation. Instead, some parts of the production/consumption sequence of a pot are more often affected by change, while others tend to remain constant over time. By observing the formal and technical features of ceramics it is then possible to distinguish which events in the life of a vessel are characterized by significant fluidity as opposed to stability.

As briefly mentioned before, there are multiple characteristics that enable us to trace different degrees of variation within artefacts technology, thus materialising the choices of both producers and consumers. However, these characteristics have different degrees of visibility and therefore require different analytical methods in order to be detected. The surface of a pot preserves visible traces of certain tempering methods, forming and finishing techniques as well as some post-firing treatments. As rightly pointed out by Gosselain, the visual characteristics produced by these techniques connect the maker and the user in a mutual relationship, as users can see the material evidence of the maker's behaviour and therefore his/her choices will largely depend on the consumers' reaction to the end-product. The interdependency between maker and user triggered by visual characteristics makes them the most likely to display fluctuations over time. Visual attributes are then key means of materialising aesthetic, economic, and symbolic meanings within society and their variability mirrors the instilled knowledge and practices of individual makers learning within an encircled community.[30]

Contrary to the manufacturing steps named above, the selection, extraction and mixing of clay, as well as primary forming and firing techniques are hard for a non-trained eye to detect on the finished product. These activities are likely to be less dependent on the customer's approval and more so on the shared practices established within bounded community of potters.[31] As mentioned earlier when commenting on the pottery traditions of Papua New Guinea, we have noticed that among the Azera potters the act of collecting clay follows strict rules - only women are allowed, wearing a traditional dress and carrying a specific type of container - and more importantly no external people are admitted all along the process. The case of the Azera potters illustrates well how the selection and extraction of raw materials are a collective endeavor during which potters assist each other and work in close collaboration. The same applies to the firing process, which often takes place in shared facilities whose preparation and supervision usually requires the involvement of potters from a whole village over a few days. On the other hand, the last invisible manufacturing step, i. e. the primary forming or "roughing out" in Courty and Roux's terminology[32], is an operation potters carry out individually. The gestures performed by a potter to fashion the roughout are typically learned through repetition, and trial and error during his/her apprenticeship period. Once they become a routinized practice, these internalized motor habits will tend to remain unchanged throughout a potter's life time, being so firmly grounded in the way-of-making and knowledge of his/her peers.

FLUCTUATION AND STABILITY AMONG SATRICUM POTTERS: THE CASE OF RED SLIPPED WARE

Through the study of the technical characteristics of ceramics, whether visible or not, we can gather fundamental information about the mutual influence that producers and customers exert on each other, thereby revealing established economic, cultural and symbolic values. We can also gain a greater understanding of the learning process, knowledge transmission, kinship, and social identity shared within the bounded craft communities. A good example to assess the potential of such an approach is provided by the red slipped ware vessels produced at Satricum during the late Archaic and Early Republican period (5th – 4th BC).

*Of Terminology, Chronology and Typology*

Scholarly research dealing with Archaic settlements in Etruria and Lazio usually provides accounts of the so called *Red Slipped Ware* group within the wider category of fine and semi-fine wares (ceramica figulina) commonly attested in domestic, sacred and funerary contexts. Characterized by a distinctive red/orange coloration evenly present on the whole surface, vessels attributed to the group of red slipped ware do not occur consistently across the Etrusco-Latial region, nor over the same time span. In addition, the high degree of intraregional and interregional variability in terms of surface treatment and shape repertoire makes the task of assigning specimens to the class quite challenging, resulting in uneven attention in relevant literature, hence the impression of a scattered geographical and chronological frequency. The variations in the way the red color finish is achieved by potters adds especially to the elusive nature of this class:

vessels show a very diverse range of surface treatments, from lustrous to matt, in some cases obtained not by coating their surfaces with a layer of paint or slip, but by burnishing and then adding a diluted clay emulsion, which is an artisanal trick known also in the manufacture of bucchero.[33] The differences detectable in this visual attribute led to inconsistencies in the terminology used to refer to the class: from red matt slipped (ceramica a vernice rossa opaca),[34] red glazed ware,[35] slipped fine ware (ceramica depurata verniciata),[36] to red bucchero,[37] the existing range of names possibly indicating similar objects is puzzling to say the least. In this work, I will rely on the terminology commonly used at Satricum to indicate this category of objects, which is also the closest to the denomination formulated by M.C. Biella in her work addressing the materials belonging to the Collection Feroldi Antonisi De Rosa in display at the Archaeological Museum of Civita Castellana (*Falerii*). To date the red slipped ware specimens retrieved at *Falerii* are the closest parallel to those produced at Satricum.[38]

At Satricum, the earliest specimens date to the second half of the 6th century BC. However, red slipped bowls and jars most commonly occur in 5th to early 4th century BC contexts and gradually decrease until their final demise at the end of the 4th century BC. This timeframe follows Bouma's reconstruction based mainly on the material retrieved from the two sacred deposits excavated on the acropolis of Satricum, dated respectively to the 7th – 6th century BC (Votive Deposit I) and 5th – 4th century BC (Votive Deposit II).[39] However, the identification of both instances as primary, open votive deposits as well as the chronology of the second deposit have been questioned by M. Gnade in her analysis of the stratigraphic evidence available, thus casting reasonable doubt on the timeline inferred by Bouma for part of the findings.[40] In particular, the earliest recorded specimens of red slipped ware, two bowls which were found in the most superficial layers of the so called votive deposit I (sealed between 540/530 BC), do not seem to provide conclusive evidence to assign the beginning of the production at Satricum to the second half of the 6th century BC.[41] On the other hand, the consistent quantity of red slipped ware found in contexts dating to the 5th – 4th century BC such as the Southwest Necropolis, the Votive Deposit II, the road and the necropolis in the lower settlement, confirms a flourishing production activity during the post-Archaic and early Republican periods.[42] It is worthwhile noting that extant evidence in Satricum differ from the trend recorded elsewhere in Lazio and Etruria where red slipped wares generally do not appear earlier than the mid-5th century BC. Data about the demise of this material are less contrasting, showing a clear decrease at the turn of the 3rd century BC when the competing production of black gloss starts to spread in the whole Etrusco-Latial area.[43]

The shape repertoire of Satrican red slipped ware is limited to jars (in most cases with a perforated lip), but the great majority are open forms, more specifically bowls, demonstrating a shallow linear or variably carinated profile with ring-foot or stemmed base attached (*fig. 1*). In the surroundings of Satricum, morphologically similar vessels are known in Cisterna and Lavinium, while in the rest of Lazio they have been found at Sezze, Velletri, Ficana Tivoli, Fidene, *Crustumerium* and Anagni.[44] However, closer comparisons in terms of typology and surface treatment come from Rome (the southwest and northwest slopes of Palatine hill and the temple of Castor and Pollux), *Veii* and *Falerii*.[45] As mentioned earlier, Faliscan red slipped bowls strongly resembles those found at Satricum, both in the normal sized and miniaturistic versions. Despite the lack of

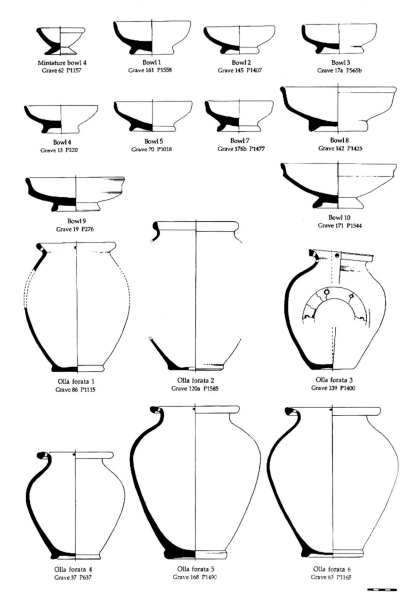

*Fig. 1. A selection of red slipped bowls and jars recovered from the Southwest Necropolis at Satricum (after Steures 1991, 210).*

contextual information, which prevents the author from narrowing down the wide chronological span of these vessels, Biella's typological analysis provides solid arguments to relate Faliscan red slipped bowls to the late bucchero production.[46] The author highlights that morphologically both ring-foot and stemmed base bowls can be compared most convincingly with 5th century BC bucchero specimens, confirming an observation mentioned only in passing by L. Murray Threipland for Casale Pian Roseto.[47] This is also the point raised in the 90s by D. Steures in his overview of the red slipped ware found at Satricum in the Southwest necropolis. Here, he also extends the parallel to the method possibly used by Satricum potters to coat the surface of these artefacts (by burnishing and then by adding a clay emulsion),[48] a procedure which was experimentally assessed by Vallesi in his reproduction of the bucchero technological sequence (*fig. 2*).[49] That being said, the possible morphological analogies are not limited to bucchero. Part of the bowls analysed by Biella at *Falerii* also find clear comparisons in the local repertoire of black gloss, in particular the earliest production dated by Schippa to the end of the 4th century BC (320/300 BC).[50] The remark of C. Angelelli follows the same line, when commenting on the red slipped wares retrieved from the southwest slope of the Palatine as possible antecedents of the later Campana B and Campana C production.[51]

Drawing on the typological observations gathered so far, red slipped ware - spanning over the 5th and 4th centuries BC, stemming from late bucchero prototypes and anticipating black gloss specimens - has been taken to reflect either a transitional moment in pottery manufacture or a long phase of experimentation preluding to the more successful black gloss production. This is a fascinating hypothesis, which in my view fails to address the question of the alternating fashion of black vs. red containers, a visual attribute certainly hard to ignore in the eye of a potter and even more so of a customer. Can red slipped bowls all be just firing trials and errors?[52]

*Of Technology, Fluctuating Practices and Inculcated Knowledge*

We saw that the shape repertoire of red slipped ware documented at Satricum becomes limited to two types of containers, bowls and jars with a perforated lip (*olle forate*). Usually the latter occur less frequently than the bowls, however, the amount retrieved from the Southwest necropolis (49 specimens) attests to a consistent production. This type of jar, featuring four equidistant rounded holes pierced in the lip before firing, has no parallels outside Satricum. The intended use of this unusual container is still a matter of debate: the possibility that the perforated lip could function as a hanging device has been ruled out due to the absence of any wear trace observable around the holes. It seems a more viable option that the holes were somehow instrumental to allow air inside the jar when closed with a lid, hence the suggestion of connecting these vessels to the process of fermentation, most likely of dairy products.[53] Unfortunately, the lack of data from residue analysis does not allow for further speculation on the function and use of these containers, which would also stray from the purpose of this paper, but certainly opens an interesting path for future research.

Turning now to the technological aspects of red slipped ware, jars with a perforated lip and bowls both remain consistent in their visual characteristics along their two-century long life span, conveying an impression of overall standardization. Jars almost invariably show the same dimensions (approx. 25 cm high), 4 holes on the outturned lip, a high shoulder, an attached ring foot and a red coating. Bowls also contribute to the impression of red slipped wares as being a fairly standardized material with their shallow profile, which is only carinated in few instances, attached base, straight rounded rim, and the red finish. However, on a closer examination both jars and bowls reveal a greater variability especially in three visual attributes: the rim, the base and the

*Fig. 2. Bucchero bowl found in the necropolis of Poggio dei Cavallari at Satricum (SA10 TXXV P905): detail of the traces of slip left on the outer surface, and close up of the fresh break.*

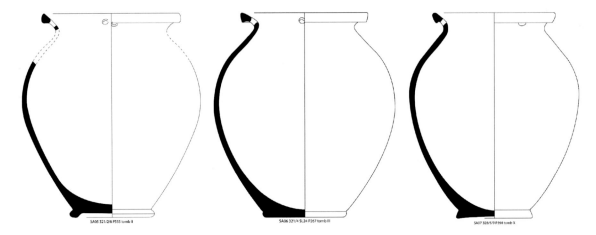

*Fig. 3. Three specimens of perforated jars recovered from the necropolis of Poggio dei Cavallari (SA05 321/2/6 P555 Tomb II; SA06 321/4 SL4 P267 Tomb III; SA07 328/5/9 P398 Tomb X, drawings by L. Opgenhaffen).*

matt red color applied on the surfaces. Among the jars, for instance, the range of micro variations recorded in the morphology of rims and ring-bases led to the identification of six different types (*fig. 3*); among the bowls, the disparities documented for lip/base/profile shapes is wider and led to the identification of 10 different types.[54] Lips in particular show the greater spectrum of variability in shape and style, highlighting this as the manufacturing step which better materializes the dynamic interaction between inculcated practice and bodily gestures, individual expression and shared aesthetics (*fig. 1*). A combination of learned behaviors – i.e. how much pressure to exert on the clay or how long to polish the upper part of the lip – and the lack of strict norms dictating the exact morphology of the rim along the technological sequence of shaping for instance a bowl result then in a range of acceptable rim types spanning from thickened to not thickened, tapered to rounded, outcurving to incurving etc. The heterogeneity of such differences suggests that each and every variation was perceived as an appropriate shape for a rim, even though they were all visibly different in the eye of both the potter and the customer. The act of modeling a rim testifies to a relatively high degree of variability within the process of making a red slipped bowl, disclosing at the same time the potter's choices (i.e. complying with socially accepted rim aesthetics) as well as their individual motor habits learned through bodily practice.

The methods used to apply the red coating also indicate that potters put in place different strategies to obtain the red color distinctive of this class. Even though the final goal is the same (to coat the surface with a red slip) the ceramic record shows detours from the original idea. Leaving aside the firing mistakes causing unintentional discolorations and cloudy patterns, the techniques used to apply the color varied according to the individual knowledge and experience of the potter, resulting into a range of different visual outcomes (*figs 4-5*): in some instances the layer is thin, matt and flacking, probably due to an overly watery clay emulsion and applied on not perfectly polished surfaces. In other instances, the slip becomes more compact, thicker, shinier and homogeneous revealing either the practice of burnishing the surface before applying the slip, or the use of intermediate substances to enhance the grip between the clay and the coating layer. Some specimens show stroke traces on the surface indicating that the potter used a brush instead of dipping the objects directly in the slip. As for the lip shapes, customers could clearly distinguish such variations in the coating at a glance, and could also possibly discriminate between high and low quality artefacts. However, we find them interchangeably offered as funerary goods, and so we might infer that small variations in the overall look (and quality) of red slipped wares were perceived as acceptable within the community. The variations in slipping techniques do not only illustrate to what extent the technological choices of potters and personal variations on an agreed design were socially accepted, but they also reflect the time and labor invested into the final product, thus contributing to a better understanding of both the skills and workflow of the potter.

To complete the overview of red slipped ware technological features, we shall consider another fundamental component that is invisible to the

*Fig. 4. Rim fragments of red slipped bowls recovered from Poggio dei Cavallari (road area) showing a range of different slipping techniques.*

customer, i. e. the clay recipe utilized to actually shape bowls and jars. The petrographic data gathered from the integrated analysis of ceramic thin sections and geological samples of the raw sources available at Satricum and its surroundings indicates that the clay used most likely originated from the micaceous deposits located in a 3 km radius from the acropolis of Satricum.[55] More specifically, from the littoral sand weathered sediment sampled at Le Ferriere – Villa (*fig. 6*, n. 6 on the map; *fig. 7a-b*) and the fluvial deposit sampled in the vicinity of the bridge on the river Astura (*fig. 6*, n. 7 on the map; *fig. 7c-d*). These micaceous clays are invariably mixed with quartz and plant fibers, such as dried grass and hay: when examining a fresh break, it is always possible to spot the dark halo left by the combustion of the organic matter in the core of each ceramic fragment (*fig. 7e-f, g-h; fig. 8*). This clay recipe characterizes the whole class, with no distinction between open or closed forms, and is therefore a constant within the operational chain of red slipped wares. As rightly pointed out by Gosselain, the choices operated by potters when it comes to clay selection and processing greatly depend on collectively learned knowledge and practice and usually express communal views on where to extract the most suitable raw materials and how to mix them to obtain the best outcomes. These technical behaviors are indeed the least

*Fig. 5. Red slipped bowl showing a flacking layer of slip found in the necropolis of Poggio dei Cavallari (SA10 P431 Tomb XXII).*

139

susceptible to change, and the stability in clay recipe observed in Satrican red slipped wares seems to confirm such trend.

CONCLUSION

To conclude, the case of red slipped ware from Satricum, although limited to a quantitively minor class of ceramic material, successfully demonstrates the potential of approaching the material record by reconstructing the production sequence in all its aspects: deterministic and mechanical as well as social and cultural. The analysis of visible (shape, decoration) and invisible (clay recipe) attributes of red slipped jars and bowls enabled us to trace the itinerary (echoing Fontijn's felicitous definition)[56] of these vessels from their origin point in the clay deposits of Satricum to their final use in the kitchen, on the table or as votive/funerary offering. Along this journey, it has been possible to suggest where potters had more space to express their individuality and creativity, and where they acted collectively sharing learned practices and technical knowledge. Moreover, we could also gain an insight into consumer behavior and attitude toward the possible variations occurring into the design and outlook of a category of objects that were both used in their everyday life and ritual activities. By merging two traditionally opposing interpretations of technology, respectively rooted in materialistic and structuralist standpoints, it is possible to increase the quality and quantity of information contained in the material record. At the same time such an approach enables us to reconstruct craft traditions and technological innovation among artisanal communities, and more importantly to unravel the complex interaction between practice and knowledge, and materiality and social values within society at large.

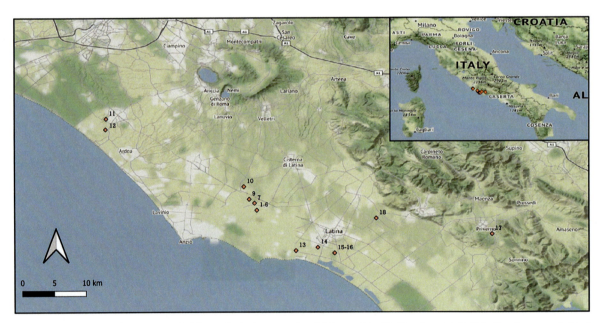

*Fig. 6. Map showing the sites sampled for geological prospection (elaborated by D. Derzhavets): 1-6) Le Ferriere, area behind the acropolis along the Astura river; 7) Le Ferriere, in the vicinity of the bridge on the Astura; 9) Le Ferriere/Campo Verde – next to the road Le Ferriere-Campo Verde; 10) Campo Verde, Laghetto Monsignore; 11) Lavinium 1 (Pomezia)– 1ˢᵗ brick factory; 12) Lavinium 2 (Pomezia) – 2ⁿᵈ brick factory (Laterizi Tacconi); 13) Borgo Sabotino; 14) Cerreto Alta 1 – Old Beach Ridge; 15-16) Cerreto Alta 2 – Old Beach Ridge/Gravel Pit; 17) Fossanova; 18) Agri Villa Franca.*

*Fig. 7. Microphotographs of thin sections (XPL on the left, PPL on the right column; scale bar 200 mm): a-b) clay outcrops sampled at Le Ferriere in the area behind the acropolis, site 6 on the map; c-d) clay outcrops sampled at Le Ferriere in the vicinity of the bridge on the river Astura, site 7 on the map; e-f) rim fragment of a red slipped bowl (SA07 340/2/1-70/P98); g-h) rim fragment of a red slipped perforated jar (SA09 314A/1/1-75-P62).*

*Fig. 8. Close up pictures of red slipped fragments (Dinolite 30x): on the fresh break it is possible to distinguish the leftover traces of burnt out fibres (elongated voids showing dark contours, highlighted in red).*

## Notes

* This work stems from my years spent as pottery specialist within the framework of the Satricum project and PhD fellow at the University of Amsterdam. I owe much to prof. Gnade for having supervised my work all along the way, for having welcomed me as a researcher in her team and more importantly as a member of the extended Satricum family since the very beginning of my involvement in the project.
1. Latour 1991, 2000; Lemmonier 1993; Dobres & Hoffman 1994; Kohring et al. 2007; Dobres 2009.
2. Dobres 2009.
3. Overview in Dobres 2000, 35-44.
4. Kohring 2006, 100-101.
5. Skibo et al. 1999.
6. Sahlins 1976; Conkey 1993.
7. Moore 1986.
8. Olsen 2013, 43.
9. Binford 1965, 209.
10. Overview in Preucel 2001, 15647-52.
11. See for example Bleed 2001, 152-154; more examples in Dobres 2000, 35-44.
12. Schiffer and Skibo 2001; Bleed 2001.
13. Ingold 2001, 17.
14. Dobres 2009, 106.
15. See respectively May and Tuckson 2000 on pottery traditions in Papua New Guinea, Ortega 2005 for New Mexico, and Geedh and Nadgauda 2013 for Madhya Pradesh.
16. May and Tuckson 2000, 14 and 130-36.
17. Ortega 2005, 3.
18. Ingold 2001, 20.
19. Hodder 2014, 31.
20. Kohring 2006, 105.
21. Martinón Torres 2002, 30.
22. Cresswell 1990, 46.
23. Sellet 1993; Grace 1996; Sillar and Tite 2000. A recent overview in Maldonado 2018, 13-16.
24. Dobres 1999, 124.
25. Whether objects do possess innate agency remains a matter of debate. Among the advocates of things as agents see Hoskins 2006 and Tilley 2001, contra Knappett 2005 (11-34). Discussing the terms of the question here would stray from the purpose of this paper, however, it is unanimously acknowledged that objects and their subsequent actions and legacies are dependent upon human interaction and societal intentions. We do, indeed, imbue objects with a certain purpose; whether or not this purpose can be considered as true agency depends, ultimately, on an individual's perception of the state of materiality in the world.
26. Respectively Hodder and Mol 2016; Roux 2003; Curta 2008 and Cresswell 2010.
27. Gosselain 2000, 190.

[28] Gosselain 2018, 2.
[29] Gosselain 2000, 190.
[30] Kohring 2006, 101.
[31] Gosselain 2000, 192.
[32] Roux and Courty 1995, 20.
[33] Vallesi 2004, 317-318.
[34] Ferrandes 2019, 91.
[35] Murray Threipland 1970, 78.
[36] Angelelli 2001, 256.
[37] Steures 1991, 207-210.
[38] Biella 2011, 137-148.
[39] About the chronology of both deposits see Bouma 1996, 61-62.
[40] Gnade 2000, 25-42.
[41] Bouma 1996, 315-316.
[42] Overview of Late Archaic contexts in Gnade 2000, in particular on the ware class p. 90; about the lower settlement area see also the updates in Gnade 2011 and 2013.
[43] A synthesis in Angelelli 2001, 256.
[44] See relevant references in Bouma 1996, 315-316.
[45] Southwest slope of Palatine hill Angelelli 2001, 256 (type 2); northwest slope of the Palatine hill Ferrandes 2016, 81-93 (fig.8-12-18-19, specimens dated to 360-330 BC); the temple of Castor and Pollux, Slej 2008, 153-154 (plain polished ware bowls type VII,1); *Veii* Murray Threipland 1970, 78 (cat. 3,4,5, plts. 16.Q e XIV b-c) and Vagnetti 1971, 140, 196, (plts. LXII, D); *Falerii*, Biella 2011 137-148 (cat. II.a.9.4 – II.a.9.31, figs. 16-17-18, plts. L-LI-LII).
[46] Biella 2011, 137, 139, 145.
[47] Murray Threipland 1970, 75.
[48] Steures 1992, 74.
[49] Vallesi 2004.
[50] Biella 2011, 138, 145.
[51] Angelelli 2001, 256.
[52] As suggested by D. Steures in his review of the red slipped ware found in the Southwest Necropolis, where he argues that "the reddish colour of bowls and other shapes from the Southwest Necropolis is the result of a potter's laziness" (1992, 74).
[53] Steures 1992, 63-66.
[54] Steures 1992, 66 (Dendrogram 6, perforated jars), 56 (Dendrogram 2, bowls).
[55] A summary of the results in Revello Lami 2017.
[56] Fontijn 2013.

BIBLIOGRAPHY

Angelelli, C. 2001, Ceramica depurata, in P. Pensabene/S. Falzone/C. Angelelli (eds.), *Scavi del Palatino 1. L'area sud-occidentale del Palatino tra l'età protostorica e il IV secolo a.C., scavi e materiali della struttura ipogea sotto la cella del tempio della Vittoria*, Roma, 247-256.

Biella, M.C. 2011, *La collezione Feroldi Antonisi De Rosa: tra indagini archeologiche e ricerca di un'identità culturale nella Civita Castellana postunitaria*, Pisa.

Binford, L.R. 1965, Archaeological Systematics and the Study of Culture Process, *American Antiquity* 31.2 (1), 203-210.

Bleed, P. 2001, Artifice constrained: what determines technological choice, in Schiffer 2001, 151–162.

Bouma, J.W. 1996, *Religio Votiva: The Archaeology of Latial Votive Religion* 1-3. PhD Dissertation, University of Groningen.

Conkey, M. 1993, Humans as materialists and symbolists: Image making in the Upper Palaeolithic, in T. Rasmussen (ed.), *The Origin and Evolution of Humans and Humanness*, Boston, 95-118.

Courty, M.A. /V. Roux 1995, Identification of wheel throwing on the basis of ceramic surface features and microfabrics, *JASc* 22(1), 17-50.

Cresswell, R. 1990, "A New Technology" Revisited, *Technology and the Humanities. Archaeological Review from Cambridge* 9 (1), 151-175.

Cresswell, R. 2010, Techniques et culture: les bases d'un programme de travail, *Techniques & Culture. Revue semestrielle d'anthropologie des techniques* 54-55, 20-45.

Curta, F. 2008, The Earliest Avar-Age Stirrups, Or The "Stirrup Controversy" Revisited, in F. Curta/R. Kovaled (eds.), *The Other Europe in the Middle Ages. Avars, Bulgars, Khazars, and Cumans*, Leiden/Boston, 297–326

Dobres, M.A. 1999, Technology's Links and Chains. The processual Unfolding of Technique and Technician, in M.A. Dobres/C.R. Hoffman (eds.), *The Social Dynamics of Technology. Practice, Politics and World Views*, Washington, 124-146.

Dobres, M.A. 2000, *Technology and Social Agency: Outlining a Practice Framework for Archaeology*, Oxford.

Dobres, M.A. 2001, Meaning in the making: agency and the social embodiment of technology and art, in Schiffer 2001, 47–76.

Dobres, M.A., 2009, Archaeologies of technology, *Cambridge Journal of Economics* 34, 103–114.

Dobres, M.A./C.R. Hoffman 1994. Social Agency and the Dynamics of Prehistoric Technology, *Journal of Archaeological Method and Theory* 1 no. 3, 211-258.

Ferrandes, A. F. 2016, Sequenze stratigrafiche e facies ceramiche nello studio della città antica. Il caso delle pendici nord-orientali del Palatino tra IV e III secolo a.C., in A.F. Ferrandes/G. Pardini (eds.) *Le regole del gioco. Tracce, archeologi, racconti. Studi in onore di Clementina Panella*, Roma, 77-112.

Fontijn, D.R. 2013, Epilogue: cultural biographies and itineraries of things: second thoughts, in H.P. Hahn/H. Weiss (eds.), *Mobility, meaning and transformation of things*, Oxford, 183-95.

Geedh, S./T. Nadgauda 2013, Contemporary Traditional Pottery Practices at Archaeo-Historically Important Sites, District Khargone, Madhya Pradesh, *International Journal of Modern Physics*, Conference Series vol. 22, 93-98.

Gibson, K.R./T. Ingold (eds.) 1994, *Tools, language and cognition in human evolution*, Cambridge.

Gnade, M.1992, *The Southwest Necropolis of Satricum. Excavations 1981-1986*, Amsterdam.

Gnade, M. 2002, *Satricum in the post-archaic period: a case study of the Interpretation of Archaeological remains as Indicators of Ethno-Cultural Identity*, Leuven.

Gnade, M. 2012, Satricum 2011: il proseguimento delle ricerche, *Lazio & Sabina* 8, 451-457.

Gnade, M. 2013, A New Burial Ground Form Satricum. Preliminary Results of the Excavations in 2010, in A.J. Nijboer et al., *Research into pre-Roman burial grounds in Italy* 8, Leuven.

Gosselain, O.P. 2000, Materializing Identities: An African Perspective, *Journal of Archaeological Method and Theory* 7 no. 3, 187-217.

Gosselain, O.P. 2018, Pottery chaînes opératoires as historical documents, in *Oxford Research Encyclopedia of African History*, Oxford, 1-41.

Grace, R. 1996, Use-wear Analysis: The State of the Art. *Archaeometry* 38, 209-229.

Hodder, I. 2014, The entanglements of humans and things: A long-term view, *New literary history* 45(1), 19-36.

Hodder, I./A. Mol 2016, Network Analysis and Entanglement, *Journal of Archaeological Method and Theory* 23, 1066–1094.

Hoskins, J. 2006, Agency, Biography and Objects, in C. Tiller et al., *Handbook of Material Culture*, London, 74–84.

Ingold, T. 2001, Beyond Art and Technology: The Anthropology of Skill, in Schiffer 2001, 17- 32.

Kohring, S. 2006, Let's NOT talk technology? Bringing production into a discussion of technological knowledge, *Archaeological Review from Cambridge* 21(1), 98-116.

Kohring, S./C.P. Odriozola/V.M. Hurtado/S. Wynne-Jones 2007, Materialising 'complex' social relationships: technology, production and consumption in a Copper Age community, in S. Kohring/S. Wynne-Jones (eds.), *Socialising complexity: Structure, interaction and power in archaeological discourse*, Oxford, 100-117.

Knappett, C. 2005, *Thinking through material culture: an interdisciplinary perspective*, Philadelphia.

Latour, B. 1991, Technology is society made durable, in J. Law (ed.), *A Society of Monsters: Essays on Power, Technology and Domination*, London, 103-131.

Latour, B. 2000, The Berlin key: Or how to do words with things, in P.M. Graves-Brown (ed.), *Matter, Materiality and Modern Culture*, London, 10-21.

Lemonnier, P. 1993, Introduction, in P. Lemonnier (ed.), *Technological choices: Transformations in material cultures since the Neolithic*, London, 1-35.

Maldonado, B.E., 2018, *Approaches to the study of technology and craft production*, in: *Tarascan Copper Metallurgy: A Multiapproach Perspective*, Oxford.

Martinón Torres, M. 2002, Chaîne Opératoire: The concept and its applications within the study of technology, *Gallaecia* 21, 29-44.

May, P./M. Tuckson 2000, *The Traditional Pottery of Papua New Guinea*, Honolulu.

Miller, D. 2005, Materiality: An introduction, in D. Miller (ed.), *Materiality*, London, 1-50.

Moore, H. 1986, *Space, Text, and Gender. An Anthropological Study of the Marakwet of Kenya*, Cambridge.

Murray Threipland, L./M. Torelli 1970, A semi-subterranean Etruscan building in the Casale Pian Roseto (Veii) area, *BSR* 38, 62-121.

Olsen, B. 2013, *In defense of things. Archaeology and the ontology of objects*, Plymouth.

Ortega, F.V. 2005, Ceramics for the Archaeologist. An Alternative Perspective, *Engaged Anthropology: Research Essays on North American Archaeology, Ethnobotany, and Museology* 94, 1-5.

Preucel, R.W. 2001, n.d. Theory in Archaeology, in *International Encyclopedia of the Social & Behavioral Sciences*, Amsterdam, 15647-15652.

Revello Lami, M. 2017, Evidenze dirette, indirette, o circostanziali? Topografia e archeometria della produzione ceramica a Satricum durante il periodo arcaico, *ScAnt* 23(2), Roma, 389-412.

Roux, V. 2003, A dynamic systems framework for studying technological change: application to the emergence of the potter's wheel in the southern Levant, *Journal of Archaeological method and Theory* 10, no.1, 1-30.

Sahlins, M. 1976, *Culture and Practical Reason*, Chicago.

Schiffer, M.B. (ed.) 2001, *Anthropological perspectives on technology*, Dragoon/ Albuquerque.

Sellet, F. 1993, Chaîne Opératoire; the concept and its applications, *Lithic Technology* 18, 106–111.

Sillar, B./B. Tite 2000, The challenge of the technological choices for materials science approaches in archaeology, *Archaeometry* 42, 2–20.

Skibo, J./J.M. Skibo/G. Feinman (eds.) 1999, *Pottery and people*, Salt Lake City.

Skibo, J.M./M.B. Schiffer 2001, Understanding artifact variability and change: A behavioral framework, in Schiffer 2001, 139-149.

Slej, K. 2008, Plain Ware, in K. Slej/M. Cullhed (eds.), *The Temple of Castor and Pollux II.2. The Finds and The Trenches*, Rome, 139-200.

Steures, D.C. 1991, Reddish Bucchero from Satricum, in M. Gnade (ed.), *Stips Votiva. Papers Presented to C. M. Stibbe*, Amsterdam, 207-210.

Steures, D.C. 1992, Bowls and Jars, in Gnade 1992, 53-68.

Tilley, C. 2001, Ethnography and Material Culture, in P. Atkinson et al., *Handbook of Ethnography*, London, 258–272.

Vagnetti, L. 1971, *Il deposito votivo di Campetti a Veio. Materiali degli scavi 1932-1950*, Firenze.

Vallesi, M. 2004, Produzione sperimentale di buccheri, in A. Naso (ed.), *Appunti sul bucchero. Atti delle giornate di studio*, Florence, 315-328.

# Produzioni di ceramica a vernice nera nell'area costiera del Latium Vetus

*Alessandro M. Jaia*

*Abstract*

*Departing from the technical features of two groups of black gloss ceramics that come from Ardea and Lavinium, two of the most important cities on the Tyrrhenian coast, this paper discusses aspects of the original production site for each of them. These productions closely follow forms and types of the so-called "Gruppo dei Piccoli Stampigli" and can be attributed to local workshops, rather than known Roman ones. This article presents several technological elements that have permitted to identify these newly discovered production centers.*

Le produzioni specializzate attestate nella fascia costiera compresa tra Ostia ed Anzio costituiscono certamente un campione adeguatamente rappresentativo per tentare di inserire letture di tipo tecnologico nei contesti storici di riferimento e, di rimando, per rintracciare in particolari applicazioni tecniche elementi che possano supportare interpretazioni di carattere più generale. Al riguardo, le ampie acquisizioni derivanti da imprese di scavo di lunga durata, come la missione della Sapienza Università di Roma a *Lavinium*, permettono di spaziare nelle problematiche connesse alle produzioni ceramiche utilizzando campioni particolarmente significativi. Per rimanere nell'areale costiero, naturale parametro di confronto potranno essere i dati derivanti dalla storica impresa di scavo a *Satricum*, diretta da M. Gnade.

Come per gli altri centri laziali, anche a *Lavinium* è ben distinguibile un'ampia e assai risalente produzione ceramica locale, per quanto riguarda sia forme di uso comune, che tipi destinati ad usi specializzati come il banchetto o la ritualità funeraria. Laddove compaiano espressioni vascolari particolarmente complesse, è desumibile, se non il luogo di produzione, almeno l'areale di circolazione, sempre piuttosto circoscritto. É il caso, ad esempio, delle produzioni in impasto sottile e in impasto rosso dell'Orientalizzante recente. La grande quantità di *kantharoi* di piccole dimensioni in impasto sottile con decorazione incisa a motivi differenti, talvolta con riempitivo di pasta di colore rosso documentati nelle sepolture lavinati, come la tomba a cassone sotto l'*Heroon* di Enea e le coeve o, poco più recenti, sepolture della necropoli orientale, trovano non un semplice confronto, ma una sostanziale identità con produzioni del tutto analoghe nella necropoli di Castel di Decima. Tale "identità", rilevabile non solo nel rigido schema rappresentato dalla combinazione tra il tipo di decorazione e la foggia dell'ansa, ma anche nella qualità dell'impasto e nei caratteri generali dei vasi, permette di ipotizzare una comune origine di produzione. Altra cosa, con buona evidenza, è identificarne con certezza il luogo e da qui far discendere ragionamenti di tipo economico o di rapporti tra insediamenti basati sulla distribuzione areale.

Allo stesso modo, il corredo della Tomba 2 della necropoli orientale di *Lavinium* presenta un *set* completo da banchetto di impasto rosso comprendente, oltre a sei olle globulari costolate, un grande piatto, un *foculum* a tre piedi e, soprattutto, un imponente sostegno a quattro registri con calderone decorato da grifi.[1] Si tratta di un complesso di vasi del tutto simile a quello del famoso servizio da banchetto di Ficana. Le analogie tra i due *set*, a livello di tecnica produttiva, appaiono evidenti e anche in questo caso ci si può domandare se essi non siano opera di botteghe operanti nel medesimo centro. Tuttavia, come ben noto, l'orizzonte di circolazione di questo genere di prodotti è assai limitato.

E' del tutto evidente che, in rapporto a tali tematiche, il quadro è assai complesso e bisogna fare riferimento a studi specialistici e ad analisi molto approfondite. Un ulteriore fattore di complessità, del resto, viene introdotto dalla necessità di prendere in considerazione l'eventuale coinvolgimento di manodopera itinerante, come ormai ampiamente dimostrato in relazione ad alcune specifiche produzioni già a partire dall'età arcaica e tardo arcaica. Al riguardo, è ben nota la discussione relativa ad alcune manifatture in terracotta di ambito santuariale, spesso identificate come "greche" o magno greche, ma probabilmente più spesso campane ed etrusche, come nel caso della coroplastica templare di alcuni casi notissimi, da Roma Sant'Omobono, a *Satricum*. A *Lavinium*, i frammenti di statue acroteriali e, più in generale, le terrecotte architettoniche di seconda fase del santuario costiero di *Sol Indiges* sono nettamente distinguibili per ispirazione stilistica o (ed è il caso più interessante) per tecnica di manifattura rispetto alle statue del Santuario di Minerva.[2]

Nel caso dei frammenti delle statue probabilmente poste a coronamento del colmo del tetto del tempio di *Sol Indiges* nella fase degli inizi del V secolo, lo strato superficiale esterno è notevolmente meno ricco di smagrante rispetto agli esemplari di offerenti, genericamente databili al V sec. a.C. e provenienti dal Santuario di Minerva, fatto che denota un orizzonte produttivo diverso a livello di tecnica manifatturiera. E' ovvio che possono esserci motivi di carattere economico alla base di alcune scelte tecniche di realizzazione dei prodotti, come la necessità di fornire, nell'ambito del santuario, prodotti diversi, sia sotto il profilo della qualità che dal punto di vista delle modalità di realizzazione, in rapporto alla destinazione d'uso e/o alla committenza, a seconda che si tratti di elementi di decorazione o di offerte. In questo caso, però, sembra più verosimile pensare a due diverse tradizioni tecniche nella realizzazione dei prodotti.

Il caso del complesso coroplastico del Santuario di Minerva a *Lavinium* rappresenta di per sé uno straordinario laboratorio per lo studio della tecnologia della terracotta e delle produzioni di alto livello qualitativo, per il quale rimando ad un prossimo lavoro di Maria Fenelli, che spero possa raccogliere l'enorme quantità di osservazioni originali di chi, come lei, da tanti decenni ne cura la ricomposizione (*fig. 1*). L'elemento interessante su cui ci si può al momento soffermare è, però, la sostanziale limitazione areale della diffusione della statuaria in terracotta lavinate, prodotta da alcune botteghe che lavorano intensamente, e con un livello qualitativo assai alto, per quasi tre secoli. Evidentemente, al di là di semplici

*Fig. 1. Lavinium, Santuario di Minerva. Esemplificazione di tracce lasciate da utensili usati nel corso della lavorazione e soluzioni per ricomporre giunture e parti delle statue.*

problemi relativi alla casualità delle attestazioni, strettamente correlate agli interventi di scavo, entrano in gioco altri fattori, come la trasportabilità delle statue o, più in generale, dei prodotti di realizzazione particolarmente complessa, le tradizioni locali relative agli attributi tipici delle statue, la tipologia della committenza, la diffusa capacità di produrre manifatture anche di pregio, la circolazione di operatori specializzati, ecc.

Con chiara evidenza, queste semplici osservazioni fanno riferimento a problematiche ben note, altrove discusse approfonditamente da specialisti del settore; in questa sede si è solo voluto accennare alla complessità in cui ci si muove nel trattare di produzioni in terracotta, anche solo da un punto di vista tecnologico. Tale complessità emerge anche in un periodo cruciale nella storia del Lazio costiero, come quello della prima romanizzazione, tra il 338 a.C. e il primo quarto del II sec. a.C.

Agli inizi di questa fase, nel settore più settentrionale del Lazio costiero, le realtà urbane sono autosufficienti e indipendenti e trovano il presupposto economico di sussistenza nella combinazione tra il controllo degli approdi, anche in rapporto ai centri dell'entroterra, e lo sfruttamento delle risorse connesse al sistema lacustre paracostiero e dell'immediato retroterra collinare. I territori dipendenti dalle singole entità appaiono non particolarmente estesi e la tipologia delle risorse disponibili comprende aree adatte a colture specializzate, ma meno consone alle produzioni di base. Tali compagini, nel IV sec. a.C. sono in piena crisi per una articolata serie di motivi: rapporti generalmente complessi con Roma da un lato e i Volsci dall'altro, frammentazione statale non più adeguata al livello degli scambi interregionali, retroterra altrettanto statico (Colli Albani). La circolazione limitata delle manifatture specializzate non genera *surplus* di ricchezza, come nel caso della coroplastica lavinate e più in generale delle manifatture ceramiche e della produzione di tegole. In tutto l'areale costiero, poi, non è nota alcuna fornace di anfore, fatto che sembra suggerire una scarsissima propulsività anche a livello di attività agricole specializzate.

Con la riorganizzazione *post* 338 a.C., il quadro di riferimento viene modificato: deduzione di colonie di diritto romano (Ostia, Anzio e *Tarracina*), probabile attribuzione dello *status* di municipio a *Lavinium*, assegnazioni viritane, apertura dell'Appia nell'immediato retroterra, consolidamento della viabilità di collegamento con i Colli Albani. Viene superato, in questo modo, il limite della frammentazione delle comunità costiere del *Latium Vetus*, con ampliamento e unificazione dei mercati di riferimento, a cui si collega il retroterra. Tale apertura non riguarda solo le produzioni agricole o le manifatture, ma anche la circolazione di materiali da costruzione, come sembra indicare, ad esempio, l'avvio dell'impiego massiccio del peperino dei Colli Albani nei santuari della fascia costiera (*Sol Indiges* a Lavinio e *Castrum Inui* ad Ardea).[3]

In tale quadro, i segnali forniti da indicatori fondamentali come le manifatture in terracotta sono contrastanti tra loro per tutto il III sec. a.C. e vanno interpretati utilizzando anche parametri di valutazione di tipo tecnologico (*fig. 2*).

La coroplastica lavinate sembra concentrata su modelli standardizzati e di minore qualità artistica. Le tegole cominciano in alcuni casi ad essere bollate, pur restando un prodotto di circolazione locale.[4] Si continua a non produrre anfore.[5] Segnali relativi alla presenza di manifatture specializzate sembrano però provenire dalla possibile individuazione, ad Ardea, di un *atelier* che, nel corso del III sec. a.C., realizza una serie di *askoi* ad otre, acromi, rientranti nel cosiddetto *Gallonios Group*, firmati da un *P. Caesius*.[6] L'attestazione di tali *askoi* in Etruria, nel Lazio (Ardea, *Lavinium*), a Lilibeo e, al contrario, la presenza a *Lavinium* di anfore e materiali ceramici prodotti nella Sicilia occidentale o veicolati attraverso gli scali di Solunto e Lilibeo sembra indicare che anche gli approdi del Lazio costiero siano pienamente inseriti nella rotta tirrenica nord-sud che si consolida nel corso del III sec. a.C., probabilmente prima, ma con maggiore certezza dopo la prima guerra punica.[7] In tale panorama, la ceramica fine figurata, in continuità con quanto noto per il IV sec. a.C., proviene ancora, in genere, dall'Etruria meridionale e soprattutto da Roma, con bassa incidenza di produzioni magnogreche.

All'interno del quadro così delineato, un caso che non sembra inutile approfondire è l'imponente presenza, in tutti i contesti del Lazio costiero, di ceramica fine da mensa a vernice nera, in passato attribuita alla fabbrica romana dell'*Atelier des petites Estanpilles*, ed attualmente suddivisa in diversi areali di produzione, pur sotto la comune denominazione di Gruppo dei Piccoli Stampigli.[8] In particolare, la massiccia presenza di questa tipologia ceramica è verificabile nei contesti santuariali (Casalinaccio ad Ardea, Minerva a *Lavinium*), in ambito urbano (*Lavinium*), nei territori ardeatino e laurentino, ma anche in quelli di Anzio, *Satricum* e *Tarracina*. A questa affermazione di forme ceramiche tipiche della produzione romana a vernice nera, corrisponde nei medesimi territori l'improvvisa e consistente proliferazione di insediamenti agricoli, con un picco nel secondo quarto del III secolo.[9] La sensazione è che tale, possibile, correlazione

*Fig. 2. Lavinium, Santuario di Minerva. Classi di materiali ceramici prodotti localmente tra età tardo-arcaica ed età medio-repubblicana; in basso a destra ceramica di importazione (Roma ed Etruria meridionale).*

non dipenda dall'apertura sistematica di nuovi mercati per le produzioni romane dopo il 338 a.C., ma che vada piuttosto letta in relazione a una specifica richiesta dei nuovi coloni dedotti nel territorio costiero e delle elites "romane" che probabilmente sostituiscono, almeno in parte, quelle locali all'interno dei centri urbani (*fig. 3*).

Una possibile conferma di questa ipotesi può derivare dal fatto che sono attestate, nell'area, produzioni locali che riproducono quelle romane. Ad esempio, tra i materiali del deposito votivo del santuario di Casalinaccio, ad Ardea, sarebbe stata individuata una manifattura locale di ceramica a vernice nera, in parte stampigliata. In questo caso, sono i dettagli tecnico-produttivi che sembrano indirizzare verso una fabbrica locale, attribuita all'ambito del santuario. Le caratteristiche dei vasi sono: vernice a volte opaca, evanide e facile a scrostarsi; argilla in genere di color camoscio; processo di cottura imperfetto; livello qualitativo complessivamente piuttosto basso.[10] Si tratterebbe, dunque, di un'officina non tecnologicamente avanzata quanto quelle romane, che in questa fase propone le medesime forme, con gli stessi tipi di stampigliature. Il pezzo più antico attribuito all'*atelier* ardeate è un piattello tipo Morel 2222, ascrivibile ancora al IV sec. a.C.[11] Segue poi un esemplare, forse locale, vicino alla serie Morel 2923 (coppa emisferica su piede). Anche un consistente nucleo di coppe ad orlo rientrante di piccole dimensioni, riferibili alle forme Morel 2787e, 2765a, 2783c e 2734d (a cui si aggiunge un numeroso gruppo di fondi stampigliati[12]), e un altro, relativo alla forma "Morel 96", sono attribuiti ad una produzione locale di ambito santuariale; di queste forme, infatti, sono stati rinvenuti alcuni scarti deformati.[13] Non mancano patere miniaturistiche.[14]

A *Lavinium*, un caso-campione significativo, relativo ad una possibile produzione locale di ceramica a vernice nera, è rappresentato da un notevole scarico di materiali scavato nel 1985-86 all'interno dell'area urbana, presso il cosiddetto "Capannone", la rimessa agricola della tenuta Borghese.[15] Nello scavo furono messe in luce parte di un edificio con zoccolatura in opera quadrata di età almeno medio-repubblicana, un tratto di via basolata e alcune strutture relative ad un impianto di età imperiale. Nei pressi, ma all'esterno dell'area di intervento, doveva sorgere un

*Fig. 3. Territorio Laurentino. Confronto dell'entità dl popolamento tra età tardo-arcaica ed età medio-repubblicana (stralcio della carta archeologica).*

edificio con settore termale. Infatti, lavori di sistemazione del terreno eseguiti presso un piccolo rudere in opera laterizia posto nelle immediate vicinanze portarono in luce numerosi mattoni bessali. Uno degli ambienti dell'edificio in opera quadrata risultò riempito, forse al fine di rialzarne il piano di calpestio, da un imponente scarico di materiali ceramici. Si tratta di centinaia di vasi relativi a diverse classi ceramiche (in particolare impasto grezzo tornito, impasto chiaro sabbioso, ceramica a vernice nera anche suddipinta, anfore greco italiche, puniche e rodie[16]) databili tra la fine del IV e la fine del III secolo a.C., con qualche scivolamento verso il secondo quarto del II secondo secolo, limite più basso di datazione del complesso.

In questo contesto, sono stati individuati, in base alle caratteristiche tecniche, diversi gruppi di produzioni di ceramica a vernice nera stampigliata. Tra questi, due nuclei spiccano per consistenza numerica; entrambi probabilmente attribuibili a manifatture di area romana, sono distinguibili per le evidenti differenze nella consistenza e nella diversa dinamica di decadimento della vernice; all'interno del complesso è stato poi riconosciuto un terzo nucleo, rappresentato da circa un terzo dei vasi (si tratta di diverse decine di contenitori), anch'esso nettamente riconoscibile per impasto e caratteristiche della vernice. Per questo terzo nucleo di materiali è possibile ipotizzare una produzione locale o forse, per meglio dire, allo stato attuale delle ricerche, una produzione di tipo areale all'interno del settore costiero (*fig. 4*).

Il primo gruppo, di probabile produzione romana, è riconoscibile in base all'impasto, ben depurato, tendenzialmente sempre rosato in diverse gradazioni di colore. La vernice, in genere con riflessi metallici, spessa, coprente, molto omogenea, appare raramente soggetta ad azioni abrasive meccaniche. Il secondo gruppo, presenta caratteristiche simili al primo per quanto riguarda l'impasto, con vernice di tono omogeneo, ma meno spessa della precedente. Tale vernice sembra caratterizzata dalla tendenza a subire alterazioni non solo per azioni abrasive meccaniche, ma anche secondo modalità particolari, osservabili anche in materiali simili di altri contesti romani e laziali. Si nota, infatti, una frequente perdita di vernice in modalità puntiforme ed in maniera diffusa, a piccole scaglie subcircolari, anche nelle sezioni che non presentano punti di debolezza dovute ad articolazioni della superficie e non direttamente e più frequentemente esposte ad usura meccanica. Al riguardo, allo stato attuale degli studi e in base ad un esame autoptico, tale

Fig. 4. *Lavinium, area urbana. Esemplificazione delle caratteristiche della vernice dei tre gruppi di ceramica a vernice nera rinvenuti nello scavo del cosiddetto Capannone.*

modalità di caduta della vernice sembra essere associabile al fenomeno della migrazione dei sali solubili in superficie e, in questo caso, essere connessa alla tipologia delle materie prime utilizzate nelle varie fasi di produzione più che al contesto di giacitura, comune evidentemente a entrambi i due gruppi ceramici in esame (*fig. 5*). Se questa ipotesi venisse confermata dalle analisi archeometriche sarebbe possibile dedurre che i manufatti furono prodotti in due atelier differenti poiché il fenomeno dipenderebbe dall'utilizzo di materiali di caratteristiche diverse.[17]

Il terzo gruppo di vasi si distingue nettamente per il colore dell'impasto, sempre di tono camoscio chiaro, spesso con gradazioni tendenti verso l'estremo più chiaro della tonalità. La vernice tende con facilità a distaccarsi a larghe placche su gran parte del corpo del vaso; non infrequenti, i casi di perdita quasi totale; il colore varia dal nero al rosso cotto (*fig. 6*).[18]

La seriazione delle forme è sostanzialmente la stessa per tutti e tre i gruppi individuati, con alcune, lievi, ma forse significative differenze. Nei primi due gruppi sono attestati piatti da pesce, coppe delle serie più comuni e piatti. Gli stampigli associati, quando presenti, coprono le fasi GPS GPS II-III, con particolare addensamento nelle fasi GPS GPS III. Nel terzo gruppo, mancano i piatti da pesce; sono presenti soprattutto coppe di tipo comune e piatti, con predominanza delle rosette per gli stampigli, associate talvolta, nei piatti, a rotellature. L'assenza dei piatti da pesce, l'attestazione di stampigli multipli a palmetta orientati nella stessa direzione o di stampigli di ispirazione magnogreca restituisce l'impressione che si tratti di una produzione sviluppatasi in corrispondenza di un momento avanzato della *facies* 5 (GPS II-III), con addensamento a partire dal secondo quarto del III sec. a.C. (*facies* 6, GPS III), ovvero nel periodo in cui sembrano aumentare i nuovi insediamenti nel territorio lavinate. Al contempo, la predominanza di forme con stampigli a rosetta (soprattutto singola), sembra indicare che questa produzione continua con inalterato successo nella *facies* 7. Alla fine di tale periodo, le attestazioni sembrano scomparire o, almeno, diminuire drasticamente. Tra i materiali rinvenuti a *Lavinium*, nel santuario di Minerva, sono presenti *oinochoai* e *skiphoi* in vernice nera suddipinta che presentano caratteristiche simili per quanto riguarda l'impasto, ma differenti per la vernice, molto sottile e tendente a decadere in maniera progressiva (*fig. 7*). Al riguardo potrebbe trattarsi comunque di importazioni.

In conclusione, le caratteristiche tecniche del terzo gruppo di vasi di ceramica a vernice nera del Capannone sembrano suggerire l'esistenza di una produzione locale che imita in maniera pedissequa i tipi romani più diffusi. Se si confrontano tali caratteristiche con quelle della manifattura individuata ad Ardea, si notano elementi di estrema vicinanza.[19] Nel caso di Ardea, almeno per quanto riguarda il tempio di Casalinaccio, la produzione sembra essere riferibile ad un ambito santuariale, ma la presenza di più *atelier*, operanti a fini commerciali generalizzati, non appare implausibile, se, come sembra, vasi con le stesse caratteristiche sono presenti anche nello scalo portuale di *Castrum Inui*. Al riguardo vale la pena di ricordare che, a *Lavinium*, esistono produzioni di ambito santuariale vicine per certi versi a quelle in vernice nera. Infatti, il fossile guida dei votivi del Santuario delle XIII Are è rappresentato da craterischi a colonnette di argilla depurata con fasce dipinte a vernice nera o rossa, rinvenuti in elevata quantità, ma relativi soltanto alla frequentazione del santuario.[20] Alcuni dei caratteri produttivi del gruppo dei craterischi, in parte risalenti rispetto al contesto del Capannone, sono simili alla produzione

150

*Fig. 5. Lavinium, scavo del cosiddetto Capannone. Particolare delle modalità di distacco della vernice dei vasi del gruppo 2 a piccole scaglie subcircolari.*

*Fig. 6. Lavinium, scavo del cosiddetto Capannone. Esemplificazione delle modalità di distacco della vernice dei vasi appartenenti al gruppo 3.*

*Fig. 7. Lavinium, Santuario di Minerva. Vasi suddipinti con particolare tecnico della vernice.*

individuata nello scavo dell'area urbana: impasto colore camoscio molto chiaro o beige e vernice nera, in quel caso a fasce.

Riassumendo, appare dimostrabile che sia ad Ardea, sia a *Lavinium* sono presenti manifatture locali di ceramica a vernice nera nel corso del III sec. a.C., attivate probabilmente sotto la spinta del riassetto istituzionale *post* 338 a.C. e del conseguente apporto di popolazione romana. Il problema nasce nel momento in cui ci si domanda se

151

l'insediamento di tali manifatture sia da attribuire ad uno solo dei due centri, o ad entrambi e come tali produzioni si rapportino con quelle individuabili in altri settori, limitrofi, della costa laziale. Per il momento è forse preferibile pensare ad un generico areale produttivo costiero, anche se tendenzialmente la soluzione di più luoghi di produzione appare plausibile.

Note

[1] Notizia del ritrovamento in Fenelli 2003, p. 189, figg. 2-3.
[2] Per le decorazioni tardo arcaiche del tempio del Santuario di Sol Indiges vedi Jaia 2010.
[3] Sull'intera tematica vedi le proposte di chi scrive in Jaia 2013 e Jaia 2019.
[4] Si segnala il caso di *Satricum*, al riguardo vedi Nonnis 2016, p. 519.
[5] L'unico atelier di anfore che inizia a produrre nel III sec. a.C. noto lungo la costa del *Latium vetus* è quello delle Grottacce, presso Torre Astura, che vira precocemente verso forme riferibili ad ambiti campani (Piccarreta 1977, nn.11-14-15, fig. 145; Hesnard 1989, pp.24-26).
[6] Al riguardo vedi Nonnis 2016, pp.523-525 con ampia trattazione. Esemplari di questi *askoi* sono stati rinvenuti, oltre che ad Ardea (Santuario di *Castrum Inui* e presso l'area urbana), a *Lavinium* (area urbana), a Vulci (Tomba *François*) e Tarquinia (scavi presso la porta nord). Due esemplari provengono dalle necropoli di Lilibeo.
[7] Per le importazioni di anfore e ceramica punica sulla costa laziale vedi Jaia 2019; Per i materiali etrusco-laziali in contesti della Sicilia Occidentale vedi Michetti 2007.
[8] Per il punto sull'intera problematica con particolare riferimento al Lazio costiero vedi Olcese-Coletti 2016.
[9] Jaia 2013, pp.475-489.
[10] Ceccarelli - Di Mento 2005, pp. 301-315.
[11] Ceccarelli - Di Mento 2005, p.198, n.13, tav. 22.13.
[12] Ceccarelli - Di Mento 2005, p. 242.
[13] Ceccarelli - Di Mento 2005, pp.212-213 e 220.
[14] Ceccarelli - Di Mento 2005, p. 224.
[15] Per il contesto di scavo e il corpus dei materiali vedi Jaia 2020.
[16] Per le anfore puniche rinvenute nei contesti lavinati vedi Jaia 2019; le anfore rodie riportano bolli riferibili al periodo III e IIIe (Jaia 2020, pp.252-253).
[17] Ringrazio Agnese Livia Fischetti per alcuni chiarimenti di carattere tecnico sulla lavorazione della ceramica e sulla tipologia e trattamento dei materiali utilizzati.
[18] Per una prima caratterizzazione di questa produzione vedi Jaia 2020, 81-98.
[19] Tale vicinanza mi è stata confermata da Angela Arena, che ringrazio, che ha scavato a lungo nell'ambito del santuario costiero ardeatino di *Castrum Inui*.
[20] Per i craterischi vedi P. Sommella 1975, pp. 30-34 e figg. 27-28.

Bibliografia

Ceccarelli, L./M. Di Mento 2005, Ceramica a vernice nera, in F. Di Mario (ed.), *Ardea. Il deposito votivo di Casarinaccio*, Roma, 201-215.
Fenelli, M./M. Guaitoli 1990, Nuovi dati dagli scavi di Lavinium, *Archeologia Laziale* 10.2 (Quaderni del Centro di Studio per l'archeologia etrusco-italica, 19), Roma, 182-193.
Fenelli, M. 2003, Scavi e ricerche topografiche nella fascia costiera tra Lavinium e Anzio, in *Lazio & Sabina* 1, Roma, pp.189-196.
Hesnard, A. et al. 1989, Aires de production des Gréco-italiques et des Dressel 1, in *Amphores romaines et histoire economique. Dix ans de recherche*, Actes du colloque (Siena, 22-24 mai 1986), Rome, 21-65
Jaia, A.M. 2010, La decorazione plastica tardo arcaica del santuario di Sol Indiges – Lavinium, in P.S. Lulof/C. Rescigno (eds.), *Deliciae fictiles* 4. *Immagini di dei, mostri ed eroi* (21-25 ottobre 2009 Roma – Siracusa), Oxford, 188-193.
Jaia, A.M. 2013, Le colonie di diritto romano. Considerazioni sul sistema difensivo costiero tra IV e III secolo a.C., *ScAnt* 19, 475-489.
Jaia, A.M. 2019, Aspetti economici della fascia costiera in età medio repubblicana in F.M. Cifarelli/S. Gatti/D. Palombi (eds.), *Oltre Roma Medio repubblicana: il Lazio tra i Galli e la battaglia di Zama* (Roma 7-9 giugno 2017), Roma, 53-65.
Jaia, A.M. 2020, *LAVINIUM III. Saggi di scavo presso la rimessa agricola della tenuta Borghese (1985-1986)*, Roma.
Michetti, L.M. 2007, Scambi e interferenze culturali tra ambiente etrusco-italico e mondo punico: alcuni esempi nell'artigianato artistico di età recente (IV-III sec. a.C.), *AnnFaina* 14, 325-363.
Nonnis, D. 2016, A proposito degli *askoi* del Gallonios Group: un nuovo esemplare da *Lavinium*, in F.Mainardis (ed.), *Voce concordi. Scritti per Claudio Zaccaria* (Antichità Altoadriatiche 85), Trieste, 519-530.
Piccarreta, F. 1977, *Astura* (Forma Italiae, 13), Firenze.
Sommella, P. 1975, Lo scavo stratigrafico delle platee, in *Lavinium* II. *Le tredici are*, Roma, 7-87.

# Ironworking between the Early Iron Age and the Archaic period
## *A view from the Middle-Adriatic region*

*Valeria Acconcia, Serafino Lorenzo Ferreri*

INTRODUCTION

The Middle-Adriatic region (including Marche and Abruzzo) provides a quite rich documentary dossier about the ancient bronze and iron metallurgy.[1] In comparison to the local bronzeworking, iron productions have been considered much less attractive in the history of the studies, due to their lower diagnostic value.[2] This paper will explore the relationship between the local ironworking and the earlier bronzeworking practices, in comparison to other contemporary metallurgical spheres in Italy; the natural metal deposits effectively exploitable with the ancient extractive techniques as well as the circulation of both artifacts and technological skills.

To this purpose, some methodological premises must be pointed out, regarding the general topic of ancient ironworking and its development in the Middle-Adriatic area:

1. as archaeometallurgists know very well, there is not only one kind of iron in nature. This metal is rarely found in a "pure" native status: it is often variously combined with other minerals or rocks and requires highly skilled workers in extracting and producing it. Thus, the identification and exploitation of iron ores in ancient times were strictly connected to the level of knowledge gained by miners and craftsmen.

2. Although there is no need to establish direct relationships within metal production and the natural availability of raw material, and although for later periods the historical and archaeological sources prove that iron or semi-finished artifacts circulated along the Tyrrhenian coast and in the inner Italian peninsula (see, further, 2),[3] it is highly probable that during the 2nd and the first half of the 1st millennium the metal supply was mainly practiced on a local scale.

3. In the area and for the period under consideration, neither archaeological research in extractive/productive sites, nor exhaustive metallographic analyses have been carried out. Accordingly, we can only hypothesize about the provenance of raw materials and about the technical skills. Thus, the study of the Middle-Adriatic ancient metallurgy has been based on the morphological characters of finished artifacts, which were prevalently found in funerary contexts. Especially for ancient Abruzzo, we lack a clear framework of the pre-roman inhabited sites: therefore, it is very difficult to connect the settlement pattern to the natural availability of metal ores.[4]

IRONWORKING AND METALLURGICAL SPHERES IN ITALY BETWEEN THE FINAL BRONZE AGE AND THE BEGINNING OF THE ROMAN PERIOD

The origin and diffusion of ironworking in ancient Italy are still widely debated by scholars, who have underlined (and sometimes emphasized) the prevailing role of the Middle-Tyrrhenian mining district (the Colline Metallifere and the Elba Island in Tuscany; the Monti della Tolfa in Latium; *fig. 1, A*).[5]

As widely known, since the 6th century BC the town of Populonia (*fig. 1, 1*) promoted an intensive iron production based on the exploitation of the Elba island hematite ores, and progressively increased it until the Roman Republican times. The raw mineral and the semi-finished iron circulated in the Tyrrhenian basin and in the inner peninsula. This "*Etruria Mineraria*/Mining Etruria" pattern has frequently traced back also to the starting phase of iron metallurgy in Italy, reducing the relevance of the connections between the highly varied framework of the local resources and the Aegean/Near Eastern influence.[6]

The "first" iron in Etruria appears during the Final Bronze Age, as small artifacts, in shape of production wastes or "patinas" on bronze objects. It is still matter of debate if these examples can be interpreted as intentional products or "accidental events" obtained by iron ores used as flux in the copper extracting process. It is highly probable that this iron was exploited by limonitic outcrops

*Fig. 1. Mining district and natural ferrous ores in ancient Italy (map red. from STRM DEM; V. Acconcia). A: the "Etruria mineraria" district (Elba Island; Colline Metallifere and Monti della Tolfa); B: the Monti Peloritani in Sicily; C: the Gargano area; D: the Aspromonte basin; E: iron ores of the Karst region. 1) Populonia (LI); 2) Coppa Nevigata (FG); 3) Broglio di Trebisacce (CS); 4) Castellace (RC); 5) Torre Galli (VV); 6) Torre del Mordillo (CS); 7) Santa Maria d'Anglona (MT); 8) Incoronata di Metaponto (MT); 9) Gorzano (MO); 10) Satricum (LT); 11) Piazza d'Armi di Spoleto (PG).*

naturally present in sulphide ores, as those in the Tolfa region.[7]

At the beginning of the EIA (9th century BC in traditional chronology), in Etruria but also in *Latium Vetus* and Campania, iron was used mainly to produce a small number of ornaments, swords, knives and spears, found in graves of adult males, probably to underline their social status.[8] The use of iron increased during the second phase of EIA (8th century BC) and, since the 7th century onwards, it was widely worked to produce all kinds of weapons and tools.[9] This development overlaps the "three stages" pattern hypothesized by A. Snodgrass for ancient Greece.[10]

C. Giardino has suggested that iron exploitation and production technology were transferred across Etruria at the end of BA by Sardinian craftsmen, probably influenced by Cypriot metalworkers since the 13th century BC. It is still debated if the increase of iron artifacts during the first half of the 8th century BC in the Middle-Tyrrhenian area should be ascribed to an autonomous improvement by Etruscan metalworkers or to the collapse of the Nuragic production system.[11] In this case, the opening of the Upper Tyrrhenian sea to the circulation of Phoenician and Euboean traders should have promoted the transmission of new metalworking skills. Above all, the recognizing and exploiting parameters for the Elban hematite ores. It could be no coincidence that the earliest indirect traces of their exploitation relate to the 8th and 7th century BC Euboean settlement in Pithecusa.[12]

Although this "Middle-Tyrrhenian pattern" represents undoubtedly an early and exceptional experience, it is not isolated in the archeological framework of ancient Italy, as scholars have identified other contemporary metallurgical spheres.

Substantial concentrations of iron artifacts have been found in Sicily, some of them probably imported by Myceneans traders since the middle of the 2nd millennium BC. Giardino has connected this early evidence to the exploitation of the Monti Peloritani metal deposits, densely settled since the FBA onwards (*fig. 1, B*).[13]

The Gargano area is rich in iron oxides and hydroxides (the fossiliferous deposits of the *Terre Rosse*/"Red Soils"), exploited almost in the FBA, as shown by the iron slags and artifacts found in the so-called "iron workshop" at Coppa Nevigata (FG) (*fig. 1, C; 2*).[14]

Similar evidence has been identified in Calabria and Basilicata, connected to the iron ores located in the Aspromonte basin, although their ancient exploitation is still uncertain (*fig. 1, D*). A forge, probably dated to the FBA, was brought to light at Broglio di Trebisacce (CS),[15] and an FBA/EIA iron spearhead was found at Castellace (RC) (*fig. 1, 3-4*). The clearest evidence for a local well-established iron metallurgy comes from the EIA cemeteries of Torre Galli (VV), Torre del Mordillo (CS), Santa Maria d'Anglona and Incoronata di Metaponto (MT) (*fig. 1, 5-8*).[16]

Scholars have hypothesized a direct relationship between the early interactions with the Aegean/Near Eastern area and the development of local ironworking spheres in Southern Italy, possibly also recalled in the problematic passage of the Odyssey about the metal exchanges at Temesa (I, 180-184). Recently, A. Nijboer has underlined that the *orientalia* of Torre Galli suggest a Phoenician origin for the local metallurgy. Likewise, at Huelva in the Iberian Peninsula, the earliest use of iron coincides with the establishment of the Phoenician *emporion* during the first half of the 9th century BC.[17]

In Northern Italy, iron rings dated to the M/FBA have been found in the Gorzano *Terramara* (MO) (*fig. 1, 9*) and, at the beginning of EIA, ironworking was adopted in the eastern Alpine area, based on the exploitation of the limonitic ores in the Karst region, crossed by the routes which connected the internal Balkans to the Adriatic coasts (*fig. 1, E*).[18]

The development of iron productions, adapted to the availability of ferrous minerals on a local scale, can be recorded also in later times. For instance, the metallographic analysis carried on Satricum (LT) iron artifacts and iron slags (7th-4th century BC) shed light on the probable exploitation of the bog ores of impure limonite, easy to smelt, localized in the Pontine region (*fig. 1, 10*).[19]

The rich limonite hardpans at Monteleone di Spoleto (PG) could have been exploited in surface as well, although ancient mining activities can be hypothesized only on the basis of the rich local metallurgical tradition, as shown for instance by the high-level funerary items buried in the princely graves at Piazza d'Armi in Spoleto (PG) (7th–6th century BC), realized with a skilled technique of bimetallic working (*fig. 1, 11*).[20]

*Valeria Acconcia*

Tracing resources: characters and diffusion of ferrous minerals in the Middle-Adriatic area and especially in Abruzzo

Before analysing the topic of ancient metallurgy in the Middle-Adriatic area, with a particular attention to the Abruzzo, it seems necessary to deal with the issue of local metal resources and the history of their exploitation during modern times, comparing the metallic potential of iron ores with the ancient exploiting skills. In general, the geology of this region is mainly characterized by sedimentary processes and lacks the huge metal deposits of volcanic soils typical, as mentioned above, of the Middle-Tyrrhenian region. However a quite good amount of ferrous minerals is recorded in Abruzzo, whereas the cupriferous ores are extremely rare.[21]

The iron ores in Abruzzo are too scarcely productive for the modern mining methods, although they were exploited almost since the Late Medieval period, by applying the same empirical skills that could effectively have been used in previous times too in order to localize, mine, select and process of minerals. This topic has been valorised only marginally in the relevant scholarship so far.[22]

In this section, the characters and problems of the iron minerals supply in Abruzzo will be synthetically discussed, summarizing what is recorded in the geological maps and by the scientific literature.

Firstly, it must be underlined that the presence of ferrous minerals in the region must be consi-dered as a residual geological phenomenon, deriving from karst erosion, by the dissolution of limestone host rocks, which contained iron as an impure element. The residual state of these rocks did not preclude their aggregation as earthy masses of iron oxides and hydroxides (limonite) in quite thick deposits. Frequently, these accumulations are unequally composed by the above-mentioned limonite aggregates (ca. 15,5-50 %), silica (ca. 2,5-7,5 %), titanium oxides (ca. 3 %) and aluminium silicates (ca. 40-67 %) that, where they are prevalent, compose bauxite deposits. In general, they are formed by concretions (pisolites) and earthy masses of various dimensions, also known as "red soils" (*terre rosse*) for their typical colour: the more bright, the larger is the percentage of iron oxide (hematite).

At the surface level, they look like lens or veins of various extensions (a few meters to hundreds), whose depth is not easily measurable (a few cm to several metres) and, for their karst origin, they fill up paleo-dolines or hollows in rocks dated to the Cretaceous (for bauxite) or to other geological periods (for limonite). The best-known examples are sub-aerial deposits, formed and still present in continental environment (in some cases, they have been subsequently covered by marine sediments).

At natural state, they could be hidden by soil and vegetation. Considering this scarce surface visibility and the uneven character of the geological research (carried on intensively only in the better exploitable areas), the knowledge about limonite and bauxite ores in Abruzzo is still substantially incomplete.[23]

In order to define an almost updated distribution chart of the metal resources and mining activities, the author has implemented a GIS platform, mapping by point-like elements the extractive sites recorded in the geological studies, and the extension of every deposit.

A first review of the 19th century naturalistic/mineralogic research has evidenced a huge and exclusive presence of ferrous minerals as limonite hardpans.[24] Although much of these reports cannot be punctually verified for their scarcely accurate level of description and for the lacking of mineralogic characterization analysis, on the other hand it must be underlined that the sole mention of limonite during the same century is connected to the delay in the discovery of the bauxite in Abruzzo, which occurred only at the beginning of the 20th century, even if some samples already circulated since 1857 (with the wrong and almost homophonic reference to *"Bruzio"*, namely Calabria). Later on, a lot of "red soils" deposits were properly recognized as bauxites, thanks to specific analyses which verified their percentage of alumina, higher than the ferrous content.[25]

For instance, if we compare the 1854 mineral survey of the area between Lecce nei Marsi and Gioia dei Marsi (AQ) in the Fucino basin (*fig. 2*),

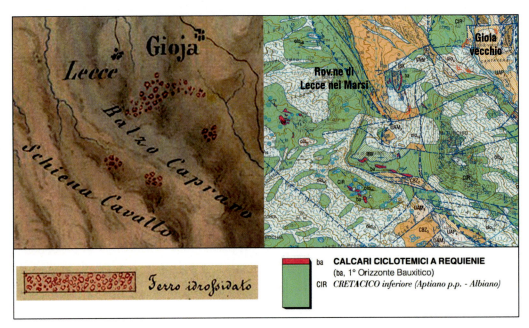

*Fig. 2. Lecce nei Marsi, Gioia dei Marsi: comparison between a geognostic survey in 1854 and a geological map in 2010 (ISPRA; elab. S.L. Ferreri).*

with a recent edition of the Geological Map of Italy (2010), the same deposits nowadays identified as bauxites, were previously described as "hydroxide iron" (*ferro idrossidato*).[26]

Therefore, the research carried on since the beginning of the 20th century and collected in the geological maps, give a completely different framework of three wide bauxite basins (the Sirente-Velino range, the mountains south of the Fucino between the Giovenco and Liri valleys; and the Maiella massif), coinciding with the Cretaceous rocks which they were originated from.[27] On the contrary, only around ten of properly iron deposits have been localized, in addition to the already known Vallelanci (Gagliano Aterno; AQ) and M. Pietre Fitte (Acciano; AQ).[28] The other iron ores reported during the 19th century has not been verified, since until the '60 of '900 the scientific and industrial interests displaced towards the exploitation of the bauxite, while mining research during the previous century was concentrated on the development of iron industry, under the impulse of Bourbonic government (since 1852).

Taking into account this framework, in *fig. 3* the limonite (or whatever iron minerals) has been evidenced in orange with a smaller symbol if not verified by analysis, with a bigger one if verified or newly recovered. Bauxite deposits have been divided into three groups: those already recognized as limonite during the 19th century (in blue); the bauxite deposits properly recognized and documented in scientific reports (in scarlet) or represented in the geological maps (in brown).

The overlapping of the above-mentioned three bauxite basins to the ferrous deposits is particularly relevant, considering that some of them were initially exploited to produce iron and, later, aluminium. This conversion is recorded in Abruzzo since 1907, at Bussi sul Tirino (PE), where the Italian Aluminium Society was founded as the main supplier in Italy for the first 20-30 years of the 20th century.[29]

Ferrous minerals which raised the 19th century mining prospectors' interest, could have been previously exploited. A brief analysis of the regional toponymy, based on the database of the IGMI (which collects the toponyms registered in the maps from the 19th century, largely with an older origin), evidences the frequency of names as *Vena Rossa/Vene Rosse* ("Red Vein/Veins"), *Rava del Ferro* ("Gorge of Iron"), *Ferrarecce* etc. (*fig. 3, A-C*).[30] The last one, noticed only in a mountainous area near Tornimparte (AQ), probably derives from *ferrariciae* (*fossae*) used in the Early Middle Ages to define iron extracting caves.[31]

The earliest written sources about the exploiting of the "red soils" iron content in Abruzzo raised up to the Late Middle Age. Waiting for a more extensive analysis of the archive documents and sources, only the ironworking plants already known in the history of the studies have been pointed out on the map at *fig. 3*, with the nearby iron sources (the connection is represented as a dashed line). Thus, the exploitation of the mine of Rocca Pia (AQ) started in the 15th century, near bauxite lenses (*fig. 3, 1*).[32] An ironworking plant was set up during the last quarter of the 18th century at Morino (AQ), in the Roveto Valley, supplied by a nearby mine and by those on the Arunzo mountain (between Capistrello and Tagliacozzo - AQ; *fig. 3, 2*).[33] Particularly, the *Ferriera Marsicana* ("Marsican Ironworks"), started in 1843 at S. Sebastiano di Bisegna (AQ) and initially exploited the "limonite" ores of Lecce nei Marsi (curiously, the same which supplied most part of the Italian aluminum for the first quarter of the 20th century, see above, 155-156) and also the limonite ores of Vallelanci, after having been taken over by a well-known weapons supplier for the royal army (*fig. 3, 3*).[34]

These plants were not maintained after the Italian Unity process: mainly because of the lack of investments on fossil fuels, since the local forest coverage had been highly depauperated, also by the massive ironworking.[35] Furthermore, although the relevant diffusion of these deposits and their high ferrous content (around 15,5-50%), the mining activities could have been ceased for the high cost of the transports and for their seasonal trend (due to the quite thick snow-covering, typical of the Appennine range winter). For the same reasons, the local bauxite mines were closed at the end of the '60 of the 20th century.[36]

These problems concerned only marginally the pre-industrial societies, as the protohistoric communities.[37] It cannot be excluded that the iron deposits in Abruzzo above mentioned could have supplied a local ironworking, as recently

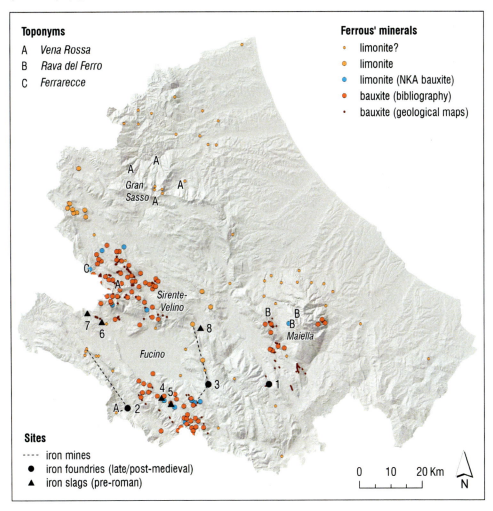

*Fig. 3. The Abruzzo metal resources. Syntetic map: 1. Rocca Pia; 2. Morino; 3. Bisegna-S. Sebastiano; 4. Collelongo-Fond'jò; 5. Collelongo-Paretella; 6. Magliano de' Marsi-Casale di Stefano; 7. Magliano de' Marsi-Sante Marie; 8. Castelvecchio Subequo/Castel di Ieri-Colle Cipolla (elab. S.L. Ferreri).*

proposed for the bauxites in the Salento area.[38] The "red soils" are empirically exploitable: they can be easily localized thanks to their recurrent altitude and to their color; their exploitation can be open-air carried on, with scarcely skilled methods, also because of the friable texture of their matrices, that allows the manual separation or the sieving of the metallic fractions. The disposability of dense forest as a fuel and limestone covers to lower the melting temperature shouldn't be overlooked.

Although the scarcely developed knowledge of the inhabited sites, the archaeological framework of Abruzzo gives back some traces of ancient ironworking. For instance, bronze and iron slags have been recorded at Collelongo (AQ)-Fond'jò, settled since the MBA up to the EIA2 (in traditional chronology, the second-third quarters of the 8th century BC).[39] Unless they are intrusive elements in earlier levels, they can be ascribed to a local metallurgic production.[40] The settlement is localized nearby dense bauxite lenses, as in the Vallelonga, which could have had exploited in ancient times (fig. 3, 4).[41]

In the same valley, at Paretella, a relevant number of iron slags have been surveyed nearby an area frequented during proto-historical times, contiguous to another bauxite deposit (fig. 3, 2, 5).[42] Similar traces have been recorded at Magliano de' Marsi (AQ), dated to the EIA (Casale di Stefano and Sante Marie), at the edge of a hill characterized by bauxite lenses (fig. 3, 6-7).[43]

Iron slags have been found also in the hillforts of the inner Abruzzo region, by the École Française de Rome (which has carried out a long-term survey project). For instance, slags were surveyed inside the hillfort of Colle Cipolla (AQ), dated to the EIA and abandoned at the end of the 6th-beginning of the 5th century BC:[44] even in this case, the proximity with the limonite deposits of Vallelanci is significantly interesting (fig. 3, 8).[45]

These evidences should be better characterized not only from a chronological point of view, by extensive excavations of the settlements mentioned above, but also on a mineralogic one, analyzing the slags to verify the presence of bauxite components.[46] The topic of the iron supply should be treated also by an experimental approach, reproducing the different phases of its cycle: exploiting the local metal deposits with ancient technological skills.

In conclusion, the identification of local ferrous deposits can enrich the discussion about pre-roman metallurgy and help in recognizing the characters of ironworking in later periods, up to the 18th and the 19th century plants (as industrial archaeology). On a more general note, the metal resources integrate our knowledge of the broad spectrum and versatility of natural resources, typical of the mountainous habitats, which marginality has recently focused the archaeological debate on the resilience of communities settled in inner areas.[47]

*Serafino Lorenzo Ferreri*

METALLURGY IN THE MIDDLE-ADRIATIC REGION BETWEEN THE BRONZE AGE AND THE ARCHAIC PERIOD

As mentioned above, the Middle-Adriatic area is characterized by an early rich bronzeworking since the 2nd millennium BC. In the Marche, at Offida (AP), a bronze smelting furnace (dated by N. Lucentini to the EBA) was found with 20 bronze slabs and a mould (fig. 4, 1).[48] At Osimo (AN), a crucible was excavated in the inhabited area and a small mould for rings from Cartofaro (AP) is dated to the M/RBA (fig. 4, 2-3).[49] In Abruzzo, moulds and slags were found in the Grotta a Male (AQ) and at Coccioli (TE); a certain number of semi-finished bronze artifacts and slags come from the Fucino area and crucibles from Fonte Tasca (CH; fig. 4, 4-6). In general, the inner Fucino district is supposed to be the core of the bronze metallurgy in Abruzzo in the R/FBA (fig. 4, A).[50]

Based on archaeometallurgical analyses, Giardino has hypothesized that bronze was imported here from other regions, as ingots or recycled materials, and then worked locally. The narrow similarities between local bronze artifacts and those produced in the Central Tyrrhenian region during the FBA, suggest that bronze objects to be re-smelted should be imported from Tuscany or Latium.[51]

Since the beginning of the EIA, the productive patterns of ancient Marche and Abruzzo diversified, along with the changes in the settlement's pattern and social organization. The "Picene"[52] bronzeworking achieved and preserved high quality levels, thanks to the ability of local workshops to catalyze the exchanges with the Tyrrhenian area and with the Trans-Adriatic region.

The topic of trades to-and-from the Balkans can be just mentioned here due to its complexity. The diffusion of common patterns for pottery and metal artifacts has been interpreted by scholars as the trace of commercial or also "individual" exchanges in the Adriatic basin since the end of the BA.[53] The diffusion of artifacts from the Picene and Southern Italy in the Balkan area during the 7th and 6th century, and the corresponding diffusion of Eastern Adriatic goods along the Italian coasts, have been interpreted as markers of a route connected to the search of

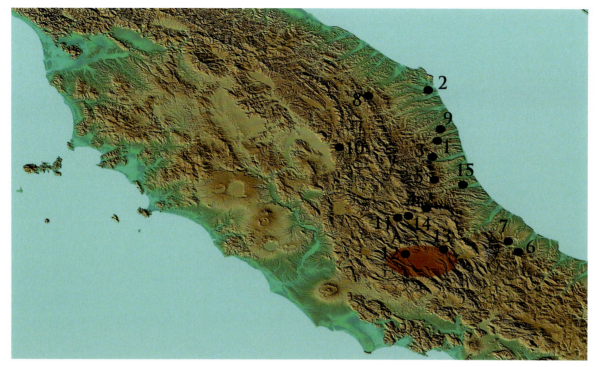

*Fig. 4. The Middle-Adriatic area. A: the Fucino district (map red. from STRM DEM; V. Acconcia). 1) Offida (AP); 2) Osimo (AN); 3) Cartofaro (AP); 4) Grotta a Male (AQ); 5) Coccioli and Campovalano (TE); 6) Archi - Fonte Tasca (CH); 7) Guardiagrele – Comino; 8) Matelica (MC); 9) Fermo (FM); 10) Colfiorito di Foligno (PG); 11) Fossa (AQ); 12) Avezzano – Cretari (AQ); 13) Castel di Ieri (AQ); 14) Bazzano (AQ); 15) Atri (TE).*

metals alternative to the Etruscan one.[54] The inner Balkans are rich in metal ores: iron, copper and especially tin. Although the artifacts exported from Italy are diffused prevalently along the coast of Slovenia, D. Yntema has hypothesized that the Eastern Adriatic coastal communities could have acted as intermediaries towards those who directly exploited the metal ores in the inner Balkans.[55]

The Abruzzo region, instead, was excluded from this circulation process, which involved only marginally its northern and coastal communities.[56] Since the beginning of the EIA, the local bronzeworking decreased and bronze was mainly used for fibulae, belts or small basins, most of them probably imported from the Picene territory. On the other hand, the local workshops (and mostly those of the inner mountainous area) concentrated on the prevailing use of iron.

A certain number of iron ornaments found in the necropolis of Guardiagrele (CH) and dated to the end of the 9th- beginning of the 8th century BC represents the earliest evidence of ironworking in the Abruzzo territory (*fig. 4, 7*).[57] The oldest iron artifacts in the cemeteries of Brecce at Matelica (MC), Fermo and Colfiorito di Foligno (PG) can be ascribed to the end of the 9th-8th century BC as well (*fig. 4, 8-9; fig. 5, 1-7*).[58]

The small chronological delay after Etruria and Southern Italy suggests that the ironworking cycle skills could have been introduced in the Middle-Adriatic area from the outside. Nijboer suggests an Etruscan origin for local ironworking, on the basis of imported artifacts from the Middle-Tyrrhenian area and the lack of Greek imported goods.[59]

During the 8th century BC, in the inner Abruzzo area iron weapons increased markedly in funerary contexts, replacing the bronze equipment of the previous period. Local workshop started a sort of "experimental" production of iron ornaments and tools usually realized in bronze. A good example for this practice is represented by the tomb n. 551 in the necropolis of Fossa (AQ), dated around 750 BC according to traditional chronology (*fig. 4, 11*).[60] In particular, among the grave goods do feature: two iron knives with a *"lingua di fiamma"* blade, which imitate bronze models diffused in Etruria and *Latium vetus*; two drilled iron fibulae which reproduce bronze types well known in Campania and in the EIA necropolis of Terni (*fig. 5, 8-9*).[61] Always from the necropolis of Fossa

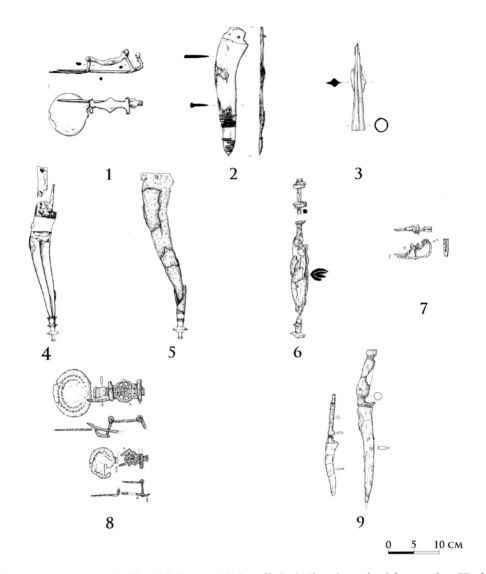

*Fig. 5. EIA iron artifacts in the Middle-Adriatic area. 1-3) iron fibula, knife and spearhead from tomb n. 77 of the Brecce necropolis at Matelica (Sabbatini 2008, cat. 8-10); 4) iron knife with a bronze scabbard from tomb n. 75 SmIII / 1957 of Fermo (Drago Troccoli 2003, fig. 11, 1); 5) iron knife from tomb n. 75 / 1956 of Fermo (Drago Troccoli 2003, fig. 17, 1); 6) iron sword from tomb I B / 1956 of Fermo (Drago Troccoli 2003, fig. 12, 1); 7) iron fibula from tomb n. 78 sm VI / 1957 of Fermo (Drago Troccoli 2003, fig. 19, A2); 8-9) iron drilled fibulas and knives from tomb n. 551 of Fossa (Fossa II, tav. 189).*

and in the same period, iron hairpins (so called "*Fermo*" type) are attested, along with iron pendants and a small iron vessel too (probably a *pyxis*; *fig. 6, 2-3, 5-6, 7, 9-10*).[62] Ornamental drilled disks, made in iron and mounted amber, found in female graves dated to the end of the 8th-beginning of the 7th century BC at Fossa, Cretaro near Avezzano (AQ) and Castel di Ieri (AQ), clearly reproduced bronze prototypes, spread in a wider area within Marche, Umbria and Abruzzo (*fig. 4, 12-13; fig. 6, 1, 6*).[63] This experimental phase, when shapes typical of the bronze production (already attested in the local repertoire) were adopted by iron craftsmen, was extremely lively for the local workshops: they developed technological skills and produced precious iron artifacts, which originally should have had the color and shininess of silver, resulting therefore very different from their current state of conservation (heavily damaged by oxidation process). Metallographic analyses have also revealed the use of the damascening technique for fibulae, which involved the use of bronze decorations on iron artifacts, transmitted by foreign workshops (Etruscan? Southern Italic?).[64]

Then, starting from the 7th century BC, the use of iron became predominant in the Abruzzo region: iron artifacts were produced in standardized shapes, widely diffused and adopted by the local communities with small variants, eventually self-identifying, interpreted by E. Benelli and J. Weidig as a "Middle-Adriatic metallurgic koiné".[65] Local workshops kept on imitating high-quality level bronze models too, such as the sword scabbard caps. The only bronze example currently known in Abruzzo is that found in tomb n. 81 at Navelli (AQ), obtained by two bronze drilled sheets, probably imported from Etruria (or the Faliscan region) at the end of the 7th century BC.[66] It could be no coincidence that all the other scabbard caps of the archaic period in Abruzzo are made of iron and dated to a slightly lower chronological horizon (since the first half of 6th century BC, as those from Campovalano): they could be interpreted as local reproduction of higher models.[67] A single case of iron belt is known from tomb 232 of Fossa (*fig. 6, 8*).[68]

FUNCTION AND SHAPE: QUANTITATIVE DATA FROM SOME FUNERARY CONTEXTS AND METAL SUPPLY IN ABRUZZO.

The relevance of the iron metallurgy in Abruzzo since the end of the 8th century BC onwards, can be better understood comparing the statistical value of iron artifacts with that of their bronze counterparts. The personal ornaments provide useful evidence for this: if the weapons are made of iron for strictly practical purposes, the use of iron or bronze for fibulae, rings, pendants etc. is instead much more problematic (scarce availability of bronze? clothing trends?).

The following comparison has been realized based on the 8th-5th century BC funerary items from the widely known cemeteries of Fossa, Bazzano, Campovalano and Atri (*fig. 4, 5, 11, 14-15*). The 145 graves taken into account for this period in Fossa, and the 469 in Bazzano, represent very well the archaic material culture of the inner mountainous area of Abruzzo; as the 257 in Campovalano and the 40 in the Petrara necropolis at Atri (though on a minor scale) do for the coastal area.[69]

The metallic shapes with the highest diagnostic value, mostly bronze items (such as belts, basins and other bronze vessels) have been excluded from this evaluation, taking into account instead the most frequently occurring metallic shapes: fibulae, bracelets, rings and pendants (pendants are often made of iron and bronze elements).[70]

The fibulae represent most of the personal ornaments in this sample, perhaps because of the clothing trends: they are prevailingly made of iron and outnumber all the other shapes by far (*fig. 7, A*). Conversely, the abundancy of bronze bracelets and rings could be explained by the mechanical properties of this alloy, much more ductile and "wearable" in direct contact with parts of the body. Alternatively, it can be explained by "aesthetical" or symbolic reasons, as for the quantitative variations of every shape among gender and age classes.

The *a drago, sanguisuga, traforo, due pezzi* and *arco rivestito* bronze and iron fibulae of the EIA and of the early Orientalizing period, during the 7th and the 6th century BC were replaced by *ad arco semplice, rialzato* e *ondulato* shapes, with local variations that can be ascribed to the already mentioned "Middle-Adriatic koiné" (*fig. 6, 11-18, 27-33*). The bronze types (as the San Genesio, Grottazolina and "pre-Certosa" types, see *fig. 6, 22-25*), imported or inspired by the Picene workshops, were mostly diffused in the northern coastal Abruzzo, and only the less elaborate Loreto Aprutino and Certosa types circulated in the inner area of the region (*fig. 6, 17, 19-21*), as well as a few number of specimens probably imported or influenced by the Campanian metal production (*fig. 6, 26, 34*).[71]

Such evidence is quite clear for Bazzano and Fossa,[72] were the iron fibulae exceed 90% of the whole amount, although in Campovalano and Atri (closer to the Picene area) their percentage decrease under 80% (*fig. 7, B*).

The abundance of iron artifacts can be explained in various ways, without excluding the impact of a local appreciation for the silver-like appearance of wrought iron (as bronze originally resembles gold). Another key to interpretation can be identified in the natural availability of metal resources. As already mentioned, although the lack of archaeometric analyses makes it difficult to connect the artifacts to iron deposits possibly exploited in ancient times, such an intensive production could hardly have flourished only on imported iron from other mining districts, as the Etruscan or the Balkan ones.[73]

As S.L. Ferreri explained above, iron deposits in Abruzzo are concentrated in the mountainous inner area, especially in the Fucino region (Monte Ventrino, Gagliano Aterno, Molina Aterno, Acciano, Val Rovereto-Cappadocia, Lecce dei Marsi, Gioia dei Marsi, San Sebastiano di Bisegna e Collelongo) and nearby Latium (Morino, Canneto, Campo di Grano, San Donato Val di Comino).[74] They are prevalently surface limonite outcrops with poor ferrous content, between Ovindoli

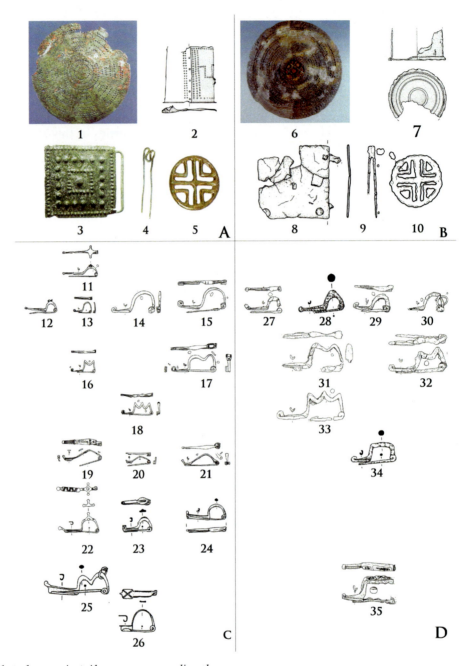

*Fig. 6: artifacts from ancient Abruzzo: corresponding shapes.*
A: Bronze Artifacts. 1) drilled disk from the necropolis of Camerino (Lecce dei Marsi; AQ; d'Ercole-Cairoli 1998); 2) vessel from the tomb n. 191 of Fossa (Fossa I); 3) belt plaque from tomb n. 198 of Fossa (Fossa I); n. 4) "Fermo" type hairpin from tomb n. 445 of Fossa (d'Ercole-Martellone 2007); 5) pendant from tomb n. 190 from Fossa (Fossa I).
B: Iron artifacts. 6) drilled disk from the tomb n. 365 of Fossa (d'Ercole-Martellone 2007); 7) vessel from tomb 57 of Fossa (Fossa I); n. 8) belt plaque from tomb 232 of Fossa (Fossa II); 9) "Fermo" type hairpin from tomb n. 523 of Fossa (Acconcia, d'Ercole 2012, fig. 3); 10) pendant from tomb n. 582 of Fossa (Acconcia, d'Ercole 2012, fig. 2).
C: 7th – 6th century bronze fibulae shapes in the Abruzzo territory (most common: nn. 1-21; only in Campovalano and in the northern coastal region: nn. 22-26). 1-21) types D2, F3, G3, I1-var. a, I2, L1-var. b, N2-var. b, N1, O1 from Bazzano (Weidig 2014, tavv. 70-71); 22) Grottazolina type fibula, from tomb 75 of Campovalano (Campovalano I, tav. 64, 11); 23) San Genesio type fibula, from tomb 47 of Campovalano (Campovalano I, tav. 43, 5); 24) "pre-Certosa" type fibula from tomb 212 of Campovalano (Campovalano II, tav. 99, 2); 25; "pre-Certosa" type from tomb 75 of Campovalano (Campovalano I, tav. 64, n. 9); 26) fibula from tomb 158 f Campovalano (Campovalano II, tav. 84, n. 3).
D: 7th – 6th century iron fibulae shapes in the Abruzzo territory. 27, 29-33, 35) types F2, G1, G2, H1, I1, M1 from Bazzano (Weidig 2014, tavv. 70-71); 28) fibula from tomb 100 of Campovalano (Campovalano II, tav. 38, n. 4); 34) fibula from tomb 75 of Campovalano (Campovalano I, tav. 66, n. 9).

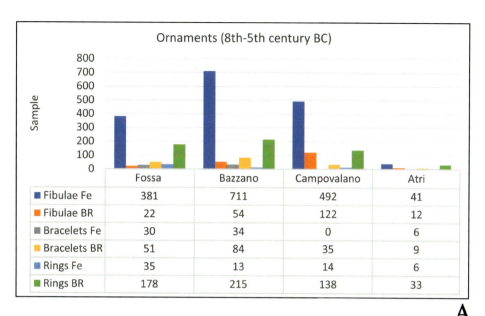
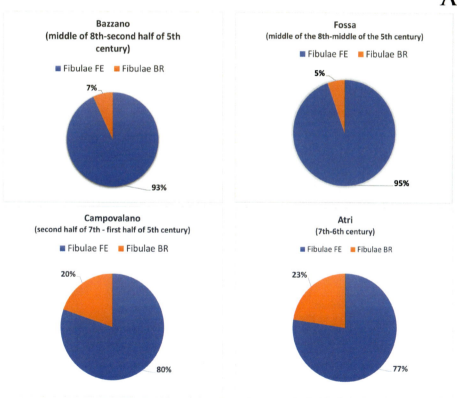

Fig. 7: A) Percentages of bronze and iron ornaments in the Fossa, Bazzano, Campovalano and Atri graves ($8^{th}$-$5^{th}$ century BC).
B) Percentages of bronze and iron fibulae in the Fossa, Bazzano, Campovalano and Atri graves ($8^{th}$-$5^{th}$ century BC).

and Caprasecca and along the Aterno river, and were exploited in the 18th and 19th century by the Bourbon Government, which production plants and mining tunnels were dismantled after the unification of Italy (see, further, 2-5). Relevantly, the Marsica bauxite deposits area exploited in modern times before being closed, have a chemical composition very similar to that of the already mentioned "Red Soils" in Puglia. Still we do not have archaeological evidence to verify the ancient exploitation of these deposits, which could have provided small amount of iron. In this respect, it is significant that the only results obtained by metallographic analyses on iron artifacts from Abruzzo (realized by G. Ingo on a sword, a nail and a slag from Bazzano) has suggested scarcely skilled productive processes, probably finalized to realize standardized and utilitarian tools, weapons and ornaments, requested by small communities, characterized by a scarce level of internal complexity, as those of Abruzzo in the first half of the 1st millennium should be.[75]

*Valeria Acconcia*

## Notes

[1] A first report about this topic was presented during a workshop about craft and production in the European Iron Age, held in Cambridge in 2015.
[2] The ancient iron artifacts of the pre-roman period are usually recovered in a very precarious state (covered by corrosion agglomerations, with fragile metallic bodies splitting apart in thin plates etc.).
[3] Acconcia/Milletti 2017, 333.
[4] Acconcia 2015.
[5] Giardino 1995, 7-15, 109-133; Acconcia/Milletti 2009, 141-143.
[6] Acconcia/Milletti 2009; 2017.
[7] Giardino 1995, 118-119; Delpino 1988; 1997; Acconcia/Milletti 2015, 242. Iron patinas also on a sporadic axe from Giulianova (TE; Bietti Sestieri/Giardino 2003, 426).
[8] De Marinis 2004, 68; Nijboer 2010, 12.
[9] Hartmann 1985; Corretti/Benvenuti 2001; Giardino 2005, 499.
[10] Snodgrass 1971; 1980; De Marinis 2004, 65.
[11] Giardino 1995, 147-148; Giumlia Mair/Maddin 2004, 56.
[12] Zifferero 2002, 181; Nijboer 2008, 11. With regards to Pithecusa and the Euboean settlement, Giardino has related the first ironworking traces to the exploitation of local ferrous sands (2005, 499).
[13] Giardino 1995, 134; 2005, 496; De Marinis 2004, 65-66.
[14] Giardino 2005, 500; Giardino/Spagnolo 2011.
[15] Vanzetti/Vidale 1999; doubts about the chronology of this forge have been expressed in De Marinis 2004, 66.
[16] Pacciarelli 1999, 61-62; 2004; Nijboer 2010, 11; Chiartano 1994; 1996; Frey 1991.
[17] Nijboer 2008; 2010, 11. See also Pacciarelli 1999, 58-59.
[18] Giardino 2005, 494, 498.
[19] Nijboer 1998, 237, 245-247.
[20] Zifferero 2001, 112; Manca/Weidig 2014.
[21] Amary 1854, 2; Jervis 1874, nn. 1545-1546; Letta 1972, 21; Mattias/Guidi Giolj 1999; Presutti et al. 1863, 376, n. 8; Speranza 1955, 19; Weisse 1973.
[22] Fortini 1988, 61-63; Letta 1972, 21; Zifferero 2001.
[23] Ranieri 1974, 45-86.
[24] Adamoli et al. 2010, 64; Amary 1854, 2-3, 10, 38; Bonanni 1875, 10, 38; Carelli 1859, 7; Corcia 1843, 65, 110, 140, 165, 168, 288; Del Re 1835, 69, 164, 195; Jervis 1874, nn. 1478, 1480-1481, 1489-1490, 1539-1540, 1549-1550, 2043, 2098; Jetti 1978, 11, 83; Letta 1972, 21; Pascetta 2008, 165-166; Ranieri 1974, 85; Rozzi 1838, 213-215; Scibilia 2015, 138, 140, 159, 160; Speranza 1955, 9; Tenore 1864, 52; Valignani 1729, 131.
[25] Formenti 1902; Mattirolo 1901; Vespasiani 1904.
[26] http://opac.apat.it/sebina/repository/catalogazione/immagini/jpg/null084.jpg; http://www.isprambiente.gov.it/Media/carg/378_SCANNO/Foglio.html.
[27] Cassetti 1901, 173; 1902, 172-173; 1906, 45, 51; Catenacci 1974, 70-71; Centamore et al. 2006a, 43-44, 46, 49, 54, 115; 2006b, 39-40, 105; 2006c, 43-44, 143-144; Centamore/Dramis 2010, 45, 47, 119; Chelussi 1903, 73; 1906, 48; Colecchia/Agostini 2014, 228; Crema 1912, 63; 1917, 4-5; 1926, 334; Jetti 1978, 82-83; Letta 1972, 21; Miccadei et al. 2010, 44-45; Moschetti 1927, 66; Praturlon 1968, 65-66; Scibilia 2015, 140-141, 159; Speranza 1955, 7-9; http://193.206.192.231/carta_geologica_italia/centro.htm (ff. 145-147, 152-153).
[28] Centamore et al. 2006c 144; Ranieri 1974, 86; Scibilia 2015, 83, 138, 140-141, 159-160; Speranza 1955, 8.
[29] Gribaudi 1931; Mastrostefano 2009; Moschetti 1927.
[30] Pascetta 2008, 165-166; https://www.igmi.org/it/descrizione-prodotti/cartografia-digitale/database-toponomastica.
[31] http://ducange.enc.sorbonne.fr/FERRUM1#FERRUM-1-33 (s.v. *ferraricia fossa*).
[32] Pascetta 2008, 165-166; http://193.206.192.231/carta_geologica_italia/centro.htm (f. 153).
[33] Del Re 1835, 203, 265; Leosini 1863, 119-120.
[34] Aune 1843; Brocchi 1819, 370; Jervis 1894, n. 2097; Leosini 1863, 120; Mastrostefano 2009, 63, 65.
[35] Del Re 1835, 203; Tenore 1864, 62.
[36] Ranieri 1974, 62-65.
[37] Giardino 1998, 194-195.
[38] Giardino, Spagnolo 2011.
[39] Gatti 2004, 111-112; Grossi/Irti 2011, 93, 95.
[40] Gatti 2004, 127; Grifoni Cremonesi 1973; Grossi/Irti 2011, 70, 133, n. 3; Letta 1972, 21.
[41] Crema 1926; Praturlon 1968, 66; Speranza 1955, 7-8.
[42] Grossi/Irti 2011, 70, 133, n. 4; Crema 1926, 334, n. XV.
[43] Grossi/Irti 2011, 139, nn. 1, 3; http://193.206.192.231/carta_geologica_italia/centro.htm (f. 145).
[44] Acconcia 2014, 194; Bourdin 2010, 431, fig. 1; Cosentino/Mieli 2006, 500-502.
[45] Centamore et al. 2006c, 144; Scibilia 2015, 83, 138, 140, 159-160.
[46] Giardino, Spagnolo 2011, 272.
[47] Colecchia, Agostini 2014; Stagno/Montanari 2015. Taking into account the versatility of the "red soils", they could have been used also as dyes and as pozzolanic additive to prepare binding agents (Gribaudi 1931, 629; Mozzetti 1845, 156).
[48] Lucentini 1987, 477-484.
[49] Naso 2000, 62.
[50] Giardino 2001, 110; Bietti Sestieri/Giardino 2003, 411, 418, 421, 427.
[51] Peroni 1961; Peroni et al. 1980; Giardino 2001, 110; Bietti Sestieri/Giardino 2003, 419-422.
[52] "Picene" is used here to generally define the material culture in the Marche territory since the beginning of EIA.

[53] Bietti Sestieri/Lo Schiavo 1976; Yntema 1985. About the circulations of artifacts since the FBA-EIA, Naso 2000, 52, 88; Gatti 2005; Lucentini 2007; Blečić 2007; Iaia 2007; Nijboer 2010, 6.
[54] Peroni 1976.
[55] Yntema 1990; D'Ercole 2002, 189.
[56] Bietti Sestieri, Giardino 2003, 421. As already mentioned, the datings in this paper are on a traditional chronological basis, for a discussion of the absolute and relative dates in ancient Abruzzo, see Acconcia 2019, 8-9.
[57] Iron artifacts are in tombs 59 and 65: Ruggeri 2003, 122; 2010; Ruggeri et al. 2009, 43.
[58] Matelica, Brecce, tomb 77: Sabbatini 2008, 60-61, nn. 8-10; Fermo, Misericordia, tombs 75 SmIII / 1957, 75 / 1956, I B / 1956, 78 sm VI / 1957: Drago Troccoli 2003, 52, 56-57. Colfiorito di Foligno, tombs 39 and 40: Bonomi Ponzi 1997, 237.
[59] Nijboer 2010, 13. Although we have evidence of contacts with the Campanian/Oenotrian metallurgy, as shown by the well-known bronze fibula from Pizzoli (AQ) or by the four spirals bronze fibulae diffused along the coastal area of the Abruzzo (Cosentino 2010, 298; Acconcia/d'Ercole 2012, 27, nt. 76).
[60] *Fossa II*, 229-232; Acconcia 2014, 32; Acconcia 2019, 12.
[61] Acconcia/d'Ercole 2012, 22.
[62] For the "Fermo" type, see *Fossa I*, 169, type 1 ; Acconcia 2019, 22. For the iron vessel in tomb 57, see *Fossa I*, 86, n. 4. Another iron vessel was found in the necropolis of Camaia at Navelli (AQ; Ferreri in Acconcia et al. 2017, 65, n. 7).
[63] Ceccaroni 2010, 343-344; Acconcia/d'Ercole 2012, 31, ntt. 98-99; Acconcia/d'Ercole 2018, 33; Acconcia 2019, 20.
[64] E.g., *Fossa I*, 75 (tomb 21, n. 6).
[65] Benelli/Weidig 2006.
[66] Di Sabatino in Acconcia et al. 2017, 76.
[67] Weidig 2014, 122-124.
[68] *Fossa II*, 93, n. 3.
[69] *Fossa I-II*; *Campovalano I-II*; Weidig 2014; Baldelli/Ruggeri 1982. For the sample selection, see Acconcia 2014, 22-23.
[70] The rings could have had much more uses than the ornamental one: so those used as suspension elements for knives of swords, or those used as decorative ornaments (for clothes or other artifacts) have been excluded.
[71] In general, for the fibulae types diffused in Abruzzo, Weidig 2014, 229-284.
[72] With regard to this, preliminary research in other cemeteries of the inner Abruzzo region (as Capestrano, Navelli, Peltuinum) provide similar percentages.
[73] A. Naso hypothesized the provenance of an iron slag found in Fortellezza at Tortoreto from the Slovenian ores and dated it to the Iron Age, although it was part of coating soil ("*terreno rimosso*"; Benelli/Naso 2003, 186).
[74] Zifferero 2001; Giardino 2001, 111; Bietti Sestieri/Giardino 2003, 427-428.
[75] G. Ingo in Weidig 2014, 865-876.

BIBLIOGRAPHY

Acconcia, V. 2014, *Ritualità funeraria e convivialità. Tra rigore e ostentazione nell'Abruzzo preromano* (= Officina Etruscologia, 10), Roma.
Acconcia, V. 2015, L'Abruzzo: sedi e percorsi degli uomini in armi, in M. Rendeli (ed.), *Le città visibili. Archeologia dei processi di formazione urbana* I. *Penisola Italiana e Sardegna* (= Officina Etruscologia, 11), Roma, 143-180.
Acconcia, V. 2019, Some Remarks on the Periodization of the First Phase of Fossa (AQ) and its Absolute Chronology, *Mediterranea* 16, 7-29.
Acconcia, V./V. d'Ercole 2012, La ripresa delle ricerche a Fossa (2010). L'Abruzzo tra il Bronzo Finale e la fine dell'età del Ferro: proposta di periodizzazione sulla base dei contesti funerari, *ACl* 63, 7-53.
Acconcia, V./V. d'Ercole 2018, La necropoli de Le Castagne a Castelvecchio Subequo (AQ): cultura materiale e inquadramento territoriale. Gli scavi 1983 e 1989, *BArch* 5-42 (https://bollettinodiarcheologiaonline.beniculturali.it/wp-content/uploads/2018/12/2018_1_Acconcia_d_Ercole.pdf; l.a. 08.05.2021).
Acconcia, V./M. Milletti 2009, Pratiche metallurgiche e circolazione di saperi all'origine di Populonia, in F. Cambi/F. Cavari/C. Mascione (eds.), *Materiali da costruzione e produzione del ferro: studi sull'economia populoniese*, Bari, 141-147.
Acconcia, V./M. Milletti 2015, Il ripostiglio di San Martino e la metallurgia elbana tra Bronzo Finale e Prima età del Ferro, *RivScPreist* 65, 217-251.
Acconcia, V./M. Milletti 2017, La gestione degli spazi urbani a Populonia: artigiani e metallurgia del bronzo e del ferro, *ScAnt* 23.2, 333-350.
Acconcia, V./L. Di Sabatino/S.F. Ferreri/F. Properzio 2017, Rituale funerario e cultura materiale nell'Abruzzo interno: il caso di Navelli, *Mediterranea* 14, 63-82.
Adamoli, L./F. Calamita/A. Pizzi (eds.) 2010, *Note illustrative della Carta Geologica d'Italia alla scala 1:50.000: foglio 349, Gran Sasso d'Italia*, Firenze.
Amary, A. 1854, *Storia naturale inorganica della provincia teramana*, Aquila.
Aune, Ch. 1843, *Scavo di miniere e fabbricazione del ferro in Abruzzo*, Napoli.
Baldelli, G./M. Ruggeri 1982, Necropoli dell'età del Ferro di Atri, in *Studi in onore di Ferrante Rittatore Vonwiller*, Como, 631-651.
Benelli, E./A. Naso 2003, Relazioni e scambi nell'Abruzzo in epoca preromana, *MEFRA* 115, 177-205.
Benelli, E./J. Weidig 2006, Elementi per una definizione degli aspetti della conca aquilana in età arcaica. Considerazioni sulle anforette di tipo aquilano, *Orizzonti* 7, 11-22.
Bietti Sestieri, A.M./C. Giardino 2003, Alcuni dati sull'industria metallurgica in Abruzzo, in *Preistoria e Protostoria dell'Abruzzo*. Atti della XXXVI Riunione Scientifica IIPP; Chieti-Celano 2003, Firenze, 411-430.
Bietti Sestieri, A.M./F. Lo Schiavo 1976, Alcuni problemi relativi ai rapporti fra l'Italia e la penisola balcanica nella tarda età del bronzo inizi dell'età del ferro, *ILIRIA* 4, 371-402.
Blečić, M. 2007, Reflections of Picens impact in the Kvarner Bay, in M. Guštin/P. Ettel/M. Buora (eds.), *Piceni ed Europa. Atti del Convegno*; Piran 2006 (Archeologia di Frontiera, 6), Trieste, 109-122.
Bonomi Ponzi, L. 1997, *La necropoli plestina di Colfiorito di Foligno*, Perugia.
Bonanni, T. 1875, *Quale fu, qual'è, quale potrebbe essere la Provincia del 2° Abruzzo Ulteriore: memoria dell'officio di statistica provinciale*, Aquila.
Bourdin, St. 2010, I centri fortificati nel territorio dei Vestini e Peligni Superequani, *QuadAA* 2, 429-437.
Brocchi, G.B. 1819, Osservazioni naturali fatte in alcune parti degli Appennini nell'Abruzzo ulteriore, *Biblioteca*

*italiana o sia giornale di letteratura scienze ed arti* 4, 14, 363-377.

Campovalano I: C. Chiaramonte Treré/V. D'Ercole (eds.), *La necropoli di Campovalano. Tombe orientalizzanti e arcaiche* I (BAR Int. Ser., 1177), Oxford 2003.

Campovalano II: C. Chiaramonte Treré/V. D'Ercole/C. Scotti (eds.), *La necropoli di Campovalano. Tombe orientalizzanti e arcaiche* II (BAR Int. Ser., 2174), Oxford 2010.

Carelli, G. 1859, Esplorazioni disposte dal Real Governo per la ricerca di nuove miniere negli Abruzzi e nel Contado del Molise, *Annali civili del Regno delle Due Sicilie* 65, 60-70.

Cassetti, M. 1901, Dalla Valle del Liri a quelle del Giovenco e del Sagittario. Rilevamento geologico eseguito nell'anno 1900, *Bollettino del R. Comitato geologico d'Italia* 32, 164-178.

Cassetti, M. 1902, Dal Fucino alla valle del Liri. Rilevamento geologico fatto nel 1901, *Bollettino del R. Comitato geologico d'Italia* 33, 168-177.

Cassetti, M. 1906, Osservazioni geologiche nel Monte Sirente e suoi dintorni, *Bollettino del R. Comitato geologico d'Italia* 37, 41-60.

Catenacci, V. 1974, *Note illustrative della Carta Geologica d'Italia alla scala 1:100.000: foglio 147, Lanciano*, Roma.

Ceccaroni, E. 2010, La necropoli in località Cretaro-Brecciara di Avezzano (AQ): primi dati e nuove prospettive, *QuadAA* 2, 341-346.

Centamore, E./F. Dramis (eds.) 2010, *Note illustrative della Carta Geologica d'Italia alla scala 1:50.000: foglio 358, Pescorocchiano*, Firenze.

Centamore, E./U. Crescenti/F. Dramis (eds.) 2006a, *Note illustrative della Carta Geologica d'Italia alla scala 1:50.000: foglio 359, L'Aquila*, Firenze.

Centamore, E./U. Crescenti/F. Dramis (eds.) 2006b, *Note illustrative della Carta Geologica d'Italia alla scala 1:50.000: foglio 368, Avezzano*, Firenze.

Centamore, E./U. Crescenti/F. Dramis (eds.) 2006c, *Note illustrative della Carta Geologica d'Italia alla scala 1:50.000: foglio 369, Sulmona*, Firenze.

Chelussi, I. 1903, Sulla geologia della conca aquilana, *Atti della Società italiana di Scienze naturali e del Museo civico di Storia naturale in Milano* 42, 58-87.

Chelussi, I. 1906, Alcune osservazioni preliminari sul gruppo del Monte Velino e sulla conca del Fucino, *Atti della Società italiana di Scienze naturali e del Museo civico di Storia naturale in Milano*, XLIV, fasc. 4, 34-53.

Chiartano, B. 1994, *La necropoli dell'età del ferro dell'Incoronata e di S. Teodoro* (Quaderni di Archeologia e Storia Antica, 6), Galatina.

Colecchia, A./S. Agostini 2014, Economie marginali e paesaggi storici nella Maiella settentrionale (Abruzzo, Italia), *Post-Classical Archaeologies* 4, 219-258.

Corcia, N. 1843, *Storia delle Due Sicilie* I, Napoli.

Corretti, A./M. Benvenuti 2001, The Beginning of Iron Metallurgy in Tuscany, with Special Reference to Etruria Mineraria, *MeditArch* 14, 127-145.

Cosentino, S. 2010, La tomba 45 della necropoli Scentelle-Capaturo di Pizzoli, in I. Franchi dell'Orto, L. (ed.), *Pinna Vestinorum e il popolo dei Vestini*, Roma, I, 298-305.

Cosentino, S./G. Mieli 2006, Insediamenti della prima età del ferro in Abruzzo: la struttura abitativa di Cansano (L'Aquila). Scavi 2005, *RivScPreist* 56, 483-504.

Crema, C. 1912, Abruzzo aquilano. Foglio 145 (Avezzano), *Bollettino del R. Comitato geologico d'Italia* 34, 61-68.

Crema, C. 1917, Nuovi affioramenti di bauxite nell'Abruzzo aquilano, *La Miniera italiana* 1, 2, 71-72.

Crema, C. 1926, I giacimenti bauxitici della Vallelonga nel bacino di Avezzano, *La Miniera italiana* 10, 11, 333-334.

Delpino, F. 1988, Prime testimonianze dell'uso del ferro in Italia, in G. Sperl (ed.), *The first iron in the Mediterranean* (Proceedings of the International Symposium, PACT 21), Strasbourg, 47-68.

Delpino, F. 1997, La metallurgia, in A. Zanini (ed.), *Dal Bronzo al Ferro. Il II millennio nella Toscana centro occidentale* (Catalogo della mostra; Livorno 1997), Pisa, 23-27.

Del Re, G. 1835, *Descrizione topografica fisica economica politica de' reali dominj al di qua del faro del Regno delle Due Sicilie* II, Napoli.

De Marinis, R.C. 2004, La metallurgia del ferro nella protostoria italiana, in W. Nicodemi (ed.), *La civiltà del ferro, dalla Preistoria al III millennio a.C.*, Milano, 63-82.

D'Ercole, M.C. 2002, *Importuosa Italiae litora: paysage et échanges dans l'Adriatique méridionale à l'époque archaïque*, Naples.

Drago Troccoli, L. 2003, I rapporti tra Fermo e le comunità tirreniche nella prima età del Ferro, in *I Piceni e l'Italia medio-adriatica. Atti del XXII Convegno di Studi Etruschi e Italici*; Ascoli Piceno-Teramo-Ancona 2000, Pisa/Roma, 33-84.

Formenti, C. 1902, Analisi di vere bauxiti italiane, *Gazzetta chimica italiana* 32, I, V, 453-461.

Fortini, P. 1988, Nuovi insediamenti preromani nell'area laziale del Parco Nazionale d'Abruzzo e del pre-parco, in *Il territorio del Parco Nazionale d'Abruzzo nell'Antichità. Atti del Convegno*; Villetta Barrea 1987, Civitella Alfedena, 51-63

Fossa I: S. Cosentino/V. d'Ercole/G. Mieli, *La necropoli di Fossa I: Le testimonianze più antiche*, Pescara 2001.

Fossa II: V. d'Ercole/E. Benelli, *La necropoli di Fossa II: I corredi orientalizzanti e arcaici*, Pescara 2004.

Frey, O.-H, 1991, *Eine Nekropole der frühen Eisenzeit bei Santa Maria d'Anglona* (Quaderni di Archeologia e Storia Antica 1), Galatina.

Gatti, D. 2004, *L'insediamento di Collelongo-Fond'jò nel quadro della sequenza culturale protostorica dell'Abruzzo* (Grandi contesti e problemi della Protostoria 9), Firenze.

Gatti D. 2005, I rapporti transadriatici nella prima età del Ferro sulla base della diffusione della ceramica d'impasto, in P. Attema/A. Nijboer/A. Zifferero (eds), *Papers in Italian Archeology VI. Communities and Settlements from the Neolithic to the Early Medieval Period*, Proceedings of the 6th Conference of Italian Archaeology /Groningen 2003 (BAR Int. Ser. 1452), Oxford, 482-487.

Giardino, C. 1995, *Il Mediterraneo Occidentale fra XIV e VIII secolo a.C. Cerchie minerarie e metallurgiche* (BAR Int. Ser. 612), Oxford.

Giardino, C. 1998, *I metalli nel mondo antico. Introduzione all'archeometallurgia*, Roma/Bari.

Giardino C. 2001, La metallurgia in area medio-adriatica, in *Eroi e Regine. Piceni Popolo d'Europa* (Catalogo della mostra; Roma 2001), Roma, 110-111.

Giardino, C. 2005, Metallurgy in Italy between the Late Bronze Age and the Early Iron Age: the Coming of Iron, in P. Attema/A. Nijboer/A. Zifferero (eds.), *Papers in Italian Archeology VI. Communities and Settlements from the Neolithic to the Early Medieval Period*, Proceedings of the 6th Conference of Italian Archaeology, Groningen 2003 (BAR Int. Ser. 1452), Oxford, 491-505.

Giardino, C./V. Spagnolo 2011, L'estrazione del ferro dalle bauxiti del Salento: le evidenze da Salice Salentino, in C. Giardino (ed.), *Archeometallurgia, dalla conoscenza alla fruizione. Atti workshop*; Cavallino 2006, Lecce, 271-279.

Giumlia Mair, A./R. Maddin 2004, Le origini delle leghe di ferro, in W. Nicodemi (ed.), *La civiltà del ferro, dalla Preistoria al III millennio a.C.*, Milano, 35-61.

Gribaudi, G. 1931, La produzione italiana dell'alluminio, *Bollettino della R. Società Geografica Italiana* s. VII, VIII, 8-9, 611-633.

Grifoni Cremonesi, R. 1973, Prime ricerche nel villaggio dell'età del Bronzo di Collelongo nel Fucino, *RivScPreist* 28, 495-524.

Grossi, G./U. Irti 2011, *Carta archeologica della Marsica* I, Avezzano.

Jervis, G. 1874, *I tesori sotterranei dell'Italia 2. Regione dell'Appennino e vulcani attivi e spenti dipendentivi*, Torino.

Jetti, G. 1978, *Cronache della Marsica (1799-1915)*, Napoli.

Hartmann, N. 1985, The use of Iron in 9th and 8th century Etruria, in C. Malone (ed.), *Patterns in protohistory*, Papers in Italian Archaeology IV.3 (BAR Int. Ser. 245), Oxford, 285-294.

Iaia, C. 2007, Identità e comunicazione nell'abbigliamento femminile dell'area circumadriatica fra IX e VII secolo a.C., in P. von Eles (eds.), *Le ore e i giorni delle donne. Dalla quotidianità alla sacralità tra VIII e VII secolo a.C.* (Catalogo della mostra; Verucchio 2007-2008), Verucchio, 5-36.

Leosini, A. 1863, La provincia d'Aquila, *Rivista italiana di scienze, lettere ed arti* 4, 127, 117-121.

Letta, C. 1972, *I Marsi e il Fucino nell'Antichità*, Milano.

Lucentini, N. 1987, Note per la viabilità nell'ascolano meridionale in età protostorica, in *Le strade nelle Marche. Il problema nel tempo*. Atti del convegno; Fano, Fabriano, Pesaro, Ancona 1984, Ancona, 437-494.

Lucentini, N. 2007, Riflessi della circolazione adriatica nelle Marche Centromeridionali, in M. Guštin/P. Ettel/M. Buora (eds.), *Piceni ed Europa*. Atti del Convegno, Piran 2006 (Archeologia di Frontiera, 6), Trieste, 95-116.

Manca, L./J. Weidig (eds.) 2014, *Spoleto 2700 anni fa. Sepolture principesche dalla necropoli di Piazza d'Armi*, Spoleto.

Mastrostefano, R. 2009, Esiste la bauxite in Calabria? Le miniere di Lecce nei Marsi e gli errori degli ingegneri francesi, *Bullettino della Deputazione Abruzzese di Storia Patria, Supplemento. Incontri culturali dei soci* 16, 62-66.

Mattias, P./F. Guidi Giolj 1999, La mineralizzazione a malachite di Lama dei Peligni (CH) - Maiella sud-orientale, *Mineralogica et petrographica acta* 42, 145-154.

Mattirolo, E. 1901, *Bauxiti italiane*, Rassegna mineraria metallurgica e chimica 16, 15, 229-230.

Miccadei, E. et al. 2010, *Note illustrative della Carta Geologica d'Italia alla scala 1:50.000: foglio 378, Scanno*, Firenze.

Moschetti, A. 1927, Giacimenti di bauxite negli Abruzzi, *L'industria mineraria. Bollettino mensile della Federazione nazionale fascista dell'industria mineraria* I, II, 63-66.

Mozzetti, F. 1845, Su delle Limoniti, de' Peperini e delle Grauwacke, rinvenute in diversi luoghi dell'Aquilano, *Il Gran Sasso d'Italia. Opera periodica di Scienze naturali ed economiche* 8, 10, 155-157.

Naso, A. 2000, *I Piceni. Storia e archeologia delle Marche in epoca preromana*, Milano.

Nijboer, A.J. 1998, *From household production to workshops. Archaeological evidence for economic transformation, pre-monetary exchange and urbanization in central Italy from 800 to 400 BC*, Groningen.

Nijboer, A.J. 2008, A Phoenician family tomb, Lefkandi, Huelva and the tenth century BC in the Mediterranean, in Sagona, C. (ed.), *Beyond the Homeland: Markers in Phoenician Chronology* (Ancient Near Eastern Studies Supplement Series, 28), Leuven, 297-309.

Nijboer, A.J. 2010, Italy, its Interconnections and Cultural Shifts During the Iron Age, in *Meetings between Cultures in the Ancient Mediterranean*, Roma 2008 – International Congress of Classical Archaeology, in *BArch* on line, www.archeologia.beniculturali.it/pages/pubblicazioni.html.

Pacciarelli, M. 1999, *Torre Galli. La necropoli della prima età del Ferro (scavi Paolo Orsi 1922-23)*, Catanzaro.

Pacciarelli M. 2004, La prima età del Ferro in Calabria, in *Preistoria e Protostoria della Calabria*, Atti della XXXVII Riunione Scientifica (Scalea, Papasidero, Praia a Mare, Tortora 2002), 447-474.

Pascetta, C. 2008, Riflessi toponomastici delle attività estrattive in Abruzzo, in Fuschi M./Massimi, G. (eds.), *Toponomastica italiana: l'eredità storica e le nuove tendenze*, Atti della Giornata di studio (Pescara, 2007), Roma, 161-177.

Peroni, R. 1961, Bronzi dal territorio del Fucino nei musei preistorici di Roma e di Perugia, in *RivScPreist* 16, 125-205.

Peroni, R. 1976, La koiné adriatica e il suo processo di formazione, in *Jadranska obala u protohistoriji* (Atti del simposio di Dubrovnik, Zagabria, 1972), Zagabria, 95-114.

Peroni, R./Carancini, G.L./Bergonzi, G./Lo Schiavo, F./von Eles, P. 1980, Per una definizione critica di facies locali: nuovi strumenti metodologici, in *Archeologia, Materiali, Problemi* 1, 9-87.

Praturlon, A. 1968, *Note illustrative della Carta Geologica d'Italia alla scala 1:100.000: foglio 152, Sora*, Napoli.

Presutti, D./Giordano, G./Laurenzano, N./Marone, A./Costa, O.G. 1863, Rapporto sulle miniere esistenti nelle province meridionali del Regno Italico, in *Atti del R. Istituto d'incoraggiamento alle Scienze naturali di Napoli* X, 369-384.

Ranieri, P. 1974, *Le risorse minerarie ed idriche dell'Abruzzo*, L'Aquila.

Rozzi, I. 1838, Cenni statistici sulla natura del suolo del secondo Abruzzo ultra, in *Il Gran Sasso d'Italia. Opera periodica di Scienze naturali ed economiche* I, 14, 209-216.

Ruggeri, M. 2003, La necropoli di Comino a Guardiagrele, in *Genti e culture dell'Abruzzo in epoca preromana* (Actes de la journée d'études; Roma 2001) *MEFRA* 115, 109-127.

Ruggeri, M. 2010, Accessori ed ornamenti femminili, schede nn. 1-2, in *S.O.S. Arte dall'Abruzzo, una mostra per non dimenticare* (Catalogo della mostra; Roma 2010), Roma, 75.

Ruggeri, M./Cosentino, S./Faustoferri, A./Lapenna, S./Sestieri, A.M./Tuteri, R. 2009, Dai circoli ai tumuli: rilettura di necropoli abruzzesi, in *QuadAA* 1, 39-52.

Sabbatini, T. 2008, La tomba 77 in località Brecce, in Silvestrini, M./Sabbatini, T. (eds.), *Potere e splendore. Gli antichi Piceni a Matelica* (Catalogo della mostra; Matelica 2008), Roma, 60-62.

Sabbatini T. 2008b, La tomba 3 del tumulo di Santa Maria in Campo, in M. Matelica/Sabbatini, T. (eds.), Potere e splendore. Gli antichi Piceni a Matelica (Catalogo della mostra; Matelica 2008), Roma.

Scibilia, C. 2015, *L'olimpiade economica. Storia del Comitato nazionale per l'indipendenza economica (1936-1937)*, Milano.

Snodgrass, A. 1971, *The Dark Age of Greece*, Edinburgh.

Snodgrass, A. 1980, Iron and Early Metallurgy in the Mediterranean, in Wertime, T.A./Muhly, J.D. (eds.), *The Coming of the Age of Iron*, New Haven-London, 335-374.

Speranza, U. 1955, Notizie sui giacimenti minerari in Abruzzo, in *Rivista abruzzese* 8, 1, 1-22.

Stagno, A./Montanari, C. 2015, Archeologia montana e archeologia delle risorse ambientali: approcci 'marginali' di studio alle aree montane italiane nel periodo post-classico, in Moscatelli, U./Stagno, A. (eds.), *Archeologia delle aree montane europee: metodi, problemi e casi di studio* (Il Capitale Culturale 12), Macerata, 479-501.

Tenore, G. 1864, Sui minerali e rocce utili del 2° Abruzzo Ulteriore, in *Annali dell'Accademia degli aspiranti naturalisti* s. III, IV, 50-63.

Valignani, F. 1729, *Chieti: centuria di sonetti storici*, Napoli.

Vanzetti, A./Vidale, M. 1999, La forgia, in Peroni R./Vanzetti A. (eds.), *Broglio di Trebisacce 1990-1994. Elementi e problemi nuovi dalle recenti campagne di scavo*, Soveria Mannelli, 17-19.

Vespasiani, T. 1904, L'Abruzzo e le miniere di alluminio, in *Rivista abruzzese di scienze, lettere ed arti* XIX, II, 72-75.

Yntema, D. 1985, *The matt-painted pottery of Southern Italy*, Utrecht.

Yntema, D. 1990, *The matt-painted pottery of Southern Italy. A general survey of the matt-painted pottery styles of Southern Italy during the final bronze age and the iron age*, Lecce.

Weidig J. 2014, *Bazzano, ein Gräberfeld bei L'Aquila (Abruzzen). Die Bestattungen des 8.-5. Jahrhunderts v. Chr. Untersuchungen zu Chronologie, Bestattungsbräuchen und Sozialstrukturen im apenninischen Mittelitalien* (= Monographien des Römisch-Germanischen Zentralmuseums, 112), Mainz.

Weisse, J.G. 1973, Quelques considerations sur les bauxites des Abruzzes et sur la présence de cuivre dans un gisement, in Proceedings of the 3rd International Symposium ICSOBA - International Committee for Studies of Bauxite, Oxides and Hydroxides of Aluminium (Nice 1973), Paris, 63-71.

Zifferero, A. 2001, Le risorse minerarie, in *Eroi e Regine. Piceni Popolo d'Europa* (Catalogo della mostra; Roma 2001), Roma, 111-112.

Zifferero, A. 2002, Attività estrattive e metallurgiche nell'area tirrenica. Alcune osservazioni sui rapporti tra Etruria e Sardegna, in *Etruria e Sardegna centro-settentrionale tra l'età del Bronzo finale e l'Arcaismo*, Atti del XXI Convegno di Studi Etruschi e Italici; Sassari, Alghero, Oristano, Torralba 1998, Pisa-Roma, 179-213.

Zifferero 2009: A. Zifferero, Attività minerarie e trasferimento dei saperi metallurgici nell'alto Tirreno: conoscenze attuali e prospettive di ricerca, in F. Cambi/F. Cavari/C. Mascione (eds.), *Materiali da costruzione e produzione del Ferro. Studi sull'economia populoniese fra periodo etrusco e romanizzazione*, Bari 2009, 149-156.

# Technology and tradition of textile production during the first millennium BC in southern Etruria

*Romina Laurito*

*Abstract*

*We are all very familiar with the high quality of Etruscan textile production thanks to the famous frescoes from Tarquinia and a very rich record of statuary and vascular production unearthed across Southern Etruria (central Italy). Numerous iconographies testify to the wide variety of fabrics, their elaborate manufacture and the attention paid to their realization. On the contrary, we know very little about the tools used to spin and weave such fabrics. This was the starting point and the background of the European research project TexSEt (Textiles in Southern Etruria) 2014-2016, which had as main aim to combine the analysis of textile instruments with the study of archaeological fabrics. The research coupled microscopic use-wear analysis carried out on the objects with experimental archaeology and ethnographic investigation, in order to explore the pre-Etruscan and Etruscan tool-kits to evaluate the different qualities of fabrics produced, and to highlight patterns of continuity and change within the archaeological record. In this contribution, I will focus on the results obtained so far within the framework of the TexSEt Project, placing particular emphasis on the tradition that characterizes the technology and production of textiles in the first half of the first millennium BC in Southern Etruria.[*]*

## Current state of textile studies in archaeological research across Italy in the first millennium BC[1]

In ancient times, textile production was practiced at every social level and constituted one of the most complex activities. Being an activity of relevant cultural and economic importance and, as such, it should be considered among the evaluation parameters of the ancient economic system. Over the last twenty years, studies on fabrics have developed a new important branch in the archaeological field, demonstrating how much we can learn about culture, society, technology and economy of the ancient world throughout the study of textile finds recovered from archaeological contexts.[2]

In fact, a fabric, even being a simple binary system of spun or twisted fibres, is actually the result of a complex interaction between resources, technologies and society.[3] The engines of this interaction are the needs, desires and choices of each ancient society that in turn influence the exploitation of resources and the development of technologies. The availability of resources and the technological level create a close and reciprocal conditioning between these elements. The resources necessary for textile production include plant and animal products used for fibres and dyes. Therefore, also agriculture, sheep farming and the exploitation of environmental resources and the territory are closely related to textile production.

Considering that the Italian environmental conditions do not generally preserve organic material, the study of the Italian textile culture has been significantly neglected until few decades ago compared to contemporary sites in central and northern Europe. Currently the main problem is not the quantity of the textile findings, but the lack of scientific analysis and synthetic works on these finds.

In Italy, part of the most ancient textile finds was recovered in pile dwelling and terramare in northern Italy and are dated between the 3rd and the beginning of the 2nd millennium BC. Among the most ancient Italic textiles, are those of Molina di Ledro,[4] often quoted in literature for their technical complexity and similarities with Neolithic Switzerland textiles.

The spectacular Iron Age findings of Verucchio[5] have changed our approach to the technology of the pre-Roman textile materials in Italy. The cloaks and other textiles found folded or wrapped around the funeral urns in the tomb of Verucchio not only give an idea of how prehistoric costumes were dressed but it is also the direct evidence that the fabrics were integral part of the complex funeral ritual and, most likely, reflected the status and identity of the deceased. The fabric fragments from the Caolino necropolis at Sasso di Furbara (8th century BC) probably referred to similar garments.[6] Wool socks and gaiters (6th-4th century BC) were found in Vedretta di Ries in the Aurine Alps[7] and in Padua.[8]

Textile material was used not only for clothing and for ceremonial and daily uses (i.e. the sails of ships, of which we know very little from an archaeological point of view), and also for the sacred books, the so-called Etruscan *lintei* books. Perhaps the most famous Etruscan artefact is the linen book that wrapped the mummy of Zagreb, preserved by the dry climate of Egypt.[9]

Most of the Italian fabric finds, however, have been preserved in small mineralized traces observable on metal surfaces, often on *fibulae* and other metal objects of grave goods (*fig. 1*), for example in Santa Palomba,[10] Poggio Aguzzo di Murlo,[11] Monte Bibele,[12] and in many other sites.[13] These mineralized formations are created when the metal (bronze or iron) forms corrosion products in or around the fibres maintaining almost unaltered their morphology and dimensions.[14] In some cases, textiles are preserved also in a mineralized form with calcium salts, this is the case of fabrics found in the Strozzacapponi necropolis at Perugia.[15]

If the fabric surveys allow us to understand how and which raw materials were used, for the reconstruction of the production process we must refer to other sources of information. The high quality of the Etruscan fabrics is well known, eloquent are the Tarquinian paintings and the vascular and statuary productions made in Etruria, which show the variety and sometimes the richness and care, even in the details, of the clothes worn. In this sense, the now classic of Larissa Bonfante, *Etruscan Dress* (1975/2003), proved forty years ago, the wealth of information available on fabrics throughout iconographic sources.

To the direct investigations on the fabrics themselves and the iconographic sources, analyses on the textile tools are certainly to be added and have a great impact on the understanding of textile production.[16]

"Production" is "the blend of operations necessary to transform an asset into another one different from the first one".[17] Archaeological markers of production and activities are, in addition to finished products, raw material, semi-finished

*Fig. 1a. Mineralized textile on bronze cinerary urn from Cuccumella at Vulci (6th cent. BC); 1b. Small textile fragment from the Tomb of Aryballos at Tarquinia (6th cent. BC).*

products, remains, tools, and fixed installations. The process of producing textiles (*châine opératorie*[18]) can be traced back to:

• *Collection of fibres.* Several different types of fibres – vegetal and animal - can be spun. The procurement of these fibres is substantial for textile production.
• *Fibre preparation.* Turning raw material in fibre involves a number of manual steps, both for plant and animal fibres.
• *Spinning.* The production of yarn is the fundamental step for textile production. The yarn can be produced in several different ways and many methods of spinning are archaeologically and ethnographically well attested.
• *Weaving.* A textile is obtained weaving together two threads or set of threads. Textile is usually woven on a loom. Other methods to produce fabric are knitting, crocheting, felting, and braiding or plaiting.
• *Finishing.* In textile production, finishing refers to the processes performed after dyeing the yarn or fabric to improve the look, i.e. in Etruria the application of buttons or tiny rings on cloths.
• *(Dye).* Dyeing can take place in different stages of processing both when the fibre has not yet been worked, when it has been spun, and in the final stage when the fabric has been woven.

All these phases require specific equipment. Spinning and weaving tools are the most attested from the archaeological point of view and the most easily traceable to textile activity, even if they are still little known and studied from a techno-functional point of view.

The European project *Textiles in Southern Etruria* – TexSEt[19] – has been focused precisely on the textile equipment and fabrics of southern Etruria and Agro Falisco between the 10th and 5th centuries BC. On this occasion we focus on the main *corpora* of tools analysed for the project, tools coming from the necropolis of Cerveteri (materials almost exclusively from the 7th century BC), of Vulci (9th-7th century BC) and of Narce and Falerii (8th-7th century BC).

As known, the most attested textile tool in Etruscan funerary contexts is the clay spindle whorl, in different shapes and decorations, engraved or imprinted (*fig. 2*).[20] The presence of spindle whorls in the graves - almost exclusively female – implies the presence of the spindle itself which was made of perishable material, probably of wood. The nodal point, from a technological and functional point of view, is how these spindle whorls were used and what their productive potentials were.

*Fig. 2. Some spindle whorls from southern Etruria. a-b: Necropolis of Osteria at Vulci; c: Necropolis of Banditaccia at Cerveteri; d: Grotta Gramiccia at Veio.*

Traditional crafts and experimental archaeology are other important methodological approaches for textile research, even better is the combination of the two.[21] In fact, the results of experiments on textile instruments create an important basis for the interpretation of their function and for the evaluation of fabrics produced using the instruments in question.

The experimentation performed for years on textile tools by the European Centre for Textile Research (CTR), University of Copenhagen, has established - on the basis of a solid program of experimental archaeology - that the weight and the maximum diameter of the spindle whorls are the real parameters to evaluate the instrument from a techno-functional point of view.[22]

To these parameters, the recent experience conducted in Italy for the TexSEt project, has confirmed another element, the importance of the starting quality of the vegetal or animal fibre spun.[23] This aspect, in fact, had already been considered within the experiments carried out in the past at the CTR in Copenhagen.

Generally speaking, what has been noted is that lighter and smaller spindle whorls are more suitable for thin yarns, while heavier ones with a larger diameter would seem more adapt for thicker yarns. When dealing with materials from southern Etruria, specific occurrences emerge clearly. The most ancient spinning tools from Vulci (10th-8th century BC) show a wider weight range: both light and the heaviest ones, even more than 30 g are present, with the majority concentrated between 10 and 20 g. The more recent spindle whorls coming from Cerveteri (7th century BC), are small and light, ranging between 3 and 21 g and with concentration between 7 and 12 g. Narce's spindle whorls - chronologically close to those of Vulci - have similar dimensional features, no specimen exceeds 28 g.

The shapes found are: conical, biconical, with three variants (a first type with the maximum central diameter, a second with the maximum diameter in the upper part, and a third with the maximum diameter in the lower part), and finally the spherical one. Also the relationship between the shape of the spindle whorl and the size allows to identify some associations. In Cerveteri, for example, in the more recent phases (7th-6th century BC) in which the smallest and lightest spindle whorls occur, only the conical and biconical shaped are attested (type 2, the one with the maximum diameter in the upper part); the biconical type 1 are completely absent (*fig.* 3). In the other Etruscan sites, on the contrary, there are numerous biconical spindle whorls and indeed the heaviest ones are only biconical in shape. A final note regards the few spherical types, which are the only ones made of glass paste and never in clay.

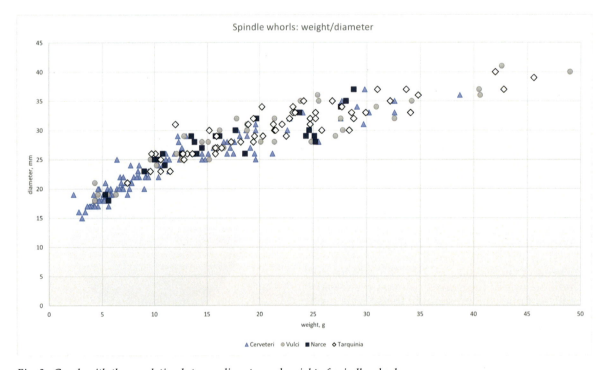

*Fig. 3. Graph with the correlation between diameter and weight of spindle whorls.*

An important point to be ascertained is how the spindle whorl was inserted into the spindle shaft. The rare bronze spindles with the inserted spindle whorl help to clarify this issue. The bronze spindle certainly did not have to be in the norm, but suggests several techno-functional details. The spindle was placed at the bottom, at the opposite end there was a small offset or protuberance useful to hook the fibre. Moreover, a thickening in the middle of the spindle shaft makes the instrument heavier. From a technical point of view this is an important precaution, also detected by artisans/spinners Assunta Perilli and Elena Ciccarelli,[24] considering the lightness of the spindle whorls. The iconography, - i.e. the spinning scene represented on the *tintinnabulum* of the Arsenal of Bologna[25] - assures the use of the spindle with the spindle whorl placed at the bottom. Even the study of traces use on clay spindle whorls would seem to confirm this.[26]

However, many spindle whorls show no sign of their actual use. This is one of the most interesting aspects, and it clearly suggested that in the funeral ritual both objects daily used and symbolic ones made specifically to accompany the deceased were deposed.[27]

The spindle is often associated with the distaff, a rather simple tool used to contain a certain amount of raw fibre to spin. The long distaff with forked top is typical of the Agro Falisco area; very rare specimens have been found in Veio and Osteria dell'Osa.[28] It is a very useful and practical object, since the spinner can lock it under one arm or at the waist, inserting it into a belt, and able to stretch the fibre with both hands (*fig. 4*).

In all southern Etruria and in the rest of central Tyrrhenian Italy, however, the short hand-held distaff is prevalent (*fig. 5*).[29]

The reason for using such dissimilar tools remains to be clarified. The difference can be explained by the spinning of different materials or perhaps the two typologies are symbolic expressions of specific social and/or cultural aspects. In this sense it is useful to remember that in two tombs of the Agro Falisco - tomb 2 (XXIX) of the N-NE necropolis of Montarano and tomb XLIX of the Pizzo Piede necropolis (end of the 8th century BC) - the two types of distaff were found in the same context together with some spindle whorls.[30] It is also true that the metal distaffs come from funerary contexts, even in this case, it is therefore reasonable to think that they may be the precious version to be deposited in the burial and not the practical tool daily used for the spinning process.

In addition to the spindle whorls, spools are the most attested textile tools (*fig. 5*). In many tombs of southern Etruria there is only one example, more frequent are groups of spools up to 40 or few more, with the only exception of the famous Tomb of Isis in the necropolis of Polledrara in Vulci where a group of 161 spools were found.[31] To a lesser extent, instead, they occur in the Agro Falisco. Chronologically they are attested from the 10th century BC and they rarely appear after the 6th century BC.

They have a standardized, cylindrical or hourglass shape with flattened or rounded ends or like a mushroom. In many cases they have been made accurately presenting well-smoothed surfaces and exceptionally signs are engraved or imprinted on the ends. The meaning of these signs is not yet clear.

To mention some important centres, in Vulci spools are from the 9th century BC, with cylindrical or hourglass shape. Even if they are not very numerous, if we consider their dimensional aspect - weight and maximum length - we can clearly distinguish groups of spools. The confirmation comes from the data of the Cerveteri necropolis, where they are present in both of the tombs with cremations (10th century BC) both in the later burial tombs (7th century BC). The shape is always the same, in rare cases the Cerveteri specimens have a central hole. Also in the necropolis of Cerveteri the trend is clear, different sets of spools are identified and the different groups move in a narrow range (*fig. 6*).

In this case the question is how they were used and why this variability in the tombs occurs. The presence of one or two spools should correspond to a "real situation" or are perhaps a *pars pro toto*, as already suggested by other scholars[32] and then symbolically placed to accompany the deceased.

Their simple shape clearly makes them potentially multifunctional objects. They could have been used to wrap the yarn like a modern bobbin and experimentally it has been ascertained that 20 to 30 m of yarn can be wound on similar objects.[33] The fact that they are found in a certain number in the same tomb and have roughly similar weights also suggest the possibility that they are weights for small looms.[34] Italic spools, mostly lighter than 70 g, have also been connected to the tablets weaving with the use of a spacer (*fig. 7*), a technique used to make borders and fringes.[35]

Regarding weaving activities, very little information can be obtained exclusively from the rare loom weights found in the necropolis. They do not seem to be objects pointed to be offered in the funeral ritual. The few specimens have a truncated-pyramidal shape with weight values ranging from 140-330 g. Significant is the fact that they all come from tombs chronologically later than the 6th century BC On the contrary, the practice of their deposition seems to have recent origins, since they are not attested either in the tombs of the Orientalizing period and neither in the more ancient ones.

SOME FINAL REMARKS

This brief overview of textile tools in the Etruscan funerary world offers precious insights and add some relevant elements to our knowledge about the pre-Roman craft production processes and economies. The methodological approach adopted to study such archaeological evidence combing material data, iconographic references, use wear analysis, ethnography and experimental archaeology is the best theoretical approach to produce meaningful archaeological and historical interpretations.

Spinning tools have different shapes and size that vary considerably over the centuries and from one area to another. This variability certainly suggests different textile productions and is at the same time the mirror of different traditions and demands.

*Fig. 4a. Long distaff with forked top from Tomb 15 (XXVII), Necropolis of Montarano N.N.E. at Falerii (8th cent. BC); 4b-c. the spinner Elena Ciccarelli using the long distaff (photos by Gianluca Gandini).*

*Fig. 5. Spools, one short hand-held distaff and other bronze textile tools from the Tomb HH 11-12, Necropolis of Quattro Fontanili at Veio (8th cent. BC).*

The analytical study of the spools shows that they were produced in series to form weaving sets. Here a great question arises, we should never exclude the multi-functionality of the instruments, especially in the domestic and artisan fields, as for many other artefacts of the past and as ethno-archaeology teaches us.

At this point, considering the only material from funeral contexts, it is difficult to say whether textile production was domestic, semi-industrial or industrial. Probably, according to time and place, it could have been exclusively one of these, or a combination of all three. And, it is not clear whether fabrics were made for home use or for exchange. Exchange relations seem to be attested by the diffusion of models from central Etruscan Italy towards the northern areas. However as the fabrics constitute in most cases an object of archaeologically invisible exchange, every consideration on the subject remains at a conjectural level. Although studies in the textile field are mainly concerned with how the fabrics were made and with which materials, the understanding of textile technology cannot be separated from the social "fabric".

On the basis of the available evidence, with the examination of how textile technology relies on important concepts such as urbanization, specialization of activities, exchange and socio-political development in Italy during the protohistoric period, it will become increasingly possible to reconstruct an art that has been unacceptably lost in the pages of the first Italic History.

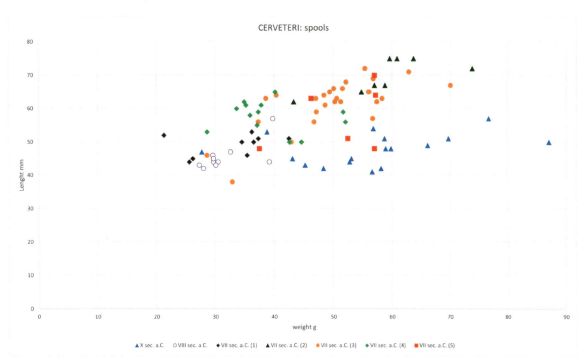

*Fig. 6. Graph with the correlation between lenght and weight of spools.*

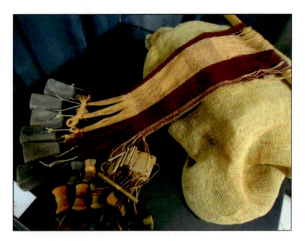

*Fig. 7. Reconstruction of a small vertical loom with loom weights and spools used with tablets and spacer to weave borders. (Museo della Preistoria "Luigi Donini" at San Lazzaro in Savena. Reconstruction and photo by Elena Ciccarelli).*

NOTES

* I sincerely thanks Margarita Gleba for the possibility to share and publish here textile data collected until now for the PROCON project and published by M. Gleba in various articles (for details see Bibliography).
1. Translation by Antonio Bongi and photos by Mauro Benedetti (Archivio Fotografico del Museo Nazionale Etrusco di Villa Giulia).
2. Barber 1991; Gleba, Mannering 2012; Grömer 2016.
3. Andersson *et alii* 2010.
4. Bazzanella, Mayr 2009; Bazzanella *et alii* 2003.
5. Stauffer 2002; 2012; Raeder Knudsen 2002; 2012; Rodriguez 2019.
6. Masurel 1982; Mames, Masurel 1992; Serges *et alii* 2019.
7. Bazzanella *et alii* 2005.
8. Maspero 1998.
9. Flury-Lemberg 1986; 1988, 344-357, 496.
10. De Santis *et alii* 2010.
11. Gleba 2015.
12. Moulhérat 2008.
13. Gleba 2008; 2012; 2017a; 2007b.
14. Chen *et alii* 1998.
15. Gleba, Vanden Berghe, Cenciaioli 2017.
16. Gleba 2008.
17. Mannoni, Giannichedda 1996, 3.
18. For the concept of *chaîne opératoire* in textile production see Andersson Strand 2012 and previous bibliography.
19. European Project FP7-PEOPLE-2013-IEF - Marie-Curie Action: "Intra-European fellowships for career development" no.187753 (https://cordis.europa.eu/project/rcn/187753/factsheet/en).
20. Gleba 2008, 81.
21. Andersson Strand 2010; 2015.
22. Mårtensson *et alii* 2006; Andersson Strand, Nosch 2015. All reports of the experiments conducted at the CTR are available online on the website of the Centre (https://ctr.hum.ku.dk/research-programmes-and-projects/previous-programmes-and-projects/tools/).
23. Laurito, Lemorini, Perilli 2014; Ciccarelli, Perilli 2017.
24. Personal communication.
25. Morigi Govi 1971.
26. Forte, Lemorini 2017; 2019.
27. Lipkin 2012.
28. Gleba 2008, 109-110.
29. Gleba 2008, 110-121.
30. Barnabei 1894, 387-389, plates IV and XII.
31. Gleba 2008.
32. Gleba 2008, 141; Lipkins 2012; Pitzalis 2011.
33. Experiment carried out by Assunta Perilli at the Experimental Center of Lejre (Denmark) in May 2015 using reproductions of Etruscan spools.
34. Mårtensson *et alii* 2007.
35. Gleba 2008, 140-150 with previous bibliography; Ciccarelli 2019.

BIBLIOGRAPHY

Andersson E.B./K.M. Frei/M. Gleba/U. Mannering/M.L. Nosch/I. Skals 2010, Old textiles – new approaches, *European Journal of Archaeology* 13(2), 149–173.

Andersson-Strand, E. 2010, Experimental Textile Archaeology, in E. Andersson-Strand *et al.*, NESAT X, 10th North European Symposium for Archaeological Textiles, Copenhagen 2008, (Ancient Textiles Series, Vol. 5), Oxford: 1-3.

Andersson-Strand, E. 2012, The Textile *Chaîne Opératoire*: Using a Multidisciplinary Approach to Textile Archaeology with a Focus on the Ancient Near East, *Paléorient* 38 n. 1-2, 21-40.

Andersson-Strand, E. 2015, L'archeologia sperimentale e la ricerca sui tessuti, *Forma Urbis* 20, n. 9: 31-33.

Andersson-Strand, E./M.-L. Nosch (eds.) 2015, *Tools, Textiles and Contexts. Investigating Textile Production in the Aegean and Eastern Mediterranean Bronze Age* (Ancient Textiles Series 21), Oxford.

Barnabei, F./A. Cozza/A. Pasqui 1894, *Degli scavi di antichità nel territorio falisco*, MAL 4.

Barber, E.J.W. 1991, *Prehistoric Textiles. The Development of Cloth in the Neolithic and Bronze Ages*, Princeton.

Bazzanella, M./A. Mayr 2009, *I reperti tessili, le fusaiole e i pesi da telaio dalla pala tta di Molina di Ledro*, Trento.

Bazzanella, M. *et al.* 2003, *Textiles. Intrecci e tessuti dalla preistoria europea*, Trento.

Bazzanella, M./R. Dal Rì/A. Maspero/I. Tomedi 2005, Iron Age textile artefacts from Riesenferner/Vedretta di Ries (Bolzano/Bozen, Italy), in P. Bichler *et al.*, *Hallstatt Textiles: Technical Analysis, Scienti c Investigation and Experiment on Iron Age Textiles* (BAR Int. Ser. 1351), Oxford, 151-160.

Cardon, D. 2007, *Natural Dyes. Sources, Tradition, Technology and Science*, London.

Chen, H. L./K.A. Jakes/D.W. Foreman 1998, Preservation of Archaeological Textiles through Fibre Mineralization, *JASc* 25, 1015-1021.

Ciccarelli, E. 2019, Sperimentare i rocchetti piceni: alcune osservazioni sull'impiego dei rocchetti a foro obliquo nella tessitura a tavolette, in M. Massussi/S. Tucci/R. Laurito (eds.), Trame di storia: metodi e strumenti dell'archeologia sperimentale, *Archeofest* 2017, Roma, 227-248.

Ciccarelli, E./A. Perilli 2017, Tracing the thread: spinning experiments with Etruscan spindle whorl replica, *Origini* 40, 155-164.

De Santis, A.O./M. Colacicci/R. Giuliani/B. Santoro 2010, Il processo storico nel Lazio antico tra la tarda età del bronzo e la prima età del ferro: i protagonisti, in

N. Negroni Catacchio (ed.), *Atti XI. Preistoria e Protostoria in Etruria. L'alba dell'Etruria. Fenomeni di continuità e trasformazione nei secoli XII-VIII a.C. Ricerche e scavi*, Milano, 311-326.

Esposito, A.M. 1999, *I principi guerrieri. La necropoli etrusca di Casale Marittimo*, Milano.

Flury-Lemberg, M. 1986, Die Rekonstruktion des Liber Linteus Sagabriensis oder die Mumienbinden von Zagreb. *VjesMuzZagreb* 3 s., 19, 73-82.

Flury-Lemberg, M. 1988, *Textile Research and Conservation*, Bern.

Forte, V./C. Lemorini 2017, Traceological analyses applied to textile implements: an assessment of the method through the case study of the 1st millennium BCE ceramic tools in central Italy, *Origini* 40, 165-182.

Forte, V./C. Lemorini 2019, L'analisi delle tracce tecnologiche e d'uso di strumenti in ceramica per la tessitura e la filatura: lo sviluppo di una metodologia di indagine applicata a contesti del I millennio a.c. in italia centrale, in M. Massussi/S. Tucci/R. Laurito (eds.), *Trame di storia: metodi e strumenti dell'archeologia sperimentale*, Archeofest 2017, Roma, 69-87.

Gleba, M. 2008, *Textile Production in Pre-Roman Italy* (Ancient Textile Series 4), Oxford.

Gleba, M. 2012, Lo sviluppo delle fibre di lana nell'Italia preromana, in M.S. Busana/P. Basso (ed.), *La lana nella Cisalpina romana: economia e società*, Padova, 351-363.

Gleba M. 2015, Production and Consumption: Textile Economies in Mediterranean Europe 1000-500 BCE, in K. Grömer/F. Pritchard (eds.), *Aspects of the Design, Production and Use of Textiles and Clothing from the Bronze Age to the Early Modern Era* (NESAT XII), Budapest, 261-270.

Gleba, M. 2017a, Tracing Textile Cultures of Italy and Greece 1000-400 BCE, *Antiquity* 91,1205-1222, doi:10.15184/aqy.2017.144.

Gleba, M. 2017b -Textiles in pre-Roman Italy: from qualitative to quantitative approach, *Origini* 40, 9-28.

Gleba, M./R. Laurito 2019, Tessuti e loro produzione dell'età del Ferro e arcaica nell'Italia continentale. Metodi di ricerca, riscontri ed esiti sperimentali, in M. Massussi/S. Tucci/R. Laurito (eds.), *Trame di storia: metodi e strumenti dell'archeologia sperimentale*, Archeofest 2017, Roma, 41-67.

Gleba, M./U. Mannering (eds.) 2012, *Textiles and Textile Production in Europe from Prehistory to AD 400* (Ancient Textiles Series 11), Oxford, 242-253.

Gleba, M./E.I. Vanden Berghe/L. Cenciaoli 2017, Purple for the Masses? Shellfish purple dyed textiles from the quarry workers' cemetery at Strozzacapponi (Perugia/Corciano), Italy, in H. Landenius Enegren/F. Meo (eds.), *Treasures from the Sea*, Oxford, 131-137.

Grömer, K. 2016, *The Art if Prehistoric Textile Making*, Wien.

Laurito, R./C. Lemorini/A. Perilli 2014, Making Textiles at Arslantepe in the 4th and 3rd Millennia BCE. Archaeological Data and Experimental Archaeology, in C. Breniquet/C. Michel (eds.), *Wool Economy in the Ancient Near East and the Aegean: From the Beginnings of Sheep Husbandry to Institutional Textile Industry*, Oxford, 151-168.

Lipkin, S. 2012, *Textile-Making in Central Tyrrhenian Italy from the Final Bronze Age to the Republican Period*, Oxford.

Mamez, L./H. Masurel 1992, Étude complémentaire des vestiges textiles trouvés dans l'embarcation de la nécropole du Caolino à Sasso di Furbara, *Origini* 16, 295-310.

Mannoni, T/E. Giannichedda 1996, *Archeologia della produzione*, Torino.

Märtensson, L./E. Andersson/M.-L. Nosch/A. Batzer 2006, Technical Report. Experimental Archaeology. Part 2:2 Whorl or bead?, https://ctr.hum.ku.dk/research-programmes-and-projects/previous-programmes-and-projects/tools/technical_report_2-2__experimental_archaeology.pdf.

Märtensson, L./E. Andersson/M.-L. Nosch/A. Batzer 2007, Technical Report. Experimental Archaeology. Part 4 Spools, https://ctr.hum.ku.dk/research-programmes-and-projects/previous-programmes-and-projects/tools/technical_report_4__experimental_arcaheology.pdf.

Maspero, A. 1998, I resti di tessuto, in E. Bianchin Citton et al., *"Presso l'Adige ridente..." Recenti rinvenimenti archeologici da Este e Montagnana*, Padova, 62-67.

Masurel, H. 1982, Les vestiges textiles retrouvés dans l'embarcation, *Origini* 40, 381-414.

Morigi Govi, C. 1971, Il tintinnabulo della 'Tomba degli Ori' dell'Arsenale Militare di Bologna. *ACl* 23, 211-35.

Moulhérat, C. 2008, Les vestiges textiles de la Nécropole Celto-Etruscque de Monte Tamburino à Monte Bibele (Monterenzio – Bologne), in C. Alfaro/L. Karali (eds.), *Purpureae Vestes* II. *Vestidos, Textiles y Tintes*, València, 89-99.

Pitzalis, F. 2011, *La volontà meno apparente. Donne e società nell'Italia centrale tirrenica durante l'orientalizzante antico*, Roma.

Raeder Knudsen, L. 2002, La tessitura con le tavolette nella tomba 89, in P. von Eles (ed.), *Guerriero e sacerdote. Autorità e comunità nell'età del ferro a Verucchio. La Tomba del Trono*, Firenze, 220-234..

Raeder Knudsen, L. 2012, The tablet-woven borders of Verucchio, in Gleba/Mannering 2012, 254-265.

Serges, A./E. Pizzuti/M. Gleba 2019, Analisi preliminari e ipotesi ricostruttiva del bordo a tavolette rinvenuto al Sasso di Furbara: nuove prospettive di studio, in M. Massussi/S. Tucci/R. Laurito (eds.), *Trame di storia: metodi e strumenti dell'archeologia sperimentale*, Archeofest 2017, Roma, 157-171.

Stauffer, A. 2002, I tessuti, in P. von Eles (ed.), *Guerriero e sacerdote. Autorità e comunità nell'età del ferro a Verucchio. La Tomba del Trono*, Firenze, 192-220.

Stauffer, A. 2012, Textiles from Verucchio, Italy, in M. Gleba/U. Mannering (eds.), *Textiles and Textile Production in Europe from Prehistory to AD 400* (Ancient Textiles Series 11), Oxford, 242-253.

# The core formed glass from Satricum
## *An overall assessment*

*Artemios Oikonomou*

*Abstract*

*Glass, one of the latest pyrotechnological products, was first manufactured in the form of beads and minor decorative objects around the mid of the 3rd Millennium BC. The earliest glass vessels were manufactured with the so called core forming technique and first appeared in Mesopotamia and Egypt during the mid of the 2nd Millennium BC. The revival of the technique in the Early Iron Age brought to light the largest numbers of glass vessels produced in the Mediterranean area during the 1st Millennium BC, the Mediterranean core formed bottles. In this paper, state-of-the-art analytical techniques were used for the study of 53 glass fragments of core formed vessels and 3 beads found in the Hellenistic Votive deposit, also known as Votive Deposit III, associated with the sanctuary of Mater Matuta, in the archaeological site of Satricum, in central Italy. The results of this study showed that the chemical composition of the assemblage is homogeneous, but small differences in major, minor and trace elements indicate the use of different types of raw materials, suggesting therefore diverse manufacturing technologies/traditions. The new data set provides new insights into the nature of the glass used in the central Italian region during the Hellenistic period allowing us to explore technological and possible provenance interpretations.*[*]

Main objectives of the study

During the last twenty years the history of glass has been the focus of an increasing interest, especially the application of state-of-the-art analytical techniques to interpret key archaeological questions.[1] Archaeometrical investigations have been aimed primarily at reconstructing the operational sequence (chaîne opératoire) of ancient glass making, (identifying raw materials, reconstructing the production technology, defining melting conditions etc.)[2] and secondly, during the last decade, identifying the origin of glass (provenance, trade routes, reconstructing economic systems etc.).[3]

The main objective of this study is to offer an overall assessment of the technology of both the glass used to manufacture the main body of the vessels as well as the characterisation of the glass used for the decorative trails. In addition, it is of crucial importance to establish the link of the chemical composition to production areas so as to answer provenance questions.

Archaeology of the core formed vessels

The core forming technique is the earliest method to manufacture glass vessels. The earliest examples of such vessels were discovered in Mesopotamia and date back to the mid of the 16th century BC.[4] However, the production of core formed vessels stopped during the transition period between Late Bronze Age and early Iron Age. Between the 9th and 7th century BC the Eastern Mediterranean experienced a cultural revival. As part of this, the core forming industry rebounded, too, and reached its zenith as three successive industries produced a vast amount of bottles intended to hold scented oils, unguents, perfumes and cosmetics. These bottles/vessels were widely distributed all around the Mediterranean from the Black Sea and Asia Minor in the East, to Italy and the Iberian Peninsula in the West. In the archaeological record such bottles are often found in funerary contexts since the content of the vessels was used to anoint the dead and the empty bottles were discarded in the grave. In addition, the vessels were also used as votive offerings in sanctuaries and deposits.[5]

These bottles, as a whole, have been generally considered as a unique corpus because not only they share a common function and technology but also most of their forms were inspired by the shapes of Greek ceramics and metal ware of archaic, classical and Hellenistic periods.[6]

The glass bottles, which circulated in the Mediterranean for half a millennium, can be divided in three broad categories: Mediterranean Group I, II and III. These three groups have succeeded one another, with Group I dating from late 6th to early 4th century BC, Group II from the mid-4th to late 3rd century BC and finally Group III from the mid-2nd century BC to the first decade of the 1st century AD. In each of these periods, we witness new forms, decorative motifs, handle types and colour combinations which replaced those of the earlier period. The factory/workshop locations of the three industries are still a matter of debate, and no solid evidence is known (no workshops have been uncovered); however, according to recent studies Group I is considered to have been manufactured in the Levant,[7] Group II in Italy or/and Macedonia and Group III in Cyprus or/ and the Syro-Palestinian coast.[8]

Among the three industries, Group I has produced the biggest number of vessels and four different forms: *alabastron, oinochoe, amphoriskos* and *aryballos*. The Group II industry, on the other hand, even though it introduced three new forms, *stamnos, hydriske* and *unguentarium*, produced far fewer vessels than Group I industry. Finally, a radical change happened in Group III industry, where five of the previous forms ceased to be produced and only two of them were produced, the alabastron and the amphoriskos.[9]

According to the archaeological data, the Satricum assemblage, investigated in this paper, belongs as a whole within the Group II industry.

CORE-FORMED MANUFACTURING TECHNIQUE

The core forming technique involved various stages/steps (*fig. 1*).[10] In the first stage the glassmaker manufactured the core (*fig. 1a*) which was made from relatively rough material (soil, sand, animal dung etc.) and formed to the desired shape of the vessel around a metal rod. In the second stage the core was covered by glass in three different ways as it is suggested by various scholars:

- By trailing molten glass around the core (*fig. 1b*).[11]
- The glassmaker immersed the core directly in a pot of molten glass which was placed in the furnace.[12]
- The core was coated with crushed and powdered glass which then was positioned in the furnace and both were heated.[13]

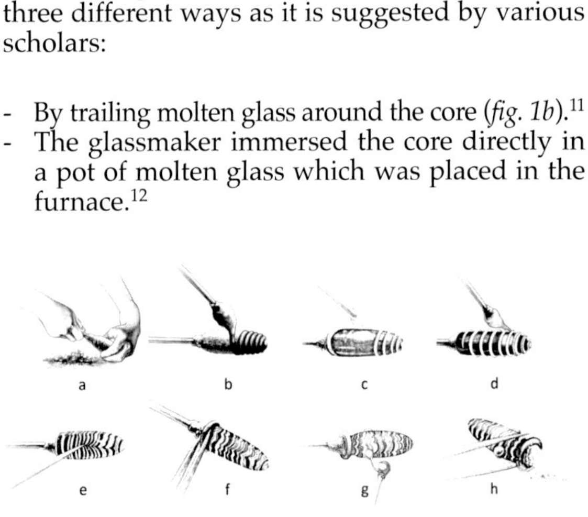

In the third step decorative trails of coloured opaque glass were applied on the main body of the vessels (*fig. 1c-d*) and were pressed into the vessel's surface by marvering. The decorative motifs, such as zig-zag, feathers, festoons etc., were made using a metallic pin or a hook (*fig. 1e*). The decoration of the vessel was followed by the formation of the rim and by adding the handles on the vessel (*fig. 1f-g*). Finally, in the last step the metal rod was removed, the vessel was annealed and, after cooling, the core was scraped out leaving a rough, pitted, often grey or reddish interior surface (*fig. 1h*).

MATERIALS

This paper focuses on the glass finds from the Latin settlement of *Satricum* which is situated ca. 60 km south of Rome. The site of *Satricum* is probably best known for its sanctuary dedicated to *Mater Matuta*, the goddess of dawn which is situated on top of the acropolis; it incorporates three successive temple buildings from the Archaic period onwards. The importance of offering practices in *Satricum* is attested by three substantial votive deposits associated with the sanctuary of *Mater Matuta*. Among them is the so-called Hellenistic Votive deposit, also known as Votive Deposit III, discovered in front of the temple.[14] Among the rich finds of the deposit some 140 fragments of core formed glass flasks and several glass beads were discovered. So far this is the largest corpus of Hellenistic core formed glass vessels known in Latium. The fragments of the core formed vessels belong to the Mediterranean Group II industry, dating between mid-4th to 3rd century BC.

In the present study 53 glass fragments from core formed vessels and 3 glass beads are investigated by combining two techniques, namely Scanning Electron Microscopy (SEM/EDS) and Laser Ablation Inductively Coupled Plasma Mass Spectrometry (LA-ICP-MS), in order to identify the major, minor and trace element chemical composition of the samples. In addition, the decorative trails of part of the assemblage (in particular in 19 vessels and in 1 bead) were studied with the same techniques.

The assemblage consists of 25 alabastra, 8 oinochoai, 7 amphoriskoi, 4 hydriskoi, 1 aryballos and 8 unidentified glass vessels.[15] The beads are separated in 2 eye beads and 1 bead with decorative trails. There is a combination of colours in

*Fig. 1. The various stages of the core forming technique (Wight 2011, 27).*

the decorative trails. There are white-yellow, only yellow and only white decorations, while there are two examples of white-yellow-turquoise and yellow-turquoise trails. We also notice four different types of the decoration and in particular zigzag, zig-zag and straight, straight, feather and festoon trails (*fig. 5, table 1*).

METHODS

The sample preparation and the operational/experimental conditions of the two techniques have been described in detail in previous publications.[16] The SEM/EDS instrument was used to identify the major and minor elements while it provided high resolution and high magnification images of the structure of the samples (especially of the decorative trails) and the LA-ICP-MS instrument was used to identify trace elements. Both instruments were calibrated using established geological and glass standards and the error was within the accepted limits for both techniques. The analytical results and the calibration data have been published recently.[17]

| Decoration | | Cluster A | Cluster B | Cluster C | Total |
|---|---|---|---|---|---|
| | "Zig-zag" | 1 alabastron (W.) | 8 alabastra (W.Y.) 2 oinochoai (W.) 2 amphoriskoi (W.Y.) 1 bead (Y.) | - | 14 |
| | "Zig-zag & straight" | - | 1 alabastron (W.Y.) 2 hydriskoi (W.Y.) | - | 3 |
| | "Straight" | 1 alabastron (Y.) | 1 oinochoe (W.Y.) 1 oinochoe (Y.) 1 oinochoe (Y.T.) 1 amphoriskos (W.Y.) 3 amphoriskoi (Y.) | - | 8 |
| | "Festoon" | 1 aryballos (W.Y.) 1 oinochoe (W.Y.T.) | - | - | 2 |
| | "Feather" | 1 alabastron (W.Y.) | 6 alabastra (W.Y.) 1 alabastron (Y.) | - | 8 |
| n.d. | "No decoration" | 3 unidentified | 4 alabastra 2 hydriskoi 2 oinochoai 2 beads | 1 alabastron 1 amphoriskos 6 unidentified | 21 |
| Total | | 8 | 40 | 8 | 56 |

*Table 1. The type of the decoration witnessed in the Satricum assemblage in correlation with the typology, the three identified clusters and the colour of the decoration. W.: white; Y.: yellow; W.Y.: white and yellow; W.Y.T.: white and yellow and turquoise; Y.T.: yellow and turquoise; n.d.: no decoration.*

## Results and discussion

All samples recovered in Satricum belong to the general soda-lime-silica category.[18] Silica ($SiO_2$) is the main glass former, and in the *Satricum* samples, varies from 68.6 % wt. to 74.0 % wt. with a mean value of 70.6 % wt. The main source of $SiO_2$ could be either sand or quartz pebbles. Sand, as a less pure source than pebbles, exhibits elevated amounts of impurities such as alumina ($Al_2O_3$) and iron ($Fe_2O_3$).[19] In the present study the mean values of $Al_2O_3$ and $Fe_2O_3$ are 2.1 % wt. and 0.2 % wt. respectively, close to the typical values of such impurities found in sands.[20] For example, sand from Belus river which is thought to be a suitable sand source during antiquity, contains 2.8 % wt. $Al_2O_3$ and 0.3 % wt. $Fe_2O_3$, values that do not change significantly in the final base glass composition (after the firing procedure).[21] Potassium ($K_2O$) and magnesium ($MgO$) are found in concentrations below 1% wt., indicating the use of natron as a flux.[22] Natron also introduces soda ($Na_2O$) in glass which averages at 17.6 % wt. Lime ($CaO$), with a mean value at 6.9 % wt. can be introduced in the glass either but unlikely as a deliberate additive or usually as in this study as an impurity in the form of marine shells which form part of coastal sands.[23] Two main colorants were detected, cobalt (Co) and copper (Cu). The combination of both provided the deep blue colour of the majority of the samples while elevated amounts of solely Cu were responsible for the turquoise colour in four samples. The amber glass samples did not exhibit significantly high values of colorant elements such as iron (Fe), manganese (Mn) and copper (Cu), and therefore it can be suggested that their coloration is probably due to varied furnace atmospheres.[24]

As mentioned above alumina is found in glass as an impurity in the sand, therefore the correlation between silica ($SiO_2$) and alumina ($Al_2O_3$) can reveal differences between primary sand sources and help in provenance studies. It has been demonstrated in previous studies[25] that the glass from *Satricum*, which belongs to the Mediterranean Group II industry, can be divided in three different clusters; this differentiation is due to the particular levels of both $SiO_2$ and $Al_2O_3$, and at least two different sources/locations of the primary raw materials have been proposed.[26] According to Oikonomou et al.[27] a small cluster (Cluster A) of *Satricum* glass has an Egyptian origin while the majority of *Satricum* glass[28] (Cluster B) have an Italian origin.[29] The third cluster (Cluster C) is from a yet unknown source, but rather different than Cluster A and B samples. This is evident when plotting the mean values of

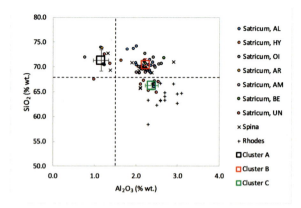

*Fig. 2. The correlation between silica ($SiO_2$) and alumina ($Al_2O_3$). The squares represent the mean values of $SiO_2$ and $Al_2O_3$ for the corresponding clusters of Satricum glass and the crosses the standard deviation for each oxide. The glass from Satricum is also compared with coeval core-formed vessels from Spina, in Italy and from Rhodes, Greece. AL: alabastron, HY: hydriske, OI: oinochoe, AR: aryballos, AM: amphoriskos, BE: bead, UN: unidentified.*

$SiO_2$ and $Al_2O_3$ for each cluster on the same graph (*fig. 2*) which are well separated.

The majority of glass objects from Satricum are alabastra (at least for Cluster A and B) (*fig. 2*). This typological form is the most common in the archaeological record. This has already been pointed out in other studies, e.g. in Cyprus the Group II alabastra are 46% of the total core formed vessels found on the island.[30] Either there was a specific reason to choose alabastra to keep the perfumes, oils and unguents against the other typologies or it was a matter of fashion/trend. At Satricum, the vessels imported from Egypt (Cluster A-low $Al_2O_3$) do not show any particular preference in typology (*fig. 2*). On the other hand, there is a form preference for the Italian Cluster B samples (50% of the samples are alabastra, while the other 50% splits in oinochoai, amphoriskoi, hydriskoi and beads, Table 1.

Regarding the provenance and the manufacture of the Satricum glass there are two possible scenarios:

- primary and secondary glassmaking happened somewhere in Italy, probably close to the location of the raw materials e.g. close to the sand deposits.
- primary and secondary glassmaking happened in two different, maybe distant, locations either in Italy or elsewhere in the Eastern Mediterranean.

There is no archaeological evidence suggesting primary and/or secondary glassmaking in Italy

182

during the Hellenistic period. However, it has been suggested that a possible origin of Group II core formed bottles must be sought in Italy.[31] According to recent archaeometrical studies there are only three specific locations in Italy where the sands can be possibly used in glassmaking.[32] In particular, there is a sand deposit (Sand 1) between the mouth of the River Basento and the River Bradano in the golf of Taranto (in Basilicata region, SE Italy); in the south east coast of Italy (Sand 2) near Brindisi (in Puglia region, SE Italy); and the western part of the Follonica Gulf (Sand 3), between Piombino and Follonica (in Tuscany region). The composition of these sands regarding the two oxides under investigation is typical (Sand 1: $SiO_2$: 76.5% wt., $Al_2O_3$: 2.7% wt.; Sand 2: $SiO_2$: 80.3% wt., $Al_2O_3$: 1.3% wt.; Sand 3: $SiO_2$: 79.5% wt., $Al_2O_3$: 2.8% wt.) and slightly changes when they are fused into glass (glass deriving from Sand 1: $SiO_2$: 69.6% wt., $Al_2O_3$: 2.4% wt.; Sand 2: $SiO_2$: 72.6% wt., $Al_2O_3$: 1.1% wt.; Sand 3: $SiO_2$: 71.4% wt., $Al_2O_3$: 2.6% wt.). This slight change, especially in the $SiO_2$ content, happens due to certain physicochemical procedures which are out of the scope of this paper. Among these three sand deposits only Sand 1 from the Basilicata region and Sand 3 from Tuscany when fused can produce a typical soda-lime-silica glass composition similar to the composition of the majority of the glass from Satricum (Cluster B samples). Sand 3 has similar composition to Cluster A samples, but the latter are imported according to Oikonomou et al.,[33] and should be excluded as possible raw material. Whichever sand was used (sand 1 or sand 3 or both) there are strong indications that the Cluster B glass has an Italian origin. This confirms the archaeological interpretation according to which the location of the glass workshops responsible for the production of Mediterranean Group II core formed vessels should be sought in Italy. Therefore, the idea of a primary glass workshop in the Gulf of Taranto or in the Tuscany region where the glassmakers had access to the sand deposits cannot be excluded; this needs to be confirmed either by archaeological evidence or isotopic analysis.

*Trace elements*

Trace element characterization can provide solid evidence for the use of different sand sources.[34] There are specific trace elements found in sands as impurities and which are not affected significantly from the firing process and the colorants used in glass making.[35] In particular, strontium (Sr), barium (Ba), neodymium (Nd) and zirconium (Zr) are present in the sand raw material and are often used as discriminants in glass studies.[36] Specifically, Sr is associated mainly with calcium, and by implication primarily derived from shells in the sands;[37] Ba can be related to the alkali feldspar found in sands[38] or/and to barite which is a heavy mineral found in sands.[39] In addition, barium can be connected to the carbonate fraction of the beach sands.[40] Nd is incorporated in the glass with the source of silica and originates from the heavy or non-quartz fraction of the sand raw material;[41] Zr is generally concentrated in associated accessory minerals such as zircon which is present in sands.[42] Differences in the Nd/Sr and Ba/Zr ratios could reflect use of sands with different proportions of "contaminant" minerals and therefore provide provenance information. The Satricum samples are directly compared to published analytical data of core formed vessels from Italy (Adria)[43] and Greece (Macedonia and Epirus).[44] Both published assemblages belong to Mediterranean Group II and III industries and therefore offer a secure and direct comparison to the Satricum assemblage.[45] According to *fig. 3* Cluster A samples are clearly distinguished from Cluster B samples indicating sand raw material with different geological characteristics. The same behaviour is also noticed in few samples from Adria and Epirus which according to the authors have an Egyptian origin.[46] In addition, according to Freestone et al.[47] late antique glass from Egypt (Tel el-Ashmunein) shows low strontium and high zirconium content. This is also obvious in Cluster A samples reinforcing the idea of the Egyptian origin. Regarding the origin of Cluster B samples in *fig. 3b* we notice an overlap of the Italian sands with the Cluster B assemblage supporting the suggestion of the Italian origin of this particular group.[48]

*Colorants*

Regarding the coloration of Satricum glass, glassmakers used three different cobalt bearing minerals to provide the deep blue colour at least for the majority of the glass from Satricum (Cluster B samples). There are various minerals rich in cobalt such as trianite, cobaltite, absolane and skutterudite.[49] Another common source of cobalt is cobaltiferous alums which are found mainly in Egypt but there are alum ores also in Iran, Turkey and Germany.[50] Therefore, there are various elements that can be associated with the cobalt minerals and act as discriminants for possible different sources of cobalt.

The glass samples fall in three different manganese to cobalt (Mn/Co) ratio groups (*fig. 4*). In

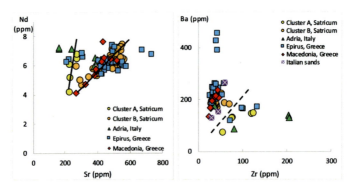

*Fig. 3. a. The correlation between neodymium (Nd) and strontium (Sr). Cluster A and B samples are divided in two groups with differing slopes. Few samples from Epirus and Adria overlap with Cluster A samples; b. The correlation between barium (Ba) and zirconium (Zr). The two clusters are distinguished with the dashed line. The Italian sands overlap with Cluster B samples.*

particular, Cluster B samples can be distinguished in three groups:

- a group of samples having low Mn/Co (below 0.4),
- a second group having mid Mn/Co (between 0.5 and 2) and
- a third group having high Mn/Co (over 2).

It is difficult to make any suggestions about the provenance of these minerals, but there are some indications that they have an Iranian origin.[51]

Regarding the manufacturing procedure, Cluster B glass was produced in two stages:

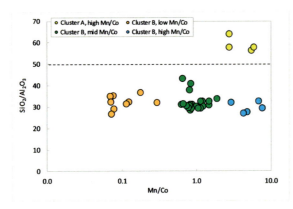

*Fig. 4. The correlation between the ratios $SiO_2/Al_2O_3$ and Mn/Co. The first ratio is associated with the primary raw material of the sand and the second with the secondary raw material of the colorant. The Cluster A samples have characteristically higher $SiO_2/Al_2O_3$ ratio (because of the low $Al_2O_3$ content) while the Cluster B samples are clearly distinguished in three groups with low, middle and high Mn/Co ratio.*

*Stage 1*: In the first stage the glassmakers in a single firing event produced the base glass composition (all Cluster B samples form a solid cluster in the upper right quadrant of *fig. 2*);

*Stage 2*: In the second stage they produced the blue colour glass by remelting the base glass and adding one of the three different colorants (the Cluster B samples now are separated in three groups according to the Mn/Co ratio which is connected to the cobalt mineral (*fig. 4*)). The second stage most likely happened in three different firing events, otherwise, if the glass was coloured in stage 1 or in stage 2 but simultaneously with the three different colorants then Cluster B samples in *fig. 4* would form one broad group. It is also interesting to note that Cluster A samples have high Mn/Co ratio (more than 2.5). Interestingly, the Cluster B, high Mn/Co samples (low right group in *fig. 4*) are solely oinochoai. This could be an indication of a specialized workshop which produces a specific type of core formed vessels with specific raw materials.

*Decorative trails*

The vessels under study have, as expected, various glass decorative trails which vary both in shapes and colours. They present four different decorative motifs, such as zig-zag, feather, festoon and straigth (*fig. 5, table 1*), and three different opaque colours: yellow, white and turquoise. Yellow and white trails can be either simultaneously or separately applied on the vessel and there are only two examples having turquoise trails. Due to sampling creteria only a proportion of the samples having decorative trails were investigated. In particular, from the total of 56 samples (53 vessels and 3 beads), 19 vessels and

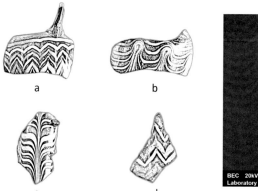
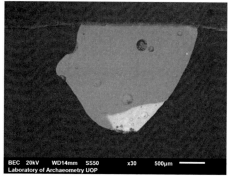

*Fig. 5. On the left, sketches of the different decorative designs witnessed on the samples under study. a. zig-zag and straight decoration; b. festoon decoration; c. feather decoration; d. zig-zag decoration. On the right, a back scattered electron microscopy image of a deep blue glass with yellow decoration in cross section. Various sized undisolved particles of lead antimonate were identified in the yellow decoration in the lower part of the image.*

1 bead were chosen for analysis providing sufficient data for the decoration trails.

As already shown (*fig. 1c-d*) a thin opaque glass was trailed around the body of the vessel and then was marvered on a flat surface. This particular step required a glass with different working properties (e.g. higher viscosity, lower melting/working temperature etc.) thus this is reflected to its chemical composition. In addition, the opacity of the glass trails offered a contrasting effect over the often deep blue glass achieving a unique polychromatic result.

The glass used for the decorative trails (yellow and white) belongs also to the general category of soda-lime-silica glass. The main raw material is sand with mean value of $SiO_2$ for the yellow glass at 57.6 % wt. and for the white glass at 69.6 % wt. In addition, the $Al_2O_3$ and $Fe_2O_3$ for the yellow and white glass is 1.7% wt. - 1.4 % wt. and 1.9 % wt. - 0.6 % wt. respectively which is characterised as typical for impurities found in sand. Both glasses were fused with natron since the $K_2O$ and MgO content is lower than 1 % wt. (yellow: mean values $K_2O$: 0.4 % wt., MgO: 0.4 % wt.; white: mean values $K_2O$: 0.5 % wt., MgO: 0.4 % wt.). The SEM examination showed that the decorative trails were opacified with lead and calcium antimonate crystals (*fig. 5 right*). In particular, the mean value of PbO in yellow decorations is 21.7 % wt. and the $Sb_2O_3$ 2.0 % wt. and therefore the use of a lead antimonate opacifier such as $Pb_2Sb_2O_7$ compound can be suggested. $Pb_2Sb_2O_7$ was used in the past both as a colorant in glazes and as opacifier in glass in Egypt and Mesopotamia in the 2nd Millennium BC.[52] It was also used as a colorant and opacifier in the Roman world.[53]

On the other hand, the mean value of PbO and $Sb_2O_3$ in white glass is 1.81 % wt. and 4.20 % wt. respectively indicating a calcium antimonate opacifier, such as $CaSb_2O_6$, which is a well-known material used as a white colour pigment/opacifier since ancient times.[54]

These differences described above are presented in the graphs of *fig. 6*. According to *fig. 6a* there is a clear distinction between yellow and white glass. In addition, yellow glass has slightly lower $SiO_2$ and $Al_2O_3$ values as it is shown in Fig. 6b. There are two samples showing very low $Al_2O_3$ (below 1% wt.) (*fig. 6b*). It is interesting to note that these two samples belong to ClusterA glass as discussed above, therefore both the main vessel and the decoration glass were manufactured with a sand having low levels of $Al_2O_3$ and is clearly distinguished from the rest of the glass.

CONCLUSIONS

According to recent studies Satricum glass can be differentiated/categorized into three clusters based on the relative elemental concentration.[55] The mean values of these three clusters for the corresponding elements occupy distinct positions on the respective graph (*fig. 2*). The samples belonging to Cluster A most likely have an Egyptian origin. In addition, Cluster B samples correlate well with sand raw materials suitable for glassmaking, which are found in Italy, indicating a possible Italian origin. The above assumptions are reinforced by the trace element study. Taking into consideration and comparing specific trace elements a clear distinction between the two clusters (A and B) is noticed and their origin is also

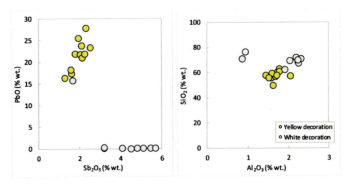

*Fig. 6. The correlation of the main oxides found in the decorative trails. a. On the left there is a clear distinction between the yellow and the white decorations due to the different amount of the corresponding opacifiers, lead and calcium antimonate respectievely. b. On the right the yellow decorations show lower $SiO_2$ and $Al_2O_3$. Interstingly, the white decorations with low $Al_2O_3$ content belong to Cluster A samples.*

confirmed (i.e. Cluster A shows similar characteristics with Egyptian samples and Cluster B correlates well with the Italian sands).

Although there is not any archaeological evidence for primary or/and secondary glass production during the Hellenistic period in Italy, it has been suggested that the production of the Mediterranean Group II core-formed vessels took place somewhere in southern Italy.[56] It has been also demonstrated that Satricum glass (Cluster B) and other Italian glass (e.g. Adria glass) have similar compositions with Italian sands providing a solid indication for glass production in Italy. Therefore, the primary or/and secondary glass workshops should be sought close to the sand sources.

Regarding the coloration of the Satricum glass, three different Co bearing colorants were identified for the majority of samples (Cluster B) which can be attributed in three different sources. This is clearly shown in the respective graph (*fig. 4*) and suggests a two stage manufacturing process. In the first stage the basic glass composition was produced and in a second stage colorants were added to the glass melt producing the final glass composition. Interestingly there is a connection between a specific typology and one of the three colorants indicating specialization of the glass workshop responsible for the production of the particular type.

Finally, the investigation of the decorative trails showed that they were manufactured using a "special" soda-lime-silica glass recipe with a composition appropriate to suit the special workability properties needed for this glass. This glass was opacified with the addition of two compounds, namely lead and calcium antimonate, which were responsible for the yellow and white colour respectively.

## Notes

* I would like to thank the Soprintendenza Archeologica del Lazio e dell'Etruria meridionale and the Satricum-Project (University of Amsterdam) for giving permission to study the glass samples; Prof. M. Gnade for entrusting me with the analysis of the Satricum assemblage; Prof. N. Zacharias for providing access to the Scanning Electron Microscope facility at the laboratory of Archaeometry, Department of History, Archaeology and Cultural Resources Management of the University of the Peloponnese; many thanks also go to Dr S. Chenery for providing access to the Laser Ablation ICP Mass Spectroscopy facility at the Centre for Environmental Geochemistry, in British Geological Survey, Keyworth, Nottingham. This project was part of the *Glasstech2013-Continuity and change in the emergence of the Hellenistic Glass industry in Greece* project, funded by Marie Curie Actions, Project number: 623645, FP7-PEOPLE-2013-IEF.

1. Nenna 2015, 1-2 and references therein.
2. Brill 1999, 277-300; Freestone *et al.* 2000, 69-71; Rehren 2000, 1226-1227; Rehren/Pusch 2005, 1756-1757; Brill/Stapleton 2012, 191-192; Henderson 2013, 83-106.
3. Degryse *et al.* 2009, 15-19; Degryse 2014; Smirniou *et al.* 2017, 11-13.
4. Barag 1970, 133.
5. Grose 1989, 109.
6. Grose 1989, 109.
7. Blomme *et al.* 2016, 5-8.
8. Grose 1989, 116, 122; Cosyns/Nys 2010, 241-242.
9. Grose 1989, 109-125; Stern/Schlick-Nolte 1994, 38-39.
10. Wight 2011, 27.
11. Schlick-Nolte 1994, 39-40.
12. Gudenrath 1991, 214.
13. Giberson 2004
14. Gnade 2002, 31 n. 76; Heldring 2007, 78-81.
15. Oikonomou *et al.* 2018, 99.
16. Oikonomou *et al.* 2017, 48-49; 2018, 99-100.
17. Oikonomou *et al.* 2018, 100-102, tables 2-4.
18. Sayre/Smith 1961, 1825.
19. Nicholson/Henderson 2000, 197.
20. Degryse 2014, see Appendix A.
21. Brill 1988, 270.

[22] Henderson 2013, 92-97 and references therein; Devulder/Degryse 2014, 87.
[23] Henderson 2013, 64-65.
[24] Paynter/Jackson 2018, 568-569.
[25] Oikonomou et al. 2017, 49-50; 2018, 101.
[26] Oikonomou et al. 2018, 107-108.
[27] Oikonomou et al. 2018, 108.
[28] Arletti et al. 2011, 2097.
[29] Triantafyllidis et al. 2012, 536-538.
[30] Cosyns/Nys 2010, 236, Fig. 11-3.
[31] Grose 1989, 116.
[32] Brems et al. 2012, 2902-2903; Brems/Degryse 2014, 32-34.
[33] Oikonomou et al. 2018, 108.
[34] Brems/Degryse 2014, 70-72.
[35] Shortland et al. 2007, 787.
[36] Shortland et al. 2007, 786-787.
[37] Brems et al. 2014, 52-53.
[38] Brems/Degryse 2014, 71.
[39] Wedepohl/Baumann 2000, 131-132.
[40] Brems/Degryse 2014, 78.
[41] Degryse/Schneider 2008, 1999; Brems et al. 2014, 53-54.
[42] Brems/Degryse 2014, 71.
[43] Panighello et al. 2012, 2949-2950.
[44] Blomme et al. 2017, 139-140; Oikonomou 2018, 517.
[45] Trace element data for Mediterranean Group I vessels have been published in Shortland and Schroeder (2009), but were excluded from this study for consistency purposes.
[46] Arletti et al. 2011, 2097; Oikonomou 2018, 521-522.
[47] Freestone et al. 2000, 73.
[48] Due to sampling criteria, none of the Cluster C samples were analyzed by LA-ICP-MS therefore there are no available trace element data. However, I believe that they would show a distinctive behavior. Furthermore, there are no available trace element data for the Spina (Arletti et al. 2011) and Rhodes (Triantafyllidis et al. 2012) assemblages therefore they are excluded from the corresponding graphs.
[49] Henderson 2013, 69.
[50] Kazmarczyck 1986, 373-374; Henderson 2013, 70-72.
[51] Abe et al. 2012, 1805; Oikonomou et al. 2018, 106.
[52] Oppenheim et al. 1970, 116-118.
[53] Zacharias et al. 2018, 21.
[54] Artioli 2010, 293-295; Nicolopoulos et al. 2018, 5-7.
[55] Oikonomou et al. 2018, 101.
[56] Grose 1989.

BIBLIOGRAPHY

Abe, Y./R. Harimoto/T. Kikugawaa/K. Yazawa/A. Nishisaka/N. Kawai/S. Yoshimura/L. Nakai, 2012, Transition in the use of cobalt-blue colorant in the New Kingdom of Egypt, *JASc* 39, 1793-1808.

Arletti, R./L. Rivi/D. Ferrari/G. Vezzalini 2011, The Mediterranean group II: analyses of vessels from Etruscan contexts in Northern Italy, *JASc* 38, 2094-2100.

Artioli, G., 2010, *Scientific methods and cultural heritage, An Introduction to the Application of Materials Science to Archaeometry and Conservation Science*, Oxford.

Barag, D., 1970, Mesopotamian Core-Formed Vessels 1500-500 BC, in A.L. Oppenheim et al., *Glass and glassmaking in ancient Mesopotamia*, Corning, NY, 131-199.

Blomme, A./P. Degryse/E. Dotsika/D. Ignatiadou/A. Longinelli/A. Silvestri 2017, Provenance of polychrome and colourless 8th-4th century BC glass from Pieria, Greece: A chemical and isotopic approach, *JASc* 78, 134-146.

Blomme, A., Elsen, J., Brems, D., Shortland, A., Dotsika, E., Degryse, P., 2016. Tracing the primary production location of core-formed glass vessels, Mediterranean Group I, *Journal of Archaeological Science Reports*, 5, 1-9.

Brems, D./P. Degryse 2014, Western Mediterranean sands for ancient glass making, in P. Degryse (ed.), *Glass making in the Greco-Roman world. Results of the ARCHGLASS project*, Leuven, 27-49.

Brems, D./P. Degryse/F. Hasendoncks/D. Gimeno/A. Silvestri/E. Vassilieva/S. Luypaers/J. Honings 2012, Western Mediterranean sand deposits as a raw material for roman glass production, *JASc* 39, 2897-2907.

Brems, D./M. Ganio/P. Degryse 2014, The Sr-Nd isotopic fingerprint of sand raw materials, in P. Degryse (ed.), *Glass making in the Greco-Roman world. Results of the ARCHGLASS project*, Leuven, 51-67.

Brill, R.H., 1988, Scientific investigations of the Jalame glass and related finds, in G.D. Weinberg (ed.), *Excavations at Jalame, Site of a Glass Factory in Late Roman Palestine*, Columbia, 257-294.

Brill, R.H., 1999, *Chemical analyses of Early glasses 1-2. The Corning Museum of Glass*, New York.

Brill, R.H./C.P. Stapleton 2012, *Chemical analyses of Early glasses. 3. The Corning Museum of Glass*, New York.

Cosyns, P./K. Nys 2010, Core-formed glass vessels on Cyprus reconsidered, in S. Christodoulou/A. Satraki (eds.), *POCA 2007: Postgraduate Cypriot Archaeology Conference*, Cambridge, 231-261.

Degryse, P. 2014, *Glass Making in the Greco-Roman World: Results of the ARCHGLASS Project*, Leuven.

Degryse, P./J. Henderson/G. Hodgins 2009, *Isotopes in vitreous materials*, Leuven.

Degryse, P./J. Schneider 2008, Pliny the Elder and Sr-Nd isotopes: tracing the provenance of raw materials for Roman glass production, *JASc* 35, 1993-2000.

Devulder, V./P. Degryse 2014, The sources of natron, in P. Degryse (ed.), *Glass making in the Greco-Roman world. Results of the ARCHGLASS project*, Leuven, 87-95.

Freestone, I.C./Y. Gorin-Rosen/M.J. Hughes 2000, Primary glass from Israel and the production of glass in the late antiquity and the early Islamic period, in M.D. Nenna (ed.), *La route du verre. Ateliers primaires et secondaires de verriers du second millénaire avant J.C. au Moyen Age (Travaux de la Maison de l'Orient Méditerranéen 33)*, Lyon, 65-83.

Giberson, D.F. 2004, *Dudley Giberson's Core Vessel Video*, Warner, N.Fl.

Gnade, M. 2002, *Satricum in the post-archaic period: a case study of the interpretation of archaeological remains as indicators of ethno-cultural identity*, Leuven.

Grose, D.F. 1989, *Early Ancient Glass: Core-formed, Rod-formed, and Cast Vessels and Objects from the Late Bronze Age to the Early Roman Empire, 1600 BC to 50 AD, The Toledo Museum of Art*, New York.

Gudenrath, W. 1991, Techniques of Glassmaking and Decoration: Vessel core-forming, in H. Tait (ed.), *Five Thousand Years of Glass*, London, 214-215.

Heldring, B. 2007, Il deposito votivo III: una cisterna prima, un deposito votivo dopo, in M. Gnade, *Satricum. Trenta anni di scavi olandesi*, Amsterdam, 78-81.

Henderson, J. 2013, *Ancient Glass, an Interdisciplinary Exploration*, New York/Cambridge.

Kazmarczyck, A. 1986, The source of cobalt in ancient Egyptian pigments, in J.S. Olin/J. Blackman (eds.), *Proceedings of the 24th International Symposium on Archaeometry*, Washington, DC, 369-376.

Nenna, M.-D. 2015, Primary glass workshops in Graeco-Roman Egypt: Preliminary Report on the Excavations on the site of Beni Salama, Wadi Natrun (2003, 2005-9), in L. Freestone et al., *Glass in the Roman world, in honour of Jennifer Price*, Oxford, 1-22.

Nicholson, P.T./J. Henderson 2000, Glass, in P.T. Nicholson/I. Shaw (eds.), *Ancient Egyptian materials and technology*, Cambridge, 195-224.

Nicolopoulos, S./P.P. Das/P.J. Bereciartua/F. Karavasili/N. Zacharias/A.G. Pérez/A.S. Galanis/E.F. Rauch/R. Arenal/J. Portillo/J. Roqué-Rose/M. Kollia/L. Margiolaki 2018, Novel characterization techniques for cultural heritage using a TEM orientation imaging in combination with 3D precession difraction tomography: a case study of green and white ancient Roman glass tesserae, *Heritage Science* 6:64, 1-12.

Oikonomou, A. 2018, Hellenistic core formed glass from Epirus, Greece. A technological and provenance study, *JASc Reports* 22, 513-523.

Oikonomou, A./M. Gnade/J. Henderson/S. Chenery/N. Zacharias 2017, The provenance of Hellenistic core formed vessels from Satricum, Italy, in S. Wolf/A. Pury-Gysel (eds.), *Annals of the 20th Congress of the International Association for the History of Glass*, 48-53.

Oikonomou, A./J. Henderson/M. Gnade/S. Chenery/N. Zacharias 2018, An archaeometric study of Hellenistic glass vessels: evidence for multiple sources, *Journal of Archaeological and Anthropological Sciences* 10, 97-110.

Oppenheim, A.L./R.H. Brill/D. Barag/A. van Saldern 1970, *Glass and glassmaking in ancient Mesopotamia*, Corning, N.Y.

Panighello, S./E.F. Orsega/J.T. van Elteren/V.S. Šelih 2012, Analysis of polychrome Iron Age glass vessels from Mediterranean I, II and III groups by LA-ICP-MS, *JASc* 39, 9, 2945-2955.

Paynter, S./J. Caroline 2018, Mellow yellow: An experiment in amber, *JASc Reports* 22, 568-576.

Rehren, Th./E.B. Pusch 2005, Late Bronze Age glass production at Qantir-Piramesses, Egypt, *Science* 308, 1756-1758.

Rehren, Th. 2000, Rationales in Old World Base Glass Compositions, *JASc* 27, 1225-1234.

Sayre, E.V./R.W. Smith 1961, Compositional categories of ancient glass, *Science* 133, 1824-1826.

Schlick-Nolte, B. 1994, Mediterrranean Core-Formed Vessels of the 1st Millennium BC., in Stern/Schlick-Nolte 1994, 37-44.

Scott, R.B./P. Degryse 2014, The archaeology and archaeometry of natron glass making, in P. Degryse (ed.), *Glass making in the Greco-Roman world. Results of the ARCHGLASS project*, Leuven, 15-26.

Shortland, A.J./H. Schroeder 2009, Analysis of first millennium BC glass vessels and Beads from the Pichvnari Necropolis, Georgia, *Archaeometry* 51, 947-965.

Shortland, A.J./N. Rogers/K. Eremin 2007, Trace element discriminants between Egyptian and Mesopotamian late Bronze Age glasses, *JASc* 34, 781-789.

Smirniou, M./Th. Rehren/B. Gratuze 2017, Lisht as a New Kingdom Glass-Making Site with Its Own Chemical Signature, *Archaeometry* 60, 3, 502-516.

Stern, E.M./B. Schlick-Nolte 1994, *Early Glass of the Ancient World. Emesto Wolf Collection*, Ostfildern.

Triantafyllidis, P./I. Karatasios/E. Andreopoulou-Magkou 2012, Study of core-formed glass vessels from Rhodes, in: N. Zacharias et al., *Proceedings of the 5th Symposium of HSA*, University of Peloponnese Publication, 529-544, (in Greek).

Wedepohl, K.H./A. Baumann 2000, The use of marine molluskan shells for Roman glass and local raw glass production in the Eifel area (Western Germany), *Naturwissenschaften*, 87, 129-132.

Wight, K.B. 2011, *Molten Color. Glassmaking in Antiquity*, Los Angeles.

Zacharias, N./F. Karavassili/P. Das/S. Nicolopoulos/A. Oikonomou/A. Galanis/E. Rauch/R. Arenal/J. Portillo/J. Roque/J. Casablanca/I. Margiolaki 2018, A novelty for cultural heritage material analysis: transmission electron microscope (TEM) 3D electron diffraction tomography applied to roman glass tesserae, *Microchemical Journal* 138, 19-25.

# Visualizing Technology

# Identifying past building practices through 3D modelling
## *The case of the late Archaic temple of Satricum*

*Loes Opgenhaffen*

*Abstract*

*This paper proposes an innovative integrated methodology that combines the chaîne opératoire approach with digital 3D modelling. The methodology is demonstrated through the reconstruction of the late Archaic temple of Mater Matuta at Satricum, specifically the phase that goes by the name 'Temple II', dating to 500-480 BC. Studying technology through the lens of a chaîne opératoire approach enables to break the complex sequence of building activities into several steps, and 3D modelling applied during research enables to virtually re-build the temple step by step, or stone by stone. Additionally, the integrated technology assesses and combines both traditional and digital datasets from a different perspective, which generates new information. Ultimately, the bottom-up perspective to architectural technology allows to enter the previously intangible building site of the past, revealing how multiple craft communities and foreign workshops were organized and how they communicated about construction matters.*

1. INTRODUCTION

Temples in Late Archaic Central Italy are the silent witnesses of a turbulent era. By the end of the sixth century the last king of Rome was expelled resulting in the installation of the Roman Republic, while increased expansion to Latium and a growing tension with the southern Etruscan cities led to wars; tribes from the mountains invaded. At the same time, the technological and artistic progress that developed over the course of the sixth century BC gained momentum, and ground-plans and decorative systems of temples changed drastically to monumental dimensions. Tyrannical rulers controlled (forced) labour and commissioned public and private buildings by prominent workshops. These workshops often featured artisans coming from the Greek world who brought with them innovative artistic and technological knowledge.

Analyses of major transformations in the design of similar-looking temples from various sites tend to be attributed almost exclusively to political events and elite activities, preferably of a dominant centre that ideologically ruled all: Rome. Regrettably, by focusing scholarship on similarities in temple buildings in a wide region and relating this to the politics of a dominant centre and its foreign influences, local variation and difference are largely overlooked. Fifty years ago, Boëthius (1970, 31) remarked that '[...] scholars have assumed that all the variations of Etruscan temples were derived from Vitruvius' two types – an unfounded conclusion, which has given rise to strained categorization and arbitrary reconstructions. The obvious approach to our material seems to be an empirical description of common features and an unbiased classification of the various types [...]'. So, when scales are shifted from central politics to local practices, a new set of aspects is revealed.[1] A bottom-up perspective to architectural technology facilitates this shift because it identifies and explores these local practices by placing focus on the building site of a temple itself, as will be demonstrated with the reconstruction of the Late Archaic temple of Mater Matuta of Satricum ('Temple II', ca. 500-480 BC, *fig. 1*). In order to examine the technology of Archaic temple construction, this paper proposes an innovative integrated methodology that combines the *chaîne opératoire* approach with digital 3D modelling.

While the strength of the *chaîne opératoire* approach has long been advocated, particularly by the French School and in Bronze Age Aegean studies – as it was originally formulated by prehistorian André Leroi-Gourhan and elaborated by ethno-anthropologists such as Valentine Roux and Olivier Gosselain – it has not yet fully landed in research to Archaic Central Italic architecture. Full understanding of technology is essential before exploring the organisation of craft com-

*Fig. 1. 3D reconstruction of Temple II, dedicated to Mater Matuta. Parts of the temple decoration are terracotta coloured and/or are not fully modelled in 3D, because there is no information or publication available to reconstruct them completely (image L. Opgenhaffen).*

munities participating on building sites, especially in the case of poorly preserved built environments. More specifically, the *chaîne opératoire* approach enables scholars to break the complex sequence of building activities into several steps, and through this to illustrate the social environment where technological activities took place. Actions and performances on material during these processes are associated with knowledge and know-how, which can now be reconstructed with this approach.[2]

The addition of innovative visualisation methods such as 3D scanning and modelling, buildings from the past can be materialised on the basis of tangible data to visualise the inherent intangible processes. Complex sequential architectural procedures are reconstructed virtually by re-building the temple step by step, or stone by stone. Every aspect of construction reflects the actions, habits and choices of craftsmen (and the archaeologist/3D modeller). Simultaneously, the material is acting on the craftsmen as well. This detailed reconstruction process may therefore provide insights into the social organisation and communication on the building site between craftsmen, local building material suppliers and foreign artists. What is more, a multi-scalar perspective allows one to zoom in on details of materials and zoom out to intra-regional connections of technological transmission, without losing sight of the building site itself. In doing so, modern technology can reveal old technologies and practices within their social context.

3D modelling compels one to reconsider traditional data from a different perspective, which itself generates new information. Therefore, the history of the temple's excavation and study is analysed from this new perspective, forming the basis of the reconstruction of the late Archaic Temple of Mater Matuta shown in section 3. This is followed by a reflection on the approach and suggestions for future research.

2. BRIEF HISTORY OF RESEARCH TO THE TEMPLES IN SATRICUM

The first excavations of the temples of Mater Matuta started in 1896, under the auspices of the Frenchman H. Graillot, and quickly lead to the discovery of a rich votive deposit, which attracted a fair share of attention. In order to prevent the exportation of the finds to overseas countries, the Italian archaeologists soon took over the excavations. A. Cozza and R. Mengarelli directed the excavations from 1896 to 1898 under the auspices of F. Barnabei. They reconstructed seven phases and published them in preliminary reports, whereas Graillot had identified only four different phases for the temple, but soon reduced the number of phases to four as well. E. Petersen, the secretary of the German Institute at Rome, visited Satricum at the end of the excavations in 1896, and he disagreed with the phasing as reconstructed by Cozza and Mengarelli.[3] He published his own findings in the same year accompanied by drawings, stating that there were only two phases. In the course of the 1950's, after a few decades of archaeological inactivity, the Soprintendente of the Villa Giulia Museum, M. Santangelo, carried out small excavations at Satricum, with as main objective reaching the oldest layers and the *terra vergine*. She identified the 'temple hut' as being the first phase of the sanctuary,[4] followed by the first rectangular structure in stone, the *sacellum* or Temple 0.[5] After Santangelo's intervention, all remained quiet in Satricum until the arrival of Dutch archaeologists in 1977. Under the direction of C. Stibbe, vice-director of the Dutch Institute at Rome (NIR), the remains of the temples that were left out in the open and severely damaged by erosion and creeping vegetation caused by years of neglect, were cleaned and further excavated.[6]

The Dutch never left. Excavations were continued from 1991 onwards by the University of Amsterdam under the direction of M. Gnade. During these years, significant publications about Satricum and specifically the temples appeared. Additionally, the archive of excavation documentation from Mengarelli and others was made available by the Villa Guilia to Gnade. Among the documentation are field notes and sketches with measurements of eight building phases as reconstructed by Santangelo, based on both her own observations as well as Mengarelli's notes and drawings.[7]

In 1981 J. De Waele published the first reconstructions of three building phases of the Temple of Mater Matuta. He carefully studied and assessed the scant evidence the original excavators published, and agreed with the (written) reconstruction and reasoning of E. Petersen that Temple II was erected in a single episode. De Waele recorded all the remains of the temples and reproduced the drawing of Mengarelli to meet modern standards. As such, he could make a comparison of what was lost over the years. This comparison between the past and present state of the remains showed that most of the column bases and parts of the eastern wall of the *sacellum*, or Temple 0, that Mengarelli recorded, had disintegrated or completely vanished. Besides cleaning and recording the remains, he carried out stratigraphic research at a few undisturbed locations within the temple walls. These descriptions of the simple layering between the temple walls were not further interpreted, but may provide interesting clues about the foundation of the temples. The foundation techniques and the actual fill and floor level received little attention at that point. Only recently, M. Gnade investigated possible foundation techniques of Temple II.[8] Lastly, a general study of the architecture of Temple II was carried out by E. van 't Lindenhout (2010), which provides a summary of previous research.

In the course of the 1980's attention shifted upwards from the foundations, ground plans and construction; R. Knoop and P. Lulof devoted doctoral research to the architectural terracottas that once protected and decorated the temple roofs. Knoop was the first to publish the antefixes of the the first two temples, and Lulof the reconstruction of the ridge-pole statues that adorned the roof of Temple II. Multiple publications about the architectural terracottas were published over the years by Knoop and Lulof.[9] The final publication of all architectural terracottas from all phases of the temple has yet to be published.

Lulof and Knoop were the first to modify the reconstruction of De Waele. They adjusted the slope of Temple II. In 2004, Lulof produced a digital 3D model of Temple I to test the visibility of the terracotta decoration of the roof. Although these reasons to create a 3D model are valid, and the immersive VR reconstruction as a visual portal provoked productive discussion, the archaeological establishment dismissed the utility of the 3D model.[10] Lulof was a pioneer, but was apparently too early in adopting the new technology for archaeological practice.[11] Recently Lulof also completed, in collaboration with the author, a 3D reconstruction of Temple 0.[12] This leaves the monumental Temple II with its exuberant decoration as the final challenge for 3D reconstruction. The previous works of De Waele, Lulof and Knoop are invaluable and form the cornerstone of the reconstruction of Temple II, from foundations to terracottas.[13]

3. 3D MODELLING AS RESEARCH TOOL

*3.1 Material and techniques*

Research on construction and building practices in Archaic Central Italy is usually limited to the study of ground plans and terracotta roof decoration.[14] When the structure between these two is considered, it is often restricted to only mentioning the possible application of a particular material. What is more, materials are usually taken for granted in 3D reconstructions of architecture. They act merely as a 'texture' to colourise the structure rather than being thoroughly interrogated for their properties. But real materials have affordances, and they affect how people use material and transform it into a finished product, since the properties of material limit or allow a certain use and application. Building a temple of massive dimensions requires immense organisation. This includes arranging a sufficient work force as well as understanding location, quantities and qualities of construction materials. This section assesses materials, their sources and the associated techniques that could have been applied in the construction of Temple II.

*Wood*
Wood was, alongside clay and stone, the main building material in Archaic Central Italy. It was widely available in the direct vicinity of Satricum, though not every type of wood was suitable for construction, as the 'architects' and building supervisors were well aware. Different species are suitable as timber for indoor or outdoor use as well as specific constructive application. Specific applications may call for carrying or distributing weight, flexibility, soft- or hardwood, pulling or bending qualities, resistance to cracking or splitting, and so forth. The 'architects' and building supervisors must also have been well aware the quantities of timber required for such a structure, and what type of wood was available from a not too great distance.

Pollen-analysis is useful to find indications of local timber sources. The vegetation in the Pontine region consisted of, among other species, pine (in the dune area), evergreen or holm oak (*quercus ilex*), alder, walnut, and chestnut (at the tufa and alluvial-colluvial depositions). On the foothills of the calcareous Monti Lepini grew kermes oak (*quercus coccifera*) and Turkey or Austrian oak (*quercus cerris*), while hornbeam and ash grew on the mountain slopes.[15]

The holm oak produces extremely hard and heavy wood, albeit in modest dimensions – the tree only reaches a total height of between 21-28 m and the trunk an average height of 6 m. Since ancient times it was a favoured wood for its strength and the capacity to carry heavy loads. Hesiod (*Works and Days* 429) mentions that holm oak was popular for the construction of pillars, wagons and tools. Although the Turkey oak can grow even taller and the tree trunk can reach a diameter of 1,5 to 2 m, the wood tends to split and crack, and would be – aside from the fact that it had to come from farther than the holm oak – a less suitable candidate for a use of building material, and was better suited for boards, fencing, or fuel.[16] This leaves a logical choice for holm oak trunks to serve as outdoor columns, which therefore were restricted to a maximum height of 6 m. The traveling distance would not have been more than 10 km. Holm oak must have been used for the ridge beam and large purlins as well, in order to carry the heavy ridge pole statues as well as to reach the extensive cantilever at the front and back of the temple.

The pines from the dunes are too wet to use as building material, therefore the Satrican carpenters were most probably in favour of the pines of the Monti Lepini, at a distance of ca. 25 km. Pine grows quite tall and its soft wood and length makes it ideal for roofing and flooring. However, it survives poorly outdoors when exposed to the elements (only 12-18 months), which explains the protection of the roof with terracotta plaques. Pine makes an excellent candidate for the large spans that needed to be covered by the tie beams, the principal and common rafters, the purlins and wall plates of the roof construction, as well as the wooden framework of the cella walls which contained the mud-bricks. Finally, as Theophrastus stated in the fourth century BC, it was the first choice of the architect for roofing and the best wood for timber.[17]

*Earth*
Building with earth is something that humanity has done since a sedentary way of living emerged, and is still practiced today, both in developing countries and in sustainable modern architecture. Although no remains of building material have been reported by the first excavators, there are many indications for earthen construction material from recent contexts both within Satricum and contemporary cities.

Many ways to build with earth co-existed in the Archaic period.[18] Wattle-and daub – a framework of wooden beams with a wickerwork of reeds which was then covered with daub – is the oldest and most common technique particularly applied in (local) hut building. Clay deposits for local pottery production were not far (3-7 km), since Satricum is located on a sandy-clayey marine 'terrace', although not every clay is suitable as building material.[19] The sources of the substantial amounts of silt (ca. 70%) and a lesser amount of sand (ca. 20%) necessary to prepare the daub in order to make it plastic and spreadable are not yet identified, but both silt and reeds[20] were likely found in the alluvial deposits of the Astura and the nearby swamp area of the Agro Pontino.[21] The wattle-and-daub technique was not applied much in the construction of Temple II, but may well have been applied to enclose the frontons because of its light structure.

The walls of the cella were erected with mud-bricks,[22] held together with a framework of wooden posts and horizontal beams. The raw material needed to produce mud-bricks – clay (15-18%), silt (10-28%) and sand (55-75%)[23] – like the wattle-and-daub, was extracted in the immediate vicinity. Enough sand should be added to avoid shrinkage and to make it pressure-proof, but in balance with enough clay to bind the materials.[24] Mud-bricks are made by filling square wooden moulds with a plastic daub mixture or throwing lumps of earth into the moulds. Throwing lumps creates greater compaction, which makes the brick strong and able to carry its load.[25] Depending on the climate (temperature and humidity), mud-bricks of average size (30 cm) dry in between 14 (humidity 44%) and 30 days (81%).[26] About 300 blocks a day could be produced with the throwing technique by only one person,[27] which includes the paste preparation if the raw materials were already to hand.

Another major application of earth is foundation works. In order to stabilise the relatively narrow foundation walls of the stylobate[28] underneath the columns, and to create a solid floor level, the extracted soil from the digging of the construction pits for the walls was used to refill the pits along the foundation walls. To make this filling solid and compact the soil was probably mixed with clay (at least 15%) and perhaps silt.[29] On top of this a pavement layer of clay mixed with flakes of tufa and rubble (broken pottery) could have been placed.[30]

Daub was also applied in roof construction to create an even and binding surface to position the roof tiles and to stabilise them. Lastly, the light-coloured clay (*impasto chiaro sabbioso*) source that probably was used to produce the roof tiles (and pottery too) has been recently identified as, surprisingly, Lavinium – a distance of 40 km from Satricum.[31]

*Stone*

Stone was another major building material, in the case of the second phase of the temple *tufo lionato*, with in some occasions a white tufa (re-used from the previous building phase). *Tufo lionato* quarries were identified along the Astura, some of which were still used in the eighties, and on the hill east of the acropolis,[32] indicating that this particular building material did not travel far: less than 1 km. In the next section about building techniques more attention will be given to the processing of the blocks.

*Techniques*

*Ashlar masonry*

While closely studying the foundation walls, several observations were made. The podium walls consist of three superimposed rows of blocks.[33] The walls were two blocks thick, and courses alternated between rows of headers and stretchers. The cella walls are constructed of at least four superimposed rows of rectangular blocks (excluding the rows of blocks of the foundation). The fifth, lowest row, founded in a trench in the *terra vergine*, consists of predominantly headers, which extend towards the inside of the cella wall. The two uppermost rows rose above stylobate level. The blocks are of irregular dimensions, probable due to the crumbly nature of tufa it was hard to cut the blocks precisely.[34] To move the heavy blocks into position a form of mechanical lifting was probably deployed. On several locations (at least 12) shallow, rectangular holes, rounded at the short sides, are visible in the blocks, which could be identified as lifting holes in which metal levers would fit (*fig. 2a*). Several rectangular cut-outs were identified as well, in which wooden poles could have been fixated, as to form a lifting device that was known in Etruria in the Archaic period (*fig. 2b*).[35] Cranes, a technology that was known by Greek architects in the late sixth century and in the shipping ports to move goods with either metal levers or with ropes, could have been deployed as well.[36]

In the western foundation wall, which is on the entrance side of the temple, there is a series of blocks (12 in total, spread over two different rows) which are hewn as to form a flight of steps. The blocks do not run across the entire wall. At other apparently random locations, square shallow shafts or dug outs are carved at the side of the blocks, which may have been to embed wooden poles for the superstructure or for purposes during construction, such as scaffolding or to anchor levers.[37] Elsewhere, also apparently at random, ledges are chiselled, but it is hard to reconstruct a building practice or determine constructional use from these ledges.

Most blocks have cut marks of pickaxes. On the interior of the cella walls, the marks run crisscross over the surface. The blocks were hewn neatly on site to fit the course of placing. A few other, reused blocks of another harder type of tufa stone, are believed to be sawn, leaving a smooth surface.[38] Deep parallel running lines cut in a block of *tufo lionato* seems to confirm the use of saws (*fig. 2c*).[39]

*Fig. 2a. Possible lifting holes in which metal levers would fit; 2b. Rectangular cut-outs to fixate wooden poles of the lifting device; 2c. Possible sawing marks (photos by L. Opgenhaffen).*

*Foundation techniques*
The raised stylobate of the temple was composed of multiple rows of superimposed tufa blocks of varying size,[40] of which the lowest row was founded in a trench in the *terra vergine*.[41] The stylobate is not solid, but has an open character instead with foundation limited to only walls and columns. This form of foundation is found in most temple ground plans in Latium and Etruria, but slight variation can be discerned. In most occasions the foundation walls of the cella and ante-cellae are extended to the external foundation walls.[42] Sometimes this is to carry columns, but in most cases this compartmentalisation serves to stabilise the stylobate and prevent the fill from shifting. A divergent type – to which Satricum can be attributed – is a foundation with non-extending walls and separately founded column bases which seems to be mostly employed in Latium.[43]

This type of light and non-solid foundation suggests a light superstructure with the ability to carry a heavy load that is not distributed vertically into the walls. The superstructure would be kept low too, for a too high building would be susceptible to tilt. Thus, although the peripteroid layout of columns is inspired by its Greek counterparts, the foundation technique could be regarded a local tradition.

*Construction technology*

*Roof construction*
In mainland Greece, with its great temples with massive foundations and stylobates, a stone superstructure usually carried a prop-and-lintel system roof. In this system the large span of the roof was supported by inner walls and columns, with principal rafters resting directly on the walls and not physically connected to cross-beams. In the Western Greek colonies in Sicily, however, evidence of sockets hewn in the stone architraves indicate that some of the stone temples received a wooden trussed roof as early as the 6th century BC.[44] Religious architecture in Central Italy was by contrast erected of light, perishable materials, resulting in a truncated appearance which was distinct from their elegant Greek counterparts. This type of construction demanded a light roofing system to carry the new building technology of terracotta roof tiles that was introduced by the Greeks, combined with local traditions of heavy ridge-poles and terracotta roof decoration. A post-and-lintel system could not have been supported by the insubstantial Central Italic way of foundation, nor could a superstructure of perishable materials carry the load. Given the abundance of good timber in the region, the natural solution to cover the wide span of the Italic temples would be the tie-beam truss.[45] In Central Italy the technique of the truss was already known and applied as early as the 6th century BC in Poggio Civitate (Murlo).[46] Recenty a discussion was raised whether the truss was used in the Jupiter Optimus Maximus temple on the Capitol Hill at Rome, of which the presence was convincingly demonstrated by J.N. Hopkins.[47] Another argument for the presence of a trussed roof is the fact that the insubstantial single wall foundations of the cella could support the heavy weight of its superstructure if the thrust was divided evenly and converted vertically on its walls. If this were a post-and-lintel system, the walls would risk toppling sideways or sagging.

The inhabitants of Central Italy show a peculiar taste for immense ridge beams, as is best demonstrated by the extremely large *columen* plaque from Temple B at Pyrgi[48] that covered the end of the beam (ca. 1.20 x ca. 1.40 m). Also, the *columen* from Temple II at Satricum itself proves to be of enormous dimensions (ca. 1.25 x 1.10 m), as well as numerous other examples of large ridge beams from other contexts, such as miniature terracotta temple models. It seems to be a tradition that originated from hut-building, visible in Iron Age 'hut-urns'. The continuation of this tradition within new building methods demanded a strong construction system such as the truss. An additional argument for the presence of the enormous ridge poles and purlins is the need to support the weight of ridge pole statues and the recessed roof in the fronton (see below). The purlins – or *columen* and *mutulus* beams – were supported by props placed on the tie-beam. The two most outer purlins were placed directly on the tie beam.

*The technique of the truss*

The timber roof truss consists of two rafters joined at their lower ends to the tie-beam, so as to form a triangle. The tie-beam works in tension and compression but hardly bends, and counters the lateral thrust of the rafters and transforms it into vertical thrust; it is therefore self-supporting, preventing the substructure from experiencing significant strain.[49] As a result, it can carry considerable weight, spans greater distances and causes little sagging (*fig. 3*).

*Carpentry techniques*
Because the protective terracotta elements have a flat surface at the back, the wooden timber that

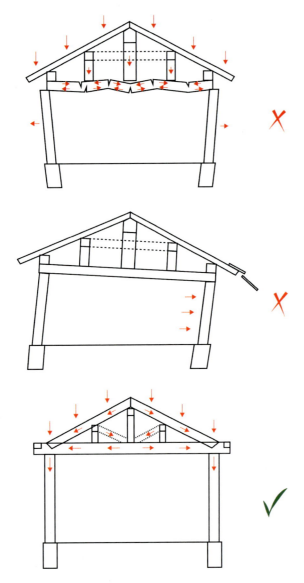

Fig. 3. The distribution of thrust in a post-and-lintel system (upper) vs. a truss system (lower) (image L. Opgenhaffen).

they covered must have been cleaved or sawn to square beams. Sawyers, as is known from building inscriptions Greece, were highly specialised and fairly expensive.[50] It remains unknown, though, if the timber of Temple II was cleaved or sawn. What is certain is that the terracotta elements were attached to the roof construction with nails, evidenced by the present nail-holes in the terracottas. Another important detail of these nail-holes is that they were pierced at fixed positions in the plaques before firing.[51] This implies that the coroplasts were informed at forehand about beam sizes and tailored the terracotta plaques to the woodwork.

Little direct evidence exists for timber connections and joints, but indirect contexts – such as contemporary shipbuilding, wooden furniture and architecture in Magna Graecia – provide valuable insights. Ancient ships may be considered valuable technical comparatives;[52] the triangular shape of a composite frame and beam assembly recall roof construction. The central keel (or ridge beam) is kept in place by floor timbers (rafters) which in turn are anchored in deck-level beams (tie-beams). The planks of Archaic Greek 'lashed' ships were connected with dowel pins and pegs, and sewn together with laces.[53] Archaic Greek religious architecture in Magna Graecia shows that wooden beams of the roofs were anchored in the stone sub-construction by sockets hewn in the architraves.[54] These can be translated to (half-) lap joints (heel joint) and mortise-and-tenon joints.[55] The rafters of the truss must have been connected with the first type of joint: a socket in the tie beam embedded the rafter firmly (*fig. 4a*), and at the other end the rafters were connected by mitre joints (the ends being bevelled at a 45-degree angle, see *fig. 4b*). Small sized purlins and jack rafters were stabilised by lap joints. Large dowel pins or a mortise-and-tenon could have been used to secure the tie beam to the columns (*fig. 4c*). Mortise-and-tenons were also applied for the construction of door-frames.

  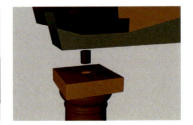

Fig. 4a. The principal rafter is connected to the tie beam by a heel joint (the sockets), and the purlins to the rafter by lap joints; 4b. At the other sides the rafters are connected by mitre joints; 4c. the tie beam is secured to the column by a dowel pin (images L. Opgenhaffen).

*Terracotta production and laying tiles*
The production of architectural terracottas is a well-studied subject and therefore only a few relevant techniques of terracotta production shall be mentioned here, as they were produced by foreign, travelling workshops locally.[56] Although the exact locations of the workshops and kilns remain unknown, the presence of foreign artisans reveals some hints about the communication between different crafts on the building site, being the most evident line of communication the dimensions of the wooden elements from the master builder or 'architect' to the master-artisan: the plaques needed to be adjusted to the beam sizes, and the painters had to know how much the soffits of the roof tiles were protruding in order to decorate the projecting part.[57] The focus is placed here, however, on the constructive implications these decorative elements contain; the type of terracotta element reveals what particular constructive element they protected, and the dimensions of the elements, especially the nail-holes but also the variation in types with differing heights, reveal the sizes of the constructive elements behind them (i.e. the size of the ridge beam, rafters, tie-beams, wall-plates, purlins etc.). To illustrate with one example: the revetment plaques, or anthemion plaques, that covered the rafters were 43 cm in height and ranging in width (35, ca. 50, ca. 63, ca. 64.5 cm) and were assembled by three bands from multiple moulds.[58] They received several nail holes before firing: two in the upper band of tongues (in the 3$^{rd}$ and 8$^{th}$ tongue) and two in the lower band at W. c. 9,5 and H. 16 cm from below. This indicates a rafter of at least 30 cm in height.

All terracotta protective elements except the ridge pole statues, acroteria and palmettes, were produced with moulds. Lumps of tempered clay were thrown into moulds, and nail holes were pierced in the still-wet clay, indicating that the dimensions of the wooden construction elements were already calculated and communicated to the terracotta workshop.

Pan tiles were produced by throwing clay into wooden frames and flattened with a wire or wooden straightedge. It is uncertain if the raised borders were then added by hand or pre-modelled in the wooden frame and then manually finished.[59] Cover tiles were manufactured by wrapping a slab of clay over a wooden shape.[60] The diameter of the cover tiles were, of course, determined by the height and width of the raised borders of the pan tiles. What remains to be determined, however, is whether the same clay sources were used for the production of the terracotta decoration and the other applications of clay/earth elsewhere in the construction of the temple.[61]

The low pitch of 11.4 degrees[62] enabled the roof tiles to stabilise themselves by their own weight, preventing them from slipping off the roof.[63] The low pitch was ideal to carry away water.

Placing the roof elements such as the raking simas and revetment plaques along the short ends must have begun at the corners and then placed one plaque after the other up to the apex.[64] Once reaching the apex, the sima blocks and revetment plaques were cut obliquely, *at the time* of laying, *after* firing.[65] This implies that neither the architect nor the coroplasts knew in advance where to cut exactly. The laying of the roof then proceeded from the eaves of the roof onwards to the ridge and centre. Because part of the soffits of the pan tiles were painted, these particular tiles were projecting from the edge of the roof, and were thus visible from the floor level of the temple. They were painted before they were placed, indicating the laymen must have started laying pan tiles from the eaves heading to the ridge, and not vice versa. Although not documented so far in Satricum, pan tiles were often 'chipped'[66] or 'nicked'[67] at the raised borders to 'tailor'[68] the interlocking with the adjacent tile (*fig. 5*).

*Fig. 5. Nicked edges of rooftiles (photos by L. Opgenhaffen).*

*3.2 The reconstruction process: a matter of choices, recording and data transparency*

The materials and techniques in the section above constitute the raw data of the digital 3D reconstruction of Temple II. But raw data are not the only data scholars use. As archaeologists are inherently concerned with the technological choices about how things were made in the past, this can be extended to the choices that have been made in the present by the digital archaeologist to reconstruct that same thing from the past. It is therefore an ethical obligation to document this process of research and modelling, while keeping the agency of the modern archaeologist in mind too.[69] Such a detailed account of the process of modelling encompasses the research, the options given and choices made (paradata) by the scholar-modeller to reconstruct something, elevate the 3D reconstruction to a 'transparent' level; it reveals the data (research), metadata (technical details) and paradata (intellectual data, choices and certainty) from which it is created.[70] Once the 3D reconstruction is connected to the data, it will reach its actual denotation of a model, a model that can be queried, interrogated, and even used to predict and produce multiple outcomes. Unfortunately, a straightforward solution to easily connect 3D models with data does not yet exist.[71] Massive reconstructions and huge datasets restrict good connection too; the models are often simply too large to publish online, hence preventing it to be accessible. Small research budgets are another limiting factor, let alone unpublished archaeological material. But it is not the aim nor within the scope of this paper to solve these difficulties. As a consequence, the reconstruction of Temple II is published in a 'traditional' format: a written paper with 2D images of the 3D model. But as adversative this may seem, it is ultimately the archaeologist, and not the 3D model itself, that does the interpretation and actual reconstruction. 3D modelling is regarded here as a research tool to structure data and guide the reasoning and interpretation process that is shaping the reconstruction.[72]

*The process in steps*
The process of reconstruction of Temple II is presented step-by-step, starting at the foundations and ending with the roof tiles and terracotta protective elements. This forms the framework of a new methodology to employ 3D modelling as an active scientific research tool in the study to ancient architecture in combination with the *chaîne opératoire* approach. These steps also show how additional, unanticipated research is continually carried out while modelling. This research is broadly described in the previous sections.

Generally speaking, the only tangible certainties are the temple foundations and the decorative elements of the roof. This give the dimensions of the stylobate: 20.40-21.05 x 33.90-33.80 m, the various dimensions of the terracotta plaques that protected the wooden structure and subsequently the minimal height of the wooden beams, the dimensions of the roof tiles, and the inclination of the roof of 11.4 degrees. This data, together with the background research, forms the starting point of the reconstruction of Temple II. All precise data such as dimensions and quantities, sources and provenance, and distance to sources can be found in Table 1.

*Step 1: Digitalisation of analogue data*
Digitising the ground plan of Mengarelli and the plans, sections and reconstruction drawings of De Waele in Adobe Illustrator and import these in the 3D modelling software Maxon Cinema4D R17 (*fig. 6a*).

*Step 2: Import of other data*
Import the modern orthophoto and 3D model[73] of the remains in Cinema4D and position and compare these with the drawings (*fig. 6b*).

*Step 3: Reconstruction of the landscape*
Produce a landscape to assess how the temple was situated in its surroundings. Import a digitised isoline map and reconstruct the landscape in 3D (*fig. 6c*).[74]

*Step 4: Assessment*
Analyse and compare the modern 3D model and orthophoto of the foundation walls with the reconstructed plans of De Waele: these and other reconstructions can now be tested. Further assessment of the ground plan and building phases is realised by comparative analysis of the phases proposed by E. Petersen, the drawings of Mengarelli and the sketches of Santangelo, and old photographs of the first excavations, supplemented by personal observations of the remains. This provided insights in the phasing of Temple II, which shall become clear in the coming steps.

*Step 5: Digitalisation of the terracottas*
Digitising the drawings of the terracotta elements made by Lulof and Knoop in Illustrator and import in Cinema4D. Produce basic 3D models of the terracotta elements with textures of the drawings. The most important part are their dimensions, in order to position them in the temple construction.

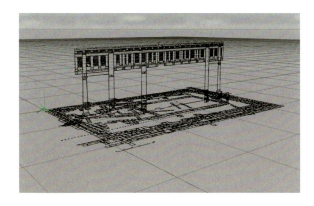

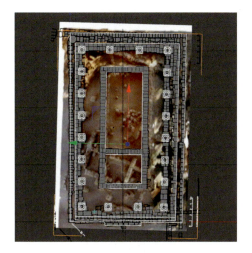

*Fig. 6a. The drawings of Mengarelli and De Waele were digitalised and imported into 3D modelling software Maxon Cinema4D; 6b. The orthophoto and 3D model of the temple remains are imported into Cinema4D as well; c. the original landscape is based on the map produced by Guaitoli (images L. Opgenhaffen, landscape based on Guaitoli 2003, pp. 283-287, fig. 519).*

- 5A. 3D scanning of the original material in the Museo Nazionale di Villa Giulia and virtually restore the antefixes where needed (*fig. 7*).

*Step 6: Modelling the foundation*
Modelling the individual blocks of the foundation and podium walls. The fill and floor level are simple cubes with a texture, but researched and reasoned in full detail in the process description. At certain locations the foundations and podium walls are reconstructed, especially around the foundations for the column bases. As the stylobate is warping a little (20.40-21.05 x 33.90-33.80 m), the possible starting point of measuring the temple perimeter could be determined. Assuming that the temple was aligned along the Via Sacra at the front, the departing point of calculation must have been at the west side. One would expect the least deviation in the beginning, and this would be the south side with a deviation of 7.85 degrees. The east side deviates 7.9 degrees and the north side 8.6 degrees, leading to the conclusion that the architect must have started measuring from the southwest angle of the stylobate.

*Step 7: Reconstructing columns*
Placement of the columns, based on the reconstruction drawing by De Waele, but carefully investigated if the remains of foundation blocks indeed correspond to 4 x 8 columns and research to available wood sources.[75] The intercolumniation was 3.80-3.85 m at the lateral sides, with the exception of the two intercolumniations at the western short side which measure ca. 4.40 m. The four columns at the short side had a different intercolumniation: in the centre the columns stood ca. 5.40 m apart and the outer columns ca. 4.60 m.

The foundations suggest a maximum width for the column basis of 1.26 m. The reconstruction of the column is not only based on De Waele is reconstruction, but also by additional research to contemporary representations of columns in other contexts, such as miniature architectural elements and terracotta temple votive offerings and Etruscan wall-paintings in tombs. Based on this information, a column can be reconstructed consisting of a square stone base with a torus on top (to prevent pests crawling under the shaft as well as water seeping under, causing rot and disintegration), supporting a shaft of holm oak of a diameter of ca. 1 m at the bottom and tapering to a diameter of 0.7 m at the top. The shaft itself is 4.24 m in height (*fig. 8*). Unknown is if the abacus and echinus are carved from the same tree trunk, so part of the shaft, or added separately.

*Fig. 7. 3D scan and virtual restoration of the Siren antefix (image L. Opgenhaffen).*

If added separately, this would decrease its stability and potential to bear the permanent load of the roof. The trunk of a holm oak can reach a diameter of 1-1.2 m and an average height of 6 m (of solid trunk). The total height of the reconstructed column including the base (0.37 m), echinus (0.23 m) and abacus (0.23 m) is 5.17 m.[76] Restricted by the affordances of holm oak, a greater height for a column is impossible. The dried weight of holm oak is 800 kg/m3, which means the column shaft had an approximate weight of ca. 2760 kg. This could explain the additional founding at the locations of the columns.[77]

Step 8: The reconstruction of the cella walls.
What material was used and how was this supported? The cella walls are an auxiliary support for the trusses that carried the roof construction. The cella walls were elevated from the podium level by at least two rows of tufa blocks.[78] It is impossible to say if the cella was erected entirely of tufa blocks. Mud-bricks, on the other hand, found on several other contemporary residential dwellings around the temple, were most probably used to build to cella walls. The mud-bricks were kept in place by a framework of wooden posts. The space between the square mud-bricks

*Fig. 8. Reconstruction process of the columns and the mudbricks. The space between the mud-bricks and rounded wooden posts is filled with daub (image L. Opgenhaffen).*

*Fig. 9. Reconstruction process of the roof structure (image L. Opgenhaffen).*

and the round posts would have been filled with daub to stabilise the construction (*fig. 8*). For the mud-bricks, size was reconstructed of 0.3 x 0.2 x 0.15 m,[79] which could fit in all irregular shaped cella and pronaos walls. The height is arbitrary but fits the reconstructed building module that De Waele calculated (3:2). A total amount of approximately 24,700 mud-bricks would have been required to erect the walls.[80] The width of the entrance and door-posts could at this point not be decided yet.

*Step 9: The reconstruction of the roof structure (fig. 9)*
- 9A. The beams of the roof construction could not be placed directly on the columns, because it would cause instability. Wooden wall-plates were positioned on top of the columns, varying in size from ca. 3.80 to 4.40 m long and 0.6 m thick. The thickness of the beams is derived from the revetment plaques and their nail-holes that covered the architrave, to which the wall-plates connected. The wall-plates did not receive terracotta protection because they were not directly threatened by weather conditions. The beams would have been from holm oak because of its natural resistance to humidity.
- 9B. On top of the wall-plates, eight trusses were positioned, directly above the columns.
- 9C. Small purlins are positioned on top of the principal rafters every 0.70 m and secured with lap joints, spanning a distance between 3.80 and 4.40 m. Jack rafters of pine are positioned on top of the purlins and fixed with lap joints, each separated the width of a roof tile.
- 9D. The lateral overhang to protect the substructure from weather conditions is provided by the elongation of the tie-beams of the trusses. The overhang projects ca. 1.35 m from the wall-plates.
- 9E. To create the overhang at the front and back of the temple, the wall-plates and purlins were elongated with 1.70 m at the front and ca. 1.40 at the back side.

*Step 10: The reconstruction of the recessed roof/fronton*
Many Archaic miniature votive temples demonstrate the presence of a recessed roof in the fronton. Also, a particular type of smaller antefixes of Silen and Juno Sospita heads is thought to have decorated the eaves of this recessed roof.[81] This requires a strong and stable construction. To this end, the wall-plates and purlins are elongated and connected to architraves, so as to form a triangle. The recessed roofs could only incline into the temple until the first truss. To carry the architrave and roof, two wooden beams are positioned on top of the two centre columns and wooden doorposts of the pronaos, firmly embedded into the architrave by lap joints. The weight of two trusses and the roof covering prevented the beams from tilting. Parallel to the outer trusses runs an extra beam. Between this beam and the architrave, planks are fixed to receive the roof tiles (*fig. 10*).[82] The inner, uppermost row of roof tiles lack two cover tiles because of the protruding *mutuli*. De Waele did not reconstruct a recessed roof at the back. However, to prevent the building from swerving due to un-even weight distribution, a shorter roof of two rows of roof tiles is reconstructed.[83] The frontons are closed by a light-weight construction of wattle-and-daub finished with stucco.

*Step 10A: The reconstruction of the columen and mutulus plaques*
Out of a tradition to build with enormous purlins and a need to support heavy ridge-statues and cantilevers, the light weight truss was the only option to divide the weight of these gigantic beams. Two beams of pine of ca. 15.5 m spanned the length of the temple. The *columen* measured at least W 1.25 x H 1.10 m, and the *mutuli* ca. W 1.10 m.[84] Two additional purlins are placed at the inside of the corners of the trusses. The purlins carry rafters at their ends, fixed by tenons and mortises.

*Step 11: Laying roof tiles*
The usual reconstruction to place the roof tiles is wooden sheeting of the entire roof, but sawing or cleaving wood for such an enormous surface was probably not desired. An economic solution of plaited mats smeared with daub was selected in modelling to stabilise the roof tiles. Plait work of reeds was a technique very well known in con-

*Fig. 10. The construction of the recessed roof. The large extended ridge-pole and purlins to carry the columen and mutulus plaques are also clearly visible (image L. Opgenhaffen).*

temporary house building with the wattle-and-daub method, and therefore a technique within reach.[85]

*Step 12: Installing the terracotta protective elements*
The 3D models of the terracottas in this reconstruction lack detailed relief for they only serve here to indicate the dimensions and nail-holes. For that reason, they are left as original coloured drawings. Some elements are left white because they are not published yet.
Restore virtually the 3D models of the scanned terracottas in Cinema4D and place the digital surrogates on the roof (*fig. 11*).

*Step 13: Creating the Level of Certainty model*
All the different elements in the reconstruction will receive a colour according to the Level of Certainty Index (LoC)[86] that was created along the guidelines of the London Charter to demonstrate the balance between actual remains, thorough study, and sheer imagination to fill the gaps (*fig. 12*).

4. Preliminary insights gained from the 3D reconstruction process

The virtual re-construction allowed to analyse the temple in its original surrounding in combination with on-site observation of the remains, and detailed comparative analysis of the previous proposed building phases, strongly indicate that Temple II underwent at least two building phases. The reconstruction process demonstrates that the original layout, say 'first phase' of Temple II, had a podium of 17.30 x 30 m. The disorderly positioning of the tufa blocks of varying sizes and reused blocks of older building phases,[87] together with the somewhat tapering ground plan, gives the impression that Temple II has been erected in a hurry.[88] Particularly the walls of the pronaos appear irregular as opposed to the more well-arranged walls of the cella and they do not seem to interconnect. This is an odd choice and a constructional disadvantage, and leads to the idea that the pronaos was constructed in a later stadium and that the temple initially possessed a second row of columns *in antis*, on the tufo lionato blocks at the entrance of the later pronaos.[89] There are a few examples of contemporary temples that testify to a presence of two extra columns in front of the cella: the temple of Torvaianica at Lavinium[90] and Temple B at Pyrgi. The peripteral layout of Temple II of Satricum is unique in Latium Vetus. Therefore, one might not look for parallels for double rows of columns in 'Tuscan' models, but in the southern equivalents of the Greeks. Here, double rows of columns in front of the cella is quite common.

In the 'second phase' Temple II was extended to the dimensions De Waele used, to 20.30 x 33 m. The two extra columns of the first building phase must have been started to tilt or sink due to the weight of the recessed roof in the fronton, and were subsequently replaced by a pronaos. The construction of the recessed roof was stabilised now by the solidity of the pronaos. The addition of the pronaos could have been part of a larger renovation plan that included the widening of the stylobate with additional rows of blocks,[91] on the north and south sides interpreted as gutters; the function of the massive extension on the east side remains unclear. After more than a century of research in Satricum, it seems that the first excavators were at least partly right in the phasing of the temple of Mater Matuta.

The presented methodology combining the *chaîne opératoire* approach with 3D reconstruction revealed that the un-Greek truss was applied in Satricum, however it has been suggested that Greek artists found their way to Satricum too.[92] The analysis of the construction practices so far, on the other hand, suggests that no Greek 'architect'[93] could have been responsible for the construction design of the temple, for they had little experience with building in wood, the huge lateral overhang and recessed roof in the frontons, ridge-pole statues and large *columen* and *mutulus* plaques, the type of foundation, or the truss. The columns however, do give it a Greek appearance, but not make a constructive difference; the columns could also have been made invisible in walls and subsequently called posts. Another insight obtained from the analysis of the step-by-step production is that indeed if the temple was built in a hurry, it could have been erected in only a few months by not that many people, opposing the idea of 'large controlled workforces by tyrannical rulers.'

5. The future of visualising the past

The detailed reconstruction of a temple carried out within the *chaîne opératoire* framework allows one to enter the previously intangible building site of the past, revealing how multiple craft communities and foreign workshops were organised and how they communicated about construction matters. Future comparative and in-depth analysis between these organisations and transfer of technology between communities on a larger scale, could ultimately help explain why Archaic religious architecture in Central Italy received their distinct appearance.

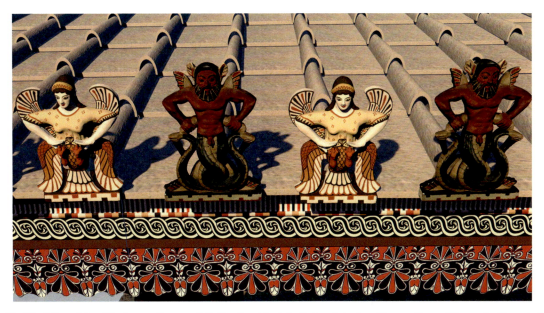

*Fig. 11. The 3D models of the terracottas are digitally placed back in their original position on the roof (image L. Opgenhaffen).*

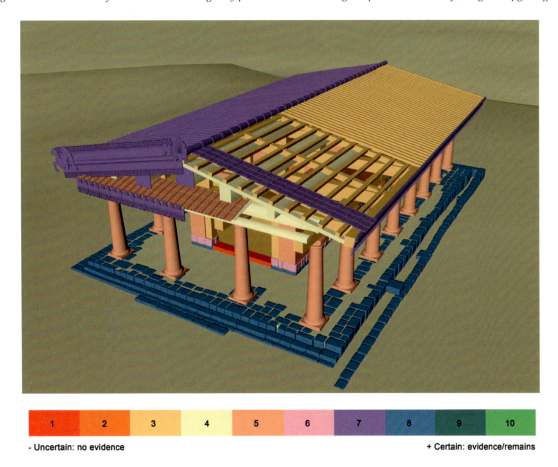

*Fig. 12. The Level of Certainty (LoC) model. Red is an educated guess, and green represents the actual remains, albeit digitally reproduced (image L. Opgenhaffen).*

205

| Construction element | Material | Amount | Dimensions (cm) | Total weight kg | Source/provenance | Distance |
|---|---|---|---|---|---|---|
| Tufa blocks | tufo lionato/bianco | 2401 | | 720300 | Satricum region | < 1 km |
| Foundation fill | clay (15%) with backfill | | 1012m3 | 2024640 | Satricum/Pontine region | <10 km |
| Columns | holm oak | 20 | 100-71x576 | 55200 | Pontine region | >10 km |
| Wall posts cella | fir | 13 | 60x60x448 | 1001 | Monti Lepini | >25km |
| Door posts cella | fir | 4 | 51x65x391 | 279 | Monti Lepini | >25km |
| Mud-bricks | loam | 24706 | 20x30x10 | 237177 | Satricum region | 3-7km |
| Wall plates cella long | fir | 4 | 32x30x2116 | 4384 | Monti Lepini | >25km |
| Wall plates cella short back | fir | 2 | 32x30x780 | 810 | | |
| Wall plates cella short pronaos | fir | 4 | 55x35x825 | 3434 | Monti Lepini | >25km |
| Wall plates | fir | 4 | 30x30x926 | 1794 | Monti Lepini | >25km |
| | fir | 4 | 30x30x1174 | 2290 | | |
| | fir | 4 | 30x30x1025 | 1987 | | |
| Beams fronton front | fir | 4 | 30x30x490 | 950 | Monti Lepini | >25km |
| Beams fronton back | fir | 4 | 30x30x630 | 1232 | Monti Lepini | >25km |
| Boards fronton | fir | 79 | 20x1x178 | 151 | Monti Lepini | >25km |
| Fronton architrave | fir | 2 | 16x15x1576 | 410 | Monti Lepini | >25km |
| Fronton support beam | fir | 2 | 48x30x1576 | 2452 | Monti Lepini | >25km |
| Connection beams | fir | 12 | 15x15x355 | 516 | Monti Lepini | >25km |
| Truss | fir | 8 | | | | |
| tie-beam | fir | 8 | 48x48x1961 | 17920 | Monti Lepini | >25km |
| rafter | fir | 16 | 24x24.5x850 | 4234 | Monti Lepini | >25km |
| rafter overhang | fir | 4 | 22x23x903 | 992 | | |
| Ridge-pole | fir | 2 | 109x100x1560 | 18360 | Monti Lepini | >25km |
| Mutulus big | fir | 4 | 100x88x1560 | 2964 | Monti Lepini | >25km |
| Mutulus small | fir | 4 | 50x56x1560 | 940 | Monti Lepini | >25km |
| Queen post | fir | 16 | 17x37x62 | 346 | Monti Lepini | >25km |
| King post | fir | 8 | 54.5x37x100 | 864 | Monti Lepini | >25km |
| Purlin | fir | 37 | 21x24x1570 | 15762 | Monti Lepini | >25km |
| Purlin lateral | fir | 4 | 38x38x1570 | 4904 | Monti Lepini | >25km |
| Jack rafter | fir | 132 | 15x15x1015 | 16368 | Monti Lepini | >25km |
| Pan tiles | terracotta | 2477 | 45-49.5x68.4-70 | 49540 | Lavinium | 40km |
| Cover tiles | terracotta | 2466 | 14-18x9-12x63 | 49320 | Lavinium | 40km |
| Kalypters | terracotta | 34 | 44x33x97 | 1190 | Lavinium | 40km |
| Sima blocks | terracotta | 60 | 37.5x68.5x5-8 | 1800 | Lavinium | 40km |
| Pedimental cresting | terracotta | 68 | 20x62x2.5-3 | 1020 | Lavinium | 40km |
| Anthemions raking | terracotta | 60 | 59.5x64x2.5-3 | 1200 | Lavinium | 40km |
| Revetments architrave | terracotta | 50 | 55x63.5x5x3 | 750 | Lavinium | 40km |
| Lateral revetments | terracotta | 92 | 64x59.5x2.5-3 | 1840 | Lavinium | 40km |
| Columen and mutulus plaques | terracotta | 6 | | 380* | | |
| Antefixes | terracotta | 138 | | 2760* | | |
| Acroteria | terracotta | 5 | | 150* | | |
| Ridge-pole statues | terracotta | 6 | | 300* | | |
| Total weight on the foundations, trusses and columns | | | | 168160 | | |

*Table 1. Data on building materials and their dimensions, quantities, sources and distance to sources. * Clay source from Lavinium, but probably produced locally by a foreign workshop.*

The 3D reconstruction of Temple II is still under development; some of the new insights such as the columns *in antis* of the first phase, have yet to be processed into the model. Due to the fluid, flexible and momentary nature of 3D modelling as data-structuring research tool, the 3D reconstruction should be continuously adjusted and updated according the latest insights and standards.[94] Therefore, a scientific 3D model is never finished but is always subject to change and scientific progress.

The process of modelling Temple II in 3D did not produce new data by itself, instead its greatest power resides in its ability to structure extensive heterogeneous datasets and guide the reasoning process during research. 3D modelling as a tool during research forces the archaeologist to keep searching for additional evidence, parallels and explanations to connect the present remains with past practice. Therefore, this completely new way of technological analysis in combination with innovative 3D technology enables to materialise buildings from the past and to socialise old technology and practices, hence peopling the past.

Notes

[*] I wish to express my gratitude to Prof. M. Gnade and M. Revello Lami for inviting me to present and publish this project on the Tracing Technology conference. I also thank my supervisor Dr J.R. Hilditch and esteemed colleague Dr C.J. Jeffra for not alone the proof reading, but also their support to realise this paper.
[1] This paper therefore deliberately omits historical sources for explanations that were written in a later stage and which may obfuscate the analysis of what is actually in front of us - unless they inform about materials and building practices.
[2] Audouze 2002, 287.
[3] Waarsenburg 1998, 59.
[4] See Gnade infra.
[5] The first rectangular structure with stone foundations and tiled roof. The Roman numbering of the three successive building phases of the temple was agreed upon at the conference in Rome in 1992 on the occasion of 25 years of excavation in Satricum (*MededRom* 52, 1992). For the phasing and various dating proposals for the temples, see *Satricum* 2007, 32-36.
[6] See also Gnade infra.
[7] Gnade kindly shared these drawings with me.
[8] Gnade 2017.
[9] A selection: Lulof 1993, 1996, 1997, 2006; Knoop 1987; Lulof and Knoop 2007 and forthcoming.
[10] Ratto 2006.
[11] Over a decade later, however, Lulof started a new project, 'The Art of Reconstruction', in which she successfully integrated 3D modelling into archaeological research (Lulof, Opgenhaffen and Sepers 2013). This became the pilot project of the 4D Research Lab of the University of Amsterdam, which she directs.
[12] Lulof and Opgenhaffen in press. The interpretation of the terracotta roof decoration and proposal for a second phase of Temple 0 stems entirely from Lulof. The author is responsible for the creation of the 3D models as well as research to construction methods and building materials.
[13] I am in indebted to Patricia Lulof and Riemer Knoop, who kindly shared the draft manuscript comprising all architectural terracottas and their reconstructions. With the manuscript, I could look for technological clues about the wooden construction which the terracottas once protected.
[14] With a few exceptions of course: Cifani (2008, 2010) carried out extensive research to early Roman and Latin architecture, but not from a truly technological perspective. Also, Winter (2009) provided some details about the production of roof tiles.
[15] Kamermans 2000, 135. Joolen (2003) mentions that the deforestation of the oak forest began before 400 BC.
[16] Joolen (2003) mentions that the *quercus coccifera* from the foothills vanishes vastly from the Archaic period as a consequence of use as fuel and building material. The latter is an unlikely option since the *coccifera* is not more than a shrub of a few meters tall.
[17] HP 5.7.4-5, in Meiggs 1982, 443.
[18] Many fragments of wattle-and daub, that is secondary fired lumps of daub with imprints of wooden poles and reeds, are encountered during recent excavations in the lower city area of Satricum (belonging to late Archaic contexts); see Gnade infra.
[19] Revello Lami 2017, 401.
[20] Reeds growing along present-day Astura were compared with the archaeological remains and matched the imprints.
[21] Kamermans 1991.
[22] Relatively little evidence for mud-brick building is found in Satricum, except for a burnt mud-brick attributed to a late 6th century BC structure and a concentration of burnt/baked mud-bricks found in trench 340/333 (Gnade infra). Both Mengarelli and Santangelo suggested a superstructure of mud-bricks (see note 29). Cifani (2008) remarks that there is only scant evidence for mud-bricks in Rome, aside from the abundant presence of mud-bricks on the podium of the Temple of the Dioscouri. The Archaic temple of San Omobono in Rome was built with mud-brick as well (Brocato *et al.* 2016). Elsewhere in Etruria, such as Pyrgi, Rosellae and Veii, mud-bricks measuring 31-33x41-46x7-8 cm are found (Belelli Marchesini infra; Cifani 2008, 244).
[23] Minke 2006, 65; Houben 1990.
[24] http://www.joostdevree.nl/shtmls/leem.shtml (accessed 10 February 2019).
[25] Minke 2006, 62.
[26] Minke 2006, 28; Cifani 2008, 245.
[27] Minke 2006, 62-63.
[28] Under stylobate the entire platform is understood and shall be referred to as such throughout the remainder of the paper.
[29] Santangelo noticed a clayey layer on top of the *terra vergine* that, according to her, was from collapsed walls of the older temple. This clayey layer was later interpreted by Dutch archaeologists as belonging to the levelling layer for the construction of Temple I (Waarsenburg 1998, 107; De Waele 1981, 20, 22).
[30] Cifani 2008, 245. There are no traces of pavement left in Temple II, but in the notes and sketches of Mengarelli at least two pavement layers were identified in

the cella. Unfortunately, the sketch was not accompanied by a description of the composition of the layer. Elsewhere in Satricum (in PdCII, field 3), floor levels similar to the description of Cifani, attributed to the Archaic period, were identified.
31 Revello Lami 2017, 401.
32 Maaskant-Kleibrink 1987, 34-35.
33 The podium walls are the outer walls directly supporting the columns. The most outer rows of blocks flanking those walls on the outside are not attributed to the original ground plan of the temple.
34 Bernard 2012, 10.
35 See for an excellent overview of early lifting technology: Belelli Marchesini infra.
36 Belelli Marchesini infra; Bernard 2012, 103. Bernard proposes that the blocks must have been positioned using earthen ramps, for which evidence has been found in the Archaic layers of the San Omobono excavations (Bernard 2013, 100), but such evidence lacks for Temple II of Satricum.
37 Colonna 2005, 112.
38 These blocks are attributed to the monument of the Lapis Satricanus. Stibbe, in Stibbe *et al.* 1980, 29.
39 Incisions, although mostly present on blocks of earlier phases, may cautiously be identified as building marks. In two specific blocks from Temple I, are carved rows of horizontal lines crossed by a single vertical line. These may inform us about building practices but more research is necessary to confirm this.
40 The average dimensions of the blocks measure ca. 75 x 50 cm, the largest ca. 60 x 90 cm.
41 De Waele 1981.
42 Examples of this type of foundation are the Temple of Jupiter Optimus Capitolinus (Rome), Pyrgi temple B, Velletri, Piazza d'Armi (Veii).
43 More research has to be done to support his notion. Parallels of this type of foundation are the temples of Torvaianica and Iuno Sospita in Lavinium and Le Salzare in Ardea.
44 Hodge 1960, what he called 'Gaggera'-roofs; Klein 1998.
45 Meiggs 1982, 227; MacIntosh Turfa 2000, 113.
46 The Orientalizing Complex Building 2/Workshop (Winter 2009, 505) and the Upper Building (Hopkins 2010, 23). MacIntosh Turfa (2000, 113) makes an interesting suggestion that the origin of the truss may have derived from Etruscan ship-building.
47 Hopkins 2010, 21-26, for a concise discussion on the presence or absence of the truss in Archaic Central Italy, with bibliography.
48 Belelli Marchesini infra, for the building techniques applied to Temple B; Ulrich 2007, 133.
49 Hopkins 2010, 23.
50 Meiggs 1980, 348, 435.
51 Lulof 2016, 338; Winter 2009, 510, as common practice.
52 This has been suggested by MacIntosh Turfa 2000.
53 Polzer 2011, 366.
54 Hodge 1960.
55 Hodge 1960; Adam 1984; Ulrich 2007, 62-63;
56 Lulof 2016; Knoop and Lulof 2007, 41.
57 The actual production was located probably at the periphery of the town instead at the building site itself, as Nijboer suggests for the pottery workshops (1998, 194-195). Lack of space on the acropolis in Satricum caused a problem too: the temple is cramped between the processual road and residential buildings, preventing on-site production.

58 Class 18.1-4 of Lulof and Knoop forthcoming.
59 Ö. Wikander 1993, 27-28; Winter 2009, 513. Experimental reproduction and analysis of macrotraces could give a decisive answer. The huge variation in raised border types, which is not atypical in pan tile production (Meyers, Jackson and Galloway 2010, 311), on the other hand, suggests manual assembling.
60 Winter 2009, 513.
61 It has been observed that the same fabric used in the production of roof tiles, was also used to produce large ceramic vessels such as mortaria (*impasto sabbioso chiara*), which is believed to have been produced locally using the same large kilns (Winter 2009, 525). The use of local clay but stylistically distinct rendering of the terracotta decorative elements were produced locally as well, albeit by non-local, perhaps Greek, travelling workshops (Lulof 2016, 336; Strazzulla 2011, 32; also Winter 2005, 250).
62 The exact sloping angle of the roof is known because fragments of these cut apex pieces are found in Satricum (Knoop 1997; Knoop 2018, 17).
63 Cooper 2008, 240: when positioned between 11 and 27 degrees, roof tiles could stabilize themselves. Damgaard Andersen goes even further and demonstrated experimentally that roof tiles stayed in place until 30 degrees (2001, 255).
64 Winter 2009, 530.
65 Winter 2009, 530.
66 Ö. Wikander 1993, 125-126. Wikander documented 30% of the tiles to be chipped.
67 Meyers, Jackson and Galloway 2010, 315.
68 Sapirstein 2008, 313-314. Sapirstein's doctoral research on the emergence of ceramic roof tiles in Archaic Greece revealed that '[i]f the tiles were laid directly on the rafters, a moveable wooden platform would have been required to support the workmen as they tailored the tiles on the roof. However, a solid decking over the rafters would have made the job much easier, and the tiles might have been securely supported on a bed of unfired clay.' The clay bed would furthermore absorb much of the blows of the nicking of the pan tiles on the spot. The author found some indication of chipped corners of pan and cover tiles, but additional research is needed to confirm this practice. The clay was smeared on reed mats attached to the jack rafters.
69 Earl 2013; Dallas 2015. The author is aware of the Extended Matrix (EM), developed by Emanuel Demetrescu (2018). The EM is a stratigraphic approach that is exactly designed for this purpose: a system that documents the scientific process while acknowledging the role of the visualizer in this process as well. However, the EM was launched after the author started with the reconstruction of Temple II in 2016 and its presentation on the Tracing Technology conference.
70 Ryan 2001; Denard 2012; Huvila 2012; Bentkowska-Kafel *et al.* (eds.) 2012; Bentkowska-Kafel 2013; Apollonio 2015; Demetrescu 2018.
71 For a general overview of projects that tried, see Von Schwerin *et al.* 2016 and for successful projects: Noordegraaf *et al.* 2016; Piccoli and Huurdeman in press..
72 Increasingly the use of heritage 3D visualisation is broadly considered as such (Hermon 2008; Bentkowska-Kafel 2013, 41; also Beale and Reilly 2017).
73 Produced by Jitte Waagen, with a UAV with go-pro camera, 3D model reconstructed with Agisoft Photoscan.
74 The author is aware that modern LiDAR data is freely available (cf. García and Waagen this volume), but

75 since Temple II is modelled in its original environment, the reconstructed landscape of Guaitoli 2003, pp. 283-287, fig. 519, was preferred.
75 De Waele and many others rely on Vitruvius' formula. This use should be reconsidered as it was designed almost half a millennium later than Satricum's Temple II, for a Tuscan temple. Availability and affordance of building material should instead form the starting point.
76 Van 't Lindenhout (2010, 131) suggested a height of ca. 7 m based on the reconstruction drawing of De Waele (1981, Folio 15 and 17). This is an incorrect calculation. In the present reconstruction the digitised drawings were imported in Cinema4D and set scale 1:1. The columns of De Waele must have been ca. 5.20 m, just as they are in the present reconstruction.
77 A freshly felled oak however, was far heavier and not yet fully processed, having an estimated weight of 3800-4000 kg. An ox (they were smaller before the Middle Ages) can pull two times this weight, which is about 750 kg. To move one oak from the Pontine region to Satricum a team of 6 oxen would have been required. Important to keep in mind though, is that timber needs to season for at least one year before it can be safely as building material. This suggests that specialised logging existed in the Archaic period. It does not lie within the scope of this paper to elaborate in great detail about energy expenditure of materials and construction techniques, but to stress the possibility of the wide range of crafts and labour involved in an ancient building project, and the level of detail one can reach through the application of the *chaîne opératoire* approach combined with 3D modelling, the example is given for the columns and mud-bricks (see below and note 80).
78 Van 't Lindenhout (2010, 129) reconstructs at least three rows of blocks rising from the podium, which is simply not the case; the blocks are protruding only 1.5-2 blocks above the level of the podium. This is also visible on De Waele's section drawings and reconstructions.
79 Based on a mud-brick fragment measuring W 0.21 x H 0.15 m (min. L 0.23) and other large fragments found in the lower settlement area (PdCII), see note 24. The blocks of the walls in the lower settlement area are of the same type as the those of Temple II (Gnade 2002, 10). Ethno-archaeology and modern mud-brick production indicate similar dimensions. Elsewhere in Satricum (cf. Gnade 2007, 129. Inv. nos. 222-224) mud-bricks are even smaller. The mud-brick from PdCII and the reconstructed dimensions fit perfectly on the cella walls of Temple II.
80 One person alone could produce ca. 300 mud-bricks a day (Minke 2006, 62-63). One person could then produce enough bricks in 83 days. One may expect that a small workshop of 5-8 people could produce the required amount of bricks in 7-10 days.
81 Class 20.1 and 20.2 of Lulof and Knoop forthcoming.
82 99 pan tiles and 93 cover tiles in three rows and 32 antefixes.
83 66 pan tiles and 61 cover tiles in two rows and 32 antefixes.
84 Class 19 of Lulof and Knoop forthcoming.
85 A similarity between daub and Roman roof building material can be identified, where a layer of mortar was applied to stabilise the roof tiles. On the placement of the rooftiles itself see note 69.
86 This LoC index was developed and published by the author in Noordegraaf et al. 2016.
87 Gnade (2017: 252) calculated that ca. 500 white tufa blocks from Temple 1 were reused, and ca. 1500 new blocks of brown-red tufa were quarried.
88 Also observed by Gnade 2017. Rendeli (1989), who suggests rivalry and competition between local communities as an explanation for hastily erected edifices in this period of time.
89 Already observed by Barnabei in 1896, but dismissed by Petersen (1896, 166) and De Waele (1981, 19, 39).
90 Ceccarelli and Marroni 2011, 243.
91 Lulof and Knoop (forthcoming) found a small amount of deviating types of terracotta architectural plaques and antefixes, pointing to these further renovations, as possible replacements for restored or altered parts with different beam sizes.
92 Lulof 2016 mentions Greek architects and itinerant foreign, possibly Greek, workshops.
93 Strazzulla (2011) also refers to itinerant workshops, but from the surroundings of Rome (possibly led by Greek coroplasts); Winter (2005, 250) on the other hand suggests that workshops in Veii, Cerveteri and Campania were commissioned by Tarquinius Superbus, who might also have been responsible for the building of Temple II at Satricum. However, Winter points out at the same time that '… the special character of the Etruscan roofs […] has nothing to do with Greek architectural traditions.'
94 Hodder 1997.

BIBLIOGRAPHY

Adam, J. 1984, *La construction romaine: Matériaux et techniques*, Paris.

Apollonio, F.I./E.C. Giovannini 2015, A paradata documentation methodology for the uncertainty visualization in digital reconstruction of CH artifacts, *Scires.it*, 5 (1), 1-24.

Audouze, F. 2002, Leroi-Gourhan, a philosopher of technique and evolution, *JArchaeolRes* 10 (4), 277-306.

Barnabei, F./A. Cozza 1896, Conca. Nuove scoperte dell'area dell'antico tempio presso le Ferriere, dove si pone la sede della città di Satricum, *NSc*, 23-48.

Barnabei, F.R. Mengarelli 1896, Conca. Nuovi scavi nel tempio satricano di Mater Matuta scoperta sulla colina presso le Ferriere di Conca, *NSc*, 190-200.

Beale, G./P. Reilly 2017, After virtual archaeology: Rethinking archaeological approaches to the adoption of digital technology, *Internet Archaeology*, (44,

Bentkowska-Kafel, A. 2012, Processual scholia: The importance of paradata in heritage visualization, in A. Bentkowska-Kafel et al., *Paradata and transparency in virtual heritage. Digital research in the arts and humanities*, Farnham, 245-260.

Bentkowska-Kafel, A. 2013, I bought a piece of Roman furniture on the internet. It's quite good but low on polygons. Digital visualization of cultural heritage and its scholarly value in art history, *Visual Resources* 29 (1-2), 38-46.

Bernard, S.G. 2013, The transport of heavy loads in Antiquity: Lifting, moving, and building in ancient Rome, in S. Altekamp et al., *Perspektiven der Spolienforschung* 1. *Spoliierung und Transposition* (Topoi. Berlin Studies of the ancient world 15), Berlin/Boston, 99-122.

Bernard, S.G. 2012, Continuing the debate on Rome's earliest circuit walls, *BSR* 80, 1-44.

Boëthius, A./J.B. Ward-Perkins 1970, *Etruscan and Roman Architecture*, Harmondsworth.

Brocato, P./M. Ceci/N. Terrenato 2016, *Richerce nell'area dei templi di Fortuna e Mater Matuta* (Roma, Ricerche – Collana del Dipartimento di Studi Umanistici, Sezione Archeologia, 10), Arcavacata.

Ceccarelli, L./E. Marroni 2011, *Repertorio dei santuari del Lazio*, Roma.

Cifani, G. 2008, *Architettura romana arcaica: Edilizia e società tra monarchia e repubblica*, Roma.

Cifani, G. 2010, I grandi cantieri della Roma arcaica: Aspetti tecnici e organizzativi, in G. Camporeale et al., *Arqueología de la construcción II. Los procesos constructivos en el mundo romano: Italia y provincias orientales, Siena 2008* (Anejos de archivo español de arqueología 57), Madrid/Mérida, 35-49.

Colonna, G. 2005, Tra architettura e urbanistica. A proposito del tempio di Mater Matuta a Satricum, in S.T A.M. Mols/E.M. Moormann (eds.), *Omni pede stare: Saggi architettonici e circumvesuviani in memoriam Jos de Waele*, Napels, 111-117.

Cooper, F.A. 2012, *Greek engineering and construction*, Oxford.

Courty, M.-A./V. Roux 1995, Identification of wheel throwing on the basis of ceramic surface features and microfabrics. *JAS* 22, 17-50.

Dallas, C. 2015, Curating archaeological knowledge in the digital continuum: From practice to infrastructure, *Open Archaeology* 1(1), 176-207.

Damgaard Andersen, H. 2001, Thatched or tiled roofs from the early iron age to the Archaic period in Central Italy, in J. L. Rasmus Brandt et al. (eds.), *From huts to houses: Transformations of ancient societies*. Proceedings of an international seminar organized by the Norwegian and Swedish institutes in Rome, 21-24 September 1997, Stockholm, 245-262.

Demetrescu, E. 2018, Virtual reconstruction as a scientific tool: The Extended Matrix and source-based modelling approach, in S. Münster et al., *Digital Research and Education in Architectural Heritage*. 5th Conference, DECH 2017, and First Workshop, UHDL 2017, Dresden, Germany, March 30-31, 2017, Cham, 102-116.

Denard, H. 2012, A new introduction to the London Charter, in A. Bentkowska-Kafel et al., *Paradata and transparency in virtual heritage*, London, 57-71.

Earl, G. 2013, Modelling in Archaeology: Computer Graphic and other Digital Pasts, *Perspectives on Science* 21(2), 226-244.

Gnade, M. 2002, *Satricum in the post-archaic period: A case study of the interpretation of archaeological remains as indicators of ethno-cultural identity*, Leuven.

Gnade, M. 2007, *Satricum: Trenta anni di scavi olandesi*, Amsterdam.

Gnade, M. 2017, Satricum nel periodo di Tarquinio Superbo: Cambiando prospettiva, in P.S. Lulof/C. Smith (eds.), *Proceedings Of The Conference The Age of Tarquinius Superbus: A Paradigm Shift? Rome, 7-9 November, 2013*, Leuven, 249-258.

Gosselain, O.P. 1992, Technology and style: Potters and pottery among Bafia of Cameroon, *Man* 27 (3), 559-586.

Guaitoli, M. 2003, Satricum, in M. Guaitoli (ed.), *Lo sguardo di icaro: Le collezioni dell'aerofototeca nazionale per la conoscenza del territorio*, Rome, 283-287.

Hermon, S. 2008, Reasoning in 3D: A critical appraisal of the role of 3D modelling and virtual reconstructions in archaeology, in B. Frischer/A. Dakouri-Hild (eds.), *Beyond illustration: 2D and 3D digital technologies as tools for discovery in archaeology*, Oxford, 35-44.

Hesiod: R.S. Hamilton 1988, *Hesiod, Works and Days*, Bryn Mawr.

Hodge, A.T. 1960, *The woodwork of Greek roofs*, Cambridge.

Hopkins, J.N. 2010, The colossal temple of Jupiter Optimus Maximus in Archaic Rome, in G. Camporeale et al., *Arqueología de la Construcción* II, Madrid-Mérida, 15-33.

Hopkins, J.N. 2012, The Capitoline temple and the effects of monumentality on Roman temple design, in M.L. Thomas/G.E. Meyers (eds.), *Monumentality in Etruscan and early roman architecture. ideology and innovation*, Austin, 111-138.

Huvila, I. 2012, The unbearable complexity of documenting intellectual processes: Paradata and virtual cultural heritage visualisation, *Humanit* 12 (1), 97-110.

Kamermans, H./A. Voorrips/S.H. Loving/H. Kamermans 1991, *Faulted land: The geology of the Agro Pontino*, Amsterdam.

Klein, N. 1998, Evidence for West Greek influence on mainland Greek roof construction and the creation of the truss in the Archaic period, *Hesperia* 67, 335-374.

Knoop, R.R. 1987, *Antefixa Satricana: Sixth-century architectural terracottas from the sanctuary of Mater Matuta at Satricum (Le Ferriere)*, Assen.

Knoop, R.R. 1997, The Satricum corpus of architectural terracottas, in P.S. Lulof/E.M. Moormann, *Deliciae Fictiles II: Proceedings of the second international conference on archaic architectural terracottas from Italy, held at the Netherlands Institute in Rome, 12-13 June 1996*, Amsterdam, 113-122.

Knoop, R.R. 2018, Ich bau dir ein Schloss. *Satricum Nieuwsbrief* 24 (1), 16-18.

Knoop, R.R./P.S. Lulof 2007, L'architettura templare, in Gnade 2007, 32-42.

Lulof, P.S. 1993, Reconstruction and architectural setting of large terracotta statues in Late Archaic Central Italy, in Rystedt, E., Wikander, Ch., Wikander, Ö. (1993, *Deliciae Fictiles: Proceedings of the first international conference on Central Italic architectural terracottas at the Swedish Institute in Rome, 10-12 December 1990*. Skrifter utgivna av Svenska Institutet i Rom. Stockholm: Åström, 277-286.

Lulof, P. S. 1996, *The ridge-pole statues from the late archaic temple at Satricum*. Amsterdam: Thesis Publishers.

Lulof, P. S. 1997, Myths from Greece. The representation of power on the roofs of Satricum. *MededRom*, 56, 85-114.

Lulof, P. S. 2006, Roofs from the South. Campanian architectural terracottas in Satricum. Edlund-Berry, I., & Greco, G. (Eds., *Deliciae Fictiles III: Architectural terracottas in ancient Italy: New discoveries and interpretations: Proceedings of the international conference held at the American academy in Rome, November 7-8, 2002*. Oxford: Oxbow Books, 235-242.

Lulof, P. S. 2010, Manufacture and reconstruction, in D. Palombi, *Il tempio arcaico di Caprifico di Torrecchia (Cisterna di Latina): i materiali e il contesto*, Rome, 79-111.

Lulof, P.S. 2016, Networks and Workshops. Construction of temples at the dawn of the Roman Republic, *AEspA* 77, 331-342.

Lulof, P.S./R.R. Knoop forthcoming, *Three central-italic roof-systems. Architectural terracottas from the sanctuary of Mater Matuta at Satricum*.

Lulof, P.S./L. Opgenhaffen in press, Connecting Foundations and Roofs: The Satricum Sacellum and the Sant'Omobono Sanctuary, in C. Potts (ed.), *Custom Made: The Connected World of Central Italic Architecture*, Cambridge University Press.

Lulof, P.S./L. Opgenhaffen/M.H. Sepers 2013, The Art of Reconstruction. Documenting the process of 3D modeling: Some preliminary results, in A.C. Addison et al., *Proceedings of the 2013 Digital Heritage International Congress (DigitalHeritage)* 1, Marseille, 333-337.

Maaskant-Kleibrink, M. 1987, *Settlement excavations at Borgo Le Ferriere "Satricum"* 1. *The campaigns 1979, 1980, 1981*, Groningen.

Macintosh Turfa, J. 2000, The Technology of Wooden Structures: Etruscan Temples and Shipbuilding, *EtrSt* 7(1), 113-116.

Meiggs, R. 1982, *Trees and Timber in the Ancient Mediterranean World*, Oxford.

Meyers, G.E./L.M. Jackson/J. Galloway 2010, The production and usage of non-decorated Etruscan roof-tiles, based on a case study at Poggio Colla, *JRA* 23, 303-319.

Minke, G. 2006, *Building with earth. Design and technology of a sustainable architecture*, Basel.

Nijboer, A.J. 1998, *From household production to workshops: Archaeological evidence for economic transformations, premonetary exchange and urbanisation in Central Italy from 800 to 400 BC*, PhD dissertation, University of Groningen.

Noordegraaf, J./L. Opgenhaffen/N. Bakker 2016, Cinema Parisien 3D: 3D visualisation as a tool for the history of cinemagoing, *Alphaville* (11), 45-61.

Petersen, E. 1896, Funde. *RM* 11, 157-184.

Piccoli, C./H.C. Huurdeman in press, *3D Reconstructions as Research Hubs: Geospatial Interfaces for Real-Time Data Exploration of 17th-Century Amsterdam Domestic Interiors*, Open Archaeology.

Polzer, M.E. 2011, Early Shipbuilding in the Eastern Mediterranean, in A. Catsambis et al., *The Oxford Handbook of Maritime Archaeology*, Oxford, 349-378.

Ratto, M. 2006, Epistemic commitments and archaeological representation, in L. Oosterbeek/J. Raposo (eds.), *Proceedings of the International Union for Prehistoric and Protohistoric Sciences XV*, (*Lisbon, 4-9 September*) 1, Oxford (available on https://www.researchgate.net/publication/236000195_Epistemic_commitments_and_archaeological_representation)

Rendeli, M. 1989, "Muratori ho fretta di erigere questa casa" (Ant. Pal. 14, 136, Concorrenza tra formazioni urbane dell'Italia centrale tirrenica nella construzione di edifici di culto arcaici, *RIA* n.s., 12, 49-68.

Revello Lami, M. 2017, Evidenze dirette, indirette, o circostanziali? La produzione ceramica a Satricum durante il periodo arcaico tra topografia e archeometria, in R. Biella et al., *Gli artigiani e la città. Officine e aree produttive tra VIII e III sec. a.C. nell'Italia centrale tirrenica*, Rome, 389–412.

Roux, V. (2003, A dynamic systems framework for studying technological change: Application to the emergence of the potter's wheel in the southern levant, *JArchaeolMethod Th* 10(1), 1-30.

Roux, V./D. Corbetta 1989, *The potter's wheel: Craft specialization and technical competence*, New Delhi.

Ryan, N. 2001, Documenting and validation virtual archaeology, *Archeologia e Calcolatori* 12, 254-273.

Sapirstein, P. 2008, *The emergence of ceramic roof tiles in Archaic Greek architecture*. PhD dissertation, Cornell University.

Stibbe, C.M. (ed.) 1980, *Lapis Satricanus: Archaeological, epigraphical, linguistic and historical aspects of the new inscription from Satricum*, The Hague.

Strazzulla, M.J. 2011, Gli altorilievi tardo arcaici tra Roma e Lazio, in P.S. Lulof/C. Rescigno (eds.), *Deliciae Fictiles IV. Images of Gods, Monsters and Heroes*. Proceedings of the Fourth International Conference on Architectural Terracottas from Ancient Italy (Rome, Syracuse, 21-25 October 2009, Oxford, 32-44.

Turfa, J.M./A.G. Steinmayer 1996, The comparative structure of Greek and Etruscan monumental buildings, *BSR* 64, 1-39.

Ulrich, R.B. 2007, *Roman Woodworking*, New Haven.

Van Joolen, E. 2003, *Archaeological land evaluation: A reconstruction of the suitability of ancient landscapes for various land uses in Italy focused on the first millennium BC*. Unpublished PhD dissertation, University of Groningen.

Van 't Lindenhout, E. 2010, *Bouwen in Latium in de archaïsche periode*. PhD dissertation, University of Groningen.

Waarsenburg, D.J. 1998, *Satricum. Cronaca di uno scavo*. Rome.

Waele, J.A.K.E. 1981, I templi della Mater Matuta a Satricum, *MededRom* 43, 7-68.

Waele, J.A.K.E. 1997, Cronologia ed architettura dei templi della Mater Matuta di Satricum, *MededRom* 56, 69-84.

Wikander, O. 1993, *Acquarossa VI.2: The roof-tiles. Typology and technical features* (Skrifter utgivna av Svenska Institutet i Rom 4, 38, 6.2), Stockholm.

Winter, N.A. 2005, Gods walking on the roof: The evolution of terracotta statuary in Archaic Etruscan architecture in light of the kings of Rome, *JRA* 18, 241-251.

Winter, N. A. 2009, *Symbols of Wealth and Power: Architectural terracotta decoration in Etruria and Central Italy, 640-510 B.C*, Ann Arbor.

# Built environment in Satricum
## *Tracing technology and Archaic society using Remote Sensing tools*

*Jesús García Sánchez, Jitte Waagen*

*Abstract*

*The aim of this paper is to bring forward new geospatial and remote sensing methods that are available for archaeological research, but have been only rarely applied to the research on Archaic cities and their landscapes in the Latium Vetus. We will focus chiefly on the recently available LiDAR (Light Detection and Ranging-Airborne laser scanner) data and its combination with other tools as Low Altitude UAS Photogrammetry (LAUP) and historical aerial imagery. We rely on the capabilities of remote sensing methods to enhance the understanding of known sites and the social use of the ancient landscape. One of the main points we want to raise is the possibility of applying these techniques to generate insights on ancient technology, manmade interventions in the landscape, and the social implications beyond the construction of site features (walls, trenches, urbanism) and the appropriation of landscape.*

INTRODUCTION

The study of Airborne Laser Scanner or LiDAR is not a new archaeological technique.[1] Research conducted in several Italian archaeological regions and on various sites have demonstrated the capabilities of this technology and its impact in archaeological projects oriented on scales of both landscape and site. The publicly available Italian data has largely contributed to projects with a strong interest in landscape dynamics, human interaction in the environment and particularly, and more important to the scope of this paper, to the traceability of ancient technology using the most up-to-date techniques.

The aim of this paper is to highlight how ancient technology has left a persistent imprint in the present-day landscape and how modern archaeological methods are capable of tracking down this footprint using geospatial methods of remote sensing, a mature discipline in Mediterranean and Landscape Archaeology. Going beyond the modern debate on the capabilities of digital archaeology,[2] we would like stimulate the discussion on how these digital approaches are capable of shedding light on the social agency behind the detected archaeological features and ancient enterprises of landscape modification. Thus, we should ask ourselves about the type of empirical data we are currently creating in a massive way and how to connect increasingly large datasets to new interpretative frameworks of such data, at the threshold of "big data" in archaeology.

Social agency is driven by forces within a particular ancient society in which the social organization and engagement with technology is fundamental.[3] One of the most appealing cases where social agency at a large scale can be seen is when environment has to be adapted to specific requirements of a given human group. This social agency in the landscape could be ephemeral or long lasting, but in all the cases the effect of application of knowledge and technology could be seen in a variety of forms, from construction techniques, to the material culture and the settlement patterns of such societies. Archaeological enquiries on technology has often lead to evolutionary and diffusionist paradigms; and more recently to post-colonial approaches to knowledge-transfer which stresses the role of indigenous societies without oversight the importance of early Mediterranean colonialism in the spread of technics, technologies and technicians. One of the most relevant cases of technological improvement is the so-called Mediterranean connectivity, which highlights the role of overseas cultural contact beyond mere economical schemes without neglecting the role of indigenous communities in Central and Western Mediterranean in the interpretation and appropriation of Eastern Mediterranean architectural and decorative programs, often linked also with religion and ideology.[4]

In line with the publication of the Proceedings of the conference celebrating the 40th anniversary of Dutch excavations in *Satricum* we want to reflect on the usefulness of new geospatial and remote sensing data to understand Archaic technological evolution, social agency involved in the building programme of *Satricum* and the relevance of Airbone Laser Scanner– LiDAR in the improvement of archaeological knowledge about the city and its landscape.

First, we will contextualize the LiDAR approach to landscape research in *Satricum* within the research framework in Italy, explaining briefly the history and the provenance of such new datasets and the most recent research done with it, highlighting the link of modern and ancient technology. Secondly, we will present the latest work done in the field of remote sensing in *Satricum* and its very surroundings, emphasising potential and limitations, as well as including insights of forthcoming digital work to promote local heritage.

AIRBORNE AND LASER SCANNER IN ITALY

As presented recently,[5] LiDAR is not new to Italy. In the early 2000s, a couple of projects sharing strong links with UK-based institutions and companies first started creating LiDAR visualizations of Italian territory, one of these was the *Ager Faliscus* project in which the project team aimed at detecting large scale Etruscan infrastructural works done in the territory of *Faleri Novii*.[6] These works were very relevant for the state-of-art of Etruscan world. The main point raised by these works was to underline the interrelation between society/culture and enterprises with a strong degree of technology and organization. The authors stress that point despite the fact that the knowledge about building techniques was not new to Etruscology. In the paper presented by Cifani and his collaborators the focus was oriented to the understanding of the scale of such projects which of course has to do with the technology itself and the social organization. The second Italian research project where remote sensing based in LiDAR data was applied, were the surveys in territories of Siena and Grosseto[7] and the Brebemi project, in order to study the construction of new road facilities in Po valley.[8] Furthermore, the researchers at the Brebemi project promptly realized the capabilities of LiDAR data to improve archaeological gazetteers over large territories, even in flat terrains as the Po valley or the *Agro Pontino*. Eventually the application of LiDAR in these environments was not really useful because the main requirement for these LiDAR data to be useful is the preservation of topographic expressions of the archaeological features, and in this case there was limited topographical variability, and therefore only very generic features were visible in the LiDAR derived DTMs. To counter the limitations of feature recognition in flat areas a series of methods have been developed, namely a whole range of visualization techniques that highlights almost invisible archaeological features.[9]

From 2008, a series of publicly available LiDAR datasets have been generated in Italy in order to manage the extraordinary hydrogeological risk that affects large parts of the country, especially those areas without rocky soils and severe agricultural exploitation in clayish slopes. The products generated by the Italian authorities illustrate very well those areas which have to be monitored with stronger emphasis, not for heritage purposes but to control a real threat for the human population. The LiDAR coverage led by this official landscape monitoring project has been improved thanks to several phases for data gathering different official programs which enlarge the original coverage, from the coast line and the main rivers (Astura, Arno, Tiber, Biferno, Bradano, etc.) to an almost full coverage which includes the secondary river's network and areas subjected to very acute landslide risk. Nevertheless, the result of this environmental-oriented LiDAR survey is the absence of continuous data over the entire Italian territory (both islands and mainland). The last phase finished in 2011 provides a quite extensive coverage in some regions, but regretfully not complete and not for the whole of Italian territory (both mainland and islands) (*fig. 1*).

Parallel to the creation of this LiDAR coverage, Italy signed the European Inspire directive thanks to which it is possible to access and use the geospatial data created by the government institutions. Thus, an already processed DTM was available to the public through the geoportal at the Italian Geoportale Nazionale. Nevertheless, we consider this new product only illustrative of the big capabilities of this data for archaeological research. The useful grey data is also accessible via request to the Ministero dell'Ambiente, allowing to carry out your own filter and classification algorithms as well as different visualization techniques to maximize the extraction of archaeological data or landscape information. The access to not only the final products but also the raw data is key to achieve a direct control over the created datasets and the subsequent archaeological information.

Following that working principle, several projects have recently started to use these available datasets in order to enhance the understanding of different aspects of their case-studies. We can divide the scope generally in two big groups.

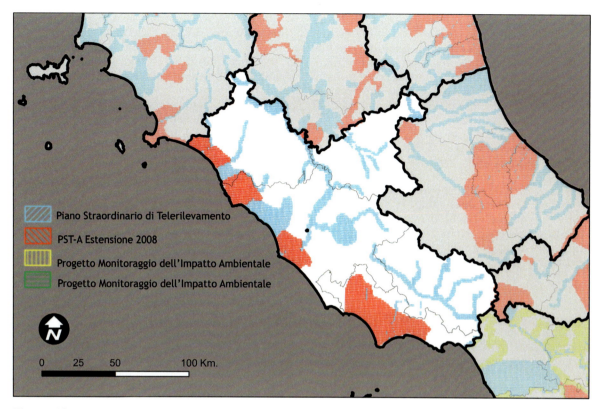

*Fig. 1. Lidar coverage in Central Italy-Lazio region (colours indicate different recognisance flights).*

First those interested in specific sites, aiming at detecting new archaeological features or structures, i.e. archaeological anomalies in the surface and terrain models; and secondly those projects with a broader interest in human-made landscapes and past processes that have shaped it. In case of the latter, it is not so much about the detection of archaeological features and structures, i.e. discrete physical entities, but more about studying continuous general spatial patterning of human behaviour that is made possible by creating very fine filtered DEMs. It is worth mentioning that in many occasions, these two big aims and related techniques do overlap, and that the dichotomy presented here is a bit simplifying LiDAR research, but we feel that it is illustrative for explaining the approach presented in this paper. We reflect mainly on the former projects, those with a clear archaeological oriented scope. In occasions both types overlap, but regretfully this is often difficult due to the partial Italian coverage. Therefore alternative sources for environmental reconstruction are preferred such as photogrammetry either with new aerial series or with historical reconstructions.[10]

Among the first group of projects we can mention the recently published Potenza valley project (Marche), where key sites have been explored using LiDAR elevation data.[11] Another case is the recent research on the Archaic site of *Muro Tenente* (Puglia) where the LiDAR derived DEM has been compared to other archaeological data collected in the past, through excavations and artefactual survey.[12] That comparison has allowed the creation of new reconstructions of the ancient topography of the site, including the extensions of its nucleus, as well as the construction and course of the city walls.[13] LiDAR is also complementary to reconstruct the defensive wall, and even to track the location of old excavated features in Serra del Cedro (Tricarico, MT), and thus to the up-to-date understanding of this relevant Lucanian oppidum.[14]

The Landscapes of Early Roman Colonization (LERC) Project[15] and the Tappino Area Archaeological Projec[16] led by Tesse Stek, has proposed a systematic remote sensing survey of the hinterland of Aesernia (Isernia, Molise) and Venusia (Venosa, Basilicata) and the Hellenistic landscapes alongside the Tappino Valley using some of these tools, chiefly aerial photography and LiDAR datasets. That work has resulted in an increasing awareness and renewed understanding of the fortification of Italic (Samnite) hillforts and hilltops. In particular a recent multi-scalar project in Montagna di Gildone (CB, Molise)[17] has revealed a complex system in which a large and fortified hillfort interacts with secondary settlements devoted to landscape exploitation, agriculture, husbandry and with an also significant sacred landscape structured around the sanctuaries of Cupa[18] and possible Sant'Andrea (both in the territory of Gildone).

Despite the amount of research groups aware of the possibilities that LiDAR could offer to regional oriented projects it is still difficult to find comprehensive application of LiDAR surveys over large territories. That situation is due mostly to the lack of extensive coverage of the Italian territory (mentioned above). that prevents regional scale projects benefit from a technology fruitfully applied in archaeology in the rest of the EU and beyond.[19]

*LiDAR, technology and ancient society*

Mlekuz's reflection (2013) on LiDAR and landscape is relevant to the main aim of this chapter. Mapping and landscape-environmental studies form the core of research on regional scales. In that context LiDAR plays a major role on tracing landscapes as a whole, as a social and multi-temporal result of successive and parallel engagements of environment and society.[20] Ancient technology is the means by which society transforms landscape. We believe in the possibilities of tracing the role of technology in the long-term landscape evolution in the *Agro Pontino* from the 1st millennium (construction of the Archaic cities and the appropriation of territory) to the 20th century incarnated in Mussolini's "*bonifica Agricola*"– land reclamation[21] and contemporary land movements.

A digital LiDAR approach to *Satricum* and its environment could allow us to tap into the conceptual approaches to building spaces and society. The description of built environment offered by Lawrence and Low[22] engage with contemporary archaeological understanding of (pre-) historical landscapes, also termed as total landscapes, messy landscapes or historical palimpsests. Using the author's own words on how we see a built landscape, ranging from site to off-site contexts:

> *It refers in the broadest sense to any physical alteration of the natural environment, from hearths to cities, through construction by humans. Generally speaking, it includes built forms, which are defined as building types (such as dwellings, temples, or meeting houses) created by humans to shelter, define, and protect activity. Built forms also include, however, spaces that are defined and bounded, but not necessarily enclosed, such as the uncovered areas in a compound, a plaza, or a street. Further,* *they may include landmarks or sites, such as shrines, which do not necessarily shelter or enclose activity.*[23]

In the near future, we would like to explore the possibilities brought forward by anthropological scholarship on built environment[24] and its relationship with current archaeological research on Archaic and Hellenistic fortifications, or landscape appropriation. This interest on the social meaning of build environment is the main reason why we approach the seminal works edited by Rapoport.[25] In this volume, a series of contributions aim to demonstrate that the built environment is culture-specific and its form results from the interaction of many different material, social, cultural and psychological factors.[26] Obviously, we should add technology as one of the main forms of interaction of mankind and the act of "building environment". We could also frame this interaction as the distinction between tools in restricted sense (tools) and tools in its extensive sense (land or countryside). Thus, we have technological concepts and a set of tools, building techniques, style, etc. and the capabilities of applying it (knowledge creation and knowledge transfer between generations or between foreign masters to local workers) and a frame where to apply conceptual and physical set of tools, i.e. a fortification, the setting of a Roman estate, or the city's hinterland as a comprehensive projection of the social organization.[27]

Archaeology is already well aware of this subject[28] both from the perspective of the Archaeology of Architecture[29] and from the long-established Landscape Archaeology. The former offers insights into the human constructions from a stratigraphical point of view by looking at standing remains or at excavated features, the latter aims to understand the dialectic relationship between nature and mankind from the earliest exploitation of landscape to more complex forms of social organization, with special interest in the diverse procedures of reclamation, appropriation and transformation of the physical space (this perspective intersect the scope of our research on LiDAR and other remote sensing approaches). In both site-oriented and landscape-focused views, the common denominator of research is the social background of any human action and construction, the social agency. We shall not address such debates here but it is important to acknowledge the criticism. The ultimate aim of this paper is not to discuss the nature of social evolution or complex societies organization, however, we seek to open new grounds of research which will allow comparative perspectives of remote sensing approaches bridging archaeological and anthropological scholarship.

This work will not offer a characterization of the Archaic society (*Latini* and *Volsci*) who inhabited *Satricum* and the conflictive succession of historical episodes so relevant for the configuration of the city. The core of this work lies in exploring the methodology used and seeks to demonstrate the potential of remote sensing and digital archaeology to engage in such debate by tracing technological decisions in the construction of specific urban features and other "scars" in the hinterland. In this light, the wealth of data yielded in decades of systematic research at *Satricum* provide a particularly apt case study.

INTERSECTIONS OF LIDAR AND SOCIAL TECHNOLOGY IN *SATRICUM*

We will focus on two case-studies to bring forward the possibilities of remote sensing to engage in the ongoing archaeological research at *Satricum*. The first case will be a comparative study of LiDAR data and low-altitude UAS photogrammetry (LAUP).[30] In the *Satricum* area the extant archaeological remains of an early 1st C. AD Roman Villa have been excavated in 1984, which brought parts of the *pars urbana* and *pars rustica* to light. Using trial trenches, the main road of ancient *Satricum* running from east to west through the Archaic town has been identified in the area as well. The area is since 2018 under renewed interest and is examined by various remote sensing techniques and new excavations, making it ideal for testing the methodological potential of LAUP (JW). The second will be the defensive system of the Archaic city, especially at the west and south of the research area (JGS). This combined approach enhances the multi-temporal dimension of our proposal.

## 3.1. LiDAR and low-altitude UAS photogrammetry

LiDAR and LAUP offer unique possibilities to produce high-resolution 3D models[31] and thereby study the morphology of the terrain in very high detail. The main question for this case study is to what degree LAUP can offer a similar or improved visualisation of morphological traces that can be expected in the area; backfilled excavation and trial trenches and possibly surface contours related to the archaeological remains of the villa or the main road of ancient *Satricum*.

The deployed LAUP workflow leans heavily on recent developments in Structure from Motion techniques that more widely fall under the Image Based Modelling moniker, in which 3D data is generated from photographs. Technicalities and workflows have been covered extensively by others and will not be dealt with here.[32] A LAUP model of the terrain has been derived by deploying a UAS with a 1/2.3" CMOS, f1/2.8 and 12 MP sensor, capturing images of 4000x3000 pixels, and processed into a model using AgiSoft Photoscan 1.4.4. The accuracy of the measurements derived through LAUP elicits the tracking of even minor alterations of the terrain, as long as they resulted in some sort of recognizable deformation. Due to the modest resolution of LiDAR, i.e. 1 point every 0.5 metres, as well as the nature of LiDAR data processing,[33] there are likely still features on ground level that remain elusive in studying LiDAR data. Essentially, LiDAR ground sample distance, or GSD, the ground in mms covered by a single pixel, is here 500 millimetre; in contrast, the model of the terrain derived through the low-altitude UAS photogrammetry has a GSD of 18.4 millimetre, an improvement of 27 times (*fig. 2*). Surely, the enhancement in resolution is considerable and presents the opportunity to look in much more detail at the surface in search of traces of human behaviour in the past.

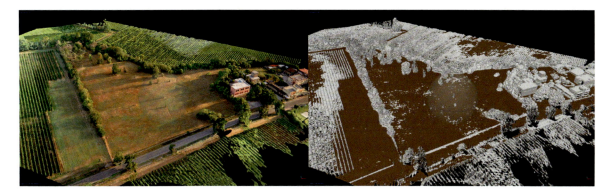

*Fig. 2. Photogrammetric model of the villa terrain (l), dense cloud classified in 'terrain' and 'other' (r).*

To assess the benefits of the LAUP approach, we have to establish first whether the photogrammetrically derived data is actually not just high precision but also of sufficient accuracy, i.e. are the projected points a good representation of the true morphology. We will forego on explicitly dealing with error estimations, for which there is extensively material on similar techniques by other authors,[34] and limit ourselves to stating the reprojection error, which is 0.941 pixel (i.e. the pixel difference between a point on the photo and the same point acquired through its 3D projection). Actually, at this point, the production of a highly accurate geometric model of the LAUP data is not really our main concern; more importantly, it is the assessment of its usefulness through direct comparison that interests us. Therefore, the accuracy of the model in comparison with external data sources will be examined. To do this, the general surface trend between the LiDAR datasets and LAUP datasets will be compared. Evidently, they should follow roughly similar trends, and where the LAUP data deviates, it should ideally be as a result of improved resolution.

In order to make a good comparison, the LAUP data needed to be classified similar to the LiDAR data, as in the separation of terrain coordinates as opposed to vegetation, structures etc. Clearly there is a difference between the techniques, in that the LiDAR data that we will use is generally last-return, i.e. only the part of the pulse that actually reaches ground level is used for the terrain reconstruction. Photogrammetry is usually comparable to the 'first-return', in that it is very unlikely to 'penetrate' thick vegetation and generate coordinates on ground level, but rather reconstruct the surface at canopy level, although in some circumstances it is known to perform better than laser scanning due to the advantage of multiple camera orientations.[35] The classification of the LAUP dense pointcloud was done using Agisoft (*fig. 2*). Points that are likely belonging to trees or upstanding structures can be filtered out by defining a tolerance threshold for differences in altitude and angle between adjacent points. Although there is a trade-off between the efficiency to filter out all low vegetation and the risk of removing bumps in the terrain that one may wish to keep, the approach works quite well. Since the histograms of the two rasters follow a similar progression, it is reasonable to suggest that they generally reflect similar trends in the terrain (*fig. 3*).

The absolute altitude of the LAUP model is derived through the coordinates of the cameras, which have been established through the uncorrected GPS readings of the UAS, and is therefore quite inaccurate. To bring the LAUP model at the same level as the LiDAR data, the average difference in elevation is measured for the two datasets and the mean difference between them is added to the LAUP raster.

Directly overlaying the two datasets made clear that they were slightly off; in the western part of the area, the LiDAR data was on average

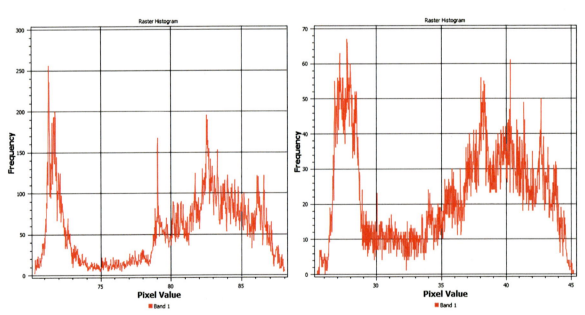

*Fig. 3. Histograms of z-values of LiDAR (l) and LAUP (r).*

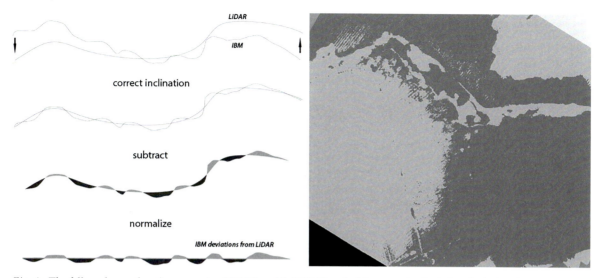

*Fig. 4. The followed procedure in comparing LiDAR and LAUP (l) and a binary raster depicting deviations between LiDAR and LAUP. lighter shade of grey is where LiDAR is 'on top' of LAAP data, darker shade of grey vice versa (r).*

just lying 'on top' of the LAUP data, and in the eastern part vice versa (*fig. 4*). This is not unexpected; although the internal geometry of the photogrammetrical model can be expected to be of high quality, as mentioned earlier, the absolute coordinates of the resulting model are based on inaccurate GPS coordinates. Where for the internal geometry that is not a problem, since it is corrected by estimations of relative camera positions, the model itself is still dependent on the GPS data.

This problem can be solved using total station measurements that have been taken in the field; adding these points as a reference to AgiSoft Photoscan as Ground Control Points (GCPs), and regenerating the model, the LAUP dataset can be matched to the inclination of the LiDAR dataset. As an estimation of accuracy, the deviations between the two datasets have been compared. It is not useful to compare both models in their totality; edges of vegetation are left in LAUP as a result of the classification method, as well as some bumps in the terrain have been removed for the same reason and there is an edge-effect due to decrease in number of photos towards the edges. To be able to get a good look at both files, three bounding boxes were defined where such deviations were thought to be absent, and there the terrain was directly compared (*fig. 5*). The average deviation in three bounding boxes is 7 cm, with a 19 cm standard deviation.

That there still is a deviation is not very surprising; there is no reason to assume that the LiDAR and LAUP will have an average deviation close to 0. Differences can be expected due to LiDAR penetrating vegetation that LAUP cannot on the one hand, and LAUP will capture more and smaller fluctuations in the shape of the terrain. Due to different capturing moments, such differences can be quite substantial. In addition, poor classification of LiDAR data is not uncommon, resulting in the removal of terrain parts that are not vegetation or building.[36] Finally, and most vital of course, is that deviations are actually reflecting the increased detail of the LAUP data. In order to study that detail, the general trend of the LiDAR data can be subtracted from the LAUP data, leading to 'normalized' LAUP data, so only the deviations from the LiDAR data are visualized (*fig. 3*). These then, are the basis of studying

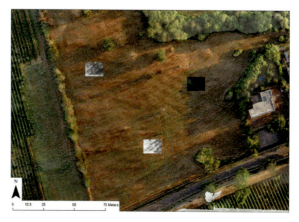

*Fig. 5. Three bounding boxes projected on LAUP orthophoto and Analytical Hillshade model, used for assessment of LAUP accuracy.*

the landscape in more detail and understanding where LAUP can add to our understanding.

Overall, the LAUP data seems quite good and certainly very useful due to its quality in capturing details. The increase in resolution is apparent (*fig. 6*). The question then is what we can identify that we could not before. We produced various visualizations that enhance elevation variability to be able to study anomalies, i.e. the Sky View Factor (SVF), especially optimized for

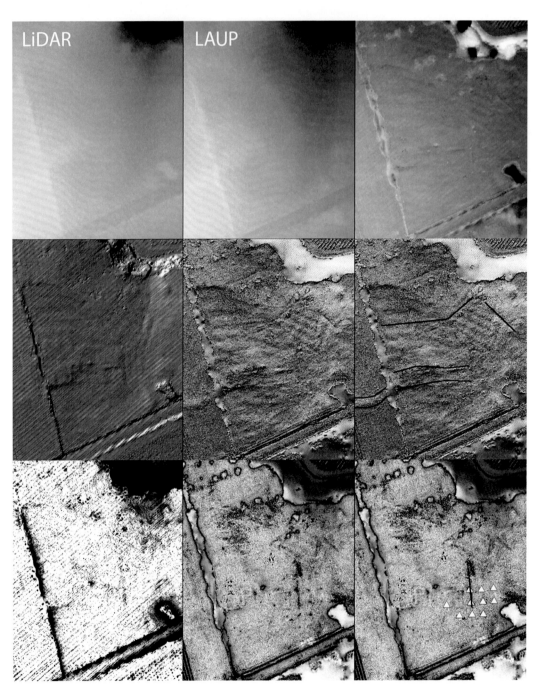

*Fig. 6. LiDAR and LAUP visual comparison. Upper row, LiDAR DTM (l), LAUP DTM (m), difference between LiDAR and LAUP (r); middle and lower row, Analytical Hillshade and Sky View Factor, with identified features (r).*

local contrast, and the Analytical Hillshade (ANHS) visualized using histogram equalization, which are both optimized for enhancing global contrast, both visualizations produced using SAGA 6.4.0). The visualisations allowed us to identify a couple of features that were not, or at least much less pronounced, visible on the LiDAR model.

Quite prominent are the excavations executed in various stages from 1984-2005 in which the main road of ancient *Satricum* has been excavated, the very rough delineation of the features marked on the ANHS, central-east of the area. Although crudely visible on the LiDAR model as well, the edges of the original excavation trenches are very pronounced on the LAUP model (I). Moreover, on the LAUP SVF a fossa running in front of an original earthen rampart, that was left in place between the clearly visible measuring gridpoints towards the western area, is distinctly visible (II). Regarding terrain morphology, the elongated bulge to the east of the excavations is most interesting (III). On the Google aerial photographs (*fig. 7c*) the continuation of the road is evident by discolorations here, and the bulge is very physically related to the road; this could e.g. be due to a different soil matrix here as a result of ancient deposition or structuring as part of the local road construction, or a natural depression that has been followed by the road and has not been levelled. This marked feature is not clearly discernible in the LiDAR models, its faint reflection in the ANHS very likely to be passed over. In the northern part of the villa terrain (*fig. 6*), in the east the contours of three trial trenches dug in 1997 are plainly visible on both LAUP ANHS and SVF (IV), and on neither of the LiDAR models. Finally, a bit north of these trial trenches, we can discern a straight line that is not clearly connected to anything modern, terrain morphology or vegetation line, and acould be representing some buried feature (V). Since its orientation is similar to the walls of the excavated villa, this could surely be an interesting anomaly to explore further. Evidently, as the archaeological layers in this part of the site are buried under a thick layer of moved sediment, features that can be traced are predominantly those with an effect on the upper layer of soil, i.e. recent intrusions such as digging and ploughing, and everything that affects those activities physically. It is patent though that LAUP can add significantly to our study of landscape morphology, and allows the tracing of manmade interventions in the present and in the past similar to LiDAR study, but at a much finer resolution.

*Agger and Fossa in Satricum*

Recent literature on defensive constructions both on a regional and on a Mediterranean scale reflects on the relevance of the social aspects of constructions.[37] This approach aims to counter the traditional interpretations of the mere defensive purposes of constructed city limits. We acknowledge the wide scholarship on conceptualizing fortifications beyond straightforward interpretations of defensive constructions. Nevertheless, we should not fall in a deconstructive loop and try to incorporate a complex social dimension to the interpretation of walls, which of course may have served as limit between locals and foreigners, urban space and countryside, safety and wilderness.

The fortification of *Satricum* has been studied extensively.[38] This was done using both excavation with deep trenches through presumed fortifications and non-invasive techniques as interpretation of legacy data using the maps created by R. Mengarelli in the early 20th century[39] maps, historical aerial photography from the various photographic series collected by the British army in 1936 and 1939 during the Second World War, modern aerial photography of the terrains nowadays covered by intensive vineyards, and artefactual surveys over selected areas within the Archaic city and around the fortification (*agger* and *vallum* or *fossa*) (*fig. 7*). In 1997 an excavation took place to confirm the presence of the fortification and to gain understanding about its construction from a stratigraphical point of view despite the scarcity of material remains and the difficulties for excavation due to problems such as the risk of collapse. In the same paper M. Gnade presents some clues that render our remote-sensing proposal very useful. Firstly,[40] she treats the work of Guaitoli[41] and his studies on urbanism and defensive systems of Latial cities, of which perhaps most remarkable point of criticism was the lack of systematic study of the topography. Secondly[42] she brings forward the question of the origin of the *fossa*, and the two main hypothesis to explain its origin. The *fossa* could be either natural, adapted to the gentle slopes over the Astura river, or anthropically built, a question that remains open in her paper.

Our remote-sensing proposal is based mainly in the publicly available LiDAR data to accurately model the present-day topography in Satricum. This product may help us to trace the construction of the *agger* and *fossa* system in non-explored areas of the city, especially the areas nowadays covered by vineyards. The results of the LiDAR exploration can be easily visualized

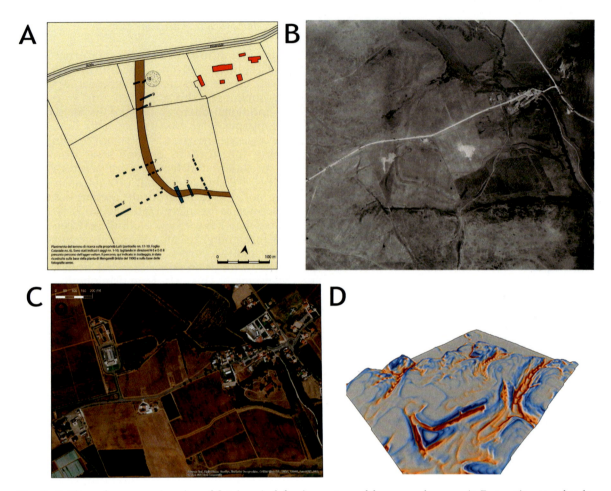

*Fig. 7. Evidence for a reconstruction of Satricum's defensive system of fossum and agger. A: Excavation trenches by M. Gnade (2017); B: RAF aerial photography from 1939, before land levelling; C: ESRI base map with the fossum still visible as soil mark; D: 3D rendering and Resampling filter performed over a DTM calculated with 1934's contour lines.*

through a wide range of techniques that exploit the mathematical composition of raster datasets. Beyond these, a quantitative comparison of LiDAR-DTMs with DTMs derived from the photogrammetry using RAF 1936 and 1939 aerials is possible[43] but yet unexplored. Such a methodology could increase the understanding of the radical landscape transformation within and in the hinterland of *Satricum*.

The remote sensing materials used here to study the fortifications of Satricum are as follows: the 1910's map, and before the beginning of Mussolini's project of reclamation of the marshes in the *Agro Pontino*; the RAF aerial imagery taken during the Second WW when the *Bonifica* was already done; the LiDAR coverage; and the most recent aerial photographs from the commercial company ESRI. The combination of all these elements is possible using a desktop GIS and the WMS capabilities of the modern repositories. The only material processed manually is the LiDAR data, which has been classified and filtered using Lastools, ArcGIS and SAGA software, and RVT for visualization.

Many features prevent us from obtaining a quality product (LiDAR-derived DTM) as the large soil movements which took place in 1960's, the intensive viticulture and kiwiculture, and quality of the LiDAR data in itself. The last two elements could be combined in even a larger bias. Kiwi trees are arranged in line with its canopies grouped horizontally, creating a continuous and dense surface. Therefore, very few laser beams from the already scarce beam density are able to reach the actual ground.

The main results of this remote sensing approach could be seen in *fig. 7*. The 1910's map[44] and the RAF aerials provide the clues to understand the features visible in the ESRI aerial photographs and in the LiDAR visualization of the modern topography. Only the Archaic road and the southwestern ramparts are visible in the LiDAR images, both apparently using the natural slopes to reinforce its position. It seems reasonable that the Archaic city employed exploited natural features in the landscapes such as undulating slopes to create earthen ramparts and ditches as delimiters of the city in its western part, which was the easiest area to access considering the presence of Astura river at East and steeper slopes in the northern part of the area. The 1998 excavation[45] suggest that use of the natural terrain for the construction of a fortification based on a series of trenches (*fossa*) and earthen works (*agger*). The massive operation and the use of the natural features of the terrain helped to preserve any topographic expression of archaeological features, still visible by the early 20th century archaeologists and in the RAF aerials. Only the large-scale levelling operations undertook in the 1960s destroyed the still-standing features, nevertheless the soil substrate still reveals traces of the excavated fossa. That was the main clue that lead the Amsterdam team to operate in the area in 1998, and which is still visible as a soil mark (depending on the date of the picture) in the ESRI aerial image.

To the east we encounter the Astura river and the elevated acropolis (see LiDAR derived topography of the *Acropolis* and immediate surroundings in *fig. 8*). To the north, the very steep slopes of the platform Poggio dei Cavalari are well preserved and help to establish a limit of the upper inhabited platform and the bottom of the Astura river valley.

CONCLUSIONS

The aim of this paper was to explore the capabilities and the diversity of approaches of publicly Italian LiDAR data to enhance both site- and landscape-oriented research in the Archaic city of *Satricum*. Our first example deals with a specific sector in *Satricum*; in that area a high-resolution terrain model has been derived applying UAS photogrammetry. This new terrain model has been compared to the Italian LiDAR data to examine the capabilities possibilities of both to detect hidden archaeological feature, or to document some of the main features of the Archaic city, such as the *agger* and the fossa. Indeed, the complementary potential of LAUP in LiDAR studies are a key topic within our research within

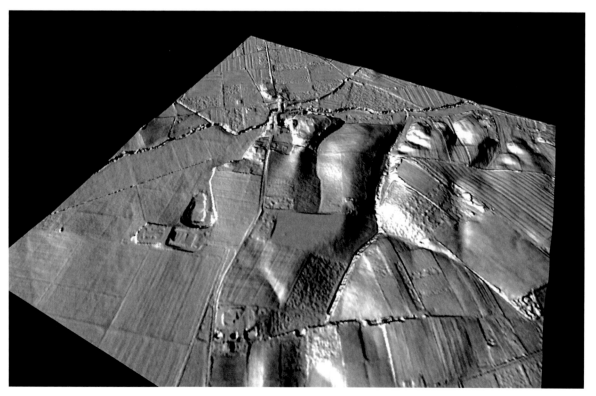

*Fig. 8. DTM-Lidar and Resampling Filter (visualized in SAGA). The depression fits well with the so-called Strada Antica in Mengarelli's map.*

the *Satricum* project. In the second example we have shown the importance role of LiDAR visualization to extract information about individual archaeological features such as the fortification system (including *fossa*, earthen works and gaps in the track of the fortifications), and relationship of such monuments with the natural topography as pointed to by the director of the archaeological project. The area of *Satricum* is very challenging due to the intense landscape transformations which took place all through the 20th century, with the *Bonifica* and the land levelling. Nevertheless, our work has demonstrated that despite such massive transformations, it is still possible to visualize the footprint of the largest Archaic monuments, as a scar in the urban landscape of *Satricum*. Moreover, it is even more relevant for us, and for the sake of research in the forthcoming years, that our remote-sensing (LiDAR) and non-destructive approach enables us to engage in debates about the rise of social complexity and the role of monuments and monumentalization in political organization in Ancient times, as discussed extensively by Osborne[46] and by many others (see different approaches to the topic in the volume edited by Osborne,[47] i.e. monumentalization, from a social and political significance of the phenomenon, Childe's link of monument construction and social surplus, the role of hegemonic culture represented by those monuments, or other modern points of view that highlight the role of common people as monumental agents– it's not the scope of this paper to address such deep theoretical approaches).

We have argued that old (aerial photography) and modern (LiDAR and LAUP) remote sensing approaches have a huge potential as complementary sources. We have thoroughly exposed that our understanding of the interrelation of nature, topography and diachronic evolution of *Satricum* could be improved by combining several of these products. One of the most interesting outputs of this approach to the *Satricum* scenario is the comparison of LiDAR and LAUP, which demonstrates the potential of both techniques for the research of ancient features in the micro-scale provide by the highly accurate DTMs, and might serve as basis to produce products to engage in other debates as heritage visualization in the digital era. Finally, our LiDAR approach to the defensive system is affected by the long-history of land reclamation, landscape changes and modern land-use. However, the remarkable works carried out in Archaic times are still visible in the landscape as cropmarks and soil marks, and the reconstruction of the landscape using photogrammetry with aerial imagery will provide some clues for a better understanding of the defensive system and its relationship with the natural and culture scenario where *Satricum* is inserted.

Notes

[1] Masini and Lasaponara 2013.
[2] Barceló/Pallarés, 1996; Djindjian, 1998; García Moreno *et al.*, 2012; Hacigüzeller, 2012
[3] see current thoughts on the topic of cultural evolution in the volume of Cofani *et al.*, 2013.
[4] Broodbank 2013; Düring/Stek 2018.
[5] García Sánchez 2018.
[6] Cifani *et al.* 2007a, 2007b.
[7] Campana 2011, 36.
[8] Campana/Dabas 2011.
[9] Ziga/Hesse 2017.
[10] Pérez Álvarez *et al.* 2013; Sevara *et al.* 2018, Tarquini *et al.* 2012.
[11] Vermeulen *et al.*, 2017
[12] Waagen 2019b.
[13] Waagen 2019a.
[14] De Cazanove 2016.
[15] Stek *et al.* 2015; Stek/Pelgrom 2013.
[16] Stek 2018.
[17] García Sánchez/Fontana 2016.
[18] Pelgrom/Stek 2004.
[19] Forte/Campana 2017; Opitz/Cowley 2013.
[20] For a recent reflection on environment and society engagement see Bryen 2017; Kearns 2017
[21] Armiero 2014, 242.
[22] Lawrence/Low 1990.
[23] Lawrence/Low1990, 454.
[24] See papers on Part IV - Landscapes and the built environment in Hicks and Beaudry 2010)
[25] Rapoport 1976.
[26] Rapoport19766.
[27] Brog Attema 1993
[28] see the theoretical introduction of Azkárate/Solaun 2012,103–104.
[29] Brogiolo *et al.* 1996; Ayán Vila *et al.* 2003.
[30] Gruszczyński et al 2017.
[31] Waagen 2019b.
[32] e.g. Chandler/Buckley 2016, Sapirstein 2016, 2017.
[33] cf. Holata et al 2018, 2.
[34] e.g. , Gruszczyński et al 2017, Sapirstein 2016, 2017.
[35] Chandler & Buckley 2016, 2, Gruszczyński et al, 2017,170, Chiabrando *et al.*, 2017, 94-95.
[36] cf. Holata et al 2018.
[37] Ballmer *et al.* 2018; Fontaine and Helas 2017; Frederiksen *et al.* 2016.
[38] Waarsenburg 1995/Ginge 1996.
[39] A short description of Mengarelli's work in Satricum in Tufi, 2008, 38.
[40] Gnade 2017, 217.
[41] Guaitoli 1984.
[42] Gnade 2017, 220-225.
[43] Blanco-Rotea *et al.* 2016; Pérez Álvarez *et al.*, 2013.
[44] Gnade 2017, fig. 1, and footnote 7 for an explanation of its origin.
[45] Gnade 1999, 36-40, fig. 4.
[46] Osborne 2014.
[47] Osborne 2014b.

## Bibliography

Armiero, M. 2014, Introduction: Fascism and nature, *Modern Italy* 19(3), 241-245. https://doi.org/10.1080/13532944.2014.926698

Attema, P. 1993, *An archaeological survey in the Pontine Region. A contribution to the settlement history of south Lazio*, Groningen.

Ayán Vila, X./R. Blanco-Rotea/P. Mañana-Borrazás 2003, *Archaeotecture: Archaeology of Architecture* (BAR Int. Ser. 1175), Oxford.

Azkárate, A./J.L. Solaun 2012, Tipologías domésticas y técnicas constructivas en la primitiva Gasteiz (País Vasco) durante los siglos VIII al XII d.C., *ArqueolArqui* 9, 103–128.

Ballmer, A./M. Fernández-Götz/M. Mielke (eds.), 2018. *Understanding Ancient Fortifications: Between Regionality and Connectivity*, Oxford.

Barceló, J.A./M. Pallarés 1996, A critique of GIS in Archaeology. From Visual seduction Seduction to Spatial Analysis, *Archeolia.e Calcolatori* 6, 313–326.

Blanco-Rotea, R./J. Fonte/M. Gago Mariño/J.M. Costa-García 2016, A Modern Age redoubt in a possible Roman camp. The relationship between two defensive models in Campos (Vila Nova de Cerveira, Minho Valley, Portugal), *JASc Reports* 10, 293–308.

Broodbank, C. 2013, *The Making of the Middle Sea: A History of the Mediterranean from the Beginning to the Emergence of the Classical World*, London.

Brogiolo, J.P./T. Mannoni/R. Parenti. (ed.) 1996, *Archeologia dell'Architettura* (Supplemento Archeologia Medievale 1), Firenze.

Bryen, A. 2017, Environment and society in the ancient world: New perspectives, *History Compass* 15(10), https://onlinelibrary.wiley.com/doi/epdf/10.1111/hic3.12427.

Campana, S. 2011, From space to place or from site to landscape? Mind the gap, in: P.M. van Leusen et al., *Hidden Landscapes of Mediterranean Europe* (BAR Int. Ser.), Oxford, 35–45.

Campana, S./M. Dabas 2011, Archaeological Impact Assessment: The BREBEMI Project (Italy). *Archaeological Prospection* 18, 139–148.

Chandler, J.H./S. Buckley 2016, Structure from motion (SFM) photogrammetry vs terrestrial laser scanning, in M.B. Carpenter/C.M. Keane (eds.). *Geoscience Handbook*, 5th ed., Alexandria, VA, Section 20.1.

Chiabrando, F./S. Spanò/G. Sammartano/L.T. Losè 2017, UAV oblique photogrammetry and LiDAR data acquisition for 3D documentation of the Hercules Fountain, *Virtual Archaeology Review* 8 (16), 83-96.

Cifani, G./R. Opitz/S. Stoddart 2007, LiDAR survey in southern Etruria, Italy: a significant new technique for the study of cultural landscapes, *European Archaeology* 2007, 2–4.

Cifani, G./R. Opitz/S. Stoddart 2007b, Mapping the Ager Faliscus road-system: the contribution of LiDAR (light detection and ranging) survey, *JRA* 20, 165–176.

De Cazanove, O. 2016, Programme Ignobilia Oppida Lucanorum. Fouilles, prospections, études à Serra del Cedro, Civita di Tricarico et Rossano di Vaglio, *Chron. Act. Archéologiques L'École Fr. Rome*. Online document -no pages-https://doi.org/10.4000/cefr.1793.

Düring, B./T. D. Stek (eds.) 2018, *The Archaeology of Imperial Landscapes: A Comparative Study of Empires in the Ancient Near East and Mediterranean World*, Cambridge. doi:10.1017/9781316995495

Djindjian, F., 1998, GIS usage in worldwide archaeology, *Archeologia e Calcolatori* 9, 19–30.

Fontaine, P./S. Helas (eds.) 2017, *Le fortificazioni arcaiche del Latium vetus e dell'Etruria meridionale (IX-VI sec. a.C.)*, Brussels/Rome.

Forte, M./S. Campana (eds.) 2017, *Digital Methods and Remote Sensing in Archaeology. Archaeology in the Age of Sensing*, New York.

Frederiksen, R./M. Schnelle/S. Muth/P. Schneider 2016, *Focus on Fortifications New Research on Fortifications in the Ancient Mediterranean and the Near East*, Havertown.

García Moreno, A./J. García Sánchez/A. Maximiano/J. Ríos-Garaizar (eds.), 2012, *Debating Spatial Archaeolgy. Proceedings of the Internal Workshop on Landscape and Spatial Analysis in Archaeology*, Santander.

García Sánchez, J., 2018, Archaeological LiDAR in Italy: enhancing research with publicly accessible data, *Antiquity* 92, 1–10; https://doi.org/10.15184/aqy.2018.147

García Sánchez, J./G. Fontana 2016, In search of Montagna di Gildone: developing an optimal workflow for the application of LIDAR in central Italy. Presented at the Joint Chapter Meeting CAA-DE and CAA-NL-FL, Ghent, Belgium (24 - 25 Nov 2016), Ghent.

Ginge, B. 1996, *Excavations at Satricum (Borge Le Ferriere) 1907-1910: Northwest Necropolis, Shouthwest Sanctuary and Acropolis*, Amsterdam.

Gnade, M. 2017, Le fortificazioni arcaiche dell'antica Satricum. Indagini archeologiche nell'area urbana inferiore, in Fontaine/Helas 2017, 213–230.

Guaitoli, M. 1984, Le città latine fino al 338 a.C. L'urbanistica, *Archeologia laziale. QuadAEI* 8, 364–381.

Gruszczyński, W./W. Matwij/P. Ćwiąkała 2017, Comparison of low-altitude UAV photogrammetry with terrestrial laser, scanning as data-source methods for terrain covered in low vegetation. ISPRS J, *Photogrammetry Remote Sens* 126, 168-179.

Hacıgüzeller, P., 2012. GIS, critique, representation and beyond, *Journal of Social Archaeology* 12, 245–263.

Holata, L./J. Plzák/R. Světlik/J. Fonte 2018, Integration of Low-Resolution ALS and Ground-Based SfM Photogrammetry Data. A Cost-Effective Approach Providing an 'Enhanced 3D model' of the Hound Tor Archaeological Landscapes (Dartmoor, South-West England). *Remote Sens*, 10.

Kearns, C. 2017, Mediterranean archaeology and environmental histories in the spotlight of the Anthropocene, *History Compass* 15 (10). https://doi.org/10.1111/hic3.12371

Lawrence, D.L./S.M. Low 1990, The built environment and spatial form, *Annual Anthropological Review*, 453–505.

Masini, N./R. Lasaponara 2013, Airborne Lidar in Archaeology: Overview and a Case Study, in B. Murgante et al., *Computational Science and Its Applications – ICCSA 2013*, Berlin/Heidelberg, 663-676.

Mlekuz, D. 2013, Messy landscapes; lidar and the practices of landscaping, in R. Opitz/D. Cowley (eds.), *Interpreting Archaeological Topography*, Oxford, 90–101.

Opitz, R./D. Cowley 2013, *Interpreting Archaeological Topography: 3D Data, Visualisation and Observation*, Oxford.

Osborne, J.F. 2014, Monuments and monumentality, in Osborne 2014, 1–19.

Osborne, J.F. (ed.) 2014, *Approaching monumentality in archaeology*. New York.

Pelgrom, J./T. D. Stek 2004, *Sacred Landscape Project: Campagna di ricognizioni marzo 2004. Schede dei siti archeologici dell'agro di San Giovanni in Galdo e Gildone (CB)*. Soprintendenza Archaeologica Molise. https://pure.uva.nl/ws/files/3644922/33945_Pelgrom_Stek_2004_Schedatura_dei_siti_archeologici.pdf

Pérez Álvarez, J.A./V. Mayoral Herrera/J.A. Martínez del Pozo/M.T. de Tena 2013, Multi-temporal archaeological analyses of alluvial landscapes using the photogrammetric restitution of historical flights: a case study of Medellin (Badajoz, Spain), *JASc* 40, 349–364.

Rapoport, A. (ed.), 1976, *The Mutual Interaction of People's and Their Built Environment*, The Hague.

Richerson, P.J./M.H. Christiansen/J. Lupp 2013, *Cultural Evolution: Society, Technology, Language, and Religion*, Cambridge.

Rinaldi Tufi, S. 2008, Raniero Mengarelli dopo Sentinum, in M. Medri (ed.), *Sentinum. Ricerche in Corso*, Rome, 36–42.

Sapirstein, P. 2016, Accurate measurement with photogrammetry at large sites, *JASc* 66, 137-145. doi: 10.1016/j.jas.2016.01.002

Sapirstein, P./S. Murray 2017, Establishing Best Practices for Photogrammetric Recording During Archaeological Fieldwork, *JFieldA* 42:4, 337-350. doi: 10.1080/00934690.2017.1338513

Sevara, C./G. Verhoeven/M. Doneus/E. Draganits 2018, Surfaces from the Visual Past: Recovering High-Resolution Terrain Data from Historic Aerial Imagery for Multitemporal Landscape Analysis, *Journal of Archaeological Method and Theory* 25(2), 611-642. https://doi.org/10.1007/s10816-017-9348-9

Stek, T.D. 2018, Exploring non-urban society in the Mediterranean: hill-forts, villages and sanctuary sites in ancient Samnium, Italy, *Antiquity* 92, 1-7.

Stek, T.D./E. B. Modrall/R. Kalkers/R.H. van Otterloo/J. Sevink 2015, An early Roman colonial landscape in the Apennine mountains: landscape archaeological research in the territory of Aesernia (Central-Southern Italy), *Analitical Archaeology*. 1, 229–291.

Stek, T.D./J. Pelgrom 2013. Landscapes of Early Roman Colonization: Non-urban settlement organization and Roman expansion in the Roman Republic (4th-1st centuries BC), *Tijdschrift voor Mediterrane Archeology* 50, 87.

Tarquini, S./L. Nannipieri/M. Favalli/A. Fornaciai/S. Vinci/F. Doumaz 2012, Release of a 10-m-resolution DEM for the whole Italian territory: a new, freely available resource for research purposes. Presented at the EGU General Assembly Conference Abstracts, 6666. https://meetingorganizer.copernicus.org/EGU2012/EGU2012-6666.pdf.

Vermeulen, F./D. Van Limbergen/P. Monsieur/D. Taelman 2017, *The Potenza Valley Survey*, Roma.

Waagen, J. 2019a, LiDAR for Italian archaeology. High-resolution elevation data to enrich our understanding of the defensive circuits of a protohistoric site in Southern Italy, *AARGnewsletter* 58, 15-25.

Waagen, J. 2019b, New technology and archaeological practice. Improving the primary archaeological recording process in excavation by means of UAS photogrammetry, *Journal of Archaeological Science* 101(2): 11-20.

Waarsenburg, D.J. 1995, *The Northwest Necropolis of Satricum. An Iron Age Cemetery in Latium Vetus*, Amsterdam.

Ziga, K./R. Hesse 2017, *Airborne laser scanning raster data visualization. A Guide to Good Practice*, Ljubljana.

# Tracing protohistoric technology using geophysical techniques in Italy and the Crimea

*Wieke de Neef, Burkart Ullrich*

*Abstract*

*This paper demonstrates how geophysical techniques contribute to archaeological research on technological traditions and production strategies in protohistoric societies. Two levels of human technology in such societies are discussed: large-scale operations requiring the effort of a community, and medium-scale operations at a household level. These two aspects are illustrated through different case studies in Italy and Crimea: Bronze Age / Early Iron Age house building techniques in the Raganello basin (Calabria, South Italy), the construction of a large defensive ditch at protohistoric Montarice (Marche, Central Italy) and the spatial arrangement of pastoral sites in north-western Crimea. In all three cases, large-scale geophysical surveys were combined with surface collections and soil studies to reveal complex processes of construction and production. We used these data to reconstruct the capacity, activity, end-product, and preservation involved in the different stages of making, including those that did not produce actual structures.*

## INTRODUCTION

This paper aims to bring together two types of technology: first, technology developed by ancient communities, and secondly, present-day near-surface geophysical techniques used to detect archaeological remains. Both present two aspects of technology that seem difficult to integrate: those related to tangible, artefactual technology, and those related to a more abstract, digital technology. Archaeology as a discipline is firmly rooted in tangible data, therefore the study of past technologies is often based on direct materialist approaches. Geophysics, on the other hand, presents archaeologists with digital datasets that are material only in a secondary sense. Geophysical techniques such as ground penetrating radar, magnetometry, and electric resistivity record the spatial variations in physical properties of materials to map contrasting elements preserved below the surface. The resulting binary data are made readable through a range of data processing and visualization steps. In this paper we argue that these two aspects of technology, ancient and modern, analogue and digital, can well be combined in present-day archaeological research to reveal aspects of ancient *chaînes opératoires*.

Before moving forward, it is necessary to elaborate on our understanding of technology for its aspects to be recognizable in archaeological and geophysical data. We describe technology as an interaction between social, material, and spatial factors within the production sequence of goods or information – in short, the process of 'making'.

We discern four major components that allows us to retrieve information on past technologies from archaeological and geophysical data (*fig. 1*), integrating the apt formulation by Auyang[1] with a fourth concerning the detectability of archaeological traces:

- Capacity: this defines spatial aspects of technology such as the access to resources, demand and scope of production, but also technical knowhow which allows to work on a large, medium, small, or micro-scale;

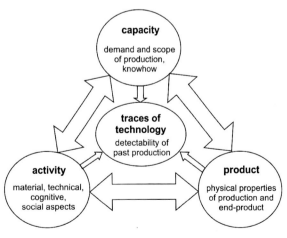

Fig. 1. Components relevant for the recognition of past technologies in archaeological and geophysical data. After Auyang (2004, 18).

- Activity: this covers the material and non-material aspects of the production chain or *chaîne operatoire*, including technical processes but also the cognitive capacities and social frameworks involved in 'making';
- Product: this concerns the physical properties of the final result but also the by-products of the production process, such as the accretion and depletion of resources and tangible traces of specific production stages, such as workshops, kilns, and waste deposits;
- Preservation: the conservation and detectability of past technology as affected by local post-depositional processes, a crucial element to the recognition of the previous three aspects in archaeological and geophysical data.

These four components all highlight tangible and non-tangible aspects of technology: there are objects and products that can be studied empirically, but also the social relationships between the individuals and groups who produce them. Moreover, there are production steps which do not produce artefactual traces, but which are crucial to the final result. The emphasis on the social aspects of technology is pivotal here as they embed the cognitive frameworks where demands for goods and information are developed and expressed, knowledge is transferred, ideas are developed, and innovation happens. In this we follow recent scholarship characterizing materiality and technology as a *quality of relationships* instead of merely a *quality of things*.[2] 'Making' is essentially a process that takes place between people and thus an expression of cognitive and social values, or, as Gauntlett[3] calls it, of 'community glue'. This idea fits well in the current attention that archaeological technology studies devote towards the concept of 'communities of practice'[4] to explain material tradition, knowledge transfer, and learning environments within the social frameworks behind the tangible archaeological record.

In the following sections, we demonstrate how geophysical datasets can help illuminate both material dimensions of past technologies as well as the 'community glue' underlying production practices of ancient societies. We do so by looking at physical properties in geophysical datasets and the spatial patterning in such data. We argue that we can extract information on past productive cycles from non-invasive prospection data by interpreting them in terms of social aspects such as collaboration, planning, tradition, and effort. We focus on two scales of human technology in late prehistoric contexts: large-scale operations which require the effort of a community, and medium-scale operations at a household level. After a short introduction on near-surface geophysical survey in archaeological research, we illustrate our approach with case studies from Italy and the Crimea.

NON-INVASIVE PROSPECTION USING GEOPHYSICAL TECHNIQUES

In the past three decades, near-surface geophysical techniques have become stable components of the archaeological prospection toolkit. The most common techniques applied in archaeology are magnetometry, ground penetrating radar (GPR), electrical resistivity (ER) and to a lesser extent electromagnetic induction (EMI).[5] These techniques record local variations in the physical properties of materials in response to electromagnetic interactions, either related to wave propagation (GPR, EMI) or stationary potential field (magnetometry, ER) principles. Using these principles, contrasts in specific physical parameters between anthropogenic deposits and natural background can be mapped. The spatial patterning in these contrasts and the strength of the recorded parameter, expressed by the amplitude of the signal, are used to interpret such data in terms of archaeological relevance. Because archaeo-geophysical prospection is based on the detectability of often subtle contrasts between natural background and anthropogenically altered materials, the applicability of a geophysical technique and its suitability depends on the local circumstances including *inter alia* depth of burial, volume and dimensions of features, and post-depositional processes. Taking these circumstances into account, not all archaeological remains produce a physical contrast that can be detected, whereas some evidence produce a contrast that can be recorded with one technique but not with another. The range of archaeological remains and their post-depositional histories are so diverse, that not all aspects of human technology can be detected by geophysical techniques. This is an important point to make, since whole stages within ancient *chaînes operatoires* may be invisible to geophysical prospection.

Nevertheless, there are good examples of pre- and protohistoric (construction) technology being recognized in non-invasive prospection data: for instance the water management system in the Kopais polder surrounding the Mycenaean fortress of Gla in Greece,[6] a Late Bronze Age canalization system surrounding the Terramare settlement at Santa Rosa di Poviglio in northern Italy,[7] Neolithic ditched village enclosures and hut foundations on the Tavoliere plain,[8] Bronze and

Iron Age architecture at Mitrou in Greece[9] and at Kalavasos-Ayios Dhimitrios in Cyprus,[10] Iron Age furnaces and workshops at the Scythian settlement of Belsk in Ukraine.[11] In the following sections, we focus on three case studies where geophysical surveys have revealed aspects of Bronze Age 'making'. In the conclusion, we return to the contribution of geophysical data to the research of the capacity, activity, products, and preservation of ancient technology.

MONTARICE (MARCHE, ITALY): COMMUNITY LABOR EFFORT AND THE CONSTRUCTION OF LARGE STRUCTURES

The first case study investigates the large-scale construction of a defensive ditch as an example of community effort. Montarice is a plateau of ca. 4.2 hectares on a marine terrace overlooking the lower valley of the river Potenza and its river mouth on the Adriatic coast.[12] So far the hill escaped expansions of the present-day coastal town Porto Recanati, but its western side, which connected the plateau to the adjacent hill of Colle Burchio, has been destroyed during the construction of the Adriatic motorway (fig. 2; left). In 1976 Delia Lollini of the regional cultural heritage authorities (Soprintendenza Archeologia, Belle Arti e Paessagio delle Marche / SABAP-Marche) recorded Bronze Age levels in several test pits. This research is still unpublished and the precise location of Lollini's trenches were not recorded, but photos in the SABAP archive help us to reconstruct their location.[13] The multi-period occupation of the plateau was established by intensive field walking survey by Ghent University in 2002,[14] during which Paleolithic tools, a dense Middle Bronze Age pottery concentration, and Iron Age, Roman, and post-antique traces were recorded.[15] The exceptional preservation of the site was established by the discovery of distinct cropmarks indicating anthropogenic features, recorded during an airborne reconnaissance in May 2003 (fig. 2, right). These include large curvilinear structures and a range of circular, rectangular, and linear positive cropmarks related to deepened features. Further detail on the buried features was obtained through a magnetic gradiometry survey of the entire plateau and part of its northern slope (fig. 3).[16] A high-resolution re-survey in 2019 provided new information on the spatial arrangement, extent, and chronology of the various occupation foci.

Without invasive research, the chronology and character of single features on the settled plateau of Montarice remain uncertain, but spatial trends in its occupation history can be derived from the surface artefact record. Activity in the Middle and Recent Bronze Age phases appears to have concentrated on the NW corner of the present-day plateau, but some caution is warranted because this is also the area of one of Lollini's 1976 trenches and probably of associated spoil heaps. The large curvilinear feature which demarcates the western last of the plateau appears, however, to be associated with the protohistoric occupation phase.

The characteristics of this remarkable feature in both aerial photography and magnetometry data suggest that it is a ditch cut in the conglomerate subsoil, enclosing the western part of the plateau. The positive crop marks suggest that the feature should be interpreted as a ditch rather than a wall;[17] this observation is underlined by the positive magnetic amplitude indicating that the geophysical anomaly is caused by magnetically enhanced deposits rather than standing architecture. The vicinity of archaeologically relevant magnetic anomalies on both sides and the flat present-day surface suggest that the ditch was not accompanied by a fence or earthwork,

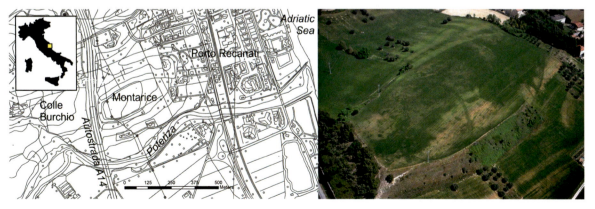

Fig. 2. Left: The location of Montarice on the Carta Tecnica Regionale (CTR; source: Regione Marche) map of Marche (Italy). Right: oblique aerial photo of the plateau with cropmarks (photo F. Vermeulen; Vermeulen et al. 2017).

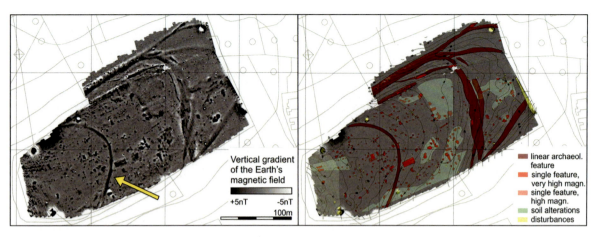

*Fig. 3. Montarice (Marche, Italy). Left: results of the magnetic gradiometer survey. The ditch discussed in the text is indicated with a yellow arrow. Right: interpretation of the magnetometry data (maps B. Ullrich/Eastern Atlas for Ghent University).*

but this may also be obscured by levelling in later phases. Large enclosures are widely known from pre- and protohistoric settlements in Italy, for instance the Neolithic villages in the Tavoliere plain in Puglia, the Late Bronze Age Terramare settlements in the Po Plain, and the large defense works of Iron Age central settlements such as Satricum[18] and Ardea.[19] Iron Age examples are usually twinned with an *agger* or large earthwork, for which there is no visible evidence at Montarice. Also, the enclosed area of ca. 1 hectare is much smaller than the defended areas in Iron Age examples,[20] and we have relatively little artefactual evidence on the plateau between the Recent Bronze Age and Late Iron Age. Therefore, we hypothesize that the curvilinear feature is associated with an earlier, Bronze Age, occupation phase.

The construction of an enclosure of this size would require the labor input of a consistent group of people. This effort can be estimated on the basis of the prospection data. Although invasive research on the curvilinear feature is pending and we do not know its construction in detail, we can propose a minimal calculation of its volume on the basis of the magnetometer data. The ditch has a length of 170 m and a width between 4-5 m (*fig. 3*). Magnetic gradiometry data does not permit an estimation of the depth of the feature, but we assume a depth of at least 2.25 m considering its width and the strength of the magnetic signal. If the ditch has a u-shape, this would mean that its section can be calculated as a half-circle of approximately 8 m². The volume of the ditch at these estimated dimensions would be $8 * 170 \text{ m}^2 = 1351 \text{m}^3$. There have been many attempts at calculating the labor effort of digging such volumes of soil in past societies. If we take the more conservative ones based on experiments with reproduced prehistoric tools, it would cost an adult an hour to extract 0.142m³ to 0.25m³ of soil (as opposed to approximately 0.48m³ with modern picks, shovels, and buckets). These numbers are based on controlled experiments: archaeology students working with antler picks managed to remove 0.142m³ of soil in an hour at the Experimental Earthworks Project at Overton Downs (UK) in the 1960's,[21] while the skilled laborers in General Pitt-Rivers' experiments managed 0.25m³ an hour.[22] Based on these numbers the total labor effort of the Montarice ditch would be between 5000-9600 man hours. Assuming that 8 hours of prehistoric shoveling is feasible, this would mean a total of 625-1200 individual days' work. Even for a small community living off small-scale subsistence farming and thus bound in many other seasonal workloads, a ditch this size could be constructed within a season.[23]

The Montarice ditch is a good example for the suitability of non-invasive prospection data to investigate aspects of ancient technology. The feature can very well be interpreted in terms of the four major components of technology mentioned earlier: capacity, activity, product, and preservation (*Table 1*). The scale of the feature is such that it served the purposes of a group of people and could be constructed by them. The activity of digging a trench itself is not technically complex but the feature's oval shape and dimensions express careful planning and decision-making. The required workload of such a large-scale operation could be supported by a small community with a number of physically fit people, but hardly by a single household involved in subsistence farming. The planning and effort spent on the ditch thus express social integration or, in the words of Gauntlett, of the 'community glue' behind the making process, probably steered by situational leadership.[24]

THE TARCHANKUT PENINSULA (CRIMEA):
HOUSEHOLD TRADITIONS AND SPATIAL ORGANIZATION

Our second case study illustrates how geophysical data throws light on the scale of construction and building tradition in agro-pastoral groups in Bronze Age Crimea (Russia). Geophysical surveys were carried out on the Tarchankut Peninsula in north-western Crimea (now Russia) as part of the Dzarylgac Survey Project (DSP) in 2007 and 2008. The project focused on the diachronic reconstruction of the settlement history of the hinterland of the short-lived Greek coastal town Panskoe near present-day Cernomorskoe.[25] Systematic artefact surveys were conducted in five landscape zones: the lowland ridge, the pediment, the area around the coastal lakes, the inland slopes, and the uplands / plateaus. Total field magnetometry surveys using an Overhauser GSM-19WG system were conducted by Tatiana Smekalova for the detailed mapping of areas of high archaeological potential in the coastal zone and the hillsides.[26] In 2008, large-scale magnetic gradiometry surveys using a flexible cart system mounted with 5 to 6 Foerster gradiometer probes were added to map unknown areas in the sloping inland, with a focus on the ridges endangered by the construction of a large wind power plant.[27] The combined archaeological and geophysical surveys revealed previously unknown rural aspects of settlement in this landscape, as well as the diachronic occupation of all landscape zones between the Bronze Age and the Early modern Tatar period. In contrast to models in which the hillsides and upland plateau were occupied only by nomadic pastoralists, a number of well-preserved single and clustered farmsteads were discovered on the presently uncultivated and artefact-poor inland slopes.[28] In some cases, they were associated with other features such as enclosures and pits. Here we present traces of protohistoric technology preserved at two of these inland settlements, discovered at survey areas Hill 1 and Hill 12 (fig. 4).

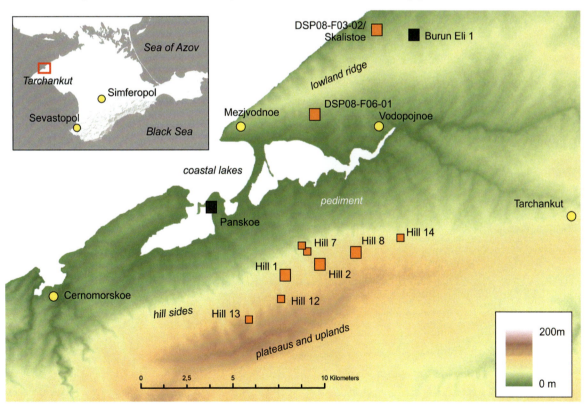

Fig. 4. The Dzarylgac Survey Project research area in the Tarchankut peninsula (Crimea) outlined in red (inset). Location of complex (large orange squares) and simple (small orange squares) Bronze Age settlements documented by the Dzarylgac Survey Project (after Guldager Bilde et al. 2012). Known archaeological sites mentioned in the text are indicated with a grey square; present-day towns with a yellow dot. (Maps W. de Neef; elevation data USGS/ESRI).

231

The site on Hill 1 (DSP07-H01-01) provides an exemplary case to understand the contribution of geophysical prospection to landscape archaeology. While the surface record consists of a few diffuse pottery fragments dating to the Bronze Age and Late Classical / Early Hellenistic period, the subsurface features mapped by magnetometry reveal a relatively well-preserved settlement with buildings, household pits, and enclosures (*fig. 5*). There is a clear spatial arrangement: the pits are located away from both the buildings and enclosures. One of the enclosures is imposed over another, indicating different occupation phases but also a persistent location preference. A nearby ash heap (Russian *solniki*), a typical settlement feature in Crimea and beyond, was identified in aerial photos.[29] Ash hills are usually interpreted as settlement refuse and occur from the Late Bronze Age to the Early Modern Tatar period.

The negative magnetic amplitudes (white) of the buildings and enclosures are produced by the magnetic contrast between the natural loess subsoil and the diamagnetic limestone wall foundations, while the household pits appear as positive anomalies (black) related to organic fills. The cause of the magnetic signal was confirmed by two test pits in rectangular building feature 5 and in a household pit in feature cluster 18 (for numbering see *fig. 5*). The pit in feature 5 revealed a shallow foundation of loosely laid limestone at a depth of maximum 50 cm below the present-day surface.[30] It sat on top of a culture layer and bordered on an ash layer to the SW. The test pit in feature 18 exposed a 1 m deep piriform pit interred in the loess subsoil, probably used for

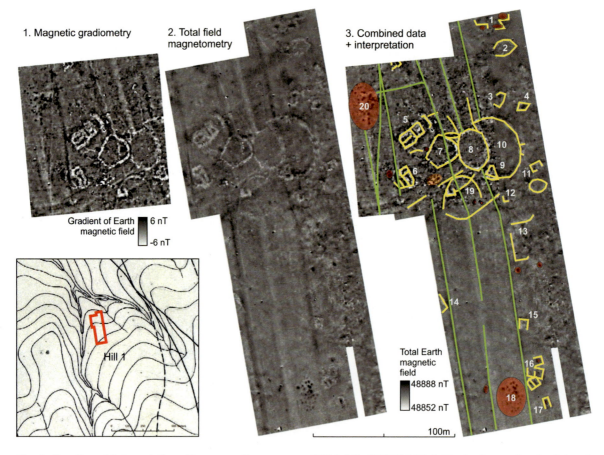

*Fig. 5. Results and interpretation of two magnetic surveys on Hill 1 (site DSP07-H01-1, Tarchankut peninsula, Crimea). 1: Magnetic gradiometry data (Eastern Atlas, 2008). 2: Total field cesium magnetometry data (T. Smekalova, 2007). 3: Both datasets overlain with interpretation (yellow: walls/negative magnetic amplitudes; red: pits/positive magnetic amplitudes; green: recent disturbances/modern land use traces). Inset: location of the magnetometry survey areas on a detail of the late 19th century topographic map of the Crimea. Based on Guldager Bilde et al. 2012: figures 4.147, 4.149, 4.151, and 4.152; interpretation by W. de Neef.*

household storage. It had a diameter of approximately 1 m and was filled with an organic cultural layer and an ash layer.[31]

Similar constellations of pits, enclosures and structures were detected at Hills 2, 6, and 8. In all cases, the surface record consisted of both Bronze Age and Late Classical / Early Hellenistic pottery fragments, which hindered the precise dating of the structures. The occurrence of Bronze Age material alongside pottery from Late Classical / Early Hellenistic phases in most of these sites indicates that these hillside promontories were the preferred settlement locations over long periods, which can be explained by their sheltered position in the windy steppe of Northwestern Crimea. An enclosure on Hill 8 showing similar dimensions and magnetic signal to those on Hill 1 was dated to the Bronze Age based on a test pit.[32] The enclosures on Hill 1 may thus also date to the Bronze Age, but it was impossible to verify this data.

So far, enclosures are only found on the hillsides, but such evidence may be biased because no magnetic prospection was attempted at (Bronze Age) sites in the cultivated lowland zones. However, the site densities in the different landscape zones point to different land use strategies: north of Lake Dzarylgac Bronze Age sites are substantial and spaced 4-5 km apart,[33] whereas on the hillsides they are smaller but more densely distributed at 0.7 – 2 km intervals (*fig. 4*). The ubiquitous presence of animal enclosures on the hillsides indicates that their inhabitants were settled (agro-)pastoralists. They may be seasonal shepherd camps linked to the lake settlements, similar to Greek *stani*, or year-round pastoral barns such as the Greek *mandria*.[34] The size and spatial distribution of the hillside settlements suggests that each of them was used by a small group of people, probably an (extended) family, a system that continued from the Bronze Age to pre-Soviet periods.

The animal enclosures in the hillside sites were integral part of pastoral subsistence strategies of their occupants. Enclosures have multiple functions including milking, shearing, separating of animals and overnight stabling. Moreover, the dung produced in animal enclosures provided an important energy source in an environment such as the steppe that does not offer a wealth of fuel; the ashes produced by the combustion of dung probably ended in the numerous *solniki* associated with the settlements (see above). To monitor the secondary products including the important dung, building and maintaining animal enclosures would have been a crucial occupation in the Bronze Age societies of the Tarchankut peninsula. Local limestone is the obvious building material in this treeless landscape and an important indicator for the capacity of the technology involved. Resource management can also be deduced from the traces of limestone quarries near Hills 12, 19, 22, and 24.[35]

The similarities between the enclosures in the magnetometry data of the hillsides reveal a standardized repertoire or building tradition of smaller and larger pens adapted at their multiple functions. Moreover, the similar arrangements within the investigated sites of enclosures, household (storage) pits, buildings and ash heaps are evidence for optimized spatial organization. The limited variation in size between the detected pens and the limited distance between the hillside sites show that animal herding was practiced at a small scale household level. Accordingly, the wall construction technique of the pens is not complex: non-mortared accumulations of stones to animal height; preserved are only the lower levels of loosely placed stones. Although prior knowledge of the ideal dimensions of animal pens is required for planning, the construction itself could be managed by a household with resources available in the direct vicinity of the site. This is underpinned by the experimental construction of a 1 m high and 1 m wide stone corral wall mimicking the prehistoric Fort Sage Drift Fence (Nevada, USA), where an estimated 0.66 m stone fence per person per hour was accomplished.[36] The construction of the animal pen at Hill 1, with a diameter of ca. 30 m and a total circumference of 94.2 m, would thus require a total of 142 person-hours or 17 person days. The animal enclosures mapped on the Tarchankut peninsula can therefore be interpreted as evidence for a small-scale level of making as part of a wider pastoralist 'community of practice' (*Table 2*).

CONTRADA DAMALE AND PORTIERI (CALABRIA, ITALY): BURNING DOWN THE HOUSE?

Our third case study continues the focus on small-scale production but also highlights the technology involved in the last stages of the 'biography of things',[37] namely Late Bronze Age buildings. The agricultural areas of Contrada Damale and Portieri in Calabria host a dense record of Late Bronze Age / Early Iron Age surface artefact scatters. These scatters were mapped during fieldwalking surveys (2000-2010) by the Groningen Institute of Archaeology (GIA), and studied intensively in the Rural Life in Protohistoric Italy (RLP) project between 2010-2016 (*fig. 6*). The RLP project aimed at a better understanding of the many small protohistoric pottery

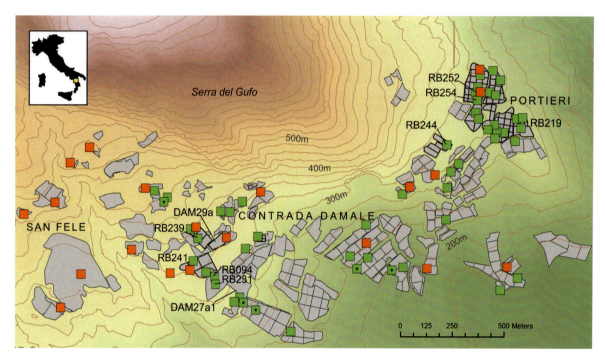

*Fig. 6. Protohistoric sites recorded in Contrada Damale and Portieri (municipality of Cerchiara di Calabria) and San Fele (municipality of Francavilla Marittima), Calabria, Italy. Green squares: simple surface scatters with Late Bronze Age/Early Iron Age dolio a cordoni o scanalature; dotted green squares: rich surface scatters with dolio a cordoni; orange squares: simple surface scatter. Fieldwalking survey areas investigated by GIA are in grey; sites mentioned in the text are labelled (map W. de Neef).*

scatters in the Raganello river basin through an interdisciplinary approach of archaeological (re-) surveys, geophysical prospection, targeted test pits and coring, and soil studies.[38] The majority of the 64 sites in Contrada Damale and Portieri yielded a wealth of *dolio a cordoni o a fasce* fragments, a large storage vessel often compared with Aegean pithoi. Previously, these vessels were associated with central Late Bronze Age / Early Iron Age settlements. However, with a total surface of 2 km² Contrada Damale and Portieri are much larger than any of the previously known central protohistoric settlements in this part of Italy and lack their typical morphological features, such as defendable slopes and limited access. Instead, Contrada Damale and Portieri are situated in open, undulating sloping land at the foot of a south-facing limestone bluff, which shelters them from the northern winds. The artefact scatters in these gently rolling fields are typically small, at a couple of meters in diameter, and spaced at intervals of some 150 m. The RLP team tentatively interpreted this cluster of sites as an open agricultural village, a site type previously unknown in southern Italian protohistory likely related to a sudden demographic explosion or resettlement, and which disappears just as sudden again at the end of the Early Iron Age.

The RLP program subjected representative examples of site types in the Contrada Damale and Portieri to a range of high-resolution prospection techniques including magnetometry, ground penetrating radar, electrical resistivity, manual augering, and artefact surveys. Magnetic gradiometry proved to be most effective in the detection of buried features associated with the surface archaeological record.[39] These include pits, ditches, and structural remains which offer new insights in the architecture and spatial organization of Late Bronze Age / Early Iron Age communities in northern Calabria. Remarkable are the (semi-) rectangular features of strongly magnetic materials which occur throughout the Contrada Damale and Portieri and which have been confirmed through targeted test pits to be associated with the Late Bronze Age / Early Iron Age surface scatters (*fig. 7*). Their obtained magnetic properties inform us about the life cycle of these features: the materials and techniques used to construct them, but also the events marking the end of their biography.

The rectangular features are characterized by strong magnetic amplitudes typical for thermore-

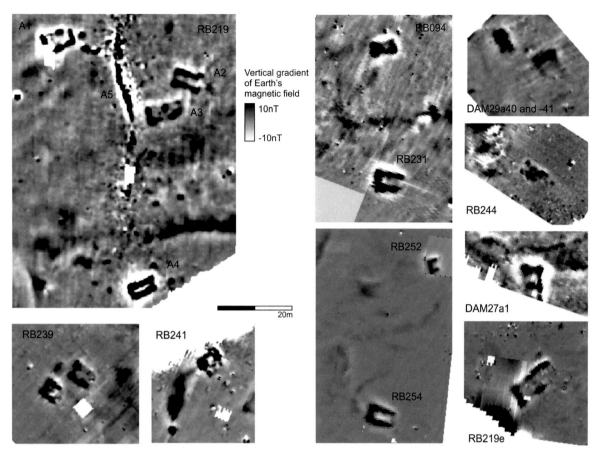

*Fig. 7. (Semi-)rectangular features in magnetic gradiometry data of Contrada Damale and Portieri (Calabria, Italy). All data in the same spatial and magnetic scale except DAM29a40 and -41 (+/-17nT) and RB252 (total field magnetometry, +46040/-45740nT). Locations of sites are indicated in figure 6. Geophysics by B. Ullrich/Eastern Atlas (RB219) and K. Armstrong/GIA (all other sites). (Maps W. de Neef/based on De Neef 2016).*

manent magnetism. This type of magnetic enhancement is caused by heating a material at a specific temperature above which it loses its inherent magnetic properties, the so-called Curie point, and subsequent cooling below this point, after which the magnetic domains in the material adopt the alignment of the Earth's magnetic field. By using such effects strongly heated materials can be detected through their remnant magnetization.

This is exactly the case of the structures at Contrada Damale and Portieri. Test pits in three of these rectangular features confirm that they are burnt cob constructions probably with lowered floors.[40] Although the test pit dimensions were too limited for detailed interpretation and reconstruction of the structures, the dimensions of the thermoremanent magnetic features indicate that these were huts of ca. 9 x 5 m. Laboratory analysis carried out on the burnt cob material of the walls including fractional conversion tests confirm that the material has been indeed burnt and therefore must have reached temperatures above 700°C, the typical Curie point for clays.[41]

Interestingly, in prehistoric cob buildings such high temperatures are only reached through repeated firing, since structures with simple wooden or dry vegetation roofs will burn quickly and most of the energy will escape vertically. This has been established through experiments with the burning of reconstructed Iron Age houses in Lejre (Denmark) and Butser Hill (UK).[42] With the rooftile generally introduced in Central Italy in the 7th or 6th century BC,[43] Late Bronze Age / Early Iron Age huts are commonly assumed to have been thatched and thus susceptible to quick vertical burning. The high temperatures reached in the cob of the lower walls of the huts in Contrada Damale and Portieri are therefore most likely the result of repeated, intentional firing. Indeed, temperatures of more than 700°C were only recorded in an experimentally ignited reconstruction of a Chalcolithic wattle-and-daub hut in Bulgaria after intentional refueling with straw.[44]

The combined results of magnetometer surveys, test pits, and laboratory analysis reveal aspects of protohistoric making, but also of deliberate un-making. The many and evenly distributed examples of thoroughly burnt cob houses in the Contrada Damale and Portieri suggest that these were not accidental fires, but the result of intentional action. Abandonment rituals including the intended irreversibility of burning down a house are known from various societies around the world.[45] Such rituals place abandonment in the intricate and dynamic relationships between buildings and their users, as a symbolic act performed by the people who outlive the structure. The Calabrian examples bring together the capacity, technology and product of a distinct architectural tradition of semi-interred cob buildings, but also the deliberate actions at the end of their life cycles which make them detectable for modern prospection techniques (*Table 3*).

Conclusion: Spatial and material aspects of technology in protohistoric societies

Geophysical surveys can contribute to archaeological research of protohistoric technology through the detection of specific material and spatial aspects of buried traces. In this paper, we have illustrated how such aspects can be interpreted in terms of production effort and the social framework of the making process. Where excavations provide information on the tangible traces of past production, geophysical data can place them in larger spatial contexts. Such spatial information on the dimensions and placement of particular features allows us to better estimate the effort spent on them, but also how unique they are in a specific situation. For instance, the construction of the curvilinear ditch at Montarice was a singular, labor-intensive event. On the other hand, the multiple animal pens in the same locations on the Tarchankut peninsula are the result of recurrent episodes of activity and evidence for persistent building traditions and the stability of socio-economic systems centered on livestock management. In the Contrada Damale and Portieri, geophysical surveys were instrumental to interpret the burnt huts not as local accidents, but as regional phenomena. The recurrence of striking thermoremanent rectangular features throughout Contrada Damale is an indication of standardized architecture and construction techniques, but possibly also of abandonment practices.

With recent technological developments including larger mobile equipment with several sensors, more powerful computers, and accurate positioning using GNSS, high resolution geophysical prospections are now commonly applied to map large scale areas. This allows us to investigate more in detail the different dimensions of ancient technology as opposed to traditional archaeological strategies such as excavations and field walking. Moreover, the examples of Crimea and Calabria show that locations with diffuse and ephemeral-looking surface records can host surprisingly complex and well-preserved traces of past activities. Without geophysical surveys, we would not have been able to interpret what people did here and how they arranged their activities.

The three case studies presented in this work are particularly well placed to illustrate the potential of geophysical data, however, we acknowledge that the success of geophysical detection depends on a range of conditions including measurable physical contrasts, post-depositional processes, and accessibility as well as from the experience and knowledge of specialists. Within the limits of detectability, however, there are specific types of archaeological remains that are better-suited for geophysical prospection, such as stone structures, ferrous objects, heated and/or burnt features, organic fills, and water-bearing deposits. Taking these limitations in account, there are specific stages of past production that we can expect to be able to identify using geophysical prospection techniques:

- Architectural end products such as walls, moats, canals, storage pits;
- Metal products;
- The remains of productive stages such as kilns, fireplaces, and postholes;
- Secondary production waste such as middens, waste pits, slag heaps, briquetage pottery;
- Areas of material depletion such as quarries;
- Areas of material accumulation such as stone cairns, clay heaps.

Detection of such features dating to (late) prehistoric phases is often more difficult than those dated to historical phases due to the scale and nature of pre-industrialized production, and also to location preferences and long-duration post-depositional processes. Such circumstances help to understand why pre- and protohistoric traces remain underrepresented in geophysical prospection surveys as compared to traces of later, historical phases, especially in the Mediterranean and Black Sea areas. We are convinced that it is possible to unravel aspects concerning the capacity, activity, products, and preservation of (late) prehistoric technology by interpreting modern prospection data in terms of complexity, specialization, knowledge transfer and energy input of production. Therefore, by combining tangible traces of past technology with state-of-the-art prospection techniques, the 'community glue' of making can be approached in a new way.

| Table 1. Montarice (Porto Recanati, Marche, Italy). Technological aspects to build a curvilinear ditch. |||
| --- | --- | --- |
| Capacity | Demand, scope, knowhow | Community; estimated labor 5000-9600 person-hours |
| Activity | Technical process, cognitive and social aspects of making | Not complex but requires planning and decision-making |
| Product | End-product and by-products | Ditch of 170 m long, 4-5 m wide, estimated 2 m deep; filled with organic material and settlement debris |
| Preservation | Conservation and detectability | Exemplary; detectable through magnetic contrast between ditch infill and natural conglomerate subsoil. No evidence for accompanying rampart, but this may be due to postdepositional effects. |

| Table 2. Hill 1 and 12 (Tarchankut Peninsula, Crimea, Russia). Technological aspects of animal pens. |||
| --- | --- | --- |
| Capacity | Demand, scope, knowhow | Household; estimated labor 142 person-hours for a pen with a diameter of 30 m |
| Activity | Technical process, cognitive and social aspects of making | Not complex but requires planning and decision-making according to multiple functions of pens |
| Product | End-product and by-products | Animal enclosure made with local limestone; typical diameter 20 - 40 m |
| Preservation | Conservation and detectability | Exemplary; detectable through magnetic contrast between diamagnetic limestone and loess subsoil |

| Table 3. Contrada Damale and Portieri (Calabria, Italy). Technological aspects of burnt structures. |||
| --- | --- | --- |
| Capacity | Demand, scope, knowhow | Household/community |
| Activity | Technical process, cognitive and social aspects of making | Multi-person project; requires planning and multiple resources; intended burning of complete structure upon abandonment |
| Product | End-product and by-products | Single structure of ca. 9 x 5 m with lowered floor, wooden frame with cob walls, thatched roof; end product: lower part of burnt walls |
| Preservation | Conservation and detectability | Exemplary; detectable through thermoremanent magnetic contrast between burnt cob walls and natural subsoil |

## Notes

1. Auyang 2004, 18.
2. Jones 2004, 330; Jones 2007, 36; Gauntlett 2011, 2, 25; Brysbaert 2017, 15-16.
3. Gauntlett 2011, 21.
4. Lave and Wenger 1991; Wenger 1998; Wendrich 2012.
5. Gaffney/Gater 2006.
6. Kountouri *et al.* 2012; Lane *et al.* 2016.
7. Cremaschi *et al.* 2015.
8. Gallo *et al.* 2011.
9. Tsokas *et al.* 2012.
10. Urban *et al.* 2014.
11. Zöllner *et al.* 2008.
12. Goethals *et al.* 2005.
13. Work on the protohistoric phases of Montarice, including the reconstruction of Lollini's trenches, is part of the first author's current postdoctoral research at Ghent University.
14. Boullart 2003; Vermeulen/Boullart 2005.
15. Vermeulen *et al.* 2017.
16. Ullrich 2013.
17. 'Positive' cropmarks are higher and /or greener vegetation as compared to the surroundings. They are connected to improved nutrition of a crop as the result of deeper and/or more organic deposits; 'negative' cropmarks are the opposite (Gojda/Hejcman 2012).
18. Gnade 2016.
19. Cipriani 2010.
20. Such a limited enclosed area resembles an unpublished example of Bronze Age levels at Numana on the Adriatic coast (pers.comm. Andrea Cardarelli).
21. Jewell 1963.
22. Grigg 2018.
23. Di Gennaro and Guidi (2010) estimate a community living in a 1-hectare area to be around 100-150 people of all ages. This number is based on the Italian censuses of the 17th century. Grigg (2018) estimates that adults in pre-modern societies would not be available for communal works during 100 days per year when they were needed for various subsistence activities, but he proposes 200 days for more cautious researchers.
24. There is little evidence for hereditary status in Italy until the Late Bronze Age and the social organization of Bronze Age communities is commonly thought to be based on kinship.
25. Guldager Bilde *et al.* 2012.
26. Smekalova *et al.* 2016.
27. Meyer *et al.* 2012.
28. See also Stolba and Andresen 2015 for recent discoveries on inland settlements.
29. Guldager Bilde *et al.* 2012, 87.
30. Guldager Bilde *et al.* 2012, figures 4.156-158.
31. Guldager Bilde *et al.* 2012: figures 4.154 – 155.
32. Guldager Bilde *et al.* 2012.
33. Large Bronze Age sites North of Lake Dzarylgac include DSP08-F06-01 and the previously known sites Skalistoe 2, Burun Eli 1 and Severnoe 1.
34. Chang/Tourtelotte 1993.
35. Guldager Bilde *et al.* 2012, 148.
36. Hockett *et al.* 2013, 70.
37. Kopytoff 1986; see also Fontijn 2013 for an update on the use of the term.
38. De Neef 2016; De Neef *et al.* 2017; De Neef/Van Leusen 2016.
39. De Neef *et al.* 2017; Van Leusen *et al.* 2014.
40. Test pits in rectangular features A1 and A4 at site RB219 (Portieri) and at site RB231 (Contrada Damale; De Neef 2016; De Neef/Van Leusen 2016).
41. Kostadinova-Avramova/Kostanova 2013; De Neef/Van Leusen 2016.
42. Rasmussen 2007; Harrison 2013.
43. Van 't Lindenhout 2016.
44. Cavulli/Gheorghiu 2008, 40-41.
45. Schiffer/LaMotta 1999.

## Bibliography

Auyang, S. 2004, *Engineering – an endless frontier*. Cambridge, MA.

Boullart, C. 2003, Piceni settlements: untraceable or neglected? *Picus* 23, 155-188.

Brysbaert, A. 2017, Artisans versus nobility? Crafting in context: introduction, in A. Brysbaert/A. Gorgues (eds), *Artisans versus nobility? Multiple identities of elites and "commoners" viewed through the lens of crafting form the Chalcolithic to the Iron Ages in Europe and the Mediterranean*, Leiden, 13-36.

Cavulli, F./D. Gheorghiu 2008, Looking for a methodology burning wattle and daub housing structures. A preliminary report on an archaeological experiment, *Journal of Experimental Pyrotechnologies* 1, 37-43.

Chang, C./P.A. Tourtellotte, 1993, Ethnoarchaeological survey of pastoral transhumance sites in the Grevena region, Greece, *Journal of Field Archaeology* 20(3), 249-264.

Cipriani, G. 2010, *Ardea: le fortificazioni urbane e del Castrum Inui*, PhD thesis, Università degli Studi di Roma Tor Vergata.

Cremaschi, M./A. Mutti/G. Baratti/F. Borgi/F. Brandolini/N. Donati/P. Ferrari/G. Fronza/T. Lachenal/A. Zerboni 2015, La Terramara Santa Rosa di Poviglio: strutture tra Villaggio Piccolo e Villaggio Grande. Nuovi dati dallo scavo 2015, *Fasti Online* 349, 1-13.

De Neef, W. 2016, *Surface <> Subsurface. A methodological study of Metal Age settlement and land use in Calabria, Italy*. PhD thesis, University of Groningen.

De Neef, W./K. Armstrong/P.M. Van Leusen 2017, Putting the spotlight on small Metal Age pottery scatters in Northern Calabria (Italy), *Journal of Field Archaeology* 42(4), 283-297.

De Neef, W./P.M. Van Leusen 2016, Devilish Details. Fine-tuning survey techniques for ephemeral sites, in H. Kamermans/W. de Neef/C. Piccoli/A.G. Posluschny/R. Scopigno (eds), *The Three Dimensions of Archaeology. Proceedings of the XVII UISPP World Congress (1–7 September 2014, Burgos, Spain), Volume 7/Sessions A4b and A12*, Oxford, 121-131.

Di Gennaro, F./A. Guidi 2010, Lo stato delle anime come mezzo per la ricostruzione della popolazione dei villaggi protostorici, *Arqueologia Espacial* 28, 1-9.

Fontijn, D. 2013, Epilogue: cultural biographies and itineraries of things: second thoughts, in H.P. Hahn/H. Weis (eds), *Mobility, meaning and transformation of things: shifting contexts of material culture through time and space*, Oxford, 183-195.

Gaffney, C.F./J. Gater 2003, *Revealing the buried past: geophysics for archaeologists*, Stroud.

Gallo, D./M. Ciminale/M. Pallara/R. Laviano 2011, Susceptibility measurements, optical and X-ray analysis to explain the origin of archaeological magnetic anomalies in Tavoliere lowland (Southern Italy), *Journal of Archaeological Science,* 38(2), 399-407.

Gauntlett, D. 2011, *Making is Connecting. The Social Meaning of Creativity, from DIY and Knitting to YouTube and Web 2.0,* Cambridge.

Gnade, M. 2016, Le fortificazioni arcaiche dell'antica Satricum. Indagini archeologiche nell'area urbana inferiore, in P. Fontaine/S. Helas (eds), *Le fortificazione arcaiche del Latium vetus e dell'Etruria meridionale (IX-VI sec. a.C.) : Stratigrafia, cronologia e urbanizzazione,* Bruxelles-Roma, 213-231.

Gojda, M./M. Hejcman 2012, Cropmarks in main field crops enable the identification of a wide spectrum of buried features on archaeological sites in Central Europe, *Journal of Archaeological Science,* 39(6), 1655-1664.

Goethals, T./M. De Dapper/F. Vermeulen 2005, Geomorphology and geoarchaeology of three sites in the Potenza Valley Survey Project (The Marches, Italy): Potentia, Montarice and Helvia Recina, *Revista de Geomorfologie* 7, 33-49.

Grigg, E. 2018, *Warfare, Raiding and Defense in Early Medieval Britain,* Ramsbury.

Guldager Bilde, P./P. Attema/K. Winther-Jacobsen (eds) 2012, *The Dzarylgac Survey Project. Black Sea Studies 14,* Aarhus.

Harrison, K. 2013, The application of forensic fire investigations in the archaeological record, *Journal of Archaeological Science* 40(2), 955-959.

Hockett, B./C. Creger/B. Smith/C. Young/J. Carter/ E. Dillingham/R. Crews/E. Pellegrini 2013, Large-scale trapping features from the Great Basin, USA: the significance of leadership and communal gatherings in ancient foraging societies, *Quaternary International* 29,7 64-78.

Jewell, P. 1963, *The Experimental Earthwork on Overton Down, Wiltshire, 1960: An Account of the Construction of an Earthwork to Investigate by Experiment the Way in which Archaeological Structures are Denuded and Buried,* London.

Jones, A. 2004, Archaeometry and materiality: materials-based analysis in theory and practice, *Archaeometry* 46, 327-338.

Jones, A. 2007, *Memory and Material Culture,* Cambridge.

Kopytoff, I. 1986, The cultural biography of things: Commoditization as process, in Appadurai, A. (ed) *The social life of things: commodities in cultural perspective,* Cambridge, 64-91.

Kostadinova-Avramova, M./M. Kostanova 2013, The magnetic properties of baked clays and their implications for past geomagnetic field intensity determinations, *Geophysical Journal International* 195, 1534-1550.

Kountouri, E./N. Petrochilos/D. Koutsoyiannis/ N. Mamassis/N. Zarkadoulas/A. Vött/H. Hadler/ P. Henning/T. Willershäuser 2012, A new project of surface survey, geophysical and excavation research of the Mycenaean drainage works of the North Kopais: the first study season, in *IWA Specialized Conference on Water and Wastewater,* London, 467-476.

Lane, M.F./T.J. Horsley/A. Charami/W.S. Bittner 2016, Archaeological geophysics of a Bronze Age agricultural landscape: the AROURA Project, central mainland Greece, *Journal of Field Archaeology* 41(3), 271-296.

Lave, J./E. Wenger 1991, *Situated Learning. Legitimate Peripheral Participation,* Cambridge.

Meyer, C./D. Pilz/T. Smekalova/B. Ullrich 2012, Geophysical Surveys, in P. Guldager Bilde/P. Attema/ K. Winther-Jacobsen (eds), *The Dzarylgac Survey Project. Black Sea Studies 14.* Aarhus, 26-28.

Rasmussen, M. 2007, *Iron Age houses in Flames: testing house reconstructions at Lejre. Studies in Technology and Culture 3.* Lejre.

Smekalova, T.N./E.B. Yatsishina/A.S. Garipov/A.E. Pasumanskii/R.S. Ketsko/A.V. Chudin 2016, Natural science methods in field archaeology, with the case study of Crimea, *Crystallography Reports,* 61(4), 533–542.

Stolba, V./J. Andresen 2015, Unveiling the hinterland: a new type of Hellenistic rural settlement in the Crimea, *Antiquity* 89, 345-360.

Tsokas, G.N/A. Van de Moortel/P.I. Tsourlos/A. Stampolidis/G. Vargemezis/E. Zahou 2012, Geophysical survey as an aid to excavation at Mitrou: a preliminary report, *Hesperia* 81 (3), 383-432.

Ullrich, B. 2013, *Geophysical surveys for the Potenza Valley Survey.* Internal Report, Eastern Atlas Gmbh &Co KG, Berlin.

Urban, T.M./J.F. Leon/S.W. Manning/K.D. Fisher 2014, High resolution GPR mapping of Late Bronze Age architecture at Kalavasos-Ayios Dhimitrios, Cyprus, *Journal of Applied Geophysics* 107, 129-136.

Van Leusen, P.M./A. Kattenberg/K. Armstrong 2014, Magnetic susceptibility detection of small protohistoric sites in the Raganello Basin, Calabria (Italy), *Archaeological Prospection* 21(4), 245-253.

Van 't Lindenhout, E. 2016, Taking courage: from huts to houses. Reflections on changes in early archaic architecture in Latium Vetus (Central Italy), in P. Attema/ J. Seubers/S.Willemsen (eds), *Early states, territories and settlements in protohistoric Central Italy. Corollaria Crustumina 2,* Groningen, 143-151.

Vermeulen, F./C. Boullart 2005, The Potenza Valley Survey, *BABesch,* 76, 1-18.

Vermeulen, F./D. Van Limbergen/P. Monsieur/D. Taelman (eds) 2017, *The Potenza Valley Survey (Marche, Italy). Settlement dynamics and changing material culture in an Adriatic valley between Iron age and late antiquity. Academia Belgica Studia Archeologica 1,* Rome.

Wendrich, W. 2012, Archaeology and apprenticeship. Body knowledge, identity, and communities of practice, in Wendrich, W. (ed), *Archaeology and Apprenticeship. Body knowledge, identity, and communities of practice,* Tucson, 1-19.

Wenger, E. 1998, *Communities of Practice. Learning, Meaning, and Identity,* Cambridge.

Zöllner, H./B. Ullrich/R. Rolle/S. Makhortykh/M. Orlyuk 2008, Results of geophysical prospection in the Scythian settlement of Belsk (Bol'šoe Belskoe Gorodišče), in A. Posluschny/K. Lamberts/I. Herzog (eds), *Layers of Perception. Proceedings of the 35th International Conference on Computer Applications and Quantitative Methods in Archaeology (CAA); Berlin, Germany, April 2–6, 2007. Kolloquien zur Vor- und Frühgeschichte, Vol. 10,* Bonn, 1-4.

# Posters

# Manufacturing *tubuli*
## *An experimental reconstruction of the chaîne opératoire based on archaeological evidence*

*Sadi Maréchal, Nathalie de Haan, Tim Clerbaut*

*Abstract*

*Tubuli (box tiles) were widely used in the wall heating systems of Roman public and private baths and villas from the early imperial period onwards. Various experiments have shown that wall heating made an important contribution to the rise in room temperature due to the most efficient radiant heating of tubulated walls. Despite the large number of surviving specimens of tubuli from sites all over the Roman Empire, little is known about their production. The experiments presented here shed more light on the manufacturing of tubuli, including the production time involved per tubulus for a trained worker. As for the successful firing, more experiments accounting for varying circumstances of drying (location, duration) and the size of kilns remain a desideratum and are planned as future research by the same team.\**

THE ROMAN BOX TILE (TUBULUS)

Wall heating was an essential part of the Roman hypocaust system. Hot gasses circulating in a hollow space within the wall both insulated and actively heated a room. From the different types of wall heating systems that were invented from the second century BC onwards, the system with hollow terra cotta box tiles (*tubuli*) was probably the most effective and definitely the most popular.[1] Even if the first prototypes of *tubuli* seem to reach back to the early second century BC (baths of *Fregellae* in *Latium*),[2] large-scale use only began from the first century AD onwards, when *tubuli* were introduced in the heated rooms of (bath) houses. Just as other types of wall heating, such as tiles with protruding knobs (*tegulae mammatae*) or flat tiles distanced from the walls by terra cotta studs or spacers, *tubuli* enabled an efficient radiant heating of larger spaces. Moreover, stacked *tubuli* formed a sturdy construction which could be clad with marble panels, whereas the construction with *tegulae mammatae* was not strong enough to carry the weight of marble slabs. Since marble veneer for wall decoration came into vogue by the middle of the first century AD, the rise in popularity of box-tiles can be directly linked to this development. Both literary sources and archaeological evidence confirm this date.[3]

The success of *tubuli* can be measured by the very fact that they were employed for many centuries until the period of Late Antiquity in all regions of the Empire. Several studies – including experiments in recreated hypocaust systems – have investigated the function of these *tubuli* within the Roman heating system, suggesting that wall heating was indispensable for reaching a high temperature in *caldaria*, damp and warm rooms (steam baths, max. 40°C), or *sudatoria*, characterized by dry heat, reaching room temperatures up to 60°-70°C.[4] It is therefore remarkable that so far only a minimal amount of research has focussed on *tubuli*, their production, and development over time.

OBSERVATIONS ON THE ARCHAEOLOGICAL MATERIAL

As *tubuli* were hardly ever stamped, it is difficult to find out by whom and where these building materials were produced. In the absence of any known production sites specializing in the production of *tubuli*, we assume that the production of *tubuli* took place in workshops where other types of brick and tile were manufactured. Decisive for the choice of production sites would have been the local availability of high quality clay and connectivity by road or water to ensure a swift distribution.

The specific shape of a *tubulus* required a more elaborate production process than, for example, a simple one-foot brick. Moreover, its more complex form required the use of high quality clay. By observing examples of *tubuli* found in Italy (Ostia) and the Roman province of *Gallia Belgica*, we have observed two types of possible production methods. For the 'Ostian' specimens, we observed a single 'seam' in one of the corners of every single *tubulus*. This means that a single slab of clay was wrapped around a (presumably wooden) core and 'closed' in a single seam. As a seam could be considered the 'weak point' during the firing process, the single-seam technique would have been the most obvious choice from a technical point of view. In the group of 'Gaulish' *tubuli*, however, some of the examples show traces of four seams, one in each corner. This would imply that four separate slabs of clay were joined around a (wooden) core. These observations formed the basis of our experimental production process. A third type of *tubulus*, which seems to have been made as a cylinder on a potter's wheel, will not be discussed in this article. This type is mainly found in the eastern Mediterranean.[5]

EXPERIMENTAL PRODUCTION

The experiment took place in three distinct phases: producing, drying and finally firing the *tubuli* (*fig. 1*). For the production, we used a pure ready-made potter's clay, fine riverine sand and hand-made pegged wooden frames and a wooden core. The timeframe of the experiment was as follows: February 2017, production of 7 *tubuli*; February – June 2017, drying of the produced *tubuli*; July 2017, baking of 5 *tubuli* (2 *tubuli* were not suitable for baking).

The first step of the production process consisted of producing a workable clay. We soon discovered that this process may have necessitated a separate production role on site, as this took us a considerable amount of time. For a volume of around 7 kg of clay, it took an average of six minutes before the clay became soft and malleable. As a second step, we moulded the clay into a wooden frame (internal dimensions: 56 x 36 cm; 2 cm deep), or four frames for the 'Gaulish' type (12 x 36 cm; 2 cm deep), ensuring the same dimensions for every *tubulus*. Spreading the clay into the frame (step 2, *fig. 1*) took an average of two minutes. It proved to be a daunting task to achieve a homogenous, smooth clay slab with no internal seams. Thirdly, we dusted the inside of the slabs with sand so that the clay would easily be detached from the core. Subsequently, we flattened the edges that would make up the seam, as to facilitate the overlap (step 3, *fig. 1* and *fig. 2*). For the fourth step, we wrapped the slab around a wooden core (8.5 x 11 x 36 cm), making sure the clay did not tear (step 4, *fig. 1*). This required delicate handling when wrapping the slab around the edges of the core. The process of dusting, trimming and wrapping took another three to four minutes. For the 'Gaulish' type, we used two wooden L-shaped moulds to press the separate slabs against the core (*fig. 3*). We paid special attention to joining the edges that made up the seam, as this would be the most vulnerable point of the *tubulus*. For the 'Ostian' type of *tubuli*, we positioned the seam in one of the corners (as observed in some archaeological examples) or in the middle of one of the long sides. For some of the *tubuli*, we cut out openings in the small sides using wooden knives or round metal shapes. Such openings are often found in *tubuli* of *Gallia Belgica*, but are non-existent in the Ostian contexts. These may have enabled a lateral gas circulation between neighbouring rows of *tubuli*, providing the openings were placed at the same height. With the same wooden knife and with a wooden comb, a net pattern was then incised on the outer side of some *tubuli*, as this enabled a better grip of the *tubulus* into the mortar of the outer wall or of plaster (for wall painting) or mortar (for marble veneer) on the side of the *tubulus* facing the inside of the room. Lastly in step 5 (*fig. 1*), we removed the wooden core, which was remarkably easy due to the sand. The process, starting from step one to step five, took us an average of 11-12 minutes, regardless of which type was produced.

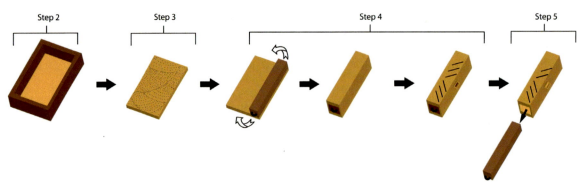

*Fig. 1. Schematic representation of the production process (image by the authors).*

*Fig. 2. The 'Ostian' type during production (photo: authors).*

## Observations on the experimental production

The experimental *tubuli* showed the same sort of smear marks in the internal corners as those observed in the 'Ostian' examples (*fig. 4*). These marks were made when the wooden core was pulled out of the *tubulus*, while the clay was still soft. This shows us that the 'core wrapping technique' could have been a viable option for creating 'Ostian' *tubuli*, but also that the core was removed before the drying. Moreover, we noted that transporting an unbaked *tubulus* was rather difficult and should best be done with the core still in place. This gives the greenling additional stability. Therefore, it seems reasonable that the *tubuli*, weighing around 8 kg each (including the core), were produced in close proximity to the drying area of the workshop. When we arranged the *tubuli* for drying, we placed them in an upright position, which seemed the most logical solution to dry all the surfaces of the *tubulus*. After the period of drying, we noted that the rims of the bottom end of some *tubuli* slightly protruded outwards. This was a result of the weight of an entire *tubulus* resting on these rims, thus creating an 'elephant foot'-like end when the clay was a bit too soft.

## Drying and baking

In this first experiment, we produced seven samples. These were dried for four months, in a room with a constant temperature, until the clay was 'leather-hard'. During this process, one of the *tubuli* made with joining four separate slabs (the 'Gaulish' type) cracked along the seams. All other samples survived the drying process, regardless of where the seam had been located or which technique ('Ostian' or 'Gaulish') was used. The surviving samples were then baked in a small,

*Fig. 3. The 'Gaulish' type during production (photo: authors).*

traditional up-draught kiln with a mixed content including pottery.[6] After several hours of heating, the temperature attained a maximum of 950°C. Unfortunately, several of the *tubuli* of both types were damaged during the firing process, leaving this stage of the experiment inconclusive. The

*Fig. 4. Detailed observation of a* tubulus *from Ostia (left) and of the longitudinal section of an experimental 'Ostian'* tubulus *(right) with the white arrow indicating the internal smear mark after removal of the core (photo: authors).*

clay was possibly still too wet when fired, meaning remaining water inside the clay turned into gas, causing some of the *tubuli* to explode. The flying debris possibly damaged other samples.

CONTEXTUALIZING THE FIRST RESULTS AND
REMAINING QUESTIONS

This experiment added some interesting new insights into the production process of *tubuli*. For the first phase we noticed how time-consuming the preparation of the clay could be. To achieve a homogenous and malleable lump, there is need for a strong pair of hands and a considerable amount of time. This phase of the production process may well have been a separate job on the production site. Once a worker could be supplied with a continuous supply of such malleable lumps, we could easily imagine a single person making up to ten *tubuli* in one hour. A production of 70-80 *tubuli* per person per day could then easily be imagined. If, on the other hand, the preparation of the clay was done by one and the same worker, the production would be considerably lower, more or less half the number. The costs (expressed in time invested by workers), however, for the workshop owner would be the same (70-80 produced by two persons = 35-40 *tubuli* made by one person a day).

The greenlings that were produced during our experiment show identical features as observed on archaeological finds. This proves at least that the techniques are suitable for the production of Roman *tubuli*.

For the second phase, we experienced that the drying space should best be near the production site, to minimize the risk of damaging the greenlings. For the same reason, the removal of the core could best be done once the greenlings had arrived in the drying area. Our experiment showed that the process of drying involves expertise as well as experience. The speed of drying would vary considerably according to the circumstances: inside (e.g. in a shed) or outside (under a roof or not), exposed to sun and/or wind or not, the time involved for the drying process etc. All these factors determined the optimum moment for firing the greenlings. Ancient writers show glimpses of the knowledge and experience that was needed for the production of brick and tile, for both the unbaked and baked variants of *lateres* ('bricks'). M. Cetius Faventinus, for example, states in his treatise on building "You are to cut your bricks in spring, so that they may dry slowly", echoing a passage in Vitruvius written some three hundred years earlier.[7] Likewise, Palladius (an author of the late fourth or early fifth century) explains that the production of brick should take place in May, June or September. During the hot summer months the drying process would proceed too quickly and eventually cause cracks.[8]

The third phase turned out to be most problematic. Examples of both the 'Ostian' and the 'Gaulish' type survived the firing, demonstrating both techniques could be used. For the 'Gaulish' type with four seams, this was somewhat surprising, especially as one sample had cracked along the seams during the drying process. However, several samples exploded during the firing process, stressing the importance of a long period of drying.

The well-known Price Edict of Diocletian (early fourth century), fixing maximum prices for goods and services in an attempt to stop inflation, sets the price for four two-feet bricks or tiles (*lateres pedum v(=b)inum*), including the preparation of the clay, at two *denarii*.[9] The same Price Edict fixes the price for a *tubulus* (or perhaps a number of *tubuli*?) at 6 *denarii*, whereas the price of an ordinary one-foot brick or circular brick (used in hypocausts), or an equal number of them, were apparently cheaper with a price fixed at 4 *denarii*.[10] Even if the Price Edict has limited value for our knowledge of ancient price-levels, given the fact that prices could vary from region to region in the same period or according to different periods, these prices do tell us something about relative values. The higher price of a *tubulus* could be explained by its more time-consuming production process, the higher quality of clay needed for its successful production, or, alternatively, the higher risks involved in drying and firing *tubuli* compared to ordinary brick and tile.

To gain further understanding of the efficiency and the actual logistics of the production of *tubuli*, further experiments are being planned. We intend to fire more samples in a reconstructed Roman open-topped tile kiln in Saalburg in the near future, hoping for more insight into the firing of larger numbers of *tubuli*, also experimenting with the duration of the drying process.[11]

## Notes

\* We would like to express our gratitude to the editors of this volume, Professor Marijke Gnade and Martina Revello Lami, for organising an inspiring conference and for offering us the possibility to publish these first results. We warmly thank the volunteers of De Gallische Hoeve in Destelbergen (Belgium) for help and advice, and Dr. Claire Stocks (Newcastle), who has been so kind as to read and correct our English text.

[1] Degbomont 1984, 135-158; see also Schiebold 2010, 18-24; Yegül 2010, 87-89; Lehar 2012, 181-232.

[2] Tsiolis 2013, 95.

[3] Literary sources: Sen. *Ep.* 90.25: "*Quaedam nostra demum prodisse memoria scimus, (…), ut suspensuras balneorum et inpressos parietibus tubos per quos circumfunderetur calor, qui ima simul ac summa foveret aequaliter.*" (We know that certain devices have come to light only within our own lifetime (...) such as baths with hypocausts and tubes let into their walls for the purpose of diffusing the heat which maintains an even temperature in their lowest as well as in their highest spaces." Translation adapted from the Loeb Classical Library edition, 1920.) For archaeological evidence of *tubuli* used at an early stage in the Vesuvian area, and the relation between the rise of *tubuli* and the use of marble veneer as wall decoration in public and private baths, see De Haan 2010, 67-68.

[4] Kretzschmer 1953; see also Rook 1979; Yegül/Couch 2003; Yegül 2010, 89; Grassmann 2011; Lehar 2012.

[5] For the *tubuli* in Ostia, see Maréchal 2020, 112. For the *tubuli* in the eastern Mediterranean, see Reeves/Harvey 2016.

[6] The small pottery kiln was built by the non-profit organization 'De Gallische Hoeve' in Destelbergen, near Ghent.

[7] Marcus Cetius Faventinus, *De diversis fabricis architectonae*, 10: "*Ducendi autem sunt lateres verno tempore, ut ex lento siccescant.*" Faventinus' treatise dates most probably to the second half of the third century AD. For the text and an English translation, see Plommer 1973. An identical passage in Vitruvius (Faventinus' source) can be found Vitr. *De arch.* 2.3. See also Plin. *HN* 35.170.

[8] See Palladius *De architectura* 6.12 (May), 7.8 (June) and 10.15 (September)

[9] Price Edict ed. Lauffer (1971) 7.15: *lateris crudi ad lateruculos diurnam mercedem, in lateribus quattuor pedum vinum* (sic), *ita ut ipse sibi inpensam praep[a]ret, pasto. (denarii) duos.* (For a maker of bricks (tiles) ready for firing, for every four two-feet bricks (*bipedales*), including the preparation of the clay and meals: two *denarii*.)

[10] Price Edict ed. Erim/Reynolds (1973) 15.20: *laterem pudalem* (sic) *quattuor (denarii); laterem rutundum* (sic) *quattuor (denarii); tubulum sive pyrodromum [s]ex (denarii).*

[11] The first results will be published in Clerbaut et al. (Forthcoming).

## Bibliography

Clerbaut T./T. Hauck/A. Langgartner/R. Schwarz, forthcoming, Mind the gap(s): theoretical and hands-on approaches to the production of Roman brick and tile based on experiments held at the Saalburg Museum, in L. Graña Nicolaou/T. Ivleva/B. Griffiths (eds.), *The Bloomsbury Handbook of Experimental Approaches to Roman Archaeology*, London.

Degbomont, J.-M. 1984, *Le chauffage par hypocauste dans l'habitat privé : de la place St-Lambert à Liège à l'Aula Palatina de Trèves* (Études et recherches archéologiques de l'Université de Liège 17), Liège.

Erim, K.T./J. Reynolds 1973, The Aphrodisias copy of Diocletian's edict on maximum prices, *JRS* 63, 99-110.

Grassmann, H.-C. 2011, *Die Funktion von Hypokausten und Tubuli in antiken römischen Bauten, insbesondere in Thermen. Erklärungen und Berechnungen* (BAR Int. Ser. 2309), Oxford.

Haan, N. de 2010, *Römische Privatbäder. Entwicklung, Verbreitung, Struktur und sozialer Status*, Frankfurt am Main.

Kretzschmer, F. 1953, Hypokausten, *SaalbJb* 12, 7-41.

Lauffer, S. 1971, *Diokletians Preisedikt*, Berlin.

Lehar, H. 2012, *Die römische Hypokaustheizung. Berechnungen und Überlegungen zu Leistung, Aufbau und Funktion*, Aachen.

Maréchal, S. 2020, *Public Baths and Bathing Habits in Late Antiquity. A Study of the Evidence from Italy, North Africa and Palestine A.D. 285-700* (Late Antique Archaeology Supplement 6), Leiden/Boston.

Plommer, H. 1973, *Vitruvius and later Roman building manuals*, Cambridge.

Rook, T. 1979, The effect of the evolution of flues upon the development of architecture, in A. McWhirr (ed.), *Roman brick and tile. Studies in manufacture, distribution and use in the Western empire* (BAR Int. Ser. 68), Oxford, 303-308.

Reeves, M.B./C.A. Harvey 2016, A Typological Assessment of the Nabataean, Roman and Byzantine Ceramic Building Materials at al-Humayma and Wadi Ramm, *Studies in the History and Archaeology of Jordan* 12, 443-475.

Schiebold, H. 2010, *Heizung und Wassererwärmung in römischen Thermen: Historische Entwicklung, Nachfolgesysteme, Neuzeitliche Betrachtungen und Untersuchungen* (Schriften der Deutschen Wasserhistorischen Gesellschaft Sonderband 3), Siegburg.

Tsiolis, V. 2013, The Baths at Fregellae and the Transition from Balaneion to Balneum, in S.K. Lucore/M. Trümper (eds.), *Greek Baths and Bathing Culture. New discoveries and approaches* (BABESCH Supplement series 23), Leuven, 89-111.

Yegül, F. 2010, *Bathing in the Roman world*, New York/Cambridge.

Yegül, F./T. Couch 2003, Building a Roman bath for the cameras, *JRA* 16, 153-177.

# Buried in Satricum
## *A bioarchaeological examination of isotopes ($^{87}Sr/^{86}Sr$ and $\delta^{18}O$) and dental nonmetric traits to assess human mobility in a Post-Archaic context*

*Amanda Sengeløv, Giswinne van de Wijdeven, Marijke Gnade, Andrea Waters-Rist, Jason Laffoon*

*Abstract*

*A recent study (Sengeløv et al. 2020, JAS Reports) combined oxygen and strontium isotope measurements with dental nonmetric trait (NMT) analyses to examine human mobility and population interactions during the Post-Archaic period (5th to 4th centuries BCE) at the site of ancient Satricum, Lazio (Italy). The aim of this study was to investigate a purported migration event of groups from the mountainous hinterland to Satricum. Individuals from three necropoleis in Satricum were analyzed. The results could not highlight a clear migration event but the strontium concentration data show a clear difference between two assessed necropoleis, while the dental NMT analysis suggested the presence of two different biological groups in Satricum, based on the high phenetic dissimilarity between the two necropoleis. This indicates that while it is not possible to identify a clear migration event, the Post-Archaic Period was a time of change at Satricum.*

INTRODUCTION

Over the past forty years, there has been ongoing research regarding the ethno-cultural identity of the post-Archaic (5th - 4th centuries BCE) population from the town of Satricum, situated in the Pontine Plain in Lazio (Italy), approximately 60 km southeast of Rome.[1] Scholars have proposed a change in the original Latin population of ancient Satricum as a result of migrating groups coming from the mountainous hinterland of Latium.[2] This hypothesis is based on a cultural shift visible in the archaeological record of ancient Satricum, which consist of three burial grounds, indicated as the Southwest Necropolis, the Poggio dei Cavallari (PdC) Necropolis and the Acropolis Necropolis, all of which are located within the city limits of the 6th century town (fig. 1).[3] Since the discovery of Post-Archaic burials in Satricum, questions arose if these could be attributed to the presence of the Volscians in Satricum, who according to the historical sources captured the town in 488 BCE.[4] The three necropoleis were very similar and did not match the graves found in the Latin necropolis in the northwest part of the town. In various publications that appeared since the discovery of the burial grounds, Gnade has attributed the graves to new Volscian inhabitants of Satricum who occupied the town after its destruction in the beginning of the fifth century BCE.[5] For this Gnade assessed archaeological evidence in relation to historical sources in a wider regional perspective. The literary sources and archaeological record seem to endorse each other in the case of Satricum. The three Post-Archaic necropoleis have therefore recently been the focus of isotopic and elemental analyses (strontium isotope analysis, elemental strontium concentration analysis, and oxygen isotope analysis) in order to investigate the provenance and mobility of the buried individuals.[6] In addition, dental nonmetric traits were assessed of two of the three necropoleis, to investigate the biological relatedness of these people. The two different approaches assessed whether there is any evidence for a possible different population group in Satricum during the fifth and fourth centuries BCE.

ISOTOPES AND SATRICUM

The isotopic values of strontium and oxygen in a person's body reflect local geology and meteorological conditions respectively, which makes it possible to determine where people originated from. Commonly, individuals are categorized as local or non-local to the geographic region. Radiogenic strontium isotopes are present in different amounts in bedrocks and leave the same geo-

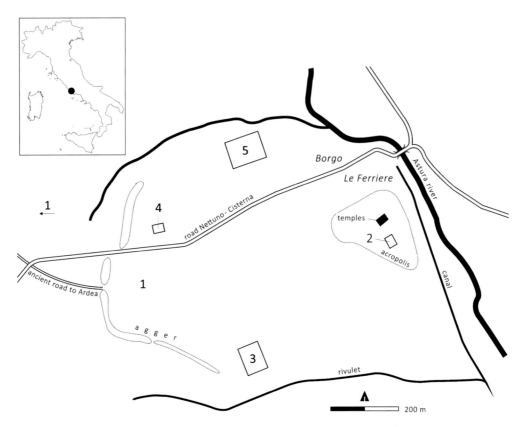

*Fig. 1. Map of Satricum with 1 = Latin northwest necropolis, 2 = acropolis (acro) necropolis, 3 = southwest (SW) necropolis, 4 = Poggio dei Cavallari (PdC) necropolis, 5 = Roman villa (Sengeløv et al. 2020, 3, fig. 1).*

chemical signature (i.e. bioavailable $^{87}Sr/^{86}Sr$ signature) in the soil and water and subsequently in the food chain.[7] In other words, strontium isotopes in the skeleton relate to the bioavailable strontium of the area where the food was produced.

Satricum is situated on a tuff mound formed by ashes of the Latian Volcano (Middle Pleistocene volcanics).[8] Therefore, the bioavailable signature of Satricum should correspond to the Roman magmatic province strontium isotope signature (0.7090 - 0.7110).[9]

Next to strontium isotope values, elemental strontium concentrations can also be used to gather information on diet and possibly geographical origin. The strontium concentrations in human bone and teeth reflect the strontium concentrations of the food an individual consumed, which in turn reflect strontium concentrations in local geology. Concentrations vary strongly between animals and plants, the latter usually having significantly higher strontium concentrations.[10]

Stable oxygen isotopes differ geographically as a result of the isotopic composition of available drinking water ($\delta^{18}O_{dw}$), which varies regionally according to temperature, distance from the coast, latitude, altitude, and evapotranspiration.[11] In Italy, the mountainous ridge of the Apennines in Central Italy defines the oxygen values of precipitation.[12] Under most archaeological circumstances the most appropriate method for identifying migrants and establishing a local range is by using the IQR (interquartile range) method based on the population's median.[13] The local oxygen range of Satricum was defined as −8.7 to −2.3‰ $\delta^{18}O_{dw}$ VSMOW.[14]

Sengeløv and colleagues sampled a total of 43 third molars from all three sites: 28 from the Southwest Necropolis, 13 from the PdC Necropolis, and two from the Acropolis Necropolis.[15] Figure 2 displays the results of the O isotope analysis (x-axis) and the Sr isotope analysis (y-axis) compared to the expected values for Satricum. Three individuals have significantly lower $^{87}Sr/^{86}Sr$ values than the rest of the population: S136, S176b and S163.[16] The obtained $^{87}Sr/^{86}Sr$ range, including the outliers, falls within the expected bioavailable $^{87}Sr/^{86}Sr$ range of Satricum. The 43 oxygen isotope samples are distributed

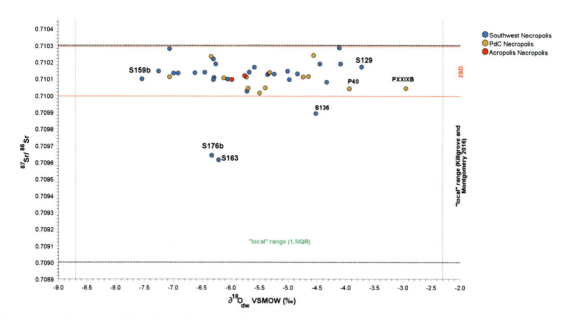

*Fig. 2. Strontium and oxygen isotope data from Satricum in comparison with estimated local $\delta^{18}O_{dw}$ and $^{87}Sr/^{86}Sr$ ranges (vertical and horizontal lines, respectively) (Sengeløv et al. 2020, 8, fig. 4).*

evenly within the expected local range of Satricum, and do not reveal any outliers. The considerably wide range of the oxygen results is likely to be a result of intra-populational variation caused by metabolism and differences in diet. Sengeløv et al. also measured strontium concentrations which revealed that the SW necropolis has statistically significantly lower strontium concentrations than the PdC necropolis, which might be caused by different subsistence strategies, catchment areas, or diet preferences.[17] In addition, the three samples that had the lowest strontium isotope ratios (S136, S163 and S176b) are the three samples with the lowest strontium concentrations. The question rises if these individuals are non-locals.

THE POSITION OF THE "NON-LOCALS" WITHIN THE NECROPOLIS

It is difficult to establish differences in the burial record because the graves are quite homogeneous in grave features, lay-out and material culture. The only differences that can be noted are differences in orientation, number of vessels, and grave type. The spatial organization of the tombs in the SW necropolis however shows a certain pattern. Where in the north-eastern section the distribution of the graves is rather orderly and well-spaced, with separate individual graves placed in clear alignment, the density of the graves increases towards the central part of the necropolis. Here the majority of the overlying or intersecting graves and multiple burials in a single grave are present (*fig. 3*).[18] This lay-out probably was chronologically determined, in the sense that the orderly organization in the higher northeast section corresponded with the first graves of the burial ground. In time the lay-out of the necropolis followed the slope down towards the south and southwest showing a denser pattern of groups of graves which expressed family ties.[19]

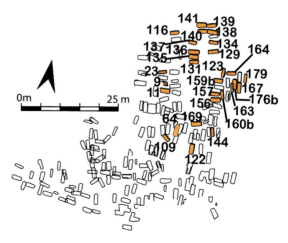

*Fig. 3. Lay-out of the southwest necropolis with sampled graves highlighted (by Giswinne van de Wijdeven).*

251

It seems likely that a first generation of deceased, when assuming the hypothesis of a migrated population, was buried in the northeast section. The fact that the three outliers (S136, S163 and S176b) are present in this presumably older northern part of the necropolis of the SW necropolis seems to support the idea of this spatial evolution. One outlier (S163) is also the only roof tile grave found in the north-eastern part of the necropolis.[20] Whether this indicates a difference in hierarchy or a distinct temporal phenomenon is difficult to validate. Interestingly, this grave belongs together with the other outlier in grave 176 to one of the few intersecting pairs in the northeastern part of the necropolis. They have been interpreted as burials of members of one family.

DENTAL NONMETRIC TRAIT ANALYSIS

Teeth exhibit morphological and metric traits that vary within and between populations.[21] Nonmetric dental traits are to a large extent controlled by genetics, which means phenetic similarity within populations provides some indication of genetic relatedness.[22] A dental NMT study of the Satricum teeth was therefore part of the research of Sengeløv *et al.* (2020) and assessed how similar or dissimilar the assemblages of SW and PdC were. By doing this, it could be assessed if it was a single, small gene pool burying their dead in the necropoleis or if it is more consistent with different populations being buried there. The comparison between the Southwest Necropolis and the PdC Necropoleis yielded interesting results. Although both sample sizes are relatively small (PdC = 17 individuals, SW = 22 individuals), which could mean the results are easily affected by outliers, they have very different trait frequencies. The SW necropolis clearly shows more trait elaboration and presence than the PdC necropolis (*fig. 4*). This could possibly indicate two different gene pools, and by extension, two different biological populations.[23] The performed mean measure of divergence (MMD) analysis confirms this statement, giving a statistically significant biological distance of 0.7879 between the two, which indicates high dissimilarity (quantified on a scale ranging from 0 to 1, where proximity to 0 indicates high similarity and proximity to 1 indicates low similarity).[24] It is important to note that two biologically different populations do not reflect two culturally different populations per se. It can be hypothesized that the SW group are perhaps individuals who settled in Satricum over time, and that the PdC group represents the subsequent mixed population of locals and nonlocals. It can be proposed that the distinct gene pool of the SW necropolis interacted with other gene pools from other regions due the increased potential for regular gene flow, resulting in a new mixed gene pool being buried in the PdC necropolis, i.e. a biological population that changed over time as a result of gene flow. Another hypothesis which explains the marked gene flow between

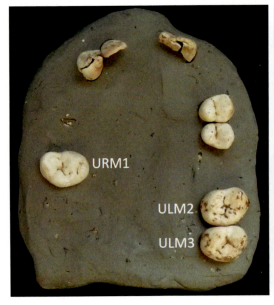 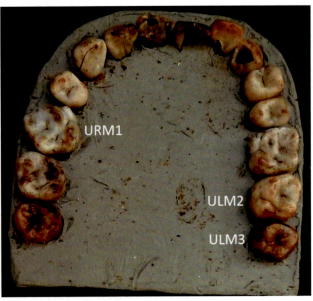

Fig. 4. Comparison between a "typical" PdC (left) versus SW (right) maxilla. Differences can be seen between the trait expressions of the molars.

the two necropoleis could be a population that contained different kin groups which used different necropoleis.

CONCLUSION

While a local origin cannot be excluded by isotope analyses, both the strontium concentration results and dental non-metric trait data show a significant difference between the individuals of PdC and those of SW necropoleis. The Sr concentrations, which are generally high for all sampled individuals, are significantly higher in PdC than in SW, which might be caused by different subsistence strategies, catchment areas, or diet preferences. In the SW necropolis three individuals stand out based on both their strontium isotopes and concentrations (S136, S163 and S176b). The results suggest that these three individuals could have originated from a different location. Two of the outliers (S163 and S176) are intersecting graves, interpreted as burials of members of one family. A biodistance analysis of the dental non-metric trait frequencies of the SW and PdC necropoleis suggest that the necropoleis contain different gene pools (MMD score of 0.789). It is hard to determine if these data suggest (1) a population that experienced fast and marked gene flow between use of the necropoleis, or (2) a population with large, distinct kin groups using different necropoleis. Future aims include the analysis of more samples for isotopic research from Satricum and other 'Volscian' sites located in the mountainous hinterland (e.g. Frosinone) and an extended dental nonmetric trait analysis of Satricum, with a larger sample size and including all three necropoleis as well as burials from the inland sites.

NOTES

\* This research is based on two MSc master theses by Amanda Sengeløv and Giswinne van de Wijdeven (Sengeløv 2017; Van de Wijdeven 2017) written at the Faculty of Archaeology of Leiden University under supervision of dr. Andrea Waters-Rist and prof. Marijke Gnade, and additional research conducted in the following years at the Faculty of Science of Université Libre de Bruxelles, which is published in Sengeløv et al. 2020.
1. Gnade 1992; 15-16; 2002, 102-103; 2007; for a reaction see Attema et al. 1992; Bouma 1996, I, 194-200; Maaskant-Kleibrink 1992, 101-105, for the acropolis burials.
2. Gnade 1992; 2002; Stibbe 1984.
3. Gnade 2002, 157-161.
4. Ibid. 143-145, 160.
5. Ibid.
6. Sengeløv et al. 2020.
7. Slovak and Paytan 2012, 744.
8. Attema et al. 2011, 47; Duivenvoorden 1992, 432.
9. Killgrove and Montgomery 2016, 11.
10. Montgomery 2010, 328.
11. Longinelli 1984; Longinelli and Selmo 2003; Luz et al. 1984, 1689.
12. Giustini et al. 2016, 163; Longinelli and Selmo 2003, 87.
13. Lightfoot and O'Connell 2016.
14. Sengeløv et al. 2020, 4 for calculations.
15. Sengeløv et al. 2020, 5.
16. Gnade 1992, 346-347, for grave 136; 395-399 for grave 163; 414-417 for grave 176.
17. Sengeløv et al. 2020, 6.
18. Gnade 2002, 108-109.
19. Ibid.
20. Gnade 1992, 33.
21. Scott and Turner 1997, 2.
22. Ibid, 14.
23. Sengeløv et al. 2020.
24. Stark 2017.

BIBLIOGRAPHY

Attema, P.A.J. et al. 1992, Il sito di Borgo Le Ferriere ('Satricum') nei scoli V e IV a.C., QuadAEI 20, 75-86.
Attema, P./T. de Haas/G. Tol 2011, Archaic Period (6th Century BC), in P. Attema/T.C.A. de Haas/G.W. Tol (eds.), Between Satricum and Antium: settlement dynamics in a coastal landscape in Latium Vetus, Leuven, 53-56.
Bouma, J./E. van 't Lindenhout 1997, Light in dark age Latium, evidence from settlements and cult places, in M. Kleibrink (ed.), Caeculus III, Groningen, 91-102.
Giustini, F/M. Brilli/A. Patera 2016, Mapping oxygen stable isotopes of precipitation in Italy, Journal of Hydrology: Regional Studies 8, 162-181.
Gnade, M. 1992, The Southwest Necropolis of Satricum, excavations 1981-1986, Amsterdam.
Gnade, M. 2002, Satricum in the Post-Archaic Period. A Case study of the Interpretation of Archaeological Remains as Indicators of Ethno-Cultural Identity, Leuven/Paris/Dudley.
Killgrove, K./J. Montgomery 2016, All roads lead to Rome: exploring human migration to the eternal city through biochemistry of skeletons from two imperial-era cemeteries (1st-3rd c AD), PLoS One, 11(2).
Lightfoot, E./T.C. O'Connell 2016, On the use of biomineral oxygen isotope data to identify human migrants in the archaeological record: intra-sample variation, statistical methods and geographical considerations, PloS one, 11(4).
Longinelli, A. 1984, Oxygen isotopes in mammal bone phosphate: A new tool for paleohydrological and paleoclimatological research?, Geochimica et Cosmochimica Acta 48, 385-390.
Longinelli, A./E. Selmo 2003, Isotopic composition of precipitation in Italy: a first overall map, Journal of Hydrology 270(1-2), 75-88.
Luz, B./Y. Kolodny/M. Horowitz 1984, Fractionation of oxygen isotopes between mammalian bone-phosphate and environmental drinking water, Geochimica et Cosmomachimica Acta 48, 1689-1693.
Maaskant-Kleibrink, M. 1987, Settlement Excavations at Borgo Le Ferriere (Satricum) I, Groningen.
Maaskant-Kleibrink, M. 1992, Settlement excavations at Borgo Le Ferriere (Satricum) II, Groningen.
Montgomery, J. 2010, Passports from the past: Investigating human dispersals using strontium isotope analysis of tooth enamel, Annals of human biology 37(3), 325-346.

Scott, G.R./C.G. Turner 1997, *The anthropology of modern human teeth: dental morphology and its variation in recent human populations*, Cambridge.

Sengeløv, A. 2017, *Buried in Satricum: A bioarchaeological examination of the Post-Archaic (5th-4th C. BCE) skeletal assemblages of Satricum (Lazio, Italy) using strontium isotope analysis of human enamel and dental nonmetric trait analysis*. MSc thesis, Leiden University.

Sengeløv, A. *et al.* 2020, Understanding the post-Archaic population of Satricum, Italy: A bioarchaeological approach, *Journal of Archaeological Science: Reports* 31, 102285, 1-13.

Slovak, N.M./A. Paytan 2012. Applications of Sr Isotopes in Archaeology, in M. Baskaran (ed.), *Handbook of Environmental Isotope Geochemistry*, Berlin/Heidelberg, 743-768.

Stark, R.J. 2017, *Ancient Lives in Motion: a bioarchaeological examination of stable isotopes, nonmetric traits, and human mobility in an imperial roman context (1st-3rd C. CE)*. Unpublished Ph.D. thesis McMaster University, Hamilton.

Stibbe, C.M. 1984, *Satricum en de Volsken*, Hollandse Rading.

Van de Wijdeven, G. 2017, *The origin of Satricum's people. A study to assess Volscian migration from the Lepini mountains to Satricum in the early 5th century using stable oxygen isotope analysis of human enamel*. MSc thesis, Leiden University.

# Vasai di montagna
*Ricostruire i modelli di sapere condiviso tra le comunità artigianali dei monti della Tolfa nel Bronzo Finale. Spunti di ricerca*

*Agostino Sotgia*

*Abstract*

*This short contribution illustrates the theoretical framework underpinning a pilot research into ceramic production systems and communities of potters in Bronze Age Southern Etruria. In particular, the notion of "community of practice" applied to the pottery production typical of the Tolfa Mountains enables us to profile in more detail the social dynamics underlying that system. By comparing the technological aspects of this distinctive ceramic material to neighbouring assemblages, it is possible to outline a more elaborate and meaningful picture of the communities involved in the manufacture, use and discard of such objects. This work is a first attempt in this direction for the area under study, and illustrates the results of a sample-study conducted on the ceramic material retrieved from Luni sul Mignone (Blera, VT) in comparison with the extant archaeological data known for this territory.*

INTRODUZIONE

*L'Etruria Meridionale nel Bronzo Finale: nel posto giusto, al momento giusto!*

Il tema della produzione ceramica dell'Età del bronzo finale in Etruria Meridionale è stato - ed è - l'oggetto di numerosi studi di Protostoria in Italia. Tuttavia, la maggior parte di questi lavori ha applicato alle proprie analisi prevalentemente un approccio crono-tipologico mirato più alla definizione delle fasi temporali degli insediamenti presenti nell'area che alla descrizione dettagliata della produzione vascolare in termini tecnologici, sociali e storici.[1] Questo a causa della mancanza di chiare evidenze direttamente legate ad aree produttive all'interno dei siti esaminati[2] e di sistematiche analisi archeometriche necessarie alla definizione degli aspetti tecnologici e delle aree di approvvigionamento delle materie prime.

Tuttavia, non si è mai considerata la produzione vascolare delle comunità dell'Etruria Meridionale nel Bronzo Finale come una vera e propria "produzione sociale", nonostante nel processo di manifattura siano rappresentate non «solo una particolare configurazione economica» (o tecnica) «ma anche un insieme composto di forme di vita, una costellazione sociale, antropologica e etica»[3]

L'idea alla base di questa ricerca è quindi quella di concentrarsi su questa dimensione "sociale" della produzione ceramica, applicando al tema il concetto di "Communities of practice" di Étienne Wenger.[4] Con questo termine si intendono infatti tutti quei sistemi auto-organizzati fondati e soprattutto definiti da una serie di conoscenze, abilità tecniche e soprattutto know-how condiviso all'interno del gruppo. In italiano il termine potrebbe essere tradotto con i termini: modelli di intelligenza condivisa, saperi comuni o comunità di pratiche e apprendimento, cercando di allargare il più possibile lo spettro dei comportamenti ivi compresi.

La produzione vascolare, nello specifico, rientra appieno tra questi sistemi, poiché ogni membro ha libero accesso alla memoria comunitaria, ed è costante il "mutuo aiuto" e i ruoli sono assunti in base alle competenze dei singoli. Tuttavia il portato della comunità all'interno del fenomeno produttivo non si conclude solo con l'atto di creazione, ma si esplica anche nelle fasi di utilizzo, circolazione e distruzione dell'oggetto stesso, in altre parole durante l'intero ciclo di vita di un manufatto che va dalla sua produzione alla sua distruzione, passando ovviamente per il suo uso e consumo.

Attraverso uno studio dei resti materiali di tutti questi processi, quindi, sarà possibile a ritroso ricostruire le entità sociali che li hanno prodotti e caratterizzare ancora più puntualmente le società da queste entità formate.

Ad oggi la produzione vascolare dell'Etruria Meridionale dell'Età del bronzo finale è definita come una produzione molto articolata caratterizzata sia da una notevole varietà morfologica, con 256 Tipi vascolari, che da complesse decorazioni organizzate in 91 tipi.[5] In altre parole, si conoscono molto approfonditamente gli oggetti della cultura materiale solamente da un punto di vista formale e –solo in parte- tecnologico; l'organizzazione produttiva, le conoscenze tecniche e soprattutto il complesso dei saperi necessari alla loro fattura rimangono ancora largamente inesplorati.

Poiché la maggior parte dei materiali utilizzati per gli studi precedentemente citati sulla produzione vascolare dell'Etruria Meridionale durante il Bronzo Finale proviene da un'area specifica, la zona dei Monti della Tolfa,[6] anche questa ricerca utilizzerà quest'area come caso studio.

D'altronde la quantità di materiali provenienti da questa zona è tale che persino le due facies archeologiche identificate per l'intera Etruria Meridionale nel Bronzo Finale sono chiamate Facies di Tolfa e Facies di Allumiere, utilizzando i nomi di due importanti località dell'area.[7]

Una volta definito il repertorio condiviso di una comunità (i tipi ceramici esclusivi), frutto delle diverse interazioni/conoscenze dei membri (riconoscibili nelle caratteristiche comuni a più tipi tra loro geneticamente o dialetticamente imparentati - Cfr. *famiglia tipologica*[8]) saranno riconosciute le entità sociali che hanno prodotto gli oggetti, grazie anche all'identificazione delle norme frutto della collaborazione reciproca tra i membri del gruppo, e dei rapporti tra entità diverse ma tra loro connesse (le particolari fogge ceramiche di un'area o di una regione).

Si utilizzeranno anche alcune tecniche di *Landscape Arcaheology* come stumenti d'indagine per raggiungere lo scopo prefissato, poiché è anche nel paesaggio[9] che si colgono alcune delle tracce più importanti delle "communities of practice" degli artigiani dei Monti della Tolfa nel Bronzo Finale, soprattutto attraverso la circolazione dei diversi tipi ceramici tra le diverse comunità.

Il presente contributo, attraverso un piccolo caso studio, illustra un progetto di ricerca che tenta di verificare se è possibile analizzare la produzione ceramica sotto questo nuovo punto di vista, contestualizzandone la tecnologia utilizzata e ricostruendo le "communities of practice" dei "vasai di montagna" che l'hanno prodotta.

DATASET

*Un mondo di vasi … e non solo*

Per l'area oggetto del lavoro si dispone di una grande ed eterogenea "massa critica" di dati.

Tale insieme è composto, innanzitutto, dai materiali archeologici raccolti attraverso: le numerose ricerche di superficie condotte, a partire dagli anni '70 del secolo scorso, soprattutto dal gruppo della *Scuola Romana di Protostoria*; le ricognizioni delle scuole straniere; intense attività di associazioni non professionistiche; gli scavi di alcuni importanti siti svolti sia da istituzioni italiane, che internazionali.[10]

Queste ricerche hanno permesso anche l'acquisizione anche di resti archeo-zoologici e paleobotanici, recentemente studiati, catalogati e pubblicati da Claudia Minniti in maniera sistematica e completa.[11] Tale lavoro non solo permette di avere gli elenchi completi dei resti faunistici e botanici presenti nei principali insediamenti dei Monti della Tolfa, ma illustra anche una prima interpretazione delle dinamiche economiche della regione.

I numerosissimi dati da ottenuti da tutte queste ricerche, nel corso degli anni sintetizzati all'interno di importanti studi regionali e lavori interpretativi generali,[12] sono la base ideale su cui organizzare il lavoro proposto.

METODI

*Una cassetta degli attrezzi … particolare*

Per analizzare i dati nel dettaglio e allo stesso tempo rendere immediatamente visibili i risultati, lo strumento d'analisi principale che si propone d'utilizzare per la ricerca è un sistema GIS. L'utilizzo di questi software – costruiti per essere interattivi ed in grado di relazionarsi tramite *queries* ai database – permetterà di generare i modelli interpretativi necessari alle analisi territoriali in oggetto, e nello stesso tempo di mostrare in maniera chiara ed immediata i risultati ottenuti attraverso una specifica rappresentazione cartografica.

La procedura d'indagine che si vuole attuare si sviluppa attraverso i seguenti passaggi:

- Creazione di una mappa di distribuzione dei tipi ceramici esclusivi dell'aria dei Monti della Tolfa[13] (*figg. 1-2*) all'interno degli insediamenti considerati. In questo modo sarà possibile individuare se esistono tradizioni artigianali differenti tra le comunità e allo stesso tempo testare se esse rispecchino o meno l'organizzazione cantonale o federativa dei villaggi così come proposta in letteratura.[14]
- L'individuazione di ipotetiche aree d'approvvigionamento di materie prime, soprattutto argilla, usate per la realizzazione dei vasi da confrontare con quanto emerso dall'analisi archeometriche sui materiali archeologici. Qualora i fondi lo permettessero, infatti, si procederà a campionare sistematicamente tanto il materiale archeologico quando quello geologico per caratterizzare la produzione vascolare anche dal punto di vista delle scelte

tecnologiche e artigianali atte alla sua realizzazione.

Ottenuti questi dati si procederà al confronto con quelli generati mediante l'analisi dei sistemi politico-territoriali e con quelli relativi alle altre produzioni delle comunità del Bronzo Finale, con particolare riguardo per la produzione primaria. Attraverso analisi di *Land Evaluation* infatti, per la zona dei Monti della Tolfa è stato proposto un modello di sfruttamento agro-pastorale che permette di caratterizzare anche in senso demografico queste comunità.[15]

Tramite tutta questa serie di analisi sarà possibile ottenere un'immagine articolata e realistica delle comunità dei Monti della Tolfa produttrici di vasi oggetti della ricerca, che non saranno più semplicemente descritti come artigiani.

Un esempio concreto, della metodologia che s'intende applicare, può essere quello di seguito riportato relativo alla produzione vascolare del sito di Luni sul Mignone (Blera, VT).

La distribuzione dei tipi ceramici (*fig. 3*) presenti in maggior quantità nel sito di Luni – quindi presumibilmente da questo originari – mostra chiaramente come la comunità artigianale di questo sito faccia circolare i propri modelli formali in tutta la regione. La circolazione di tali modelli è altresì da mettere in relazione con una qualche specie di contatto tra comunità che sembra quindi presumere l'esistenza di una dimensione comunitaria superiore ai singoli villaggi.

Tale spunto di riflessione sembra confermato anche dai dati relativi alla ricostruzione della dimensione agro-pastorale. Il modello di sfruttamento agro-pastorale del paesaggio, generato per il sito di Luni e per l'area dei Monti della Tolfa (*fig. 4*), riporta per il villaggio in esame una demografia massima sostenibile tra le circa 482 e le 697 persone, grazie ad un uso agricolo del proprio territorio. Ovviamente, come riportato in letteratura[16] il numero di abitanti per l'insediamento poteva essere di almeno il doppio, per cui è evidente come il sito di Luni sul Mignone non possa esser definito autosufficiente dal punto di vista dell'economi primaria e che vada necessariamente inserito all'interno di un sistema (politico) di dimensione più ampia per garantirne una valenza storica.

Ecco, quindi, che anche la circolazione dei modelli formali della ceramica acquista una nuova chiave di lettura: testimonia l'esistenza di legami tra comunità diverse.

Possiamo parlare, in definitiva, dell'esistenza, di confederazioni cantonali tra insediamenti caratterizzate non solo da reti di relazione, ma anche da una vera e propria divisione produttiva, tra centri prevalentemente agricoli e pastorali, che poi condividevano i prodotti, che archeologicamente lascia una traccia nel paesaggio anche tramite la circolazione di specifici "tipi vascolari", che come detto testimoniano un avvenuto contatto.

CONCLUSIONI

*Come direbbe Joe Strummer: «the future is unwritten.»*

Come si evince dal piccolo esperimento fatto per il sito di Luni sul Mignone, le metodologie d'indagine proposte sembrano idonee a definire meglio le comunità artigianali attive nei Monti della Tolfa tra X e IX secolo a.C., non solo da un punto di vista tecnologico e produttivo, ma anche politico-sociale.

Ovviamente, ampliando il campione analizzato, comprendendo cioè tutti gli insediamenti dell'area e i rispettivi tipi ceramici, queste tecniche d'indagine verranno ulteriormente testate, comprendendone appieno le potenzialità.

Anche grazie alle analisi archeometriche e alla disamina delle caratteristiche tecnologiche della produzione vascolare, inoltre, sarà possibile comprendere alcuni degli aspetti artigianali fondamentali per la realizzazione di questa particolare classe di reperti, presente – per dirla alla Binford– in "tremende quantità"[17] negli scavi.

Tuttavia, già da questo primo test pilota, appare evidente come l'utilizzo del concetto di "communities of practice" consenta di superare la dimensione puramente tecnico-artigianale e inserire la produzione vascolare nella più generale indagine storica circa le comunità umane, in un momento di fondamentale importanza quale il passaggio dall'Età del Bronzo alla Prima Età del Ferro in Etruria Meridionale.

Il progetto presentato mira, quindi, attraverso la revisione dei dati circa la produzione vascolare e la loro integrazione con le nuove informazioni provenienti dallo studio del territorio e dalle analisi archeometriche su campioni selezionati, a proporre una ricostruzione delle dinamiche produttive dei Monti della Tolfa, da inserire nella più generale investigazione delle dinamiche socio-economiche ed organizzative di questo territorio durante l'Età del Bronzo Finale.

Questo permetterà di comprendere meglio lo sfondo umano in cui si compirà la cosiddetta "Svolta Protourbana" ossia il fenomeno di sinecismo che ha portato dall'assetto policentrico del Bronzo Finale basato su centinaia di villaggi alla concentrazione degli abitanti nei grandi centri proto-urbani di Volsinii, Vulci, Tarquinia, Caere e Veio nella Prima età del Ferro.[18]

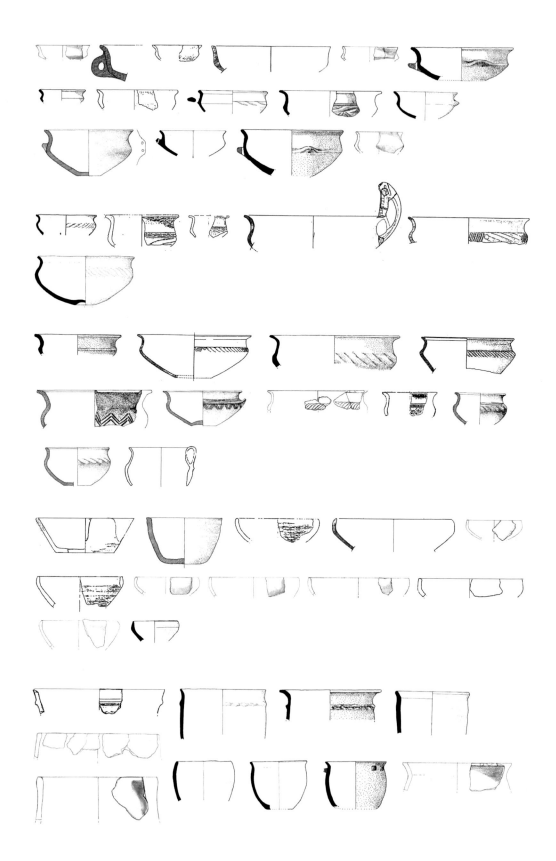

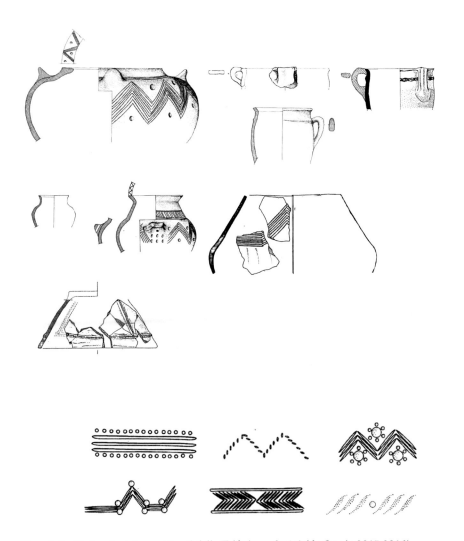

*Figg. 1-2. Tipi esclusivi area Monti della Tolfa in scala 1:6 (da Sotgia 2015-2016).*

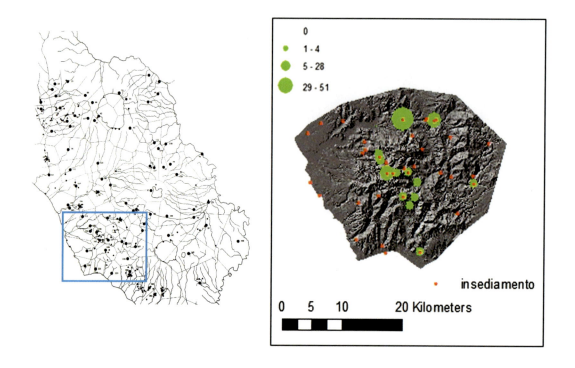

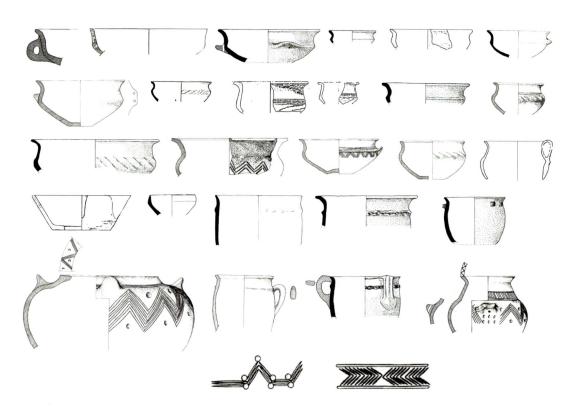

*Fig. 3. Tipi ceramici di Luni Sul Mignone (scala 1:6) e relativa distribuzione all'interno dell'area di studio.*

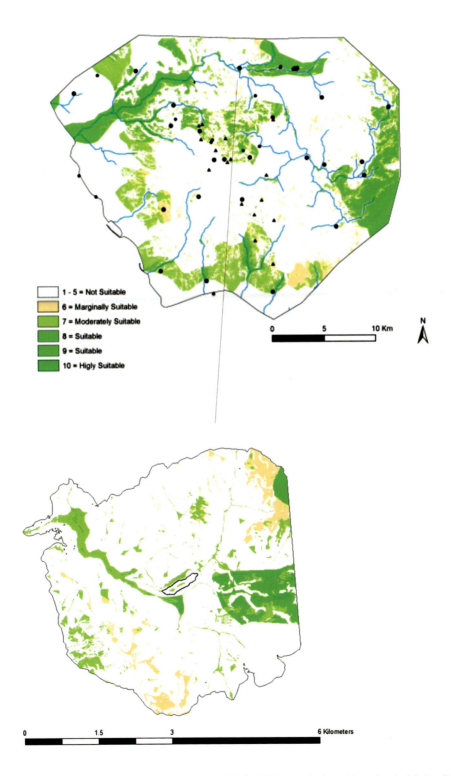

*Fig. 4. Modello di sfruttamento agro-pastorale dell'area dei Monti della Tolfa e particolare del territorio del sito di Luni Sul Mignone (da Sotgia 2020).*

NOTE

1. Gli studi cronologici sul Bronzo Finale in Etruria Meridionale cui si fa riferimento sono: Domanico 1998; Negroni Catacchio 1998; Pacciarelli 2001; Barbaro 2010; De Angelis 2010; Sotgia 2015-2016. La maggior parte di questi lavori prende le mosse dalla metodologia d'indagine crono-tipologia proposta da R. Peroni in Peroni 1998.
2. Per una disamina puntuale delle aree artigianali legate alla produzione vascolare ceramica nell'Età del bronzo in Italia si rimanda a Sotgia 2019a, 2019b.
3. Il termine di produzione sociale si deve alle riflessioni di A. Negri e M. Hardt in Negri/Hardt 2009. La citazione è invece di P. Virno in Virno 2014, p. 25.
4. Wenger 1998.
5. Sotgia 2015-2016
6. L'area dei Monti della Tolfa risulta caratterizzata da una serie di colline, frutto di un'intensa attività vulcanica, poste tra la costa tirrenica e i Monti Sabatini. Tra Tolfa e Allumiere l'orografia dei rilievi appare marcata e il settore ospita le alture più elevate; Il cosiddetto gruppo della Tolfaccia, tra Tolfa e Civitavecchia, appare invece caratterizzato da alture non troppo elevate ma con pareti molto ripide, infine attorno a questi due settori si sviluppa un'ampia zona collinare caratterizzata da lievi pendii che degradano dolcemente verso la valle del Mignone. Nel corso del Bronzo Finale risulta un'area fortemente frequentata dalle comunità umane, come testimoniato da 34 insediamenti, 18 sepolcreti un ripostiglio ed una cava.
7. R. Peroni nel 1996 definisce "Facies di Allumiere" il momento iniziale e pieno del Bronzo Finale (BF 1-2), mentre chiama "Facies di Tolfa" il momento avanzato e finale (BF3) del periodo.
8. Peroni 1998, p. 12
9. Il paesaggio, come ben noto, non va inteso solamente come uno sfondo neutro su cui proiettare la produzione ceramica, poiché col suo essere determina e influenza ogni tipo di produzione umana.
10. Per quanto riguarda una descrizione delle principali ricerche di superficie svolte nella zona si rimanda a Cardarelli et al. 1980; di Gennaro 1986; Corazza et al. 2014. Mentre per un repertorio bibliografico aggiornato degli interventi delle singole istituzioni italiane e straniere è in Barbaro 2010.
11. Minniti 2012.
12. I lavori di sintesi sull'Etruria Meridionale durante il Bronzo Finale sono Belardelli et al. 2007; Barbaro 2010; Pacciarelli 2001.
13. Tra i "tipi esclusivi" dell'area dei Monti della Tolfa si annoverano le seguenti classi e forme: a) Ciotole e Tazze carenate con carena pronunciata o con costolature oblique all'altezza della carena; b) Tazze a profilo sinuoso con costolature aventi un diametro all'orlo maggiore o pressoché uguale punto di massima espansione; c) Tazze a collo con costolature venti un diametro all'orlo maggiore o pressoché uguale punto di massima espansione; d) Scodelle troncoconiche con vasca profonda, scodelle con vasca a calotta bassa e scodelle con orlo rientrante a profilo arrotondato o angolare; e) Olle e Ollette troncoconiche, cilindriche o ovoidi (con orlo svasato e a volte decorate con cordoni o bugne) e olle di grandi dimensioni piriformi; f) Calderoncini a corpo globulare schiacciato e labbro inspessito, Boccali a corpo cilindrico o ovoide decorati con cordone; g) Vasi a collo a corpo ovoide, vasi a collo troncoconico fortemente rientrante e corpo globulare, Vasi Biconici con spalla distinta; i) Coperchi troncoconici alti decorati con cordoni formanti un reticolo.
   Sono presenti anche le seguenti decorazioni: motivi a nastro con fascio di solcature compreso tra due file di punti; motivi angolari a zig-zag continuo con fasci di solcature isolate contrapposti (impresse a cordicella); fascio di solcature a zig-zag con cuppelle di medie dimensioni circondate da cuppelle di medie dimensioni negli spazi liberi tra i vertici; Fascio di solcature orizzontale che piega ad intervalli regolai a formare elementi angolari stanti con cuppelle di medie dimensioni tangenti ai vertici e agli angoli interni, sia superiormente, sia inferiormente; Banda orizzontale con fasci di solcature a spina di pesce con vertici contrapposti entro due solcature; Serie di costolature oblique interrotte da una cuppella (Sotgia 2015-2016).
14. Una disamina delle varie forme organizzative presenti nell'area si ritrova in di Gennaro 1986; Barbaro 2010; Alessandri 2015; Pacciarelli 2016.
15. All'interno di un più ampio progetto di dottorato (A. Sotgia, *Abitare i villaggi, dissodare i campi ... prima delle città*. in co-tutela tra la Sapienza Università di Roma e la Rijksuniversiteit Groningen) è stato generato un modello di sfruttamento agro-pastorale del territorio in grado di fornire un'ipotetica base produttiva per sito, su cui calcolare la demografia massima sostenibile, utilizzando le stime note a partire dall'Età del Bronzo (Bietti Sestieri 2002; Carra et al. 2012, 2015; Cardarelli 2009; Cazzella/Moscoloni 1991) fino all'epoca arcaica (Pucci 1989) e preindustriale (Montanari 1985) utilizzate coerentemente in letteratura per questo genere d'analisi. Per quanto riguarda l'area dei Monti della Tolfa i primi risultati sono editi in Sotgia 2020.
16. Di Gennaro/Guidi 2010; Sotgia 2020.
17. Binford 1962, p. 224.
18. Pacciarelli 2001, 2016.

BIBLIOGRAFIA

Alessandri, L. 2015, Exploring Territories: Bubble Model and Minimun Number of Contemporary Settlements. A Case Study From Etruria and Latium Vetus from the Early Bronze Age to Early Iron Age, *Origini* 35, 175-199.

Barbaro, B. 2010, *Insediamenti, aree funerarie ed entità territoriali in Etruria Meridionale nel Bronzo Finale* (Grandi contesti e problemi della Protostoria italiana 14), Firenze.

Belardelli C. et al. 2007, *Repertorio dei siti protostorici del Lazio: province di Roma, Viterbo e Frosinone*, Firenze.

Bietti Sestieri, A.M. 2002, L'agricoltura in Italia nell'età dei metalli, in G. Forni/A. Marcone (ed.), *Storia dell'Agricoltura Italiana. L'Età Antica* I.1. *Preistoria*, Firenze, 205-217.

Binford, L.W. 1962, Archaeology as Anthropology, *American Antiquity* 28.2, 217-225.

Cardarelli, A. 2009, Insediamenti dell'Età del Bronzo tra Secchia e Reno. Formazione, affermazione e crollo delle Terramarei, in A. Cardarelli/L. Malnati (ed.), *Atltante dei Beni Archeologici della Provincia di Modena* III, Firenze, 33-65.

Cardarelli, A. et al. 1980, Le ricerche di topografia protostorica nel Lazio, in *Archeologia, materiali e problemi*, Manduria, 91-103.

Carra, M./M. Cattani/F. Debandi 2012, Coltivazioni sperimentali per una valutazione della produttività agricola dell'Età del Bronzo nell'area padana, *Ipotesi di Preistoria* 5 n.1, 79–100.

Carra, M./M. Cattani/F. Debandi 2015, La sussistenza nell'età del Bronzo in Italia Settentrionale. Archeologia sperimentale e analisi dei contesti di abitato come casi studio per un calcolo demografico, in *Preistoria del Cibo. L'ambiente fonte di risore alimentari.* 50ma Runione Scientifica dell'Istituto Italiano di Preistoria e Protostoria. Sessione 2, Roma, 1-12.

Cazzella, A./M. Moscoloni 1991, Aspetti dell'economia di sussistenza durante l'età del bronzo a Coppa Nevigata e nell'Italia Meridionale, *ScAnt* 5, 233-264.

Corazza, V./A. Di Renzoni/F. Ferranti 2014, Tutti a spasso: dal Crati al Po passando per il Tevere, cinquant'anni di camminate per campi, in A. Guidi (ed.) *I 150 anni di preistoria e protostoria in Italia* (Studi di Preistoria e Protostoria 1), Firenze, 515-512, 543-549.

De Angelis, S. 2010, L'inquadramento cronologico dei complessi funerari del Bronzo finale in Etruria meridionale, in B. Barbaro, *Insediamenti, aree funerarie ed entità territoriali in Etruria Meridionale nel Bronzo Finale*, 107-112.

Di Gennaro, F.1986, *Forme di insediamento tra Tevere e Fiora dal Bronzo Finale al principio dell'età del Ferro* (Biblioteca di «Studi Etruschi» 14), Firenze.

Di Gennaro, F./A. Guidi 2010, Lo stato delle anime come mezzo per la ricostruzione della popolazione dei villaggi preistorici, *Arqueología Espacial* 28, 351-358.

Domanico, L. 1998, Analisi degli indicatori cronologici dalle necropoli del Bronzo Finale in Etruria, in *Atti Preistoria e Protostoria in Etruria* III, Milano, 53-78.

Minniti, C. 2012, *Ambiente, sussistenza e articolazione sociale nell'Italia centrale tra Bronzo medio e Primo Ferro* (BAR Int. Ser. 2394), Oxford.

Montanari, M. 1985, Tecniche e rapporti di produzione: le rese cerealicole dal IX al XV secolo, in B. Andreolli/V. Fumagalli/M. Montanari (ed.), *Le campagne italiane prima e dopo il Mille*, Bologna, 44-68.

Negri, A./H. Michael 2009, *Commonwealt*, Harvard.

Negroni Catacchio, N. 1998, Proposta di una scansione cronologica del Bronzo Finale nel territorio tra Fiora e Albegna, in *Atti Preistoria e Protostoria in Etruria* III, Milano, 79-87.

Pacciarelli, M. 2001, *Dal Villaggio alla Città – La svolta protourbana del 1000 a.C. nell'Italia tirrenica* (Grandi contesti e problemi della Protostoria italiana 4), Firenze.

Pacciarelli, M. 2016, The earliest processes toward city-states, political power and social stratification in middle Tyrrhenian Italy, *Origini* 39, 169-207.

Peroni, R. 1996, *L'Italia alle soglie della storia*, Bari/Roma.

Peroni, R.1998, Classificazione tipologica, seriazione cronologica, distribuzione geografica, *Aquileia Nostra* 69, 10-27.

Pucci, G. 1989, I consumi alimentari, in A. Momigliano/A. Schiavone (ed.), *Storia di Roma* IV. *Caratteri e morfologie*, Torino, 369-388.

Sotgia, A. 2015-2016, *L'abitato di Monte Rovello e la produzione vascolare del Bronzo Finale in Etruria Meridionale*. Tesi di Laurea Magistrale, Cattedra di Protostoria Europea, "La Sapienza" Università degli Studi di Roma.

Sotgia, A. 2019a, Italian pottery kiln and production areas from Bronze Age to Archaic Period (2200-500 BC). A typological approach, in D. Gheorghiu (ed.), *Architectures of fire: processes, space and agency in pyrotechnology*, Oxford, 48-67.

Sotgia, A. 2019b, Fornaci per ceramica ed aree produttive in Italia tra Età del Bronzo ed Età del Ferro, *IpoTESI di Preistoria* 12, 301-318.

Sotgia, A. 2020, Abitare i campi. La dimensione agricola dei Monti della Tolfa durante il Bronzo Finale, in *Atti Preistoria e Protostoria in Etruria* XIV, Milano, 382-400.

Virno, P. 2014, *Grammatica della moltitudine. Per una analisi delle forme di vita contemporanee*, Roma.

Wenger, E. 1998, *Communities of practice: learning, meaning and identity*, Cambridge.

# List of Contributors

| | |
|---|---|
| Acconcia, Valeria | Istituto Centrale per l'Archeologia (ICA) - Direzione Generale Archeologia Belle Arti e Paesaggio (DGABAP)<br>valeria.acconcia@beniculturali.it |
| Alessandri, Luca | Groningen Institute of Archaeology (GIA), University of Groningen<br>l.alessandri@rug.nl |
| Attema, Peter | Groningen Institute of Archaeology (GIA), University of Groningen<br>p.a.j.attema@rug.nl |
| Belardelli, Clarissa | Istituto Italiano di Preistoria e Protostoria (IIPP)<br>clarissa_belardelli@hotmail.com |
| Belelli Marchesini, Barbara | Sapienza University of Rome<br>barbara.belellimarchesini@uniroma1.it |
| Bernard, Seth | University of Toronto<br>seth.bernard@utoronto.ca |
| Cifani, Gabriele | Tor Vergata University of Rome<br>cfngrl00@uniroma2.it |
| Clerbaut, Tim | Ghent University<br>tim.clerbaut@ugent.be |
| Cortese, Francesca | Tor Vergata University of Rome<br>francesca.cortese@uniroma2.it |
| Ferreri, Lorenzo | Sapienza University of Rome<br>s.l.ferreri@gmail.com |
| García, Sánchez, Jesús | Insituto de Arqueología, Merida - Consejo Superior de Investigaciones Cientificas - Spanish National Research Council (CSIC) - Junta Extremadura<br>j.garcia@iam.csic.es |
| Gnade, Marijke | ACASA University of Amsterdam<br>m.gnade@uva.nl |
| Gorp, van, Wouter | Groningen Institute of Archaeology (GIA), University of Groningen<br>wouter.vangorp@gmail.com |
| Haan, de, Nathalie | Radboud University Nijmegen<br>n.dehaan@let.ru.nl |
| Haas, de, Tymon | Faculty of Archaeology - Leiden University<br>t.c.a.de.haas@arch.leidenuniv.nl |

| | |
|---|---|
| HELAS, SOPHIE | Rheinische Friedrich-Wilhelms-Universität Bonn<br>shelas@uni-bonn.de |
| JAIA, ALESSANDRO | Sapienza University of Rome<br>alessandro.jaia@uniroma1.it. |
| LAFFOON, JASON | Faculty if Archaeology - Leiden University<br>j.e.laffoon@arch.leidenuniv.nl |
| LAURITO, ROMINA | Museo Nazionale Etrusco di Villa Giulia, Rome<br>romina.laurito@beniculturali.it |
| MARÉCHAL, SADI | Ghent University<br>sadi.marechal@ugent.be |
| NEEF, DE, WIEKE | Department of Archaeology - Ghent University<br>wieke.deneef@ugent.be |
| OIKONOMOU, ARTEMIOS | Science and Technology in Archaeology and Culture Research Center (STARC), The Cyprus Institute<br>a.oikonomou@cyi.ac.cy |
| OPGENHAFFEN, LOES | ACASA University of Amsterdam<br>l.opgenhaffen@uva.nl |
| REVELLO LAMI, MARTINA | Faculty of Archaeology, Leiden University<br>m.revello.lami@arch.leidenuniv.nl |
| ROLFO, MARIO FEDERICO | Tor Vergata University of Rome<br>rolfo@uniroma2.it |
| SENGELOV, AMANDA | Faculty of Science, Université Libre de Bruxelles<br>Amanda.sengelov@ulb.be |
| SEVINK, JAN | Institute for Biodiversity and Ecosystem Dynamics (IBED), University of Amsterdam<br>j.sevink@uva.nl |
| SOTGIA, AGOSTINO | Sapienza Univeristy of Rome - Groningen Institute of Archaeology (GIA), University of Groningen<br>agostino.sotgia@uniroma1.it |
| ULLRICH, BURKART | Eastern Atlas Gmbh & Co. KG<br>b.ullrich@eastern-atlas.de |
| WAAGEN, JITTE | ACASA University of Amsterdam<br>J.Waagen@uva.nl |
| WATERS-RIST, ANDREA | Department of Anthropology, The University of Western Ontario<br>awaters8@uwo.ca |
| WIJDEVEN, VAN DE, GISWINNE | Indepent Researcher<br>giswinne@outlook.com |
| WITMER, EVELIEN | RAAP Archeologisch Adviesbureau<br>evelienwitmer@gmail.com |